THE FREEDOM FIGHTER

The ability of terrorist groups to inflict death and destruction has markedly increased with technological advances in the areas of communication, transportation, and weapon capability. Using these new tools and networks, terrorists now seek to inflict mass casualties worldwide. Given these realities, it is essential to research the factors that underlie a terrorist group's origins, grievances, and demands. Such insights might help others respond more effectively to insurgencies, especially when military campaigns to capture or kill every terrorist have proven unsuccessful.

The Freedom Fighter: A Terrorist's Own Story explores why so many Kurdish people—especially young adults—join the Kurdistan Workers' Party (PKK) and conduct terrorist acts. Inspired by the groundbreaking classic, *The Jack-Roller: A Delinquent Boy's Own Story*, by Clifford R. Shaw, the author explores the issue of radicalization into terrorist organizations through the life-history method, enabling a PKK terrorist—or "freedom fighter"—to tell his story. Over a five-month period, the author interviewed "Deniz," a high-level PKK terrorist in a Turkish prison, who during his time in the PKK rose from the lowest level to near the top in terms of terrorist operations.

This riveting life history, told in Deniz's own words, provides unique insights into why someone becomes a "freedom fighter" and what such a life entails. The account provides extensive information on the PKK, including the group's recruitment, ideological and military training, armed strategies, internal structures and code of ethics, treatment of women, and goals for peace. Deniz's story not only explains why more Kurdish "freedom fighters" will be recruited to engage in terrorist acts, but also facilitates understanding of how "normal people" can become involved in conflict and organizations that are designated as "terrorist groups." A foreword by renowned criminologist Francis T. Cullen helps contextualize the material. This book will interest students of criminology, terrorism/counterterrorism, political violence, and security.

Murat Haner received his Ph.D. in criminal justice from the University of Cincinnati. He is currently a Visiting Professor in the Department of Social Sciences, Program of Criminology, at the University of South Florida, Sarasota-Manatee. He teaches courses in counterterrorism, homeland security, radicalization, the Middle East, criminal justice, and intelligence science. Previously, he was a ranked officer with the Turkish National Police, at various departments. He worked undercover on counterterrorism and similar areas across Turkey. He has also traveled to Hungary, Israel, Sudan, Azerbaijan, Greece, Syria, and Germany for security training and education programs under the auspices of European Union and Turkish state funds.

Deniz—Northern Iraq

THE FREEDOM FIGHTER

A Terrorist's Own Story

Murat Haner

Routledge
Taylor & Francis Group

NEW YORK AND LONDON

First published 2018
by Routledge
711 Third Avenue, New York, NY 10017

and by Routledge
2 Park Square, Milton Park, Abingdon, Oxon, OX14 4RN

Routledge is an imprint of the Taylor & Francis Group, an informa business

© 2018 Taylor & Francis

The right of Murat Haner to be identified as author of this work has been asserted by him in accordance with sections 77 and 78 of the Copyright, Designs and Patents Act 1988.

Library of Congress Cataloging-in-Publication Data
A catalog record for this book has been requested

ISBN: 978-1-138-10450-1 (hbk)
ISBN: 978-1-138-10451-8 (pbk)
ISBN: 978-1-315-10222-1 (ebk)

Typeset in Bembo
by Out of House Publishing
Printed and bound by CPI Group (UK) Ltd, Croydon, CR0 4YY

CONTENTS

PREFACE

The ability of terrorist groups to incur widespread death and destruction has markedly increased with technological advances in the areas of communication, transportation, and weapon capability. Using these new tools and networks, terrorists now seek to inflict mass casualties worldwide. Given these realities, it is essential to research the factors that underlie a terrorist group's origins, grievances, and demands. Such insights might help us to respond more effectively to insurgencies, especially when military campaigns to capture or kill every terrorist have proven unsuccessful.

Within this context, the current book explores why so many Kurdish people—especially young adults—join the Kurdistan Workers' Party (PKK) and conduct terrorist acts. It is inspired by Clifford R. Shaw's *The Jack-Roller: A Delinquent Boy's Own Story*, a title originally published by the University of Chicago Press in 1930 that is still in print today. Employing the same approach taken by Shaw in his 1930 classic, the issue of radicalization was explored through the life-history method: having a PKK terrorist—or "freedom fighter"—tell his own story. Over a five-month period, I interviewed a high-level PKK terrorist in a Turkish prison. The subject—known as "Deniz"—proved remarkably insightful because of his diverse experiences. During his nearly two decades in the PKK, Deniz rose from the lowest level to near the top in terms of terrorist operations.

The result—a detailed life history of Deniz told in his own words—is an amazing narrative that provides unique insights into why someone becomes a "freedom fighter" and what such a life entails. This account provides extensive information on the PKK, including the group's recruitment, ideological and military training, and armed strategies, internal organizational structure and code of ethics, treatment of women, and goals for peace. In turn, using a life-course perspective, the book concludes by examining the factors that led to Deniz's onset into, persistence of, and desistance from his life as a terrorist.

Given that the Turkish government has chosen to continue to use military means to suppress the Kurds and the PKK, it is likely that the Kurdish insurrection will remain an ongoing concern. As such, the special observations offered by Deniz are likely to be of continuing value for some time regarding the terrorist conflict in Turkey. Deniz not only explains the issue of why more Kurdish "freedom fighters" will be recruited and engage in terrorist acts, but also provides a roadmap for addressing the daunting issues between the PKK and Turkey: Is peace possible? What would it take for freedom fighters such as Deniz—and the steady flow of Kurdish young adults into the PKK prepared to follow in his footsteps—to stop fighting Turkey and become peaceful?

Murat Haner
University of South Florida Sarasota–Manatee

ACKNOWLEDGMENTS

The completion of this book would never have been possible without the support, advice, and guidance of Dr. Francis T. Cullen, who not only helped with this book, but also provided invaluable assistance and numerous opportunities throughout my entire career at the University of Cincinnati. The time and wisdom you made available to me taught me much about being a quality researcher, scholar, and teacher as well as the importance of being a good human being throughout the process. The values you instilled in me I will carry with me throughout my life.

I must express my appreciation to the reviewers. To Drs. Cheryl Jonson, Travis Pratt, and Amy Thornton, thank you for your patience and willingness to help me finish this book. I am grateful for your expert advice, suggestions, and constructive criticism for crafting this book.

Finally, the completion of this book would not have been possible without the love and support of my wife. Your love and support has been so instrumental to my journey and development to this point. You have always given me just what I needed, and many times much more than I deserved. In many ways, this accomplishment is equally yours! I love you, I thank you, and I look forward to spending the rest of my life enjoying the memories that we have built together.

FOREWORD

The Freedom Fighter is a special book—a volume that could easily become a classic in the field. Dr. Haner—who I will refer to as "Murat" as I always do—has conveyed the "own story" of Deniz Koçer. Deniz was a long-time terrorist operative of the Partiya Karkerên Kurdistanê, known as the PKK and translated into English as the Kurdistan Workers' Party. The account presents detailed information on the PKK's culture, organizational structure, military operations, and socio-political ties to the larger community. It reveals members' daily lives and career patterns. And most of all, it provides deep insight into the perceived injustices and sense of honor that lead even a seemingly normal person to heartlessly murder others.

I read Deniz's life history for the first time in my role as Murat's dissertation advisor in the School of Criminal Justice at the University of Cincinnati. In the current book version, the packaging of this "own story" has been revised, and the somewhat dreary content of a formal dissertation thankfully removed. But the core of the document—Deniz's account—has stayed the same.

I read most of the story while on vacation in Hilton Head Island, sitting in a comfortable chair by a sliding door that yielded a panoramic view of the ocean. As I started to wade into the dissertation, I steeled myself for the necessary, but admittedly unwelcomed, task of reading hundreds of pages—hoping that my inspiring setting would somehow dull my pain! Soon, however, I found my interest rapidly mounting, escalating to the point where I was reading more intensely and turning pages quickly to learn more about a topic (e.g., gender relations) or about how a dramatic event unfolded (e.g., a military operation). My experience was transformed from duty to desire; I did not want to put the story down. It was now clear to me that Murat had achieved the best possible outcome: a life history that was not only informative but compelling. A classic was in the making.

All this may never have come to pass. Several years before, Murat was a student in my Ph.D. seminar on "Structural Theories of Crime." He was the ideal student—talented and hard working. I noticed that he was hovering around me, inventing transparent excuses to see me after class or in my office. As students seek out dissertation mentors, they engage in this mating ritual of academic flirting. Murat was bold enough on one occasion to ask me if I might be his advisor, which led me to ask about his area of interest. As a student funded by the Turkish government, he said that he was required to do his dissertation on terrorism—with his specific focus being the radicalization process. I informed him that "I do not do terrorism" and suggested that he wander down the hall to persuade some other kinder-hearted faculty member to guide his studies.

Suddenly, an idea popped mystically into my mind—a stray, momentary thought. I told Murat that there was "one dissertation I might be interested in advising." I reminded Murat of a book assigned in my theory course, the 1930 classic by Clifford R. Shaw, *The Jack-Roller: A Delinquent Boy's Own Story*. Published by the University of Chicago Press, the book is still in print. Shaw's delinquent from a Polish immigrant family in the slums of 1920s Chicago, Stanley, proved to be a remarkable storyteller, furnishing a very human look into the life of a wayward youth at this historical juncture. I told Murat that if he were willing to use a similar methodological approach, it might be possible and fruitful for him to undertake a life history of a terrorist. Murat immediately agreed that my idea was awesome—perhaps because the topic fascinated him or perhaps because this was the quickest way to secure a dissertation mentor! Either way, I felt appropriately brilliant and an academic partnership was formed.

I must confess that I had no idea what this kind of project would involve. I started out by requiring Murat to read every life history of offenders written by criminologists, which turned out to be quite a few. On his own, Murat decided to earn an M.A. in Political Science at the University of Cincinnati, as a way of enriching his understanding of international affairs. The result of all this—and much more—was a 250-page dissertation proposal, a document so good that I regretted not being able to give him his doctorate simply on that basis!

Still, the proposal proved to be the easy part. The more daunting challenge was how to select a subject for his life history. Murat offered to travel to Iraq and interview active terrorists in some mountainous region, a dangerously foolhardy idea that his dissertation committee vetoed immediately! We settled on his using PKK terrorists incarcerated in a Turkish prison—a population he hoped to gain access to based on his role as a law-enforcement officer in the country. We thought that if Murat conducted three to five life histories, he might find one that was suitable—or perhaps merge all the stories to form a useful mosaic of the PKK terrorism enterprise.

In a moment of incredible criminological good-luck—similar to hitting the lottery—Murat's first subject, Deniz, proved to be his "Stanley," a subject with years of experience who was a remarkable storyteller. Based on his reading of past life histories, Murat came prepared with a detailed, structured interview. This interview schedule kept the scholarly work on track to cover key topics, but Murat was wise to allow Deniz to take the discussions where he wished. Soon, it became apparent that Deniz would be Murat's only subject. In the end, Murat spent about five months traveling daily to Diyarbakır E Type Prison to conduct hours of interviews with his subject.

The resulting transcripts—first in Turkish and then translated into English—pushed beyond 2,000 pages. The work was tedious and unrelenting. For part of the time, Murat undertook this task while residing in my wife Paula and my third-floor guest room (home previously to many other famous criminological visitors to Cincinnati!). I would hear Murat start working early in the morning—my Chihuahua Lucy barking ferociously at the first sign of his movement—until late at night. Eventually, Murat used his editing magic to transform this mountain of information into a lengthy but fascinating document. He even became friends with Lucy, no easy task.

As I first read his "own story," I felt that Deniz was having a conversation with me. Almost like becoming engrossed in a good novel or good movie, I wanted to learn more about the central character of this real-life tale. I was "getting to know" him and starting to understand his choices, even the most brutal of them. For Deniz, his abiding rule in life was to act honorably, following core principles that shaped his actions as a PKK terrorist and that ultimately led to his surrender and imprisonment. When Deniz's "own story" ended, I felt rewarded for my investment of time but then soon craved for a sequel. In real life, of course, this could not occur. Deniz will remain behind bars for the rest of his life.

It is perhaps easy to downplay Murat's role in this project because, in the end, it is Deniz's words that we read. But as noted, it is one thing to have a pile of interview transcriptions and quite another to weave them into a coherent account in a way that preserves the integrity of the words and sentences that a subject has conveyed. Murat was masterful in crafting this story while not changing what Deniz relayed.

However, there was a more daunting challenge that Murat had to surmount. He was a former Turkish police officer who was raised to detest the PKK—to see all its members as brutal terrorists to be exterminated. He knew fellow officers who had died in attacks. Now, he sat across the table from a terrorist who had killed tens of Turkish security personnel. The unavoidable reality was that if Murat and Deniz had met in their previous lives, they likely would have been trying to kill one another.

I am particularly proud of Murat that he had the scholarly principles and personal integrity to see Deniz not as the terrorist "other" but as a human being who made difficult choices in life to seek freedom for his people. After reading the life history, I told Murat that Deniz seemed a lot like him—an observation that he greeted with laughter rather than with a heated denial. Although I doubt that these two men became friends, I do believe that mutual respect emerged. This bond allowed Deniz to open up and reveal in an unconstrained way details about every aspect of his life and of the PKK. This bond also allowed Murat to see the humanity of his subject and to understand why Deniz was compelled to join the PKK and to define himself as a "freedom fighter."

Publishing this book is a courageous decision. In Turkey—now more than ever—any show of sympathy for the PKK and the Kurdish minority generally is likely to be interpreted as unpatriotic. Even in a time when the country was moving toward liberal democracy, Turkish politicians and the population in general had difficulty forgiving the acts of a group that had murdered their fellow citizens. Still, in *The Freedom Fighter*, Murat shows how a cycle of violence—political oppression followed by terrorism followed by oppression followed by terrorism—will not be broken until the Turkish people truly understand why Deniz and many more Kurds like him will sacrifice their lives for their freedom. Despite his own reservations, Murat has come to realize that peace depends on his fellow Turks having the willingness to put themselves in Deniz's place and ask whether they might have followed a similar path. Murat's masterpiece makes such reflection possible—and herein lies its true value.

Francis T. Cullen
University of Cincinnati

PART I

Terrorism in Context

1

MEETING DENIZ

In 1930, the famous criminologist Clifford R. Shaw published the life history of a wayward youth he called "Stanley." The result was an amazing account, still in print today, *The Jack-Roller: A Delinquent Boy's Own Story*. After reading many works of this sort, I was convinced that it would be possible to undertake a comparable study of "A Terrorist's Own Story." The challenge, of course, was finding someone to interview. Because of his extensive criminal career, gift for poignant insights, and talent at storytelling, Stanley proved to be the perfect subject for Shaw's *The Jack-Roller*. Shaw had first met Stanley at the age of 12 in Chicago when employed as "a residential settlement house worker in a Polish neighborhood" (Snodgrass, 1982, p. 3). Later, Shaw would interview Stanley for his "own story" starting at age 16 just after he was released from the Illinois State Reformatory located in Pontiac. By that time, he had accumulated 38 arrests (Snodgrass, 1982, p. 3). Thus, I wondered where I would find a subject to interview who would have the capacity of Stanley to convey a story that would capture what it was like to become, remain, and ultimately stop being a terrorist.

I had the good fortune of working as a police officer in Turkey before departing for the United States to pursue graduate work in criminology/criminal justice. As a result, I had "connections" in my network that I hoped would allow me to gain entrance into a correctional facility where an inmate, convicted of terrorist activities, might be interviewed. In Turkey, most imprisoned terrorists are from the PKK, or the Kurdistan Workers' Party. I had a chance to consider several subjects to interview and, in fact, my original plan was to talk in depth with three to five of them. From my initial review of potential candidates, the best possibility seemed to be "Deniz," a PKK operative for nearly two decades. At the time, I did not know that I would end up interviewing him over the course of five months. Just as Shaw found the ideal delinquent to interview, I would discover that I had found my ideal terrorist to tell me his own story.

Diyarbakır E Type Prison is the place where I interviewed the main character of this book—Deniz Koçer. This old facility has such a long history of human right abuses that several times it has been ranked among the ten most notorious prisons in the world. During the 1980s, hundreds of Kurdish activists experienced horrific acts that included mental and physical torture. Tens lost their lives, and most exited the prison disabled in some way. Several other Kurdish prisoners died during the hunger strikes that they organized to protest their ill treatment at the Diyarbakır institution.

When their calls for fair treatment were unanswered, many of these political prisoners committed suicide including by burning themselves alive. These acts were a response to the torture they endured at the hands of Turkish soldiers and prison guards. The list of inhumane practices is long and disquieting: severe beating, being forced to rape each other, sexual abuse, degradation, being stripped naked, solitary confinement, being forced to urinate on fellow inmates, water and food deprivation, electric shocks, and the extraction of fingernails. Many Kurdish activists also lost their lives when shot by soldiers when they were allegedly trying to escape this facility.

On January 27, 2015, I met Deniz in this old facility—in which many innocent lives were destroyed during the 1980s—on a rainy day. As I was trying to enter the prison, I noticed that tens of people, mainly women and children, were waiting in front of the main entrance door to obtain a permit that was required to visit their incarcerated relatives. I skipped this long line and approached the main door to talk to the soldier who was handing out permits to the visitors. The soldier initially thought that I was an attorney. He said, "The entrance for the attorneys is on the other side." I informed him that I was not an attorney and then handed him the paperwork that was given to me by the Ministry of Justice officials in Ankara. I concluded from his accent that the soldier was a peasant Turk. He glanced over the document and then asked me to wait until he consulted with one of his superiors inside the main building. I was allowed to enter the facility approximately ten minutes later.

The soldier introduced me to a Kurdish guard and then said that this new person would accompany me thereafter. At that time, I noticed that the facility was protected by two types of security officials: (1) the soldiers who are responsible for the protection of the outside perimeter, and (2) the civilian guards who supervise the interior areas.

Once inside the facility, the guard instructed me to place all metal and electronic possessions in a cabinet located next to the entrance. I was then taken into a room full of guards, almost all of whom were Kurds. I was barraged with questions from each of them: "Who are you? Where are you coming from? What do you want to do? What is your purpose?" It was like I was being interrogated. Finally, the head guard ordered one of his lower-level staff to take me to the prison director's office.

I had to go through another search procedure (X-ray and pat down) before meeting the director. Finally, I was in his office. To my surprise, five other people were in the room—all drinking tea and reading newspapers. I was told that they were the assistant directors of the prison. One of them asked me to sit down on one of the empty chairs next to the window. Another one picked up the phone and called the servant to bring tea for me.

The prison director was a rude. Half mockingly, he asked what I was doing in Diyarbakır. I explained the purpose of my study and then handed over my official paperwork that I obtained from Ankara. He glanced at it and threw it on his desk. He then said to me, "Look, this is Diyarbakır. I do not care about what Ankara says. The circumstances are different here. Those officials sitting in Ankara do not know what we are dealing with here. You cannot come here every day and speak to a terrorist. You know what that costs to me? I have to assign two guards for you just to make sure that you are safe. Additionally, I cannot allow you to use prosecutor's office when interviewing the terrorists as it is stated in this paper." The other people in the room nodded their heads confirming what the director said. I was increasingly disappointed by their attitudes. It was clear that the prison officials did not want me to carry out this research inside their facility.

One of the assistant directors asked, "With whom you want to do these interviews? Do you know your study subjects by name?" I looked at my notebook and read out the names of the terrorists I wanted to interview. I also said that I would like to begin with the inmate named Deniz, because he had started his career in terrorism at a very early age and then ascended to one of the top positions in the PKK administration. He had spent almost two decades in the PKK organization and had worked across four countries—Turkey, Iraq, Syria, and Iran—when holding different ranks and positions. Most importantly, he was a close associate of the leader of the PKK, Abdullah Öcalan, when he lived in Damascus, Syria.

The director picked up the phone and called in one of the prison guards. "Bring me all the files on inmate Deniz Koçer!" Fifteen minutes later, the guard returned with a bunch of files in his hands. The prison director looked at the front page of each file and read out the summary information to all of us: "He is originally from the city of Batman, surrendered himself in 2010, has been staying here for five years, and has no infractions or violations." He then turned to me and said: "You know that he has to voluntarily agree to have an interview with you?" I said "Yes, sir. I am aware of that. I would like to meet with this inmate and tell him about the purpose of my study. I will then ask him for his consent and have him sign the forms that I brought with me."

The director then sarcastically asked: "What do you expect to find by interviewing these guys? They are terrorists…They know nothing but to kill people." I replied, "Sir, I understand your frustration, but I would still like to meet with these inmates and listen to their version of the story with their own words for the purposes of my study."

The director was annoyed by my response. He angrily picked up the phone again and ordered the guards to bring Deniz into his room. I said, "Wait! Wait! I want to talk to him in private. I cannot have all of you in the room when I explain him the procedure." I did not want the prison officials to influence Deniz in a negative way. The director rejected my request.

Fifteen minutes later, Deniz was brought into the prison director's office. I was excited to see him. He was skinny, probably in his late 40s. He was initially calm, but soon his eyes were wide open when he saw all of the top prison officials in the room. He probably thought something serious was about to occur. He was not allowed to sit down. I had just started to introduce myself to Deniz when one of the assistant directors barged in the conversation and told him: "This guy is coming from the United States, and he wants to carry out a research on terrorists by interviewing you and others."

I was disturbed by this intrusion into my explanation of my research. It is insulting to call someone a terrorist even though he is incarcerated for the act of terrorism. "Terrorist" is a pejorative term, and the incarcerated members of the PKK see themselves not as murderers but as guerillas in a war to free their people. I worried that calling this inmate, Deniz, a terrorist might inhibit his willingness to share information and to develop a trusting and close relationship with me. It was also possible that Deniz would be offended by the stigmatizing label applied to him and could simply refuse to participate in my project. I already knew that he had turned down many offers that came from various journalists and researchers before.

I immediately stood up, shook Deniz's handcuffed hands, introduced myself in a polite manner, and then asked him whether he would be interested in becoming a part of such a book project. Deniz wanted to see the official papers that I brought with me, including the ones that explained the details of the project. We all waited until he finished reading all the documents. He said, "Can I keep these documents? I need to make a couple phone calls before I decide. I will probably let you know about my decision either this afternoon or tomorrow morning." I said, "Of course, take your time!" I shook his hands again and then he was taken back to his cell.

I was heartened by the meeting taking place but also quite apprehensive. It was good that Deniz did not reject the offer outright as he did with other interested parties in the past. But

I was worried because he wanted to call someone before giving his final decision. Who was this person that he was going to call? Why could he not decide by himself? Was he going to seek permission from the PKK headquarters? My mind grew weary as tens of questions circled through my thoughts.

I left the facility burdened with these doubts. It was still raining outside, and I did not know anything about the area. It was only my second day in the city, and I was extremely nervous because I was in a place in which hundreds of my colleagues had lost their lives in the fight against terrorism. I wanted to walk around the streets and become familiar with the area and conquer my fear of being in this new place, instead of taking a cab and returning to my hotel. For an American, I think this would have been very similar to walking down the streets of Baghdad or Kabul.

Alas, I had to wait around three hours for news—but at least when it came it was good. The guards informed me that Deniz had agreed to take part in this study! I was so happy that I rushed back to the prison. It was already 3:00 p.m., and I did not have much time to start the interviews, because the main prison doors were locked down each day at 5:00 p.m. I needed to leave the facility by 4:45 p.m. Still, I was so excited that I did not want to wait a moment longer; I wanted to see Deniz so that we could begin to learn more about one other. A prison guard set up the meeting room and informed me that he would be waiting right next to me throughout the interview session.

Later, Deniz was brought into the room. Still handcuffed, Deniz stood directly in front of me. Amidst my euphoria of starting my research, I suddenly was shaken by the realization that this man had killed tens of security officials—my brethren. Deniz and I sat across from one another on the opposite sides of a table. After introducing ourselves to each other, we started slowly, discussing only general topics such as the political atmosphere in the country. These conversations would continue for the next five months and would become increasingly far-reaching and detailed. They would cover all aspects of his life, from his childhood, through his lengthy involvement in the PKK, and ultimately to his current life behind bars. It would be an amazing experience that would make this book possible. It would also, I must admit, transform my views of the PKK, terrorism, and how best to pursue a peaceful solution to the violence that plagued Turkey.

Another realization—an ironic one—also continues to press into my mind. Over our months together, Deniz and I talked pleasantly. Yet, if we had come across one another at an earlier time in life, a different reality would have been at hand. As a Turkish police officer, I might have tried to kill him; and, as a PKK terrorist, he might have tried kill me. But, in the end, as I spent time with him, I began to like Deniz—not so much as a friend but as a person who seemed much like myself.

As I will return to in the final chapter, I am optimistic that a solution to the PKK terrorist movement—which many Kurds see as freedom fighting—is possible. It will require that the Turkish leaders and public come to understand the world as experienced by and seen through the eyes of Kurds such as Deniz. I am not endorsing all their views as fully accurate or excusing the use of violence as an acceptable means of seeking freedom. But at the end of this project, I came to wonder what would I have done had I been born into the same situation as Deniz. Would I—and many of my fellow police officers—have been tempted to become a freedom fighter for our people? Sadly, at the time of writing, the thwarted coup in Turkey has placed many innocent citizens—including me because of my studies in the United States—on a list to be arrested. If I cannot return at this time to speak for peace, I hope that the insights of this book will transcend national boundaries and bring a fresh perspective on the PKK to my beloved country.

Who Is Deniz?

Deniz was born in 1973 as the third eldest son of a poor peasant Kurdish family. He has nine siblings—six boys and three girls. No one, including his own mother, thought that Deniz would survive because he was born prematurely when his mother had been pregnant for only six months.

For most of his early life, Deniz lived in a house that had no electricity, television, or refrigerator. The living conditions were so hard that Deniz's maternal grandparents, aunts, uncles, and their family members all lived in the same house. His parents earned the livelihood for the entire family through livestock breeding and agriculture in a small village located in the southeastern part of the country. Until age 15, Deniz, along with his elder brothers, helped his parents by grazing goats and sheep in the pastures of his village.

Deniz never attended school because of the negative treatment his elder brothers were subjected to by teachers' intent on imposing a Turkish language and culture on them. However he was intelligent enough to learn how to read and write by himself. He was an active child but never engaged in fights with his siblings or with children in the village. In fact, he was known to be a mature, responsible, truthful, and courageous youngster by his circle of friends and relatives.

Deniz's parents never forced their children to live a religious life, even though they themselves were very strict about adhering to the prescriptions of their faith. They gave complete freedom to Deniz and his siblings when it came to practicing religion. Deniz chose a non-religious lifestyle because he was disappointed by the atrocities committed by an Islamic religious organization—Hezbollah—during the 1990s. However, his parents were highly strict on teaching their children to adhere to universal ethical values such as abstaining from lying and stealing.

Despite witnessing injustices and cruel treatments by Turkish soldiers early in his life, Deniz did not join PKK until 1992—until his parents moved to the city of Batman. City life provided Deniz with access to experiences that further fueled his radicalization and, importantly, gave him access to the concrete opportunity to join the PKK. These included participating in mass protests and demonstrations organized by Kurdish activists, developing close relationships with new friends, and using this network to learn how to become a freedom fighter for his people.

Deniz spent almost two decades in the PKK and fought across four countries—Turkey, Iraq, Syria, and Iran—under different ranks and positions. He came close to death several times. In 1993, he was shot in his lower abdomen. In 1994, a hand grenade exploded just in front of him, seriously damaging his face and knees. His friends thought that he was dead and left him behind. In 1996, a sniper bullet stripped his skull and broke the skull bone. None of these potentially deadly injuries made Deniz consider leaving his life as a guerilla.

Almost everyone who comes to know Deniz—his relatives, parents, childhood friends from the neighborhood he grew up, and the former PKK members that he worked with—describes him as a trustworthy person who possesses the highest level of integrity. In fact, having a strong character and being guided by the positive traits of moral conviction and physical courage eventually earned Deniz one of the top positions in the PKK administration.

The clinical records that I obtained from the prison officials indicated that Deniz did not suffer from any psychological, mental, or personality disorders that would predispose him towards the use of violence. On several occasions, Deniz also stated that he became a "freedom fighter" not because of a violent propensity or to fulfill some social or psychological needs such as excitement or identity.

Rather, he became a terrorist because of the sense that he had the obligation to defend his people through armed insurrection. He was such a devoted fighter that he did not contact his own parents for an 18-year period—fearing that getting in touch with them would jeopardize his commitment to the Kurdish cause.

Again, I would have never imagined that I would have an extended conversation with Deniz over a five-month period. My original plan was to spend just a few weeks with him and then interview as many as three to five other "terrorists." But Deniz proved to be a fascinating person—my ideal subject to tell his "own story"! With almost two decades of experience in the PKK, he was able to share details on virtually every aspect of how a major terrorist group is organized, persists, and carries out its operations.

The Value of the Own Story

Within criminology, scholars have long used the life history as a means of probing the processes that lead offenders into crime and for gaining a rich, textured understanding of the lives offenders live each and over time. As noted, the life history was used to considerable benefit by members of the early Chicago School of criminology. Most notably, along with Henry McKay, Clifford Shaw had documented the concentration of crime in inner-city neighborhoods—what was called "the zone in transition"—based on a massive study that mapped where every juvenile offender resided. But early on, Shaw realized that dots on a spot map could not illuminate why the youngsters in these impoverished, socially disorganized areas turned to crime and then sustained criminal careers. Shaw was aware that he could enrich his understanding of these realities only by talking with wayward youths and having them tell their "own story." Another member of the Chicago School, Edwin Sutherland, similarly relied on a life history—*The Professional Thief*—to illuminate how access to this criminal role was limited and explained by his theory of differential association.

Subsequently, criminologists built on these early works to develop life histories of other types of offenders in the later decades of the 20th century and also in the beginnings of the 21st century. During this period, the life histories published by scholars included such titles as *the Professional Fence* by Carl Klockars (1974); *Manny: A Criminal-Addict's Story* by Richard Rettig, Manual Torres, and Gerald Garret (1977); *Assault with a Deadly Weapon* by Dianne Hall Kelly and Philip Heymann (1978); *The Jack-Roller at Seventy* by Jon Snodgrass (1982); *Harry King: A Professional Thief's Journey* by William Chambliss (1984); *The Fence* by Darrell Steffensmeier (1986); and *The Confessions of a Dying Thief* by Steffensmeier and Jeffrey Ulmer (2005).

Similar to the Chicago School studies, these later life histories all played important roles in the further explanation of criminal behavior by providing a wealth of information about the trajectory of criminal careers. By recording an individual's experiences in the subject's own words, these stories illuminated how family disruption combined with poverty, school failure, and differential associations with other criminals were key factors for the development of criminal careers for these individuals. They revealed the specific methods and tactics that the subjects developed and used during their fencing, hustling, and other types of criminal activities. Equally importantly, the later life histories also provided information on the subjects' well-established rationalization and neutralization techniques to excuse their deviant acts and criminal lifestyles. Finally, the later life histories disclosed important insights about the negative aspects of the prison environment including the lack of rehabilitation and education, the sexual vulnerability of young inmates, the furtherance of criminal skills through association with older inmates, and the cruelty of facility administrations on the inmates.

In this tradition, my project was undertaken to acquire an understanding of the process of radicalization. Why do some people—in this case, some Kurds—join a terrorist organization with the express purpose of taking the lives of Turkish security forces and, at times, innocent citizens? But beyond the initial radicalization, it struck me that relatively little is known about what it is like to live as a terrorist for a lengthy period of time. What is life like on a daily basis? What hardships are endured or successes celebrated? What relationships—organizational, personal, romantic—are forged? How are military operations carried out and what are the dangers experienced? Why does someone stay a terrorist or decide to give up this endeavor? How is a terrorist organization—in this case the PKK—organized? What are its ideology, its leadership structure, and its sources of support, economically and socially? These and many other questions can be addressed through a systematic life history. And, again, that is the goal of my securing Deniz's own story.

Doing a Life History with a Terrorist

My interview with Deniz lasted from January 27, 2015 to May 8, 2015. I never imagined that it would take almost five months to record the life history of a single subject. But, as I previously stated, Deniz proved to be a fascinating person, who had almost 20 years' experience in the PKK—from the lowest level to near the top in terms of terrorist operations.

Before traveling to Turkey to interview Deniz, I spent many months reading every life history I could, including the few that existed on terrorism. *The Jack-Roller*, because of its classic status and enduring influence within criminology, was my main guide. But I still wanted to determine what was common across all the life histories and unique to each one. The insights obtained from these life histories allowed me to develop a lengthy list of questions. These were grouped into four domains: (1) growing up, (2) becoming a terrorist, (3) being a terrorist, and (4) prison and beyond.

Beyond securing access to a terrorist, one of the most challenging aspects of this project was obtaining approval to undertake the study from the Institutional Review Board (IRB) at my home institution at that time, the University of Cincinnati. This project was developed as my doctoral dissertation in the School of Criminal Justice but, from the beginning, was envisioned by my advisor (Francis T. Cullen) and me as a book, like *The Jack-Roller*, to be read widely. During that period, I contacted well-known academics on terrorism who had previously engaged in research in which they had talked directly to terrorists, including Jessica Stern from Harvard University and Scott Atran from University of Michigan. The goal was to learn about their IRB experiences. Dr. Stern told me that she had carried out her research outside of a university environment so she did not have to apply for IRB approval. Accordingly, she could not give me much guidance on how best to negotiate the IRB process when conducting the kind of sensitive project I was proposing.

Dr. Atran was able to share a wealth of information about his experiences with the IRB process, but his account was not encouraging. Apparently, he had tried to carry out a very similar project (prison interviews with failed suicide bombers) and he had been rejected by the University of Michigan's IRB. University officials had argued that prisoners could not, in principle, freely give their informed consent. Even though Dr. Atran's subjects were willing to take part, these officials asserted that this kind of research was incompatible with the rights of human subjects and therefore never likely to be approved. Dr. Atran informed me that he was planning to move back to Europe—where IRB, in his own words, did not have dictatorial powers—to carry out his own research agenda and advised me to do the same thing.

Knowing that I had to gain IRB approval, this feedback made me worried that I might experience difficulties in the approval process—and might even have my project rejected. I imagined this impersonal, powerful, bureaucratic entity wielding a life-and-death decision over a study that I knew I had to undertake. It might have helped, however, that I was in the School of Criminal Justice at the University of Cincinnati, where faculty had conducted extensive research on prison inmates in the United States—all without incident. Still, I was talking about research with terrorists confined in a foreign nation where the commitment to human rights might seem more uncertain. So, months of planning went into the design of the interview protocol.

I also was careful to communicate how, at this particular time, the human rights of political prisoners in Turkey were protected by agreements with the European Union. Even though the imprisoned terrorists are defined as vulnerable participants by the IRB, a number of safeguards were in place in Turkish prisons at that time that ensured the safety of the subjects.

In an effort to earn the right of full membership into the European Union, Ankara had implemented various prison and judicial reforms aimed at protecting the rights of prisoners. Prisoners have been provided a basic right to inform the European Union Court of Human Rights of ill-treatment activities by the prison officials and other law enforcement agencies. These prisoners can access and consult their lawyers 24/7 through a request form. If the prison administrators do not follow these rules, then the European Union Court of Human Rights has the right and authority to hold Turkey liable for compensation.

In my application, I explicitly stated that there was no risk that coercion will be applied to force the subjects to take part in this study. Subjects had access to their lawyers as well as European Union officials to complain about possible ill-treatment. In such a circumstance, the Turkish government would be liable to pay hundreds of thousands of Euros to prisoners as compensation. In the end, I was relieved and then excited to learn that the university's IRB approved my plan to carry out research in Turkish prisons.

After much preparation, I arrived in Turkey, gained entrance to the prison, and selected my subject. It was finally time to start interviewing Deniz! Again, I thought that I could run through the interview questions in a few weeks—a month at the most. But this did not prove to be the case. Over a five-month period, I went to the prison—on average five days a week and from 8:00 a.m. to 5:00 p.m.

Initially, the prison administration provided me with a pen and blank papers to take notes of the interview sessions. Each day, I ended up having 20 to 25 pages of handwritten notes that I had to transform into electronic format each evening. It soon became apparent that it would be a daunting task to try to record Deniz's life history by taking notes—for two reasons. First, after a week, I began to feel numbness in my fingers as a result of constantly writing at a fast pace, always trying to catch up to what Deniz told me. Second, the progress of the study was very slow. I would have had to spend more than a year in that prison if I had to continue to carry out my research by taking notes. Due to these difficulties, I asked the chief public prosecutor of the city if I could record the interview sessions. To my good fortune, this official was very understanding. He called the prison director and ordered him to allow me to use my personal laptop to speed up the process of my research.

One issue that arose was whether to conceal or disclose the identity of my subject. My original intent was not to reveal his name, which was standard practice in most life histories For example, "Stanley" was a pseudonym invented by Clifford Shaw for the jack-roller he interviewed (Snodgrass, 1982). Although my Kurdish interviewee wanted his true identity revealed, I had trepidations about doing so in a nation where some form of retaliation is always possible (e.g., against his family). My dilemma was solved because the PKK assigned a new name to all its operatives, presumably to mask their true identity if captured. My subject was called "Deniz Koçer." Accordingly, I felt comfortable using the name "Deniz" in this book.

As the interview process proceeded, I used the questions I had developed but also let the conversation take whatever path Deniz wished to explore. My goal was to record Deniz's life history and not to rigidly follow a list of questions. In fact, Deniz proved to have a strong mind and a willingness to share his experiences with me. Most of the time, I did not have to probe Deniz to reveal more detail about his past as he told his life history to me in a very detailed manner. As would be the case with any of us, he would occasionally forget to mention some incidents from his past. Thus, each morning he would start talking to me about the incidents he failed to mention during the previous interview sessions.

One thing worth mentioning is that as a police officer, it was quite frustrating for me to talk to Deniz during the first couple of weeks. This person had killed more than 100 Turkish security forces and injured many more. Now, he was sitting right across from me and telling his story. Nevertheless, despite my initial frustration with Deniz for his being a PKK terrorist, I was also aware that I had an obligation as a researcher to objectively record his story.

Over time, Deniz's story began to affect me. I was shocked to hear that his radicalization into terrorism gradually developed as a result of a number of life-course events that occurred mostly during his childhood and early adolescent years—injustices carried out by soldiers, discrimination towards his brothers at school, mistreatment and beatings by teachers, being forced to watch his father while he was beaten by Turkish security officials, and many other things. I still can never excuse his use of violence, but Deniz helped me to understand how the Kurds had been repressed culturally and militarily. Above all, I could then see Deniz's humanity. Even though my subject was a terrorist, I realized that my project would only have value if I used his "own story" as a way of showing Deniz's humanity to others—to the readers of this book.

In addition to what I heard from Deniz, being in the city of Diyarbakır allowed me to personally witness the injustices applied by the Turkish state to the Kurds of Turkey. In fact, I was forced to become a part of it. As I was interviewing Deniz, my superiors at the Turkish National Police headquarters ordered me to resume my police work. I told them that it would be difficult for me to carry out such policing duties because I was in Turkey for research purposes. My request was denied, and then I was assigned as the head of technical surveillance and intelligence collection at Diyarbakır Counter Terrorism Department. Fortunately, I was allowed to work only night shifts—from 10:00 p.m. to 6:00 a.m.

For most of the nights, I would have the time to rest so that I would have enough energy to carry out my interviews with Deniz during the next day. Nevertheless, this position would sometimes require me to provide oversight to nighttime missions that were carried out against the houses of terrorists and potential terrorist sympathizers. Such operations were not only highly dangerous but also required days and nights of planning and preparation for the police officers under my command. For these missions, the counterterrorism squads are given the addresses of the potential targets and then ordered to raid the houses around 4:30 to 5:00 in the morning when terrorist targets are expected to be sleeping deeply.

As a high-ranked officer, I was twice ordered to provide oversight to this duty while I was in the city—experiences that proved personally disquieting. In the first incident, my units raided the house in the Sur district of Diyarbakır at 4:45 a.m. Our advance teams broke open the door and entered into the house. The Kurds are usually poor people. When I say "house," I am referring to a structure that includes only a kitchen, a bathroom, and a living room that also is used as a bedroom at night. That was it. In this particular incident, the whole family—the mother, father, and their two children—were sleeping next to one other on a bed placed on the ground in the living room.

As soon as we entered into the house, the children began to cry uncontrollably. They were scared to death. The father and mother were holding their shaky hands on top of their heads and also trying to calm down their kids by trying to talk to them. The laser lights of the weapons were directed toward the whole family, pointed at their heads. I could see that the kids wetted their clothes.

We soon discovered that we were provided with the wrong address. The leader of the SWAT team apologized to the family and then we left the house. But who was going to repair the psychological damage we left on those two kids? Was that even possible? No! For a moment, I put myself in place of that father and imagined those two kids as though they were mine. I would not stop thinking that if I was their dad, I would probably join the PKK to exact my revenge—still an unimaginable choice, of course, but one that I could now empathize with emotionally.

Getting into our armored vehicles, we set off for the second address that was given to us to be raided on that same night. It was still dark, but the sun was about to rise soon. Therefore, we needed to hurry up. When we arrived, the same routine occurred—the door was broken open, guns were pointed at people, and SWAT teams yelled at the inhabitants who were sleeping on a mattress made from wool.

This time the circumstances were even more disquieting. The SWAT teams were just about to kill the father of the house because he was refusing to grovel on his knees with hands on his head. There were three children probably aged between 5 and 8 trying to protect their father by covering his body. The officers were poised to start shooting when the mother told us that her husband was bedridden and mute. One of the kids was so scared that she became unresponsive. She did not answer any of our questions but just stood still like a statue.

We searched the house to find our target—the teenager son who was a PKK sympathizer. The officers checked everywhere—the kitchen, bathroom, and the living room. Clearly, he was not at home. The Kurdish mother angrily told us that her son was serving his mandatory Turkish military service in the western part of the country. Of course, we did not believe her until I saw a framed picture in which this son was posing in his Turkish military uniform behind a Turkish flag. We phoned the military post at which the son was residing, as his mother had alleged. She was telling the truth. At the time we called the post, the supposed PKK sympathizer that we were looking for was doing his military service; in fact, he was sleeping in his bunker.

I was emotionally and psychologically devastated. All these doors broken open, the yelling in people's faces, and the scaring of children to death was for nothing. Even worse, this time we almost killed a bedridden mute person, and then one of the kids had become unresponsive because of the shock she experienced. How were we going to repair these damages that we left these people with? What might the son serving in the military do if he somehow discovered what we just did to his parents and siblings? Most importantly, for how long have mistakes of this sort occurred in this city? How many times have these people suffered at the hands of the Turkish security officials?

I saw that this Kurdish mother was putting her kids into school uniforms as the sun had risen. My officers were making their final search of the perimeter and preparing documents for the adult members of the household to sign. I also walked around the house. When I visited the kitchen, I noticed that these people were living in extreme poverty. There was not even a refrigerator. There was just a camp stove for cooking, a couple of pots, and legumes that hung on the walls in small sacks. These kids probably had never eaten meat in their lives. I was disheartened when I saw that the Kurdish mother was spreading pure tomato paste on slices of bread. The kids were excitedly waiting in front of their mother for this food. The mother fed them and then asked them to go to their school. That was probably their routine breakfast—a slice of bread with tomato paste and a glass of water.

The Kurdish mother asked us if she could serve tea to us as soon as she sent her children to school. We thanked the mother and then asked her to sign the official papers stating that no damage had occurred to anyone or to anything during the raid procedure, even though we had broken the entry door, turned the house upside down, and scared her children. I was shocked to see that she signed them all even without reading. The husband was helplessly looking at us from his bed.

We left the house. It was already 7:00 a.m., so I went directly to my home. Both of my sons were awake watching "Thomas the Train" on the television, and my wife was preparing breakfast for them. One of them was arguing with my wife that he wanted real sausage, not the fake ones made from veggies. I just looked at him, and thought of the circumstances in which the Kurdish children from earlier had to live. My heart was deeply broken.

I could not sleep but turned in the bed from one side to another. What I had witnessed at that last house had made me troubled. On that same day, I gave another visit to that house but in civilian clothes. The girl who became unresponsive after our raid opened the door for me. She was alone at the house with her aunt. Her aunt was unable to speak Turkish so I talked to this little Kurdish girl. She told me that her mother had taken her father to the hospital. The mother arrived home approximately half an hour later but by herself. She recognized that I was one of the police officers that raided her house early in the morning. Despite that, she welcomed me using kind words. She then told me that her husband was hospitalized after we left the house. The poor guy probably could not bear the treatment that his family was subjected to at our hands.

I apologized for what had happened that morning and then gave her some money so that she could buy something for the children. That was the only thing I could do for this poor family. The lady initially returned the money, but took it back when I insisted. God knows how many times these people have been subjected to these inhumane actions. She sent me off with tears in her eyes.

The only silver lining of these firsthand experiences was that they helped open my eyes to what was going on in this part of the country. I realized that the Kurdish issue (and also the related problem posed by the PKK) had been oversimplified, with the Turkish public intentionally deprived of the full truth. On top of that, the decades of the denigration of and misinformation about the Kurds had created such a sense of superiority and honor in our minds. No wonder that even most decent, good Turkish citizens showed so little respect to the Kurds and their cause.

The time flew by in Diyarbakır. The last days of the interview were particularly hard for Deniz. Not only was he telling me the most tragic incidents in his life story, but also we had become close over time and he knew that he would not be able to see me again. He gave me a beautiful oil-painted canvas and then hugged me. His last words were:

> Sometimes, I very much miss the life in the countryside; the fresh air, the silence of the mountains, peace and the atmosphere of true friendship. But, here I am, always stuck among four walls. Even worse, I know that I am going to end my life here.
>
> Despite all of these things, I never lost my hope. In fact, my hopes are the only thing that keeps me going in here. One cannot live here without hopes and dreams. I always dream of leaving here one day. The thing that I want the most is to spend time with my nephews and nieces, for at least a few days before I die.

Again, it is so ironic that although Deniz and I talked to each other pleasantly, we could have tried to kill each other if we had crossed paths earlier in our lives—he as a terrorist and me as a police officer.

I returned to the United States after finishing my interviews with Deniz. My hope was to finalize the book in about two months. I was wrong in my thinking. There was a major issue to consider when employing the life-history method that somehow had skipped my mind: the transcription of the recorded material. I had approximately 70 recordings, and it took me almost two months to transcribe them all with the help of several other people. I ended up having thousands of pages of dialogue when the transcription was completed. I am confident in the accuracy of this process—capturing what Deniz had to say. One thing that bothered me, however, was the disappearance of the expressive components of the spoken words—such as the rhythms and gestures—when Deniz's words were transcribed into text.

When the transcriptions were completed, I worked on the text to construct the foundation of the life history—short connecting passages between the paragraphs were written, duplications were eliminated, and the chronological accuracy was maintained. However, in recording the story, I stayed true to what Deniz said. I only smoothed out the text if Deniz stumbled or hesitated in his speech as my goal is to have his voice in the pages of his own story, just as Stanley's voice is heard in the pages of Shaw's *The Jack-Roller*. Everything that was reorganized was sent back to Deniz. I asked Deniz to read and approve the way his story was put together. It took another three weeks until Deniz read the whole story and approved everything.

This book employed two measures to cross-check what Deniz revealed in his story to attest the overall veracity of his account. After all, any life history raises the question of whether the subject is telling the truth or recalling events accurately. First, due to my position in the counter-terrorism department of Turkish National Police, I had access to documents—newspaper articles, court records, intelligence reports, and criminal justice records—that could be used to corroborate Deniz's statements and testimony. Deniz's descriptions of important events and terrorist missions correctly matched with the data kept by the Turkish authorities. It was interesting that Deniz was not only correct in estimating the date and time of the events that occurred years ago but also the number of casualties on both sides.

Second, using the resources at Turkish National Police, I was able to reach out and talk to two former PKK members that were mentioned in Deniz's life history. The people in this group had surrendered themselves to the Turkish security forces. After gaining their trust, I asked these people to read the life history of Deniz and inform me if they detected any inconsistency or exaggeration in any part of the study. Related to this, throughout the interview, I often cautioned Deniz that his accounts would be read by some repentant PKK members, people who know him very well, to encourage his truthfulness. I specifically told him the detection of any kind of misrepresentation would risk discrediting the whole study. Taken together, I believe that all these measures gave added confidence that what Deniz said in his account is accurate.

Then I started working on the most difficult part of this project: translating the text into English. It took me approximately another six months to complete this translation. It was quite challenging to accomplish this task, but I trust that the result is a fascinating story—which is almost like a novel—that provides a firsthand account of a PKK terrorist's experiences as he lived a life that he would see as freedom fighting.

Conclusion

Deniz's own story is presented in the book's second part. As a prelude to his life history, it is necessary to place the conflict between the Turkish government and the Kurdish people, their political representatives, and the PKK in a broader historical context. Accordingly, the next chapter addresses these issues.

2

THE HISTORY OF THE KURDS AND THE PKK

On December 10, 2016, two bombing incidents occurred outside a major football stadium in Istanbul after a match between top teams in the country. The attacks directly targeted the riot police units who were on duty in the game area. The casualties were heavy: 44 people, mostly police officers, lost their lives, whereas 155 others were badly injured during the explosions.

The Kurdish Freedom Hawks, a branch of the PKK, assumed the responsibility for the attacks. The group carried out the explosions after thousands of fans from both teams left the stadium, which was a clear indication that the Turkish citizenry were not the direct target. Nevertheless, seven civilians lost their lives during the explosions.

This attack shows how PKK terrorism is becoming even more entrenched in Turkey. Although still targeted at security personnel, the terrorist missions are now moving into the main cities of Turkey. By carrying out this attack at the heart of Istanbul, the PKK sent the message that it has the capabilities to execute similar missions whenever deemed necessary. In fact, in a statement posted on their website, PKK officials clearly stated that the Istanbul attack was a reprisal for the government's crackdown on the Kurdish politicians, including the imprisonment of mayors and deputies from the People's Democratic Party, and for the on going state violence in southeast Anatolia.

The reactions of Turkish state officials to these attacks were predictable, echoing comments made following previous incidents. As has often been the case, soon after the attack, the officials stated that they would use the military and security forces to exact revenge and crush the PKK terrorists. For example, during the funeral of the police officers, the interior minister of Turkey said, "Sooner or later, we will have our vengeance. This blood will not be left on the ground, no matter what the price, what the cost (Dolan & Gumrukcu, 2016)." Turkish President Tayyip Erdoğan also vowed vengeance after the bombing. He stated that "We are the owners of this country and will not leave it to those scum if they aim to scare us with such attacks. Nobody should doubt that with God's help, we as a country and a nation will defeat terror, terrorist organizations, and of course the forces behind them (Saheen & Smith, 2016)." This incident and the responses to it are symbolic of what is happening and what is to come. Where peace was once possible, now the cycle of violence and repression is rapidly speeding up.

At one time, I felt the same way as Turkish officials: The Kurds are terrorists and all terrorists should be annihilated. For me—as for the rest of the Turkish society—the PKK was nothing but the agent of the Western powers. Its secret agenda was to carve up our territories, steal our natural resources, and disrupt the peace and economic stability in Turkey. Thus, for any ordinary Turk, it was perfectly acceptable to beat, torture, and even kill the Kurds who would support the PKK.

But now, after interviewing Deniz, the issues seem so much more complex. The Kurdish issue had been oversimplified, and no Turkish official has paused to ask why responses that have been tried and failed previously—military operations, condemning the violence and promising to crush the PKK terrorists—would work. There is still no willingness in the country to understand why this terrorism has occurred for decades and why, now, it will worsen. Rather, after these decades of an unsolved problem, state officials are still planning to engage in precisely the actions that almost certainly would lead more Kurds to become "freedom fighters" and more Turkish forces and citizens to die. Again, the cycle of violence will almost certainly continue and many Turks and Kurds will die—in many respects quite needlessly. This insight is a central and sobering lesson to be drawn from Deniz's own story—an issue which will be discussed later in the book.

The events of today, as well as those conveyed in Deniz's life history can only be understood fully by placing them within a larger context. The current chapter presents this context in three sections. The first section describes the socio-cultural, religious, and linguistic origins of the Kurdish people. The second section discusses the long historical relationship between the Turks and Kurds. Consideration is given to the political, social, and economic factors that contributed to the Kurdish uprisings and rebellions in the Ottoman Empire and Turkey and to the salient incidents that fueled the dissolution of the Turkish-Kurdish unity in the Turkish Republic will be discussed. This section also examines the factors that played a key role in the national awakening of the Kurds during the 1980s of Turkey—the mandatory relocation of Kurdish children for educational purposes, the economic deprivation produced by the mechanization of agriculture, and the social injustices caused by the co-optation of the agha system. Finally, the third section explores the emergence and the development of PKK terrorism in Turkey. It will explain how the group's leader, Abdullah Öcalan, initiated a violent revolution against the Turks and the feudal Kurds, and how he used Marxist ideology to portray his organization as the protector of poor peasant Kurds. Special attention is given to how, over time, the PKK's armed struggle captured public attention, and made it impossible for elected officials to ignore the Kurdish problem in Turkey. This section ends by discussing recent developments related to the PKK and the Kurds in Turkey.

As a prelude to setting this context, two other matters merit consideration: First, what is meant by "terrorism"? Terrorism is conceptually complex because it involves different groups with different objectives. To date, no universally accepted definition of terrorism exists, in large part because no consensus exists on what actions should be considered as terrorism or which groups should be considered terrorist organizations. There is still a divergence of opinion among the governments, individual agencies within the governments, academic experts, and private agencies as to how the concept of terrorism should be described (Gibbs, 2012; Gupta, 2006; Horgan & Braddock, 2012; Richardson, 2006; Silke, 2003; Stern, 2003). This disagreement is mainly because "one person's terrorist is another person's freedom fighter" (Weinberg, Pedahzur, & Hoefler, 2012, p. 793; Martin, 2016, p. 33). For example, for most of the Muslim world, a Palestinian firing a rocket against an Israeli military infrastructure is not a terrorist but a freedom fighter whereas the majority of the Western countries would label the same fighter as a terrorist. As a result of this controversy, numerous definitions of terrorism can be found in the literature. Still, by selecting features of the definitions commonly used in the Western literature on radicalization and terrorism, it is possible to define the act of terrorism as follows:

(1) The use of force and violence, (2) by subnational actors, (3) through unconventional methods, (4) by targeting vulnerable civilian and passive security forces, (5) to achieve some political goal, (6) by intimidating a larger audience (Martin, 2016, p. 29; Gurr, 1989; Gibbs, 2012; Hoffman, 2006; Whittaker, 2003).

Second, terrorism is not homogeneous but heterogeneous; it does not arise from a single cause and is not practiced by a single kind of perpetrator; Vertigans, 2011). Indeed, scholars have identified at least five different types of terrorism, each of which has a distinct motivation, psychology, and organizational structure: (1) state terrorism—the use of terrorism by the governments as a means of controlling their own populations (e.g., the French Revolution, the suppression of democratic protestors in Syria by the Assad regime); (2) dissident terrorism—includes rebellious activities committed against the governments by non-state actors (ETA in Spain, IRA in England, the Tamil Tigers in Sri Lanka, Chechen terrorism in Russia, PLO in Israel); (3) religious terrorism—the practice of violence in the name of God for religious grievances and inspiration (e.g., Catholic-Protestant violence in Ireland, Islamic State, Al-Qaeda, Thuggee in India, Boko Haram in Nigeria); (4) criminal terrorism—violence committed for the goal of profit making (Narcotraficantes in Mexico, FARC in Colombia, the Italian Mafia); and (5) ideological (right and left wing) terrorism—acts committed by groups to overthrow liberal governments and capitalist democracies to establish new orders in their line of thoughts (Klu Klux Klan, Neo Fascists, Nazis in Germany, Red Army Faction in Germany, The Red Brigades in Italy, Colombian death squads) (Martin, 2016; White, 2015).

PKK terrorism would fit into the second category—dissident terrorism. However, Turkey is currently in the grips of religious terrorism as well. Aside from the battles ongoing between the government forces and PKK militants, the Islamic State has begun to target the civilian population in Turkey in retaliation for Turkey's military activities in Syria and Iraq. In fact, 2016 was a bloody year for Turkey, considering the scale of violence practiced by ISIS and by PKK terrorism, the bloody coup attempt, and the brutal crackdown that prompted the incarceration of thousands of Turkish citizens in the coup's aftermath. Facing these disparate conflicts, Turkey's future appears disquieting.

National Background of the Kurds

Kurds have lived in a region currently divided within the borders of Turkey, Iran, Iraq, and Syria—an area that is as large in size as France. Academics believe that the Seljuk Turks first used the term of Kurdistan during the 12th century to name this region as their administrative entity (McDowall, 2000; White, 2000, p. 15).

There are different theories regarding the origins of the Kurds. The most widely accepted view is that the Kurds were descended from the nomadic Indo-European tribe called Medes (McKiernan, 2006; White, 2000). Scholars also argued that the Kurds might be the people of Gutium who lived in the ancient Sumerian civilization (Izady, 1992; Waheed, 1958; White, 2000), or an ethnically new group who were formed by the mix of ancient Turkic, Persian, and Arabic people (Bois, 1966; White, 2000).

Historically, the Kurdish society has been fundamentally tribal—composed of tribes, confederations, and feudal groups (O'Ballance, 1996; van Bruinessen, 1978). Each tribe varies from approximately 500 to 3,000 families, and they are often tied to one another by blood and territorial loyalty (McDowall, 2000; O'Ballance, 1996, p. 4). Over time, some of these small tribal units ally themselves to form larger groups called confederations to provide improved security for their people (O'Ballance, 1996).

Kurdish elites have been referred to by traditional titles including agha, bey, and sheikh. Bey is a title given to the chief of a Kurdish tribe, whereas agha is a title used by rich landowners in the eastern parts of Turkey. Aghas usually control the water and land allocation, and they also maintain contact with other tribal leaders (White, 2000, p. 19). On the other hand, sheikh is a title used by the leaders of religious sects (van Bruinessen, 1978).

Kurds speak a language derived from the Iranian branch of the Indo-European language family (White, 2000). There are three major dialects of Kurdish—Kurmanji (Northern Kurdish), Sorani (Central Kurdish), and Pehlawani (Southern Kurdish). Kurmanji is the most-spoken dialect, and it is the language of the Kurds of Turkey; Sorani and Pehlawani are used by the Kurds of Iraq and Iran, respectively. The vocabulary of these dialects differ from one another, much as as Dutch and German languages differ (McDowall, 2000). Additionally, the Kurds who live in the central Turkish Kurdistan area speak a dialect called Zaza, which differs completely from the other major Kurdish dialects in its grammar and vocabulary (McDowall, 2000; Olson, 1996; White, 2000). In fact, this Zaza-speaking group do not regard themselves as Kurdish. Rather, they self-identify as a branch of the Kizilbas—a people whose origin is believed to extend to the Dailamites, Iranians inhabiting the mountainous region of northern Iran (McDowall, 2000; Waheed, 1958; White, 2000).

Approximately 80 percent of the Kurds follow Orthodox Sunni Islam similar to Sunni Turks (White, 2000, p. 30). The only difference is that Turks follow the Hanefi school of jurisprudence, whereas Kurds follow the Shafi rite (Mardin, 1989; McDowall, 2000). Fifteen percent of the Kurds are Shias, similar to the Iranians, and the remaining 5 percent of the Kurds follow the Alevi, Christian, and Yezidi beliefs (Romano, 2006, p. 3).

Kurds have large family structures. Their reproductive rate is almost three times that of Turks, Iranians, and Arabs (Ahmed & Gunter, 2005; McKiernan, 2006). Today, there are approximately 30 million Kurds living in the Middle East across Turkey (16 million), Iran (6 million), Iraq (5 to 6 million), and Syria (2 million) (CIA World Fact Book, 2017). Additionally, hundreds of thousands of Kurds live in European capitals for political and economic reasons (McKiernan, 2006).

The economy of Kurdistan has largely depended on livestock breeding and agriculture (White, 2000). Sharecropping—renting the lands of rich landlords in return for a fixed proportion of the crop—is still the principal economic activity for the Kurdish peasants (van Bruinessen, 1978; White, 2000). The decrease in the demand of labor due to the mechanization of agriculture in the 1970s forced many Kurdish families to seek new lines of employment. Some of these families moved to major Turkish cities to find industry-related jobs, whereas others started to work as seasonal agricultural workers—migrating from one city to another all across Turkey during the high-cropping seasons (White, 2000).

The identification of the Kurds as a distinct nation is a relatively new phenomenon (O'Ballance, 1996). Despite existing for thousands of years, Kurds have been unable to unify themselves as a single political entity largely due to tribal and religious divisions (McDowall, 2000). Until the 20th century, Kurdish tribes preferred to submit to and assimilate into the cultures of the central governments that surrounded their territories—Persians, Arabs, Russians, and Ottoman Turks—rather than pursuing their national interests (Romano, 2006; van Bruinessen, 1978). During those periods, the Kurdish tribal leaders were allowed to act free locally but were required to supply mercenary soldiers for the powers that controlled their lands (O'Ballance, 1996). For example, the Kurds provided troops to the Islamic armies (during the Turkish and Arabic rules) to fight against the crusades, Byzantium Empire, Armenia, and Persia (McDowall, 2000).

Today, the Kurds remain the largest ethnic community in the world that does not have a state—composed of a number of different groups, each differing in their political demands, language, and religious orientation (Kendal, 1993). Despite these existing and potentially dividing lines, Kurdish aspirations eventually came to include their own nation or, at the least, a measure of political and cultural autonomy. As will be seen, their nationalist movement and the Turkish government's response to it underlies PKK terrorism today—and, of course, the life that Deniz would pursue.

The Long Relationship Between the Kurds and Turks

The first conflict between the Turks and the Kurds occurred during the 16th century when the Ottoman Empire was preparing an offensive against Iran. With the encouragement of the Iranians, the Alevi Kurds started a large uprising against the Turks and delayed the Ottoman's plans to invade Persian territories (Izady, 1992; McDowall, 2000). One year later, in 1514, the Turks first suppressed the Kurdish Alevi threat and then inflicted a sharp defeat to the Iranians. More than 40,000 Alevi Kurds died during this offensive (de Bellaigue, 2009).

The defeat of the Iranians and the growing military strength of the Ottoman Empire encouraged the Kurds to establish close relations with the Ottoman Turks. Unlike the Iranians who appointed Iranian administrators to control Kurdish towns, the Turks appointed Kurdish rulers to Kurdistan and provided them with local autonomy (McDowall, 2000). This simple governing principle—letting the Kurds establish their autonomous administrations in return for accepting Ottoman suzerainty and promising to protect the Ottoman territories against Iranian threats—allowed the Turks to carry out their expansionist activities in Europe and Balkans during the 17th and 18th centuries (O'Ballance, 1996; White, 2000).

The First Rebellions Against the Turks

Nevertheless, towards the end of the 18th century, the decline of the military and political powers of the Ottoman Empire changed the course of the relationship between the Turks and Kurds. In 1827, the Turkish fleet was destroyed by French, British, and Russian forces. Five years later, the Greeks declared their independence. Witnessing this decline, the Kurdish tribal chiefs began to side with the new emerging powers—Russia and the European countries. In fact, only one year after the Navarino Battle, the Kurds (as well as Armenians) helped the Russian forces to invade Turkish cities in the eastern regions (McDowall, 2000).

During this period, the European and Russian powers exploited the weaknesses of the Ottoman authority and sent thousands of Christian missionaries to the areas where Kurds and Armenians lived. These missionaries gained the trust of the Muslim Kurds and the Christian Armenians—the two groups that can be provoked against the Turks when needed—by establishing hospitals as well as educational and religious institutions (de Bellaigue, 2009).

In fact, in 1831, being seduced by the promises given by the missionaries in the region, Mir Muhammad, a Kurdish confederation leader, started an uprising that killed the leaders of other dominant Kurdish tribes that were under Ottoman protection (Izady, 1992; Waheed, 1958). In 1849, another

Mir, Bedir Khan, declared his independence by aligning his power with the tribal chiefs of the Hakkari, Van, Muş, and Bitlis (Olson, 1996).

The Emergence of the Sheikhs

(Religious) Leaders in Kurdistan

The Turks took strict measures to prevent the emergence of new rebellions in the region—the Kurdish hereditary positions were canceled out and these positions were filled with governors appointed by Istanbul (van Bruinessen, 1978). However, the Kurdish society rejected the authority of their new administrators and began to visit the religious leaders, the sheikhs, to settle their disputes (de Bellaigue, 2009; Izady, 1992; Olson, 1996; Waheed, 1958). Thus, the suppression of the Kurdish rulers unintentionally resulted in the emergence of the religious sheikhs as powerful political leaders with civil administrative duties (Olson, 1996). Over time, these sheiks accumulated such religious and political influence in the region that they began to threaten the Ottoman authorities. In 1880, Sheikh Ubaydallah declared independence by starting a large uprising with the support of the British who sent him ammunition and weapons under the cover of famine relief (Olson, 1996).

Creation of Hamidiye Regiments

Beyond the danger posed by British-backed Kurdish uprisings, Russians and Iranians had also started to support the Armenian separatist activities within the Ottoman territories. By 1885, the Armenians were able to establish armed cells all over eastern Anatolia. In response to these threats, in 1891, the Turks created an irregular mountain force—the Hamidiye Regiments—in the areas that the Kurds inhabited (de Bellaigue, 2009; Waheed, 1958). By selecting the members of this force from the Sunni Muslim Kurds, Sultan Abdulhamid II strengthened the ties of nationalist Kurds to the Ottoman Empire and provided a defensive force against possible Russian and Armenian offensives in the eastern borders of the empire (Olson, 1996).

Soon, tens of thousands of Sunni Kurdish tribesmen enrolled into Hamidiye Regiments due to the economic, educational, and social advantages offered to them—exemption from tax, release from service in the regular Ottoman army, and the privilege of being trained in a special military school in Istanbul (only for the chiefs, their sons, and high-ranking commanders) (de Bellaigue, 2009; McDowall, 2000). By 1895, there were 57 Hamidiye Regiments (approximately 40,000 soldiers) in the region, which tipped the balance of power away from the Armenians and Russians to the Ottomans (Olson, 1996, p. 135).

Nevertheless, the soldiers of the Hamidiye Regiments, the armed Kurds, soon began to abuse their power over Armenians and other Kurdish tribesmen who were not enrolled in the system. The reports indicated that members of these regiments began to collect taxes on villagers, invaded their territories, forced the peasants to provide lodging and food during the winter months, and committed other atrocities under the pretext of maintaining law and order (de Bellaigue, 2009; Kendal, 1993).

The creation of Hamidiye Regiments enabled the Ottoman Empire to protect itself against the Russian and Armenian threats. However, the establishment of these forces also contributed to the reemergence of Kurdish nationalism between 1891 and 1914. During this time, the sons of important Kurdish chiefs who were trained in Istanbul (at the School for Nomadic Tribes) became exposed to nationalist sentiments as they were put into the same classrooms with the sons of nationalist Arab leaders. Thus, the Sultan's plan to convert these illiterate Kurdish youths into educated and loyal defenders of the pan-Islamic Ottoman Empire did not work (Olson, 1996; White, 2000).

Dissolution of the Ottoman Empire

In 1908, a large group of highly educated upper-class citizens called the Young Turks started a revolution and declared a new constitutional monarchy for the empire. This new administrative system not only disbanded the Hamidiye Regiments but also removed the titles of the ruling elites in Kurdistan—the chiefs, notables, and sheikhs (O'Ballance, 1996). In response, the Kurdish leaders, especially the religious sheikhs, incited the public to start an uprising against the new regime by arguing that the Young Turks were destroying the religious structure of the empire (McDowall, 2000).

Seeing the disturbance of the Kurds as an opportunity to settle into Anatolia, Russia offered autonomy to disgruntled Kurds under Russian protectorate status. Kurdish tribal leaders were promised that they would be allowed to use their own language for official and educational purposes and to adopt Islamic religious rules for the administration of justice and taxation. Obtaining the support and the lucrative promises from Russia, some nationalist Kurds openly started their resistance against Turkish rule (McDowall, 2000; Waheed, 1958). However, participation to this uprising was limited, because the Kurds were aware that Russia was offering the same promises to the Armenians, who were trying to establish an independent Armenia in the same areas in which the Kurds lived (McDowall, 2000).

World War I: Turks and Kurds Fighting Together

The start of World War I fueled the ethnic conflict within the Ottoman Empire. The Kurds sided with the Muslim Turks as the other minorities in the region—Armenians and Assyrians—declared that they would fight along with Christian Russia (O'Ballance, 1996). In 1914, the Russians defeated the Ottoman army. Then, using the help provided by the Armenian and Assyrian irregular military forces, they penetrated deep into Anatolia and invaded the major Kurdish cities (de Bellaigue, 2009). It is estimated that more than 600,000 Kurds lost their lives between 1915 and 1918 (O'Ballance, 1996, p. 10). As noted by McDowall (2000, p. 106):

> the Armenians were sweeping the countryside, massacring men, women, and children and burning their homes. Babies were shot in their mothers' arms, small children were horribly mutilated, and women were stripped and beaten.

Fortunately for the Turks, in 1917, the Bolshevik Revolution occurred in Russia and Russian troops withdrew from the Ottoman territories. Kurds and Turks collected the weapons abandoned by the Russian forces and engaged in retaliatory acts against the Armenians and Assyrians (O'Ballance, 1996; Jawideh, 2006).

Partition of the Kurdistan Region

In 1918, when World War I had ended, the victors decided to place the Kurdistan region under the control of three states: Turkey, Britain, and France (O'Ballance, 1996). This governance structure caused the Kurds to become increasingly concerned about their future. Nevertheless, as it was the case in the past, the tribal rivalry among the Kurds prevented them from unifying around a national goal (McDowall, 2000). Some Kurds favored autonomy under Turkish rule, whereas others favored the rule of the French or English. The Dersim Kurds did not want to side with either the Turks or with the Allied forces (McDowall, 2000; Olson, 1996).

In the middle of 1919, the Allied forces began to implement one of the conditions of the armistice—the partition of the Ottoman territories. Greeks landed in the Aegean region with thousands of troops, Italians took control of the Mediterranean region; and the British occupied Istanbul and Iraq. In accordance with the armistice, the Ottoman administration in Istanbul instructed the Turkish army officials to surrender themselves with their arms and weapons to the Allied forces (McKiernan, 2006). Nevertheless, a group of high-ranked Turkish military officials acted against these orders and declared a protocol that renounced the legality of the Ottoman authority in Istanbul.

The leader of this group, Mustafa Kemal Ataturk, stated that the administration in Istanbul was not legitimate anymore because it was acting according to the wishes of the Allied forces (Romano, 2006). Contrary to the armistice, Mustafa encouraged his commanders to recruit new soldiers from the local public and to prepare for an offensive against occupying forces (Lewis, 1968). Mustafa started his campaign based on Turkish and Kurdish brotherhood and focused on the importance of religious fraternity in defeating the invaders (McKiernan, 2006).

Seeing the potential for an uprising, British officials approached the Kurdish tribal leaders and promised them an independent Kurdistan if they were to fight against the Turks during the invasion of the Ottoman territories (Olson, 1996). Nevertheless, an important discovery in the region forced Great Britain to reconsider the promises given the Kurds—rich oil beds were found in Southern Kurdistan, in Suleimaniye, Mosul, Kirkuk, and Arbil (McDowall, 2000). In 1920, soon after the discovery of oil in the region, the Ottoman government was forced to sign the Treaty of Sèvres (O'Ballance, 1996). The southern part of Kurdistan was put under the control of the British whereas the northern part was given autonomy under the Turks.

The Kurds initially welcomed the signing of this treaty because it gave them the right to appeal to the League of Nations within one year, if complete independence from Turkey was desired (McKiernan, 2006, p. 90). However, later developments in the region confused the Kurds. Even though the Treaty of Sèvres promised them an independent land, the Armenians, under the protection of the Allied forces, had begun to occupy the Kurdish lands. In the context of these developments, a majority of the Kurdish tribes decided to support Mustafa Kemal's military initiative to protect their homeland from invasion (van Bruinessen, 1978).

The Kocgiri Uprising

Nevertheless, the Alevi Kurds from the Dersim region started a large uprising when Mustafa Kemal was dealing with the Armenian offensives in the eastern parts of Turkey (Romano, 2006). The rebels had blockaded the supply roads and seized a large amount of weaponry and ammunition that was being delivered to the Turks and Kurds to be used in their fight against the Armenians (Romano, 2006).

Mustafa Kemal settled the dispute by accepting the demands of the Alevi Kurds because sending Turkish troops to quell the rebellion would have weakened the Turkish army's fight against the Armenians in the eastern fronts. However, because Ankara approached the conflict in a lenient way, the Dersim Kurds increased their demands. Mustafa Kemal continued to refrain from rejecting the demands of the Alevi Kurds until the Armenian forces were defeated in 1921. After that point, Dersim was encircled with troops and the Kurdish uprising was suppressed. All Alevi tribal chiefs were imprisoned (Romano, 2006).

Treaty of Brotherhood

In the meantime, Bolshevik Russia signed the Treaty of Brotherhood in 1921—being the first country to formally recognize the legitimacy of the Turkish government in Ankara. Establishing diplomatic relations with Russia was important for Ankara for two reasons. First, in the absence of Russian support, the Armenians made a request for peace and completely abandoned their territorial claims from Turkey (McDowall, 2000). Second, guaranteed that Russia would not attack from the eastern fronts, Turkey was able to start a second offensive on its western front against the Greeks, ultimately destroying the occupying Greek forces (Olson, 1996).

British Policy Toward the Kurds of Turkey

The Kurdish issue became the main diplomatic concern between Turkey and England during the mid-1920s and onward. British officials were well aware of the discontent among the Kurdish tribal leaders due to the growing Turkish nationalistic inspirations. Therefore, some British officials favored the idea of arming and then using the disaffected Kurds to secure some political advantages from the new government in Ankara. However, another group of British intelligence officers opposed this option by arguing that such a policy not only would be very costly to Great Britain but also would antagonize the Indian Muslims (Olson, 1996).

On the other hand, three other developments had reduced British hopes of creating an independent Kurdistan in the Middle East. First, the Turks had successfully suppressed the Kocgiri rebellion in 1921. Second, the British-appointed Iraqi leader King Faysal had objected to the independence of the Iraqi Kurds by arguing that separating the Sunni Kurdish part from Iraq would place the Shias in a very strong position within the national assembly of Iraq. Third, the Ankara government had already started to develop diplomatic relations with the Soviet Union as a way of countering the establishment of a free Kurdistan under British control. Close relations between the Turks and the Russians would jeopardize the concessions obtained by Britain on the use of the Straits in Istanbul (McDowall, 2000). Weighing all these developments, Britain gave up the idea of instigating Kurds against the Turks.

Kurds in the New Turkish Republic

Before and during the war of liberation, Mustafa Kemal had promised the Kurds that the new nation would be a Muslim state based on Turkish and Kurdish brotherhood (McDowall, 2000). According to Olson (1996, p. 3), Mustafa Kemal stated that:

> As long as there are fine people with honor and respect, Turks and Kurds will continue to live together as brothers around the institution of the caliphate, and an unshakeable iron tower will be raised against internal and external enemies.

In fact, in 1922, the new government in Ankara had prepared a draft law proposing an autonomous administration for the Kurds in which they could protect their national customs and language. However, the majority of the Kurdish deputies had opposed the enforcement of this law by arguing that it was not guaranteeing the degree of autonomy they desired. As a result, the law was postponed to be discussed later but it never came to the agenda of the Turkish Grand National Assembly again (Olson, 1996).

In January 1923, Mustafa Kemal had again discussed the possibility of establishing autonomous Kurdish administrations across Turkey:

> …certainly a kind of regional autonomy is possible. In that case, in whatever province there are Kurds, they can administer themselves autonomously. Moreover, when the people of Turkey are a subject of discussion, the Kurds must be included. If we do not include the Kurds, the Kurdish Question will always be present. (McDowall, 2000, p. 190; see also Olson, 1996, pp. 214–215)

However, the Treaty of Lausanne (which was signed to replace the conditions of the Treaty of Sèvres), did not include any clause regarding the future of Kurds within the new republic (de Bellaigue, 2009). The Kurds were not even allowed to benefit from the minority rights that were provided to the Armenians, Greeks, and Jews with this new treaty (Lewis, 1968; White, 2000). Moreover, Mustafa Kemal had declared that the new Turkish Republic was going to be a secular Turkish nation state (de Bellaigue, 2009). He had outlawed the Islamic courts and rules and had forced the use of the Latin alphabet in place of Arabic script (Lewis, 1968; McKiernan, 2006, p. 92).

In fact, the new republic initiated the forced assimilation of the Kurds. Thus, official positions in Kurdistan were filled by Turks; the Kurdish names for places were replaced by Turkish names; Kurdish schools, associations, and social and political organizations were closed down; the use of the Kurdish language at public places was prohibited; and some Kurdish lands were expropriated and then given to the Turkish-speaking population (Lewis, 1968; White, 2000).

Further, in 1924, Mustafa Kemal outlawed the institution of the caliphate and so severed the last single tie between the Kurds and the Turks. The caliph was considered to be the successor of the Prophet Mohammed and also the leader of the Islamic world. The Turks had been regarded as the leaders of the Islamic world since the 15th century because this important position had only been succeeded by Ottoman sultans. The abolition of the caliphate had two devastating effects on Kurds. First, it was not race or culture but religious fraternity that had bonded the Kurds to the Turks for centuries (McKiernan, 2006). As the caliphate was abolished, there was no reason for the Kurds to live with the Turks under the same administration. Second, the abolition of caliphate caused the closure of all religious schools and institutions, which were the only source of education left available for the Kurds following the banning of the use of the Kurdish language in 1923 (van Bruinessen, 1978).

Sheikh Said Rebellion

These secularist and discriminatory policies caused great resentment among the Kurds of Turkey (Olson, 1996). As a result, the Kurds organized a clandestine group named Azadi (Freedom). Even though Azadi was a nationalist organization, a charismatic Kurdish sheikh was appointed as the leader since religion was still a much stronger driving force for the Kurds than were appeals to nationalistic feelings (O'Ballance, 1996; Romano, 2006; White, 2000).

Using his religious authority, Sheikh Said incited large crowds of Kurds to rebel against the new Turkish state for the restoration of the caliphate (Izady, 1992). Even though the rebellion was successful in defeating the Turkish forces in the region, two groups of Kurds refused to support it due to religious differences and economic concerns (Romano, 2006). First, the Alevi Kurds made it clear that they would never follow a Kurdish uprising led by a Naqshbandi Kurdish Sheikh (White, 2000). They even helped the Turkish forces to prevent the spread of the rebellion to other Kurdish cities (Romano, 2006). Second, the wealthy urban Kurdish notables rejected the call of Sheikh Said and declared that they would stay loyal to the new Turkish government—so as not to jeopardize their economic activities and privileged lifestyles in the region (White, 2000).

In the end, with the help of the Alevi Kurdish tribes, the Turkish forces suppressed the Sheikh Said uprising. To prevent the emergence of potential new uprisings, Ankara started a brutal campaign of repression in Kurdistan—Sheikh Said and his command cadre were all executed, hundreds of villages were destroyed, thousands of innocent women, men, and children were killed, and the name of the region was changed from Kurdistan to eastern Anatolia (McKiernan, 2006; Romano, 2006). The settlement law was enacted, and the Kurds who supported the rebellion were forcefully relocated to the western parts of the country.

Later, Prime Minister Ismet Inonu ordered the establishment of the Tribunal of Independence in Kurdistan and empowered judges of this court with the authority to impose capital punishment. The law was implemented for two years and approximately 700 Kurds—teachers, authors, organizers and other intellectuals—were executed without proper trial (Lewis, 1968; McDowall, 2000, p. 196; McKiernan, 2006).

In the end, the Turkish army was able to establish control in Kurdistan but had lost the hearts and mind of the people. Kurds were reduced to a second-class citizen status and a discriminatory regime had developed in Turkey. In 1926, the foreign minister of Turkey, Tevfik Rustu (Saracoglu), explicitly stated that the Kurds had to be suppressed and assimilated until they disappeared (Romano, 2006). He pronounced that the Kurds':

> cultural level is so low, their mentality so backward, that they cannot be simply in the general Turkish body politic…They will die out, economically unfitted for the struggle for life in competition with the more advanced and cultured Turks…as many as can will emigrate into Persia and Iraq, while the rest will simply undergo the elimination of the unfit. (quoted in McDowall, 2000, p. 200)

The Mount Ararat Uprising (the Khoybun Revolt)

In the meantime, the Kurdish exiles in Europe and the Middle East (Paris, Cairo, Tabriz, Aleppo, Beirut, and Damascus) met in Lebanon and established a new organization—Khoybun (Independence). Unlike the previous Kurdish organizations, Khoybun advertised itself as an Armenian-Kurdish organization and cooperated with the Armenian Dashnak Party against the Turks (White, 2000). Obtaining significant monetary help from the Shah of Iran, Khoybun formed a trained Kurdish military force in Aleppo (O'Ballance, 1996).

In 1927, the Khoybun started its first offensive in the Mount Ararat region and enjoyed success in defeating the Turkish forces (White, 2000). Ankara tried to soothe the uprising via negotiations, declaring a general amnesty, halting deportations of Kurds, and permitting already deported Kurds to return to their homes (White, 2000). Despite these concessions, the Kurds declined peace negotiations. Moreover, the Alevi Kurdish tribes who had helped Turkish forces during the suppression of the Sheikh Said rebellion were also supporting this rebellion.

In 1929, losing hope that the uprising could be settled through negotiation, the Turks first entered Iran to prevent Iranian military and economic support to the rebels. Then, Turkish air forces bombed the positions of the Kurdish and Armenian rebels and recaptured control of their lands (Olson, 1996). In an effort to take revenge for the Turks who were killed by the Kurdish and Armenian rebels, the Turkish forces exterminated thousands of rebels that were captured. Approximately 3,000 non-combatants were also reported to be killed (McDowall, 2000, p. 206).

In May 1932, a new law was enacted by the Ankara government, requiring the relocation of almost one million Kurds to the western parts of Turkey. The goal was to prevent future Sunni Kurdish uprisings by extinguishing their language and identity (O'Ballance, 1996; White, 2000).

Dersim Rebellion

Soon after suppressing the Sunni Kurdish threat, the Turks decided to focus on the Alevi Kurdish tribes that would be a potential threat in the future. The Dersim Kurds, the most serious threat to Ankara among the Kurds, were refusing to pay their taxes and rejecting the authority of the new Turkish republic. In fact, in 1926, the bureaucrats in Ankara had prepared a report that highlighted the necessity of military repression to make the Dersim people recognize the Turkish suzerainty. The report has described this thinking:

> Dersim is an abscess on the Turkish Republic and it must be removed, for the sake of the country's well-being. It is useless to try and win the allegiance of Dersimlis by building hospitals, factories, and so forth in Dersim. Only stern measures would suffice. (quoted in White, 2000, p. 79)

In 1936, ten years after this report had been prepared, Mustafa Kemal delivered a speech at the opening ceremony of the Turkish Grand National Assembly, in which he endorsed the use of military measures for the uprooting of the Dersim problem: "Our most important interior problem is the Dersim problem. No matter what cost, we have to remove this abscess at its roots" (quoted in White, 2000, p. 79).

Upon Mustafa Kemal's call for action, the name of the region, Dersim, was removed from the official records, and the region was given a Turkish name—Tunceli. Turkish troops then started their offensive. The Kurds evacuated their homes and ran into the pastures and caves in the surrounding mountains to save their lives from the heavy bombardments. Records indicated that the Turkish army destroyed the abandoned villages to make sure that the population would not return. Seyit Riza, the leader of the Dersim Alevis, asked British officials to start an international intervention in Dersim to save his tribe:

> Three million Kurds live in their country and ask only to live in peace and freedom, while keeping their race, language, traditions, culture, and civilization. Please let the Kurdish people benefit from the high moral influence of [your] government and to bring an end to this cruel injustice. (quoted in McKiernan, 2006, p. 94; see also McDowall, 2000, p. 208)

In 1937, the Turkish forces captured Seyit Riza, his two sons, and ten of his command cadre and executed them all (McKiernan, 2006; White, 2000). The local population who refused to surrender—men, women, and children—were subjected to mass killings via aerial bombings, poisonous gas, and heavy artillery shootings (Dersimi, 1992; McKiernan, 2006). Turkish soldiers killed hundreds of civilians by throwing dynamite into the caves in which they were hiding (White, 2000, p. 83). It is estimated that

40,000 Dersim Kurds lost their lives during these military offensives. Until the end of the 1950s, the area was kept under military control (McDowall, 2000, p. 93; White, 2000, p. 83).

Multi-Party System

In the 1940s, many Turkish politicians were funded to travel to Europe to examine the economic structures of the developed countries. During their visits, these officials also had the chance to observe the more participatory and democratic nature of the western countries, and, as a result, they began to criticize the authoritarian single-party system in Turkey (Romano, 2006). In 1946, these politicians separated their ties with Mustafa Kemal's Republican People's Party (CHP) and then established the Democratic Party (DP).

The DP's political campaigns revolved around the issue of lifting the bans on religious and individual freedoms that were enacted during the early years of the Turkish Republic. Many people, especially the Kurds who were harshly repressed during the Kemalist regime, viewed the DP as a protector against the current authoritarian regime and began to support it (McKiernan, 2006). Almost all of the Kurdish sheiks ordered their followers to support the DP in hopes of regaining their religious freedoms.

The DP's campaign of securing votes by exploiting the religious sentiments of the society in fact worked—the party won the 1950 general elections with a super majority (van Bruinessen, 1978). Within the same year, the DP government enacted a series of policies to revive the Islamic traditions in the country—the call for prayer was allowed to be recited in Arabic again, Islamic education became mandatory in the school curriculums, construction of more than 5,000 mosques was financed, state-controlled religious schools were established to train imams, and the sheikhs were allowed to rerun their seminaries (McDowall, 2000).

Further, the Democratic Party also allocated positions for the Kurdish tribal leaders in the party administration to benefit from the large crowd who were loyal to aghas and sheikhs. They then co-opted the agha system (which was outlawed during the early years of the republic), arguing that tribal leaders would play a more efficient role in the resolving of issues arising between the villagers and local authorities. These incentives secured another great victory for the DP in the 1954 elections (Romano, 2006, p. 40).

Revival of Kurdish Nationalism

During this term, from 1950 to 1954, the DP government, using the U.S. Marshall Plan, imported thousands of tractors into the country; the number of tractors increased from 1,750 to 40,000 in just a couple of years (Lewis, 1968; McDowall, 2000, p. 401). This sudden mechanization of agriculture proved detrimental to the well-being of the Kurds for two reasons. First, it reduced the need for agricultural labor, which resulted in thousands of Kurds relocating to the western parts of Turkey in search of jobs (van Bruinessen, 1978). Second, the small Kurdish families who were unable to buy a tractor had to rent this machinery from the aghas, allocating a portion of their crops as payment. Over the years the rental costs increased and these farmers reached a point where they were not making any profit. Thus, they sold their lands to rich aghas and left the region.

No one would have guessed that these agricultural reforms would have created the socio-economic groundwork for the revival of Kurdish nationalism in the following decades. The relocation of Kurds to western cities provided Kurdish youths with increased educational opportunities. This new generation of educated Kurds not only revived Kurdish nationalist sentiments, but also negatively judged the status of tribal and religious leaders because they were exploiting the peasant Kurds for their own political and economic gains (van Bruinessen, 1978; White, 2000).

The Military Coup of 1961

Turkey witnessed a series of economic and political upheavals between the mid-1950s and the beginnings of the 1960s. In 1955, the increasing international debt of the country led to a huge economic crisis. Further, the people had developed hostile attitudes towards one another due to the extreme partisan politics. Prime Minister Menderes also had increased his autocratic control in the country by restricting basic human rights, including freedom of the press and public meetings (McDowall, 2000; Romano, 2006).

This depressing condition of the country encouraged the Turkish military to topple the government in May 1961 (de Bellaigue, 2009). The military rule (National Union Committee) first executed the prime minister and then closed down all political party branches to prevent further polarization in the country. In this context, the titles held by Kurdish tribal and religious leaders were also outlawed because these elites had played a large role in polarizing the people by working for political parties. All Kurdish leaders were exiled to remote locations, and the lands they acquired due to the mechanization of agriculture were redistributed among the poor peasants to reestablish the economy in the region (de Bellaigue, 2009).

Mandatory Boarding Schools for Kurds

Also in 1961, the military administration implemented a law that required mandatory education for Kurdish children in distant boarding schools located in the western parts of the country. The goal was to assimilate their Kurdish identity by socializing these children with the values of the Turkish Republic. Nevertheless, contrary to what was planned, many of these Kurdish children had discovered their own national identity due to their mockery by the Turkish students during their education in the Turkish regions (de Bellaigue, 2009; McDowall, 2000).

In the following decades, many of these Kurdish children graduated from Turkish universities, obtained professional jobs, formed social organizations to discuss the future of the Kurds, and invited their siblings and relatives to follow their road to success. Soon, there emerged a well-educated and hardworking Kurdish class in the major cities of Turkey (de Bellaigue, 2009).

Co-Optation of the Agha System

The civil administration that was elected after the military rule of 1961 argued that it was easier to deal with the autocratic tribal leaders than with illiterate Kurdish peasants. Thus, the Kurdish tribal leaders were allowed to return to their homes and take back their lands from the peasants. In return for this favor, they were expected to instruct their tribes to support the ruling political party. Powerful again, the aghas began to serve as the agents of the ruling political elites in Ankara so as to protect their own privileges (van Bruinessen, 1978).

During this term, trying to please the elites in Ankara, the aghas ignored the education and the economic development of their peasants (de Bellaigue, 2009). As a result, thousands of Kurds abandoned their villages and moved to bigger cities, including Diyarbakır, Istanbul, Malatya, Adana, Sivas, and Kayseri, in hopes of finding better employment opportunities (McDowall, 2000).

Fight Against the Agha Class

The children of the relocated Kurds, and the Kurdish children who were subjected to mandatory education by the 1961 military rule, became exposed to nationalist and socialist ideas during their university years. These young Kurds embraced leftist (Marxist) ideas and argued that tribal affiliations had to be destroyed because the Kurdish tribal leaders were blocking the national revival by serving the interests of the Turkish politicians in Ankara (Romano, 2006).

Some of these highly educated Kurds returned to Kurdistan and taught communism and leftist ideas at different levels of educational settings, instead of applying the curriculum set by the Turkish Ministry of Education. In this way, the poor Kurdish youth in eastern Anatolia also became exposed to Marxism and began to criticize the agha system (de Bellaigue, 2009).

Kurdish tribal leaders found it difficult to control this new generation of Marxist nationalist Kurds. Thus, Ankara intervened and took measures to prevent the spread of this nationalist awakening. First, the Kurdish youths who were enrolled to do mandatory military service became subjected to a special training program in which they were taught that there was no such thing as a Kurd, but mountain Turks who had forgotten their own language (de Bellaigue, 2009). Thus, from then on, the Kurds in Turkey began to be described as mountain Turks (McKiernan, 2006). Second, the Turkish Radio and Television Agency (TRT) established several radio stations in Kurdish areas and spread the propaganda of Turkish nationalism. The TRT even hired some of the popular Kurdish singers to sing in Turkish (de Bellaigue, 2009).

As Ankara continued to implement these discriminatory policies, the Kurds began to join the Turkish Worker's Party—a pro-Kremlin Communist party—and then organized mass meetings to protest the oppression of the Kurdish identity in Turkey. Despite being a Turkish party, the TWP attracted many Kurds in Ankara and Istanbul because this socialist party was also against the traditional ruling elites, monopolies, and racist policies (White, 2000).

Using the material and human resources provided by the TWP, Kurdish intellectuals disseminated literary pieces in Kurdish to protect Kurdish literature from extinction. However, in 1967, Ankara enacted another discriminatory law, this time forbidding the publication of materials in Kurdish (Izady, 1992).

Ironically, while Ankara was closing down the Kurdish magazines and newspapers on the charge of encouraging separatism, nationalist Turks were given a free hand to distribute racist publications against the Kurds. For example, in 1967, two articles published on a Turkish magazine included extreme derogatory terms for the Kurds of Turkey.

> Kurds do not have the faces of human beings; they should be migrated to Africa to join the half-human half-animals who lived there. (quoted in McDowall, 2000, p. 408)
>
> Let the Kurds go away from Turkey! But to where? To wherever they like! Let them go to Iran, to Pakistan, to India, to Barzani. Let them ask at the United Nations to find them a home in Africa. Let them go away before the Turkish nation gets angry...the day when you will rise up to cut Turkey into pieces, you will see to what a hell we shall send you. (quoted in Romano, 2006, p. 110; see also White, 2000, p. 133)

A great deal of Kurdish unrest occurred in Turkey soon after the publication of these articles. The demonstrators demanded the arrest of the authors and a ban on the further publication of the magazine (White, 2000). Unfortunately, the authorities did not take any steps to find the authors (Romano, 2006). Rather, a military repression started in Kurdistan, and the founder of the first Kurdish political party in Turkey (Democratic Party of Turkish Kurdistan)—Faik Bucak—was assassinated (White, 2000).

Revolutionary Eastern Cultural Hearths

Between 1968 and 1970, there was turmoil in Turkey. Fights between the leftists and rightists had spread to universities, students from different ideologies had begun to kill each other, and the universities had suspended their educational activities due to the violent outbreaks among their students (Lewis, 1968). In this ideological conflict, the state was clandestinely helping the rightist movements to stop the spread of communism and Kurdish nationalism. Thus, the Turkish government provided rightists with arms and economic resources while also curbing the activities of legal leftist organizations (Olson, 1996). In fact, in 1970, the Turkish Worker's Party, the only political outlet for the Kurds, had been declared illegal after officially accepting the existence of the Kurds as a distinct nation in Turkey:

> There are a Kurdish people in the East of Turkey. The fascist authorities representing the ruling classes have subjected the Kurdish people to a policy of assimilation and intimidation which has often become a bloody repression. (quoted in Kendal, 1993, p. 97)

After the TWP was closed down, many leftist Turks and the nationalist Kurds traveled to Lebanon to obtain paramilitary training at the Palestinian al-Fatah military camps. Their goal was to gain the skills to fight more successfully against the state-sponsored rightist movements in Turkey. Soon, the Kurds who were trained in Lebanon returned to Turkish Kurdistan and established the Revolutionary Eastern Cultural Hearths (DDKO). Records indicate that the Turkish troops that were sent to the region to arrest these Palestinian-trained Kurdish leftists engaged in extreme inhumane tactics to extract information from the peasants.

> Since the end of January special military units have undertaken a war in the regions of Diyarbakır, Mardin, Siirt, and Hakkari under the guise of hunting bandits. Every village is surrounded at a certain hour, its inhabitants rounded up. Troops assemble men and women separately, and demand the men to surrender their weapons. They beat those who deny possessing any or make other villagers jump on them. They strip men and women naked and violate the latter. Many have died in these operations, some have committed suicide. Naked men and women have cold water thrown over them, and they are whipped. Sometimes women are forced to tie a rope around the penis of their husbands and then to lead him around the village. Women are likewise made to parade naked around the village. Troops demand villagers to provide women for their pleasure and the entire village is beaten if the request is met with refusal. (McDowall, 2000, p. 33)

1971 Military Coup

The beginning of 1971 was chaotic in Turkey. There was widespread turmoil in the country, the state institutions (schools, hospitals, and universities) were not functioning, people were being killed randomly, and the civilian government was having difficulty establishing its control. As a result, the Turkish military seized the government in March 1971 (Romano, 2006).

For the Kurds, the major consequence of the coup was the suppression of the leftist organizations. Being excluded from the prevailing political umbrella, the Kurds began to form clandestine organizations to seek out their national goals (de Bellaigue, 2009; Olson, 1996). However, these underground activities did not last long because the civilian administration, after the military rule had enacted an amnesty, freed thousands of Kurds and leftist Turks that had been arrested following the coup (Romano, 2006).

Re-Polarization of the Country

The polarization in the society occurred again in 1973. The Kurds and Turks who were disappointed by existing social inequalities joined the leftist groups, whereas the nationalist Turks grouped themselves around the far-right movements including the Idealists (Ulkuculer) and Grey Wolves (Bozkurtlar) (Jawideh, 2006).

In contrast to the 1971 insurgency, this time the bureaucracy, trade unions, professional associations, and even the teachers and police were also politicized (Romano, 2006). Parallel administrations were set up between the leftist and rightist members of these state institutions, and members of each group began to kill one another (de Bellaigue, 2009).

These ideological fights soon emerged between the leftist Kurds and nationalist Turks in the Turkish cities, where the Kurds had immigrated decades ago to find better employment opportunities. The nationalist Grey Wolves attacked the shops and houses owned by the Kurds. In return, the Kurds engaged in retaliatory acts by attacking the Turks' properties. The situation became worse towards the end of the 1970s. Approximately 4,000 people were reported to have lost their lives between 1978 and 1980 (McDowall, 2000, p. 415).

1980 Military Coup

Due to this chaos, in 1980, the army again suspended civilian authority and applied strict measures to end the polarization in society—political parties were closed down, leading political figures were arrested, media censorship was applied, ideological affiliation and activities at the universities and state institutions were prohibited, and 60,000 leftist and rightist individuals were arrested (McDowall, 2000, p. 415; Romano, 2006, p. 79).

Between 1980 and 1983, the military rule detained approximately 180,000 people (including Turks and Kurds) and arrested 42,000 of them under the pretext of restoring political stability and expelling the extremists from state institutions (de Bellaigue, 2009, p. 198). In 1983, before handing the administration back to civilian rule, the military junta officially outlawed the use of the Kurdish language in Turkey (Romano, 2006).

Kurdistan Workers' Party (PKK)

The Kurdistan Workers' Party—or, in Kurdish, Partiya Karkerên Kurdistanê—is commonly referred to by the acronym of its Kurdish name, the PKK. The PKK was established in 1974, as a Marxist Leninist organization by a group of 13 Kurdish nationalists who defined themselves as the "Apocular"—the followers of Apo (White, 2000). Abdullah Öcalan, also known popularly as Apo, was the leader of the group. He is the son of a Kurdish peasant family and the eldest of six siblings (Romano, 2006). His association with Kurdish nationalism started in the 1970s, when he was studying political science at Ankara University (McKiernan, 2006). During his university years, Apo undertook active roles in leftist groups. In fact, a leading Turkish leftist figure, Mahir Cayan, became Apo's inspiration during this time to initiate a nationalistic movement based on Marxism and Leninism (Jawideh, 2006; McDowall, 2000).

Apocular's first recruitment activities started in 1975, when Apo and his close associates traveled to the Kurdish cities in eastern Turkey and reached out to the proletariat Kurds (poor and uneducated peasants) who were disappointed by the dictatorial authority of the tribal leaders. The PKK (known as Apocular at that time) became attractive to these Kurds who had been abused by the tribal authorities for years (Romano, 2006).

In 1978, after securing a substantial number of supporters, Apo changed the name of the group first to National Liberation Army and then to the PKK—the Kurdistan Workers' Party (White, 2000). The PKK did not engage in fights with Turkish security forces until 1984. Instead, the new recruits were trained with the teachings of communism, were indoctrinated with the ideas of famous Chinese and Russian revolutionaries (including Mao Tse-tung and Alexander Bek), and then were sent back to their villages to recruit more peasants to fight for the PKK (O'Ballance, 1996; Romano, 2006).

First Attacks

The PKK's first attacks hit the Kurdish traditional ruling elites—aghas, tribal chiefs, and the sheikhs—because, according to Apo, the existence of these leaders was an obstacle for the Kurdish national awakening. Over the years, these traditional ruling elites had established close relationships with Turkish state officials to protect their authoritarian status—at the expense of the revival of the Kurdish nationalist aspirations (McDowall, 2000; Romano, 2006). Thus, Apo argued that the destruction of the traditional ties was necessary to create the new Kurdish mentality because it would save the peasants from oppressed conditions and then liberate their minds.

Aghas and chiefs were aware that the core concept advertised by the PKK ideologues—equality among all—would be detrimental to the well-being of their status among the peasants. Thus, they were hostile to the emergence of the PKK in the region. In fact, the obedience and respect to the aghas had already begun to diminish, because some of these ruling elites had lost their lives due to the missions carried out by the PKK. Many peasants, including young Kurdish men and women, started to join the ranks of the PKK to support this new nationalist movement (McDowall, 2000). Soon, the PKK had become a viable authority in the region.

Nevertheless, the 1980 military coup in Turkey halted the rise of the PKK. Apo and the other senior commanders of the party saved themselves from incarceration by escaping into Syria. However, approximately 1,800 PKK members and sympathizers were imprisoned by the military rule (McDowall, 2000; Romano, 2006).

Between 1980 and 1983, the PKK focused on training and education activities for its members. The PKK recruits who were able to avoid the repressive aftermath of the coup escaped to Palestinian paramilitary camps located in Lebanon. Once there, they were provided with extensive military and ideological training by experienced Palestinian fighters (O'Ballance, 1996; Romano, 2006). During this time, Apo also established diplomatic relations with foreign countries, including Syria, Libya, Northern Iraq, and Lebanon. In fact, history proved that it was these diplomatic relationships that saved the PKK from complete destruction when Turkey was under military rule (de Bellaigue, 2009). For example, the protocol signed between the PKK and the Northern Iraqi Kurdish administration officials, to use the Iraqi-Turkey border, facilitated the PKK's hit-and-run missions against Turkish targets in Turkey (Romano, 2006).

Even though the 1980 military coup curtailed the recruitment activities of the PKK in Turkey, the cruel and inhuman measures applied by the Turkish military forces during and after the coup played into the hands of the PKK. The state's brutal suppression campaign of the Kurds strengthened the growth of the PKK by increasing the number its recruits—people needed little encouragement to join up for revenge. The peasants, who were subjected to indiscriminate violence applied by the security forces, began to support the last remaining Kurdish political organization—the PKK (Romano, 2006).

Return of the Guerillas into Turkey

The PKK members who were trained at Palestinian guerilla camps in Lebanon were sent back to Turkey in smaller groups toward the end of 1983. The ultimate goal was the removal of the Turkish forces from Kurdistan via sudden and unexpected ambushes on important targets, rather than direct confrontation with the security forces (McDowall, 2000).

On August 15, 1984, the PKK started its first armed struggle against Turkish targets by attacking police and gendarmerie bases. PKK members occupied the town of Şemdinli (a border town at the junction of Iran, Iraq, and Turkey) for hours, disseminated the PKK's propaganda, released all prisoners, executed state collaborators, and then escaped into northern Iraq (O'Ballance, 1996). Nevertheless, the Turkish state officials ignored the emergence of this new nationalistic movement by describing these attacks as a product of a small group of bandits who were seeking economic gains (Romano, 2006).

Kurdistan Popular Liberation Front

In 1985, the PKK established the Kurdistan Popular Liberation Front (ERNK) in Turkey to facilitate the supply of provisions for its guerillas who were residing in the mountainous areas and also to increase the number of recruits via indoctrination activities. The ERNK members traveled from town to town and informed the Kurdish villagers about the PKK's goal—to establish a new state in which the Kurds did not have to learn the Turkish culture and language, in which they could give their children Kurdish names, and express and live by their customs freely (Romano, 2006). Kurds, especially those who experienced state oppression during the 1980 military coup, welcomed the preaching of the ERNK and turned into solid supporters of the PKK (McDowall, 2000).

In addition to ERNK activities, the annihilation of the Kurdish tribal leaders and the inability of the state security forces to prevent guerilla attacks had further increased the credibility of the PKK. The PKK had proved that even the Turkish security forces—despite having a larger army equipped with latest technology weapons—were unable to protect the Kurdish tribal leaders against its attacks.

As the PKK gradually became a reliable authority in the region, the local public became more sympathetic to the organization's nationalist inspirations. Kurds, including high school students, began to show their willingness to provide logistics, funds, and recruits for the guerilla fight (de Bellaigue, 2009; Jawideh, 2006). The PKK's growing authority encouraged Kurdish youths to roam the streets and forcefully shut down shops and schools to protest the brutal measures applied by the Turkish state (White, 2000).

Village Protection Guards

Soon, the PKK had turned into a widely supported organization—posing a serious challenge to the authority of the Turkish state in eastern Anatolia. An atmosphere of fear had developed as soldiers and tribal leaders lost their lives with the sudden ambushes of the guerillas. In response to this threat, Ankara enacted the village protection law in 1985 and armed the Kurdish tribes who were loyal to the Turkish political elites in the capital. Thousands of Kurds were given arms and weapons and also were paid salaries to fight against the PKK (de Bellaigue, 2009; Romano, 2006).

By 1993, it is estimated that there were approximately 35,000 Kurds serving in the village protection system. The willingness of the Kurdish tribes to fight against the PKK had two sources. First, the monthly stipend given by Ankara provided a great economic incentive for the Kurds considering the high rates of unemployment in the region. Second, by enrolling into this system, the Kurdish tribes became an ancillary force for the Turkish army so they protected themselves from the systematic harassment by the Turkish security forces (McDowall, 2000; Romano, 2006).

Despite the incentives provided by the state, some Kurdish tribes refused to serve as village protection guards. As a result, the security forces assumed that these tribes were in collaboration with the PKK and thus targeted them one by one—the peasants became subjected to arbitrary arrest, severe beatings, and humiliations (de Bellaigue, 2009; White, 2000). They were expelled from their lands, and the security forces destroyed their houses to make sure that they would not return (McDowall, 2000; de Bellaigue, 2009). Extra-judicial killings became a common issue in the region. Peasants who were suspected of being PKK sympathizers were forcefully taken from their homes for investigatory purposes. Their families often never heard from them again (Romano, 2006). Unfortunately, the reports published in Turkey at later dates revealed that there were mass graves where the detainees who died under army and police brutality were buried (de Bellaigue, 2009).

While the Turkish state was committing these atrocities against the pro-PKK villages, the PKK targeted the peasants enrolled in the village protection system because they were blocking the supply and travel routes for the organization. Thus, beginning in 1987, the PKK started to raze the villages of the pro-state Kurds. Everybody—agha families, peasants, men, women, children, and the elderly— were brutally killed so as to intimidate the village protection guards into resigning from this duty (McKiernan, 2006).

The strategy applied by the PKK—the complete annihilation of the pro-state tribes—had in fact worked. By the end of 1987, the number of village guards had dropped from 35,000 to 6,000 (McDowall, 2000). The ones that remained in the system protected themselves from PKK retaliation by providing the organization with arms and weapons, by confiding important intelligence about the movement of the Turkish security forces, and by sharing a percentage of their income (McDowall, 2000; Romano, 2006).

Bereft of the support of village protection guards, the Turkish security forces became handicapped in their fight against the PKK insurgency. In fact, the successful armed struggle of the PKK during this time had made it impossible for the Turkish political authorities to further ignore the Kurdish problem in Turkey. Apo had become the symbol of the Kurdish nation, and the Kurdish problem was carried into the international arena—not only the Kurds of Turkey, but also the Kurds of Iraq, Iran, and Syria had attached themselves to Apo as a leader of all Kurds (McKiernan, 2006).

Further, with the beginning of the 1990s, the PKK began to establish its own institutions—schools, police, and courts—parallel to those administered by the Turkish state and thus, by serving to the needs of Kurdish people in several cities, started to function as a state. The authority of Turkey was seriously challenged as the Kurds welcomed this initiative and began to visit these institutions that provided them service in their own language (Romano, 2006). According to Romano (2006, p. 89), "The number of court cases heard at Turkish civil courts declined rapidly as so-called PKK peoples' tribunals came to being. In several provinces the PKK even set up its local police and intelligence units."

Emergence of Hezbollah

In the meantime, an Islamic movement, Hezbollah Yumruki (the Fist of God), emerged in the areas where Kurds lived. The city of Batman became the headquarters of Hezbollah—a Sunni Kurdish group that should not be confused with the internationally known Lebanese Shia group. Being an extreme religious organization, the Hezbollah members did not carry out any attacks against the Turkish security forces. However, many Kurds and also some secular people in the country were executed by this group (McDowall, 2000). Especially during the 1990s, many PKK members, sympathizers, Kurdish nationalists, and secular journalists were killed in daytime assassination missions carried out by Hezbollah (McKiernan, 2006).

Even though these large numbers of deaths created a climate of fear throughout the country, the Turkish police often reported to the families of the victims that they were unable to find the perpetrators of these assassinations. In fact, until the end of 1993, no suspects were arrested for the commission of these crimes. As a result, the Kurdish nationalists began to claim that the Turkish security forces were assisting the Hezbollah by turning a blind eye to these atrocities (McDowall, 2000).

The significant support among the Sunni Kurds toward Hezbollah forced the PKK to change its hostile attitude against religion (McKiernan, 2006). The PKK cadre soon realized that Islam could be used as a potential recruiting tool. Thus, with orders from Apo, PKK ideologues began to spread the news that the religion of Islam and Kurdish national revival were not mutually exclusive (White, 2000). Further, Apo ordered a special group of PKK members to study the Koran and the science of hadith to show that the party was not the enemy of religion. In this way, Apo planned to inspire the support of religious Kurds into PKK activities (Laciner & Bal, 2004).

Change of Strategy

In 1991, the PKK changed its strategy of armed struggle by showing its willingness to start political negotiations with the Turkish authorities. Apo stated that "There is no question of separating from Turkey. My people need Turkey." (quoted in McDowall, 2000, p. 431; see also White, 2000, p. 163). Apo further announced that the PKK would accept a federalist solution on three conditions: (1) the release of all PKK prisoners, (2) the halt of the Turkish army offensives, and (3) the creation of an environment of free political activity environment for the Kurds (McDowall, 2000). Unfortunately, the Turkish political leaders did not respond to Apo's call for peace because they were fearful of how the Turkish military would respond. Seeing themselves as the protectors of the system, the Turkish generals felt entitled to use their power to intervene in the nation's politics whenever they deemed it necessary (Jawideh, 2006). In their view, heavy military measures comprised the most effective means to destroy PKK terrorism. Thus, holding negotiations with PKK terrorists was precluded as an option.

Nevertheless, the eighth president of Turkey, Turgut Özal, became the first statesperson to have the courage to respond to Apo's peace call and then publicly state the necessity of fundamental changes within the Turkish political system for the peaceful resolution of the Kurdish conflict. In 1992, President Özal publicly declared that two concessions—first, granting general amnesty for PKK members, and, second, incorporating the PKK into Turkey's political system—were essential elements for resolving this long-standing problem. However, the media and the opposition parties harshly criticized President Özal's suggestions by arguing that it was unconstitutional to make such concessions to the PKK (Romano, 2006).

Despite this criticism, Özal was able to enact two laws that allowed the use of Kurdish language among the Kurdish people and the publication of Kurdish newspapers in Turkey (White, 2000). Kurds were finally allowed to speak their languages in Turkey without the worry of police harassment. However, even though it was then legal to publish in their own language, the security forces began to harass the owners of the publication houses that printed in Kurdish.

Additionally, the Kurdish cities continued to be kept under military emergency rule—the security forces were given the right to detain anybody for 45 days without any charge and the fines for crimes were doubled (McKiernan, 2006). Extra-judicial killings of the Kurds by the security forces became common. In fact, not only the nationalist Kurds but also the journalists who presented the news from the region began to disappear. A report published in 1992 indicated that the number of journalists that were killed in the region was the highest in the world (McKiernan, 2006).

In 1992, Apo again declared that the PKK was ready to abandon the armed struggle in favor of a negotiated solution. President Özal thought that Apo's peace request was a great opportunity to end the further alienation of the Kurdish population in the region. In the same year, despite strong opposition even from his own party, Özal responded to the PKK by saying that he would offer a limited amnesty to incarcerated PKK guerillas on the condition that the PKK completely ceased its fight against Turkey (White, 2000). However, only one day after delivering this message, President Özal died of a heart attack (de Bellaigue, 2009; McDowall, 2000).

His final words on this subject were not subsequently embraced, as the new governing regimes continued to seek a military rather than a political solution. None of the parties at the Turkish Grand National Assembly showed any willingness to work with the Kurdish political party deputies—the People's Labor Party (HEP). The members of HEP were viewed as the agents of the PKK, and the members of the other parties, especially the right and far-right deputies, often opposed opportunities to conduct peace talks with the Kurdish deputies (McDowall, 2000). Many politicians and leaders of civil communities took Apo's peace offer as a sign of weakness and commented that the PKK was in fact tired of the fighting against the Turkish military. Thus, the peace settlement offers by the PKK were turned down by the Turkish authorities (White, 2000). Once again, the popular view on how to rid Turkey of the PKK became the continued application of harsh and repressive military measures.

President Özal's successor, Demirel, took no step to resolve the Kurdish question through political means. Although the new Prime Minister, Tansu Çiller, had initially argued in favor of establishing an autonomous administration in the region, her suggestions were not approved by the parliament; indeed, even her own political party opposed the idea of peace with the PKK. Thus, to prevent the loss of support for her government, Prime Minister Çiller soon became an advocate of a military solution. A new military offensive was undertaken in the region. As a part of this action, the People's Labor Party (the only Kurdish political party in the Turkish Grand National Assembly) was closed down, some pro-PKK deputies were jailed, thousands of villages and pastures were forcefully relocated, and houses were demolished to destroy the safe havens for PKK guerillas on the mountains (McDowall, 2000). Thus, Kurds again were left without a political voice in the capital. Even worse, a judicial committee formed during the 2010s later discovered that more than 5,000 civilian and pro-PKK Kurds were executed by Turkish security forces between the years of 1993 and 1996 (de Bellaigue, 2009).

After its closure, the members of the People's Labor Party (HEP) formed a new party, the Democracy Party (DEP). However, the Turkish state constitutional court stripped the members of this new party of their parliamentary immunity. In March 1994, two members of the party were arrested, and four others fled to Europe to protect themselves from police harassment. Finally, in 1994, the Democratic Labor Party was also banned from participating in the Turkish Grand National Assembly.

Former members of the DEP established the HADEP (the People's Democratic Party). Despite widespread police and military intimidation, the People's Democratic Party obtained more than 1.1 million votes in the general elections of 1995. Nevertheless, the discriminatory political actions towards the Kurdish deputies continued. In only two years, several HADEP members were barred from politics, six of their officials were killed, and 32 others were arrested by the police (McDowall, 2000; White, 2000).

In 1995, while the Turkish government was trying to crack down on the emerging Kurdish groups, the PKK wisely undertook to relinquish its Marxist-Leninist ideology to soothe its relations with Western democracies. The leaders of the party argued that the PKK's leftist ideology was reinforcing its image as a terrorist organization, rather than as an insurgent movement that was trying to protect its people. Thus, to attract the support of European countries and the United States, the party administration removed the hammer and the sickle symbols from the flag of the PKK (Romano, 2006).

Hopes for Reconciliation

In 1996, Necmettin Erbakan, the new Prime Minister of the coalition government, followed the path created by President Özal and started negotiations with the PKK administrators to find a peaceful solution for the Kurdish issue. Although meetings were held in secret, the media soon discovered them. Tansu Çiller, the co-leader of the coalition government, condemned Erbakan's approach, saying that "I have a very clear approach; the state does not talk to bandits" (quoted in White, 2000, p. 40).

Erbakan halted the peace negotiations due to the pressure applied by his fellow politicians and by military officials. In fact, two days after news of the peace talks leaked to the media, Erbakan publicly announced that: "We will not sit down at the table with terrorists. We will not give one inch in our struggle with terrorism" (quoted in White, 2000, p. 40).

The Capture of Apo

By 1998, the number of Turkish and Kurdish people who had lost their lives during the conflict had reached 35,000 (White, 2000). The PKK was struggling because the village and pasture evacuations had cut their access to food and shelter. Further, in 1998, Turkey had moved thousands of troops to its Syrian border and asked the Syrian government either to hand over Apo to Turkey or to prepare for war (White, 2000). Syria, which was vulnerable to air attacks both from Turkey and Israel, immediately banned the PKK's military and political activity within its territory and sent Apo to Russia (McDowall, 2000).

A couple of months later, Russia delivered Apo to Italy where Apo applied for political asylum. He was placed in a military hospital near Rome until the Italian authorities decided his case (White,

2000). Even though the Rome Court of Appeals initially ruled that Abdullah Öcalan, Apo, be placed under house arrest in Rome, on January 16, 1999, the Italian government expelled him back to Russia. Under pressure from Turkey and its close ally, the United States, Russian authorities sent Öcalan to The Netherlands. Nevertheless, the Dutch authorities refused to accept Apo into their country (McDowall, 2000; White, 2000). Apo was put on a plane and then sent to Greece. It was then clear to PKK administrators that neither Europe nor Russia was willing to grant asylum to Apo because doing so would jeopardize their relations with the United States and Turkey.

Greek intelligence officers sent Abdullah Öcalan to the Greek Embassy at Nairobi, Kenya. According to the plan, Apo was going to hide inside the embassy until a safe location could be found to protect him. However, on February 15, 1999, CIA operatives abducted Abdullah Öcalan from the Greeks and handed him over to Turkish security forces. Apo was brought to Turkey for trial (McDowall, 2000).

Millions of Turks were delighted, whereas the Kurds were shocked and angry. Protests soon started in the Kurdish cities of Turkey and in major European capitals (de Bellaigue, 2009; White, 2000). Large demonstrations also erupted in Iran, and Iraq, which were all organized by the non-Turkey Kurds after Öcalan was caught (Jawideh, 2006; Romano, 2006). In the meantime, Apo was placed in a prison located on Imrali Island in the sea of Marmora. On June 29, 1999, he was found guilty of treason and sentenced to death (Romano, 2006). In 2002, however, Abdullah Öcalan's execution was commuted to life imprisonment because the Turkish parliament outlawed the use of capital punishment as a prerequisite for its attempt to join the European Union.

After Apo's incarceration, instead of appointing a single person as its leader, the PKK administrators formed a ruling council consisting of its top commanders to oversee the military and political activities of the PKK. Additionally, throughout his imprisonment, Apo continued his control of the PKK by sending his directives to the PKK commanders via his lawyers.

Justice and Development Party

Holding the majority of the seats in the parliament in 2002, the Justice and Development Party (AKP) government achieved major progress in the resolution of the Kurdish conflict by enacting liberal laws, which had been unthinkable only two decades earlier. Under the leadership of Prime Minister Erdoğan, the AKP abolished the state emergency rules in Kurdish populated areas, eliminated the legal restriction on the use of Kurdish language, and lifted the ban on Kurdish publications and broadcasts (Ensaroglu, 2013; McKiernan, 2006).

To be sure, the AKP implemented these changes largely to meet the standards of the Copenhagen criterion, compliance with which was an absolute necessity for Turkey to become a member of the European Union. Regardless, these reforms inspired considerable hope for the peaceful resolution of the conflict between the Kurds and Turks (Jawideh, 2006; Romano, 2006).

The freedoms that were provided by the AKP government were substantial—considering that, in the 1990s, demonstrations were encircled by police and tens of demonstrators were killed by security forces just because they raised the PKK flag (McKiernan, 2006). Now, thousands of Kurds could gather freely and chant for their cause without the worry of police harassment. As quoted in de Bellaigue (2009, p. 252), "After the speeches there will be a concert, with songs sung in Zaza and Kurmanji. And after that, everyone will go home. No arrests; no torture; no killings. Eastern Anatolia has changed for the better…"

Official Recognition of the Kurdish Problem

Even more important than implementing these reforms, in 2005, the Turkish Republic officially recognized the existence of the Kurdish problem for the first time in its history—a history previously marked by so many years of repression, denial of identity, unaccounted murders, kidnappings, village evacuations, and forced migration (Akyol, 2015; Dalay, 2015; Ensaroglu, 2013). Under the auspices of Prime Minister Erdoğan, the AKP government declared that they would facilitate reconciliation by implementing democratic measures, including the granting of equal citizenship status to Kurds. Unlike the former governments of Turkey, Erdoğan and his cabinet rejected the view that the conflict with the Kurds was solely a matter of terrorism. Instead, they intended to apply social and democratic measures to tackle the roots of the Turkish-Kurdish conflict (Ensaroglu, 2013). For example, the AKP government enacted a new law (Social Rehabilitation Act) to allow a large number of PKK members to surrender themselves without being subject to any kind of punishment (on the condition that they were not involved in fighting against law enforcement officials) (Ahmed & Gunter, 2005; Ferhad & Gurbey, 2000).

Nevertheless, the politicians and bureaucrats failed to take into account an important side effect of this democratic peace approach. A majority of the Turks, especially those who had lost their loved ones in this fight, did not welcome the AKP's conciliatory approach toward the Kurds. Because the democratic reforms for the Kurds were applied without fully informing the public first, nationalist and Kemalist Turks began to view the peace process as a betrayal of the martyred security officials and of murdered innocent individuals who had lost their lives during this 40-year-long fight (Ensaroglu, 2013; Marcus, 2015).

In protest, thousands of Turks took to the streets of major cities to demonstrate against the AKP government. Faced with the prospect of losing the support of their political constituency, the AKP government halted the implementation of the democratic measures until the climate had become less heated—that is, until four years later (Ensaroglu, 2013).

The National Unity and Fraternity Project

In 2009—a year before Deniz would surrender himself to the security forces—the AKP government restarted the peace process under the slogan of the "Kurdish Opening." To make the reform more palatable to the Turkish public, bureaucrats later changed the name of the process first to "The Democratic Opening," then, at the request of Prime Minister Erdoğan, it was changed once again to "The National Unity and Fraternity Project" (Dalay, 2015; Marcus, 2015; Srivastava, 2016).

Unlike the peace process that was started in 2005, this initiative attempted to move forward by securing wider community support. This approach included the participation of more diverse social groups, think-tanks, NGOs, universities, public intellectuals, and other political parties. Thus, in a way, all segments of Turkish society were given the opportunity to offer their ideas and suggestions with regards to the resolution of the Kurdish problem. In the meantime, the visual media outlets were encouraged to broadcast TV shows to inform the Turkish citizenry about the possible benefits of the peaceful resolution of the conflict. Additionally, Prime Minister Erdoğan carried out several visits to South Eastern Anatolia (Kurdistan) and held meetings with the Kurds to show the warm face of the state to the neglected ones (Ensaroglu, 2013).

Attempts to Undermine the Peace Process

Unexpectedly, beginning in April 14, 2009, the Turkish National Police started to carry out operations against pro-Kurdish groups. They raided offices and homes in various cities of Turkey and arrested more than 140 people, including mayors, students, Kurdish politicians, human rights activists, and union members. Many of these people were accused of representing the urban wing of the PKK. Pictures showing these people—including mayors and Kurdish politicians—handcuffed in front of the Diyarbakır courthouse caused huge resentment and hatred across Turkey in the Kurdish society. Because the police carried out these operations during a ceasefire period, everyone, including Prime Minister Erdoğan, was shocked (Akyol, 2015; Ensaroglu, 2013).

Even though the peace process was not heavily damaged by these police operations, another development soon thereafter did undermine it. As a sign of good intentions, Abdullah Öcalan (Apo) asked some senior PKK guerillas to leave their camps in Iraq and surrender themselves to Turkish security forces (Akyol, 2015). As a result, in 2009, 34 guerillas entered into Turkey from the Habur border gate riding in an open-top bus. Approximately 50,000 Kurds from the region welcomed them as heroes, singing victory songs with PKK flags in their hands. As the Turkish media aired these celebrations, hundreds of protests and marches erupted across the country organized by nationalist and Kemalist Turks. Thousands of Turks spilled on to the streets saying that they were sold out by the AKP politicians (Akyol, 2015; Dalay, 2015; Ensaroglu, 2013; Marcus, 2015; Milliyet, 2009).

Conclusion

In the years since 2010, Turkey has become a nation embroiled in turmoil and political repression. President Erdoğan has moved to consolidate his power and, after a failed coup attempt, has engaged in a massive repression of all alleged opponents. His administration's targets are drawn from diverse sectors of the Turkish citizenry, including political opponents, members of the judicial and security forces, educators, and journalists. At the same time, the increasingly authoritarian Turkish government has revitalized its attempt to crack down on Kurdish nationalism and the PKK, with the predictable response of renewed terrorist activities. The final chapter will return to these contemporary issues and explore the challenges that will have to be surmounted if peace is to reign between the Kurds and the Turks.

The history outlined in this chapter is important for another reason: It is the context into which Deniz Koçer was born and that eventually inspired him to join the PKK. Deniz's "own story" is a biography that is bounded by disquieting conflicts and deep resentments that are rooted in a particular arch of history. It is this unique context that leads Deniz to be seen as a "terrorist" by one side (Turkish) and as a "freedom fighter" by the other side (Kurdish). For Deniz, the triumphs and tragedies of his life are a product of the long-standing inability of the parties to resolve the "Kurdish problem." By telling his story, he shows us in very personal terms how the conditions established by others shaped the choices that he made—choices that range from the brutal to the mundane to the heroic. It is to Deniz's own story that we now turn.

PART II
The Freedom Fighter's Own Story

SECTION A

Becoming a Terrorist

3

THE EARLY YEARS

My childhood was spent in a village connected to the city of Silvan. We were a family of seven boys and three girls, and I was the third child of the family. There is an average of two years between each of us, and the eldest of us is now 46. My parents are still living. They both learned to speak Turkish later in life. My mother was a housewife, and my father would help with livestock and agriculture. Until I was 15 years old, I raised animals in the pastures of our village.

Although our harvest was usually sufficient to provide for us, some years we wouldn't be able to make enough to support our large family. Those years, my father would go down to the town and seek odd jobs to provide what we were lacking. The town was also where we would buy some of our necessities, such as tea and sugar, and we often carried home several sacks of flour. Items like shoes, clothing and gas oil were also purchased in town. Because we were raising pasture animals, we could meet much of our need for meat and milk directly from them. We re-used almost everything. The clothes that were originally bought for elder siblings would become those of the younger ones later. For most of my life, I wore the cast-off clothes that my elder brothers had once worn. I don't really recall having had any new clothes bought especially for me over my whole childhood.

Village Life

Since raising animals and agriculture were the main source of living for us villagers, it was very important for a family to have a son. When a woman was giving birth, only other women were allowed in her house. The men and children would wait in another house. After the birth, one woman from the birth house would go to the father to tell him whether it was a boy or a girl. If this woman announced it was a son, she would be given a tip, but if she announced it was a girl, the father would say, "What kind of announcement is this?" and would often beat her.

Watermelon, tobacco, grapes, wheat, and almost everything else would grow in our village. However, neighboring villages had fruits like pomegranates and pears that we did not have. At harvest time, the people of the other village would load the vegetables and fruit they had collected onto their mules and bring them to us. We would trade them our vegetables, grains, and fruit that didn't grow in their village. Wheat was the most sought after product. Money was never the question. We just bartered. We might receive a bowl of pears for a bowl of wheat.

There was a large river in the village where all the villagers went fishing. We sometimes fished with dynamite; sometimes with a fishing pole, and sometimes with just a bucket. We could scoop up a lot of fish simply by dipping a bucket into the water. My elder brothers had taught me how to fish, and it was something I enjoyed very much. There was a tradition in the village that whichever family went fishing, they would share the fish they caught with the rest of the families. So, whenever any family went fishing, everyone would eat fish.

We also used this river to wash ourselves. Because there were no bathrooms in any of the houses, all the villagers would gather together at the water, once a week. The women and the children would wash themselves in a place away from the men, and the men also had their own area. However, I do remember my mother washing us in a bucket inside our home, especially in the winter. She would pour hot water on my head and my eyes would burn because of the soap. I didn't like this, but if I complained or cried, she would hit my head with the water dipper.

Our religious lifestyle depended on our living conditions at that time. We were not a wealthy village, but had only a dilapidated mosque with no imam. Later on, as a village, we built a mosque together. We pooled our money and bought an imam from another village, but he left us six months later. After that, we didn't have an imam for years, which meant we could only pray on Fridays, with no one to lead the other weekly prayers. But, as villagers, we weren't very good at applying religious discipline to ourselves, so it wasn't long before we even gave up on Friday prayers.

But my parents, and the other elders of the family, continued to pray five times a day; they just didn't go to the mosque. We children were never required to do anything we did not want to do. My father would say, "My family can pray whenever they want," and yet my parents were very strict when it came to family values and compassion, and would tell us always to ask for what we needed and never to steal anything.

My family was very sensitive about lies and theft. Of course, since we were very young, we didn't know what stealing even was. It happened that an elderly man in the village had a fig orchard. When I was five or six, we would gather with other children and eat figs from this orchard. This neighbor, Bişar, would notice us, but he wouldn't be able to do anything since he was old and couldn't chase us. Despite all the times he stood there just watching us consume his harvest, he never complained about us to our families. If our parents had learned our fig-stealing habit, I guess they would have beaten us. But we were so young, we considered it a game. We liked it: free figs! But in the following years, our families taught us how bad it was to steal something that belonged to somebody else.

We called our wise, elderly people "the dignitaries of the village," and we respected their experience and opinion. For instance, if there were a dispute between two families, they would listen to both sides and punish the wrongdoers. The punishment would always be monetary. Their word was law. If they said, "The family of the victim will be compensated with four goats and one cow!" the other side had to fulfill it. The criminal sentence was binding. Such an institution was a very good tradition for our village to have, I think. The fact that the police station was far away from our village, and that there were hardly any cars in the village, meant we relied on the dignitaries of the village for making peace between the families and preventing acrimonious incidents from getting worse.

Our family didn't practice polygamy although it is very common in the Eastern Anatolia region (i.e., Kurdistan). My mother is my father's cousin, but their marriage was not political: it was for love. Until the '90s, our family hadn't had any brides from any other family but our own, nor did we give any brides to any other families. Our marriages had mostly been between our own family members. This changed after we moved to the city in 1990.

There we had a two-story house, and we kept animals downstairs. There were all kinds of animals: goats, sheep, cows… We would stay upstairs with the uncles' families. Our house had six bedrooms, a living room, and two entrances. There was no electricity, TV, fridge, or even a driveway. There was also no gender discrimination in our family. We were all allowed to eat together.

As relatives, we made sure to live very close to each other. That's why the relationships between us were so good. My mother and my aunts would all do the housework, cook and take care of the children together.

When I was a child, each household had a radio, and everything we learned about Turkey and the world, we heard through that radio. There was a channel called "The Voice of Erivan," which featured a Kurdish broadcast, and since it was forbidden to speak Kurdish in Turkey, they would broadcast from Armenia. We listened to this channel religiously. Many families also had tape players. We had one, and could listen to Kurdish tapes brought in from Armenia and Iraq. Şirvan Perwer was a very famous Kurdish singer at that time.

My cousin used to live in the city, and he would bring the tapes to give me and my elder brothers so that we could learn about Kurdish culture. He educated us on how to treat them: "Listen to them. Hide them well. Don't ever let the soldiers see them, or they will set your house on fire." Since I was young, I couldn't understand very well what it all meant. The only concept which I think I understood, was that the Turkish soldiers didn't like anything Kurdish.

I would ask my cousin why it was forbidden to listen to these tapes, and he told me that Kurdish geography was divided into four sections because of outside forces, and had been kept repressed. I was young and the truth was new for me, so I was very curious about what I was learning. That's why we were very careful to hide the tapes. When the soldiers performed raids, they would sometimes find these tapes, and then beat everyone in the entire household, breaking all the tapes.

School and Kurdish Language

My parents registered my eldest brother in a school that was far away from our village, and he had to walk there. But after a while, he dropped out, because of all the things he suffered while attending. Of course, he did this without letting our parents know. He would still leave the house in the morning, saying, "I'm going to school." However, he would then hide around the farms and gardens or just wander around until the school was finished for the day. When my parents received his school report, they saw that he hadn't attended the school at all, after the first three weeks.

This made my father furious. When he asked my brother why he had done this, my brother complained that he didn't understand the language spoken there, saying, "I don't understand any Turkish. I speak Kurdish at home, at work, and in the marketplace through the evenings. I understand nothing in that school." But then, he also him told how strict his teacher had been. "They beat the children in the school. They make us stand on one foot for minutes at a time, and they rap us on our knuckles until I can't even feel my fingers." Because of all of those bad experiences, my elder brother didn't even finish primary school.

I never went to school. I never liked school. It had no charm for me, and I had been affected by my brothers' experiences as well. The language they spoke in the school wasn't the same language we spoke at home or in the village. That language was only spoken by soldiers or teachers, who treated people badly. Both groups were cruel. Thankfully, my parents didn't force me to go to school. My father never approved of us going to school because of the treatment my brothers had received, and naturally, they weren't successful at school. Our community was handicapped in their minds because of the understanding that, "We are Kurds, and would never be rewarded by the unyielding state, no matter how hard we might study in school." In the following years, as we moved to the city of Batman, some of my siblings studied only until middle school and a few until high school. But no one in my family had a chance to study at university level…

My Childhood and Parents

My family was very attached to their children, especially to me. More than all my other siblings, they valued me a great deal. I think it was mostly because of the fact that I was born prematurely. Another reason that they valued me so much was that my family didn't hear from me for 18 years after I joined the Kurdistan Worker's Party (PKK). My father got so depressed during that period that he had two heart attacks because of it, followed later by tuberculosis. He couldn't endure my absence, even though he had nine other children.

My father struggled a lot in his life. The poor man was always restless, because of my absence or because of all the incidents which happened in the village. That's why I feel much closer to my father than my mother. He has always been so sensitive. He never physically abused any of his children, through his entire life.

In the culture of our family, children should never be beaten; neither girls nor boys. Discipline in the family was maintained through discussion. Our elders would always caution us, saying "Do this like that, or don't do that. That's bad, or, don't let anyone talk poorly about us. Don't tarnish the name of the family!"

I used to hang out with my uncle's son, although, in my opinion, he was totally clumsy. He was always getting in trouble for no good reason and getting himself beaten up. It was as if he never knew how to act, under any circumstances. We would wander around together, day and night. We would either play soccer or play marbles, when we weren't taking the animals to pasture. I loved soccer. I've been a Beşiktaş team supporter since my childhood. When I was a kid, there was no field in our village where we could play soccer, so we would play it in flat pastures.

I would leave home, taking the animals with me, around 4:00 to 5:00 a.m., and come back before sunset. My elder brothers would take the goats and sheep to pasture, and I would take out the kids and lambs. I was always exhausted when I returned home, so I would go to bed immediately after dinner. I was never a calm kid, however, I kept true to the values my parents had taught us. I never caused any neighbors to talk badly about me—in any of the places we lived. I never had a fight with my siblings, or with the neighbors' children. I always kept myself away from such problematic situations. When someone swore at me or humiliated me, I would never retaliate at that time. I would leave the scene and look for something to occupy my mind, and although I was furious, I would hold my tongue, bottle my anger and try to keep command of myself. I would make peace, leaving no ill-will behind.

Contrary to my brothers, I would comprehend incidents and learn quickly from prior experience. Although I had never attended any school, I learned reading and writing before my elder brothers, which caused my father to get angry with them. He would say, "Sons, you've been attending school for many years now, but you neither know how to read nor write. This kid," pointing to me, "knows how, though he's never been to school."

While I was growing up, I had the reputation of being mature and responsible. Throughout my childhood, I had never lied. I had always been honest. Even if I made a mistake, I always confessed it.

For example, there was an incident from when I was young: there were many wild pigs in our town. Therefore, every night, one of our big families would always stay in our vineyards, keeping guard with a gun. One afternoon, when one of our relatives went to keep guard, he forgot to take his gun with him. In the evening my mother gave me a gun and told me, "Take this to him, as thieves or the pigs might hurt him without it."

Well, I started to play with the gun on the way. I loaded it by mistake and pulled the trigger, and the gun fired. When our relative received the gun, he said, "This has recently been used. I smell the gunpowder!" I told him what had happened, even though I could have lied if I had wanted. Although I knew my mother would chew me out, I also told her the whole truth. My mother said, "Son, if you were curious about the gun, why did not you tell me? Just let me know if you're interested, and I will show you how to use it." My mother was expert with a gun, and it was a tradition in our village back then that each household had two rifles and a few guns. There were, without any exceptions, two Mauser rifles and a few guns in every house.

Since I never lied, I could not stand hearing others telling lies. Once, when my elder brother was telling a huge lie, I was so upset by it that I told my father everything that had really happened. My elder brother had filled our rifle with too much gunpowder, and consequently, when he fired the rifle, the barrel split in half. My father had often warned us not to fill the rifle with too much powder. My elder brother thought our father would get angry with him, and did not tell him the truth. So, when I heard him lying, I couldn't endure it and I said, "Dad, my brother put two or three extra grains of powder into the rifle, so that it would fire more powerfully." My father turned to my brother and asked, "Is your brother telling the truth?" When my brother said, "Yes," my father got angry. "Son, why didn't you tell the truth? Why this lying? Haven't I told you many times that you shouldn't tell lies?" My brother was punished verbally, but not physically.

Meeting Soldiers

I had never seen a Turkish soldier until the coup of September 12, 1980. When I was a child, my father and my uncles used to tell us of memories from their military service, but I still didn't know what the presence of Turkish soldiers meant to us Kurds—the military coup gave us our first chance to see and know them.

The soldiers set up a big camp with many tents, right at the entrance to our village. They remained there for about two months. Absolutely no one would dare to get close to their camp. Every two days, those soldiers would gather up all the males in the village, into the village square, except for the very young boys. We had no idea what they were planning. Even as children, the one thing we understood clearly, was that whenever soldiers arrived, they brought beatings along with them. First, they would force all the men they had gathered into the square, to lie down on the ground. Then they would beat them with rifle butts or their boots, smashing their heads until they lost consciousness. The women and the children weren't subjected to such treatment, but they were forced to watch this cruelty, screaming out at what they witnessed. No matter what happened, no one was allowed to leave the scene until the Turkish military commander allowed them to leave.

The raids of the village would always take place in the middle of the night, while we were asleep. A few soldiers would climb onto the roof of each house, while the rest would take all of us outside in groups, while they searched inside the houses, and surveyed the surroundings to ensure their own safety. While "searching" inside our houses, they would trash everything, and inventory all of our private belongings. However, to be fair, it is necessary to state as well that no Turkish soldiers ever took anything from us by force. There was never any seizure by violence.

Since the soldiers' arrival was always unpredictable, and usually at night while everyone was asleep, the men in the village had no time to hide. Eventually, the male elders became so fed up with beatings that they would sleep in the barns, hidden inside the straw, to avoid the assaults. It was a confusing situation in the village, and although our people hadn't done anything wrong, we hid to avoid these attacks, which lasted about two months.

When the soldiers' raids of our village became routine, the villagers began to develop some evasive tactics. For example, when soldiers set off for a certain village, we devised various ways for the neighboring villages to inform the target village. Those who saw the military convoy would climb the nearby hill and inform the other village, and then they, in turn, would do the same for us.

"Wolves" was our code names for these soldiers. When soldiers approached a village, people would shout, "The wolves are here!" At that warning, all the men who could would run out of the village. Although they hadn't committed any crime, they ran away simply to avoid getting beaten. Their wives and children got left behind.

Ironically, we first heard of a group known as "Apo Sympathizers" as a result of these raids. When Turkish soldiers arrived in the village, they would ask, "Have you seen the Apo Sympathizers? Have you fed any of those men? Have they passed by the village?" At that time, we didn't know what the term even meant. We first learned of the existence of Apo, and his group of Kurdish Freedom Fighters, from the Turkish soldiers trying to eradicate them.

During this time, there was one other detail that struck me as odd. When soldiers arrived, the commander would already have a list of suspects. One by one, he would call out the names of the people on the list. It was not a discovery, but rather like an inspection. The list would consist of the names of all the male villagers. If one of the names were absent, they would ask his family and relatives where he was. If they had no good answer, each relative would be beaten. However, by this point, even beatings wouldn't scare anyone into breaking their silence. Neither the women nor the elderly would ever give away the hiding place of the men, no matter how violently they were punished for not answering. The curious thing is that, at that time, our village didn't have a census or any other official state registration of our inhabitants, so how had the soldiers come to form such accurate lists? We had no idea.

It is important to note that the Turkish soldiers didn't kill anyone during these raids. But the beatings were extreme. True beatings! No soldier knew how to speak Kurdish. The commander generally communicated with the village through translations by the Kurdish villagers who knew Turkish. Another interesting fact, I noted during these inspections, was that soldiers never hurt the headman of the village or his family. All the regular villagers were routinely beaten, but the headman and his family were never abused.

There was the economic toll on the village of the sudden appearance of a military camp on our doorstep. Sometimes a village animal disappeared during grazing time. As a herding village, this is something we were used to discovering. When the flock came back to the village, it was common to find that a few of them had accidentally been left behind in the mountain pastures. The shepherd only notices the lack once he returns to the village. Normally, the shepherd and a few other people would return to the mountain and take recovery of the missing animals. But, when the soldiers came to the village, they declared a nighttime curfew, causing the shepherds not to be able leave and look for their missing animals. Any money, meat, or milk the animal was worth, was simply lost along with the animal.

These were really bad days. Being forced to watch my father, my elder brothers, and the other respected men of the village getting severely beaten, broke my heart as well as the hearts of all the other boys in the village. But, being just a few, and young, there was nothing we could do. We could only stay silent, or weep in despair. If there were a hundred people in the village, there was a thousand soldiers. We were helpless. And that helpless suffering planted the seeds of hatred in our hearts. We had begun to learn to hate. We hated not only the soldiers, but our hate grew to include the Turkish people, and even the Turkish language.

By that time, I had not personally been beaten by the Turkish soldiers. But the soldiers' treatment of the other members of our village was more than enough to spark my desire for revenge, and this spark grew rapidly. Remember, we had no concept of a Kurdistan, or even that we were Kurdish, and certainly no idea about any "Apo Sympathizers," until the soldiers came to our village and told us. So by beating all the men in the village over and over, simply on the suspicion of sympathizing with this "Apo," the Turkish soldiers, themselves, educated us about this group that stood in defense of villagers like ourselves. It was obvious that the Turkish military felt threatened by them.

So, all of us got very clear on one point. We were going to get revenge for what the soldiers had done. And we were going to get it by joining with these Apo sympathizers who were such a threat that the Turkish soldiers felt compelled to hunt them down everywhere. In other words, because of their inhumane and unjustified attacks, the Turkish military had spontaneously caused neutral villagers, such as ourselves, actively to seek to find and join this group of rebels, whose name we had never heard, except from Turkish soldiers.

The Feud

The oppression and the torture from the soldiers wasn't the only problem we had at that time. Our family had been in a lot of trouble long before this. Due to a feud, my family had been forced to flee our village in the early 1980s. I don't remember why it started, because I was only six years old. But, originally, the other side attacked my family and killed three people. Then we attacked, and killed seven of them. Every day, the fighting was ferocious, and gunfire was so loud and frequent, that we couldn't even leave the house.

During one battle, a wounded neighbor was carried into our place. A group of women gathered and began to clean his wound. When they extracted a bullet from his chest, they realized he had been shot in the back, and so must have been running away. The women instantly stopped taking care of him. One of them even said, "This coward has sold out his friends, he was shot while leaving them, let's just let him die." I remember this very, very well.

Over time, my personality began to be altered by the repetition of incidents such as this. Although I did not yet participate in the violence myself, the beatings, blood, and gun battles had become an ordinary part of my environment. Gunshots no longer caused me panic. Everyone in the village used guns. It became so common, that it no longer seemed to be a crime, but just a fact of life. So, then, even if a gunshot were heard right in the center of the town square, nobody would investigate. In addition to this important lesson on the power of apathy, I also learned the value of courage. The fact that the women in the village had refused to treat our wounded neighbor, once they decided he was a coward, inspired me to act bravely.

As a result of this feud, many people from the opposing families were killed. Therefore, on the night of the incident, we fled the village. We left behind every animal, and all of our belongings. We ran to a different village, very far away, and settled there for our safety. The people in this new village protected us for six years.

Raising livestock and a little farming was still our livelihood. So, though we arrived in our new village as empty-handed guests, we soon resurrected our family trade. We struggled a lot in the first three years. For one thing, my father was off living in the mountains as a fugitive, and although he sometimes came home to see us in the evenings, he would leave before sunrise. My father couldn't stand with us when we needed him the most. My mother and elder brother earned the bread for our home. Thankfully, the villagers and some distant relatives also helped us.

So that feud forced 20 people, including my father, to live as fugitives from 1980 to 1983. They hid in the mountains, generally 30 or 40 kilometers from the village, and trusted shepherds were their messengers. For instance, they would say, "Tell our households that we are here and they should send us food." As excited as we would be to hear from our father, and sometimes get to see him, we always did our best not to get him caught. The coup had forever impressed upon us what would happen to outlaws who were discovered. So, I always worried that my father might be caught and brutalized.

Nonetheless, I would occasionally take the chance of bringing food to my father. A group of us would set off in the early morning, when it was still dark outside, so as not to tip off the villagers. I would set off first, and 15 to 20 minutes later my cousin would follow. Then, either my brother or another cousin would leave another 15 to 20 minutes after that. Since we worked as shepherds, leaving home early raised no suspicions. Still, we would never leave the village all at one time. Instead, we would meet at a certain predetermined abandoned place, 3 or 4 kilometers from the village, and then walk the rest of the way together. Our regular shepherd lunch bags would have been filled with food before we left home, and so, if someone asked us why our food bags were full, we would reply, "We are shepherds!"

Every time I got to see my father, I always wanted to stay with him, and each time I would ask to live in the mountains with him. But he never let me. After only a few hours of any visit, he would force me to go back to the village. I was always shocked and amazed at the weapons I saw on him during those short visits! The fugitives sometimes had weapons that we didn't even have in the village. I loved weapons, and I envied the people who used them. In my father's absence, my uncle had taught me how to use an AK-47. I had learned everything about it; how it worked, how many bullets could be loaded into it, and how it was cleaned. Everything.

Feud Trial

Eventually the legal trial for the feud began, and 17 people from our family were arrested. I was around seven or eight years old by then. Two of these 17 people were sentenced. Justice was meted out in a strange way at that time. Although the whole group committed the crime, only one or two people would receive the punishment, depending on the size of the group. The rest would be set free. My mother's uncle and another relative of hers bore this punishment. If I remember rightly, they stayed behind bars for years, and were only set free during the period of amnesty that took place in Turkish Prime Minister Özal's era.

Settling to the City of Batman and Meetings

Due to these trying circumstances, my mother took on all the responsibility of doing the housework and taking care of us when we were young. This greatly increased my father's respect for her. Although the community is mostly male-dominant in our hometown, as far as I remember my father never raised his hand against my mother. So, though my father was very emotional, he never resorted to brute force against her. I suppose this was also because my uncles lived close by. As I have mentioned before, my mother is my father's cousin. My mother's family was also much better off financially than my father's. During this time, my uncles had cars and tractors. My mother's father was very wealthy, and owned eight or nine buffalos, dozens of cows, and hundreds of other small livestock. He used to help us monetarily from time to time. I remember quite well how my grandmother would make a show of giving at least two lambs to each of her grandchildren every year. So, in terms of finances, my mother's family simply dominated my father, and in this way, they maintained authority over him.

But before the feud, our family was also very well off financially. We always got quite a good amount of money whenever we sold off our animals. From these same animals, in the meantime, we could also meet our needs for food. In addition, we owned some medium-sized fields for farming, where we would plant wheat and tobacco. This also brought in a good amount of money. In addition to all these sources of income, my father was also responsible for providing security for the official meteorology institution, located right beside the village. So, in addition to the revenue from our family business, he also had this side income. When the feud forced us to flee our village, we, of course, were severed from all these sources of support. We left everything we owned; everything we earned, all to prevent the loss of any more blood. Once we re-settled, all our family members pooled their money and bought 50 to 60 new goats and three new cows; once again beginning our livestock herd. We stayed in this second village from 1980 to 1987, and then we had to move to the city of Batman. Because, even though the people of this new village had welcomed us, it wasn't our village. We didn't have a field of our own. So, while the people protected our lives, they could not provide sufficient livelihood, and so we weren't able to remain there very long. Therefore, when I was 13 or 14, my family divided and relocated again. Some of us moved to Silvan, some of us to Diyarbakır, and the rest—including my immediate family—moved to the city of Batman.

It was a huge struggle to adapt to the city. It was such a totally different life. One of the most difficult cultural changes was realizing that people in the city didn't help each other. People there didn't care about each other. Everyone's struggle was personally their own. If your house collapsed; if you were starving to death; if you ran out of money, nobody cared. It was as if no one had ever heard of asking after a friend's well-being, or visiting one another. In contrast, when a family in the village had suffered a crisis—perhaps their livestock had perished—all the other villagers would gather together immediately and give the family more animals than they'd had previously. They would give gifts of money until the financial loss was covered. But in the city, there was nothing like that. There was no community feeling at all.

So, at first, we hawked a lot, in the city of Batman. We began by selling produce to meet our needs. My family would purchase fruits and vegetables from the marketplace, then walk from one neighborhood to another, selling them from a pushcart. But it was soon evident that we couldn't earn enough money from this alone, so I and my elder brothers started to work in a bricquette-making factory. We three siblings from the same family worked in this factory for a long time.

After we moved to the city, my father couldn't work, because of serious health issues, so we lived in a rental house for some time. The working conditions in the factory were terrible, and my father initially tried to endure the heavy work of the briquette factory alongside my brothers and me, but he simply could not manage it. Therefore, we elder children took financial responsibility for our family.

So, we men of the family would go to work in the early morning, and return home late at night. Our social life was non-existent. Even family members had no time to visit each other, since it was such tiresome work. We would hit the pillow as soon as we had finished dinner. Then, the next morning, we would arise early, have a quick breakfast, and set off back to work.

Certainly, the city had its benefits. Undoubtedly, the hospitals, health services and such-like were better there. All the same, I just couldn't get used to the city. First of all, nothing there had anything to do with nature. It was crowded and noisy, and people didn't even greet one another. I was continually perturbed. Batman disquieted my soul. Nearly every family member had the same complaints. Because we all shared the same dream, at every opportunity we would go to the green fields, far away from the city.

I remember, in those city days, the demonstrations held before the 1991 elections. Big Kurdish names, such as Leyla Zana and Nizamettin Tonguç, would gather the masses and deliver powerfully influential speeches. People from every neighborhood and district would join these demonstrations and listen very carefully to what was being said. We came to understand from the speeches that there was an ethnic minority population in Turkey called the Kurds, and that we, ourselves, were members of this population. We learned that this minority population had been consistently oppressed. Only Turks had had the right to speak on the record at the highest levels of Turkish Parliament. These speeches declared that we Kurds also needed access to the parliament, and from now on, we wanted to be there, to be heard, and to be given the right to affect decisions that influenced our own region.

So, while I spent most of my time those days working long hours in the factory, I was also being influenced by the content of these speeches. The incidents we'd had back in the village seemed to prove what had been said during the demonstrations. The way the teacher had beaten up my elder brothers because they didn't speak Turkish; the oppression and torture against our male villagers, after the military coup, and even in the present day. Although we were in a major city like Batman, because of the language barrier, we couldn't communicate when we went to the hospital, or couldn't even express ourselves when we went to court. Consider what that is like! We speak Kurdish at home and throughout our villages, but we can't communicate with any part of the state, because no one with whom we need to speak, in any official capacity, understands what we are saying. Every individual who gave us beatings, who oppressed us, who tortured us—from police officers to teachers to soldiers—all spoke Turkish. Suddenly, we clearly understood the differences between us. Turks were not Kurds, and they did not like us. We became more aware of our isolation. We, as the Kurdish populace, had been alienated, and I began to absorb the meaning of my identity as a Kurd. During this time, we began to gather into groups and listen for hours to Kurdish-language tapes. But all of this had to be in secret, because speaking Kurdish or even listening to something in Kurdish was forbidden.

Soon, I was going to the demonstrations whenever I had an opportunity. I was very young, so I was easily influenced by what was said. But, because I was young, no police officers or soldiers ever bothered with me. Although tea houses were forbidden for anyone under 18 at that time, we still would go there to gamble or to watch a movie, and always to listen to the others. Of course, there were police raids from time to time, but the police officers would just send us kids home, after slapping each of us in the face a few times.

I soon developed a very close circle of friends in Batman; about six or seven people, and we were spending most of our time together. We were all smoking back then, but never used alcohol or drugs, and never committed even petty crimes, like theft. As I said before, such misbehavior was very frowned upon in our Kurdish culture.

The only thing I liked about the urban period was that, as my awareness of this group who protected us Kurds grew, living in the city gave me opportunities to meet some sympathizers of this group in person. Thanks to demonstrations held in the city, and the television and radio programs broadcasting the speeches given in the tea houses, I had the chance to be better acquainted with the PKK.

Meanwhile, a new phenomenon had begun. The neighborhood friends with whom we always met and played suddenly started to disappear, and we never saw them again. Gradually we understood that they had all joined the PKK. So, we then came to see the disappearance of our youth as ordinary. For most families, it became a point of pride in the fact that their children had joined the PKK. Sometimes a single person, or at times, a few people would disappear all at once. This impressed us a great deal, as we grew older.

We started talking about these issues within our circle of friends, and began thinking and discussing together what we could do for the cause of helping secure the freedom of our Kurdish people. We knew that PKK participation was high in the regions of Silvan and Hasankeyf. We began exploring these regions, in our time off from work, in order to get more information about the PKK. We talked to people there, and tried to understand why they left daily life in favor of heading up into the mountains.

My family didn't know that my friends and I discussed such topics. I would never say the first word to them about it. My family always kept themselves strictly, and deliberately distant, from politics. But, when the youth started disappearing more frequently, my mother's warnings to us also increased in tempo. She would say to us, "Now this family's son or daughter has gone missing. They have probably gone up into the mountains. I agree that there must be a separate Kurdish state, a new Kurdistan, and the oppression should decrease against us Kurds. But, rather than joining a rebellion, it is more important that we should stay together as a family. So, my sons, please do not ever go up to the mountains. Don't ever join the organization." So no one else from my family joined the organization, though all my family members felt Kurdish nationalism.

My mother's constant warnings did not work on me. Within our friends' circle, we had already decided to go up to the mountains and join the organization. In preparation, we decided not to participate in any more illegal activities until we reached the countryside. Our goal was no longer to attract any attention from the police. We were successful. Never again did we join in a demonstration or a protest. Still, police officers would sometimes stop us and check our IDs, when we were out in the evenings. But they would have to set us free, since we had no criminal history. And because we hadn't joined in any of the recent demonstrations or protests of that period, the police began to believe we had become disinterested. Meanwhile, to cover our fact-finding journeys, we always traveled to tourist sights. We often visited places such as Silvan and Hasankeyf to get information. Although there were checkpoints all along the way, due to our frequent sightseeing trips, the police already knew us. They always believed that we were just on another trip, and our frequent conversations, as well, helped us overcome our fear of the police.

4

JOINING THE PKK

Our passion to better understand the PKK, and fight as their guerillas, was not only due to the oppression and torture in Turkey; the issue was much larger than any one country. For example, consider the Halepçe Massacre, which took place in 1988 in Iraq. The impact of that massacre lasted for years. Kurdish television channels, transmitting from abroad, were constantly showing the massacred victims—the women and children, and elderly Kurds in Iraq who had been tortured. Many had been killed by chemical weapons. Though this was a war in Iraq, still the Kurdish people were the ones suffering the most horrific casualties, and this affected us deeply.

My male cousin also played a large part in encouraging us to join the organization. He had grown up amidst all these things, since a child. He was smart. He had graduated from a university. In those years, to study at a university was a great success for a Kurd. Therefore, I gave great weight to his opinions. I was also quite impressed by all he had endured while at the university.

He was once thrown into jail because he joined a demonstration. He was placed in Diyarbakır Penitentiary and was constantly tortured while there. All his teeth were removed with a pair of pliers! He didn't have a single tooth left inside his mouth. Yet no amount of torture had made him change his beliefs. One day he gave my friends and me a very effective speech: "We are Kurdish, and we own our Kurdish lands, so why don't we have someone from our people representing us in the decision making levels of state affairs? Why can't those officials who are obliged to serve us Kurds actually speak any Kurdish themselves? Why do they always treat us so poorly? Why can five or six soldiers gather all our villagers and beat up all the men in front of their wives and children?"

Hearing of all these injustices, as well as experiencing them personally, hurt us deeply. When we looked around, we realized that those who were oppressed, beaten, and killed were always Kurdish. Kurds were the ones killed with chemical gases by Saddam in Iraq. Kurds were the ones tortured by soldiers in Turkey. Kurds were the ones who were suppressed by the regime in Iran. Kurds were the minority who lived in Syria, but did not even have their own ID cards—their own ethnic identity. These brutal regimes were also conducting a systematic anti-Kurd slandering campaign in the press and through broadcasting. On Turkish television news, they created the perception that, "This many Kurdish terrorists were killed in this place, while in that place this many Kurds were taken into custody." So, the general public started to consider all Kurds to be terrorists. If a few of our people disappeared in a neighborhood, it would hit the news with a deliberate spin against us. "Those who have gone up to the mountains are either the Armenians' unacknowledged children or bandits. They are irredeemable. They are traitors." Such messages of slander were all over the written and visual press (TRT 1, 2 and 3 back then). Can you imagine it! Those who went up to the mountains were labeled as being Armenian Christians and scorned. And, sure, perhaps some people with Armenian roots joined the resistance, but most of them were Kurdish Muslim youth. And, even if they were of Armenian descent, they had been raised in this region. They, too, had been subject to the same injustice, and all the doors must have been closed in their faces. Why else would they have turned to this path of resistance?

We decided upon this path of our own free will. The indifference of the state towards the people of our region; our torture; the oppression and torture in the neighboring countries against Kurds—collectively created our natural desire for revenge. In the neighborhood, and especially in the tea houses, we had learned that the PKK's purpose was to save Kurds from exactly this oppression and torture. Their purpose was to establish an independent and free state for Kurds, where we could live peacefully. We agreed, saying, "Since the Turkish Government does not recognize our national identity, and since it either ignores us or oppresses us, then why shouldn't we join this organization which fights for us?"

The Turkish Hezbollah

During that time, there was also the issue of Hezbollah. This organization appeared and began making religious propaganda. Since the PKK was a leftist-based organization, many battles occurred between the liberal PKK and conservative religious Hezbollah. Many PKK members and sympathizers were killed by Hezbollah during this time. Soon, we realized the technique behind their success: Hezbollah was killing Kurds with the support of the Turkish police. The police were using Hezbollah to get the PKK under control.

It was one of the armed attacks against a PKK's anti-police mission during that time that made us realize how the police were cooperating with Hezbollah. There were few, distinct makes of cars used by the police in the 1990s, including the Renault Toros or Şahin. Either white or red. One day, the PKK attacked a police car fitting this description. Both people in the car lost their lives. In the local news, it was reported that one of those who died had been a police officer, and the other was a member of Hezbollah. In other words, the police officers were touring around with Hezbollah. This really affected us. During that time, Hezbollah had killed many of our friends. They practiced many kinds of nastiness then, from unidentified murders and kidnapping to literal back-stabbing. The fact that Hezbollah committed those murders with the support of the state was yet another factor that pushed us into the arms of the PKK. We had started to think that we could cope with these horrors, only if we joined the PKK.

Soon, the Turkish state made its position crystal clear. They visited every kind of oppression on us in the Yurtsever Gençler ("Patriotic Youth," that is, PKK members). For example, say you were carrying a knife. They would "measure it" between your fingers. If the knife blade was longer than the height between two fingers, you would be brutally beaten. Yet, while the Patriotic Youth were subject to such oppression and torture, the members of Hezbollah could go around freely carrying anything they liked—knives, cleavers, or guns. The police did nothing to Hezbollah members, even if they were found with these weapons. I witnessed in person how the police would never intervene with Hezbollah.

The police strongly backed up Hezbollah. No matter what type of incident Hezbollah was involved in, the police never started an official inquiry against them. Many Hezbollah members that we killed were found to be carrying the same makes and models of guns and weapons that the police and soldiers used.

The Hezbollah group actually had nothing to do with true religion. They would regularly make religious propaganda, of course, but they would not practice what they preached. They would commit evil, then turn and talk loudly about religion. In fact, Hezbollah was the main factor that turned me from religion. I don't remember exactly what age I was, but in my adolescence my father had told me, "Son, look how old you are now! You must begin praying five times a day, and you must fast." I answered him by saying, "Dad, if this religion in which we believe; of which we are part, is exemplified by the members of Hezbollah and their actions, then I will have no part of this religion."

I mean, can you even imagine! The members of this organization called Hezbollah would behead people. When killing us, they would always approach from behind and shoot the members of Patriotic Revolutionary Youth Movement in the back of the neck. They would never approach directly and attack us like men. During this period, there were so many "unsolved" murders that everyone knew were down to Hezbollah, if the manner of death were a cleaver or a beheading.

Going up to the Mountains

The date was January 7, 1992. In our group of friends we talked for hours, and finally decided that it was high time to go up to the mountains. We all strongly believed that we had to do something for our oppressed people. We were all the right age, each between 17 and 19 years old. It all happened very quickly. We made our decision during the day, and by evening we were gone. Though we didn't have a leader, I knew better than my friends what was involved. Not only did I know the intermediaries who would take us to the mountains, but also I had once lived in the villages. Since I had been a shepherd from when I was little, I knew the conditions in the mountains very well. The other members of the group had all grown up in the city, and had always enjoyed a comfortable environment. They knew nothing about roughing it, or had no idea where to take shelter; what to eat, or where to find clean water in the mountains. The fact that I was experienced gave my friends confidence.

Not one of us told our parents that we were going up to the mountains. According to the plan we had made, only four of us were going to set off at first. I was in that first group. If we managed to reach members of the organization in the countryside safely, then the other three friends would come to join us.

Once our decision was made, I got in touch with the people who were going to take us to the mountains. I knew someone from another neighborhood who made these sorts of arrangements. I informed him, "We are seven people and we all want to join you voluntarily. Just tell us whatever we have to do to join the organization." I later learned that the father of this guy had been killed by Hezbollah. He was reliable, and we weren't afraid.

As an aside, there is an issue I would like to clarify. For years, Turkey had disseminated state propaganda claiming that Kurdish young people were deceived, and that they were promised money and women. They were then double-crossed, and taken away to the mountains. This is a lie! You could never force someone to stay in the mountains. In some camps, there were hundreds of PKK members; in some of them, thousands. There were a great many chores and a lot of work to be shared. Now tell me, how would you force people to stay in a working camp like that? Would you follow them 24/7? It is impossible. What was true was that it wasn't easy for anyone in Turkey to earn money during that time. Our economic situation was bad. Our family was leading a poor life, but no one came to us to make any promises. We weren't offered money or authority in return for joining the organization. This is what I want the state and then the Turkish people to understand. What do they think someone would prefer; to leave the compassion of their parents and family, and all the comforts of home, in favor of a challenging life in difficult conditions? For people to choose this kind of life voluntarily, there must definitely be a strong reason behind it. I still don't understand how Turkish people could not grasp this.

I still remember the day of my leaving quite well. My friends and I had been out since morning. I came home in the evening, and had something to eat, trying to act completely normal, as if there were nothing out of the ordinary. After dinner, I told my mother that I was going to the tea house. I remember my mother asking me, "Will you come home early, son?" I replied, "Yes, I will, mom." I left my ID at home on purpose. If we got caught on the way, I didn't want the police to learn who I was. But while I was leaving the house, my mother said, "You've forgotten your ID! If you are going to the tea house, take it with you, so that you won't get into trouble with the police." So I had to take it. At 8:00 p.m., I met my friends at the place which we had agreed earlier. It was the next street over from the tea house. Everyone was there, as planned.

Half an hour later, the intermediary joined us. We got into a small truck. They took us to a neighborhood where we had never been before. The intermediary met someone else there. While we waited in the truck, they were talking about something outside. The intermediary came back to the truck after 10 or 15 minutes, and said, "You will continue your journey with this person from now on." When we learned that our first contact wasn't coming with us, we, of course, became a bit nervous. We said to the intermediary, "We know you. We trust you. You are the one we sought out, and you are the one who has brought us this far. Why are you passing us off to someone else? We don't like this change." He answered, "This man is completely reliable. You can trust him just as much as you trust me. There's no reason to worry. The place you're going is his home area. He knows it better than I do." So, we had no choice but to trust him.

As we had planned, there were four of us in that initial group. The rest returned back to their homes, and would join us a few days later. Actually, it made everything easier, since the three remaining friends returned home as normal. If we all had disappeared at the same time, our parents might have worried and called the police. But these three friends told our parents that the four of us, who were going up to the mountains, had simply gone to the market, and that we were going to come back home late. Because of this, none of the families, including mine, went to the police to report that we were missing.

The new intermediary took us to the city of Siirt. If I am not mistaken, it was about 3:00 a.m. that we settled into a hotel. The behavior of the hotel owner led me to believe that he understood we were going up to the mountains. He welcomed us as if he were welcoming heroes. He didn't ask for money as we left. We learned later that those going up to the mountains always stayed at this hotel first, and without payment. We had breakfast in the early morning. Before leaving the hotel, the intermediary had us get in touch with someone else and said, "You will continue with these people now."

So, having left the hotel, we went to a house in the city center. We stayed there for one night. We were now seven volunteers, as three new ones had joined us. The next day, we set off by minivan for the countryside. The intermediary took us as far as vehicles could possibly go. When we reached the end of the road, we got out, and the guides told us then that we were going to continue the rest of the way on foot.

So, it was after an exhausting journey in the countryside that we reached the militants. Now, you might call up a negative image when you hear the word "militant," but I would like to point out that for us the term "militant" stood for the leaders of the public. A small group of seven militants welcomed us. We were so overjoyed to see them! These were the first guerillas we had met. Figuring we must be hungry and tired by now, they had brought us some food, and all of us sat down to eat together. They spoke with us a bit, mostly asking questions like "Where is your hometown?" and "From where have you just come?" Then, they asked us whether or not we knew Turkish. This whole time the entire experience was barely sinking in. We were so overjoyed. None of it felt real, in the exact way that time flies away quickly, when you are truly happy.

After our meal and a few hours' rest, we were taken to a valley where another militia force, much more crowded, was located. When we arrived there, we saw female guerillas in the militia force. They were all armed. We asked ourselves why had we waited for so long to join, as there were even armed females already serving the organization.

There was a total of 35 to 40 people in that valley, and at least eight or nine of them were women. Soon, the leader of the group gathered us together and gave a short speech. He caught our attention from his very first question. "Comrades, is there anyone among you who wants to go home? You see the conditions here in the mountains. Don't say tomorrow that you can't cope with it. If you want to go, go now! You don't yet have a criminal record. Neither the police nor the soldiers know you yet. You still have a chance to lead an ordinary life. You can go back home."

None of us wanted to go back home, so then he gathered information from us, by asking each of us some questions that enabled him to get to know us better. "Where are you from? What does your family do? Why have you joined us?" When it was my turn, I answered, "I have heard the name of this organization in the city and have searched for you. The reason I have joined is the same as yours." The commander of the camp smiled at me. I continued, feeling more relaxed. "If you have any doubt about me, you can conduct your own search. You have militants in the city, and they can provide you with information about us."

Turning to the entire group, the commander inquired, "Whom do you know? Through whom have you come here?" My friends and I gave the name of the intermediary in the neighborhood. The commander didn't recognize his name. Then, we gave the name of the second intermediary. This one he did recognize. We figured that everyone probably had a nickname, and maybe not everyone knew all the nicknames.

Turning back to the group, the commander asked, "Where do you want to stay?" We all said, "If possible, we want to stay in this camp!" He answered that we could not stay there now. We first had to join the camps in Iraq and get military and political training. But then he amended that, saying we could stay there for a few days, in order to have a rest. New arrivals were joining the camp regularly. So, the commander decided to wait for a week for anyone following us, to send everyone to Iraq together, instead of sending us in smaller groups. With the additions, we were now a total of 40 new volunteers. The goal for our group was to reach the Gabar Mountain. About ten experienced militants were assigned to protect the group, which included me and the new arrivals, from potential dangers.

We proceeded on foot. It was an exhausting journey, but at least we had no problems with food. There were all kinds of bread, rice, beans, and cheese. In addition to this, we would drop by the neighboring villages on our way. Generally, we had our dinners in these villages. We were newbies back then, and didn't understand why the villagers prepared food for us, as if they were throwing us a feast. Then, we figured out that in advance of our arrival in the villages, four or five people from the group would visit them and inform them of our coming. "Be ready. There is a new group of 45 people arriving." And, of course, there was no coercion in play.

When we arrived in the villages, we would be sent to different houses in groups of five. Since the villagers knew that we were new in the organization, they would offer whatever they had. Because there was no transportation out this far, or simply because the state neglected these villages in the mountainy areas, soldiers generally wouldn't stop by these villages. They only came and provided general discipline, once every three months. Therefore, the organization pretty much had control there.

Mountain of Gabar

After each dinner, we would get up and leave immediately, moving as much as possible under cover of darkness so as to avoid getting caught. During our travel, our seniors in the organization informed us about the region through which we were passing. "Those lights over there are a police station, so watch out." "Over here is a sympathetic place, where you can find food and rest." "This landmark indicates one depot where we cache our weapons."

During a break in our journey, before we had made it to Gabar Mountain, our group leader turned to us and asked us loudly, "Who here knows how to use weapons? Raise your hands!" About 20 people raised their hands. He asked them, one by one, which weapons they knew how to use. I knew how to use almost every weapon he listed. The experienced militants gave Kalashnikov weapons (AK-47s) to those who knew how to use them. But, they warned everyone, "No one will use them without an order, and if there is an incident, you will be put under the jurisdiction of the older militants." Then we continued on our way.

We walked for days. Following a long and exhausting journey, we arrived in Gabar. At the end of the journey, we who had started as seven people, were now 60. The camp at Gabar was very crowded. Besides us, there were about 120 guerrillas. The very first thing they did was to assign an older and experienced militant to every ten people. Then, they sent us to the ward tents, telling us that we were going to be wakened at 4:30 a.m.

It was our first day in Gabar, when the senior militants first taught us to call each other "heval" (comrade). We were going to call everyone "comrade," no matter what authority or rank they had, out of respect. Then they informed us about the specific rules. For instance, when we had a problem, we were to inform the person whom they appointed as the squad leader. If he wasn't available, we were told who to contact next. Also, while traveling during the day, or waiting in place, we were to leave nothing behind that might sparkle or capture attention, such as a mirror, food cups, or brightly colored fabric. We were all given military camouflage tents, and advised to hide our possessions in them. Also, when we saw a helicopter or a plane in the air, we were to remain still and not move. If we were to leave our group and join another one, we were to inform the leader of the group. Meals were to be eaten at specific hours. If we smoked, we were to be careful with the lighters in the evening. We were to light cigarettes inside the tents and we were not to leave there until we had finished smoking. However, we were also only to smoke when it was allowed.

In short, we were all to obey what we were told, word for word. But I want to add that this wasn't blind discipline with no understanding. If something was forbidden, we were told why it was forbidden. In other words, rules and orders were given in clear language.

They were also always helping us in many ways. There was a powerful atmosphere of friendship and brotherhood. Some of the newcomers frequently got tired and lost their motivation, but no one would yell at them. On the contrary, they would be approached in a friendly manner, and asked, "What's the matter? Is this too much of a load for you to carry? Are you ill? If you want, we can give your burden to someone else."

There was one overweight comrade. He had come from the city, and didn't realize at all what life in the mountains was like. He knew no Kurdish whatsoever, and his eyesight was so bad that he couldn't walk at night. We newcomers were criticizing him—questioning why he was even here. But the older ones weren't like that. They were very patient and did their best to make sure this guy reached the camp.

Weapons training started the first day. We were so excited. Some of the students in that first class immediately wanted to learn how to use bombs. The leaders rejected this idea saying, "Bombs are dangerous. We can't teach you that here, but you will learn about that in Iraq."

A huge noise woke us up on the second day. Of course, we didn't yet understand everything, since we were new, but, we were terrified. The experienced ones warned us, "Fighter jets! Air attack!" After the sorties of the [Turkish] planes were over, the helicopters started to blow up the camp field. Although the Cobras (deadly attack helicopters) burned down their target, we were already in the shelters beneath. The experienced ones were so relaxed and were telling us that we shouldn't have panicked. The shelters were really durable and safe. By this time, everywhere was covered in snow. Therefore, there was a large visual splash at the impact site of the bombs. Soon the older ones started to answer the Cobras with anti-aircraft weapons. We had lost two people, and we had eight injured. At around 7:00 a.m., the helicopters withdrew.

We thought this meant the attack was over and that we could pack up. But just then, the watchmen informed us that they had seen some soldiers get off the helicopters about 1 kilometer away. So, we were about to be attacked by land, to follow up their air attack. At around 1:00 p.m. the battle started. We were new, so initially we weren't allowed to participate in the fighting. The senior guerillas weren't very worried about this ground battle, because they estimated there were more than enough guerrillas in our camp to defeat the Turkish soldiers. They figured it would be a head to head battle. The militants knew the details of the area better than did the soldiers. That turned out to make the difference. The soldiers just showed off, but couldn't even get any closer to the camp.

The following day, we held a guerilla funeral ceremony for our two comrades who had died. Once we had buried them, the camp leaders told us that 15 experienced guerrillas were going to be assigned to guard our newbie group. Our new recruit group still consisted of 60 people, including myself, and now we were going to be sent to Besler camp, which was on the border of the city of Şırnak. It had become very risky for us newcomers to stay in the mountain of Gabar. The Turkish military could start a second attack at any time, so we were relocated to Cudi, over at Besler, and from there to Iraq.

The fighter aircraft hit our camp field again that morning, before we left the camp. There were eight aircraft this time. Being taken by surprise, it cost us 12 comrades' lives, and I myself took shrapnel in both legs. The doctors in the camp immediately treated them. Back then, I was so surprised to be attended to so quickly, outside of a hospital, right there on the ground. But I soon found out that there were at least three surgeons in each camp.

Right after the attack, we were sent off for Besler camp. We rested in two villages on our way. The villagers took very good care of us, since some of their members had joined us in the resistance. They not only gave us food but also helped us pass specific points of danger on the way. When we reached the first village, the villagers told us there was a Turkish military outpost located very close to the village. It had been hit by an avalanche, and around 40 Turkish soldiers had been buried and killed. The villagers suggested that if we could make it there, we could collect all their weapons and ammunition.

The experienced ones among us criticized this offer harshly. "A natural disaster happened, and it would be against the morals of the organization to profit from the spoils in such a situation."

In the second village, which was in the foothills of Cudi Mountain, we stayed for two days, due to the severity of the blizzards. All the roads were covered in snow. Visibility was zero. The villagers here gave us 15 pairs of snowshoes, so we wouldn't sink down into the snow when we walked. The 15 guerrillas who we fitted with these snowshoes were going to clear the path for us, and we would follow. On the fourth day, the villagers—those who survived on smuggling—took us from Cudi Mountain to Iraq.

The Camp of Haftanin

By the end of February, we reached the Haftanin region, in Iraq. Haftanin is an area under Kurdish control, in the north of Iraq. There are 250 to 300 militants in each camp. Our troop consisted of 260 people.

In this region, there were a total of four camps. The training in three of these camps was held in Turkish, and the fourth camp in Kurdish. The Kurdish-language camp was mostly for the Kurds who came from Syria and Iraq. The other three camps were for Turkish Kurds who came from Turkey and Europe.

The general commander of the camps in Iraq, and of the all four Kurdistan states, was Cemil Bayık. Bayık controlled the PKK activities in Turkey, and he also directed actions by the organization in Syria, Iraq and Iran. But Bayık wasn't there once we got to Haftanin. We were told that he was in Iraq, visiting all the camps to give political and ideological lectures. If I have the timeline right, one week later he visited our camp. He gave us training in two different areas. The first one was the historical development of the organization. He lectured us on how, where, and when the organization was established; what kind of incidents it went through during its founding; and gave us details and dates. The other training was about President Apo, and his beliefs.

Cemil Bayık's oratory was very influential. Some people just truly impress you when they speak, and he was one of them. I made it no secret throughout the organization that I was more committed to Cemil Bayık than to President Apo. Bayık has a power that charms people, draws all their attention, and channels it into a specific direction. I will talk more about this once we begin discussing the later years. After Apo was caught, there was only one reason the organization wasn't disbanded: Cemil Bayık's persuasiveness and impressive tone. His nickname in the organization was Cuma.

Apo also loved Comrade Cuma. He was the right hand of Apo, in terms of executing strategy. In other words, Apo would determine the political strategy, and Cemil Bayık would make this strategy applicable for daily use, determining which political and military tactics were to be applied, according to this strategy.

Of course, surrounding Cemil Bayık, there were other effective and experienced names. Bayık would take these people with him to the camps in Turkey and Iraq to provide motivation and moral support to the militants there.

After the lesson on "The History of the Organization," we had a training called "The Truth about Apo." This was all about Apo and the inception of the organization, such as from where Apo came, how the skeleton crew of the organization was formed, and how Apo gathered this team. Each set of training lasted approximately ten days. The eleventh day was a "question and answer" session. Any student could ask any question at all, so long as it related to the training, and we could ask anyone, even Cemil Bayık himself. We had at least 300 people in that class, so the question and answer session went on for hours, but Cemil Bayık answered every single question without ever getting frustrated or showing weariness. Moreover, he would continue explaining one answer and responding to all the follow-up questions until the student he was answering was completely satisfied. If, despite all of this, the questioner still wasn't satisfied, Cemil Bayık would send for him after the lesson and clarify any remaining details.

Bayık stayed with us from March to mid-May, during which period I got several chances to address him in person. Each time, I asked him, "How had the organization expanded so fast in such a short period of time?" The answers he gave were all surprising to me. Bayık told me many times that the organization owed its current condition to the Turkish militants. "This movement reached this level, thanks to the Turks. Almost everyone who established this organization with our President Apo—Hakkı Karer, Duran Kalkan, and Kemal Bir—were all influenced by the old Turkish revolutionaries: Deniz Gezmiş, Mahir Cayan and Hüseyin İnan, who were called the "Three Saplings," and had become the idols of the founders of PKK. Cemil Bayık once said, "This revolution is not only the Kurds' revolution. It will also be the Turks' revolution."

Other lessons we received included, "The History of the PKK," "Leadership Philosophy," "Modern Turkish and Global Politics," and "Our Leadership's Goals for the PKK." Each guerilla who completed his training in Haftanin camp left having read every book written by Apo. As I stated before, the training didn't impose anything on anyone by force. If a subject was lectured about for two hours, the next two hours were spent answering guerillas' questions, so that they didn't have any doubts. Any doubts were dismissed by the detailed explanations of the training Commission.

Political Training

Political training was very significant in shaping our thoughts. At first, many of us had joined the organization out of passion and emotion alone. Most militants were acting purely from the bloodlust of "When do we get our weapons? When do I get my revenge?" But, our training wasn't on military tactics alone. The experienced leadership knew they had first to convince us to understand the aim and purpose of the organization. Only in this way, would all of our actions align with the organization's goal.

In 1992, the year I joined the organization, the main purpose of the PKK was to establish an independent Kurdish state. In other words, it was to set free the Kurdish areas in Turkey, Syria, Iran and Iraq. The guerilla was always motivated by this purpose. But, despite the strength of our mission to establish an independent Kurdish state, the senior PKK executives were always emphasizing that we had no problems with Turkish people. Even if we succeeded in becoming physically separated from Turkey and declared our independence, we would never remain enemies with the Turks. The reason for our fight with Turkey was just the current fascist system. In other words, no matter what, we were going to stay friends with Turkish people forever.

This is why no hostility or hatred towards Turks themselves, or the Turkish ethnic identity, was ever incorporated or tolerated in any of our political or ideological training. The problem for the organization was the system, not the people. In other words, the PKK's only issue was with the political authorities who didn't recognize the democratic rights of the Kurdish people. So, our training included absolutely nothing about seeing Turks as enemies. However, some individuals among us would act emotionally from time to time. In the period during which I joined the organization, most Kurdish patriots were joining because they had been subject to violence at the hands of the Turkish police or soldiers. We all had friends with the view that "Turkish soldiers tortured my innocent family, and my relatives. Why shouldn't I take my revenge on the innocent Turks?" These people were objecting to the doctrine that we must stay friends with Turks, as we were being told in the training. But the organization was strictly against such anti-Turk sentiments and would prevent them as much as possible. The senior executives were always calming down our friends who joined the organization for revenge. They told them, "We can't solve the problem by acting from the desire for revenge and killing innocent people. On the contrary, if we used such a method, we would lose the validity of our own struggle. So, although it is right that we fight for our own people, we should never include innocent people in this war. We must respect others."

The reason for this was pretty clear. Turks and Kurds weren't separated like the other nations in Europe. We had intermarried with one another so that the Turkish and Kurdish identities were mixed. The national identities were combined through affinity, and it was now very difficult to change that. Also, in every major city, the Kurds and Turks were living side by side. Our trainers knew this and framed their political and ideological training within this reality. Even in the military training, the instructors were sometimes emphasizing that we were to be merciful to the enemy. For example, during a battle, if we were eye to eye with an enemy, we were told that we could kill him if he was going to kill us. However, it was impressed upon us that an injured enemy would be hurt no further, but rather be taken captive and be treated.

The purpose of taking them as captives was to swap them in the future with the PKK members who fell into the hands of the Turkish Government. Were we ever successful in this? No. Turkey had such a political and bureaucratic structure that they would never sit at a negotiation table with us, even if we took all the police officers in the city of Hakkari as captives, and then asked them to set free at least ten imprisoned guerillas. Their own government considered their police and soldiers to be worthless to them. Look at Israel—that as a country, the Turks were always criticizing. Those men who were derided for being Jewish swapped hundreds of Palestinians to save one or two Israeli soldiers on many occasions. It happened again in 2011. In return for one Israeli soldier, thousands of captives were set free.

The other purpose of taking captives was to use their release as propaganda later. It made us look very good if we released our prisoners even if the Turkish Government did not accede at all to our demands to negotiate. In the 1990s, when the Prime Minister was Mr. Erbakan, Haşimi came from his cabinet to the PKK camp field in Iraq, and brought back to their families the soldiers who had been taken as captives by the PKK. The Turkish families were grateful for this act by the PKK. Erbakan had sent a letter to Apo after this incident and indicated that he wanted to solve the Turkish-Kurdish problem through political means, without shedding any blood. I remember it quite well. The letter had this sentence: "Let the weapons be silent, and let's solve this through democratic methods."

With such firm steps taken towards peace, the leadership of the PKK had impressed upon us that our dispute with the Turkish Government could, ultimately, only be resolved through negotiation. Our violent missions were only justified because that's what it took to bring the state to the negotiation table. The hints of success appeared in the spring of 1993. Stopping this fight, and solving the problem through political means or through dialogues, was now inevitable.

One of our trainers in the camp had told us that the guerilla fights all over the world had three stages: Active defense, fight for equality, and attack. Most of these fights were solved before the last stage. The PKK entered into the fight for equality with the Turkish Armed forces in 1992. Although the military didn't completely withdraw from East Anatolia, in those years it had largely lost its dominance in the countryside. They had gathered their power in specific stations and headquarters, and they weren't able to leave these places. The organization, by and large, dominated. Besides the countryside, the PKK even had the power to besiege some cities! The military stations in these cities were being kept under siege sometimes for days and sometimes for weeks. In the spring of 1992, the military stations of Nerwe and Rubarok were blockaded by the organization. At that time, all the soldiers in the Nerwe Station were killed. The President at the time, Süleyman Demirel, had even paid a visit to the station after this incident.

Then the military finally understood that we guerillas even had the power to capture their bases. That's why the bases in the unsafe regions were abandoned, one by one, and the military force was gathered in specific central locations. At the start of 1993, the organization and the government declared a mutual ceasefire. During this ceasefire, the organization made a big change in its main purpose and goals.

According to the leadership of PKK, the conditions in the world had changed. The real socialism was dispersed at the beginning of the 1990s, and there was no longer any alliance of power among militant organizations, as there had been. In other words, it no longer made sense to create an independent Kurdish state, as had been the case in the 1960s and 1970s. Therefore, the leading figures in the organization started to impose upon the guerillas that PKK's main purpose wasn't to establish an independent Kurdistan anymore, but was to live together with the Turks under a democratic roof. There was no objection raised to this re-purposing from the lowest level to the upper authorities within the organization. Every militant in the organization had adjusted themselves to this new policy. So, I don't know what happened behind the scenes, but in 1993, both the organization and the Turkish Government mutually destroyed this peace process.

5

MISSION TRAINING

The camp life was physically exhausting. We would wake up at 4:30 a.m. each morning, with a muster at 5:00 a.m. After the muster, physical training, and then we would have breakfast at around 7:30 a.m. Between 8:00 and 11:00 a.m., we would receive three hours of political training. Break time came at 11:15 a.m. and we would then have lunch. After lunch, we would have a short rest period of 45 minutes. At 1:00 p.m. we would start the military training.

Both men and women enjoyed the military training. We could never understand how time flew by so quickly, and it would be 5:00 p.m. before we knew it. First, we received weapons training, which included how to hold, aim, fire, and reload properly. Then, we learned how to clean and care for our weapons. Training was given on many different kinds of weapons, such as the Kanas assault rifle, the bazooka, the heavy machine howitzer, anti-aircraft weapons, and many kinds of guns, including Kalashnikov (AK-47), BKC, and heavy automatic anti-aircraft weapons.

This basic weapons training was given to everyone, no matter how young or old they were, and included both men and women. In addition to the weapons training, we also received extended practical training on guerilla war tactics (assault, ambush, raid, infiltration, attack, extended siege, forestallment, and mining). This training was given mostly by people with practical experience—those who had been playing an active role in the organization for years, and had proven themselves in the field of military battle.

Assassination Missions

The sniper assassination missions were individual actions made against specific people. The target could be a relatively high-ranking military commander or a politician. Someone with enough individual authority, who could make trouble for us. These characteristics of the target are what made the difficulty of staging an assassination mission worth the risk. One wouldn't go through all this effort to take out any ordinary civilian, or foot soldier. How would that be worthwhile to the organization?

This action could be carried out either with weapons or explosives. For instance, you could carry out an attack by placing a bomb inside of a package. Our assassin team consisted mostly of professionals, since it took such a large investment of both time and money to fully train each sniper. They would never be risked on the front lines during battle. They would be situated at some distant place, sometimes sneaking into enemy lines and targeting those who were coordinating the operation on the side of the enemy. The targets were usually high-ranking people, for the simple reason that, if you leave a military force without a commander, you can easily disable the soldiers.

I witnessed this quite a lot in the ensuing years. Once a commander, at the head of a military force (squadron leader, lieutenant colonel, corps commander) was assassinated, the guerilla's mission was not finished. You might ask, how do you determine who the high-ranking officials are during an operation? We learned, by experience, that the fighting soldier and the commander never stayed at the same spot. The commander was always located somewhere strategic from where he directed his soldiers. This strategic area would generally be on a high hill. There would always be four or five guards near the commander. In this way, the location of the commander could be detected and then disabled by the assassins. The high-ranking officers would sometimes remove their rank insignias and pretend to be soldiers, in order to make it more difficult to be discovered. Then, we needed to try and detect who they really were from their behavior.

Ambush

We would carry out the ambush tactic to narrow the movement area of the soldiers. We would bottleneck the movement area, which panicked the enemy. The ambush was normally executed in the travel area between two travel routes. For instance, the ambush could be on the way between the military base and the town to which it was connected, or the road between two military bases.

Ambush is a short-duration action. It takes 15 minutes at most. If you remained in the area of an ambush any longer, it would turn into a battle. A battle meant losses for us, because the [Turkish] soldiers were greater in number and had support from both air and land.

But, despite taking so little time, an ambush is a very effective guerilla tactic, if you plan it well. It doesn't even take a very large group. You can create an effective ambush with only five guerrillas. One of the significant elements of ambush is that the proper conditions and sufficient time for withdrawal must be set, and the retreat route must be pre-determined. You can't use the ambush tactic in the morning, and so it is usually carried out in the evening. After the action, you retreat and disappear into the pitch darkness. We used Kalashnikovs, bixi, anti-tank weapons, mines, and bazookas while carrying out ambushes.

Infiltration

Meanwhile, infiltration tactics are made to shock the enemy unexpectedly by penetrating their territory. The number of guerrillas involved in the infiltration missions would vary, according to the nature of the target, but the maximum was six people, because as the size of the group increases, so does the risk of being noticed. But, if your plan is to stage a raid to destroy an entire enemy encampment, the night after an infiltration mission, it would make more sense to include a larger number of guerrillas in the initial infiltration, so that more of them would be familiarized with the enemy's layout, by the second mission.

Any guerrilla who participated in an infiltration, must be small, alert, and calm. First of all, it is preferable that they have a tiny body structure. Next, excellent judgment and awareness, and lastly, there needed to be a calmness, because being calm in these types of missions was most important. Someone who cannot control their fear might panic ahead of the infiltration and make the enemy team aware of our presence. Another important factor regarding infiltrations was that the people who participated in these kinds of actions set off for the mission only after saying goodbye to all of their family and friends. The likelihood of being martyred in such a mission was very high, so one does not volunteer for these missions expecting to survive. You volunteer as the ultimate proof that you hold the ideals of the organization, and the freedom of your comrades, to be of greater importance to you than your own life.

No one was forced. There was never any pressure to join an infiltration action. In fact, it was essential to have the participants be volunteers. Guerillas who wanted to participate in such an action would make the offer. The senior executives would then evaluate the offers and allow the individuals they considered to be appropriate to become part of the mission team. Not just anyone who wished could participate in an infiltration action. You couldn't join if you had never been on any other missions, and you needed to have experience living in and patrolling the countryside. You also had to have participated in the surveillance of that particular target. Rank wasn't the basis of selection in such missions. Sometimes, two high-ranking officers or two regular guerillas could carry out an infiltration mission at the same time.

We had many missions that resulted in the death of the whole infiltrating team. Thus, the guerillas who were going to participate in such missions would be carefully chosen and become completely focused on the action. Each detail was important. There was nothing like having surveillance in the morning and infiltration in the evening. The surveillance on the target would last for days and absolutely everything would be noted, including when the change of guards took place, how many soldiers were on the sites, what the precise distance was between two military posts, what kind of weapons they were using, whether they had night vision, whether there were any night patrols, and whether there was an exit or entrance to the target area. Every detail was noted.

I joined infiltration missions many times in the following years. On such missions, dogs and the wind were two risky factors that could not be in your favor. We learned, in time, that you definitely need to factor them into your plans. If you failed to notice that you're upwind of the target, the breeze could bring your scent to the dogs, ensuring that your target would be alerted to your presence entirely too soon.

Raids

The raid mission tactic was our most frequently used tactic in the guerilla war, performed with a large force and heavy weapons, and the chance of a raid turning into a battle was very high. A raid can sometimes take 15 to 20 minutes and sometimes an hour or more, depending on the target. Likewise, the raid mission could be performed with a force of 50 people, or it could be performed with 500 to 1,000 people.

All the preparations for the raid mission took place at night. The armory that was to be used during the raid was taken close to the target at night, and surveillance took place for days before the raid. During these surveillance missions, both technical and physical information is gathered. If the raid is performed with a large group, intelligence is not gathered by one particular group during a surveillance. In other words, the area subject to the raid is watched with binoculars and camera by at least three or four surveillance groups over different times. Then, through militants pretending to be villagers, the force strength in the region is studied from both close and hidden sites. Factors tallied were how much power the target had, the capacity of their weapons, and the point where their closest backup force could reach. Everything, including whether the backup force would come from the air or by land, was taken into account.

Since the backup/reserve forces couldn't easily reach the Turkish military bases situated in rocky sites, and the arrival of help would take time, we would generally make raids at such points. In a raid mission, the attacking groups were placed in three or four flanks. The support group was placed behind the attacking group. Behind the support group, the medical group was placed, which had a few doctors, nurses, and first-aid kits. Finally, at a dominant spot where the target could clearly be seen, the coordinating group was placed. It consisted of three or five high-ranking commanders. A ready team would be waiting near this coordinating group, ready to move forward to provide reinforcements.

In the raid mission, combat experience and voluntarism are essential. More experienced, active militants join these attack and support groups. Those with less experience join the defense and other groups. There were definitely two commanders at the head of each group. If something happens to one, the other commander takes over the duty. Every group participating in the mission carries small radios with channels pre-set to our intelligence wavelengths. Our coordinating team was always in touch with every guerrilla involved. As I mentioned before, the coordinating group consisted of three or five people. Those people shared the duties, and each of them took charge of two or three groups. For instance, one commander might take charge of the ambush and defense groups; one commander take charge of the reinforcements and defense groups and the remaining one would take charge of the health and replacement groups.

In the raid missions, our attack group would usually use Kalashnikovs, bombs, grenades, and bazookas. Deep within the valleys, the defense groups would have hidden heavy machine guns, Dochkas, howitzers, and missiles. The size of the arsenal depended upon the size of the target. Mines and ambushes were laid the night before the planned raid. These were to destroy land-based reinforcements. Then, reinforcements can only come by air, reducing the soldiers to only two remaining methods of harm. They could either try to bring Skorsky helicopters close enough to us to land more foot soldiers, in which case we start firing on those helicopters, long before they reach us, or their second option was to attack us with combat aircraft, shooting and bombing us directly from fighter jets and attack helicopters. Then, their problem was that the weapons employed by these combat aircraft were intensely powerful but not very precise. So, while the probability of eliminating us this way would be high, so would their probability of murdering their own forces. Even though these aircraft-based weapons were completely capable of shooting at us from their own safe distance, long before the aircraft themselves were within range of our weapons, they were blocked by their own ground troops from being very effective.

Also, in mountainous and rural areas, Turkish fighter aircraft cannot easily hit a target. There were a few reasons for this. First of all, our groups were scattered and situated far away from each other. In addition, in mountainous areas, the planes cannot get an accurate reading from their laser sights. For a fighter plane to shoot the target without missing it, there must be a laser fix on the ground or in the air, and these planes cannot achieve that in mountainous areas. Therefore, if we attacked military bases in these mountainous areas, we were generally successful.

Having a spare armory in a raid is mandatory. The reinforcement group carries the spare armory of the attack group. In addition, the general coordinating group also has a large armory, in order to supply ammo to any groups that are in need. On these missions, the schedule of which precise action will take place and at which time was determined in advance. Everyone knew the start and end times of the mission before it began. Even the routes through which the enemy would withdraw were determined beforehand. Our groups gathered at the predetermined points and moved towards the last determined point. The basic rule of guerilla warfare was to attack and retreat. No guerilla group, except in exceptional cases, remained where it was and continued to fight.

If we had any losses in any missions, the survivors brought back as many of the remains of our fallen as was possible. If the circumstances were unfavorable, we had to leave the corpses of our friends on the battlefield. Medical teams brought mules for the purpose of transporting the dead and the injured. In such missions, the commanding officers would already have estimated how many losses there might be, according to the scope of the mission, even before starting the action. For a very large mission, ten guerillas seemed to be a possible loss.

If the mission was successful, the amount of losses wasn't as devastating to us (unless, of course, you lost a close friend whom you had known for years). Because we were always aware that we were in a war, we never lost sight of the fact that we could lose a friend at any moment, as well as our own life.

Another issue that was very important, but easy to overlook by the guerillas participating in any raid or other tactics, was never to carry any information concerning the organization: no documents, no CDs, and no USBs. The reality was that these documents could get into the hands of the enemy at any time.

After each mission, every guerilla, whether ranked or not, would gather, and we would evaluate the mission together. Had we performed the mission as planned? Did anything unfavorable happen? Had the groups moved in the ways in which we had needed? Everything was evaluated. If a group hadn't followed the plan, they would be punished. I frequently witnessed this firsthand. One time a commander with 20 years' experience was dismissed from duty and his rank was lowered to that of a regular guerilla, because he had led a failed mission. It was possible for a top commander to be reduced to a foot soldier, after just one mission. War cannot accept mistakes. Therefore, we could not accept mistakes on the part of our commanders, without sanction. It could set a precedent which allowed others to be neglectful, and that would allow a crack in the very values system which formed the foundation of our organization.

Basic Training

From time to time, instructors of war tactics from foreign states would come and give us some training about combat, such as when we established a new organization to fight Iran (PJAK) between the years 2003 and 2004. Interestingly, the American authorities contacted us in Iraq and said, "We want to train PJAK." The organization didn't accept their first proposal, but when they requested the second time, we agreed to a trial. I wish we hadn't. American soldiers came and began training us as if we were their regular army. What they taught us was so basic, we quickly realized our training program was harder and more professional than theirs. Granted, Americans know a lot more than we do, technically, and their weapons are much better, but our training is guerilla training. If we exchanged our tough, environment-adapted training in favor of the Americans' standardized military training, we would only lose. When we realized we had nothing to learn from them, we thanked them and sent them home.

What Americans taught was all based on technology. Our fighting is not like that, but is directed towards improving one's fighting ability by increasing one's self-control. You saw the efficacy of our style in the battles for Kobane. ISIS had all kinds of advanced weaponry: tanks, cannons, and rifles—all with the very latest technology. Yet, the PKK would save Kobane from ISIS, without any such weapons, because ISIS members were not motivated by a righteous goal; only money interested them. The Peshmerga of Barzani also had weapons of the latest technology but were unable to fight ISIS. They simply ran away. So, the main motive was the development of self-control and courage, as well as the passion of fighting for a cause. Without this personal development and conviction, soldiers were unable to gain victories no matter how good their technology.

At heart, the guerilla being trained must have a spirit and a will. That's why we didn't often need the training of others, except on how to use special weapons. Then, specific training was received from Russia, Armenia, Greece, and some European countries.

Our basic training lasted for a few months. We practiced with weapons over and over. We were taught the theoretical underpinnings, and then drilled on the practical. For instance, the people who were trained as assassins had to shoot their sniper rifles in training at least 1,000 times. And after this three- to four-month basic training, each militant was appointed to the general branches, according to their skills and capacity. There were two main groups: saboteurs and operations.

The saboteur group was divided into three sections: the miners, the assassins, and those using heavy weapons. Women comprised the majority of this group (approximately 60 percent). Sabotage, in assassin work, takes great patience. In assassination, expertise with your weapons is extremely important, with self-discipline the only trait being more important. You need to utilize the weapon flawlessly. Most of the men in the organization fail at assassination for one reason: because they smoke. The most significant thing in an assassination, is to control one's breathing and finger sensitivity. Smokers can't breathe, so they can't get into that zone and can't squeeze the trigger space precisely. Female guerillas are more patient and calm. Men were always in an impatient rush. A man won't wait 3 hours at the same spot to shoot a target, but a woman will. Therefore, female snipers were preferred.

The other group is the operation team, which constitutes the attacking teams battling with the Turkish military. Their tasks included raids, attacks, and ambushes. The assassins also participate in battles but remain behind. Their aim is to protect the operation team by disabling distant enemy teams. They never get within the enemy's weapon sights. The military in Turkey mostly use G-3 rifles. An assassin takes the sight range of the enemy's weapons into account when choosing their location. The range is longer, so the assassin sets up their sniper nest outside of the range of the enemies' weapons, because no one can easily shoot under fire.

Military training ended around 5:00 p.m. every day. So, after the day's final military muster, everyone was set free about 5:30 p.m. You were then allowed to go to bed or participate in other social activities. You could even leave camp, with permission, but you had to be back in the camp by the end of the rest period. In general, I used to spend my free time reading books. I was mostly reading Turkish books, because there were almost no books written in Kurdish.

Many memories, both good and bad, were made during training. For example, the day that grenades were the topic of the lecture, when we were in the Haftanin training camp, everyone in our group of 25 was going to throw a grenade. We had all gathered at a large rock formation, and now we were pulling the pins of grenades and throwing them over to the opposite side. I will never forget when one of the comrades threw the pin to the other side, and dropped the grenade next to him. Thank God, the trainer was professional and grabbed it immediately, and threw it to the other side. We all had a good laugh at this comrade. It was so natural. I had no nerves around weapons, since I was no stranger to them since childhood.

Division of Labor at the Camp

Until I saw them with my own eyes, I had never thought that women would want to join the fight. Yet, almost one third of the camp consisted of female guerrillas. We asked our more experienced friends why there was such a high percentage of participation of Kurdish women in the organization. The most obvious reason, which they stated unanimously, was that the PKK had taken steps towards the social liberation of women. In Kurdish society, the dominant, patriarchal culture repressed women, as a way of life, but this was certainly not the case for the PKK. The organization, with no room for argument, stated that no one was allowed to treat a woman with anything but respect. Manners towards women were very important in the PKK and rules were strict. You would certainly catch criticism if you used bad language toward a male guerilla, but if you used the same language toward a woman guerilla, you would get penalties such as no smoking or extra watch keeping. These penalties were meted out according to the severity of your behavior. Meanwhile, despite the positive attitude and approach regarding discrimination against women guerrillas, the division of labor recognized no gender. So, the women were required to do all the same tasks as the men.

There was a huge division of labor at the camp. There were squads just for kitchen and bakery duty. If one unit of ten people was insufficient, they would enlist a second unit. Those guerillas would be responsible for cooking and baking for the day. Our camps cooked a wide variety of food. Washing-up and cleaning were also their responsibility.

We had three meals a day, but that could be flexible. For example, if we got hungry at night, we could get a midnight snack. It was up to the supply officer of the camp to decide about the menu every day. The dietician and the supply officer would make a monthly meal list, and the appointed group would then cook the meals on this list. The food was generally good, with legumes and meat products, which were available at all times, though there were instances when fruits and vegetables were in short supply.

Newcomers weren't allowed on kitchen duty for the first two months, because they needed to learn, alongside the former guerrillas, how the food was cooked and how the kitchen works were managed. After they reached a certain level of skill, they could start helping. Meanwhile, everyone, ranked or not, had to enter the rotation for the kitchen labor. No one could say, "I'm a commander, so I shouldn't be cooking meals!" Rank earned you no privileges. So it was no surprise to see a commander washing-up the dishes. At the end of the day, the squad on duty would carry the kitchen to the logisticians, after all the tasks were completed. Then, the supply officer checked all the materials, the cleanliness, and other things and assumed responsibility for the kitchen. The next day, he would pass the duty and the kitchen to a new squad.

Everything was based on the commune system in the organization. No one was salaried. Let's say there were 50 people in a battalion. For this battalion, there would be one comrade in charge of logistics. This comrade was then tasked with managing all income and expenses. This logistician calculated everything, from how many cartons of cigarettes were needed to what type of food supplies the kitchen required.

This supply officer also visited every guerilla and asked whether they needed anything special. He noted down everybody's needs, from shoes, clothes, and underwear to socks. The camp supply officer then delivered this list to the master supplier of the region, who was in charge of purchasing. Each region had a very efficient purchase unit. All needs reached the requesting region in a maximum of two days, so there was no shortage of money. No one but the commander carried money on him. In other words, the leader of a team didn't even have one Turkish lira. For possible supply emergencies, the battalion commander had 3,000 to 4,000. That's all!

The safety of the camp had also to be ensured. The security group responsible for its protection was called "Hillers." They were so named because they were generally located on a high hill. There were two kinds of hillers. One group was fixed in place, while the second group was changed every day. The fixed group stayed at a permanent observation area and consisted of 15 professional guerrillas. This group was responsible for the heavy, emplaced weapons, such as rockets and mortars. For the duration of their two to three-month assignment, they would never leave that post; not even to come down to the camp for food. All their needs were brought to them. On the other hand, the other type of group was rotated daily. This type of hillers would go to the fixed group and receive training from them. The stable, professional group and the rotating trainee group encampments were always located at least 500 meters from one another.

Types of Penalties in the Guerilla Life

The camp had a strange custom, which I originally found quite odd. Each night we were all asked to give an oral statement, evaluating the content of our daily life. All the members of the squads were gathered together and would give an oral report on their opinion of the chairmanship of their individual squad commander. At first, we could not understand any possible purpose for this meeting, since you could say anything here related to the camp about the daily life or the people. If your friend had a quirk that you didn't like, you could criticize them in front of everyone. At the beginning, I found this weird, because it felt like whistleblowing. Then, we understood that it was not that way. The aim was for everybody to help each other's personal development by highlighting mistakes. That oral report was made to correct the mistakes by stating the person's shortcomings. We could criticize anyone for the same mistake three times. If he continued doing the same thing, despite repeated criticism by various people, he would be penalized.

The penalty was decided by a majority vote of the group. In this town-hall-style meeting, we could even criticize the commander of the squad and impose penalties on him. For example, three times, a friend had left his equipment behind in his barracks and forgotten to take it to training. Besides, he hadn't woken up for the muster, and it appeared he simply could not adapt to camp life. So, we communally gave him the penalty of cleaning all the squad's weapons.

All the rules and their penalties were clearly predefined, and we were continually being updated about them. Fleeing and/or abandoning an injured comrade during a battle had serious penalties. This type of behavior could result in up to a three or six year suspension from the organization. Suspension of membership from the organization was the most severe sanction for a guerrilla. A member with a suspension could not participate in our meetings; could not speak in any of our parliaments; lost his right to vote; could not criticize others, and could not ask anything from anyone until his penalty was over. In other words, though he was allowed to stay among us, he was ostracized, and considered to "not exist". If he repeated the same offense for a second time, he would be dismissed. The theory was, "If you do not improve; if you don't spruce up your behavior, then just leave before your bad behavior starts rubbing off and damaging the other members of this organization."

The expulsion decision was only made at the end of a long process. Before making such a decision about a person, a commission of three would be formed. The commission would consist of one battalion commander and two guerrillas. Their judgment was rendered publicly, and the guerrillas, in general, had their opportunity to give an opinion about the person under discussion. The battalion commander would make a brief disclosure, stating this person had committed such and such a crime. Then, that person was given the right to speak to defend himself. If the person directly admitted his guilt, his crime would be somewhat mitigated. But, if he did not plead guilty, the commission of inquiry would investigate the incident in every minute detail, listen to all the witnesses present, and then create a report. This report would be read in front of the entire battalion, and then, if found guilty, his penalty would be announced.

Now, you may be asking yourself: "Wouldn't a person, who got fired so publicly, run straight to the Turkish security forces to reveal their location, as revenge? Wouldn't you worry about him giving out intelligence about you?" I can tell you, we never worried. The security forces in Iraq already knew exactly where we were. Almost every day, journalists, politicians, guests, and other civilians from foreign states were coming to the camp area. Therefore, if a consistent screw-up didn't make a dedicated effort to change himself, he could be easily dismissed.

There were some behaviors that were actually punishable by death. For example, if someone caused the death of another comrade, unless it was an innocent mistake, he could get the death penalty (although in 1994, the death penalty within the organization was removed during the 5th Congress by orders of Apo). I witnessed the execution of such a death sentence. The commander of a group had acted completely irresponsibly. He constantly forced his militants to march in water and snow. The militants warned him many times. "Look, if we keep marching like this, our feet might get frostbitten. We had better take some rest and dry our feet," they requested, but the commander did not listen to them. As a result, two guerillas had their feet amputated below the ankle, because of this walk. When that group came back to the camp, the commander went under investigation and was sentenced to death. First, three guerrillas dug his grave, and then the commander was brought into the excavated pit and one of the guerillas shot him in the head. After this incident, we understood that there were certain rules which are essential for the proper functioning of the organization, and that if we didn't comply with these rules, the sanctions that were invoked might cost us our lives.

Apart from killing comrades for a specific infringement, the death penalty was generally reserved for those in sexual relationships. The organization was founded on equal companionship between every body. Gender did not matter. Everyone considered one another a friend. And yet the heart does what it wants. So, it was understood that you might become fond of a woman, or a woman of a man. It was not forbidden to love, but only on the condition that this love was not to interfere with your labor in the organization. A possible scenario might be: "I'm in love with a female militant, but after a certain time in Iraq my orders sent me to Iran. In such a case, I can't ask the organization to send the woman I love with me. I do not have the right." When you had a duty, you couldn't fulfill it properly, while spending half of your time in love, and half of it for the task in front of you. That's why they would always warn us: "You can love one another, but ensure it will not be an obstacle to your work for us."

Last Days in the Camp of Haftanin

The day after Nowruz Day, the beginning of Spring, in 1992, a Turkish soldier came to our area loaded with weapons, which was not normal at all. He told us that during the Nowruz celebrations in the town of Cizre, in Turkey, his commander had given the order for his soldiers to fire into the public crowd. Following this stern order, he and his friends had obediently opened fire on the Kurdish public. He used an Mg-3. About 60 Kurdish civilians were killed that day, and this soldier couldn't handle the guilt of what he had done. He fled from his barracks and went straight to the villagers, who loaned him a guide that brought him to us. He told us his story in great detail. Our anger exploded against the Turkish military upon hearing this! We just didn't understand it! Why would an armed group want to kill a group of unarmed civilians? Moreover, their own citizens! This soldier stayed in our camp for a few days and was then sent to Apo in Damascus, Syria. I do not know what happened after that. I never heard from him again.

The PKK administration wanted to send me to Damascus, around that same time, for advanced ideological training. I refused. I was new in the organization, and I wanted a little more military experience before I left Haftanin. After four months, we were asked to say where we would like to go and have a proposal drafted. We had come to the end of our training and would now be sent to our new duty locations, based on our proposals. We were to write on a piece of paper the name of the region to which we would prefer to go, and give the reason why we wanted to be transferred there. Then, we also wrote down what kind of job we could do there. In general, most everyone selected the regions they had come from. When the new guerillas offered their reports, they listed the benefits they'd bring to their new camp, which included the fact that they knew both the region and the people well and could contribute to the organization by sharing this knowledge with senior officers. The senior officers generally would send the militants to the regions they requested. At the end of the three-day evaluation period, we finally found out where we were to be sent.

The obligation of constantly writing reports was one of the issues I had to force myself to get used to in the PKK. After the end of basic training, we were asked for a report on the training we'd had before we could be transferred to new regions. So, every militant was obliged to write, in detail, all their criticism and opinions about the training they had received. Reports were then sent to Damascus and were stored electronically in the main archive repository of the organization. Even though I knew how to read, I was not very good at writing. I was too slow. Back then, Sakine Cansız, who was killed in Paris in 2013, was a member of the leadership in our camp. She was someone who valued the new young comrades and was constantly trying to help them. In particular, she would handle comrades plagued by psychological distresses and would try to solve their problems by talking with them. She had already told me that she would write the report for me. I gave her just a few main points. She was able to write a report which was about four pages in length, just using my brief information. When she finished the report, she read it to me from beginning to end. "If there is anything in here that you don't want to say, tell me what it is, so that I can remove it," she said. "Leave it just as it is. It's good," I said.

Before being shipped to the new regions, we were faced with a stunning fact. Not everyone could become a guerilla, even if they strongly wished it. The physical characteristics of some organization members and the status of their health did not allow them to fight as guerrillas. A group of people with such handicaps, would instead, be sent to a group called ERNK (Kurdistan National Liberation Front). The goal for everyone under that roof was to have good political experience. Therefore, ERNK included not only handicapped militant-wannabes but also people with sound political knowledge.

Unlike other units, ERNK had no hierarchical structure among its members. ERNK group members staged political activities in major cities in European countries and in Syria, Iran, Iraq, and Turkey. Currently, there are ERNK members in almost every country around the world, from the Arab states to Europe and America.

Many countries were in a close relationship with the PKK, though officially they labeled us as a terrorist group, so as not to jeopardize their current political and economic interests with Turkey. Today, the PKK can easily get any kind of support, in any form, from left and socialist organizations in any state in Europe. Especially, diplomatic jobs in Europe are decided via the ERNK. Some of these countries tried keeping the PKK under control from time to time. In Syria, during his reign, Hafez al-Assad had thought he would control the PKK. The Syrians didn't realize that the PKK was able to handle all of its military and political attacks easily, thanks to the opportunities Syria, itself, had provided us.

Regardless, towards the middle of that May 1992, everyone received their orders regarding where they would be transferred to. Although the city of Diyarbakır had been my first choice, the organization had found me proficient in military training, so they sent me to the town of Garzan. This actually was a point of pride. I knew nothing about the region, but I knew that only people with great skills would get sent to Garzan. Therefore, I didn't complain. Yet, I had met a female comrade called Sevin during the training in Haftanin camp. For a few months, we stayed at the same camp. Over time, we fell in love. Fortunately for us, we were both sent to Garzan.

On the Way to the Town of Garzan

Our Garzan journey was full of disasters. We found ourselves in the middle of a minefield, just as we passed the Iraqi border into Turkey. We had a large number of people in that group (120), and we had already known there was a minefield at the border. We figured we would be safe because we had taken the necessary precautions in advance. Specifically, we told the villagers, so, ahead of our arrival they swept the area with detectors and cleared it of mines. We planned to proceed safely into Turkey through this corridor they had cleared.

But, as we set off in the dark, our guide missed the marker for the safe area by a good 20 meters. Three mines exploded as soon as the front group passed the border. Nine people were seriously wounded, including the battalion commander. Someone barked, "Everyone stay in place! Don't move!" The commander in the back of the group marched to the front to help the injured and stepped on a mine before he got to them.

We were new, and we had no idea what was happening. I thought there was a Howitzer mowing everyone down. But when the deputy commander of the battalion stepped on the mine and blew himself up, we were suddenly instantly clear on the precarious situation we were in. The senior officers began strategizing how to get us out of there. They decided we would retreat carefully, with a few of us carrying the wounded. Advancing to reach the wounded, another mine exploded. This was the most devastating one yet, because it had exploded where four guerillas were gathered, waiting to lead out the wounded. The casualties were heavy. The mine completely severed the feet from the nearest three people. Two more of our comrades lost their eyes from the shrapnel, and five people sustained serious wounds in various parts of their bodies.

We removed the wounded by stretcher, and dragged ourselves back to the camping area. On the way, we encountered the other group, the Amed (Diyarbakır) group, which had been trailing behind us for their own safety. We warned them about what had happened. The next day, we were appointed another battalion commander. Our first battalion commander had had a sincere and gentle personality. He had been Kurdish, of Syrian origin. Apo himself had appointed him. Therefore, his death really took a toll on our morale. Meanwhile, those with the amputated feet were sent to Apo, in Damascus, to serve the organization from the background.

Of course, the minefield disaster had alerted our enemies as to our intended location for passing into Turkey. So our new battalion commander radioed our comrades in the Cudi region and instructed them to hold the strategic locations, before the enemy could reach them. The next day we passed to

Cudi over Hezil Stream by cable car. For two days, we rested in Cudi. Finally, we reached Herekol Mountain, in the region of Besler. The Turkish security forces had about 2,000 soldiers holding this region, whereas we were now 250 people in total. Our battle with them began around 3:00 a.m. It lasted until 12:00 p.m. The soldiers never left the region. They had surrounded the area, figuring that nobody could escape the mountain, and if anyone had tried, the soldiers intended to destroy them.

But they had not taken into account that guerrillas were more versatile than conventional soldiers, for a few reasons. First of all, the difference between our mentality and the soldiers' was our greatest advantage in battle. Mentally, the soldiers were family men. They wouldn't take any risks. They spent their downtime counting the days to return home. Even during a battle, they were inevitably thinking of their homes, families, and their children. We were exactly the opposite. We had left our families in order to fight. Any militant who joined the organization had already abandoned all hope that he would ever go back home. That's why we were brave. We had already given up everything. This was a big disadvantage for the military and a great advantage for the organization.

Being accustomed to the terrain was also a plus for us. There was a big difference between a city-raised, briefly trained Turkish soldier and the village-born guerilla, who had survived off the land and its harsh conditions for many years.

The Turkish soldier was also obligated to carry so much more gear, like his rucksack, materials, and equipment. At the end of the day, they had been burdened with so much weight, that they had no strength to fight. Consider their ridiculous invention called "the helmet." It was very heavy, but had zero practical benefit. Maybe it would protect you against a rock, but it couldn't protect you against weapons. A bullet hitting a helmet would kill a soldier by concussion, as surely as if it had passed through his skull. So, we had absolutely no idea why our enemies bothered using helmets.

Finally, we were much more nimble. Our ability to move was much greater than conventional soldiers. This was the entire point of our fighting style. To thwart a blockade, for example, we divided ourselves into small contingents of just 15 to 20 people. This dramatically increased our ability to maneuver and attack. Had we attacked in a large group, it would have been impossible to go unnoticed. But, in small units, and in the darkness of night, we could all pass undetected through a narrow corridor. We had brought experienced friends with us who knew the details of the terrain very well. They calculated the best route for us; where we could outmaneuver the enemy and get an ambush.

While we used our expertise to our advantage, the regular Turkish soldiers were acting like rank beginners. They were continuously attacking only the main point of the siege. This left some very quiet areas on the margins of the battle. Naturally, one would expect us to go towards these quiet areas, but we already knew their tactics. They were inviting us into an ambush. So, we acted contrary to their plans, and we never once headed to these quiet points. To the experienced among us, it was all just a game. In small groups, we advanced directly on the area where they were firing. So, while a small part of our force was drawing their attention from the quiet places where they expected us to be, the actual main body of our force was silently leaving the siege and sneaking directly down their line of fire. Then, once we were clear of the siege, those units which had stayed behind and bought us time, hid themselves somewhere safe.

So, from our force which was 250 strong at the outset, we took a total of four losses in this Battle of Herekol Mountain, and we acquired eight weapons from the opposite side. The total of our weapons didn't imply that we had caused that many enemy losses, because any soldier might have become frightened and retreated, or his friend could have gotten wounded, and he may have dropped his gun to leave the field to go help him.

"Acceptable losses," according to the rules of guerrilla war, equal one loss for every ten deaths inflicted. If we killed ten soldiers and lost three guerrillas, this would be an unacceptable loss for us. In which case, the guerrilla commander in charge of such a fiasco would be dismissed.

We sustained these losses and still managed to enter the territory of Turkey. Before making it to Garzan, we waited in the countryside to the east of the city of Siirt. But the security forces expected us to cross to Siirt from the countryside. We were going to have to find an alternate route. The Turkish soldiers held almost all the passes in the countryside. Therefore, our commander said that we were going to have to go through the city. He believed the city was the strongest and most reliable option left.

So, according to the new plan, we came to a spot near the city at night, where 16 trucks were awaiting us. We boarded these trucks in groups, and were taken through the city. Without further incident, we passed through Siirt, headed straight to Bitlis. I found it interesting that all the trucks that came to pick us up were official vehicles of the city. So, thanks to the help of the city itself, we were transported in three or four hours—the same distance that would have taken us two or three days on foot. No explosions, no further casualties, and we didn't get caught.

The organization had harsh penalties for traveling by vehicle and normally this was strictly forbidden. But considering the minefield experience, and the lack of other options, our battalion commander made the call. He accepted full responsibility.

SECTION B

Being a Terrorist

6

RANGERS AND MY FIRST MISSION

When we reached the area of Bitlis, at the beginning of the summer, we found out that the commander of Garzan province had made a new arrangement for us. The body of our force, who had arrived safely, were now to be distributed into four different regions. My group was to be sent to the Şirvan district of Siirt. Our new task area was enormous, and our area of responsibility would include the central province of Bitlis, the city of Siirt, the region of Şirvan, Baykan district of Siirt, and the city of Bitlis. Our entire force would be only two platoons of 49 men and eight women in total.

There existed at that time a ranger program called the village protection system. Through this system, certain Kurdish villagers would be armed and trained by the Turkish state to seek out and destroy PKK members. These village protection guards had already been armed by the state in order to fight more effectively against us in rural areas like this. In these regions we had been assigned to control, the villagers had been officially registered in the state's bounty hunting system for tracking and killing PKK members. But the official policy of the organization at that time was that there would be no action taken against the rangers. It wasn't our mission. The sole purpose for our presence in that region was to act against the police and military stations there, which we believed was a critical area in order to shake the authority of the state. Therefore, every guerrilla serving there had been especially selected.

As a troop, we couldn't take any action until the autumn. There were so many rangers in the region that it was almost impossible to pass through them and reach the security forces. There was no way to do our job without somehow disabling all these rangers. At first, we started gently, by trying conversations and dialogue. For three months, we repeatedly had talks with the leaders of the rangers in the villages. Despite all this, we were unable to get them to agree to a ceasefire. Moreover, these rangers, even while we were trying to negotiate, were still patrolling the mountainsides for any trace of us to report to the Turkish security forces, so they could collect their reward money. Consequently, our troop of militants couldn't stay in one place for two days in a row. Our entire troop was physically exhausted from constantly being on the move.

Yet, we engaged in a total of five battles during this three-month period. Of course, the rangers helped the security forces during these battles. Actually, the rangers antagonized us the most, because the security forces acted with the logic of a regular army; collectively, and dependent on orders from the hierarchy. This made them very slow, because, in a regular army no individual has the right to act based on their own initiative. All movements are connected to, and hindered by, the chain of command.

So, all we had to do with a conventional army was to take our precautions until some soldier made a decision in the chain of command. But, the rangers were not like that. They were more like us. They would move on their own initiative and shoot at us at every opportunity. Most damaging, they were very aware of our policy towards them in our organization. They knew we would not take any action against them no matter what they did to us. So they were continuously engaging us, harassing us, and generally abusing our party policy of doing them no harm.

I did not know the terrain of Şirvan, as I did the lands around my own village or the training camp. I was new in the organization, so I didn't know where it was safe; where the Turkish troops hid; which paths through the mountains were reliable, and so much more. This lack of knowledge made us very vulnerable. When we were staying at a point near the region of Tatvan, a blizzard began. It was December, and we carried no gear for winter camping. We had not known to prepare for this. There were nearly 1.5 meters of snow. We had to leave our hiding place and go out straight into the storm. The visibility was less than five meters, and the weather was so bone-chillingly cold. We were prevented from leaving the area but wouldn't have known where to go if we could.

We feared we had gotten too close to a road, because we thought we heard the sound of a car. It was the absolute worst thing not to know where we were, but we rather figured we were probably on the Silk Road. As soon as we approached the road, we realized it led to a village very close by. There was a military post right at the village entrance, meaning we had probably just stumbled straight into a village full of rangers. What choice did we have? The soldiers didn't notice us as we entered the area from above. In two groups, we entered the first two houses. We arrested the people in these houses, and we didn't let them out. We asked them, "Is this a village of rangers? Answer honestly!" With considerable courage, considering the rebels they faced in their own homes, the men admitted, "Comrade, yes, we are rangers." The name of the village was Qesrè in Kurdish and Narlıdere in Turkish.

We explained our situation to those people. It was something like 3 p.m. We would meet our needs until it got dark and set off again. The rangers said, "Comrade, you can stay, but we need to inform one of the leading figures of the village." The head ranger came over and greeted us very pleasantly. There were about 80 rangers in the village. We were around 55 to 60 guerillas. "You are our guests," he said. "You can stay here as long as you want. Just let us know when you want to leave. We will help you escape the village."

I was new and absolutely could not understand why these men who had fought us alongside the Turkish soldiers were now treating us so well. Our region commander asked, "How will you get us out of here without the military station finding out?" The head ranger said, "I will take care of it, comrade. Without my consent, no one can talk to the soldiers here in this village."

And that is how we enjoyed three nights of rest in the village of Narlıdere. The rangers actively protected us. Not only had they placed three guards at three fixed points overlooking the town, but they also kept tabs on the soldiers' patrols. If the soldiers come close to the houses where we were hiding, our new ranger friends would notify us immediately.

We began preparations to leave the village on the third night. As I have said, there was a military station right at the entrance of the village. To leave the village, we had to cross the bridge close by the station. To cross over the Bitlis River, we had to use that bridge. We considered trying to pass through the water, but the weather was very cold, with a high chance that all our feet might freeze after coming out of the water.

But the head ranger said, "Do not worry, you will pass safely over the bridge. We will handle it." Then, he went straight to the military station and told them, "A group of us rangers has some business in the opposite village. We will use the bridge to get over there, just to let you know." We passed within 50 meters of the soldiers in their station that night. They thought we were rangers. There we were, with 58 Turkish soldiers at the station, and only 15 to 20 rangers with us. Initially, the rangers weren't going to accompany us, but as it was snowing, we were aware our footsteps would become visible as soon as the sun rose. We didn't want to give the commander of the military station the chance to wonder about the number of the footprints. That's why the ranger group accompanied us.

But, when we did reach the opposite village, the rangers were in a rush to return. Later, we learned that one of the villagers had ratted us out to the security forces. The station commander decided not to call the villagers to account until spring. I mean, of course the soldiers pretended like nothing had happened. But when it got to be spring, 80 rangers in the village were detained. The security forces were really bent out of shape that the government had given them all those weapons, all that salary, and then the rangers went and hosted the terrorists and didn't even tell the state. In their pique, they took back the weapons of 40 rangers.

So, this incident caused the rangers of Narlıdere to lose all their credibility in the eyes of the security forces. So, when all the security forces ostracized them, where did they turn? They joined the PKK, the Patriotic Front. They even told the local leader of the PKK, "We have always wanted to take part in the birth of the state of Kurdistan from the beginning, but we had no choice. We were told by the security forces that we could either accept weapons and become rangers for them, or we would be ousted from our own village and forced to relocate to the West."

Inspired, we sent two comrades, as messengers, to other nearby villages in June, in hopes of persuading these other village rangers to lay down arms. The rangers killed them without letting them speak. This news rocked our whole troop. We were in such a lather that nearly all of us wanted to mutiny against the company commander.

Instead, we held a sober meeting to evaluate our activities over this three-month period. Normally, our status meetings were held monthly, but these had been hampered due to the difficult conditions, since we first came to this region. So, this time, for about five or six hours, we talked about the village rangers. After our meeting, our troop commander was going to take our findings directly to the meeting of the PKK Provincial Government. Chaired by the provincial commander, the provincial government meeting was the gathering of the commanders of each of the four regions of Garzan for a situation report on the region as a whole. We wanted the company commander to convey our "request" to the regional commander: Either give us permission to attack the rangers in this region or watch us abandon the region.

After assessing the case, the company commander gave us leave to undertake one single mission against one single ranger village. We were even left the choice of which village to attack. There was only one village for us; the one to which we had reached out for a ceasefire. The one which had killed our messengers of peace. That was the village we chose to destroy.

It was 1992, a clear autumn day, around 2:00 p.m., when we laid our siege on the village. We did give them a chance, though. We first tried again sending peace messengers. Three comrades went. They were going to warn the villagers not to fight. All the village had to do was give us the weapons the state had given to them, and we would leave the village without killing anyone. But if they didn't obey, we were going to kill all the men of the village and anyone we found holding weapons. The rangers' bullets struck our messengers before our friends even entered the village. One of them was shot in the head and instantly martyred. The other two were heavily wounded. And yet our commander still tried diplomacy and spoke with the head ranger by radio. He tried to convince him to lay down the weapons. The head ranger could not be convinced. A Turkish military outpost, of 60 to 70 soldiers strong, was about an hour and a half from this village. I guess that's why these villagers could act so macho. They had put their faith in the military outpost. They thought those Turkish soldiers would save them.

This was my first opportunity to lead a mission. Since I was good at weapons, I was given a Bazooka. I was comfortable with it, should the battle escalate. And here was the villager's head ranger on the radio, refusing to negotiate. Our squadron commander gave the order to attack. As I have said, we had a grudge against this village. No, actually, it was a hatred! They had treacherously killed two of our friends. Then another. Then wounded two more. They had fueled a very strong hatred in us, but this mission would release all of that hatred. We had no desire for restraint, so we decided to destroy the whole village; men, women, children, the elderly. It didn't matter. Everyone.

We started by firing at the rangers. Some of them took positions near their homes, while some shot at us from the doors and windows of their very houses. The conflict lasted for nearly four hours. The villagers, themselves, prolonged the conflict, trying to buy themselves time. They still believed that reinforcements from the nearby Turkish soldier station would come and save them. How could they know our comrades had already executed an ambush on the road from which the help would come, and 13 Turkish reinforcement soldiers already lay dead. After this ambush, no help could reach the village. It was now to our advantage to prolong the fight. Leisurely, we worked our way through the village until the entire village was destroyed.

The completed action was now a horror for the other ranger villages to suffer. Now, the fate of whoever defied us would be the same. We had never taken any action against rangers until that time. We had never disproven the popular theory that the guerilla would never kill their own people. Now, everyone knew we would execute missions against soldiers and rangers, if we so chose.

Around 6:00 p.m., we finished the mission. A total of 23 weapons were seized from the village. We also seized around a half-dozen weapons from the reinforcement troops. We killed everyone except those who had hidden successfully, or those inhabitants who hadn't been in the village that day. Then we shouldered the bodies of our dead comrades, and withdrew to a safe area. As usual, we had scouted out this location long beforehand. We had already determined that it would be easy to defend, in case a counteraction had been taken against us. But neither rangers nor soldiers came after us. This was our first mission in the region. They were all in shock at what we were capable of doing.

Then, after the mission, we started to be a bit concerned. What if the senior party management didn't like what we had done? Such devastating missions were generally considered only appropriate as a counteraction or a disavowed action. At first, the party leadership said nothing. Then, they learned that we had killed the women, children and elderly. Immediately they sent a written order to the region. Such a mission was never to happen again, no matter what. It was a very long directive, but, in brief, it said that these kinds of actions could damage the image of our movement and turn both domestic and foreign public opinion against us. The Turkish media was broadcasting images of the deceased, which was as good as ready-made propaganda against us. They said all the necessary damning things against us.

But this mission had skyrocketed our troop morale, besides securing our revenge. Leveling that village provided extra benefit beyond our original purpose. All the village rangers in the area fled to the cities, leaving behind virtually all their belongings, even their livestock. Every abandoned village increased our freedom of movement. We did not need to struggle as before. Sometimes, we could even stay in the same spot for five or six days.

Winter Camp

Now it was time slowly to start preparations for the winter. We hadn't known that, in winter, we remained in the same camp for at least four months. Winter camp was the time for spiritual renovation and rest for the guerrilla. This is the time for political and ideological education to resume. This was also the time for us to self-assess the incidents which had taken place during the combat summer season. If mistakes had been made, we were to discuss what could be done the following year to prevent the recurrence of such mistakes. Thus, the self-improvement we invested in during the winter ensured that we would enter the following season better prepared and better equipped.

The winter camping areas were determined in autumn. Geographic conditions were considered. Winter camps were usually set in steep and wooded areas. But you cannot just camp anywhere. It is very important to take into account how much snow falls on the area, before you plan to set up camp there. It was beneficial to choose an area where there was no risk of avalanches in winter.

There was one other important safety detail. While determining the campground, you must keep in mind that you were at the same time selecting suitable ground for a battlefield. You must be somewhere that is defensible, if the military found you. Our first winter camp was at a very steep and high place— somewhere the terrain and winter weather deterred the military from reaching us.

Once we were all ensconced in camp, we all knew that, short of an emergency, nobody could leave. Thus, we had to predict accurately all our needs and lay in the correct supplies, during the season before. Enough food, clothes, fuel, ammo, training materials, weapons, and all other materials had to be cached in the place where we were going to stay. Our suppliers in the cities were able to procure all these essentials for us at the beginning of each cold season, and then it was up to us to transport them to our winter camp. This meant buying everything we needed all at one time from our militias in the urban centers, and then finding a way to cart all of it back to our campsite.

We lived underground in squads in the winter campground. Each squad consisted of ten people. Each squad was responsible for digging their own temporary quarters. An underground bunker of around 15 square meters, on average, was needed for ten people. There were also some winter camps in the caves, though not in every region. In addition to that, cairns of stones were also built—and in public areas too. Camouflage was essential in such cases, and the camouflage must be so good that it also disguised the cairn from the air.

Every aspect of camp life followed these strict precautions. Each squad had heating stoves. For warmth, we could light the stoves both day and night, but only when it was rainy and foggy. To avoid detection in clear weather, we could only light them at night. Otherwise they would make excellent beacons for the enemy to discover our location. The worry back then was the visible smoke from the stoves, and nighttime or fog was sufficient to obscure it. Please remember, technology in the nineties was very rudimentary. There were no such things yet as portable thermal cameras, night vision systems, or unmanned aerial vehicles. So, as long as we accounted for physical and visual giveaways, we could move with relative comfort. Back then, the game was completely different. As soon as we noticed the surveillance aircraft, we had to freeze in place. I remember having to stay completely motionless for 15 minutes at a time.

And yet, even in these circumstances, our education continued. Every morning after breakfast, we would convene with the other squads to receive political and ideological training. The training lasted until 11:00 a.m. Then lunchtime and rest between 11:00 a.m. and 1:00 p.m. After lunch, the political and ideological education resumed from 1:00 p.m. to 4:00 p.m. In these courses, we would read and discuss the founding documents of the organization. Militants were assigned different courses and topics in turn, and each expert commission was giving training to many groups. That was how training would proceed, either in a lecture format or a discussion.

Obviously, there was not sufficient space underground to conduct physical training, so winter camp was heavy on more theoretical education—for instance, strategy. They taught us everything about guerrilla warfare styles but also gave us expertise in regular army tactics, so we might better know our enemy. But, most often, we were studying the strategies and tactics of other guerrilla warriors from around the world. We analyzed the strengths and weaknesses of different resistance movements from different eras and regions, and adapted those lessons to our conditions. Our reading list included the autobiographies of important figures such as Mao Tse-Tung, who led the Chinese Revolution; legendary Vietnamese commanders, and the inspirational guerilla leader of Cuba, Che Guevara.

Several times, we had wanted to examine currently active revolutionary organizations, such as ETA and the IRA in Europe, but further review made us nix this idea. The rural warfare tactics of these organizations were too weak. They were inexperienced compared to us. So, we abandoned the idea of incorporating their operational styles into our strategies. In fact, a decade later, their senior officials would come to our camp to receive wilderness guerilla training from us! But, there was no question that these organizations were better in urban warfare and suicide bombings than were we. So, part of our education was the close study of the training materials prepared by these organizations in order to gain their expertise on these tactics.

In addition to these studies, each member of the organization was comprehensively trained in Russian revolutionary war tactics. We all had to read the true story, *Volokolamsk Highway* by Aleksandr Aleksandrovic Bek, regarding Russian guerillas' successful repulsion of advancing German soldiers. *The Art of War* by the famous Chinese commander, Sun Tzu, was also required reading. As our own comrades became experienced and specialized in guerilla warfare, we benefited from their expertise as well. No matter what we read, we were already well versed in the golden rule of guerilla warfare: time and place. No mission could succeed unless time and place had been researched and correctly predetermined.

Once more, I would like to underscore how different the style of regular armies was from our own. Conventional soldiers act in a systematic and coordinated manner. Also, technology matters a great deal in a regular army. They use all kinds of advanced weapons. But personal resilience and strength of character are diminished. We knew this, and used it to our advantage. How else could we have ever engaged a regular army brigade of 2,000 to 3,000 soldiers in battle with just one platoon of about 50 to 60 guerrillas? However, we could defend ourselves against such a large force without any loss of efficacy, because guerrilla warfare is "irregular warfare," according to the philosophy of the regular army. We are able to move in small groups; are highly maneuverable, and each squad commander is empowered to use his own initiative.

The regular army behaves nothing like this. No company commander or battalion commander can act on their own initiative. In fact, they cannot act at all, without the approval of their superiors. This strategic bottleneck was a big advantage for us. The bureaucratic delay induced by the enemy's hierarchy, often postponed their utilization of long-range artillery or airstrikes, because they needed to get permission for everything. Their hierarchy was that strict. So, their unwieldy decision chain frequently spared us casualties, since we were able to flee conflicts during the intervals while standard soldiers were awaiting the order to attack.

Then there was our practice of publicly assessing each individual at the finale of every winter training, before leaving the guerrilla camp to start the battle cycle anew with the approaching spring. A stage would be built. One by one, each comrade would put themselves on display and recite for all of us an account of their deficiencies, mistakes, and negative aspects. After this disclosure, everyone in the compound would respond with their own rendition of all his mistakes and failings. The purpose of this wasn't to discourage people. On the contrary, it was for their own good. His comrades showed him his deficiencies in order to help him overcome them.

After he has heard all the critiques from his comrades, the recipient is given the right to speak again. In this final rebuttal, that person would tell each critic which judgment he accepted; the ones he did not, and why not. Whether he rejected one criticism or many, there was no such thing as forcing him to agree with his comrades' assessment of him.

All the officers and commanders were assessed during these platforms, as well. If the organization, by consensus, didn't like the personality, war tactics, or skills of a commander, it could elect to dismiss that commander. This is how simple it was to change the roster of team and squad commanders. The company commanders were exempt from assessment at this level. But, if the personality, approach, or skills of a company commander were not appreciated, an infraction report was written to the party leadership calling for his dismissal. The senior management would review this report, and if the accusations turned out to be factual, the commander would be dismissed.

So, when someone made a written complaint about the provincial management, we were obliged to report it to headquarters. There were pre-existing criteria for the dismissal and appointment of higher-ranking officials, which had been established in advance by the organization. These are the measures and criteria by which the performance and rank of senior-level officers were systematically evaluated. These served as regulations in every command. Interestingly, these regulations contained articles regarding the acceptance and embodiment of party ideology. So, while appointing someone, the regulations dictate an investigation of how much that person has embraced the mission and the ideals of the party, how experienced he was, and how committed he was to his people…

Esprit de corps was a very important issue—and not just between members of one unit or between guerillas and their commander. There must be rapport between each and every comrade. An individual doesn't have the luxury of saying, "I like that commander, but I do not like the other one." For the organization to function, it was required for you to be close to everyone and never "on the out" with anyone. Because the advent of personal discrimination in the organization begins the dissolution of the sense of brotherhood, which leads to loss of confidence—then to loss of effectiveness, and then to failure. That's why the commander must exemplify the noblest qualities. A commander should also be expert in guerrilla warfare tactics.

If a person was assigned as a commander and later couldn't fulfill all the regulations, he would be dismissed and someone else appointed in his place. But it wasn't important whether the appointee was an experienced combatant or a new recruit. The main criterion was how closely aligned that person's life was with the party line. We sometimes witnessed a newbie being appointed as a commander over those who had been in the organization for 15 years.

But to return to our timeline. It was the middle of March, and we were just preparing to leave the camp when we were attacked by an airstrike. The campground was hit every half hour by six alternating attack aircraft. After the heavy sorties were over, we came under fire by Cobra style helicopters. Despite the horrific bombardment, we didn't have any casualties. Our bunkers and caves held fast against the attacks of aircraft and Cobras. The air attacks stopped in the evening, but we were compelled to postpone our departure. Thankfully, our supplies and ammunition weren't harmed, but the camp was physically destroyed. We would not be using it again. We salvaged our gear and supplies, and then two nights later we abandoned our winter home under darkness.

In these circumstances, it was really difficult to go on living. Going up to the mountains and rebelling against the state may seem the only logical response to tyranny, or seem to some like a romantic adventure. But, it's nowhere near that simple. It takes incredible willpower to devote oneself to this cause. If you are not committed to your purpose and your target and don't have an iron will, you can't take it for very long. How do you think you could survive −20 degrees Celsius in the middle of the winter? Sometimes, water would leak into the bunker. We were getting soaked and constantly shivering. Yet, we couldn't make a fire because the Turkish military could detect us if we did. You simply cannot survive the difficulties of this lifestyle, if you can't devote yourself to the cause—with all your heart!

I have said it before, that you can't force someone to stay in those conditions. Combat aside, sometimes people just couldn't handle the difficulty of our daily life and returned back home. Whomever wanted to leave, would just depart. We would never chase those who left us. It would do us no good to arrest them. As I have said before, the conditions were terrible, and the resources simply did not exist to monitor and force an unwilling militant to perform as an acquiescent comrade. Even if you forced him to stay, he could potentially harm you and the organization, even more than if you had just permitted him the freedom that he sought.

A Hope for Peace

The spring of 1993 was a crucible for the organization—because in the autumn of 1992 the largest-scale military operation ever fought against our party had begun. Suddenly, our enemy was not only the Turkish police and security forces, but local forces in the region lent Turkey their strength, namely, in Iraq: the PUK (Patriotic Union of Kurdistan, headed by Jalal Talabani) and the KDP (Kurdistan Democratic Party headed by Mesud Barzani) had actively joined the fight against us. Even NATO supported this attack, albeit in secret. The joint offensive against the organization was conducted over a very extensive area from southeastern Turkey to the north of Iraq. An attack of this size was staged for one reason only: in order to attempt to eliminate the entire PKK. We were so effective that we were forcing our enemy's hand. We knew very well that if Turkey didn't eliminate the organization, it would have to sit at the negotiation table with us, and eventually forge a solution with us through dialogue. But apparently we were very hard to eliminate. Our precautions, our tough lifestyle, our skill at adaptation, all worked for us. We weren't destroyed in a military sense, but we suffered heavy losses. During their operation, they managed to kill about 1,500 of us.

We also fell victim to psychological warfare. During these operations, Osman Öcalan, second in command of the entire organization, was contacted by some senior officials from PUK, under the presidency of Talabani. Back then, Osman Öcalan was working in Haxkurkê camp in the north of Iraq. As I mentioned, the sole purpose of this operation against us was the complete liquidation of the PKK movement. Moreover, this goal was supported by international operations, so the PUK got to Osman Öcalan and told him that it was over for Apo. They convinced him that the combined international forces would liquidate Apo, and that Osman Öcalan (and his followers) should take this opportunity to leave the sinking ship and accept shelter in a zone controlled by the PUK. They lured Osman Öcalan with the promise to appoint him as the head of a new party, which they assured him they would establish. "As the PUK, we will publicly support you. We have countries friendly to you, whom you can trust," they told him. "They also want you to take the lead."

It was all a game to deceive Osman, and it worked. Osman fled with his guards to "shelter" with PUK, instead of coordinating the PKK force against the enemy in Haxkurkê camp.

Barzani's KDP (Kurdistan Democratic Party) and Talabani's PUK (the Patriotic Union of Kurdistan) were the first Kurd-supporting organizations founded in Iraq. These two Kurdish parties have often sided with Turkey against the PKK. Frankly, they were jealous of us. The PKK was a new-comer organization to them. Those two organizations—founded in the 1940s—did not understand how the PKK, an organization founded in the late 1970s, had surpassed them to capture the sympathy of the Kurdish people. What was so hard to understand? The KDP and PUK's management style was based on feudalism and a family-style authority. But we had foremost a social democratic and socialist policy. This more egalitarian form of management enticed thousands of socialists, formerly in the KDP and the PUK, to join the PKK. Barzani and Talabani could not accept the reality that so many people from their base of support chose to move on and join the PKK. In their jealousy, they wanted to eliminate the PKK as soon as possible. But neither of these two parties had the strength to fight against us. They joined in the joint operation after making an agreement with Turkey. Both Barzani and Talabani planned to destroy the sovereignty of the PKK in Iraq by consolidating their power with Turkey.

Right after this operation started, they began arresting the members of our party across all the European countries. Almost all the senior executives in Germany were arrested. Some of the Western countries openly supported this operation against us, and some did it secretly. The United States especially didn't want an organization like the PKK to get stronger and upset the balance of power in the Middle East. Because the stronger the PKK got, the greater risk we became for Barzani and Talabani, who were allies of the USA. The USA could easily manipulate Barzani and Talabani. However, it knew the PKK wasn't such a pushover organization. I mean the United States wouldn't be able to use the PKK for its own purposes and goals. Therefore, the Americans supported this operation against us, both by providing weapons and by allowing Turkish soldiers to enter Iraq.

So, the fall of 1992 was a big struggle for us. When Turkey didn't get the military results that it wanted from this operation, it started to look for a political solution. The President of Turkey during that period, Turgut Özal, sent Apo a letter which said, "All of your demands can be discussed, including self-determination and an autonomous Kurdish state, as long as there is no more warfare…" Upon receipt of this letter, our party declared a ceasefire. Until this ceasefire, the aim of the PKK had been to establish an independent Kurdish state. However, during the peace granted by the ceasefire, our party made a change in our organizational strategy. We now demanded a democratic Kurdistan, united with the Turkish public and institutions, instead of an independent Kurdish government. Although this was a radical change for us guerillas, neither the commanders nor the guerillas, themselves, objected to this change in our strategy.

There were exceptions among us, though only a few. The PKK management wanted us to prepare ourselves for the two most likely scenarios. If the ceasefire process succeeded, we were going to put down our weapons and continue our struggle in a peaceful, diplomatic way. But if the peace process was spoiled, we were going to redouble our combat and fight as hard as possible. Our commanders were constantly indoctrinating us. "If the government takes sincere and serious steps, we will give the necessary response." Because, during that period, the now-deceased Özal, had even opened discussion on the issue of amnesty. We were also aware that there was a rooted, hidden power structure that took advantage of this continuing war. No matter how sincere Özal was, he would be unable to manage the peace process before demolishing these shadowy interests.

Also in the spring of 1993, mirroring Özal's friendly and sincere behavior, Apo organized a press conference in Beqaa Valley [Syria] to announce to the Turkish public that the PKK was going to remain faithful to the ceasefire. Talabani, the president of the PUK, was the mediator during these talks. It was negotiated that the ceasefire would extend for a certain period of time. During this time, some political steps in good faith would have to be taken by the state. The release of political PKK prisoners; the cancellation of the state of emergency in the eastern Anatolia region, and the dissolution of the rangers' village protection system were requirements that the PKK demanded be adopted as soon as possible, as our precondition for a ceasefire. Once these preliminary steps were taken, the organization sought to ensure education for Kurds in their mother tongue, and the national recognition of the Kurdish ethnic identity status as distinct from Turkish. These latter issues could be discussed in future years, so long as the preconditions were met, but the Turkish government told the PKK that none of these steps could be taken within the given timeframe. Özal's government wanted a little more time to convince the more entrenched levels of Turkish nationalists in the country.

The organization extended the ceasefire period upon Özal's request, although he took none of the steps we had requested. And that was when those bizarre, shadowy disruptions began occurring, specifically to derail the peace process. First, General Eşref Bitlis was killed. He was one of the names most famous for his support of the peace process and also well-known for his close stance to Özal. In February, 1993, the plane he was on crashed for some mysterious reason. The elimination of Eşref Bitlis was spooky, because here he was, a Turkish army General who supported Özal's government, in pursuit of the peace process. So, we knew it was not the government who had killed him. His death was a huge blow. Eşref Bitlis's support had been very important for us. To have someone from a military background supporting the peace process had been so valuable. It had meant so much to us to have this leader of the military stand for our side in seeking out peace. Next to die were other high-ranking soldiers, such as Rıdvan Özden and Bahtiyar Aydın, who were both known to be very close to General Eşref Bitlis. They were also killed in a "peaceable" manner. And that was how, during our hard-won ceasefire period, peace-loving Turkish bureaucrats were eliminated, one by one.

Not only soldiers died mysteriously, but some journalists close to Turgut Özal were also eliminated. All friends of Özal—all friends of peace—were killed in turn. This led up to the crowning murder; that of President Turgut Özal himself. Two months after the death of Eşref Bitlis, President Turgut Özal suddenly died of a "heart attack," according to the press. A police investigation conducted in 2015 revealed that Özal was killed by poisoning. He had been just on the cusp of granting amnesty for the political PKK prisoners. These murders were simply "good business." The local and foreign forces, which took financial advantage of this war economically, had eliminated, one by one, the people who tried to take steps for peace. Özal was assassinated because these forces realized that he had made up his mind that Turkey had resolved at the executive level to bring itself to peace with the Kurds, by any means necessary. And so the enemies of peace elected to prevent this stability, by any means necessary.

The result was predictable. The negotiation process obviously had been sabotaged, and conflicts had to be restarted. In the Turkish government, the vacuum left by the loss of the most vocal proponents of peace now left room for the rise of hawks within the military forces to corrupt the truce from their side. Under normal circumstances, there would be no chance of military operations occurring during a truce. Of course, the toppling of the opposition's leaders for peace made way for rot to set into the foundation built towards peace, in the dark part of the PKK. Although it was contrary to the rules of guerrillas, we broke our own code when PKK forces, under Şemdin Sakık's command, killed 33 Turkish soldiers. These soldiers were unarmed and defenseless, just being transferred by bus, from one place to another. Apo had no foreknowledge of this event. We do not know from whom Şemdin received the order, or what he thought his purpose was, but we are sure that he acted on his own initiative. As shadowy as Özal's assassination, this incident is the only one in the organization that cannot be illuminated. We ourselves have no understanding of why it happened. How coincidental, that this similarly mysterious event was the one single action which ended the peace process.

Although this killing of nearly three dozen soldiers was a completely individual action on Şemdin's part, Apo first took it upon himself not to disavow his officer. Even then, Jalal Talabani intervened. "Don't shoulder official responsibility for this action. This action was performed by a renegade provincial commander. At least don't sully the reputation of the PKK by taking ownership of this act on behalf of the organization. Don't let this incident harm the trust between the government and the organization." Apo replied, "No, I won't sacrifice my commander. If he committed this action on behalf of the organization, I will take the full responsibility." And he did. Thus was the ceasefire ended.

But Apo had been deceived. He took responsibility for this action because he had been given incorrect information. Şemdin had told him, "Everywhere, military operations have been started against us. They are coming down on us for our destruction. We are undertaking this mission for the purpose of retaliation." It only became clear after the fact that this wasn't the actual case. These soldiers weren't being transferred for an operation. This case was investigated a great deal by the organization. Many commissions were established. But the sequence of events simply could not be brought to light. Şemdin undertook this cruel act against a defenseless bus. We know that. But who was it that leaked the information to Şemdin that 33 soldiers would set off unarmed at exactly that time? Although it has been 22 years since the incident, the truth is no clearer. At least, not to the PKK.

Şemdin Sakık was dismissed for his action and sent to Damascus. But the damage was already done. The peace process was now corrupted. With President Özal's death, the government had already realigned in both the political and military spheres. The leadership vacuum had been filled with minds of less refinement; hawks opposed to peace had taken over the administration. Renewed operations were vigorously launched against us, more comprehensive and extensive than before. Those operations sparked a hot war again, and the conflagration spread throughout the region. The breakdown of stability followed a helplessly predictable pattern after that. Because even if, philosophically, the organization was still committed to this strategy of peace through political means and diplomatic negotiation, in action our hand was forced. We had had to protect ourselves against military operations now actively attacking us. Defensive actions led to offensive ones. Just like that, the war was back on. What was our option? With whom were we to negotiate? What proponents of peace were left alive?

So, to put it mildly, we anticipated that 1993 would be a very difficult year, and yet our ranks and influence grew. The more the security forces used brutality throughout the countryside, the more we took dominion over rural areas. Thanks to their own heavy handedness towards the end of 1993, the government had almost lost all its dominance in rural areas. It could maintain order only in certain city centers and towns. "Order" meant that they were staying in their castles until evening and could go out in armored vehicles only when absolutely necessary.

Meanwhile, the public's support for the PKK had nearly doubled. The participation rate was higher than ever. The more the soldiers forced people to fight against the PKK, the more the people adopted the ideology of the PKK. In each region our strength had almost doubled. For example, in 1992, in Garzan province, we had 300 guerrillas. By 1993, we had nearly 1,000. Because we had gained control of the countryside and the participation of their family members in our ranks had grown so pervasive, the country folk were kindly disposed towards us. Despite all the governmental pressure on them, and on us, the support of the public became even greater. Because, at the end of the day, we guerrillas, living in the mountains, were the sons and daughters of these people, and we were fighting for their rights. In turn, the populace rose to support us—even when it cost them their lives.

Nowruz in 1993

Our leadership issued a general order in May 1993, just after the killing of Özal. That is, the instructions were for each state, each region, and each area to launch a counterattack in its own right. And this time we had no shortage of weapons and ammunition, such as had plagued us in the past. Now, our support by the Kurdish Administration in Iraq meant we could buy whatever weapons we needed. Weapons were plentiful from south Kurdistan, since Americans were providing PUK and KDP with armaments and ammunition to be used against Saddam. The Americans did not know that we also had become their customers, purchasing their supplies through middlemen to use against Turkey. On the other hand, the events of the past year had clued in both the KDP and the PUK to the fact that the PKK could no longer be easily eliminated. In their newly enlightened self-interest, they had started to support us from the shadows. On the surface, they remained sincere with Turkey, and all the while secretly signed contracts with us for weapons sales. The new weapons they unofficially provided to us were so powerful that we now had the strength to destroy an entire military outpost.

But we continued with softer means of persuasion as well. To wit: in the same period (March 1993), four people, including myself, went down from the mountains and into the villages in our region. The huge international celebration of the Spring Equinox was approaching, namely Nowruz, our "New Year." We were holding meetings with the Kurdish people in the villages in preparation for the Nowruz celebrations. In the urban centers as well, there were three militants working and making preparations for the large-scale Nowruz celebration.

In the countryside, the four of us had instituted committees in each of the villages. Each committee consisted of five to six people. Each committee had, as its area of responsibility, the village in which it was located. (This system was implemented in the city as well.) We had created such committees in almost every neighborhood, in every city in the Eastern parts of Turkey. The task of these committees was to recruit people for the organization. Constituents of these committees were taken from the countryside and educated specifically. Their education was exclusively political and ideological. These people weren't given any military training. They were, however, brought into the camps to gain first-hand understanding of the rigors of our training and living conditions, as well as a greater awareness of the purpose and dedication of the organization, by seeing it in action. They then were sent back to be used in cities and villages. Men, women, clerics, people from all sections of the community were our confederates in these committees.

We wanted a demonstration of our influence—a clear message to our enemies of how pervasive our control had become, and clear proof to our people that we were keeping our promises to bring them safety and freedom. We wanted to celebrate the festival of Nowruz with a crowd right in the center of the Kurdish city of Siirt. Hence our incessant meetings with members of our committees, both in cities and villages. The job of the committee members in the villages was to redirect all the villagers to the area of the Nowruz celebration. Our job was to ensure the safety of people during these celebrations. And if the military attacked the people as they had done in 1992, we were going to respond as a guerrilla force. The year before, Turkish troops had opened fire in volleys on their own people in Şırnak and Cizre, and almost 100 Kurdish people had lost their lives. It was a massacre. Now we were taking exacting precautions, so as to avoid such a horror again. Fifteen guerrillas were going to intermingle with the public in the plains of Siirt, and if a soldier started to fire, the PKK agents would annihilate him. In all the cities the same measures were taken. And in all the Nowruz celebrations that year, nothing untoward happened. Nothing but freedom and joy!

As soon as the celebrations were over, we began preparations to return to the countryside. I recall that five comrades were chosen to stay behind. That was when we relative newcomers learned that a guerrilla force of five or six people always stayed in cities and villages as a permanent fixture. They were "sleepers," awaiting possible crises or missions. Each force had built a hidden, underground bunker, so that in case of chaos, our militants had safe places to hide.

We were absolutely never to do battle with the security forces in any village nearby to organization outposts. The organization was constantly warning us on this issue, because if we did so, the military would retaliate on those villagers.

We would visit the nearby villages to ensure the safety of their residents. The people were always very glad to see us. We were heroes in their eyes. If soldiers came while we were in their village, they would sacrifice whatever they owned to protect us. The same was true for our friends.

In the winter of 1992, our comrades and some Turkish soldiers got into a battle in a village near to Kurtalan province. Before any gunfire started, the three PKK members shouted to the Turkish soldiers, "The villagers are innocent! If you promise not to shoot them, all three of us will surrender to you instead!" Their goal was to get all the villagers to safety. That was achieved, but as soon as the innocents had been relocated, all three of our comrades were martyred in the ensuing fight. The surviving villagers gained a lot of respect for the PKK that day. As the story of that incident spread, our stature grew in the eyes of the surrounding villages as well.

The public had realized that the PKK was no longer a danger to them. In fact, we members of the PKK would even sacrifice ourselves to protect them. Over time, we saw that they would also do anything for the PKK. Now, every single village had participants in the PKK. The villagers' uncles, brothers, and sisters were serving the organization for the patriotic Kurdish people.

The security forces heavily punished the public in the town of Lice in Diyarbakır while we were making preparations to return. "Punished" would be the wrong word, because this was clearly a cold-blooded massacre! All the entrances and exits in the district had been blocked. According to the Turkish press and military sources, they had done nothing. "It was the PKK who had besieged the town of Lice, seized all the buildings and vehicles owned by the government, and jailed all the officials. It was our organization which then committed all those murders." But in reality, in those days there were never any more than five people from the guerrilla forces stationed in Lice. As proud as I am of our militants, even I must admit that a force of only five of us lacks the power to surround an entire district. So, the government story was pure propaganda. Its purpose was only to justify the state's inexplicable action against the citizens of Lice. But there was no way to prove this to the public. They had destroyed both residential and business areas in the district with their armored tanks and heavy weapons, and they had killed 16 people from the civilian population.

The Turkish General named Bahtiyar Aydın was assassinated in front of the city gendarmerie headquarters on the same day. Of course, the media tried to blame the organization for this, but as with the President and his administration, Bahtiyar Aydın was killed because he was on the side of peace. Specifically, he was aligned with Eşref Bitlis's group which supported diplomacy. Whatever you wanted to call it: the state within the shadow government, those protecting their economic interests, or foreign forces—I didn't know. What I did know was that Bahtiyar Aydin wasn't killed by the organization. He was simply a victim of the trend. Everyone in the government or the military who had wanted to stop war and start political negotiations to cure Turkey's unrest had suffered systematic assassination, one by one. In this way, the shadow state could hit two birds with one stone. They were both getting rid of the moderate officials preventing their war, while also making propaganda to pin that war on the organization.

But we, as the organization, were continuously gathering intelligence and information about the security forces. Who stayed where? With whom did they stay when they left? Where did they eat when they hung out? Were they married or single? How many children did they have? The militants stationed in the cities provided us with this intel whenever we needed it. For instance, when our regional commander ordered us to retaliate for the massacre which had taken place in Lice, we contacted the militants in Diyarbakır and asked them if they had a mission plan ready. They told us that they did have one available and agreed that we could use it. They gave us an intelligence and information report on a high-ranking soldier living in the city center. As the surveillance was already completed, the only thing left to do was to get to the city and carry out the mission.

So, I went. The head militant in the city took me to the neighborhood where the building was located. For hours, I snuck around the alleyways and the building where this officer stayed. Over two days, I ascertained on which floor this high-ranking soldier and his family lived, and in which rooms they usually spent their time. I decided to complete my mission on the night of the third day. This would be my first assassination. For this mission, I had asked the comrades in the city to provide me with one Russian made Snayperskaya Vintovka Dragunova brand rifle. But, since I was already in the city, I had no chance to adjust the scope, and no practice shots. The proper way to set up a new rifle is to test-fire the weapon while looking through the scope, again and again. Each time a bullet hits a practice target, you adjust the focus of the scope a little closer. Bit by bit, the cross-hairs of the scope come to indicate accurately the precise point at which the bullet will hit. A millimeter difference in the focusing of the scope of the weapon can cause a miss of the target in delicate missions like this. But I had had neither enough time, nor ammo, nor a practice range on which to ensure such accuracy. That's why I had asked the weapon-bearer not once but twice whether the rifle's scope was properly adjusted. He told me that it was adjusted professionally—that there certainly would be no inaccuracy in the shooting.

So, a comrade and I drove to the destination in the darkness of the evening. The target was living on the fourth floor of the seven-story building where the officers stayed. Right across the street from it, there was a building under construction about 100 meters away. We made our sniper nest in that construction zone. We stayed there about two hours, waiting for the target to come home. Around half past ten, the officer came home with a civilian friend in tow. The fact he had left the curtains of the house open made everything easier.

I told the comrade to wait quietly for me somewhere far away. Simply because the slightest touch or sound on missions this delicate may destroy your focus completely.

The officer and his friend were watching television in the living room. Just next to the couch were sitting his wife and his daughter. The officer and his friend sat side by side. Patiently, I looked down the scope at my target. I took aim. I fired at the officer. When I checked with the binoculars I saw that his friend was shot, not the officer, which meant my sighting scope was 1 or 2 millimeters deviant in the horizontal shaft alignment, relative to the weapon and I had not been aware of it. I had made one shot. To prepare a second shot would take time and cover we did not have. We had already surrendered the element of surprise. It would have been a pointless risk. So, I grabbed the empty bullet casing and instantly left the building site. We got into the car that had brought us there and got out of the city immediately.

I was so ashamed of myself. Our squadron commander had put a lot of faith in me, to entrust me with such a delicate mission. I felt raw about this failure—even though it had technically been the failure of the scope or, more precisely, of the person who had been tasked with adjusting the scope. In normal circumstances, the assassin himself is to use the assassination weapon several times before the mission. You would perform the mission only after you have adjusted the scope yourself and are positive about the accuracy of the weapon. But I had had no opportunity to test the weapon given to me. So, this entire mission was a failure because one rifle scope had been mis-calibrated by 1 millimeter.

Ambush

I met with the comrades waiting for me outside the city, and we set off for the countryside without wasting time. I don't remember the name of the village, but as we approached, we fell into an ambush trap. One of our comrades lost his life there, and I was shot in the left of my chest. The ambush was severe and lasted for some time. The other two comrades finally found themselves in a stable location and better able to protect themselves. But one of them had seen that I'd been shot and thought I was dead. As soon as they overcame the ambush, they retreated. The next day, when they arrived at the camp, they notified the commander that two comrades had been lost during the ambush.

I was seriously injured but had not died. Crawling for about 200–300 meters, in the darkness of the night, I was able to escape. My wounds were severe, and I was not able to stand and walk. I was losing a lot of blood and had fallen unconscious from time to time. In the early morning, I saw two villagers out grazing their animals, and I asked them to help me. They took me to a nearby village, and the people there gave me some first aid; stopping the bleeding. I asked a militant in the village to go into the town and find a reliable doctor. Although the bleeding had been stopped, I was in severe pain. The bullets needed to be removed. Two militants brought a doctor from the city, who re-opened the wound

"You are heavily wounded," he said, "and I cannot do anything in these conditions. You need to be taken to a hospital immediately." It was a very risky undertaking to get to the hospital, but the doctor said it could be arranged. Two villagers, the doctor, and I got into a car and drove to the hospital. It seems incredible, but I stayed in this hospital for 25 days. During this time, only the doctor and the head physician knew I was a guerrilla. No one was allowed to see me. I was in a room alone. My treatment was personally done by the head physician and the doctor. During two operations, they removed two bullets from my body.

As time passed, I gained back my strength and was able to stand. I was ready to leave the hospital, and I was at risk of being recognized at any moment. On the evening of the twenty-fifth day, I left the hospital and went into the countryside near my comrades. When I reached there, I saw that the province managements had gathered together in our region. The operational planning of 1993 was going to be made. The meeting lasted 12 days. During that time, I had the rank of squad commander, so I participated personally in the meetings. Some regions would exhibit more activity in the military aspect. In other areas, they would carry out both military and political works. The "political work" is ensuring there are sufficient warriors, and establishing committees in the cities. These committees would reach the Kurds living in metropolitan areas and encourage those who wanted to join the PKK.

Financial Support

The committees, whose establishment was decided upon in the province meeting, were going to collect financial support for the PKK in both villages and cities. Through these committee members, the PKK had no financial problems. The financial support of the people was more than substantial. The Kurds in Turkey, as well as in Europe and many other places in the world, including America, help the organization financially. Fundraising was on a voluntary basis.

But it was occasionally reported in the Turkish media that the organization forcibly confiscated the property of innocent villagers and also held the villagers for ransom. This is nothing but a lie. For example, in the winter of 1994, we needed a heater for our winter camp. We found such a stove in one of the summerhouses, and we left twice as much money as was the value of the stove. We never had an attitude to usurp the property of the people, although I cannot vouch for everyone in this regard; because not every human being is as scrupulous. Some got what they needed from villagers and paid no money in return. But I am telling you, the overall attitude of the organization was one of honesty and fairness. If the organization heads heard something like that, you would get direct criticism or punishment, and you would be accused of being a thief. For example, if you were walking along during the day, or entered into a field at night, and saw tomatoes, watermelons or other things and took them without the owner's consent, the organization would directly accuse you of theft. Everyone knew that no one except the guerrillas travel around in the countryside, so it's enough for that family to send news to the organization. An investigation would be ordered, and some compensation paid to the family.

The organization is very sensitive of the public's property, because people have a negative response when such issues occur. Villagers would ask, "What kind of men are you? You say you are here for the public's good, but you usurp our property!"

Rangers were exceptions to this rule. From 1995 until 1999, we confiscated animals, and we used the meat from these animals in the winter camps. Sometimes we even arrested the shepherds of those animals, because the organization knew that some shepherds were simply in the countryside to provide information to the security forces.

As well as collecting voluntary contributions from individuals, the organization raised money through businesses. The organization had many factories and similar production facilities. We also had income from taxing. We received our annual tax from many kinds of manufacture and industrial facilities: thermal power plants, dams, quarry factories, and food factories located in eastern Anatolia. For example, if there were going to be a dam built in the region, we had dominance over it. The company would pay us a tax; otherwise they wouldn't be allowed to start a business there. (The tax is generally 10 percent of the cost of the work to be done.)

In addition, on the borders of Turkey, Syria, Iraq and Iran, there is excessive smuggling done by civilians. We have our own customs units on all of these borders. No smuggler can operate without paying taxes to the organization. If they didn't, they would be exposed to severe sanctions. Taxes are regularly received from these smugglers.

Although donations were done voluntarily, companies or smugglers had to pay their taxes regularly. The person who resisted would have to pay more taxes. So, for instance, if you wanted 500,000 liras tax from a company (which happened from time to time), and the owner of the company not only doesn't pay but also behaves arrogantly, you would make him pay one million liras as punishment. Taxation was essential for us, because the annual expenses of the organization were very high. When I say expenses,

I don't only mean the necessary expenses for the guerilla to stay in the mountains, but, in addition to this, there are a lot of TV and radio channels, and newspapers. None of these media bodies have advertising revenue, so our taxation method is needed in order to keep them afloat.

We would never keep a large amount of money in rural areas. There were no more than the equivalent of ten million Turkish liras in total distributed throughout the camping areas. I do not know where the organization keeps the rest of the money, but when money was needed, it came from somewhere. Every unit in the organization had a financier. They were the only ones authorized to do any spending. The rest of us would just make a list of whatever we needed and give it to the financier; he would arrange for the appropriate amount of money.

Twice each year, especially during wintertime, each battalion declared their balance sheet (the cost report) to the administration. All units had to clearly declare in these reports how much they had spent—and for what. Each battalion usually received money twice a year. When the spring came, $150,000 to $200,000 was received per battalion. The same amount of money was then also sent for the winter camp preparations. The central headquarters commander was in charge of recording who spent how much.

The organization specifically used dollars or Euros. We had no reason to use Turkish lira. Although the Turkish lira could be used in Turkey, we couldn't purchase anything with it in Iran or in Iraq. On the other hand, the dollar or Euro could be used throughout Turkey, Iraq, and even in Syria.

Whatever a guerilla needed, from shoes, to a radio to a new watch, it is bought with this money. Apart from the financiers, the only guerrillas with money were each unit commander or company commander, and only for emergencies. An ordinary guerilla had no money, nor did he require any. Every one of his needs was met by the collective.

You might not expect it, but the collected taxes, donations, and fines were reported to senior management through receipts. When we requested taxes, we had to give a receipt to the person for the amount of the tax received. You always kept a carbon copy of this receipt. We freedom fighters would dole out official receipts from the organization. On each receipt was printed the organization's emblem and seal. As a second level of protection, to keep comrades honest, no one would be sent alone to collect taxes. The organization would always send at least three people to prevent rumors, or the act, of stealing money. Such thefts had occurred several times in the organization. Sometimes, the PKK border customs agents would run away with the smuggling taxes they'd collected. The organization invested the amount of effort in their pursuit, proportional to the amount of missing money.

Here is a funny story. When I was first appointed to the region of Bitlis, the organization taxed a Kurdish man for 100,000 Deutschmark. The man was very rich. He had gas stations, supermarkets, and other incomes. He was from the tribe known as Bitlis Serekanoğulları. He sent our tax bill back to us via peasants. When we received it, we saw he had written on the back, "Do you think you can take taxes from me just because a few looters like you went up to the mountains?"

When the note was read in front of the group, of course everyone became angry. Some said we should execute that man; some said we should bomb his gas stations; and some said we should take him as a captive. Of these options, the regional commander thought taking him as a captive was the best idea. So, two of us dressed up in civilian clothes, went to the city, and showed up at the man's office. His secretary first told the comrades that the man wasn't there and that they would have to come back some other time. But the comrades heard the man saying, "Send them away, I can't deal with them right now." So, they went on inside with guns and found him. They bound the hands of the secretary and left her in the office. They took the man and his driver as captives and brought them to the countryside by car.

Let me tell you, this man was grossly obese; so much so that it pained him even to walk. Our friends contacted us via radio and asked us to send them two mules, because they couldn't proceed any farther with him in that condition. So, we brought the huge man to the camp area on mules. We didn't even put him in jail, because the man would never be able to run away anyway. He was out of breath as soon as he took six steps. We brought him in front of the leaders and made him read his note. We asked him to confirm whether he wrote it. He assented, and started to beg, saying, "I did something bad, but please don't hurt me." So our regional commander replied, "OK, we will forgive you, but your penalty has doubled. You must now pay 200,000 DM. [Deutschmark], and you will now also meet our needs for food and clothes for an additional 150,000 DM." The man accepted each penalty without any objections.

Of course, we kept the man with us until we received the money and the supplies, even though that required that he stay with us for a month and a half. The military knew we had the man, but it was summer, and they couldn't come up to the camp area. This man lost so much weight in 45 days that he became a new person.

Finally, we received all the money and supplies. Everything was in order. As we were about to set him free, he surprised us by saying that he didn't want to leave. "Believe me, to have lost as much weight as I have lost here with you, I would have spent twice as much money as I gave you. Let me stay here for a while and get even thinner." The commander wouldn't let him. Then he asked, "At least tell me how I can see you when I want to?" So, we told him just to approach the peasants, and they would take him to us. After this incident, we developed such a good relationship with the man that he was now visiting us once a month. And every year, since then, he always brings us his taxes long before we ask him!

Politics and the Public

In addition to the aforementioned duties, the members of our city committees were also responsible for all urban reconnaissance and intelligence gathering. In some cases, it was difficult for guerillas to go down to the city and carry out a mission. Those were the situations for which we relied on our implanted urban guerilas. Unlike regular PKK guerrilla units, our urban units couldn't act on their own initiative. The only exception was that sometimes, if they deemed it necessary, they could bomb the security forces but no one else. The organization leadership had very firm standing orders prohibiting missions against anyone but the security forces. This forbade acts against people such as bureaucrats, civilians, public officials, or deputies.

The organization's belief was that acts against such people could trigger a civil war. Therefore, senior officials strictly ordered us to avoid such acts. Never, as the official PKK or as any self-directed branches of the guerilla force, had we ever planned such an act against such noncombatants. There were, of course, some exceptions. But those individual guerillas, who had chosen to perform such acts, never went without punishment.

We never retaliated against Turkish civilians, despite the fact that state troops had repeatedly murdered Kurdish innocents, in massacres such as those in the cities of Şırnak and Cizre. Although, up until 1993 we consistently wanted to establish an independent Kurdistan, our people were too intermingled throughout Turkey. Now, we only wanted to live in peace with the Turkish people, with rights equal to theirs. Therefore, we didn't want to incite violence in our neighbors by attacking civilians. Believe me, we had every opportunity to do so. However, we never did. In Kurdistan towns, 70 percent of the employees who worked in state institutions were Turks (apart from the security forces). Although, many of these cities and towns were completely under our control, we never attacked these people, but their acts against our people in the city of Şırnak, and towns of Cizre and Lice, had created in us a lust for revenge. We guerillas wanted to take that revenge, not only on the security forces but also on the rangers cooperating with them, even though the rangers consisted almost entirely of Kurdish villagers. This was because with native mountainfolk as rangers, the government could reach the regions they were not able to with security forces alone. This effective strategy severely restricted the PKK's freedom of movement.

Kurdish villagers were registering for the ranger system for many reasons. The state of emergency and war in the countryside had an incredible impact on the peasants' ability to graze their animals and to farm. No one could easily feed their animals or go to the highlands to tend their fields, and without livestock, agriculture, or factories in the region, there was no other livelihood left available for these people. How would they survive? They were forced to register for the village protection system to earn their living. We had this conversation with almost each of the ranger villages. All of them admitted to this fact.

By 1993, the government had already started to apply its new strategy of evacuating all the villages of PKK sympathizers. They had come to their own conclusion that the public and the guerillas are like fish and water. A fish has no chance of survival outside the water; it dies. Likewise, they had heard that if you tear the guerilla from the public, the guerilla can't survive. Their strategies worked. By gathering the villagers into the cities, the state prevented them from supporting us and prevented us from contacting them. The government had evacuated most of the villages in the rural areas by the end of 1993. Their plan was to isolate us guerillas. Many rangers had their profits from this. The government simply did not touch the villages of the rangers who were very aggressive against the PKK.

A very cruel policy was applied to empty the villages, and people were terrified. They were left no other choice but to leave. That was the only option the Turkish government gave them. The state told them that if they were not for them, then they were against them. So, they could either move to the cities and live, or they could be killed as enemies of Turkey. They had no other choice.

When Tansu Çiller and Doğan Güreş became Prime Minister and Chief of General Staff respectively, the villager's plight worsened even further. Villagers who had not abandoned their villages were now directly targeted by soldiers. This was terrible enough, but the pressures on the Kurdish public weren't limited to this. Prominent businessmen such as Behçet Cantürk and Savaş Buldan; sympathetic politicians such as Vedat Aydın and Musa Anter, became the victims of unsolved murders, one by one. The government was employing its own terror tactics to divide the public from the organization, by fear.

The security forces killed a family in a village in a province of Muş called Altınova in Turkish and Vartinis in Kurdish. They burned this family alive. The soldiers on patrol, who found them still squatting in their own village, told them that they should have abandoned their home already, and to do so immediately or otherwise they would kill them all. The family refused. So, the soldiers locked them in the family home they loved so well and set the house on fire. Again and again they did this, in village after village. The same incidents happened in all Eastern provinces. Eleven people were killed in the province of Kulp in Diyarbakır, for refusing to leave their homes. Then, the soldiers threw someone from a helicopter somewhere to scare the public, though I don't have all the details. His body was smashed into pieces. It worked. The public became terrified. The state simply abandoned the rules of war. Tactics that had nothing to do with the Geneva Convention or humane policy were shamelessly implemented by the Turkish Government during that period. There were thousands of individual "unsolved murders."

People were disappearing. Now, people had a new, legitimate worry; if the soldiers or police took someone away, would anyone ever hear from them again?

Of course, the organization was performing its own unsolved murders during this time. It is still widely believed that all the unsolved murders in the region were committed by the government, but that is not fully accurate. The organization was very professional in this regard. Some of our incidents were so masterful that they were attributed to the government. In recent years, there was a mine explosion; four people were killed, and seven to eight people were injured. History records this incident as having been performed by the government. Well, at least the peasants thought this, but it was one of our guerrillas who laid mines on a busy street, which was the route of a regular shuttle taking soldiers from one point to another. That guerrilla actually wanted to explode the shuttle, but, by coincidence, a van of the same color and brand passed by. The passengers were peasants. It was only after the explosion that the comrades saw that all the passengers had been civilians. And many of them had been closely tied to the organization. As most of the populace knew how loyal those people were to the PKK, it wasn't difficult for the organization to throw the blame on the government.

Actually, since the government already treated the Kurdish people so terribly, it was not so difficult for the organization to convince the public that the government was to blame for every unsolved murder. Some years ago, in Yüksekova, the police were unabashedly swearing obscenities at Kurdish civilians from an armored state vehicle, even as they were on official duty. This was covered by Turkish television. Now, how are the people there supposed to trust the government after hearing its representatives degrade them? Another incident happened in the city of Van. The police used their police van to intentionally drag a minibus filled with Kurds straight into a fire. Certainly, these were individual acts, perhaps committed by renegades, but the government reputation was the one tarnished. People suffering such abuse do not care whether these were isolated incidents caused by the ignorance of individuals, rogue gendarmeries or police forces. People victimized like this, react against the entity of the government.

There were also psychologically powerful incidents, which were deliberately planned by the Turkish government to cause resentment and hatred for the organization. Killings at the hands of the government were committed in such a way as to frame the PKK for them. Unfortunately, for us, such incidents happened frequently. A non-commissioned officer was gunned down in 2014, in the city of Diyarbakır. He had been shopping with his wife in the farmers' market place. If the government were honest, it would have shed light on this murder, but it didn't, because people would then see their government for what it was. This is similar to the incident which happened in the city of Bingöl, in 2014. The chief of police was shot. Officially, no one knows who shot him. The investigation was closed without a resolution. Media coverage of the police investigation was banned. The verdict of the investigation committee was sealed. But all of this succeeded in causing more hatred in the Turkish people against the Kurds.

I hated this kind of underhanded influencing, whether it came from the government or the organization. It's disgusting to fuel public sentiment with lies. As I have said, the organization is certainly responsible for its share of incidents, but it has been almost 15 years since we used this kind of underhanded tactic. But Turkey's government utilizes it to this day, even by murdering its own police and soldiers.

There are also explicit murders the Turkish Government performed against the Kurds, such as those that occurred between October 6 and October 8, 2015. In total, 51 Kurdish civilians were murdered. Yet, somehow only four murderers were found. Coincidentally, those four people were the ones who killed the Hezbollah sympathizers. Yasin Börü, a Hezbollah sympathizer, was killed by PKK sympathizers and was mentioned on the media channels every day. But where are the perpetrators of these remaining 47 murders? Why does no one ask about them? Society is manipulated by the media. Everything is done to divide rather than unite the people. Society has become so surreal that nobody has anything to say about 47 murdered people, while weeping loudly for those Hezbollah supporters who were killed. Turks do not know anything. They believe whatever the media tells them. But the Kurdish society is different. They are much more aware of reality. Regardless of the official message broadcast by the media, they communicate the actual facts to each other and are savvy to the true tactics of the government. Here in Turkey, we Kurds are highly politicized. We are much wiser regarding politics than the Turks living in the other parts of Turkey. Nevertheless, that's pretty blatant—that you only find the perpetrators of the murders of four supporters of your cause, but do not seek for the perpetrators of the murders of 47 other people who were not important to you. The Kurdish people are not stupid. They know very well that those 47 people were killed by the security forces.

As long as such injustices continue, the Kurdish people feel more and more alienated from Turkish governance and any Turkish identity. They no longer feel loyal to Turkey. The bond is not yet completely severed. At the moment, we still have the chance to fix the rift and to live together as brothers, but this situation is getting worse. If this problem is not solved quickly, we will reach a point of no return, as did Iraq. If the Prime Minister were to come out and say, "We ask forgiveness for all the mistakes we have made in public or private. I apologize on behalf of all the security forces. Never again will we commit actions outside the rules of law," the Kurdish population would rededicate themselves to Turkey with all their hearts and souls. But if you refuse to do this—if you insist that you are always in the right—the public will drift further apart from you every day. Before you know it, they might develop loyalty to the leadership of another country.

From 1993, the government's purpose for the repression and killing of the Kurdish people was to divide the public from the organization and gain popular support for themselves. But, the opposite has happened. Although the Kurds were scared, they also developed a desire for revenge against the government. Their answer was ready-made. They could take their revenge by joining the organization. That's why our participation rate doubled in those years. The populace was joining the organization in groups of 10, 20, and even 30 people at a time.

In other words, the government wasn't successful, despite its policy of intimidation, because each of the Kurdish families had at least one family member who was serving up in the mountains. So, the public didn't give up on their own children in the organization. Risking everything, they protected the organization and, in doing so, protected themselves. They even sent their children away from home to join the PKK camps in Iraq.

The brutal, unlawful violence perpetrated by the government during this period forced the organization to be brutal in return. Now, we had to contend with both the rangers and the security forces. Although we had not carried out a large-scale mission until 1993, from this point forward our missions needed to be of grander scale and greater effect.

We forced the rangers to abandon their villages and migrate to big cities. We also committed some brutal missions against these rangers in some of the towns and villages. Women, children, the elderly; it made no matter. Everyone was killed in these missions. The villagers we murdered were Kurdish like us, but they did nothing for the Kurds, and they were serving the Turks. Therefore, we had no sympathy while killing them.

The more brutal the war became, the more power the PKK gained as a party. Every Kurd forced to leave his village by the government joined with us to fight against the government. Participation grew so rapidly that suddenly the cities of Şırnak and Hakkari, alone, boasted nearly 5,000 guerrillas. And the more the government attacked the people, the more the people wanted our protection. In those same two cities of Şırnak and Hakkari, 15,000 civilians abandoned their homes in order to travel to southern Kurdistan (Iraq) and join our camps there. Thousands upon thousands of displaced Kurdish villagers wanted to join the PKK. But the organization wouldn't accept them all. Our leadership wanted the majority of these sympathizers to stay and defend the Kurds in the general population.

This was crucial, because the government of this era knew no limits on the level of tactics it would employ against its own people. So, urban Kurds began to display their anger at this cruelty by organizing. Rallies, meetings, and peaceful demonstrations became more and more common. The public refused to surrender. They were no longer afraid of their government. Why should they be? Death had become an everyday occurrence for the people in this region. What more could the government do to them? Kill them? It was doing that anyway. So, the people lost nothing by demonstrating their rage at this treatment. Meanwhile, the fact that our own Kurdish people were organizing these kinds of revolutionary activities in the city centers, and finding their courage to stand up against the cruel acts of the security forces, was a great morale booster for us guerrillas in the field.

In fact, we were so moved that we were discussing among ourselves how this public deserves our very best. Even death can't dissuade the people any longer. As guerillas, we never dreamed of living a long life. We could be martyred any time, and we were very aware of this. Sometimes you would lose a friend who had stood by your side night and day. Therefore, death had become common for us. This outlook motivated us to do anything to fulfill our duties.

Around the fall of 1993, we secured full dominance of the countryside. We already knew very well where the security forces were located. But, in areas where we had only had 55 or 60 guerrillas, we were now 200 strong. Also, our ability to meet our needs was diminishing, as more and more villages were abandoned. It began with simple shortages. For days, we'd be unable to drink tea, simply because we didn't have any. We would finally get tea, only to run out of sugar for it. Tea and sugar would finally present themselves in sufficient quantities, and that's when we'd run out of flour to make bread. But we survived all that. Things got hard, but we all did our best to meet every challenge with fortitude.

After all, we had been well aware before even joining the PKK that life in the organization was not going to be easy. While those who could endure all of these privations became guerillas, those who couldn't bear them worked instead to support our activities behind the scenes in the European countries and in southern Kurdistan, Iran, Iraq and Syria.

We, in the mountains, on the other hand, knew that we were suffering such conditions because of the soldiers, and therefore, we were fueled with strong feelings of hatred and of revenge, and these feelings were reflected in our actions.

This was the atmosphere in which we planned to perform a mission against a military station located in the countryside between the cities of Bitlis and Siirt. This outpost was also located inside a ranger village. So, we had to disable these rangers in order to reach the station. We used the radio to guarantee to the rangers in the village that if they let us pass, unimpeded through the village to our target, we wouldn't touch anyone; we wouldn't even shoot a single bullet. The rangers agreed, promising they wouldn't stop us from attacking the station as long as we left them alone.

As we had expected, the leader of the rangers even offered us the use of his arsenal and personnel if we needed them. But we knew that these heavy weapons had been lent to them by the Turkish

Government. We also knew the Turkish Government would return and kill every villager there, if it found out they had given us government weapons to use against the government's own security forces. They would have no excuse to offer when the military asked them why they didn't fight the PKK. That's why we told the villagers to pretend to shoot at us when we entered the village.

At 11:00 p.m., we raided the station. We killed nine of the security forces and sustained no losses. We withdrew from the battlefield at about one in the morning. Our mission had been to disable the station, not to kill every last soldier.

We left an exit open. We knew the soldiers were going to see it and leave the area without making any further stand against us. The soldiers in the station knew very well that they wouldn't receive any reinforcements at this time of night. Because everyone understood we would have set an ambush on every possible route, the reinforcements couldn't take the risk of entering and would be obliged to wait for the morning.

We had wanted to give the military the message that we had changed. We were serious now. We could completely destroy any one of their stations anytime we wanted. So, our mission was simply to destroy the military station building itself. As long as that was accomplished, and our message was delivered, it didn't matter how many soldiers inside of it lived or died.

Sometimes, we would get the news that our comrades had besieged military stations closer to the national borders, and that they had been able to destroy the station buildings completely and kill everyone inside. This was because of the heavy weapons the border units could smuggle in from neighboring countries. These included Dochka brand bazookas; up to a hundred howitzers; even surface-to-air missiles made in Russia, called SAM-7s. It was just impossible for those of us stationed in the interior parts of Turkey to transport such heavy weapons with us all the time. Normally, the most we carried were bixi and bazookas. However, after occupying a military station, we would acquire more effective weapons than we had ourselves.

The morning after we performed this mission, the military in the region started a large-scale operation against us. They were furious and wanted revenge. They heavily wounded four of our comrades and martyred three more. With these heavy losses on both sides, both the soldiers and the guerrillas were eager for battle. But with our newly increased numbers, we weren't capable of moving in small groups any longer. Therefore, whenever we moved, the military would detect us, and a battle would ensue.

7

TURKISH OPPRESSION TOWARD THE KURDISH VILLAGERS

The uptick in incidents was indicating that 1994 would be even more difficult on us than 1993. The village evacuations were fully under way. During this exodus, the civilians were frequently harmed; many little children lost their lives. The evacuations were particularly focused on the villages on the borders of Turkey-Iran, Turkey-Iraq, and Turkey-Syria. Villagers there were being forced to immigrate wholesale into city centers. Some resisted. Most of the villagers on the Turkey-Iraq border, for instance, settled in places in the countryside close to PKK camps, instead of obediently moving to the metropolises.

This was possible because there were PKK camps near almost all the cities in northern Iraq. The Kurds who passed into northern Iraq came under the jurisdiction of our guerilla camp located in Haftanin. After being hosted there for a month, the commanders sent them to the villages and cities inside Iraq for their own security. Air assaults still targeted our training camps from time to time. Although we guerillas knew how to protect ourselves from such attacks, the ordinary public, such as these villagers, had no idea how even to begin to protect themselves.

To be frank, the camp management faced great difficulties trying to meet the needs of these refugee villagers. They had not been able to take anything with them while running away from the soldiers, so they came to us with no resources of their own. They had left their animals and all valuable possessions behind. We in the PKK were well aware of how brutal the military was against us, but we had never imagined they would torture the noncombatant civilians that badly—so extremely that the villagers would flee for their lives and abandon literally everything they owned.

Fortunately, the regional Kurdish administration in northern Iraq was able to assist the refugees with their basic needs. Otherwise, it would have been a very difficult task for us to support them unaided. The same thing had happened to the hundreds of Kurds in northern Iraq, who ran away from the torture of Saddam between the years of 1988 to 1991. The Kurds in Turkey had helped them. This time, Barzani, the President of the Iraqi Kurdistan region, had first established a big camp in northern Iraq, in Ninova province. The displaced families were settled there. Their basic needs, such as food and clothes, were met for the length of their stay, which was a very long time.

It was advantageous for us, in a way, that so many villagers moved to the cities. We guerillas could easily infiltrate this crowd and, through them, conduct missions in the cities. Just as the public protected the guerillas in the countryside, they also assisted them financially and spiritually in the cities. The children of these uneducated refugees were going to be registered in schools there. We hoped they would then become the representatives of the organization, after starting their education in the big cities. In all its years, the organization hadn't been successful at this strategy, even though we had urgently wanted this to happen. So, although the government harmed the organization in the short run by moving the villagers who supported us, and then forcing us to provide for their needs, in the long run, the government helped us a lot, by concentrating our young future members together and forcing them to receive free high-quality education.

Our ranks swelled so much during this period that that our camps were thronged. This was now a great disadvantage for us. We were then acting like a regular army, instead of like a guerilla one. The size of our active guerilla units was now so great that we couldn't implement the foundational rules of secrecy and covert missions by which the guerilla survives. Naturally, we had become an explicit target. We simply couldn't hide ourselves as well as we once had. As a natural result, as the number of explicit targets we presented increased, the number of air operations against us increased as well.

The enemy's force also increased. The operations, which used to be conducted with two or four aircraft, were now being conducted with 15 to 20 aircraft. Indeed, at the end of 1993, we were subject to the biggest air operation of our organization's history. A great bombardment of 56 Turkish combat aircraft attacked the Zele camp at the intersection of the Iran, Iraq, and Turkish borders.

The security forces attacked our camps because they knew very well that no matter how many guerillas they could kill in Turkey, the organization would have the ability to continue its missions so long as our camps were in service. Wherever we took a loss, these camps would furnish reinforcements to that region.

The other reason for the military to target the Zele camp, instead of our more accessible camps in Iraq, was that Cemil Bayık and other senior officials were staying at the Zele camp at that time. During this airstrike, Cemil Bayık and some senior managers were in Iraq on diplomatic missions. Just as they were finishing their meetings and preparing to return to the Zele camp, they were notified about the airstrike. When they were told not to go to the camp because of the danger, Bayık and the others didn't leave Iraq. They immediately contacted the commanders in the Zele camp by radio and told them to prepare for the Turkish airstrike.

And so, although the air operation was massive, we didn't take too many losses. The first reason was the advance warning and the precautions that resulted. The second reason was the heavy anti-aircraft weapons we had in the camp. The Zele camp was surrounded with automatic anti-aircraft weapons, preventing the Turkish aircrafts from hitting the targets they wanted. We only had 34 losses from a 56 aircraft mission.

Jalal Talabani, who was the head of the PUK back then, was appointed as the intermediary between the PKK and Turkey. As I mentioned before, Talabani had made various promises to Osman Öcalan, and Osman Öcalan had been seduced by them. So, before the peace negotiations started with Turkey, Osman Öcalan was sentenced to death. The decision was approved by Apo immediately. Apo wanted Osman Öcalan (his own brother) to be caught and executed as soon as possible. As soon as Osman Öcalan heard that he was sentenced to death, he fled from the PUK and took shelter in Iran. Osman knew that the PUK's military force wasn't strong enough to protect him from the organization.

He had made a very strategic mistake with this decision. You can't compete in politics with Iran. You can't trick them. The Iranian government isn't a simple and inexperienced government. They are devious. They have various tricks, and they show no loyalty. This is why, when Apo heard that Osman Öcalan was in Iran, he sent Cemil Bayık to Iran as an ambassador. Bayık made hard bargains for the return of Osman to the PKK. As the result of the agreement, Iran gave Osman back to Apo. As easily as that. They only had one condition, saying, "Osman Öcalan took shelter with us and asked us for help. We will give him back to you only if you don't enact the death penalty." Cemil Bayık, who participated in this negotiation, said, "I am the guarantor. Take my word for it. We won't execute Osman Öcalan. I will somehow convince Apo."

Cemil Bayık had a high rank and a certain reputation in the organization, and Iran was well aware of it. If Cemil Bayık made a suggestion, they knew Apo would definitely listen to him. Indeed, it happened just this way. The death sentence of Osman Öcalan was postponed solely upon the insistence of Cemil Bayık.

It turned out that Apo had actually been completely correct in his decision to impose the death sentence on his brother, because, as a result of his leniency and his promise to Iran and to Cemil Bayık to spare Osman Öcalan, he left himself open to a smear campaign. Now it was said that Apo would never forgive anyone who committed a crime, regardless of the pressure coming from international society and regional leaders, unless the criminal is a family member, in which case Apo does nothing at all. Apo was aware of this rumor. He had already approved the death sentence against Osman Öcalan, though he was his own brother! If he hadn't been able to sentence his own brother to capital punishment, he would have lost the authority to give a death sentence to anyone in the organization who committed the same crime.

On the other hand, Apo was also subject to the opposite criticism. The image was simultaneously created of Apo as a brutal and blood-thirsty dictator—in order to preserve his own power, he would even execute his own brother. Cemil Bayık had convinced Apo to change his mind in order to eradicate this second image and fulfill the promise that he gave to Iran.

And so, Osman Öcalan survived his betrayal. Bayık warned Osman, "If the same thing happens again, I will kill you with my own hands." Osman returned to the party, but he had lost his previous authority. He was dismissed from his post in the PKK central command, and his membership to participate in decision-making and missions was suspended until the fifth congress (until 1995). This was the most severe punishment for him. The brother of our leader was now only a civilian in the organization. During this time, he was assigned to the most basic labor forces. He dealt with kitchen chores, cooking, washing-up, baking bread, and keeping watch. He had no one's respect; neither did he have any friends. As I said before, whatever your rank or authority is, if you commit a crime, you get punished—even if you are Apo's own flesh and blood.

Cemil Bayık told Osman Öcalan, "Repair your reputation until the fifth congress. If you regain the trust of the organization, we will restore your membership." During this period, I witnessed—for the first time—a young comrade and fellow guerilla die of natural causes. I was incredibly affected by this incident. I had seen many funerals; I had carried my dead comrades in my arms. But this friend of mine who died at such a very young age touched me deeply. I told myself that no one should die this young.

He had gotten lost at night while moving with his group. You'll remember that the years between 1994 and 1997 were troublesome ones. When he got separated from his unit, he was isolated in the mountains for 45 days. He knew the location of our warehouses of food and ammunition. He knew where our caches of supplies were hidden. I don't know if he panicked or got overwhelmed by fear, but he circled that mountain for a month and a half. Our comrades found him on the mountainside, nearly unconscious, and brought him to the field camp. He was sick and weakened from hunger. He couldn't speak. We called the doctor immediately.

The doctor examined him for half an hour. He declared that our friend would only live for about three days. Of course, we were shocked. That's impossible, we said, and I argued, "He has stayed in the mountains for 45 days before he came to the camp. How can you say that he will only live for three more days?" This friend even started to speak, laugh, and make jokes with us. He was fine and appeared healthy. However, just as the doctor said, he died on the third day. We were all completely saddened. For the first time, we had actually seen someone die of natural causes, right in front of us. The doctor told us, "Comrades, this man ate raw grass in the mountains for 45 days. His stomach was always empty. He had no nutrition to process. His organs weren't able to function. He had no chance of surviving."

Platoon Command

The command structure in other organizations and militaries differed from the command structure in the PKK. If you were a commander in the PKK, you were the leader of everything: every sphere, every variable. You needed to be able to anticipate danger and hunger, as well as numerous other difficulties, because you led the way in all matters. In other commands, the higher your rank, the greater your comfort. This was certainly not the case in the PKK. With us, the greater the rank you attained, the more responsibilities you accrued. You couldn't be a commander and send your militants to the front and remain safely behind. You were the platoon commander, and you commanded! This meant that if your team went somewhere, you must lead them, and the organization responded in kind. The guerillas in the team would never jeopardize the safety of their commander. Their reasoning was: "the platoon commander is my senior, and I must do everything in my power to protect him."

There were certain criteria that must be satisfied, in order to earn promotions in the guerilla force. A leading criterion was to have self-command of the standards of the party. You must be committed to your comrades, without any discrimination. You must protect your comrades under any circumstances and think of them before yourself. You should never relinquish your air of military discipline. You must be experienced in guerilla combat tactics and styles of action and even conduct missions yourself, when necessary. Insufficiencies were especially impossible to justify in someone appointed as a commander. Finally, no one could request a certain rank or position. You had to understand that duties were only appointed to you based on your own performance and the needs of the organization.

Even if you passed these requirements, the senior commanders in the northern provinces could only stay in a position for three or four years at most, though there have been exceptions. This command echelon was then withdrawn to the southern provinces or to Damascus, and a new command echelon was appointed in their place. Fatigue was the main reason for intermittent change. The command echelon that stayed in the fight for a long time might see slippage in their focus and control. Physical and mental weaknesses might creep in and costly mistakes might take place in battles. The effects from mistakes at that level are exponential. If a random guerilla made a mistake, the mistake was limited to him. But a mistake by the commander in the fight would not only affect multiple guerillas under his control but also the reputation of the organization. It was simpler and safer merely to switch out the command echelon in the north every three or four years.

A few days before leaving the winter camp of 1994, I was appointed as a platoon commander, even though I was quite young. A platoon consisted of 27 to 30 people. Since I was pretty inexperienced, I had hard times adjusting to being in this position of authority. Almost everyone in my team was older than me, and it was very difficult for me to give orders to these people. Guerillas, who were almost the same age as my father, were under my command.

Since I was a platoon commander, the company commander was always advising me about how to act within the organization. This company commander had a big hand in shaping my personality and character. I was assigned to his squadron for a long time, and we worked together almost until the end of 1996. He never did tell me his real name, but his nickname was Orhan. I hear that he eventually died of a heart attack in Germany. But while he was my commander, I took all of his actions and demeanor to heart. I looked up to him as a role model, and I always tried to act as I imagined that he would. I so wanted to emulate him with his ability to fight; his character, and his behavior throughout daily life. He was one of the rare people in the organization who was loved by everyone. Whenever someone had a problem or had failed at something, he would talk to that person for hours. Every guerilla knew that commander Orhan was someone who would think rationally and take care of everyone.

As I was so young, commander Orhan would always advise me as if I were his own son. I clearly remember the time he told me, "Deniz, I hope you will never use the phrase 'I don't know' on the battlefield." When I asked him why, he replied, "Imagine that your platoon is besieged and you have absolutely no chance of retreat. The guerrillas under your command will be hanging on your every word, and you will become their only hope. They will be looking to you and thinking, 'Our commander will save us!' So, in the middle of that ambush, if one of your guerrillas ever asks you, 'commander, what are we going to do?' and you answer him with 'I don't know!' all of your guerrillas will lose hope. They will give up fighting and all of you will die. That is why, so long as you are a commander in the organization, you will never once use the phrase, 'I don't know' while in combat. Now, if you are asked something in the camp or during trainings, which you honestly can't answer, then you can admit that you don't know. But in battle you have no right to say that, because, under fire, you are your fighters' only hope."

I had been in the region for almost three years, and by now I was familiar with the details of the terrain, as well as with the workings of the organization and the guerilla fighters individually. But the most vital knowledge that I held was that I had already decoded the tactics and plans of the enemy, though there really hadn't been much there to solve. Those were the reasons I was appointed to the position of platoon commander, when the former one was sent to Damascus. I was so young that I rejected the assignment at first. I told the leadership that the job would be too challenging for me, and that I simply couldn't accept it.

I shared these worries of mine with my company commander. He told me, "If the organization appoints you to a position, you don't have the luxury of refusal. They think you deserve this promotion and you will do your duty. Don't worry," he added dryly, "If you don't perform well, they won't hesitate to fire you."

First Mission as a Platoon Commander

A massive land attack was launched against us in April of 1994, just as we were leaving our winter camps and entering the battle season. As we were listening to Turkish military radio conversation in the middle of the night, we found out that the military was about to hit us. This mission was very important for our region, since we wanted to go into the new fighting period with a great victory. For our own morale, we needed to finish their attack by devastating their forces but without sustaining any losses ourselves.

When the mission started, we were on the outskirts of Kuris Mountain, which is connected to the city of Bitlis. Kuris Mountain was of great strategic value for us, because there existed only two options in going up to the summit. It was also a steep mountain, and was both rocky and wooded. The forests offered little concealment, since it was the first month of spring. The snow was newly melted, and the trees hadn't yet blossomed.

Still, we knew it and its value well. So, as soon as the operation started, we deployed our entire force onto this mountain. The security forces thought that we were only a company, but we were deployed as a battalion of 130 people. The security forces knew as well as we that this mountain had only two entrances. They were planning to climb the mountain at midnight from one of those entrances and hit us while we slept.

Our scheme was to act as if we were unprepared and pretend not to know that the security forces were on the way. We left one of those entrances free, just like they wanted. This was during the time period just after the gendarmerie special operation units had been established in Turkey. So, the enemy's strength, collaborating in this operation, consisted of these special operations units. Just as we had figured, 18 members of these units climbed up to the summit of the mountain, from the unencumbered entrance, while we listened in on their radio conversations. We knew exactly where and when the Turkish soldiers were located.

The battalion commander ordered, "No one will shoot until this team reaches the summit." We knew the sun would brighten the mountaintop at around 4:30 a.m. As soon as the team reached the summit, we shot them all. All of them, except one, were killed. It was their wounded commander whom we captured. We forced the commander to speak and learned all the details of the operation, including how many days the operation would last, how many forces would participate, and whether there would be any airstrikes. We learned everything!

Our battalion commander confiscated the radio of the Turkish soldier and contacted their commander. Their entire force understood that the team they had sent to the mountain summit had been killed. As soon as they realized the situation, the battle stopped. A few hours later, our location was hit by Cobra-type attack helicopters. This battle martyred two of our friends, and three were seriously wounded. But the crippled security forces lifted their siege that evening.

At midnight, after we had treated our wounded comrades and the captive commander, we climbed down the mountain and went back to the countryside. This wounded enemy officer was sent to our camp in Iraq. As we had hoped, this battle had been a good morale booster for us since we had sustained only a few losses but had caused many causalities on the other side.

A week after this operation, one of the teams attached to our battalion was trapped in a ranger ambush while passing from one area to another. The youngest guerilla of us all was martyred in this ambush. He was either 17 or 18. As the team was in the middle of the ambush, the rangers captured his corpse. They were rangers of a village connected to the city of Siirt. I don't know for what reason, but they abused his corpse a great deal. His head was severed from his body, his organs were removed, and his feet were pulverized. He was then given to the animals in the village as food. We were enraged.

In the teahouse connected to the Baykan town, the ranger who had done this terrible thing was talking openly about how he had bashed our comrade into pieces, feeling proud of himself. He was repeating the story to anyone who would listen. "I shot the guerilla just like that and then I beheaded him like this. I did this and that!" The security forces decided to reward him because of what he had accomplished. They gave the man a G3 weapon with binoculars. This was a very important gift at that time.

All this information was passed along to us by the patriotic villagers. They gave us photos of the man who had perpetrated all the abuse on our comrade. The community's help proved that they, also, had been outraged by this situation. As we took in this information, there arose in our company a great feeling for revenge. So, it was agreed that, no matter how many losses we might suffer in the end, we were going to kill that man.

Of course, the village of these rangers wasn't an ordinary village. There was a military outpost right at the entrance. We observed those rangers closely for a long period of time. They were being armed and dispatched to ensure security along the road between Baykan district and the village. We noted they were leaving the village around 8:00 a.m., and returning about 6:00 p.m. There was a curfew that forbade anyone to use the vehicle road once it was dusk.

When we had collected sufficient intelligence, our commander held a meeting and told all of us, "Though our primary target is this man, my order is that nobody accompanying him will survive the attack. Kill them all!" Because we were only a squadron, we had asked for a reinforcement force from another region for this operation. The reinforcement squadron would besiege the village, while ours would trap the rangers who were out on security patrol. We took plenty of food provisions with us. The rangers were ensuring the road security in rotating groups of eight each day. We didn't know which of these teams that man was in; therefore, we might have to nest at one place for a few days. In this way, we, as six guerillas, set our ambush on the side of the road.

The teams on the first and second days did not include the man we were looking for. It wasn't easy to wait for him. Staying in place for two days, our movement was very limited. But, on the other hand, the feeling of revenge was very strong; very sustaining. It can make someone do most anything. We were rewarded on the morning of the third day, when we saw the man and his team leave the village. We were so ready. Our comrades were situated in readiness for the ambush in different spots along the road.

Their team queued like a rope on the road. There were 12 rangers in total. When I looked through the binoculars, I recognized the guilty man from the trophy weapon he was holding. He was the only one holding a G3. The rest had Kalashnikovs. He was walking out in front of his team. I immediately contacted my comrades waiting in the ambush and said, "The target is walking in front of the team. Everyone shoot at him first." The rangers would normally walk at a distance of 10 meters from one another. The exit to the village was winding and narrow, so, it was a difficult place to maintain team security, and they knew to be attentive there. But, when they reached the straight section of the road, they thought nothing would happen and began to walk side by side. It was a unique opportunity for us guerillas, since it would be very difficult to kill them all when there was distance between them. That is exactly why they had maintained that interval of 10 meters between them, so that some might escape if attacked. Walking side by side they were much easier targets.

Luck was with us. Just when they got in the ambush spot, they closed the distances between themselves, and our comrades began to shoot. All of these 12 village protection guards were killed at the one spot. When the village rangers heard the gunfire, they raced to save their comrades, but our backup unit fired at them and pinned them down. Under this siege, neither the soldiers in the station nor their rangers could get out of the village.

One of the men next to me said, "Comrade, if you let me, I want to bash the body of this asshole into pieces, just like he did with the body of our friend." We were all highly emotional. I told him, "Comrade, go and do whatever you want to him but don't touch the corpses of the others."

I was following his actions through the binoculars. He first cut off the nose and the ears of the ranger. Then he beheaded him. His body was already blasted into pieces because of the bullets, so our comrade didn't even touch his body. We then quickly gathered and escaped to the countryside. The security forces might ask for help from the neighboring villages, and we didn't want to be there when that happened.

Meanwhile, our company commander contacted the head ranger of that village, via radio, and said, "You can fight us; you can aid the soldiers; you can even kill us, which is fair in war. But, if you disrespect the bodies of our fallen comrades, then we will obliterate your entire village." The organization was very sensitive about this issue. We killed many soldiers and rangers; however, we never mistreated their bodies. Never! Once a person has been killed, it is unacceptable to desecrate their corpse, even if they had been the enemy.

This mission made a great impact on the region. A ranger had bashed the dead body of a guerilla into pieces, and that ranger and his team were completely eliminated, before even a month had passed. All of the rangers in the region became afraid of us after this mission. They were now more careful. From their disrespect of our fallen comrade, we had taught them complete respect.

Our company commander heard about the incident of bashing the body of the ranger into pieces. Upon our return to our region, the comrade responsible for beheading the ranger went straight to our commander and told him, "We took revenge for our friend." He had been awaiting his commander's words of appreciation, but instead heard many curses from the company commander. "How could you do something like that? Who allowed you to do that, you, idiot?" The comrade gave our commander my name.

Our company commander had joined the organization in 1986. He sent for me and chastised me. "Comrade, even if they are your enemies, you will show respect to their dead bodies. You were overpowered by your feelings and lust for revenge, and you allowed someone in your command to behead the ranger. If you can't learn to control your feelings, you will soon be in trouble. This emotional reaction of yours will only harm our party. If one bullet is sufficient to kill an enemy, there is no need to shoot three. There is no need to bash a dead body into pieces. There is nothing good in this. And, since there is no good, it will only bring harm to the organization."

Our company commander talked to me about these issues on many occasions in the following way, saying, "Deniz, if you can't better control your feelings, this might become a habit for you. Then, in each mission you command, your emotions could get the better of you."

Nevertheless, our situation was psychologically wearing on us. As the organization, we suffered a lot because of the village protection guards. They would instantly inform the military whenever they so much a spotted one of our footprints. These new patrollers didn't behave the same way as the predictable military we used to know. The military performed operations in the spring and in the fall, like clockwork, but rarely operated in the winter. When we performed a mission in the summer, they would follow us just long enough to make a good showing. Then, they returned. It was like a sport. They didn't risk going into the forest or steep areas. They were so predictable. But the rangers behaved completely differently. They were also from this region, as were we. They investigated everywhere in detail because they knew how. They'd come after us until the chase was finished. They were relentless. That's why the organization hated them. They were exactly like us! The state had ensured that the Kurd was killing the Kurd.

The Corridor

There was a lot left for us to do in the Garzan region. The organization at that time hadn't achieved full dominance in the regions in Sirvan province of Siirt and in Hizan province of Bitlis. We needed to open a corridor between Botan province and Garzan province, so first we had to terminate the dominance of the Turkish military presence there. Upon the opening of this corridor, the forces in Botan and northern Iraq could easily pass into the provinces in Turkey. This route had to be opened for the organization to receive reinforcements from the southern border. The guerillas coming from the camps in northern Iraq were going to use this route while traveling within Turkey. The other reason for the importance of this route to the organization was that the command echelon and the management echelon would use this path for traveling in Turkey—because we had training camps, called command schools, both on the southern border as well as in Damascus, in Syria. The command echelon, who graduated from these officer schools, were to be appointed in the provinces in Turkey. In order to blow open this route, I was going to lead a battalion to attack from Hizan province, while another battalion, located in Botan province, was going to launch a substantial attack from Eruh and Pervari provinces. This would ensure that the two military stations along this route, and their two ranger villages, were going to be destroyed or disabled.

Both villages had been mixed up with the village protection system since 1984. Although the reason we were going to annihilate them was to open ourselves a corridor, the guerillas also wanted to destroy these villages for revenge. Sabri Ok, who had been a central committee member of the PKK, had been delivered to the Turkish security forces by one of these villages in 1985. We decided we needed to take revenge for this incident. We were going to use this opportunity to give the message to the other villages of: "the PKK never forgets an insult made against us, no matter how many years may have passed."

So, we attacked these villages. Our intent was to disarm the rangers, without harming any civilians. Our plan was simply to take the guards' weapons. But if they resisted, we were going to kill them all. With this mindset, we simultaneously raided both villages at midnight. In fighting with the rangers, some civilians also lost their lives. The official government tally after the fact listed 35 people dead.

For months, the press used the outcome of these missions against the organization. We were aware that this could happen, our reputation being tarnished, but a guerilla might naturally lose control of his feelings and actions during a battle. People can act emotionally and kill someone without checking whether they were a woman or a child. In fact, that was what happened that night.

One of our guerillas did just that. His emotions caused him to react in a way that ruined the purpose of the mission. Some civilians ran and hid inside a certain house during the battle. The guerilla noticed this and set the house on fire, though he was fully aware that there were women, children, and old people inside. He didn't report his actions to any one of us. So we, as the PKK, got our reputation badly blemished from this mission. The senior officers of the party didn't accept the responsibility for civilian deaths in this mission. They notified the public via the press that this incident had happened without the knowledge of the PKK, so our reputation was healed somewhat. Also, after this mission, all the villagers on our route abandoned their villages and moved into the city center of Siirt. So, unintentionally, we achieved the cleared corridor we had wanted.

But for this, our commander was dismissed. This mission had created a bad image of us, not only in Turkey but also abroad. Many governments already considered us to be terrorists, and due to such incidents, they now had reason to believe the PKK actually was a terrorist group. Upon the dismissal of the company commander, everyone in the command echelon, including myself, was called in for internal review. Whether we would be fired or not, would be based on the results of the internal investigation.

But the truth remained, that the last standing military station was now alone and defenseless. And the soldiers there knew we would be gunning for them next. So, in the summer of 1994, before we could attack the station, the military evacuated their post and withdrew to the city center. In this way, a natural corridor was just about to be opened from northern Iraq to the city center of Bitlis in Turkey.

One village and its military outpost, both controlled by enemy forces, still needed to be taken care of. Compared to other villages, this village was quite populated. This wasn't a village to be eliminated or frightened with a normal attack, and this was why the entirety of our forces in Botan, along with my company, laid siege on this village and station. We brought 2,000 guerillas with us, while intentionally leaving them only one route of escape.

Our siege lasted for a week. We had closed down all the roads over which reinforcements would have come. We knew that the ammunition of the security forces would soon be consumed. They were using up so much just shooting around randomly. When their reinforcements didn't arrive and they had no way to replenish their ammunition, both the rangers and the soldiers fled down the passage we had left free. It wasn't a real fight.

After this travel corridor was opened to us, our regional force was again questioned regarding the incident of the village raid. The party had decided to dismiss everyone under the command of the provincial force and appoint a completely new group. Meanwhile, the PKK leadership sent a general memo throughout the organization, notifying us that the rangers were no longer to be harmed under any circumstances. The security forces and the police in the cities were now the only acceptable targets.

During all of these incidents, I was still in the same squadron with Sevin, the woman I loved. She was very worried about me being questioned. She was aware that I would most likely be sent from the region after the investigation's report was drafted. She told me, "If you are sent from here, I will also volunteer to leave this region." I asked her to have patience and to wait for the conclusion of the questioning.

Organizational Propaganda

During one of our road inspections, about midsummer, we met a Japanese tourist and decided to kidnap him for a few days. Our purpose was to host him for a while and tell him about our mission; our purpose, ideology, and why we fought against Turkey. We also thought to show him the broken gadgets we had: radios and other items, which were all made in Japan.

It highlights our level of global cultural illiteracy that we thought he would definitely understand the workings of all the Japanese gadgets. The comrades in the company who spoke English went up to him and asked him if he would repair the gadgets. Although the Japanese tourist checked all of our items, he said that he wasn't an electronics engineer and had no idea how to fix any of our technological problems. We insisted, "Aren't you Japanese? These are the products of your country. How could you not know anything about them?" The more the comrades talked, the more the man laughed. We hosted him for three days and took him around to our various companies.

Once we had set him free, this incident was broadcast throughout Turkish media, and as usual, they didn't tell the truth; especially not the television channels. They claimed that the tourist had been able to save his own life by escaping from us.

In those years, such incidents would often take place, especially in the city of Van. Tourists were hosted by the organization for a few days and later set free. There was definitely no mistreatment. We simply wanted to impress these tourists. We were attempting to change the opinion of the world about us, through the eyes of these people. Actually, we were crafting a kind of organizational propaganda. When they returned to their own countries, they were affecting their personal networks but also were being invited to appear on TV shows. Meanwhile, the organization was impressing on the people in those countries, as well as our own, that our only purpose was to defend the basic rights of the Kurds. Therefore, the fact that the foreign tourists were hosted as captives was a very important opportunity for organizational propaganda.

We sometimes did the same thing to the rangers. For example, in 1994, we took seven rangers as captives. They were en route to the city center by automobile, and we arrested them right there on the road. They stayed with us for 15 days. We hosted them very well, and then our comrades set them free close to their village. It was a very hardline village. The rangers there had caused the organization a great deal of loss. Nonetheless, once we set these captive rangers free, this village returned their weapons to the state and removed themselves from the village protection system.

These hardliner villagers' opinions changed completely, and they began supporting us. It was totally unexpected and even caused a domino effect. The other villages, who witnessed what that village had done, followed their example and quit the village protection system, one by one. Our Kurdish society is like that. Once you did a favor for them, they would be committed to you forever. They would also tell everyone about this little favor, as if it were something very big. But the same philosophy held for mal-treatment as well. If you beat up a villager, he would tell everyone what you had done—and embellish it with what you didn't do, but report it as if you had: "Not only did the guerillas beat me; they robbed me; they assaulted my wife, and pummeled my child."

The New Commander

The commander who had allowed the incineration of a houseful of civilians was removed. After his dismissal, the newly appointed commander had no experience in the region nor in the countryside. He was terribly inexperienced. Moreover, he arrived firmly convinced that our entire regional force was comprised of traitors. In every public platform, he scorned us saying, "It has been years since the party forbid these reactionary missions. Why are you doing such missions? Are you reactionaries?" However, as I said, this action had been the mistake of one comrade. There was no point in blaming everyone for it.

In addition to this scolding, none of our opinions would be taken into consideration during his command meetings. It was as if he were thinking, "they already made a mistake, so they would probably make it again." This attitude disturbed me and my other friends very much. We became angry with this man and resigned from the command cadre. We didn't intervene in anything. We wouldn't help him make plans. We devolved into behaving like ordinary guerillas.

The commander was very illiterate, but we were tricked into thinking that he was effective, since he had come from Damascus where Apo was. Nevertheless, he was always making mistakes. In the middle of the winter, he brought a force from another region into ours. Were already 120 strong, but, he brought in 90 more guerrillas. We began to have trouble meeting the basic needs of so many and assuring their security.

We knew the security forces would perform a land-based offensive against us every fall and spring. The reason was simple. The trees had no leaves and hadn't blossomed yet. In other words, even if we were to hide in a crowded forest, we could easily be detected, since there were no leaves to conceal us. Also, it always rained during these times of year, and we had a lot of difficulty traveling among the regions, since the rivers were so flooded. So, in general, the security forces wouldn't make attacks in other seasons than these. There were almost no operations to worry about after the trees had blossomed.

It was right when we were in such a difficult period, in terms of hiding, that this new commander brought another entire regional force to us. And, of course, the Turkish national security forces would easily be able to detect us. As we had predicted, around the end of February in 1995, a land-based security operation began in the area where we were hiding. The additional 90 guerrillas had left footprints in the snow, leading the security forces directly to our campground. The battle lasted two days. It began in the daytime and continued until dark, when both sides would stay in place and wait until morning. Five comrades were martyred. It was now very clear to everyone just how cowardly and untested was our commander.

Once the battle was over—that is, once it was too late—the commanders of our force and the new force jointly decided that keeping both forces in one place was too great a risk. The other commander decided to withdraw to his own region. It was also decided that our own force would be split into two units that would camp in two different areas.

After the other force left, our commander objected to the division, saying, "We are going to stay together. Our enemies won't come back, but if they do, we will retaliate." We knew that if we stayed at the same place, the military would recover itself and begin another land attack. No matter how many times we explained this to the commander, we couldn't convince him, and he refused to let us relocate. We continued to stay where we were. Those of us in the command echelon were very angry but decided to do nothing.

In March, when everything was under snow cover, the security forces began another land-based operation against us. Once again, we detected the situation from the radio conversations of the soldiers preparing to participate in the operation. We were quite efficient at this practice of listening to the radio conversations of the security forces 24/7. We recorded them and tried to understand what they were attempting against us. Once again, we spoke to the regional commander about dividing our squadron into two, as a precaution. Despite all our effort, we couldn't convince him. The man was so very stubborn!

Unsurprisingly, the battle started in the morning, and even though we had the advantage of knowing the area, the military had the upper hand due to the climatic conditions. Everything was covered with snow. The tops of the hills, usually very strategic for us, were covered in snow. It was well known that once you have secured the high ground at the top of a mountain or hill, it was easy to control the lower sections. So, we knew that if the security forces captured these areas, they could cause us significant losses by placing heavy weapons there. At any cost, we had to defend the hills, but the snow was restricting our ability to move about, though we had received warning and were prepared. So, the first two days, we had the initiative of the battle and took no losses; a few comrades received small wounds. Then, about the evening of the third day, we lost one of the high positions. All our forces in this line had to withdraw. We had lost a very critical position, since it was the only high ground that also had a clear path all the way to the summit. The soldiers placed five tanks in that area.

We figured that those tanks could cause us trouble during the day but would probably do nothing at night. The system was so new that we were not aware of "night vision." Suddenly, the slightest move of ours at night gave the tanks their target area. We couldn't even send reinforcements to our comrades on the summit. The enemy's tanks had divided the force in two. The soldiers were attacking from positions at the summit. With the tanks not allowing us to move, the enemy executed an intense bombardment of the summit by combat helicopters. Since we had no reinforcement, we lost our positions at the top. At least ten guerillas lost their lives and 12 guerillas were seriously wounded, waiting for death. We took the wounded to the field doctor, where they were treated, but without any high hopes.

During the evening of the fifth day, the current region commander, our previous region commander, and I had a short meeting. Actually, all the officers from the command echelons should have gathered, but since the battle still continued, those comrades couldn't leave their positions. Our previous regional commander really had no right to join the meeting due to the nature of his punishment, but this was an exceptional situation. He was simply a very experienced man, who knew the tactics and plans of the security forces very well, and that's why we needed his input to lead the offensive against the Turkish military. We had to remove the guerillas from this siege as soon as possible. Otherwise, they would all be killed.

This previous region commander told us that the only solution was for a chosen group of 30 guerillas to attack the Turkish soldiers from the rear. When the soldiers were raided from behind, their divided attention would open an escape corridor. The group of 30 guerrillas would escape through this open corridor, while the rest of us would pass to a steeper area, from where we could better defend ourselves.

So, on the night of the sixth day, this group of 30 guerrillas slipped from the circle, to cross the Silk Road, and attacked the soldiers from the rear, as we had planned. Unfortunately, the Turkish military had already prepared themselves against such a tactic. They had hidden two tanks behind a small hill, next to Silk Road. Our group of 30 was trapped in a tank ambush before they even reached the road and 16 of them were martyred. Another 13 were wounded and captured by the security forces. A female guerrilla, who had been able to flee the ambush, came back to us. We hadn't been aware of what had taken place. We thought that those 30 were already out of the circle and would be attacking the soldiers at any time. This woman was able to catch us up on everything. Now, the only strategy we had left was to hide in small groups. Obviously, the military had resolved to eradicate us completely. Their attack was continuous, with no fewer than 15 tanks and four attack helicopters.

At times, there were even combat aircraft taking dives but not hitting anything. A bomb thrown from an aircraft would not only harm the guerillas but also their own military, and so was not a resource that was used. We, the remaining 51 guerillas, were now defending ourselves.

On the eighth day of the siege, the security forces began to come inside of our area. For their safety, we had left the doctor and the wounded comrades near the mountain summit in a hidden cave that was about 200 to 300 meters deep. We thought the enemy would never discover this place, but, sadly, we had made another strategic mistake. The 13 wounded guerillas who were captured after the tank ambush, told the soldiers, one by one, all the places in which we were hiding.

Soon, we heard the doctor on the radio telling us that the security forces were at the cave entrance and only being held back by gunfire from the wounded guerrillas. We learned that two soldiers were killed during this stand-off, but when the soldiers became frustrated at not being able to enter on foot, they had one of their Skorsky helicopters fire gas canisters into the cave. At this point, there was no need for them to enter. They just bombed the cave entrance and sealed our guerrillas inside.

Not until the tenth day of the operation were the soldiers ready to withdraw. But just then, they happened upon our footprints in the snow. About 30 people and I had hidden in a very steep area, after crawling across this snow. Our area was steep enough to dissuade the soldiers from pursuing us, but they had two helicopters make an excursion over the area where we were hiding. We had camouflaged ourselves so well, that they didn't have a chance of finding us by air. So, when they got no result from the helicopters, they sent rangers to our hiding spot to look for us.

By afternoon, the rangers reached our hideout. We had camouflaged ourselves in scattered groups of five or six, yet they were able to find us, at which point we immediately threw down our weapons and began negotiating with them. We spent 20 minutes trying to convince them not to reveal us to the security forces. One of the rangers asked, "But how are we supposed to explain all these footprints leading up here?" I suggested to him to say that the footprints simply belonged to the other rangers who must have investigated this area before.

It was the head ranger who saved us. While we were standing there pleading with him, he contacted and related to the chief officer the entire assault and repeated what I had told him. So, the rangers left us there and returned to the enemy without exposing our cover. That was how we survived that battle!

But the battle had cost us dearly. We took 60 losses. This was a very serious blow to a province force consisting of volunteer guerillas such as we. After the soldiers had completely withdrawn, I took four guerrillas with me and went up to the cave where the doctor and his patients had died. It took us three hours to clear enough rubble from the mouth of the cave to create an opening, but even then we couldn't go in. A heavy smell of gas emanated from the cave as soon as the entrance was opened. Our eyes spontaneously began weeping and then swelling shut. We could hardly breathe and immediately turned back and retreated to our group. That was when we realized the military had thrown chemical weapons into the cave and blown shut the entrance to hide their crime. So, we were ordered by the regional commander to let the gas dissipate for a few days before attempting again to go inside.

The security forces had been feeding details about their operations to the press since the conflict had started. "We killed this many guerilas." "Now we are moving into this region." "We have taken this many captives, but the battles still continue."

Our province commander hand-selected a squadron and brought them towards us as reinforcements, since the news reports had told him exactly where we were besieged. He contacted us by radio as he got closer and learned from us that the enemy had already withdrawn, so he and his unit could safely come directly to our location. Unlike the Turkish forces, we didn't report any of our movements in clear language. We knew full well that the military was always listening to us, which is why we spoke in codes and passwords. Sentences we frequently used had been written out and assigned numerical designations in a list that covered two pages. There was a code for anything we may have needed. For example, everything in the #27 group of code phrases had something to do with water. The Turkish soldiers couldn't understand these numbers we used and, in fact, most of our own guerrillas couldn't either. Only PKK commanders and other senior commanders were given these codes. That way, if an ordinary guerrilla were taken captive, the enemy couldn't press him for these codes.

After such heavy causalities, our regional commander quit his post and isolated himself in shame. He wouldn't speak to anyone. He knew he was mostly to blame for our staggering defeat. He knew that all of the guerillas who were alive had been saved, not due to him, but thanks only to our previous regional commander.

The Cave

When the provincial commander arrived, we took him straight to the caves. Not only did we have to know how our comrades had died, and by what type of gas, but we also had a duty to recover their weapons and gear and to destroy the codebooks they carried.

We decided to enter the cave in pairs, and I was in the first duo. Only 6 meters in, our eyes began to burn and we immediately had to retreat. Covering my face with a wet scarf, which would at least afford me two minutes of protection, I took a flashlight and went in alone.

Once in the cave, I recovered the weapon and other equipment of the first fallen guerrilla I saw, and then I got out. The second time, another comrade and I entered together, and as he collected the gear,

I examined the corpses in order to try and determine the manner of death. I noticed one thing in particular. They all had a few drops of blood coming from their noses and ears. It had been ten days since they had died and their bodies were a bit swollen. We couldn't remove the bodies, since they had begun to rot and there was the chance they might fall apart.

But after collecting the weapons and equipment, we began to collect the empty gas capsules. The writing was in English, and one of our comrades was able to describe how the writing on the canisters indicated chemical gas, as well as instructions how to throw the canisters, and how great an area each one would affect.

When our commander came to the province, he gathered all the command echelon and said, "Although the person primarily responsible for this incident was our region commander, you are each as responsible as he." Our commander then reclaimed the weapon and the equipment of the regional commander and threw him into our jail. The other commanders, including myself, were consigned to the internal review process. The province commander also recommended jail for our previous regional commander, telling him that he should have intervened on the first day of the clash and taken the initiative, which was the party's tradition. If a commander couldn't keep command of the incidents during a battle and made mistakes that caused guerillas to lose their lives, the former commander was understood to have the right to intervene. By this precedent, our region commander was accused of not fulfilling his duty to intervene.

Trials at Garzan

The operation against us had destroyed all our food and clothing. Our entire regional force was physically and emotionally drained. Can you imagine how it would feel to lose 60 comrades all at once? For these reasons, we were ordered to be sent to another region.

We were sent first to Garzan province headquarters. We stayed there and recuperated for a month, while the command echelon wrote their after-action reports and defended each other to the ultimate level of detail that headquarters demanded. Our reports were first read by the province commander, and if there were any deficiency or some point, which wasn't fully understood, we were asked to rewrite them entirely. After they were completed, we were going to get called to the stand to defend ourselves in front of the organization, after which they would make a decision about us.

The day before the trials started, we received word that Apo wanted to speak with our province commander. We used mobile phones for this, which meant we had to climb a mountain summit, so that the phones could have decent reception for the interview.

My province commander took me with him and, as we were climbing the hill, told me that if Apo asked him something he didn't know, it was up to me to answer for him. Apo and the commander talked for 45 minutes about the battle, and then the phone was handed to me. Apparently, our leader wanted to hear an account of what had happened from someone who had actually been there.

After I told him how many mistakes the new, inexperienced commander had made, Apo answered, "But, you all had a hand in this. You all share responsibility. The fact that the commander didn't accept your advice is an invalid excuse. You even had another commander obliged to intervene, despite the fact he'd been demoted. What excuse does he have for keeping silent?" Then, Apo turned his criticism onto himself: "We sent the wrong man. We here at headquarters would never have thought that commander would prove to be so incapable of handling that region." And he hung up.

The trials started the next day with both previous and new commanders. The judge and jury were ready, and the prosecutor began by calling for the execution of both commanders. The prosecutor knew the rules and codes of the organization intimately and so presided over our law. But the judge and the jury objected to these executions and overruled him. In the end, both commanders were merely dismissed from their posts, and their party membership was suspended for a year.

The rest of the command echelon and I only stood trial at the platform level, which is to say that our sentences were decided directly by the organization and not by any judge or jury. A three-member panel arbitrated the platform, which was really a forum for all the guerillas to weigh in with their suggestions on your punishment. Once all the suggestions were given, everyone voted, and the most popular punishment was administered. In our case, the organization declared a mistrial of six months—at the end of which we were brought before another panel and questioned once again, and then given back our old duties.

As soon as we were dismissed from our posts, our replacements' orders were then obeyed instead of ours, and all guerillas were sent back to their previous areas of operation, except for myself and the other punished commanders, who were ordered to stay behind at the state headquarters. There were no rank-and-file guerrillas in the state headquarters. Everyone there was a command officer, and nearly everyone had direct combat experience. We always travel with the state commander wherever he goes. Everyone at state headquarters falls into one of two categories. They are either punished commanders, like ourselves, who there to undergo all the training from scratch, or newly minted commanders awaiting appointment to their first duty station. Obviously, then, the headquarters' detachment had a lot of powerful officers with a lot of authority. That's why our arrival always inspired the regular guerrillas of any region we visited.

We covered many, many regions, since the state commander's job was constantly to travel and check in with each province. He didn't stay anywhere for more than three days, and so we 60 officers that were assigned to him received our training while constantly on the move. (The woman I loved had also requested to be assigned to headquarters, and her request was granted—so we were able to travel together.)

When the headquarters commander planned our mission of revenge, the idea was that we were going to take our fight to the soldiers, and the military was going to be drastically shocked. Fully three of our regional forces were going to attack them simultaneously, in three different areas, combining direct attacks in some places, with raids and a forestallment in others. My group was tasked with blocking the Silk Road at three points, in order to disseminate organizational propaganda to the drivers we would stop. For this mission, two groups laid in ambush; each 2 meters apart on either side of our roadblock, as we stood in the middle taking the drivers out of their cars and preaching propaganda.

The security forces brought panzers against us that first day, but when our ambush groups destroyed the tanks, the rest of the soldiers withdrew, because the military mistakenly thought our mission would last just one day, while we had already planned to stay for three. We wanted our message to the public to be clear—that we could control any roads we wanted, wherever they were, for however long we wanted. This was not an easy feat to accomplish in 1995, and it made a strong impression on the populace.

Meanwhile, what could the military do to us? Their hands were tied. We were among the civilians so they couldn't risk attacking us from the air; they could only fly by with their combat helicopters and try to intimidate us. It wasn't until the third day of our mission that they blocked off the traffic in both directions before the cars could reach us. No vehicles certainly meant there were no drivers to propagandize, but we had planned to finish the mission on this third day anyway.

The final tally for this mission was that we lost four comrades, but the security forces lost two panzers with all hands still inside. Incidentally, we also incinerated four public vehicles.

After this mission, the headquarters unit took us to the Mutki region, which is connected to Bitlis, and we continued our retraining. Here we learned that the commanders who had replaced us in our positions were failing at their duty to control our former region. They were losing too many guerrillas during their battles. Part of the reason for this was the increase in the number of guerrillas in our ranks. Since our groups weren't as small as before, they were harder to hide and began incurring serious losses. Every mission now meant discovery, and every discovery meant battle. So, not only did the new commanders lack familiarity with the region, but the small-unit tactics they had always relied on were no longer useful. As a result, the guerrillas they commanded were suffering.

Summer of 1995

While in the state headquarters in the summer of 1995, we decided to perform a mission against a ranger village located in Muş. We didn't normally kill the rangers, but the rangers in this village were oppressing the nearby villages. They were using scare tactics to force villages to register in the village protection system by leveraging the status and the weapons they had been provided. They were so overbearing in their control tactics that they didn't even allow noncompliant villagers to feed their animals in the fields.

There was a military station only 15 minutes from this ranger village, so as a precaution we set ambushes on every road going to the village. Then, that day at 2:00 p.m., we began our mission.

Shortly after the mission started, our ambush teams all abandoned their posts. We had expected the enemy to come down the regular roads in armored panzers or by foot; we hadn't considered that they might use tanks. As soon as our ambush teams saw the tanks, they knew they were outgunned. You couldn't do much against a tank, when the village was in a flat valley and the tanks could drive anywhere. They were not restricted to the roads we had prepared. The big problem was that those of us battling in the village had no idea that we had lost our ambush teams, along with their control of the roads. We were already devastated by the fact that both of our team commanders had been martyred, and three of our comrades were seriously wounded.

We were still planning on completely demolishing the village and still believing we had the force to do it, until the tanks came into the village and changed everything. Four out of nine guerillas were seriously wounded in the tanks' initial bombardment, and we quickly understood that we needed to abort the mission and get our injured comrades to safety. The enemy would simply demolish our headquarters' force if we tried to continue the attack, so we retreated.

I was one of the senior officers who had been seriously wounded on this mission. Shrapnel had cut into my knees when a bomb had exploded near me. I wasn't as badly wounded as my other comrades; I could retreat from the battlefield. This was unfortunate, since the enemy attack was so intense that we couldn't even pause long enough to carry out the bodies of our dead friends.

A month later, the senior leadership of the party criticized this failed mission of ours. They asked, "Why would you undertake such a mission on a flat valley floor during broad daylight and not even take any measures against the tanks?"

They were right for criticizing us. We had known that there was a tank unit assigned to that military outpost, but we hadn't believed they would attack. We had mined the roads so often during previous missions that the tanks frequently avoided battles with us so that they wouldn't be disabled by our road mines. But we should have considered that this area was flat, so that the tanks had no reason to remain on the regular roads, and they hadn't. They entered the village from the fields in the valley, so the work we'd done to hide all those mines on the roads had been no deterrent at all.

The field commander, who had planned and coordinated this mission, was brought under investigation, and we all felt he had earned his punishment, since in the meeting we'd had before the mission, the entire command echelon had objected to this plan. Even when we saw that he had already made up his mind to attack this village, we told him he had to perform this mission at night, but he didn't accept this suggestion from us. "All our village missions take place at night," he had retorted. "This time we are going to attack during the day when the rangers don't expect it."

We had answered him, "Okay. Fine. Your plan is great, but this village lies in a flat valley, not in the mountainous countryside. It won't be so easy to divert the reinforcement soldiers approaching from the station." In addition, if the battle became prolonged, we wouldn't have had any cover behind which to hide. It would be difficult to miss us in the open fields of a flat valley during the day.

But no matter how we argued, we couldn't convince the field commander to abandon or update his plan. If we could have gotten in touch with the state commander, we might have had a chance, since he was a much more rational man. But he had been in a meeting at the time with five or six other people, so this mission went forward without the state commander's knowledge. The field commander had designed this mission entirely on his own.

In short, he had failed. He not only got three comrades killed, but another 12 seriously wounded. Yes, we had killed 20 rangers in return. But at our level, having three martyred and 12 wounded in exchange was an expensive disaster, since our force was a special detachment of the organization headquarters and we all held at least the rank of commander. By the traditional equation of acceptable losses, it would have been acceptable if we had lost two ordinary guerrillas, in exchange for the 20 enemy that we had killed. To lose three commanders in a single, simple mission was unacceptable. It took so much time and effort to train and teach each commander and then allow them to accrue enough combat experience truly to lead.

At our suggestion, the senior officials of the party froze all the duties and authorities of this field commander. When the state commander returned a few days later, he got incredibly frustrated when he learned what had happened. He berated us, demanding to know how we could have allowed such a flawed mission to proceed. We told him the field commander had made the decisions, and we hadn't been able to do anything about them. This made him even angrier. "You should have objected to it! You could have informed me about it! I am the commander of this unit, and nobody has the right to waste my unit on such a senseless mission," he scathed.

Ultimately, this field commander was dismissed from his position and sent to the south. We had a tradition in the organization never to keep a field or state commander in his former region of command once he was discharged. There was a strong danger that he might come to harm from the guerrillas he had wronged through his bad actions. But if anything untoward happened to an officer ranked so highly, the cost would be extreme, not only because of the loss of such a leader but in terms of all the guerrillas who would have to be punished as well. The risk wasn't worth it, and so they transferred discharged commanders as soon as possible. No one could take the risk of a former field or province commander losing his life on his own battlefield.

Dr. Süleyman

In mid-1995, the PKK leadership issued a notice that we were going to decrease the number of guerrillas present in each province, so that we would be able to move in small groups once again. To achieve this, some of the guerrillas in Turkey were going to be sent south to Iraq and Syria, where they could participate in the fight against Barzani and carry out counterattacks against the KDP.

While I was assigned to state headquarters, our field commander was Dr. Süleyman, the brother of Selim Çürükkaya, another well-known senior official in the organization. The man was a failure. Every time he planned a mission, guerrillas were killed. I had even heard it whispered that he was sleeping with some women in the organization, and I had warned him when I had the opportunity, saying "Comrade, there are some rumors about you." He didn't deny it, but looked very nervous when he saw that I had learned about it, as if he knew that I was going to notify the party at the first chance I had.

Therefore, in June of 1995, he called me to him while we were still in the field and said to me, "Deniz, I am tasking you with a sniper mission against the hill where the Turkish tanks are stationed; the one which protects the Mutki town of Bitlis. Take one guerrilla with you." This was insanity. You didn't order a sniper mission on a regular battlefield, using only two people, much less with tanks present that would surely obliterate you as soon as they noticed you. So I asked our company commander, "Comrade, do you know of any reason for this man to send me on a mission like this, especially now? Why is he doing this?" The commander replied, "He is sending you to your death. I don't know what bad blood you two have between you, but this is a suicide mission. It will be almost impossible for you to survive it." So, I said to him, "then I am writing a report about this. I will leave it in my bag. If I don't manage to make it back from this mission, send my report directly to headquarters."

From the armory, I requisitioned a Dragunov type sniper rifle. I shot it about 50 times, adjusted the scope properly, and got it ready. Before I left for the mission, Dr. Süleyman said, "Take whichever guerrilla you would like to be your partner. You should have someone go with you." So, I pointed to his beloved guard. He was shocked. He hadn't been expecting a move like that. "Why choose my bodyguard when there are so many other guerrillas here?" he asked me. "Well, you told me to take absolutely anyone I wanted," I replied. "So I'm choosing him." He couldn't deny what he had originally said. I was thinking that now surely Dr. Süleyman would cancel this ridiculous mission for me, if only in order to save his favorite guard. Instead, it became clear that he wouldn't cancel it even if I took all his guards with me. This is how determined he was to cause my death.

He also schemed to stack all the odds against me. For instance, though sniper missions are mostly always performed under cover of night, he said the assassination had to take place between 8:00 and 10:00 a.m. "Ok," I said. So, during the night, the guard and I took our places on the opposite side of the hill. There were at least ten tanks in front of us and so close that the tiniest mistake would cost us our lives. I had us wait in place until 4:00 p.m. It truly would have been suicide to perform that mission in the morning, when all the soldiers are alert and attentive and the front is thronged with them. However, by evening, if they hadn't perceived a threat, the soldiers would withdraw to their stations and leave the tanks behind.

As evening drew on, Dr. Süleyman constantly radioed me, asking why we hadn't completed the mission yet. I ignored all his chatter. His guard asked me a few times, "Comrade, why are we waiting? Why haven't we started yet?" I replied, "Just hold on a bit longer. You'll know when the time comes." And at 4:30 p.m., I fired one, single bullet. One of the soldiers in the rear guard fell to the ground. Nobody knew from where the bullet had come. The soldiers intently investigated their surroundings, but we had already retreated into the depths of the woods. When we returned safely to camp, Dr. Süleyman was shocked. He asked us if we had completed our mission. When I said yes, he didn't believe me. "Then call the guerrillas stationed in town and ask them about it," I said. So, they contacted a sympathizer who worked at the Bitlis Morgue, and he confirmed our story. There was nothing Dr. Süleyman could do to us.

Not even a week after this assassination mission, he assigned me a new mission in the center of the city of Bitlis. If he had sent me to a city I already knew well, like Siirt or its surroundings, I would have understood, but I had never been to Bitlis before. I was not familiar with the layout nor with any guerrillas or sympathizers in this city. So, I directly refused the mission. I told him to his face that I wouldn't go. Instead, I immediately got in touch with the state commander and told him everything I knew about Dr. Süleyman. Dr. Süleyman was immediately removed from duty and sent to Damascus, Syria. I only learned later that there had been many negative reports about him, and many guerrillas who had known about his immoral behavior.

Immediately afterwards, the state commander reappointed me as platoon commander of my previous province. At first, I rejected this offer as well. I had been sentenced to be punished for six months and it had only been three. It wouldn't right to have been appointed before I fulfilled the six-month sentence. My excuse wasn't considered justifiable. Headquarters were also aware of the punishment they, themselves, had given me. They hadn't forgotten. But there was a need for an experienced commander in that region, and we hadn't been directly responsible for the losses there. Therefore, the woman I loved and I were sent back to that region. Sevin was promoted as the platoon commander, and we were assigned to be in the same unit.

8

THE PKK ORGANIZATION

Around the fall of 1995, I notified the hierarchy that our company commander was insufficient in meeting his obligations, and this caused a risk in regard to the region. Therefore, this person should be discharged, and an experienced commander should be appointed. Headquarters management listened to me and reinstated our former regional commander to his post. Now, we had strong, effective leadership, in someone who not only was familiar with the region, but was very experienced in combat as well. The most significant detail was that we got along well with one other within the command echelon. After these personnel changes, our region began to avoid taking losses.

The name of the other field to which I had been assigned was "Middle Field." Apart from this, there were Northern Field, Botan Field and Zagros Field. The Middle Field covered a very large area: Bitlis, some parts of Siirt, Diyarbakır, Erzurum, Muş and Bingöl were all connected to it. The Northern Field consisted of Tunceli and Black Sea provinces, and Koçgiri. Botan Field consisted of Şırnak, Mardin, and some parts of Siirt. Finally, Zagros Field covered Serhat, Kars, Ağrı, Hakkari, and Van. The field commanders of these regions worked in direct connection to the leadership of the entire PKK.

There was a hierarchy to the zones of responsibility, which was taken into account when guerillas were selected for promotion to the level of field commander. For us, Botan Field was the most important, both because of its proximity to the south, and because it had a force of 4,000 to 5,000 guerrillas, where most other zones only had a few hundred guerrillas. Besides, the weapons depot of the PKK was in Botan. We stored various kinds of weapons there, from bazookas to howitzers.

Another significant feature of Botan Field was its location. In guerilla fights, the fronts and field were preserved while proceeding towards the target. Botan was the first field the organization preserved, then appropriated. That's why it was very important for the organization.

Equivalent in importance to Botan Field, our Middle Field was strategically crucial because all our forces used it to transfer from one field to another, such as the Northern Field and Amanoses. On the other hand, it was in the center of everything (hence its name), and the Middle Field was also our center of greatest contact with the public. All the city centers in the Middle Field were under the control of the PKK. Therefore, the most experienced and skilled commander would be appointed to this field. Halil Atac (nickname: Ebu Bekir), was one of the founders of PKK and was the initial commander of the Middle Field.

At first, the Northern Field (Dersim, Tunceli) didn't appear to be that important to us, but since the organization had recently discovered that it provided easy passage to the western parts of Turkey, it had become one of the most important fields.

To clarify: a field could consist of two or three provinces. Our field, by which I mean the Middle Field, consisted of three provinces—Garzan Province (Bitlis, Muş, and some parts of Siirt), Amed Province (central Diyarbakır and some parts of Bingöl), and Erzurum Province (Erzurum and Tunceli's Pülümür section on the west, and Serhad segment on the east). Each province's borders and delineations of responsibility were strictly determined. In addition, the most experienced and skilled commanders in each province were appointed as assistants to those commanders of their fields.

Amanoses was a province on its own. It wasn't connected to any field. Different than other provinces, it was directly connected to the headquarters of the PKK. This province was located in a spot which was very sensitive and strategic for the organization. You could easily reach the critical interior parts of Turkey, such as Antalya, Osmaniye, and Adana through Amanoses. The control of Amanoses had no field commander. Its defense was ensured directly by the headquarters.

A commander who was in charge of Amanoses, could not randomly perform a mission. The headquarters must approve each step the guerillas there would take. In every other province, any leader from the province command down to the company commander level could plan and execute their own missions. However, the province commander of Amanoses could not carry out any mission without the direct approval of the senior leadership of the PKK. This was simply because the slightest mistake in this field might have heavy consequences for the organization. There were hundreds of thousands of tourists coming from around the world to this field for vacation purposes. Any mission performed there had the potential to cause much harm and no benefit. In recent years, the organization detonated a bomb in an area in Antalya, where there were many tourists. We wanted to strike a blow on Turkey's tourism economy. However, European states began criticizing the PKK heavily since we had wounded so many of their citizens. Our financial backers in Europe began withdrawing, one by one. After that, no provincial or regional commander appointed to lead Amanoses was given the right to act on their own initiative.

Each province was divided into five or six regions; each with its own commander. One of these region commanders was appointed as assistant to the province commander to handle the administrative works when the province commander was not available. Under region commanders were battalion commanders, who were each responsible for 160 to 170 guerillas in the south, but only 100 to 110 in the north. Beneath that level were company commanders, each being responsible for 60 to 70 people. Then, there were platoon commanders under company commanders. A platoon commander was in charge of one or two squads. Squad commanders were in charge of ten guerillas. When three teams came together, the result was one platoon.

There was also a presidency council, which was the highest structure of the organization. It always consisted of about seven people, though its number was subject to change. This was the council that included Apo. Many people believe that Apo was the only party president, but that was not the case. The PKK was a truly democratic institution, which chooses its own president. The members of the council were determined by a congress, which happened every four years, but now was held every other year. The 200 to 300 congress members' first task was to choose the members of the council, which had doubled from an average of seven to 13 now that we included women guerillas on the council.

The congressional delegates first voted on the members of the PKK central executive committee. A secret ballot was held to choose those 40 to 50 people, but the vote was counted openly. This executive committee then elected the eligible voting candidates for the presidential seat election. No one in the council could nominate themselves. By the end of their session, this 50-person committee had chosen who was appropriate for the presidency.

Candidates were determined by their rank in the organization, their mastery of our political and ideological content, the extent of their military experience, and the depth of their commitment to the values of the PKK. Once these criteria were used to determine a list of eligible names, a new election was held, and the council members were chosen. I believe at that time, the line-up of the PKK Presidency Council was Apo, Murat Karayılan, Cemil Bayık, Duran Kalkan, Musa Karasu, and three female comrades, whose names I didn't know.

These seven people chose the new president of the PKK. Since Apo was the one who founded the organization and who was the most experienced and competent among us, he was always voted to be president. However, since he was in prison, every six months the presidency rotated to a new member of the council. For that six-month duration, whoever was president was in charge of all decisions and approvals. However, tradition held that no one in the council—not even the president—could finalize a decision without consulting Cemil Bayık. His opinion was certainly asked every time. He had been friends with Apo since the founding of the organization, so everyone trusted and respected him a great deal.

As far as internal friction went, if you were dissatisfied with someone's behavior in the organization, you could write a report. These reports were taken very seriously, since everyone needed to work at the optimum level for the organization to function.

The reports were private. If I wrote a report about a province commander, then that province commander could not read my report. On the front of the envelope, you wrote the name of the institution to which you were filing a complaint. Any PKK institution lower than this could not open the envelope. If so, the punishment for such an offense would be serious. Incidentally, all reports had to be detailed and specific. Let's say I had a criticism about the region commander. I had to write the reason explicitly, such as he had caused a comrade to die because of his mistake in that mission. Then, the author of the report signed his name and his unit's name at the end. No such thing existed as a report without the name of the responsible party.

If you wrote a report, it would not be lost or forgotten. Reports were treated so seriously that, if you had not received a response in due time, you could even use the regional commander's radio to ask about your letter.

Besides complaint reports like these, each province had to give a balance report each year. Every notable incident was written in this report—from which missions had been carried out to which militants had defected and asked the Turkish government for amnesty. Also which newbies had joined since the last report. We had to give reports for everything.

All these reports were read and evaluated in turn during the military conference. A report of 15 comrades surrendering to security forces in a certain province would definitely bring that province under review. Obviously, if there were so many deserters from a single province, that province was not being managed correctly. Headquarters then gathered the other reports and all were presented to the defense committee.

Headquarters Command Management (HPG) then presented their findings from all these reports to the Public Defense Committee (YPG). This is where they would announce that, in the past two-year period, there had been 150 deserters, 200 losses, and 500 newbies.

The reports were not even written on paper any longer. They were typed on a PC and saved to a memory stick, which was then transported. A report written in Diyarbakır could reach clear to Iraq in the same day. Headquarters would read the stick on their own PC, write their reply, and ship it back. Internet existed, and might be faster, but could not be used, because it allowed location detection.

Our chain of command consisted of four fields, followed by the province commands under them. Next were the regional commands and, under them, the lowest who were the company commands. Let's say the guerrillas in one company suggested the replacement of one of their commanders. They would have to go up the chain and contact their regional command. If the regional commander saw merit in the request, he could directly remove the company commander, yet he would ask the province commander beforehand, as a courtesy.

The province commander received any complaints about region commanders and would then share the issue with his field commander, acting upon his opinion. All complaints about province commanders were made to the field command. In the same way, the field commander would notify the leaders one level above him—in this case, the HPG headquarters Command—and incorporate their advice into his decision. Complaints about field commanders were made directly to headquarters command.

There were 13 people in the Headquarters Command Management (HPG). Every two years, they held an election to vote in a new headquarters commander. Whereas province commanders acted as military parliament members, field commanders comprised the HPG guerilla Parliament. The guerilla Parliament and command membership were different, with command members being of higher rank than the guerilla Parliament.

It would sometimes also happen that some of these province commanders in the HPG guerilla Parliament were also members of the PKK Headquarters Committee. In this case, if an action needed to be taken against a province commander who held membership in both groups, the HPG guerilla Parliament and PKK Headquarters Committee made the decision jointly.

The Defense Committee (analogous to a Defense Ministry) was the liaison between the guerilla force and the PKK headquarters council. So, to get an issue before the headquarters Executive council, the guerilla must contact the Defense Committee, who would then contact the HPG headquarters Command on their behalf.

Everyone in the organization (if they were not under punishment) was naturally a member of the PKK. Suspending this membership was the heaviest punishment for the guerilla. In my opinion, this was worse than death, because you were stripped of every one of your rights. If you executed a man, you punished him once. But suspending the membership is not so. It is ongoing. Everyone talked and gossiped about you. Suddenly, no matter how high a rank you held, there was no difference between you and a peasant, in terms of the organization. You had no authority, no right to make a suggestion, no right to criticize, and no one would take anything you said into consideration.

The organization also had a political infrastructure, which carried out tasks about relations with foreign states and political parties in Turkey, Iraq, Iran, and Syria. There were four political parties of the organization. There was the HDP (the People's Democratic Party) in Turkey, the PYD (Democratic Union Party) in Syria, the PJAK (Independent Kurdistan Party) in Iran, and the PCDK (Kurdistan Democratic Solution Party) in Iraq. These parties were active in the political arena on behalf of the organization. These parties had no relation to the guerilla wing (including the Defense Committee) either directly or indirectly. They were, however, directly connected to the KCK (Kurdistan Communities Unity). Otherwise, this political wing represented the PKK across Europe.

The political parties handle the relations based on the countries under their influence. For example, the PCDK handles the organization's relations with Iraq because it is their responsibility. The PJAK, on the other hand, handles the relations with Iran. If I am not mistaken, the PJAK was working through a peace process with Iran in 2012. Because of Iran's clever actions, the guerilla force was almost abolished completely and now the organization is only active in politics within Iran.

Until the Syrian war began, the PYD was only politically active with no guerilla force. When things got complicated, the organization immediately established the YPG (People's Protection Units). The rights of the Kurds in the region had to be taken care of somehow. When the ISIS problem emerged, the YPG began to protect the regions where the Kurds lived, spanning from Haseki to Arfin. The Syrian government did not react to this because the purpose of the YPG was only to protect the Kurds and Arabs who lived in the region from the ISIS threat. Not only did Syria not react to the fact that these regions were under control of the organization, it even supported the YPG personally. The salaries of most of the YPG guerillas are paid by the Syrian regime.

Besides this, the congressional works of these political parties are extremely important to the organization. Most co-presidents of these parties live within European countries. There is a board meeting held in Kandil once or twice a year where the conditions of these parties are examined. All the party representatives in Syria, Iraq, Iran, and Europe are present at these meetings. The only exception is the HDP (People's Democratic Party), which is active in Turkey. Their representatives do not attend it because Kongra-Gel (Kurdistan People's Congress) is still considered illegal in Turkey. All the members of the HDP may be expelled from their duties under the Turkish Grand National Assembly if they attend these meetings, so they simply do not go. However, they are still informed about the decisions that are made at this meeting.

So, you could think of the Kurdistan Communities Union (KCK) as being like a roof, under which all the other institutions and organizations dwell. The KCK was the top, no doubt. But under its shelter, the PKK Headquarters Committee was the brains, both directing it and determining the short and long-term policies. There could be overlap between the headquarters committee members and the executives of the Presidency Council and the management of the KCK. For example, Zübeyir Aydar was in the Presidency Council of the KCK. He lived in Europe and, at the same time, he was co-president of the KNG (Kurdistan National Congress). Remzi Kartal was also the co-president of the congress. All of these politicians were civilians. Besides them, the Presidency Council of the PKK were the functional leaders there.

In short, the committee members of the PKK headquarters constituted the brain trust of the KCK. Just like the institutions, which determine the strategies of the official state, the committee members had this same authority in the KCK. Consider the United States. In that country, the strategies were determined by specific institutions. Whether they were Republican or Democrat, each administration was, nonetheless, responsible for applying these strategies. The method and the style of the execution of these decisions could be changed, but the intent must always be to apply the determined strategy to attain the target. And, exactly so, the PKK's leadership cadre was at the helm of the KCK, and this cadre determines the short, and long-term strategies to be applied by them in Turkey and Europe. Therefore, whether Remzi Kartal or Murat Karayılan was appointed to the head of the KCK, the task never changed, because the overall strategy had been determined in advance. The purpose of the person who was appointed to lead the institution was to take the communally derived strategy to its target, and this was a simple yardstick by which to judge a leader. Unless the person who had been appointed applied the strategy, he was immediately discharged.

The PKK's headquarters committee also determines the short, and long-term strategies of the guerilla force. It analyzes and determines staffing and growth goals. Some structural plans, such as your number of guerillas, would be at this level.

Now, as may be expected, there was always a conflict between the guerilla wing and the political wing. The conflicts happened because each side showed disrespect for the other, and for the work they did. Now, it was a true statement that all the steps taken for the Kurds in Turkey and all the political declinations and the economic developments in the region occurred as they were spurred by the efforts of the guerilla wing. When there were still the old pro-Kurdish political parties present—the DEP (Democratic Party), the EMEP (Labor Party) and the HADEP (People's Democracy Party)—the Kurdish politicians could not act as freely as they do now, because there was an incredible pressure from the Turkish state. It was the same situation in Iraq and Iran. For example, at one point, there was no executive left in the PCDK who had not yet been arrested in Iraq. Both the KDP and YNK put great pressure on this party.

However, with the increase of the acts of the guerilla force against these states, Turkey, Syria, Iraq, and Iran began to refrain from exerting control over our nationalists in their governments. In order to avoid the threat of dealing with our guerilla force, these states made way for the political structures we wanted, though under duress. I can explain this situation better by using Iran as an example. There was no political formulation of the organization in Iran originally, because Tehran was simply too strict. As they shut down all the oppositional political parties that were founded there, they executed all the members as well. Therefore, the PKK eschewed forming a political party there. Instead, we started to exercise influence in Iran through our guerilla arm. These conflicts were very severe in 2008. It was not broadcast much to the public, but the PKK managed the fighting very well. Think about it! Even the general of Iranian revolutionary guards was killed.

After that incident, Iran was obliged to sit at the negotiating table and suddenly wanted to reach an agreement with us—according to our demands that we could establish a political party; that our party would conduct all the same activities as their current, dominant parties, and that it could even participate in the elections. The guerilla force of the PKK stopped all combat after this agreement and established the PJAK in Iran. So, just like the HDP did in Turkey, that group serves in the political arena in Iran now.

The conflict between the guerilla structure and the political structure was rooted in the discrepancy of the politicians living in mansions with their children (whom they had the luxury of having); once they made it there, they soon forgot the hardships that the countryside guerrillas still endured. They pretended that all the turns and changes, in the way the state related to us, happened because of themselves. The guerilla force was angry at this outlook, saying, "Look my friend, if it were not for my hard scrabbling in the countryside, you wouldn't even be able to talk to the public now. You wouldn't have been granted the right to enter the Turkish Parliament and play the role you do in the mechanisms of decision."

Another side to it was that everyone joining the PKK first stayed in the HPG camps, where their character and capacity were observed. During their stay in the guerilla force's camp, the guerilla force connives, choosing the most intelligent, the most qualified, and the most competent individuals for itself, and sends the lazy, unskilled new members to the KCK. Naturally, this pisses off the KCK.

The guerilla force seniors would join the congresses of the KCK and the PKK. Although they participated there only as an audience, they criticized the political structure a great deal. I have witnessed it many times. They called out many times, complaining, "You have no obstacles in front of you. There is nothing forbidden to you. Nothing stands in your way. So, why did you not get organized in that region? Why did you not form your public committee before now? Why don't you open public houses? Why aren't you preparing youth camps? Why are you only active in the legal field? You have billions, financially, yet despite all this, you can't be successful in achieving your mission?" The KCK always gave the same excuse in each case for the poor quality of its members as the reason. "All these failings are due to the men you gave us," they'd claim. "If you gave us men of higher quality, we could do what you ask."

The Regulations of the Organization

We did not have much trouble getting used to guerilla rules. There were some individual problems, but there is always an exception to these things. When there is no discipline, the system cannot work. For example, I love sleeping in the morning. At 4:30 to 5:00 a.m., someone on duty comes in and wakes everyone up for the morning muster. When I was with my friends, I would sometimes say that I would abolish the morning muster if I could. But, in the end, even though we found it quite upsetting, the rules were very important for the proper functioning and stability of the organization. If a guerilla got used to comfort (and sleeping late), you would not be able to make them get over it.

So, there was a strict approach to discipline within the organization. No one would take you under formal investigation simply because you made a few initial mistakes. However, they would warn you verbally. There were some moral rules that were known by everyone. For example, you had to go to bed at 9:00 p.m., but if you wanted to you could listen to the radio until 11:00 p.m. or 12:00 a.m. But you cannot disturb your comrades. So, if you wanted to listen to music, you must use earphones. Your comrades might want to have a rest because they may have things to do in the morning. You have to respect the rights of everyone. If there happens to be someone who is insistently disrespectful regarding these rules, then he gets a written warning. Normally, each rule is stable and written. The hour one must go to bed, the hour one must wake up, how you will treat a commander, etc.

There is a great culture of respect for the teachers and trainers within the organization. When an instructor enters a classroom, everyone in the class stands up. You must stand up no matter who the person is that is giving a lecture, whether they are superior or inferior to you. For instance, let's assume that three guerillas are delivering a training session. Even a battalion commander or a PKK central headquarters member does not have the luxury to stay seated when these three guerillas enter the room. Everyone must arise. Even if Cemil Bayık is in that class that day, he has to stand up when they enter. In addition, the commission has to allow you to sit down; you cannot sit down on your own without their permission.

Also, there is an obligation that each member of the organization has to write a report once a year. Sometimes, the draft arrives and the reports are written in accordance. All of them are read and evaluated without any exception. Women have to write three reports: one to the military headquarters, one to the central executive committee, and one to their own headquarters. Men have to write reports only to the first two institutions listed above. Whether you are a normal guerilla or a ranked commander, these reports have to be written once a year.

Apart from the normal obligation of writing a report, each guerilla can write reports pertaining to any issue whenever they feel the need. I mean that there is not a limitation; you do not have to write only the required reports each year. You can utter a criticism or a suggestion in these additional reports and even give your opinion about a job or mission. After writing a report, you also have the right to ask for feedback. For instance, let's say you wrote a report making a suggestion. You can ask for the conclusions on your report from the institution you wrote it to. You have to be given a reply whether it be negative or positive. For example, you have made a suggestion about wanting to transfer from one area to another. A reply must be given to you within a month.

You have the right to ask for a reply, but you do not have any rights on whether your opinion is accepted. Another issue about reports is that they can only be opened by the institution to which they were sent. No other institution of the organization can open the report. If something like that happens, then the offender can go under a heavy sanction. For example, if a guerilla wrote a report to his province commander, no one but that commander may open it. If you want to write a report to the HPG headquarters command, you can either send your report directly to the HPG or you can send it to a specific person among the seven people there, stating HPG. If you write the HPG/Bahoz Erdal, no one but Bahoz Erdal himself can read your report.

Of course, there are exceptions: if a guerilla wrote a report to the province commander and the province commander is not in the region at the time (he could be somewhere else for a meeting), then he can instruct his assistant to open the report, read it, and inform him on the issue when he returns. Or he can instruct him not to touch the letter and that he will read it himself when he comes back.

There is also an oral report system in the organization. In the north, the system is very flexible, but in the south oral reports are taken on a daily basis. Everyone on the team gives a feedback report about what has happened during the day. The commander of the team gets the oral report from everyone. You can give information about anything, whether it is negative or positive.

In addition to these daily oral reports, there is team reporting every three days. Also, this is not done alone; the team gathers and gives an oral report together. On that same day, the company commander evaluates the reports given by the guerillas. While these reports are received, anyone can state their opinions, but it is not required that you say something.

On the fourth day, battalion management gathers and evaluates all of the reports. Battalion management consists of company and team commanders. On the fifth day, the conclusion of those reports is given orally to the guerilla structure. Each commander shouts out the conclusions of the reports to their unit.

There are team meetings held every 15 days where everything that has happened is evaluated. These meetings are more extensive than the oral reporting. In team meetings, you can say things that you forgot to say in the oral reports. You can evaluate only your own team in the oral reporting system. You cannot reveal your discomfort with another team. However, in the team meeting you have the chance to evaluate the lifestyle of the three teams and give your opinion about any incident that has happened with another team.

Also, there is a company meeting once a month where the gatherings of the three teams are evaluated. This evaluation lasts from half a day up to a full day. Everything that has happened in their region and in other regions in the last 45 days is completely evaluated.

In these meetings, the commanders are not the only ones who speak, but the guerillas also have the right to say their opinions. You have equal rights with those within the commandment echelon. No commander can tell you that you have no right to evaluate an issue. First, the lifestyle of the company is evaluated in these meetings. Then, you can criticize the company commander, the battalion commander, and even the region commander. For example, a guerilla can easily criticize the specific actions or behavior of a company commander.

There is an executive meeting held once every two months. Battalion commanders, the region commander, and two of his assistants participate in this meeting. These high-ranked administrators evaluate the entire region, and then they notify their battalion about the results of the meeting. Let's say there was a particular problem in a battalion which they evaluated as such. Based on their discussion, that person would be punished because of what happened within that battalion. All these things are reported to each battalion by its commanders.

Once every two years, there is yet another conference that pertains to the guerilla force. The mostly highly ranked individuals participate in this conference. In addition to these high-ranked commanders, representatives from the political extensions in Iran, Syria, and Iraq participate in these conferences simply as observers. There is no congress of the military force; they only make a conference. There is a headquarters team that consists of 50 people who are chosen at the end of this conference. They come from within the headquarters commandment. These 50 people come together and establish a commandment council of 11 people. Finally, these 11 people choose the headquarters commander. This selected person is submitted for approval by the defense committee. The military council is subordinate to defense committee. When the defense committee approves this person, they become the headquarters commander. If they do not approve them, the commandment council will have to make another election. Apart from some exceptions, those who become candidates are generally appointed as headquarters commanders.

The present headquarters commander has the right to postpone this conference for six months in the case of an extraordinary situation. For instance, you have heard that Turkey will perform a military operation. It is risky for such an amount of people in the commander rank to gather. So, the date of the conference is postponed. The guerilla council can postpone the date of conference for six months. I mean the headquarters commander cannot postpone the conference on its own free will. They need the approval of this council of 50 people. In the same way, in the case of an extraordinary situation, the conference can be held six months early.

In extraordinary situations, the condition of all the provinces is evaluated. Four months in advance, all of the province commanders write reports telling about the situation in their provinces. These reports are read during the guerilla conference. For instance, let's say that a province commander in the north could not attend the conference due to the clashes there. That individual can send what he wanted to say at the conference as a report to the secretary of the conference and then his opinions are read there. During the meeting, answers are written to the guerilla council. The conference is over in 15 days at the earliest, but they can last up to a month sometimes.

Again, the place and the importance of the guerilla force is different to other sections of the organization. It is autonomous within itself, but its initiative area is very large. For example, a guerilla commander can easily criticize the headquarters committee of the party, officials of the KCK, or the officials of the Kongra-Gel management. But these institutions that I listed can never criticize the guerilla force directly. If they have a problem, they notify the People's Defense Committee (KCK).

There is also a reward and punishment system in the organization. What I mean is that life in the PKK is not based simply on punishment. Just like you punish someone when he makes a mistake, you also reward him when he is successful in doing something. The punishment system in the north is more flexible. It is not as strict and straight as it is in the south because the conditions in the north are worse.

It can be so bad in the north that you do not even need to give an oral report everyday if the situation does not allow for it. It may be 15 days and if things are not OK then you can miss the team meeting. In the north, the rules must be flexible based upon the conditions there.

There are written and non-written rules. And the written regulations do not include any exceptions or variations. What I mean is that there are not rules that are only for a specific region, like different rules only for the north or the south. The regulations are written in sharp sentences and define the general framework—and reveal the more concrete rules. However, the commanders in the north and south soften these rules according to the conditions of their regions.

Guerilla regulations clearly define which region the high-ranked guerilla will be on duty in and for how long they will be there. For instance, a commander would not stay in the same region for more than four years no matter how highly ranked he was. A normal guerilla can stay in a region for up to ten years. This rule is the same in the north and in the south.

There is a specific difference between a guerilla and a commander: the guerilla can make many suggestions on his own behalf, like he wants to go to a specific region. But a commander does not have such a right orally or in writing. What I mean is that after being promoted to commander, the duty is assigned, not requested.

There is such a culture within the organization that a commander would not really make a suggestion for himself. There is not such a thing as being a volunteer for a particular duty. If someone wants to become a higher rank or go to a certain place, that person will be pacified by the party and no one would trust him very much. This is because once you join, you are giving all of your free will to the organization. I mean that you are actually willing to go wherever they appoint you.

There are also some clauses in the regulations about the numerical organization of the guerilla force. For example, a squad consists of three to five guerillas. Two to three squads make up a single platoon. Then, two or three platoons make up one company. The management of a company consists of both company commander and platoon commanders. Battalion management consists of a battalion commander and also company commanders. The platoon management consists of a platoon commander and squad commanders. All of this is clearly stated in the regulations.

Each battalion, company, platoon, and squad in the organization has a name. They are usually named after the martyred. For example, the battalion of the Martyred Mahsun, the company of the Martyred Kemal, and the team of the Martyred Mehmet. Names are given according to level. You can name a team after a martyred guerilla or name a company or a battalion after its martyred commanders.

The number of female guerillas to be employed within each unit is also determined by the regulations. For example, there has to be one female company and two male companies within each battalion. As I have said, the management echelon of a battalion consists of company commanders. The organization applies a positive discrimination for female guerillas in the battalion management. Besides the female company commander, the female guerilla who is the commander of the first platoon of the female company also works in the battalion management. What I mean is that battalion management consists of two females and two males.

The guerillas determine the candidate they want to be a squad commander. In the same way, the management can also declare their candidate and ask the guerillas to determine their own. Then, the elections are held to determine the squad commanders. Once these team commanders are elected, they immediately start on duty.

The appointment of a company commander is decided by the battalion and regional managements. The appointment of a battalion commander is decided by the regional and headquarters managements. But there is such a rule that says a regional commander cannot appoint a battalion commander without the approval of the headquarters management.

Evacuation of the Hills for the Winter Camp

But to return to my own timeline, our province commander sent Sevin and me back to our former field. But, when we arrived in our former region, we learned that the state security forces had taken it over. All the strategically significant areas were now controlled by the enemy's tanks and thermal cameras. So, now, if we moved across any open areas at night, the thermal cameras would immediately detect us; thus, our movement was severely restricted.

The comrades who had taken our place had not been familiar with the region, so they suffered 15 losses in three months. Since they did not know the back roads and secret paths, they were caught up in tank ambushes in the open field.

So, by my suggestion, the command echelon went under revision. After these leadership changes, our priority was to carry out missions against the security forces in order to expand our freedom of movement. Otherwise, we would neither be able to stay safely where we were nor prepare for the winter camp in the fall. (We had to transport food to the camp field and lay in supplies all during the fall, but we could not easily stock the food and ammunition if the security forces did not leave their positions.)

There were also some teams of rangers settled in our field. In contrast to the security forces, these teams were very unstable, and constantly relocating. They were staying in a different spot every night. They were not large groups but very lean. A ranger group might have 15 people in total. Moreover, they knew the field better than we did, because they had consistently been rangers in their own lands, whereas we had been away.

The result of all these disadvantages was that the command echelon, replacing us so frequently, lost control over very many strategic areas. While these locations were under state control, the Turkish soldiers placed mines there. Now, almost all the paths were full of mines. I have said before, the fight between the years 1994 to 1995 was very brutal. Their purpose was to restrict the mobility of our regional force and, once they had softened us, to destroy us in the fall or winter. We had already been in the field for some time, when we discovered it had been mined. Five of our comrades stepped on them before we knew it. Their feet were blown off from their ankles. Three of them were martyred.

We had to do something. We decided to act against the rangers before we took on the security forces, since the security forces were staying in a stable position and would not easily abandon their location. They were predictable. But, we did not know exactly where the rangers stayed, so they were more dangerous to us.

Once, we managed to detect the location of a group of these ranger teams between the cities of Siirt and Bitlis. As I said before, they were constantly on the go. They would never sleep in the same place they had stayed the night before. They would stay in a location until evening, preparing as if they were going to stay there overnight; building positions with stones. But they then moved somewhere else in the pitch darkness of the night, trying to throw us off the scent. We followed this team for about a month. We realized they always used the same tactic. One day, they stayed stable until evening. However, they changed their location during the evening and climbed to a hill but did not encamp. They failed to dig in a defensive position, thinking no one knew that they were there.

We made our raid at around 10:00 p.m. They had a team of 12. We killed nine and left three alive. We did not bother trying to converse or to persuade them to our side. We were sick of it. Also, there was little point in it. This had been one of the most belligerent and effective teams in the region. We had made a raid, some time ago, on the village from which the team came, and had killed many of the villagers. Therefore, they were very incensed, very vengeful, and very dangerous. They were wholeheartedly joining in every operation alongside the security forces. They patrolled around our field, as an advance unit for the military. That is the reason we chose this specific ranger team to target.

Once the members of this team were killed, the other ranger teams withdrew to their own villages. They all realized that we had uncovered the strategy that they had developed. Now they were the ones who were unsafe.

And so, the time came to address the stable security forces. The military was dug in at three different points, but they had tanks at only two points. We purposely became familiar with the movement patterns of the soldiers before we attacked.

The nearby stations were meeting all their supply needs, except for food. The military vehicles would carry the goods to the furthest point that the road reached, and the items were transported from there by mule. Apart from this, we learned where they got their water, which paths they used, from where their food came, and the habits of the soldiers' shift change. There were 40 to 50 soldiers on each hill, and these soldiers were sent back on the fourth day of each month, with new ones replacing them. So, we began by planting mines on the paths they used two days before the guards were changed.

But, in order to leak into the hills where the enemies were encamped, we needed more information. So, at night, despite their thermal cameras, we would approach them at a distance of 50 meters. With small groups of two or three people, we were collecting as much intelligence as possible. The thermal camera was not as effective as it was first considered to be. It could not detect everything. We also made note of the fact that there was only one thermal camera on each hill.

We knew that after we destroyed one of the ranger teams, the rest would withdraw. Our surveillance of the permanent soldier camps revealed that the teams that retreated would sometimes race up the other hills to the aid of their fellow soldiers. What the soldiers did not know was that the ranger teams we had intimidated were now working for us. These rangers were transmitting details to us such as how many thermal cameras there were and what kind of weapons the soldiers had.

Thanks to their intel, we were able to mine the paths they used. All three hills on which the soldiers camped were now ringed with mines. It was time to draw the soldiers down into the field in order to get them to step on the mines. So, we laid down harassing fire and assassinated one or two soldiers by sniper shot. We would send three guerillas, and they would perform an assassination each and come back. After getting out of the effective shooting range of the soldiers, they would intentionally let themselves be spotted. The military was not only using howitzers, but they were also chasing our guerillas to block their escape and kill them. However, since we laid mines around the hills, the soldiers were stepping on the mines with every step in pursuit.

The military now had no will to remain in their positions—not only because of the mines, but because of the snipers we sent to demoralize them. Our men were hiding in the steep and wooded field at a distance of 150 to 200 meters. When they found an opportunity, they would shoot a soldier with a Dragunov assassin weapon and then retreat. We caused the military to feel so frustrated and disheartened, because now they were the ones unable to move freely throughout the autumn. Finally, they left all three of the hills and withdrew to their headquarters.

So, in this way, in just three months we had managed to disable both the military and all the rangers. It was a great relief for us, since otherwise, we would not have been able to lay in all our essential food and ammunition before winter. This is how important the control of our geographical area was for the guerilla. Once you abandon a position over the winter, you lose the control of that area. As I mentioned, in the previous year, we had abandoned our field for a month and a half and by the time we returned, the Turkish soldiers had taken control of the strategic positions and rangers were patrolling throughout the area. All these changes happened in six weeks. Just like that, the hills were under their control. The teams of rangers had learned the details of the field, and the mines were placed. This is why, when our command echelon was reinstated, we became so adamant about sweeping and holding our ground before winter came.

The Background of a Land Mission

It was around this same autumn, while we were finally free to prepare for winter, that we were attacked by a land assault. The leaves of the trees had already fallen, and the field visibility had become convenient for an operation. We lost two comrades in the battle. One of them was the platoon commander. This was a huge loss to us, because not only had he been very familiar with our field, but he had been on excellent terms with all the guerrillas and the civilians in the region. Consequently, we had many difficulties during the preparations for the winter camp. The platoon commander had been responsible for a number of years for supplying what we needed. He knew what to get and from whom, and he knew how to bring these supplies to the camp.

Without him, we would have to do the best that we could, so, I went down to the city of Siirt with two comrades. The journey took two nights, since we only moved after dark. I knew some of the peasants in the valley and had visited with them for the Nowruz celebrations in 1993. It was through the help of these peasants that we were supplied all our needs in 25 days. We bought all our essentials: food, flour, sugar, oil, fire, tea, meat, etc. We bought all these supplies with the money we had been given. We used Deutschmarks in those days and would occasionally use American Dollars as well, but not very often.

With the supplies purchased, now the most difficult part of the task had just begun. We had to carry all of these staples we had just secured into the countryside. For this, we bought 16 mules from the peasants. Upon taking our supplies to the countryside, we had planned to give the mules away to the peasants. They would look after these mules, use them for their own tasks, and give them back to us when we needed to once again ship our supplies out to the countryside. Since there were no drones back then, we could easily carry our supplies by mules yet still avoid detection. The military stations were only at specific locations. We decided on the paths to take simply according to which ones avoided those spots. We would travel each of these planned paths twice, without carrying anything, before loading and transporting the supplies by mule.

And the philosophy of the plains was also in our favor back then. Not all the military stations were like this, of course, but the stations on the plains held the attitude that, "If you do not interfere in our business, we won't interfere in yours." Of course this was not official, but these were the unwritten rules. In exchange, we also did not attack them.

We would never attack or perform a mission while preparing for the winter camp. During this season, when the security forces went on a mission, or entered our field, we would hide, so as not to disclose the location of our camp fields. If we made any contact with state forces in the fall, they might think, "If this guerilla army is here in this month, then they will stay here in winter as well." And they would be right. That's why we absolutely would avoid any contact in the fall.

Even if we did undertake a mission, we would perform it far away from the camp field, as a diversion. Sometimes, when we were just about to start the winter camp, I would send five teams to areas far away from the camp field and allow them to get noticed by the security forces. Sometimes, I would send these teams to the villages, because we knew there were people in each village that worked for the military. We knew who they were but pretended not to know. Our comrades would go to these villages before the winter camp and deliberately visit those households. Naturally, these military informers would run straight to the government with the information that they had seen us. When the security forces learned that we guerillas were visiting the village, they thought that we were located nearby, and their superiors would station them there throughout the season. Once we had tricked them like this, we could spend the entire winter comfortably.

When we visited these false villages in fall, we would give the villagers a list of supplies we needed, even though we no longer required any of them. For realism, the lists would contain mostly things to be used in winter such as heaters, nylon blankets, pickaxes, salt, and oil. We knew that this list would go straight to the security forces. It was guaranteed that the village informants would drop by the station before supplying us and say, "Commander, look! They have given me this kind of list. I will go and fetch these items, but, just so you know!" The commander would look at the list and see the things to be used in winter. It would be natural to conclude that we must be encamping near their town for the duration. However, what delivery of such a list actually meant was that we had finished all our winter preparations with enough time left over deliberately to fox the military. We did it to misdirect them, and we were generally successful at such ruses.

Before hunkering down for winter, the military sprang an operation on us in the area in which we were entrenched. We abandoned the area and lugged everything to another area at a distance of a night's travel away. If we wanted, we could always sneak away from a battle, but in this instance, we intentionally tried to get in contact with them. Because, again, if we contacted them in this season, they would believe that we were staying near the place of the confrontation. Indeed, six of our comrades got wounded in that particular battle, and three were in a serious condition. Each were shot in their chests. Without surgery, they would die, but there was no way to bring a doctor from a hospital to the countryside. Therefore, all these comrades did die.

Invitation to Damascus

After this battle, the security forces bragged to the media, "We killed eight PKK militants!" The executives of the organization were naturally worried. They began to wonder if it were true. But an oral report was received daily at headquarters from us guerillas in the countryside. Around 10:00 a.m. every day, one by one, all regions give information about the incidents and developments in their area of operations. When the connection was provided, I told them in codes that the news report was a lie and that we had six wounded guerillas, three of whom later became martyred.

After the daily report, headquarters would reply, "All commanders must listen out for the big radio. We will be making contact!" We thought that headquarters would make a statement. We had two distinct kinds of large radios, which we used to communicate with Iran and Syria from our location in Turkey. One of them was as big as a MacBook and could be set on a desktop and remain permanent. The other one was half its size. We had recently bought them from Japan, and both ran on batteries. Their antennae were four meters long and faced three directions: east, north, and south. There was a panel in the middle of these antennae, which could be turned towards whichever direction was needed. We turned it to the direction of Iraq and Syria. As we were waiting, we suddenly heard comrade Apo speaking.

When Apo talked on the radio, he would first contact the provinces where the greatest problems had arisen. So, this time he spoke first to the Serhad province. They had suffered many losses that season. After he finished addressing them, he talked to the Dersim field commander. It was after that, that he began to speak to our field commander. He asked whether the media battle report and the losses it claimed were true. Our field commander told him that these reports were not true. Apo asked where the battle took place and the commander answered "In the Şirwan district of Siirt." (It is worth noting that Apo did not speak in codes on the radio. He spoke clearly.) Apo asked our commander to include a commander in the conversation who had directly been in charge during these conflicts. Since our company commander was not prepared, I spoke on the radio on his behalf, just in time to catch judgment from our leader. Apo criticized the battle saying, "Why did you perform such a mission in such a season? Why did you do this in this kind of area?" He thought that we had conducted our mission in the same area as our permanent winter camp. Once I explained our strategy behind the battle, he sounded a bit more relieved and asked me, "You've been in that region for a few years, right?" I answered, "Yes, President Apo!" Then he asked me, "Have you ever come to Damascus to be trained?" I replied, "No!" That's when he invited me, saying, "Then come to Damascus when appropriate for your region. I will inform your province commander, and they'll send you at the first opportunity." Then he hung up.

When he had finished speaking with the other provinces, the interpreter, standing beside our province commander, asked him not to leave. That's when we realized he was going to give our region an encoded message. My province commander told me to keep the radio on, because the message might be about me. In code, the province commander talked to Apo's interviewer. Then, through the radio, he told me, "You are wanted in Damascus. Prepare ASAP!" But I told him, "This season is really to travel in and we're about to hunker down in our winter camp. In addition, one of our best platoon commanders just died. I'm the only leader left who really knows the area. Can we wait until spring?" Not that I did not want to go to Damascus by the personal invitation of our leader! I did. But it was even more important to me that I not abandon my responsibilities. The province commander responded by agreeing that, "Okay, we will think about it." Then I heard later that headquarters command thought I was right, saying, "It is difficult now. He is needed there, too. He can come here next year."

Torn as I was, my gut told me it would not be right for me to go to Damascus at that time. We had already lost 50 to 60 guerillas the previous spring. The entire executive board had been dismissed, and the membership of two region commanders had been suspended. Moreover, the platoon commander had just been martyred. If I had accepted Apo's invitation, despite such conditions, I would have left my company in a dire situation. If I thought about nothing but my own interests, of course I would have gone straight to Apo in Damascus! But I liked my men very much. They were very committed to me. If I left them alone in winter camp and something happened to them, I would regret it for the rest of my days.

An Unexpected Incident

The year of 1995 turned out to be a very interesting one. Many incidents occurred, one after another. To begin with, just as we were about to enter the winter camp, our company commander fled with a female guerrilla. We learned they ran away to Botan field to join the guerilla force there.

The company commander had been sentenced for a mission he had enacted. He ran away because he just could not bear his punishment. While being trained at headquarters, he had planned a mission and had been given command of it. While the mission plan could have been applied in traditional ways, this comrade was brutal and cruel in his execution of it. In short, the organization had realized that the Turkish soldiers and the rangers had been dressing up in PKK uniforms and visiting villages to ferret out the villagers' relationship with the PKK. Our headquarters unit had received intelligence about these imposters: where they had been staying; which paths they used most frequently; which villages they had already visited, and which they would visit next. With this information, our old company commander had planned an act against this deceptive team.

They laid an ambush on the path over which these soldiers and rangers most often drove their van. They killed every single person of this special team. They could easily have taken most of them captives, if they had wanted. According to some of the guerillas who accompanied this commander, a soldier and a ranger escaped their van and tried to surrender. Our comrades reported that these captives told our commander not to shoot and that they were surrendering. But the company commander had given a strict order saying that none of the members of this impersonator team would be left alive. So, the guerillas, under his command, frog-marched this group of 16 rangers and soldiers and executed them by firing squad. But even this atrocity was insufficient for the commander, because then he ordered his guerrillas to throw the corpses in the van, and light the van on fire.

As soon as they returned to headquarters, the guerillas filed a complaint about this incident with the province commander. They were very disturbed by what they had been ordered to do. The guerrillas reported that they could easily have taken all the soldiers captive alive, if the company commander had not overruled them. The province commander, himself, was shocked when he heard of this ferocity. The command team had already heard some rumors that "the PKK had burned soldiers alive," before the responsible team even returned to headquarters, but they had not believed it. They had been positive the news was a Turkish state smear campaign, since they did not use such horrific tactics. Obviously, they figured the media must be giving false information.

When I first heard of that incident, I thought to myself that it was a conspiracy. Only gradually did it become apparent that the reports had been authentic. The company commander had honestly, intentionally executed, and desecrated those soldiers. Let me assure you that the instant the province commander heard about the incident, he came down on the company commander like a ton of bricks, right in front of everyone. "Even a government agent would not do what you did. Are you an agent? Do you work for the government? Who are you, actually?" He demanded he turn in his gun and then he threw him into jail. The company commander got very angry at this dressing-down from his superior and retorted, "I earned this gun in this organization, and I will only give it back when I am dead. Nothing short of that will make me return it. If you force it from me, then do not bother ever retuning it to me." The province commander could not take his arrogance any longer and sent him to our region for us to deal with.

When he arrived at our region, I asked him if he really did what was reported. He said, "Yes, I gave the order and my guerrillas carried it out." I asked him how he could do such a thing, and he told me, "I could not forget those 60 friends of ours whom they killed this past spring. They cost us some comrades with whom I had served for a long time." I replied, "It's normal that we lose guerrillas. Whenever there is a battle, their side will lose lives, or ours will. It was our own mistakes back then that cost us so many comrades. This is no justification for your war crime. It is no excuse! You set 12 people on fire in this mission, but the real harm was to our reputation. The media is now using this incident against us, and your own reputation in the organization has been harmed as well. Which commander at province, or even company command level would trust you now to complete even the most insignificant mission?" I berated him like that for a long time, after which he said that he did not have to stay in this field and take such abuse.

An Act of Escape in the Camp

In the fall, we migrated to the area of the winter camp. The evening we were about to enter the camp, the duty officer came up to me and said, "Comrade, here is a note written for you." I took the note. The company commander had written, "I am not going to the security forces to rat you out, so you do not need to relocate your winter camp. Stay where you are!" This was in reference to the rule in the organization, which stated, for pretty obvious reasons, that you must change the place of the camp if someone deserts and knows exactly where the camp is located. This may sound like an overreaction, but relocating our field as a precaution is better than risking our entire field force. Still, to move our camp so late in the season would have been both arduous and dangerous, so the company commander had written in his note that we were not to worry nor relocate. He had gone to Botan field and he would get in touch with us in two or three days.

His defection was so troubling that it brought our regional commander straight to our location. I gave him the note and he asked me, "What do you think? Do you think he would reveal us to the security forces?" I said, "I do not think so."

The morning after his defection, our camp was suddenly attacked by cobra attack helicopters. We figured the defector had informed the enemy of our location. Then, they obliterated our mules, and we realized they had not seen us, they had only spotted the pack animals. We had only three mules, and they killed them all.

At 8:00 to 9:00 a.m., that same morning, I found a missed call on my radio. It was the company commander who had deserted us. I asked him where he was and he replied, "Do not worry about me! Are you guerrillas all right?" "No," I said. "The enemy just destroyed all our mules. Now, how did they spot them?" He answered, "It was not I! Please believe me, I am still in the countryside. I did not defect to the security forces. I am on the hill opposite your location. I can see you from where I sit," he said. So I told him, "Then come back here, since the regional commander is here now. Come back, otherwise everyone will think poorly of you." But I could not convince him to return.

I radioed to him, "Okay, if you really want to leave, a force that belongs to our region is bringing from Botan Field some grenades, bullets, and other weapons. Why don't you welcome them on the way? Here is the channel they're using. You must contact them in advance so as to avoid any misunderstanding." He could have been mistaken for an enemy and killed.

Meanwhile, our team had settled into the winter camp field. We had not changed our location. I contacted the Botan force three or four days after my radio conversation with the defector. We were using the role communication system belonging to the Turkish security forces. We used codes, of course, since the security forces were bird-dogging us 24/7.

It was through this system that I talked to the unit that was bringing us the weapons. They told us that they had our "fugitive," which is when the regional commander took the radio from me and joined the conversation. He chewed out the company commander saying, "Are you a coward? Why did you run away? You will come back this instant." There was a long silence from the company commander. Then he said, "I won't come back." The regional commander answered, "Look, if you go to Botan, the field commander there is my childhood friend and I will tell him to throw you directly into jail. He will do whatever I ask of him. You broke our rules, took a woman and fled from one place to another with her. They will keep you in jail for months."

The company commander said he was not planning to stay in Botan but was just stopping over there on his way to Damascus. The regional commander said, "What makes you think they will allow you to go to Damascus? They won't send you there. They will keep you in jail for months. It is not even certain what decision the organization will make about you. It is best for you if you face us directly and come back here as soon as possible!"

And so, six days later, the company commander, and his woman, returned to the camp with the Botan group that replenished our ammunition. We certainly could not let him keep his old job. The organization had a set of official rules, and no one is an exception. He stayed in jail for 15 days, but

I did not confiscate his weapon. This was because I knew his character. He also used to outrank me, but, in those days, I used to respect him a lot. That's why I did not treat him strictly by the book. I was appointed as the company commander, once he was put in jail. I held that position between 1995 and 1996. So, in the end, his cowardice got me a promotion.

I mentioned to you before that I was not at all comfortable about this promotion. I told the regional commander about my discontent many times. I was only 22 years old, and yet I had been given a great deal of responsibility. In order to carry out a mission, one needs to strategize for months. We were pre-occupied with the negative reaction of the public now that we had undertaken a mission against the rangers rather than the security forces. Since the field where we were located was full of ranger villages, how could we avoid battling more rangers? Our task was too challenging. That's why I found it so hard to be a company commander and so I objected to the duty.

But the regional commander was determined. I realized then, that he was not going to change his mind. So, I told him that I would accept the command but only on one condition. "You will take these older, respected commanders out of my company." The regional commander laughed. "Are you crazy? How could I afford to transfer them out in this season?" I said, "I get embarrassed when I have to order them to do something." He replied, "I will talk to them. It won't be a problem." He gathered all the wise, respected older commanders and told them, "He is your company commander, but he is shy about giving directives to you. So, if there is something to be done, please do it before he tells you." I tell you, having these experienced soldiers directing themselves sure helped me a lot.

Nearly Dead

Before we had even left the winter camp, early in the spring of 1996, the military began advancing towards the region in which we were located. One of the duty officers wakened me one night at midnight. He told me that they had noticed something on the radio, so I turned it on and listened for a while. The security forces were definitely discussing something, but they were using crypto. We could not understand the conversation, but we could tell among which stations the conversation was taking place. The notable thing was that the stations connected to one province normally would not talk directly to the province central command. But that was far from the case this time. I realized that all the stations in the province were talking to their headquarters directly and that there was a tense talk between the cities of Bitlis and Siirt.

It appeared obvious to me that they were definitely getting prepared for an attack. Otherwise, these two provinces would have nothing to do with one other. I immediately contacted the hillers, who were responsible for the security of our camp. I asked whether they had reached their intended position. The hillers were from the female cadre that day, and one of them told me that they were not at their position yet. It was almost 3:00 a.m. They were to have been on the hill by 2:00 a.m. I reprimanded this woman, saying that they were almost an hour overdue, and there was no excuse for not being there by now. She replied, "Comrade, there is something on the hill. We do not know if it is animal or human, but something is definitely moving up there." I told her, "Absolutely do not go up there! Keep two experienced people with you and send the rest back to the camp." She panicked when I gave her those orders. She asked me, "Why?" I answered honestly, and said, "Those are probably Turkish soldiers on the hill. We have overheard that they are advancing towards our camp. With the two people next to you, approach the hill about 50 to 60 meters further. Then, do not do anything till you hear from me!"

I was going to organize our guerrilla army and leave the winter camp field but now realized that we were surrounded. There was another strategic hill next to the camp, and I had been planning to go up there to make our escape. But the crafty soldiers had taken their position there during the night. Of course, we did not know that yet. It was not until they began shooting intensely at us from that hill, as we walked in the stream at 5:00 a.m., that we had the first sign that they had noticed us. I now ordered the three female guerillas that I had left on the hill to shoot the soldiers who were shooting us. "Shoot until you run out of ammunition and then retreat to a safe area."

We were surrounded and caught flatfooted, but we knew of a very steep, strategic spot that the soldiers would not be easily able to reach. In such battles, whoever gained a position in such a place, would dominate. There were only two paths going up there, and I directed my team to head there. But we again began taking heavy fire. The male advance team was the only team that could safely reach that area. The one female group, and the male unit I was in, were now blocked from any hope of crossing over.

The soldiers nearly completely surrounded us. Our probability of escape was not very good. If we were going to have any chance to make it past them, we would have to move with focus and unity. In order to ensure coordination, I took my position on the ground between our two teams. It was around 10:00 a.m. and we had not yet sustained any losses. The three female comrades caught up with us from the other mountain. There was a tense skirmish on the spot where one platoon had taken a position, and yet there was no battle on another spot where another platoon was positioned. I became suspicious of this. I asked that unit commander on the radio if there was any movement anywhere around them. She said, "No!" I noted that there was a stream opposite their position and, on the far side of the stream, there was another hill. I determined that this would be our passage of escape.

But before I directed the group there, I told the commander of the female unit, "Watch that area very closely, this silence isn't normal." She contacted me 15 minutes later, saying, "You're right! A unit of their military wants to sneak through our front line from the direction of the stream." I asked her, "Are there any soldiers on the top of the hill?" She answered, "No, comrade! I did not believe so." I told her, "Check it more carefully. It is a very strategic location. Are you positive that no soldiers have positioned themselves there?" She answered, "No, there's no one." (In the heat of battle, we naturally do not use any codes on the radio. We just speak plainly. The military does the same.)

Meanwhile, my assistant was with me. I told him, "Comrade! I will go towards the break in the line." He said, "Comrade, wait! Let's take this male platoon with us." I told him that would not be necessary. I retrieved a pair of binoculars from the female unit and started to scan the stream. A military team of 25 soldiers was just waiting there, standing in the stream. I observed them for a while and then realized that they had no intention of breaking through our line. They appeared content to stay there, just waiting. What was going on? I could not make sense of this. Although in retrospect, I should have been able see what was happening. How many times had I trained others to defend the rear flank, but now I had forgotten to check it. Instead, I had relied on the assurances of others. The guerrillas whom I had asked concerning it, had told me that there was nothing there, and that our rear was safe. Since I had performed many assassinations before, I knew to give importance to a 360-degree situational awareness. I again observed the behavior of the soldiers in the stream. I now knew for sure that they would not sneak over to where we were, but still their purpose eluded me.

Meanwhile, one of the platoon commanders contacted me and said that a howitzer had hit the male company and two guerillas had been wounded. It was now imperative that I find a way out, before it was too late. It was drizzling, and fog was settling over everything. It was unusual weather. I was still talking to the male company on the radio and directing them how to change their position. I had taken cover behind a boulder, but while issuing orders I inadvertently moved away from the rock. I suddenly felt a pain in my head. It was as if I had been hit with a very solid object. I do not remember anything after that.

[Deniz showed me the cavity on the top of his head. The sniper's bullet had hit and broken the skull bone. There was only membrane left between the brain and the skull. Doctors in Syria had later placed a piece of bone over the area.]

Just before the incident, I had been talking to the platoon commander on the radio. When my radio fell to the ground, the commander of the female company, who was with me, took the radio and told the commander of the male company that I had been martyred. Everyone was shocked. "How could he be shot? There isn't even a battle there." The female commander responded, "We do not know. But we do know there was the sound of a sniper bullet, and then he collapsed."

When I came around, I opened my eyes for a moment. I was lying there in the dirt. I saw the women around me crying. I lifted my head and asked the woman next to me, "Comrade, what happened?" She answered, "Comrade, you were martyred." I said, "If I were martyred, how could I talk to you now, you, idiot?" "You were hit on your head by a bullet. We thought you had died," she said, through her tears. I put my hand up to my head and felt the place where the bullet had struck. They made me lie back down, and I could feel I was bleeding from my head, as the blood ran down my neck. I put my hand to my neck, and it came away wet with blood. I realized at that instant that if the bullet had hit my neck, I would have really been dead. I felt around my whole neck with my fingertips. There were no wounds that I could detect and I felt an intense relief.

I immediately resumed issuing orders. "Bring me a piece of cloth immediately. I need to clean away this blood around my neck and head." After wiping off the blood, we could see that the bullet had only glanced off my skull. I took back my radio and contacted the platoon commander. He was shocked. "Weren't you martyred?" I responded, "No, just a misunderstanding." I did not tell him that I was injured. Meanwhile, when this company commander had told everyone over the radio that I was martyred, the company commander with whom I was in love (Sevin), left her position and came to where I was. When she saw me, she exclaimed, "Comrade, you are alive! Why did this woman announce that you were martyred?" I replied, "There is nothing wrong. It was just a misunderstanding."

Even though I had not stood up yet, I knew I would not be able to walk. At least now there was no longer any mystery behind the silence on the hill. The soldiers standing in the stream had only been there to draw our attention. In order to get into a vantage point from which to spy on them, and shoot them there, we guerrillas had to move out from cover and make ourselves visible. The military had cleverly engineered this and, in anticipation, had placed some snipers on the opposite hill. Their purpose was to eliminate each guerrilla who emerged from hiding, in order to shoot their friends in the stream. But I was the only one they managed to shoot, so we got off easy.

Clearly, we could not stay there any longer, so I stood, with the help of the others. I started to walk slowly, but fell to the ground after only a few steps. My vertigo was so bad that I could not walk any further. The women with me were very short and unable to support me very well. Our slapdash plan was to cross to the safe place on the steep area where our lead team had crossed before. A thick fog crept in before we tried to move that way, and the range of vision suddenly dropped to under 20 meters and it was still drizzling. When it was foggy, the battles were mutually halted, but we knew the security forces were now preparing their attack plan. Obviously, they were planning to attack and destroy all of us on the hill. I whispered, "This fog is a great opportunity for us. Under its cover, we should rush to the steep area." Thanks to that thick fog, we safely crossed over and met up with our team in that area.

It had been just in time, too, because, as soon as the fog lifted, the military began to use howitzers to shoot at the hill from where we had just escaped. They carried out a very intense bombardment of our former location with bazookas, flame throwers, and more types of additional weapons than we could ever imagine. I felt sure that they were going to sneak past our front lines after this. It seemed pretty clear that the military thought we were still there. So, the bombardment proceeded with an intense fusillade of technology, until suddenly it all cut off at once. They had been issued a stop order through the radio. They all quit because there was no counterattack from us. We heard the enemy battle commander consulting with his fellow commander. "This silence isn't good. They must be planning something," he said.

Obviously, they expected a counterattack. The commander said, "I do not like this silence. Pay close attention to the areas where those guerrillas could sneak through our lines." All the other commanders answered, "Yes sir, we are looking closely. There is no movement." Then, one of them said, "An hour ago we were in a close battle with that location, from only 20 meters away, yet now there is no movement on that hill." Their battle commander finally said, "They probably escaped under cover of the fog." Then one of our commanders said over the radio to the enemy leader, "You're too late. But if you still want to come over, I can give you the address. We will be waiting for you there." The battle continued verbally, as their commander swore at us a great deal, and our commander swore back.

They finished their attack on the evening of that same day. We incurred no losses, but three people were wounded, including myself. Our province commander, himself, visited our region after the incident. He knew how to treat wounds, such as mine. I had already been "treated" by our female doctor, but she had not cleaned the wound well. Women are more squeamish in such situations. My skull bone had been broken and chipped when the bullet hit, so there was only a skin flap left over the hole. Our female doctor had only covered the skull hole with the flap of skin. All the hair, blood, and dust had stayed packed inside. The province commander opened the wound again and cleaned it out very well. He touched the membrane against my brain with the stick of a piece of plant, and asked me, "Can you feel me touch you there?" I said, "Yes!" He told me, "If the bullet had broken this membrane too, your brain cavity would have filled up with blood and you'd be dead."

9

ON THE WAY TO DAMASCUS, SYRIA

If you recall, in 1995, before the winter camp, Apo himself had invited me to Damascus. Now, the province commander said, "Do not stay with us any longer, especially wounded as you are. We need to answer Apo's order and send you to Damascus as soon as possible. You can receive better treatment for your wound in Damascus as well." They gave me an escort team of 16 guerillas. Some of them were responsible for getting me to Damascus safe and sound, while some of them were, likewise, being sent to Iraq and Syria for training.

The regional commander told me, "First make a visit to the province commander. He is holding some reports, bound for Damascus, that you'll need to take with you." When we arrived at the province commander, he told me, "Look, only three of you 16 are going all the way to Damascus. So, when you've safely reached the south, nobody should argue with you about the right to go to Damascus also. Everyone's destination is clear." I then pulled the province commander aside and said that there was something personal about which I wanted to speak to him.

I mentioned my girlfriend's name and told him that I wanted her to come with us. (She, too, had been in the same region for four years, and was completely burned out.) The commander smiled kindly at me. "Deniz," he said. "Besides the fact she is burned out and due for a change, are you sure you do not have any other reason to ask to take her with you?" I looked at him. "You know my reason very well, comrade," I said. The commander then said to me, "I can send her to the south with you, but, after Damascus, what are you going to do?" I held my ground, "She has earned the right to go to Damascus. She has a bright future ahead of her, and she is as talented as any senior officer. Write the transfer orders that you have selected her, for higher level training in Damascus." He relented. "All right, I will. But absolutely nobody can know about this relationship between the two of you."

On my return to the regional commander, I gave him the transfer orders. He smiled as he read it. "So, you really want to take Sevin with you?" he said. "Yes, comrade," I replied. He gave it to me straight, saying, "Look, up here, we are aware of the relationship between the two of you, but in the south or in a battle zone, your entanglement with each other will do no good for either of you." He continued, "Comrade, you two have been with each other for four years. You came here to the north together. Nobody here has said anything against it. However," he warned me, "Be careful." I answered,

"You're right, comrade. I have loved this girl for four years now, and I haven't even held her hand. We truly are in love with each other. This isn't about sex." He answered, "And that's why we tolerate the two of you."

The commander's guard called out to the girl whom I loved, "Comrade, prepare! You are also going to Damascus." Sevin was elated. He told her what he had told me. "Such affairs are tolerated in a war zone but that isn't the case in the south. Nobody there would show you any mercy. Take care."

Then, as a group of 16 people (four women, 12 men), we set off on our journey. From the district of Şirwan, we were going to travel to Eruh, through the city of Siirt, and from there we planned to travel to the district of Botan. We had a one-day rest somewhere next to the Siirt stream. During this resting period, I wanted to contact the Eruh guerrilla force to decide with them on a meeting point for when we got closer to their area. I took a comrade with me and climbed up to a hill where I would have better radio reception. Before leaving, I told the rest of the group to rally at the field and meet us at the top of the hill after the sun set.

Just as we reached the hill and were speaking to the force from Eruh, we heard gunfire from the spot we had just left. The security forces had noticed our comrades and started a battle. We remained where we were. What could we do? We neither saw nor heard from any of our comrades until 10:00 p.m. We were worried. I risked making contact with them by radio around 1:00 a.m. I asked them where they were, and how they were. They said that they were okay and they had escaped from the area in the dark. But the problem was, they did not know where they were hiding now. They tried to describe their location, but we could not quite figure out where it was. We were in a vast area. Finally, I gave up. "We will meet each other in Eruh. No need to gather now," I told them.

The path we were now traveling was the same one we had used to pass from our training camp into Turkey back in 1992. It had been four years. As we proceeded, we tried to remember, "Wasn't there a boulder here? There must be a tree there. There was a village over there...." Really, we were making it all up. It was nighttime and we could not see anything, yet we walked nonstop. We did not even have drinking water left, so we were very thirsty. This whole time we had no idea where we were going.

Around 3:00 a.m., we came across a river. We tried to remember the name of the river. We could see mountains in the moonlight. They were beautiful, except we did not know which mountains they were. We got even more confused when, while walking along the edge of the river, we came to an asphalt road. In 1992, there had been no pavement on our route. At this point, though we were not aware of it, we had gone to the town of Mawa instead of Eruh. We had gone completely in the opposite direction!

While following the path, we suddenly came upon a long iron bridge. Someone on the other side of the bridge was patrolling it with a flashlight, and guard dogs were constantly barking. We figured that the people we were hearing were probably nomads, who were, most likely, grassing down their animals. This was a great stroke of luck for us, because shepherds would have no problem with us. We were more than happy to head in that direction, since we figured we could learn from them where we were. But, before stepping on the bridge, we noticed that there was a big hole which had been dug to the right of it. It looked like a foxhole; such as the military use to dig into position. I checked it over for a while, but could not understand why it had been dug.

We started to walk slowly across the bridge. We had not had any food or sleep for approximately 11 hours. We were hungry, thirsty fugitives. Just when we arrived at the end of the bridge, my companion beside me quietly tugged on my arm and pointed to something. In that instant, I realized that the set of tents I had taken to be a nomad village was actually a military encampment. They were experiencing an electrical outage, and that's why the soldiers had been patrolling in the dark with flashlights.

There were two iron guard shacks right at the beginning of the bridge, and each was manned. One soldier looked as if he were dozing off, but I told the comrade next to me, "There is no escape!" Even if we could pass by these guard shacks, those soldiers in the station would notice us. But if we went back, there was surely a soldier there as well, who probably had not noticed us before, because he had been asleep. But, to go forward was to walk directly into the military station. I looked down, and the river seemed to be deep enough, so I told my comrade that only one solution remained to us. We would have to jump off the bridge and into the river. Since there was no electricity, I figured that even if the guards heard our splash, there was nothing they could do to us.

My comrade followed my logic, and said "Okay!" We both mounted the rails. All our gear was still strapped to us—our weapons, our armor, and ammunition. The bridge was about four meters above the water. We jumped. The soldiers definitely heard the splash, and began searching the river with their flashlights. We were proceeding slowly in the water, covering ourselves by staying close to the shrubbery at the water's edge. Before we were even 80 meters downriver, their electricity came back on. By the absolute worst luck, they had aimed a very powerful spotlight right on the middle of the river, and the guards spotted us immediately.

We left the water and made a run for it. We came to the edge of a large field, and the soldiers tried to block our way onto it with panzers, each of which had its own spotlight, so we crawled to the edge of the road, in an attempt to avoid them. When a panzer headed toward us, we would hide. When it passed, we would get up and keep running. We kept that up until we vanished without a trace.

Soon, we were walking on the paved road again. My comrade asked me where we were headed, and I replied, "I do not know. We're following this road wherever it goes." He responded, "Well, what if this time it takes us right into a military battalion, and for once we do not manage to escape." We had to laugh a lot at our good fortune.

On one side of this road, there was a wooded hill. I said, "Let's hide in the woods and surveil the area. We can wait until it gets dark tomorrow night to set off again." As soon as we hid ourselves among the bushes, we passed out cold. We were so exhausted that we did not wake up until 3:00 p.m. the following afternoon. Once we were awake, my comrade stepped away in order to pee, quickly! However, he immediately came back. "There are the footprints of soldiers," he said. I checked his story. There was a path to the summit of the hill and there really were Turkish soldiers' boot prints. I thought for a while and I decided that this hill was only a security hill; I said that the soldiers would take their position on the hill during the day and at night, they would be leaving.

So, we waited where we were, smoking and chatting with each other until the soldiers began coming down the hill toward us around 4:00 p.m. They were stupidly walking in a group, and only 10 to 15 meters away from us—a convenient target. We easily could have killed them all. It was our ignorance of not knowing where we were that prevented us from taking this opportunity. If we had shot them, where would we run? Where could we hide? We did not know the area, so we could not take the chance.

My comrade was fervent that "We shouldn't miss this opportunity! Let's kill them all!" But I said, "Are you crazy? Do you have any idea where to go to escape? We have no idea where we are!" During our debate, the soldiers continued past us and down the road, where two panzers picked them up and took them all away, alive and unhurt.

Once they had left, we came off the hill and continued our journey. We came across a village, and surveyed it with binoculars for a very long time in order to ascertain whether it was a ranger village or one patriotic to Kurds. But just watching the daily life of the villagers was not showing us either way.

So, I had a brilliant plan. "Before it gets dark, let's arrest someone on the bridge and make them tell us about this place!" Just then, we saw an old lady leading a horse with a rope, headed back to the village. We were still 50 meters away, when we began to call out to her, "Auntie! Auntie!" She started to run as soon as she heard us, and so we were obliged to chase her. We absolutely had to catch her because if this were a ranger village, she would alert them and they would never let us leave there alive. When she tripped and fell, we finally caught up to her.

We asked her, "Why are you running away, Auntie? Why are you frightened?" She answered, "You must be state soldiers!" I was shocked. "State soldiers? Why would you believe such a thing?" She said, "You must have been with those soldiers! They just left by vehicle, but you're still here. They must have left you behind, right?" She was frightened and babbling. Nothing we could say was going to convince her. So, I finally just asked her directly, "Is this village a ranger village, or is it patriotic to the Kurdish cause?" She said it was not a ranger village, and we were greatly relieved. Then, we asked her the name of the place, and she responded to us with a question of her own. "Son, what are you doing here, if you have no idea where you are?" "Auntie," I said, "You are right to ask. But it is a very long story. Suffice it to say that we are quite lost. Won't you please tell us where we are?" But no matter what we tried, she absolutely would not tell us the name of the village which we had overcome so much to reach.

There was nothing to do, but take the risk and go into the village. Then, we met an old man. We trusted what the lady had told us, and we honestly told him that we were patriotic guerrillas. This man said to us, "I will test you by asking you a question. If you answer it correctly, you are what you say. If not, then I know you are state soldiers." "Go ahead and ask," I dared him. The old man's test was to ask me the name of a fellow guerrilla—and it just so happened to be a comrade whom I knew very well! I was able to describe my friend to the old man in great detail, telling he had blue eyes, was fairly short... etc. The old man embraced us. "That's right! You must be one of us." And that's how I found out my friend was this old man's son.

He was shocked when I told him the situation. "Comrade, this is Mawal, not Eruh!" he informed us. Our hearts sank. "You got so lost, you came all the way over to the Mardin side!" I asked him how we could contact representatives of the organization in that region. To our good fortune, the regional force had stopped by this village just the previous night. "When will they return?" I asked him. "They are going to come back on Monday afternoon," he told me. "They wanted certain supplies which we are now trying to collect." So, it looked best to stay in one place for two days, if there were a safe place to wait. "Do not worry," he assured us. "We will take care of you." And then he offered us a nice meal.

Once darkness fell, we were given a young shepherd to guide us to the safe waiting place. He took us to a cave about two kilometers from the village, where we were given food, tobacco, and other essentials. "You can stay here for two days," we were told. "And there are shepherds all around this mountain, so do not worry about security. They will alert you if they see any soldiers."

When darkness fell on the second day, two people from the village came to our cave and told us to stay where we were. "We have told the local guerrillas about your situation," they said, "but they do not believe us." The organization's regional headquarters had told the villagers that we must just be state soldiers trying to entrap them. So, we asked the friendly villagers what our next step should be. They described a different location and told us how to get there, saying, "Be ready there tomorrow evening. They will be waiting to meet you."

What else could we do? The next evening, we went back to the village, enjoyed a lovely dinner, and then set off once night had fallen. We were following the paved road to Eruh when the local organization contacted us through the radio, and told us they would now give us some instructions to follow. Their questions were stupid from the start: "How many in your party? Why are you here? How did you get here?" I was instantly angry, responding, "Why do not you stop asking us such stupid questions over the radio? Why do not you tell us where you are? We will come to you, and you can ask whatever questions you want of us directly." But his questions did not stop: "How can we trust you? What if you are a state soldiers?" He completely ignored anything I had said and kept replying with more questions. This made me even more angry. "If I were not a fellow guerrilla, why the hell would I have waited here for you like a target for three days? How would the villagers have given me the information that you were coming? What kind of idiot are you?" But nothing I said was going to make them trust me.

But all this time we were following their instructions. We began walking directly on the pavement like they told us to do. It was pretty pleasant, actually. The weather was lovely and the landscape was awash in moonlight. We were sauntering straight down the middle of the road because vehicles were not permitted to drive on it after dark. The whole scene was quite nice. And in all this calm and beauty, I asked my comrade, "If you were to set an ambush for us, where would you place it?" I absolutely knew that the local guerrillas were waiting in ambush for us. Their suspicious questions had made it evident. The comrade indicated the back of the hill that we were approaching. "I would lay in ambush there," he told me. "I would kill whoever arrived. Then, I would flee back into that wooded area." I agreed with him, "I bet they're waiting in ambush there for us right now."

The instant we arrived at the back of that hill, we were contacted by radio and told to back up for 80 meters. I naturally got angry over this order. I asked the speaker why we had to go back, when he had just told us to move forward. "And now I want you to go back," he replied. We had to do whatever he wanted, regardless of how angry it made us, so, of course we backed up for 80 meters.

Then, he made contact again and told us to lay down our weapons. We figured that we would be able to see the person holding the radio, being this close, but, we only learned later that the leader, speaking by radio, had stayed 50 meters away from us so we could not detect where he was. But, suddenly, we did see someone. There were six guerrillas beside the road, holding bixi, bazookas, and all sorts of other weaponry.

There was nothing for us to do but comply, so we put our weapons on the pavement, raised our hands above our heads, and walked forward, away from our weapons. The guerrillas surrounded us; three from the front and three from behind, and began body-searching us. "We already left the weapons back there!" I protested. "What in the hell are you looking for?"

I was very frustrated by now. The guerrillas searching us had been ordered not to talk to us. Their job was to take us to their leader. I asked them the name of their commander, and, coincidentally, their commander turned out to be a friend of mine from back in 1992! He was always filthy. We could never make him wash or care about his hygiene, so we had nicknamed him Dirty Mehmet.

We discovered that this company was the roaming unit of Botan province. They were sent wherever there was a need. The province commander recognized me the instant he saw me, and we embraced. But I was still angry. "You made complete fools out of us for three days straight! You called us liars, swore at us, and gave us stupid orders! And now here you are, hugging me as if we were friends!" He had the manners to apologize to me. "There are so many state soldiers here," he informed me. "Comrades who desert us and join the state military patrol in groups just like you. We mistook you for them." I asked him, "Does that make sense? Look at us. There's only two of us. We're here where we arranged to be, and we have the same types of weapons as you. And, if we were soldiers, would we ever have radioed you to tell you our location?"

"We made a mistake, comrade," he admitted. "Please forgive us. All the same, it makes no sense. What are you doing here?" I told him that we had been going to Damascus. "We were attacked, and then we became very lost." He was especially interested in how we had crossed the river. "Over the bridge," I said, and when he asked me which one, I told him, "There was a bridge downhill, with a soldier encampment on it. We crossed that one." Coincidentally, this unit had been planning out a mission to take out that same encampment. He was very curious about how we could have crossed the bridge and not been noticed. When I told him our story, he saw an opportunity. "Comrade," he asked me, "please help us with surveillance of this encampment! We truly want to destroy it."

"Go and do your own reconnaissance!" I was still annoyed. "We have to go on to Eruh as soon as possible. Contact the Eruh force for us, and ask them if the rest of our unit has already reached there." So, they contacted them, and we discovered that everyone else from our unit had arrived there safely. I said, "Tell them not to wait for us. They should move on."

We stayed with this company for a week. Then, one unit took us to another, which took us to another, all the way to Eruh. We stayed only a few days with each force and finally reached Eruh. The other group, with whom we had started, had reached Iraq by the time we arrived in Besler, despite the fact that there was a road of ten days' journey between the two. That's how far behind we had gotten.

The command echelon of the Botan management was having a meeting in Besler. They asked us to wait until the end of that meeting, so that we would take the results with us to headquarters in Syria. We accepted this request. The meeting finished, and we were about to leave when the province commander said to me, "Deniz, a unit of ours in Şırnak wants to execute a mission. Would it be agreeable with you to check over their plan, and see if it is feasible or not?" What could I do? I had to say, "Yes!" We had been their guests for two days. How could I refuse?

I went to the city of Şırnak where this unit was located, and I checked their plans. They focused on a hill, which the security guards held. It had a three-story structure on it, surrounded by smaller buildings. Their plan was simply to shoot at this hill. "But you cannot sneak through their lines with the large force you have," I told them. The unit commander said, "We have Russian made Aspinay rockets (similar to a Bazooka-type rocket launcher, about 3 meters long and shoots rockets that are 1 meter in length). We will attack them with those." Of course, I had never seen this weapon before. I did not know its impact area, specifications, or how it was used. So, I asked, "Would these rockets reach that hill from here?" The strategist answered, "Do not worry, comrade. They would reach." "Okay," I said, walking him through his plan. "Let's say they do reach. You must be effective the first time you fire. Otherwise, the entire force there will run into their shelters," I warned. "Our purpose is to demolish that three-floored military building," he replied. "Okay, if your purpose is not to leak through their lines and infiltrate them, but only to fight in terms of technology, then there is no problem with your mission planning," I said.

Finally, I asked them if they were taking any measures to protect against a counterattack. "For example, let's say you fired three or four rockets. Şırnak is in this region, as you know. There is a military unit in downtown Şırnak, and also a watch hill, plus the hill which you are planning to attack. After you have fired the rocket, you will be under fire from two, three, or even four sides with howitzers. Have you taken any measures against these?" (We very frequently encountered this situation in the north. We would fire three rockets, and get a response of dozens of cannonballs from the security guards, costing us the lives of many of our comrades.) The team commander said, "Yes, our countermeasures are shelters we have built. After we strike at them, our force will hide in these shelters."

As a final step, after all of this, I contacted the commander for the Botan province, with whom this unit was connected, and told him, "On paper, their plan is fine, but I am not familiar with this weapon they are using. So, I cannot say whether they will succeed or not." Of course, since we were now curious about how the mission was going to turn out, we stayed there on the day it was executed. While they were firing the rockets, I was watching the target building with my binoculars. They fired the first rocket, but, though I was watching the hill, I saw no rocket arrive. Nothing at all happened to the target building. We did not understand where this rocket had gone. We had heard a loud noise, but it sounded as if it came from far away. I asked the mission team where they had fired that thing. (Even the Turkish soldiers were looking around to figure out from where the noise had come.) The guerrilla who controlled the weapon said that the rocket had probably gone over and down behind the target building from above. They prepared a second rocket. As the security forces were trying to pinpoint from where the noise had come, we had time to ready an entire second rocket. This rocket reached the hill and hit the first floor of the building. Before we placed the third rocket, howitzer fire started to rain down on us. This gunfire was coming from the other hills close to the city of Şırnak. No one in our team lost their lives, but, I do not know if the military lost any soldiers, either…

The Dark Figure: Şemdin Sakık

The day following this mission, we went up to the guerrilla detachment located in the Cudi Mountains. The plan was for me to pass into Iraq, after staying with them a few days. However, once we were in Cudi, someone contacted the Cudi force by radio and said, "We are coming over, our comrade is en route to you." I asked the regional commander if he could tell me who this comrade was. He replied, "Zeki (Şemdin Sakık) will transfer to Botan Field Command, so he is on his way here from Iraq." When I asked what time exactly Zeki would arrive, the commander said they would most likely arrive by nightfall. I did not want to talk to Şemdin Sakık. I had never seen him in person before anyway and had only talked to him that once via the radio. (But he had cursed me out soundly that one time. And I had cursed him vigorously, in response.)

This animosity all stemmed from when we had been about to enter the winter camp. The military had conducted an operation against us then, and three of us had lost our lives. Şemdin had been the commander of the headquarters at that time. Instead of reaching out to the provincial or the regional commander, he had contacted me directly. "Who the hell do you think you are to plan your own missions? Who are you to send these people to their deaths?" He had sworn at me very badly, despite the fact that he did not know anything at all. The provincial commander had been the one to plan that mission. Nonetheless, after he told me off, this moron ordered me to write my report and send it directly to him. Meanwhile, our provincial commander said, "You cannot directly ask for a report from Deniz. You do not have that authority, and besides this is out of your jurisdiction. If you have a criticism of him, tell it to me. I will tell his regional commander, and his regional commander will report back to me on the situation. You just cannot directly call Deniz to account for these deaths, because I am the one who designed this battle plan." Upon hearing this, Şemdin also started to curse the province commander. Afterwards, the province commander told me to rest, and that I was not going to be writing any reports. It was then that I understood there was a standing dispute between Zeki and the seniors of the organization.

One intriguing feature of our party was that nothing remained a secret for long. Zeki had made great mistakes in the past. Apo, himself, had given Zeki the authority to visit and control the northern cities in Turkey in 1994. During that time, whichever province Zeki visited, the command echelon of that area was destroyed by the Turkish security forces. It was uncanny. After we left Garzan province to head to the south, both our province commander and their assistants got martyred. We knew that Zeki had something to do with all these deaths.

It began with the uptick in battles in our province soon after we had left it. Of course, we were still following events in our old province from over the radio. Wherever this greatly respected province commander went, the province he entered would definitely be subject to a raid. As that connection was made, everyone was surprised and thought this all could not be merely coincidence. The problem was that nobody could figure out how he was being targeted for attack. Was he being surveilled by the security forces? Was he being trailed by some other, more insidious method? The senior officials of the organization finally just ordered the province commander not to move anywhere.

One day when we were all listening to the radio, Zeki started calling out our province commander, using very provocative and insulting words. "You have no right to live, because you only live off the blood of your guerillas. How is it that our comrades died every time you went into a battle, but you have always come through with your life?" We were learning of this after my team and I had already set off for Iraq. During our journey, I told the regional commander, "Comrade, use this radio and stop him. Tell him that his tone and attitude are out of line, and that he cannot treat a province commander like that." It was just my luck that the regional commander had gotten fearful and did not want to intervene in that confrontation.

Meantime, the province commander began feeling incredibly guilty over what Zeki had said to him. This commander told the other comrades, "Do not worry. If another battle happens, I will let myself be martyred, rather than allow any of you to die." This province commander, named Kemal, was loved very well by Apo, and he always said of him, "If there is anyone after Mahsun Korkmaz (Korkmaz is still viewed as the most important spiritual commander of the HPG) whom I would have succeed me, it would be Kemal." He was elected to the PKK's Central Committee membership when he was only 22 years old. That is how talented he was. But Şemdin was jealous. That's why he was dismantling Kemal's confidence on purpose.

When we reached Mawa, they were in mid-battle. The management team had come under attack in Tatvan when the province commander had gathered them together. Because the province commander had fought on the front lines, he was the first one wounded. There were two regional commanders and two platoon commanders with him at the beginning of the fighting. They had carried him somewhere safer. The province commander had said, "Lead our detachment of new guerrillas safely out of this unexpected battlefield. Leave me here. I will ask for only two volunteers to stay behind with me, and we will fight against the soldiers until you escape." They flatly refused, saying, "We will either die with you or we will get you out of here with us." One of the former guerillas took the new ones out of the skirmish. The rest of the command echelon died. I mean a full 21 senior officers were killed there. All because Şemdin had been envious of a man better than himself and goaded him into becoming a pointless sacrifice.

As incredible as that level of treachery was, Şemdin's mistakes were not limited only to that situation. He also visited the province of Serhad around that same time. We had a force of almost 600 in Serhad. After he stayed there for a week, he went to the district of Dersim, and was put in charge there. Then, for no apparent reason, he contacted the province of Serhad and invited all the command echelon to come to Dersim for a meeting. Everyone was shocked. They pointed out that they had all just been together a week prior and wondered why he had not told them then whatever it was he wanted to share now.

So, suddenly, the entire command echelon had to move to Dersim in the middle of the winter, right at the time when such movement is hardest to conceal. During this journey, the whole company got trapped in an ambush and were martyred. Imagine! The entire command echelon! Every company commander, each of the battalion commanders, the regional commander, the province commander, and all of the province commander's assistants. Each and every one of these distinguished and rare leaders was killed there in one single ambush. Immediately after they were all killed, the entire Serhad province force of 600 guerrillas was also liquidated. The security forces had noted their opportunity. Realizing that all the commanders were dead, they took their chance to kill all the now-leaderless guerillas. Indeed, they killed almost 300 guerillas before they were stopped. This was all because of the criminally irresponsible behavior of one idiot. Zeki!

Zeki then went to Dersim, and Dersim suffered the same fate. In fact, the entire leadership cadres of Serhad, Dersim, Amed, and Barzan districts were liquidated because of him. After these incidents, he was recalled to the south to justify his actions. We guerillas did not know at the time, but Apo and the senior officers had sent Zeki to the northern provinces on purpose. Because of the incident that took place in Bitlis in 1993 (with the 33 martyred Turkish soldiers) the organization had developed its suspicions about Şemdin. Everyone was wondering whether Şemdin had any connection with the JITEM [Turkish gendarme intelligence unit] or other intelligence units in Turkey, because by this time we had heard many times that Şemdin Sakık had often spoken with Mahmut Yildirim [Code name Yeşil; a Turkish intelligent agent]. In order to clear up these doubts, Zeki was appointed with these critical missions. The organization used this strategy from its repertoire: If it suspected that one of its members was working for the government, it would paradoxically give that person even greater responsibility. Really this meant greater and larger opportunities to reveal their own weaknesses or deceptions. Oh, and how very closely organizational leadership would watch them then!

After all of these incidents, Şemdin was called back to the south and forced to remain at headquarters command for some time, but he kept on doing whatever he wanted. As the commander of our headquarters, he called a meeting of all the senior officers. Murat Karayılan, Duran Kalkan, Harun Atmaca and Halil Ataç (Bekir) were all present. Only Cemil Bayık and Apo were absent. Much to his surprise, the majority of comrades there began to criticize him directly. He had never heard their true opinions of him like this. He could not handle it and got very angry. "I did not invite you here to criticize me. I called you here to criticize yourselves!" he said. But before they could even start following his silly command, Şemdin started to pick each of them apart. He blamed one of them for being unsuccessful and a snob. He told this commander that he would destroy both himself and his province. Then, he told someone else that he was a weakling in terms of combat, and that he should have taken additional training to counter his cowardice. But the biggest load of criticism was directed at Murat Karayılan; "You want to steal my authority. You are planning to kill me and take my position. Learn your proper place, or I will teach it to you." Of course, everyone was shocked to hear such disrespectful paranoia. But there was nothing to do. Zeki was the commander of the headquarters so, nobly, they listened to him in perfect silence.

The senior officers of the party had reached their tipping point. They appointed Zeki as the field commander of Botan. How shameful. He was downgraded from the commander of all of headquarters, to the commander of a single field. In addition, our force in Botan was in a very difficult situation at that time. All the villages had been evacuated of civilians, and the guerillas were having a very hard time having all their needs supplied. Procuring a few bags of flour, cheese, and bread was almost more difficult than destroying a military station. There was also no drinking water. This was their purpose in sending Zeki to such a difficult field. It was a test of his ego. Senior officials wanted to see whether the self-important Zeki would work under such conditions. Then, as an extra insult, they appointed the comrade previously in command of Botan field (Murat Karayılan) as commander of our headquarters. Şemdin had been passing through Cudi Mountain, when he was appointed to be the Botan field commander.

For each and every one of these reasons, I hated Şemdin. And there I was in Cudi, hearing my comrades tell me that this same Şemdin was now going to visit the area. I asked them how one could pass into Iraq. It was only 9:00 a.m., so they were curious as to why I wanted to know so far in advance of my planned trip. In order to quell any doubt about my intent in the mind of the Cudi guerilla force, I said, "We will set off tomorrow evening, you had better describe the way to me during the day, so that we do not lose our path to Iraq."

Guerillas described the area to me. This is how you cross the border; this is what the passage area looks like, and so forth. We had lunch, and around 11:00 a.m. I told the Cudi commander, "Good bye. We are setting off now." The commander replied, "Are you crazy? How could you leave at such a time as this, and during the day? We have difficulty passing over the border even during the night." I said, "Look, I would rather die than see that moron, Şemdin."

Kemal, the province commander, handed us two written reports as he said farewell to us. Both envelopes were closed and officially sealed. The Kemal commander had said that no matter what happened, even if there were only one person of our group of 16 who could flee an ambush or other catastrophe, the last survivor absolutely must take these reports to the party leaders. The reports were both about Zeki, and one of them was addressed to headquarters in general while the other was written directly to Apo. I was certain that if Zeki had seen me in Cudi, he would have taken the reports and any other information I had on me, since he knew I had come from the province. That's why I rushed away in the afternoon, although that province's leadership insisted vocally that we stay.

We ran straight into Şemdin's guards, just as we approached Hezir Stream. They had left Şemdin somewhere safer, thankfully, before bringing their horses to be watered. When they saw us, they wanted to know where we were going. "We're on our way to Damascus," I told them. Then, I asked, "Where is Zeki?"—as if I wanted to meet with him. So, they told us where Zeki was, at which point, we promptly ran off in the other direction ensuring our path took us nowhere near him. I had a strong desire never to have to hear his curses again. If we met again, I was likely to kill him. My revulsion of him was so strong, it had motivated me to take my unit over a border in the middle of the day. The border was so dangerous that our comrades usually waited and surveilled for weeks before attempting to cross and then only ever at night. Yet, when we crossed, there was not a single soldier or an intelligence officer to be seen!

After crossing the border, we went directly to the PKK battalion. They interrogated us, asking, "From where are you coming?" "We have just come from Cudi, heading to Damascus," we answered. They were suspicious. The commander of the battalion asked us when we had gotten underway. I said, "We set off this afternoon and we have just arrived here now." The commander was shocked and asked again, "So are you telling me that you just now crossed the border? During broad daylight?" Again I said, "Yes!" "I swear that is an incredible tactic!", he crowed. "Why have we been sending groups over only at night for years? Let's begin sending all our units over the borders in broad daylight, since the border is apparently wide open!" I said, "Comrade, please exercise caution in imitating me on this. Honestly, I really do not know whether the border was empty or not. My aversion to Zeki was simply so strong I happily took the risk of dying."

Having safely crossed the border, we did not linger, but immediately went to Haftanin regional camp, and there we found a surprise. Zeki had contacted the Haftanin regional commander and told him to send my fellow comrade and me back to Cudi. Obviously, his intent was to take back the sealed reports from me before getting them to Apo. The commander of Haftanin could not do anything. "Comrade, we have to send you guys back. He gave us a strict order." It was our good fortune that Murat Karayılan, the headquarters commander, himself, happened to be listening in on the conversation just then. "Deniz won't go back to Cudi," we heard him say, "Because we are urgently waiting for him here at headquarters." Once headquarters spoke, there was nothing Şemdin could say against it.

Therefore, Murat Karayılan sent his own driver to fetch us from Haftanin. We had been planning to reach as far as the main headquarters in Zap, from the roads along Haftanin, Zaho, and Dohuk. If we walked, it would have taken us seven to ten days. But, it would only take six hours by car.

I suddenly decided that I wanted to drive. So, I took over the car from the driver. Just my luck, I caused an accident at the entrance of Zaho, Iraq. I had not driven for a long time. A curve appeared as I was speeding, and the car flew off the road and hit a house. The steering wheel impacted my chest very badly. Comrades immediately took me to the hospital. I was treated in Dohuk Hospital for two days. After I was released, we finally continued on to headquarters command.

The instant we reached headquarters, I found Murat Karayılan. He immediately asked me for the reports, and I turned them over to him. He was a bit angry with me because of the accident. "You had not driven for a long time and all you're used to is mules. Why in the world would you choose to drive now? Thanks be to God, you all are okay." Finally, he was able to read the reports I had taken such pains to deliver intact. After reading over the reports, he realized one was for general headquarters and one was for Apo. He said, "Take this one back. You can give it to Apo when you reach him."

Karayılan then asked me about the losses sustained in our province. "When is the last time you bought an electronic gadget in your region?" I told him the month we last bought the gadget in question and told him that everyone in all the regions bought these gadgets at the same time. "We have suspicions about these gadgets," he told me. "The enemy might have placed bugs in them."

"Comrade, these losses are not because of a secret bug, or an inefficient style of moving, or even an information leakage from headquarters. The blame for all these mistakes lie with Şemdin and with you," I said. Naturally, he got angry when I said this. He demanded to know how they could be the ones to blame. So, I enquired, "Comrade, when Şemdin was the commander of our headquarters, did not you listen to the conversation he had with Kemal?" He replied that he had not, so I said, "Please listen to that conversation, and you will find out the truth of the matter."

If that province commander had so chosen, not one single person from his leadership echelon would have been martyred that day. How could 18 inexperienced, brand-new comrades have been saved, including all their weapons, but nearly two dozen of the most experienced commanders in our organization somehow succumb to being martyred? Leaving all of this aside, a province commander would never have led a charge into a battle in the first place. Not even a company commander would fight in the front. Zeki had berated province commander Kemal so badly that his entire command staff officially committed suicide, by rushing to the front.

The Arrest of Şemdin Sakık

My friend and I were staying at the barracks of the guerilla training school in Zap region, Iraq. We were waiting for audience, for duty, and for assignments. Meanwhile, seeing as we had nothing to do, I visited the hospital in downtown Zap. The doctors checked the wound on my head, but in the end they advised me to see a professor in Damascus, Syria if I were to go there soon.

At the beginning of August, when Murat Karayılan's messenger had called me, he had also contacted 14 other guerrillas. Karayılan told us that we were being tapped for an important task, but he gave no explanation. I looked at the people around me. We were all guerillas of commanders' rank. I started to consider the importance of this task, which required so many high-level commanders. I asked Murat Karayılan, "Comrade, may I please ask you about this task? What is the nature of this mission, exactly?" "It's a chore you will love!" Karayılan said, and then laughed. That was when he informed us that we were setting out to arrest Şemdin. "Arrest! Let me emphasize that," Karayılan stressed. "I am specifically prohibiting you from killing him. Arrest only!"

We were all instantly euphoric. Meanwhile, Karayılan had contacted Şemdin and called him back to headquarters, since he was now officially under inquiry. Our entire cadre of commanders was going to Botan, straight from headquarters, to arrest Şemdin, the moment we saw him. When Şemdin first heard this from Karayılan, he began objecting strenuously, "Who do you think you are to question me? Nobody has the right to question me! I am not coming to the south, and that is the end of the matter!" Şemdin was being so insubordinate that Karayılan immediately told Cemil Bayık what was going on. When Cemil Bayık heard that not only was Şemdin resisting the trip down to the south but was even refusing to answer questioning, Cemil Bayık took the radio himself and said directly to Şemdin, "Get yourself to headquarters now, Zeki. I will meet you there."

The reason that Şemdin had rejected Murat Karayılan's direct order to return was simply his fear of the headquarters command team. Şemdin was terrified they would execute him in secret. So, when Cemil Bayık intervened, he was greatly relieved. Cemil Bayık is a symbol of reason. All guerrillas knew this, just like they knew that if Cemil Bayık promised something, he always kept his word. So, Şemdin must have thought, "If Cemil Bayık is there, then nothing underhanded will happen to me."

It was strange to be traveling in vehicles again so soon. But the fifteen of us reached Haftanin camp in three trucks. We were going to arrest Zeki in Besler region after crossing to Cudi from Haftanin. Each day, we turned on the big radio that we had, and received information regarding Şemdin's location. One night, just when we were about to reach Cudi, we got the update. "Go to the Hakkari border, Şemdin is coming through Hakkari!" This was bad news. There was no way we could get there in time. The new location was just too far from where we were. In addition to that, there were very many points along that road which were not at all safe for us.

We also moved to the new route by car. There had been a serious fight between the organization and the KDP in 1995. The KDP had received a big defeat in this fight, and had been compelled to accept every condition the organization had set for it. According to the conditions of the agreement, the PKK was going to conduct political missions in cities with the guerillas and establish guerilla stations next to Peshmerga stations. No limitations or restrictions by the KDP would be countenanced. Each and every one of the provinces and cities had accepted this agreement, except one province. The leader of that city was the chief of a tribe and was opposed to this agreement. In every public platform, he was expressing his strong opposition to it. This chief was vocally telling the guerillas that they should never again enter his region (Begova); otherwise he would order his men to kill them.

Bad luck! We had to use the Begova road to cross through the border of Hakkari, because that's where Şemdin had gone. At that time, Begova was close to declaring its independence. They left the PKK alone, and did not even recognize the authority of the KDP. Theirs was a town of only 2,000 people. Yet, at the entrance of the city they halted our trucks and told us we could not pass. No matter how hard we argued, we could not convince them to let us through. Finally, the Metina province commander told them to go and bring their chief.

When the chief arrived, our commander told him, "Listen, we are only going to use the road and go to Hakkari. We won't stay in the city. We won't conduct any political or guerilla mission at any point." Again we received a negative response, upon which our commander placed a single call. I do not know what kind of order he gave, or to whom, but instantly they opened the road. They gave us an escort of three cars ahead of us and three cars behind. This was how we reached the area of Kaşura, in other words Çukurca. There, we began to wait for Şemdin. We had already been informed by radio that Şemdin was going to cross the border that same night. It was 6:00 a.m. in the morning, when Zeki and his men crossed into Iraq. There were a full company of guards in place with Şemdin, to protect him.

Our platoon commander delivered the note to Şemdin, which headquarters had written. I did not know what was in the note, but after reading it, Şemdin asked, "You won't tie me up, will you?" The Metina commander said that he would not, but informed him that "we do need to take back your weapon." Şemdin had a Smith and Wesson brand weapon. He unholstered it and gave it to his chief bodyguard, telling him, "From now on, this is your gun. Take good care of it. It's quite expensive." Then, we prepared to leave and saw Semdin's bodyguards preparing to come with us. Our commanders approached them and said, "Your mission is over. Hang around here for a few days, and then you can go on to the headquarters." They got very angry upon hearing this. Our commander saw this, and said very calmly, "Do not resist, or we can arrest you, too, if you like. So, how about not making any trouble?" (Actually, our commander was wrong in this stance. We should not have taken Şemdin, without explaining everything to his guards, because they were the ones responsible for Şemdin's protection.)

With Şemdin secure, we drove first to Amediye, in Iraq. We decided to eat in a nice restaurant in the tourist area of Amediye. The windows of the cars were tinted dark black, not see-through. We were getting out of the cars, and Şemdin was about to get out also. But once he looked outside, he told me to call my commander and warn him, "It's a bad idea for me to get out of the car. All of those Turkish journalists know me. Trust me, it's better if they never know I'm here." Then, we also recognized Namık Durukan and some other well-known journalists, who were all waiting on the other side of the road. That was when we found out that the organization had decided to give some Turkish captives back to their families that day. The journalists were there to report the moment of delivery. There were also high-profile deputies, such as Haşim Haşimi and Fethullah Erbaş from Turkey. Our commander had to accept Şemdin's wisdom in this. "All right. Then stay in the car and we will send you food."

After the meal, we drove directly to headquarters. Rıza Altun welcomed us. He first thanked us, then told us, "Leave the comrade Şemdin [Zeki] with us and go see Murat Karayılan." He called out to two guards, "Take Şemdin to the cave and tightly bind his hands and feet." They had prepared a room in the cave just for him. And Şemdin could not utter a word against this. He just asked if he could see comrade Cuma. Rıza said, "Not now. You can see him later." (Cemil Bayık [Cuma] was in fact in Damascus, but Şemdin did not know this.)

When we went to meet Karayılan, we learned that five additional people including two senior commanders had been arrested. These two commanders had divided the forces between them when Karayılan was the headquarters commander. They had taken control of the guerrilla forces in Botan and

Zagros, while Şemdin had controlled the guerilla forces in the north. They also arrested three females, who used to work in the headquarters command. So, in 1996, Zeki and all of his confederates were arrested.

Five days later Zeki was arrested, and a ceremony was held for delivery of our Turkish hostages back to their families. The battalion in the school, the female battalion, and about 400 unassigned guerillas gathered at the ceremony Field. Fethullah Erbaş, who was the deputy in Turkey back then, made the first speech. Murat Karayılan also spoke on behalf of the party. "These soldiers have been our guests for two months. We will now return our esteemed guests safe and sound to their families," he announced. I do not remember the exact number, but I think there were about ten soldiers who were delivered to their families, one by one, to accompanying applause. Interestingly, two Turkish soldiers took the microphone to say, "We do not want to go back, we want to join the organization." One of them was a sergeant, and the other one was a new recruit in the Turkish army. (The sergeant is still in the organization. He has been serving at the administration level. I do not know what happened to the younger soldier.) Everyone went back to their families except for these two. And the journalists took pictures the whole time.

The Assassination Attempt Against Apo

It was during this same period that a new negotiation process had begun between the PKK and Turkey. The Turkish President, Erbakan, had sent Apo a letter. In this letter, Erbakan penned his wish to hold negotiations for a peace, as there had been in Özal's time. The organization accepted this offer at first, but the ceasefire was very brief. It was canceled in May of 1996. The reason for this was simply that, during the peace process, an assassination attempt was made against Apo. In response, Apo made a very sharp speech and canceled the ceasefire. He declared, "You first placate us, telling us to solve this problem with negotiations. Meantime, you also try to eliminate the leadership. Your truce is not sincere. From this point forward there is no ceasefire!"

Now, the organization runs two schools in Damascus, Syria. Education in one of them is taught in Turkish, and at the other is delivered in the Kurdish tongue. Training was also given in houses which Apo had bought in Damascus and Halep. On the day that this assassination was scheduled, Apo had intended to teach in the Turkish school, but he did not attend this class for some reason. He went somewhere else. Cuma gave the training instead. The school was located on a vast campus, surrounded with walls and wired fences, 3 meters high. There were Syrian officials stationed close to this complex. It was not a place where people could easily come and go undetected.

The security of the camp perimeter was provided by Syrian troops and their intelligence service. They patrolled around the camp 24 hours every day. Moreover, whenever Apo was in residence, a Syrian military helicopter would fly over the camp for extra insurance. Apo was extremely well guarded.

But on the day of the assassination attempt, in the entrance of a narrow street next to the school, a Mercedes full of bombs had been parked and left in front of a home where an Arab family lived. Their suspicions were aroused concerning the car, so they approached the school security guards and asked them if they had left the car there. Both security guards approached the car and inspected it. There was no one inside and the doors were locked. They came back to the compound area and informed the management. Just then, the car was detonated, and 15 meters of the wall around the camp was obliterated. Every piece of glass in the camp broke into pieces, from the force of the blast.

Much later, we learned that this cowardice was conducted by some Turkish military officials to spoil the peace process. Suddenly, two high-ranking Turkish commanders were fired, effective immediately. We became more and more shocked with every new detail we learned about this attack. The Turkish military authorities bought off the Syrian intelligence officers. Furthermore, the KDP and the YNK had supported this assassination attempt. Eventually, it came out that Turkey, the KDP, and the YNK all signed an agreement in Dublin in 1995 to destroy the PKK. They even had the blessing of the United States. This assassination plan was framed there at that time.

How interesting to watch the subsequent disputes which emerged within the government of Turkey. Prime Minister Çiller blamed the leader of the opposition party, Mesut Yılmaz, for giving Apo advance information about the operation. Rumors emerged that Mesut Yilmaz worried that Çiller would get more votes if the assassination had succeeded and had informed Apo about the assassination attempt ahead of time. I do not know how true any of the particular rumors were, but I know that Apo did not attend his class that day. There is no doubt that someone must have told him beforehand.

So, on May 6, 1996, for the first time in the history of the party, we conducted a self-sacrifice mission. I do not know what celebrations there were on June 10, but for some reason the Turkish soldiers had organized a magnificent ceremony. Maybe it was for the liberation of Tunceli. The official government report listed that seven senior officers from the Turkish Armed Forces' command echelon lost their lives that night.

Who performed this mission? A female comrade named Zeynep Kınacı (nickname Zilan) was the first self-sacrifice in the party. I would like to draw your attention to the distinction that it was not actually a suicide mission. The organization did not consider such acts to be suicide missions, and did not describe them that way. To us, a suicide attack means "dying for nothing, without any plans or goals." But a self-sacrifice mission is not so. It is strategized, voluntary, and deliberate. The mission gives a direct message. "If you attempt such assassinations against us, we have the power to perform similar targeted missions against any level of your officials that we so choose and at any place across Turkey."

Such missions had been prohibited until then. In all his orders and trainings, Apo always underscored the fact that, "We do not fight with the Turkish public. Ours is not a fight against the Turkish people. It is against the government and the system. There is no such thing as taking the civilians as captives or hurting a bureaucrat or a deputy." However, after this spiteful assassination attempt against Apo, the government needed to be sent a message. This message found its address through Zilan's courage. "If you do not obey the rules of war, neither will we. We will perform self-sacrifice missions all around Turkey."

Let's be clear. Zilan volunteered. She had written three letters prior to undertaking this mission. One was for Apo, one for her family, and one for her friends. All over the Turkish media, claims were made that Zilan had psychological problems—that the organization used her illness for its own interests and forced her into this. They lied. How could you ever force anyone to carry out such a personal mission? You cannot. The fact that this act was on the agenda of the press for days, was a sign of new tactics emerging in the organization, in response to the state. If the Turkish army performed traitorous acts anywhere in the future, the organization was prepared to retaliate with self-sacrifice missions in different cities.

Simultaneously, with this mission, another mission was performed against the security forces in Zagros. The assassination attempt against Apo enraged us guerrillas a great deal. We were fixated on somehow taking our revenge. The management of Zagros province had placed mines and bombs several months before, across a vast area, to be used in future guerrilla missions. The Zagros force had done months of surveillance to determine the locations where the security forces took their positions during their land operations. They chose their entrapment positions well, in case a land battle erupted. Mines were placed in every possible target area. Following the assassination attempt, Zagros province forces carried out a few bursts of harassing fire in order to draw the security forces into the minefield. Just as the province forces had planned, the security forces came out into the field where the guerillas had emplaced the mines. Our comrades then blew up the mines. All at once, nearly 70 soldiers were killed. This action was voted to be our best mission of the year. Before this one, our missions against the soldiers had been only simple assault missions, engaging them with only light harassment fire, or placing as few as one or two mines on their roads. When these tactics proved to be so successful, such missions and techniques were used more often in the following years. We got serious!

Duran Kalkan, the Headquarters Commander

Meanwhile, as all these incidents were taking place, I was still trying to get to Damascus. Once, while I was preparing again to go to Damascus, another conflict emerged between the KDP and the organization. The KDP martyred two of our comrades. Upon hearing this, the headquarters command ordered all the forces along the southern border to take up their attack positions. There were 210 guerillas in the school where I stayed back then. I only knew the name of Duran Kalkan. I had not yet met him, but I knew that he had been appointed as the headquarters commander back when Şemdin had been arrested and brought back there. This was the same time that Murat Karayılan had been appointed as the field commander for Botan.

So, while in the school, waiting to go to Damascus, the leadership gave me a force consisting of 20 females and 40 males. They said, "Take them to headquarters with you. They will tell you there where to go." This force consisted of company, battalion, and platoon commanders, but I would not accept them. "Look," I said, "there are more experienced comrades here than myself. They know this area better than I. They can take them wherever you want." But leadership would not accept my excuse. When I accepted the fact that this assignment was going to stick, the first thing I did was give those officers the report I carried; the one which was addressed to Apo. This would be safer, I felt, in case I ran into any fighting. I charged them to take the report to Damascus and give it directly to Apo, as soon as they possibly could.

I then took that detachment to headquarters. As I mentioned, I had never before seen Duran Kalkan, the headquarters commander. So, I asked two comrades in the headquarters to describe Duran Kalkan to me. They told me that he was tall, bald, and old. Therefore, 60 of us were sitting in the dark, patiently waiting for Duran Kalkan to arrive. We had heard that he was talking to Apo on the phone. There was a man from Syria sitting next to me. He knew that I did not know Duran Kalkan. So, whenever he saw someone old and bald, he would tap me on my arm and say, "Comrade, there is Abbas (the nickname of Duran Kalkan)." Each time, out of respect, I would shoot up to my feet. But then I would look around me, and there would be no one else standing. He was teasing me. Finally, at around 11:00 p.m., Duran Kalkan really arrived, and the Syrian pointed him out to me. Of course, I thought he was fooling me again, so I did not stand. When I saw everyone else standing up, waiting in silence, I stood up immediately.

They had turned on the generators to power the lights for the meeting room. Since I did not know Duran Kalkan in person, I told the Syrian to answer, if he asked any questions. Duran Kalkan then spoke. "You have a hierarchy right? Everyone knows his leaders and platoon." The Syrian replied "Yes!" to whatever Duran Kalkan asked. Too late I learned that he did not know much Turkish and did not fully understand what Duran Kalkan was asking him. I was thinking to myself that the Syrian was lying. We did not have any clear organization. There were no assignments into squads, teams or companies. Nothing. Everything was undefined. Duran Kalkan then said, "Okay! Then, you will go to the parade ground tomorrow. There, I will tell you the areas to which you will be assigned."

I was angry with the Syrian after Duran Kalkan left. I took our group and started to arrange the squads, teams, and company. I told them, "Look. I'm going to count you off, person by person, and whoever gets the number ten will be the unit commander. Whoever gets the number 21, will be the platoon commander." What else was I supposed to do? I did not know anyone. "One, two, three, four, five…ten," I counted. "Comrade, you are the commander of these ten people. Get to know your comrades. I give you ten minutes! Get acquainted with each other; arrange your hierarchy," I said. Through counting like that, I appointed three platoon commanders. I was the company commander. Under me, I had two male and one female platoon commanders.

This was the way things stood by the next day when we went to the meeting place and found the local forces of 150 ready and waiting. I had not known anything about this. We all sat down. Pointing to our force, Duran Kalkan said, "The leader of this force should rise." I stood. He looked at me, and said, "Unless I remember incorrectly, you were not the leader last night." "No, another comrade had stood for me," I admitted. "As I had never seen you before, I wanted to take your measure first," I confessed. Duran Kalkan replied angrily, "Who do you think you are? Do you need an interpreter or a consultant to talk to us? How could you make someone else talk to me while it was you, the whole time, who was the leader of the team?" I remained silent, waiting.

He asked me if we had a hierarchical order (unit, platoons, etc.) when we were sent from the headquarters. Somebody must have complained about us, I realized, as soon as he asked the question. There must have been some order or task we had failed, of which we had not been aware, because we were new. Obviously, we had been caught, so there was no sense in trying to cover up our mistake now. So, I loudly shouted, "No!" "Then why did your assistant say 'Yes?'" Duran Kalkan demanded. "Comrade," I replied, "he is from Syria. He does not speak any Turkish. He simply said, 'Yes!' to everything you asked." "Well, do you have a hierarchy now?" he demanded. "Yes," I told him. "We arranged it last night." He asked how that had even been possible. I told him exactly what we had done, randomly counting off. This got Duran Kalkan upset again. "What authority do you think you have to determine an entire organizational structure so haphazardly? How can you build an entire hierarchy of command in so few as 15 minutes?" he yelled at me, in front of all the guerillas.

I felt so offended at being called on the carpet in front of every single member of our forces. It would have been acceptable, had I only been dressed down in front of the force I had arranged, since they already knew the situation. But this was the entire local force of 150 people. The guerillas were forming their first impression of who I was. I needed to salvage my pride, so before Duran Kalkan even finished his speech, I interrupted with, "Comrade, just let me tell you something. This Syrian comrade replied 'yes!' to you, so as not to disappoint you. When he said yes; he committed us, so then I was forced to make such an arrangement as I did. I am not familiar with anyone in this force. I have no connection to any of them. The leadership of the school told me to take them here to headquarters, and that's what I did. I am sure their previous rank structure was pretty much the same. After all, it does not really matter which one is assigned to be the platoon commander or the team commander, so long as they each do their jobs. I had a problem, and this was my answer to it. With unfamiliar guerrillas, what else could I have done to create a new structure in the amount of time I had? Their system is more or less unchanged."

Of course, Duran Kalkan became even more frustrated. "Who do you think you are to speak to me like that?" he shouted. I could not take his attitude anymore so I addressed him again, "Look, comrade, I was told to take this force to headquarters. I brought them here safely and here they are. I am turning them over to you. My mission is now over. I do not care how you arrange them from here, or whom you will appoint to what position." With my speech done, I deliberately sat down. Duran Kalkan was furious. "Stand up!" he ordered. "How dare you sit without my permission? Who the hell do you think you are? Who gave you this mission? How could they assign someone like you to a team of 60 people?" I stood up again. "Look here comrade Abbas, if this is your approach to things, then I will leave this meeting now." There were two people from the leadership echelon who had come with him. One of them was male (Ali Sapan) and the other one was female. They called a ten-minute cigarette break for all assembled. After this break, I did not rejoin the meeting. I was just sitting alone when one of Abbas' personal guards came up to me, and said, "He is specifically calling you, so come back to the meeting area." I said, "Go and tell him that I refuse to join the meeting." And I did not go.

In five minutes, the same guard returned, and said, "You are hereby ordered to return immediately to the meeting area. He has something to tell you." This time, I went. Regardless of my personal feelings, he was the headquarters commander, and what I had done had been disrespectful. He asked me to stand and inquired as to why I had become angry. "Comrade," I addressed him. "Again, I know no one from this guerilla force. Officials at the school ordered me to bring them here, and that is what I did. Many of them, I have never seen before. How can I evaluate what rank they should have? Random assignment would be just as effective. So, I counted them, and I chose the commander of the platoon or the unit based on specific numbers, which I had assigned."

Of course, Abbas was calmer then. "Such cover-ups are wrong," he stated. "At least you should have stood up that night and revealed that the speaker did not know much Turkish, and that you did not have any rank system or orders." That was it. This was how that incident was amicably settled.

For the record, out of those 60 comrades, only two had their assignments changed. The rest remained the same. So, all that swearing and insulting and chest-beating had happened for nothing. One of those changes was a ranked officer, who was already a battalion commander, who was demoted to a unit commander that day. This had offended him, and that's why he changed places with the battalion commander. And those were the only two re-assignments.

10

WAR AGAINST BARZANI'S PESHMERGHAS

And so Abbas appointed me as the commander of this company and sent us to a hill in Zap region in Iraq, to fight against the KDP. We were having a lot of difficulty, especially in October of 1996, when the KDP was receiving support from Turkey. The Turkish aircrafts were constantly bombarding our camps. Once they saw that our southern camps were surrounded by Dochka anti-aircraft weapons, their planes would not approach as closely as they had. They would send long-range bombs at us from a distance and then turn tail. These bombs were unable to hit their targets, or they were disabled before they hit.

But, as with most things in this conflict, the situation was soon to change. The Zap area was a vast basin of 20 kilometers in length, surrounded by hills. Every hill was crowned with Dochkas. We were safe. However, this situation eventually turned against us. I may never know the truth of it, but we had received intelligence, which indicated that the Israeli aircraft were flying surveillance missions above us in league with the Turkish planes. We heard that these Israeli pilots were training the Turks in their tactics for how to disable or evade the anti-aircraft weapons we had mounted on the hilltops. In fact, 15 days after this intelligence report, an intensive air attack occurred. The aircraft were bombing the valley by running in lower than the level of our guns, and then flying back.

Since our anti-aircraft weapons were placed on the tops of the hills, we could not do anything, because Dochkas do not shoot downwards. We began taking many losses, due to this new tactic the Turks were using. On my team alone, we had three martyred, and 16 seriously wounded. Some of them had their feet ripped off and some were blinded—injuries of a type that, even if they were treated expertly, would prevent that guerrilla from ever fighting again.

We had to find a solution; otherwise we were going to lose many comrades. We began by placing four smaller-sized Dochkas inside the valley walls themselves. When the Turkish aircraft repeated their trick of diving into the valley, these four Dochkas started shooting simultaneously at one of them. When the aircraft was shot this way, it flew higher to escape, which then placed it in the sites of the Dochkas above, and these higher Dochkas shot the aircraft again. In this manner, we managed to disable the aircraft. If I am not mistaken, this particular one fell down near the city of Batman in Turkey. After this incident, the pilots stopped using this tactic they had learned from their Israeli counterparts. They still flew above the camp area a few times, but their weakened attacks were not as dangerous anymore. We knew now that such attacks were not as harmful.

By the end of October, the KDP indicated that they wanted to make peace. They informed us that two of the PKK militants they had killed were by mistake; that it had been an individual mission, and that the responsible parties had already been punished. It was just an excuse, because we knew the KDP had already been worn down by the war in 1995. The PKK had performed simultaneous missions on their 23 stations and conquered them all. Even the YNK (the military forces of Jalal Talabani) had invaded Erbil by taking advantage of the newly weakened status of the KDP. With the beginning of the peace negotiations, I was no longer needed in the field. Consequently, I finally went back to the school at the beginning of November. The leadership of the school called me on the evening that I was waiting to be sent to Damascus. Seyit Fırat and Ali Sapan, who were currently working as political activists in Turkey, were the heads of the school management back then.

They told me, "Comrade, you are to be trained for a serious mission, and you need to go to the headquarters as soon as possible." I asked them if they knew about what the mission entailed and, interestingly, they said they did not. I asked if I were going there alone, and they told me that another comrade was to go with me, naming the person. It was the woman with whom I was in love—Sevin. I was both happy and fearful. I worried for her safety, if it were to be a dangerous mission. At the same time, I was happy at this further opportunity for us to be together. Again, I asked Seyit Fırat what our mission might be. "We know nothing," he repeated. Of course, both Sevin and I began worrying in earnest about whether they had learned of our relationship.

Regardless, orders were orders. We set off in the evening. Since the location of headquarters had been changed, they gave us two guides to take us there. We reached the headquarters at midnight. When we arrived, an official directed Sevin to the female barracks and indicated that I should go to the male unit. Before this guy even finished speaking, I asked him again why they had called us there. Paradoxically, when he said it was not urgent and that we could speak about it later, it made me even more curious.

As ordered, I headed to the male barracks. There was no one inside, only a caregiver. He brought me food, made me tea, and attended to my other needs. "Comrade," I asked him, "Surely, you of all people must know why they called us here?" I was practically demanding the answer. "Comrade," he placated me. "I really do not know. All they said to me was, 'there is a guest. You should take care of him.' So, here I am." Then, a different person came up to my solo barracks on the evening of the second day. I knew this man. He had been the battalion commander in the city of Hakkari. They had told him no more than they had told me: "Go to the headquarters immediately. You have an important task." Together, we tried guessing what it could be. What kind of mission was it? Why were we they ones they had called? Had we made some kind of mistake, and this "secret mission" was their cover story to get us here to question us? We obsessed over every possibility. During our stay, two more people joined us on the evening of the fifth day. The information they had been given was identical to ours; no more, no less detail.

I do not remember precisely whether it was the sixth day or the seventh day, but while we were having breakfast in the morning, someone came inside our barracks and said, "Comrades, Abbas wants to see you." Four of us instantly got ready and left the barracks to meet with him. I saw that Sevin and another woman, unknown to me, were waiting there. Duran Kalkan, himself, turned to the group and said, "We're sending you to Damascus, but you won't say anything about this to anyone." I immediately asked, "For what reason do you want to keep our travel destination a secret?" His instant reply was, "Almost everyone wants to go see Apo in person for this training. So, to reduce the demands, we told everyone that the camp was closed, and that we no longer send anyone there. If they find out that we are sending you there, and we were lying to them, they will rebel. That's why it is a secret."

Before we left, Comrade Abbas said, "There is something else. There are six senior executives who have been arrested. Three of them are males (Şemdin Sakık, Ali Haydar Kaytan, and Hamili Yıldırım). Three of them are female. (I do not remember their names.) You will also see all these captives safely to Damascus. One of us said, "Are we six people enough to escort and guard these arrested seniors all the way to Apo? We might have trouble in terms of security." Abbas replied, "There won't be a security problem. You will travel by car. For your safety, you will be escorted by two trucks full of Peshmerga teams. [These were soldiers who fight for Barzani.] Our comrades in Syria have been informed of this as well, so another two cars will be waiting for you there."

And this is how we set off, escorting the captives, on November 7, 1996. Şemdin was very nervous. He was afraid of Apo, because Apo had given him many responsibilities, all of which he had ruined. During the last two years, Şemdin was given the authority to supervise and control all of the states within Turkey. He was assigned as the head commander of Botan Field, and he was even assigned as the leader of headquarters command. However, he had abused his authority in all of this duties. Apo was definitely going to call him to account for his sins. He was so nervous, he sounded pathetic as he spoke to us.

During this trip, Şemdin asked me if we had ever talked before. I said, "No!" I still had absolutely no desire to talk with him. He asked me from which region I came. I said, "I'm staying somewhere or other. It's not important right now." He kept insisting and was really getting on my nerves. So, I told him the truth. He asked me again if I were positive that we had not talked before. I saw no point in hiding it now. "We did have a conversation on the radio in the spring of 1996. You wanted a report from me and I would not write it," I said. He was quick, and instantly remembered the incident. Şemdin said, "It was you who berated me, was not it?" I replied, "Yes!" He asked me, "Why did you do this?" I was now angry again. "I was not going to teach you how the organization functioned. I should not have had to, since you were the one who had trained us on the rules, when we first joined. You knew you could not directly demand that I give you a report without the province commander knowing about it. I chewed you out because you made a mistake. In answering you that way, I could have been put in jail for months, but the epic scope of the mistakes you had made, gave me courage." Şemdin Sakık stopped cold for a long while. And then, laughing, he said, "So, sometimes people you bring up might be your downfall."

When we had crossed the Syrian border, we were taken to a house with the group who had welcomed us there. These people told us to stay with them that night; that they would come collect us the following morning, and we all would set off again. Around 9:00 a.m., a jeep belonging to the Syrian intelligence service came by. One Jeep! There were 12 of us! When we were about to ask them to provide us with another vehicle, they told us they would be sending an additional car in the morning.

This is how we came to stay there one more night. A Mercedes that Apo used came by the following morning, and we set off in these two cars. We were nervous. None of us had IDs, and there were checkpoints everywhere. The first time they stopped us was at the entrance of the city of Halep, in Syria. There was a Syrian man in our jeep. This man showed some special card to the police officers. It was not an ID, but I was not able to see what was written on it. When he showed it, the police officers stepped back and allowed us to pass. In this way, we sailed through all the checkpoints and reached Damascus.

We arrived at the field camp at 4:00 a.m. The guards told us that Apo was going to hold a class in the Turkish language school around 9:00 a.m., and that we should go there. So, we had breakfast and, when we were about to settle in for a rest, the guards announced that Cemil Bayık was waiting for us. The arrested officers thought Cemil Bayık would set them free. They got the opposite of what they hoped. As soon as they reached Bayık, they were all sent straight to prison.

But, with us, Bayık introduced himself. Then he turned to me, saying, "Comrade, I am thinking I remember you from somewhere." "That's right," I agreed. "I was your guard for three weeks in the Haftanin camp in 1992." He told me, "You have changed a lot. I did not realize that you were still alive." I smiled at him, and said that I was still very much alive. Then, Bayık turned to us all and said, "Apo will come here tomorrow. Be ready for him by 10:00 a.m." We all headed towards the door, and I was just about to leave when he added, "Deniz, you stay!" I went back over to him, and he asked for the situation report on my province. "Comrade, explain to me why you had so many losses from your executive echelon? We understand that Şemdin berated your province commander until he killed himself, but how could the Turkish military know where commander Kemal had gone? Do you think the headquarters had an insider agent working for the Turks, or do you think these radios that had recently arrived from Europe could have been wired with enemy surveillance devices? Is it possible?" he asked.

I said, "Comrade, do not think that these things are true." He asked me, "Why are you so sure they are not?" "Comrade," I said, "These radios were distributed to all areas over the entirety of the country. So, if it were the case that they were bugged, the security forces would be listening in on everyone. Out of so many compromised targets, why would they only follow the province commander Kemal? If a soldier found a vulnerability in us, they would never pass up a crack at a company commander, much less leave the province commander alive. And it's not plausible for there to be an insider agent in the region. Who would risk his own life to provide the military with such intelligence? No one would willingly go to their death. The only man spared by this attack was the single best officer under the province commander. We all knew him. He was a very good comrade. He was not a spy, so the two reasons you gave were not very plausible." He considered what I had said, and then asked, "Why did these deaths happen then?" I asked him if he had listened to what Şemdin had said to province commander Kemal on the radio. When he admitted that he had not, I told him everything. It was the first time he had heard any of it, and he asked if I were positive. I told him he should listen to the records. "I know which day the conversation between them took place. Ask for them to bring you the records."

Cemil Bayık was shocked to hear of all this. "Deniz," he commanded, "you will be here while we question him. I want you to stand up and tell everyone what he has done," I told him that Şemdin would answer none of my questions. "I am the chief executive of the inquisition," he informed me. "He has to answer my questions. Whatever you ask him in my presence, he is compelled to answer," he promised.

Two days after this conversation with Cemil Bayık, we were invited into Apo's presence to share lunch. We each introduced ourselves to Apo. This was the first time I had ever seen him in person. While he drank his tea, he asked me, "Are you the one who has come from Garzan province?" I replied, "Yes, sir. Sevin and I came from Garzan." I have mentioned before that Apo had loved the province commander Kemal very much. He asked me why his good friend Kemal had been martyred. I told him what I knew. He was not convinced, and said, "This story you have been telling me is not satisfactory, Deniz." "Sir," I protested, "Kemal was deeply shamed by what Zeki had said about him. If such a guilt trip had been placed on me, I would have either quit the PKK altogether or fought in the front lines in the very next battle." Apo got a bit angry when I said this. "That's the part I do not accept," he said. "How could a province commander commit suicide like this? Was it a noble solution? Who could possibly have benefited from his suicide?" He answered his own question: "Zeki would! A clever man would never have committed suicide. He would have known to protect himself, in order to inform us firsthand about Zeki's glaring mistakes. No, this 'suicide' must have been a mission against the party. Because, unless I have been deposed unknowingly, Şemdin is not the one who leads this party. If Kemal had been offended by what Şemdin said, he would have just given me a call and told me that he did not approve of this man, and then given his reasons. The idea that he committed suicide rather than address the issue itself is simply outrageous."

I interrupted him, "Sir, he had written a report to you. If it had reached you before that battle, he might still be here with us now." "The report arrived late," Apo countered, "but I made a point of talking to all provinces once a month. All the province commanders had the phone number for the direct line to Damascus. They could have called whenever they wanted, and asked for me. So, why did not my friend, commander Kemal call and ask to speak with me, since obviously Zeki was such a huge problem? My question is, did someone prevent him from doing so?" Apo was very frustrated. "Regardless, Zeki has been arrested. Everything will be revealed in the due course of time," he said. He turned to Cemil Bayık and said, "Establish a findings commission of three people and investigate this incident immediately. Clarify Şemdin's situation to the finest detail. We missed the chance to thoroughly investigate this man after that incident in 1993. If we had performed a good investigation; if we had done our jobs then, this tragedy would not have happened. Whatever sentence the committee decides on, at the end of this investigation, make it happen," he commanded. Then, he stood, and everyone left his room.

Mahsun Korkmaz Academy

I started my training in the Mahsun Korkmaz Academy in Damascus. In this academy, training is delivered to cohorts. When a cohort finishes the training, the comrades comprising that class are sent to the provinces in the north and south, as commanders, and another cohort starts their training. Each cohort consists of 180 people. I have mentioned that there were two different schools in Mahsun Korkmaz. One of them was taught in the Turkish language, while Kurdish is all that is spoken at the other. So, those who do not know Turkish still have the Kurdish school available, and are educated equally. Apo taught classes in both schools. He spoke Kurdish in the Kurdish school and Turkish in the Turkish school. There had been some propaganda, a long time before, saying that Apo was originally from Armenia, and he could not speak Kurdish. The Turkish public just swallowed that lie, without doing any research for themselves. I tell you; I was trained in both schools myself. Apo would sometimes lecture us in Kurdish for two hours.

We arrived at the camp as our future classmates were also arriving, at the start of a new cohort. Some students even came from Europe. They first had to fly into Iran, and then reach the camp field in Syria by ground routes, so as not to draw any attention. Traveling this way did not cause us as much trouble as we would have thought. We were even shipping our weapons from Europe by plane. It goes to show that you can do anything in this world, as long as you have money.

I guess it was the spring of 1997. There were obsolete Russian missiles called SAM-7s defending our southern border. We needed to replace them somehow. So, Strela brand missiles were brought from Russia. These missiles were first transported to Europe by plane, and then shipped directly to Syria. Once in Syria, they were distributed to all the other lines in the south. It turned out commercial shipping companies had few scruples.

Regarding my education at headquarters, it was just before I finally started my training under Apo and his friends in these exclusive schools, that Comrade Cuma called me in to his office. "You have a doctor's note in your file," he said. "So, now our medical team are asking if you need treatment. You're not sickly, are you?" he inquired. "No, this note is not about a disease," I assured him. "It's just that I took a wound to my skull in the last battle." "Then the first thing you will do tomorrow is to go to the hospital and get it professionally treated," he said. He assigned me a female comrade who spoke Arabic and sent us to a hospital in the city center. The organization had a prearrangement with this hospital in Syria. There was a special cadre of doctors who were reserved for us who received wounds in the countryside.

They arranged for me to be seen by a doctor who was also a professor. First he re-opened my wound as a crust had formed on it. He cleaned the cavity and then took measurements of the hole broken into my skull bone, and said, "We need to close this area, so come back in three days." Three days later, we returned. He had carved a piece of animal bone into the same size and shape as the wound-hole in my skull. He fitted this piece into the hole in my skull and closed my scalp back over it. The doctor told my comrade, "He should take precautions. If the environment gets too hot or too cold, he may feel a little vertigo." So, that is the story of how the wound on my head was treated.

They had accepted me into the Turkish school for my training. I was happy about this, because Cuma was giving most of the lectures in the Turkish school. He rarely gave lectures at the Kurdish language school.

During the training, he called for me, and I went up to his room. He asked, "How is your head wound these days? I said, "I do not have any problems. The wound on my head is much better." He announced, "We are going to appoint you as Apo's bodyguard. We have selected a group of you. You will all get trained in both close-proximity security and distant personal security. I will register you into that group." "Comrade," I answered. "I am honored, and I would love to be his bodyguard, but I have one condition. Let me first check out how difficult the training is. If I can, I will go through with it," I promised him. "But, if it is very demanding, I will give it up and come back to the camp." Cemil Bayık accepted this condition.

I had not been in Damascus even two weeks when I was reassigned to a location that looked like a farm. There were 18 of us there. All were experienced guerillas. There were two people from the Syrian intelligence service. They were Syrian, but they spoke perfect Turkish. They were our trainers, and their training regimen was intense. I could only endure it for a week. It was too heavy and tiring. For instance, consider the width of a Mercedes car. We were to open the car door for the official, then jump over the car, cross to the other side, and sweep our right and left fields of vision, using our weapon. Next, while walking on the road, in open fields, or between houses, the trainers would try to shoot us with plastic bullets, at which point we were to raise the suitcase they had given us always to carry and were to press the secret button on it. The suitcase was the armor, and when deployed, it covered the entire person's body. You also had to participate in heavy athletics to be in shape for all this work.

While I was going through this training, Comrade Cuma came by, and I approached him, admitting, "Comrade, I cannot do this training. I cannot do what they command. All this jumping over cars, opening armor… this is not my cup of tea." Cemil Bayık entreated me, "Look, do not you see that this is an opportunity for you? When you finish the training, you will be close to the Leader. You will have such access! You are worthy. That's why I chose you." I was very sorry to let him down, but facts were facts. "Comrade," I said to him. "I'm sorry, but I cannot do it. I would love to, but this is not something of which I am capable. I would feel so guilty if something were to happen to our leader, when I was his bodyguard." At this, Cemil Bayık tried convincing me a bit more, but the fight had gone out of him. When he saw that I would not change my mind, he said, "Okay, obviously you do not want it anyway."

That very day, I went back with him to the main camp. Later, I learned that only four of those 18 people had been chosen as Apo's bodyguards, and the rest had also been sent back. So, apparently the training was too hard for nearly everyone.

So, back in camp permanently, I attended the Turkish school, where Apo lectured us two or three times a week. Apo gave the lectures during the day, and sometimes would stay in the camp, and sometimes he would leave the camp after the training. On the days he was absent, the trainers he had hand-picked to run his academy gave the lectures.

Apo would casually play volleyball, and then soccer, after the training. Before I knew him, I was so worried about expressing myself around him. But the leader himself was coming up to us. He made himself so approachable that you would suddenly forget who he really was and begin to treat him as a friend. He would always care and always ask questions. We always felt free to answer. We would even have two-way discussions, just like peers.

At Mahsun Korkmaz Academy, none of the training was practical. It was all theoretical. For example, we would have a class called "Military Terms for War and the Army." Besides this, there were political and ideological lessons. Yalçın Küçük, a well-known professor in Turkey, would visit the camp once for each cohort and stay there for two weeks. He visited the camp when we were there and gave us a lesson called "The Truth About Apo." The training would take a half day, from 8:00 a.m. to 11:00 a.m. We were free after lunch. We could spend this free time reading a book or participating in social activities.

Sometimes, committees from abroad would visit the camp. They would not train us but examined how our training was delivered and asked whatever questions this brought up for them. They especially came to hear Apo's lectures. During my stay there, some official committees from England, Germany, and Greece visited. They stayed in Apo's own house with him.

This was all in the spring of 1997. One day, Apo was having a question and answer session with us trainees, instead of giving a lecture. First he would talk about a subject, then he would ask for our opinions. There were four German officials visiting during this lecture, and they were all very athletic. We were all very surprised that two of them could speak perfect Turkish. One of them raised his hand to ask a question. Apo responded, "Please ask!" The German explained, "I want to ask the room." Apo allowed, "Of course. You can ask your question to anyone and everyone you want." Now, there was a person named Selim Çürükkaya who had left the organization. While hiding from us abroad, he had written a book against Apo and the organization. The German turned to us all and asked, "Is it forbidden or allowed for you to read this book?" Apo turned to the whole classroom and said, "Whoever wants to answer this, just raise your hand." One of us stood up and said, "Let's go the library. We have the book. Whoever wants to read it can read it, of course," he said. The German then asked again, "Are you sure it isn't forbidden for you to read it?" Our comrade was surprised, "Don't you understand? If it were forbidden, why would we have it in our library? Whoever wants to read can read it, whenever he wants," he said.

The German turned back to Apo, and said that he wanted to ask another question. Apo allowed him to ask it. He said, "Under what circumstances would you forgive Selim Çürükkaya?" Then everyone understood that obviously, the German officials had come to the camp on behalf of Selim Çürükkaya. Apo was silent for a moment, but shortly said, "You had better leave and instead send the man who makes you ask this question. You do not know how we work. This organization would never leave someone alive once we have issued a death penalty in his name. Tell Selim that we have issued no death penalty. If we had, he would already be dead. He wrote bullshit about me, but that was okay. We honestly just did not have the time to waste on him."

The German interrupted once again and asked, "Then why did you kill Cemil Işık in Germany? He merely left your party. If, as you say, you have no time to waste on your defectors, then why did you execute this other guy in Germany?" Cemil Işık had been the commander of the moving battalions in the Botan Field between 1988 and 1989. He was someone who improved himself militarily. His nickname was "Hogir." Although he was a military genius, he caused the organization a lot of damage in those years. This man was the single main reason behind the increase in the number of rangers in the areas of Botan, Hakkari, Şırnak, and the surroundings. For example, in 1989, he executed two entire villages, complete with women and children, for no reason. Despite this cruelty, six tribal leaders in the region visited Cemil Işık to settle the issue and forget about all past mistakes. However, Cemil executed all of these well-respected leaders, even though they visited him as friends. Of course, the organization had no idea that any of this was going on. Moreover, his actions violated our rules. It is the policy of the organization that, if someone voluntarily visits you in peace, you cannot harm him, even if he is your enemy.

Directly after this incident, Cemil Işık was brought under internal investigation. Cemil Işık, Sarı Baran, Mehmet Şener, and Şahin Baliç had already formed a cabal against the management of the organization. While under inquiry for this, Işık ran away to save himself from the same fate befalling the rest of the cabal he had established. First, he took shelter in the Iraqi Government. While he was in Iraq, he contacted the organization twice, begging to be forgiven. Then, Cemil Bayık told him, "We do not have the luxury to give you forgiveness or not. You did not harm us, you harmed the peasants. Come back, and if the peasants forgive you, we will forgive you, too. But if they do not, we will carry out justice." But Hogir already knew that the peasants would never forgive him. That is why he left Iraq and asked the Turkish security forces to give him sanctuary. He switched sides, and between 1991 and 1992, he worked for the military units connected to the JITEM. It is well known that he had something to do with many extra-judicial killings during that period. I do not know how, but after this, he managed to run away to Germany. In 1994, he was noticed by a PKK sympathizer in Germany and was killed.

So, Apo related that story to the German official now in his classroom. "You see? There was no death penalty issued for him. We could have killed him when he was in Iraq, or in Turkey while he was working for the JITEM. A patriotic citizen noticed him and killed him without our knowledge or consent. That assassin was not from our team." The German said he was convinced, but Apo was angry at him nonetheless. "I thought you were our guest. You have abused our hospitality. If you want to visit here again, visit us as guests only. You, yourselves, are always welcome. But first you need to do your homework and get to know the organization. Do not come here again with stupid questions," he said. And that concluded class for that day. (The regular public could also visit the training camps from time to time. The local Syrian families would be our guests for a few days, touring the camp and conversing with our comrades.)

Misinformation About Admiration for Apo

During the founding years of the organization, very few Kurds were given the opportunity to study at university. Nevertheless, each Kurd who had been able to study there, and achieved a career afterwards, had joined our struggle. Apo had been a Turkish state official; Halil Ataç had been a teacher; Cemil Bayık was a historian; and Bahoz Erdal was a doctor… (There were hundreds of examples like that. Bahoz Erdal and Bashar Assad were classmates. They both studied in the same class at the same university, and

Bahoz Erdal graduated first in his class. Then, when he saw what Kurds had been through, he joined the organization. He left everything behind; money, a normal life, and his successful career.)

Sixty percent of those who joined the organization were Kurdish peasants. Most of these people had never even been inside a school. That's why Apo gave such importance to the concept of the peasantry. They were blank slates. But, thanks to the importance the organization gave to education and self-improvement, many peasants would gain enough knowledge to evaluate developments around the globe, not only in Turkey.

Apo would especially emphasize the impact of education on himself: "If I had not read Marx, I would most probably be an Imam [religious leader] now." The philosophy of the organization was Marxist, but there were people who prayed five times a day and fasted during the month of Ramadan. There were even women guerillas that wore headscarves. Everyone had freedom of choice; freedom of religion. They could believe whatever they wanted.

I witnessed this in person. In my very own unit, there were people who prayed and fasted. Also women with headscarves. On the other hand, there were guerillas who were atheists, who believed in no religion, and who ate pork without hesitation. The organization was not against religion. It was against the groups who used religion to take advantage of people. The senior officials told us many times, "Whatever religion you followed (Christianity, Islam or Buddhism), have it be transparent. Tell the public all the details about these religions. Then, let the public choose its own religion with full information, using their own will."

Especially in Turkey, our PKK organization was presented as an enemy of Islam. The reality was nothing like that. I heard Apo say many times, "Mohammed, was the greatest revolutionary of his era. No one but him could have managed to impress and transform such a tribal Arab community, and make them adopt a completely different life than the traditions they had known."

Apo used to say, "Before making a decision, learn the truth and details of everything. You should not have an unyielding opinion. For instance, today this is a tree. But tomorrow it may be firewood, or a table, a pencil, or a chair. It can change. So, there is no such thing as I was born this way and I will stay this way. Everyone changes, but the time and the style of the change is what's important." This was the main dialectic Apo adopted.

Yet, the local and the foreign media were spewing propaganda that said Apo would kill everyone who had the potential to suppress him. This was a disgusting lie! If that were Apo's goal, he would have killed Cemil Bayık. Bayık is one of the founders of this organization. After Apo, he is the man that everyone loved the most, in the organization, even though sometimes, he would not follow Apo's rules. After him came Duran Kalkan, Murat Karayılan, and so on down the leadership hierarchy. Each of these people had great authority in the organization. If Apo had not wanted anyone powerful around him, would he have left any of these people alive? If Apo were a dictator, would he not have killed Cemil Bayık before now? I personally heard Apo say many times over the radio, "I wish any one of you worked hard enough to remove this load of leadership from off my shoulders!"

Before making such accusations, one also needed to very closely investigate the executions in the organization. You cannot be enlightened by rumors alone. Apo did not approve any of the senior executions, except for three people: Şahin Baliç, Terzi Cemal (the man who had been responsible for the southwestern regions, before his direct relation with MIT—the Turkish National Intelligence Agency—was revealed), and I do not remember the third name. Apo approved the execution of those three people only. He had no foreknowledge of the executions of Kör Cemal, Adnan, Topal Nasir, or many other top PKK organizational heads.

Those assassinations aside, Apo felt highly disturbed by the executions we performed against the villagers. He once told me off harshly. While I was undergoing training at school in Damascus, I was occasionally assigned guard duty around Apo's house. There was a guard shack right in the corner of the garden. One day, while I was waiting in this shack, someone shouted, "Comrade, come here!" I looked around. The lights were on, but I could not see any one. Then, I heard the same voice saying, "I'm telling you, come down now." So, I went down to the cottage and saw Apo in front of me. He began to chat with me, asking many questions such as in which states and at which capacity had I served so far. I was giving short answers in order to brush him off and go back to my duty station. He understood what I was trying to do and asked, "Why aren't you giving proper answers to my questions?" "Sir, my duty station is empty. If you want, I can give you long answers another time." In the meantime, my superior on duty had realized that the guard shack was empty. There was a wall made of bricks, with holes in it, all around the property, and he had not seen me talking to our leader. He got angry and hollered from the other side of the wall, saying, "Why have you abandoned your duty station?" I responded, "The leader is standing here with me, and he called me down." Then the superior lost all his anger, and said, "Okay. I'm going up there, you can stay where you are."

Apo asked me tough questions about our uncontrolled missions against the rangers, back when that travel corridor was being opened into Botan Field. "Sir, in order to open that corridor, the ranger villages had to be disabled," I maintained. He got upset, and replied, "That corridor would have been opened one way or another, but how could anyone have employed such cruelty just to open a corridor? How could you kill that many people? I want to send you to the same region, but it worries me. Will you promise me that you won't do anything like that, ever again?" he entreated me. "Sir, I can promise you, on my behalf, but there will be actions which are still outside of the control of my command echelon," I explained. He got more frustrated. "You are a commander! You must know what's going on in your own unit. If any action by your unit happens outside of your control, then you are not the commander of that unit," he answered. I really took it to heart, this lesson from our leader.

One other of the biggest slanders about Apo is that he considered himself a God. Rumors existed that he had pictures of himself everywhere, from the classrooms to the corridors; from the kitchens to the restrooms. I can tell you, because I witnessed it, that before Apo was arrested, there was not a single picture of him anywhere. Not in the meeting rooms nor in the classrooms. In the meeting halls, there were only pictures of the founders of the organization, who were martyred in the early years—Cemal Bir, Mahsuni Korkmaz, Hayri Durmuş, Hakkı Karer and so on. The senior management allowed the pictures of Apo to be posted in the classrooms and meeting rooms only after he was arrested.

As I said, I attended the lectures both at the Turkish and the Kurdish schools, and I also stayed in the barracks of the Turkish school for six months. If there were a picture of Apo on the wall in a classroom, there would be pictures of the martyred founders on the right of Apo's picture, while on the left, there would be the pictures of important commanders who lost their lives in the battles. This classroom setup remained the same even after Apo was arrested.

Look, it is well known that I left the organization after falling-out with one of my fellow commanders. I firmly believe that a few individuals treated me, and the people around me, very unfairly. You would think that, under these circumstances, I would be eager to tell you that Apo was a dictator and a psychopath—someone who considers himself a God and did everything he could to prevent promotions within the PKK. Certainly, this would be one route by which I could take revenge for the poor treatment to which I felt subjected. But I would simply be lying if I said these things. If Apo really were as terrible as that, how could he possibly be loved so very much but all the Kurds of Iraq, Iran, Syria, and Turkey? My slander would make no sense.

Executions in the Organization

False propaganda can only polarize people, and there were constantly reports on national and international media, stating that Apo has been casually taking lives, destroying the commandment echelon, and executing prominent people. Problems cannot be solved by slandering the organization and making them appear evil. If Apo were like that, he would have quickly killed Şemdin Sakık, and even though execution was demanded for him twice, it was never carried out, because Apo canceled it himself. Those who circulated that slander should have been made to give an actual example of someone who was supposed to have been killed by Apo's order. But they cannot, because nothing like that ever happened. If Apo had wanted, he could have killed his ex-wife, Kesire Fatma. He could also have prevented those who fled to Europe, like Selahattin Çelik or Selim Çürükkaya, from living for even one more day, but he did not kill any of them.

I witnessed myself the German authorities who came to Damascus to ask Apo to forgive Selim Çürükkaya. Apo answered them, "Are you idiots? There is no execution order from the organization for that man! If there were, we would have already killed him. He can stay in your country, the way he is living now, but keep him away from us." Also, Osman Öcalan and Nizamettin Taş wrote some strongly worded articles about Apo, and the organization verbally warned them twice. Both of them ignored those warnings, and so the organization killed their guards in order to frighten them. After that, they kept silent and gave up their slandering.

I do not know where or how, but those people who spread propaganda about the organization, also found the names of a few people, martyred within the organization, and they ran a slanderous campaign, stating that those martyrs were executed by Apo's order. Mehmet Sevgat (nickname Bedran) was the commander of the first attack performed by the organization in Eruh, district of Siirt, Turkey, in 1984. There had been propaganda reports, saying that Apo gave an order calling for Bedran's execution. It was a lie! Bedran was martyred in a clash, and was not killed by the organization. Murat Karayılan was seriously injured twice and almost died. Murat was the headquarters commander and coordinated many of the battles himself. If he had died in one of those battles against the Turkish army, those propaganda experts would definitely have said that Apo sent him to his death.

Mehmet Cahit Şener was executed, but he was not executed for being against Apo. An American journalist shared this incident with the world, without knowing all the details. Şener had been arrested by the Turkish security forces in 1980 and imprisoned in the city of Diyarbakır. While there, a large revolt occurred on July 14, 1982 (Mazlum Doğan set himself on fire during that revolt). Şener had supported Mazlum in this resistance and staged a death fast (hunger strike) with the other imprisoned comrades as an act of political protest. At that time, all PKK prisoners were housed in separate cells, so no one knew it then but Şener had changed sides and had become an agent for the Turkish security forces. While his friends were dying, one by one, due to the death fast, Şener was eating regularly.

Mehmet Hayri Durmuş, Ferhat Kurtay (set himself on fire in this resistance) Kemal Bir, Akif Yılmaz, Şener Bir, Mustafa Karasu, and Ali Çiçek were also present in this hunger strike of 63 days. In the end, there were only two survivors of this resistance: Mustafa Karasu and Mehmet Cahit Şener. Mustafa Karasu's death fast, was terminated, and he was force fed, after he fainted from hunger.

After this incident, Cahit Şener became the leader of the PKK prisoners at Diyarbakır prison, and was immediately hailed as a hero. Everyone thought Şener had joined in the hunger strike, along with the leaders of the organization, and survived. No one realized he was actually an agent of the Turkish government, while posing with the PKK prisoners. During the following years, he was set free by the government and ordered to go to Beka Valley, in Syria, and the capture control of the PKK camp management. Of course, he could not do that at that time, so he went to Damascus, and while there, dealt with situations concerning Syria. Rumors spread that he was making connections with Turkish security forces in order to annihilate Apo, but the organization could do nothing at the time, since they had no definite proof.

However, his lifestyle and relations were different from the norm found within the organization. For example, Mehmet Şener was the first person who appointed a female close protection guard for himself, and when Apo saw his weird behavior, he sent him to countryside. He did not want to punish him directly, because the guerillas might raise their voices and oppose him, since Şener was considered to be a hero back then. That's why Apo sent him to harsh conditions of the countryside on purpose, so that his masquerade would be made known, and the cadre would discover who he really was.

Şener was planning to capture the control of the organization in the fourth congress, being united with a person named Sarı Baran. The fourth congress of the PKK took place in February 1990. During that time, Apo made strong criticisms concerning the guerillas out in the mountainous areas. Şener wanted to pacify Apo and said he would talk to each person within the commandment echelon, one by one. During the meetings, Apo used to criticize them and ask why they did not perform proper missions or use guerillas for the correct purposes. Şener took advantage of this, by gathering the guerillas in the commandment echelon and saying, "I still do not understand why Apo is criticizing you. You are giving so much of yourselves in fighting and sacrificing your lives. Despite this, Apo is leading a luxurious life in Damascus and then criticizing you!"

Of course, Şener and Sarı Baran thought that Cemil Bayık would not join the congress. Cemil Bayık had been sent to Iran and Iraq for some kind of negotiations, so when he unexpectedly did join the congress, their plan fell apart, and they both fled from where the congress was being held. Sarı Baran took refuge in KDP Management, and Şener was killed by the organization while hiding in a house in Syria.

Şener's main purpose had been to destroy the organization slowly from within. He had made a collusive agreement with the Turkish security forces while he was in prison. The security forces had set him free under certain conditions. He was to go back to the organization, leak them information, and cause discomfort in the management level. Şener was a clever person. Even Apo had said a few times, "If there were four people as intelligent as Şener among you, our struggle for independence would not last very long. We would have reached our goal much sooner." Nevertheless, he used his intelligence for his own personal goals, and he resembled another comrade, Semir, in many aspects. He wanted to take the organization abroad and continue the struggle with a marginal group and was considering using banners and social gatherings.

Terzi Cemal was the person who stayed in the organization the longest, despite being an agent working for Turkish security forces. He completely wiped out the southwest province of the organization, through his cooperation with the Turkish government. He informed the government security forces whenever large groups of guerrillas were traveling from one place to another within that area. Each time, the security forces laid an ambush and destroyed the guerillas. After those incidents came to light, Terzi Cemal was executed in Damascus in 1993.

I stayed in the same cell with Şemdin Sakık, for a few months, in Diyarbakır prison. He was no different than the Turkish media outlets in regard to spewing false propaganda, and Şemdin still blames Apo for all the bad things that happened. He told me that Apo had purposefully sent him to Amonesses, so that he would die there in one of the clashes between the guerilla forces and the Turkish security forces. This made me very angry, and I asked him, "Why would Apo send you on a death mission?" Şemdin had already been sentenced to death at that time, but the execution had been postponed by Apo in order to give him a second chance. I asked him again, "If Apo had sent you to Botan field, would you say the same thing?"

I remember that period very well. Şemdin had actually asked the organization to be sent to Amonesses, but he made foolish statements to the Middle Eastern press, soon after he was assigned as the commander there. "I will turn Amonesses into Vietnam. I will destroy anyone who stands in front of me." He even said that if the American government continued to help Turkish security forces, he would start attacking American targets, such as the embassy, consulates, and the U.S. military establishments, within Turkey. He said all of this of his own accord.

After Şemdin's ridiculous statements to the press, Apo even had to make a press briefing to defuse this ugly and stupid situation with the United States. Apo also communicated with Şemdin through the radio. We all heard it. It was clear that Apo was extremely angry with Şemdin. "Why do you cause the world to be against us? Has America ever targeted the organization directly? I know they are indirectly supporting Ankara, because they have military, economic, and political interests in Turkey, but America has never directly waged a war against us. Why are you now pissing off Americans? Why do you multiply our enemies?"

Şemdin complained in the prison also. He cried that Apo still wanted him dead, even though he was incarcerated. One of those incidents was reflected in the Turkish press in 2010. It said that Apo wanted to execute Şemdin in prison. The press indicated that one of the repenter convicts sent a model ship, made out of wood and decorated with light bulbs, to Şemdin as a gift. Word on the street was that a bomb had been placed inside the ship. I know very well the person who sent the gift. I do not remember his real name, but his nickname was Cihangir. He is probably among the Kurdish political prisoners now. As a matter of fact, the public prosecutor interviewed me to take my testimony on this incident. At that time, I said, "Mr. Prosecutor, something fishy is going on here. Şemdin was trying to re-win the favor of Turkish security forces by declaring that the organization was still trying to kill him, since he could do damage to them, with his knowledge. The repenter convict, who sent the so-called bomb, aimed to win the trust of the political prisoners by attempting to kill someone who had been sentenced to death by the organization. So, both Şemdin and Cihangir risked doing something like that in order to reach their goals." I later talked to Şemdin about this so-called "assassination attempt." I straightly told him, "You guys planned a very smart game. Whose idea was that? Yours or Cihangir's?" Şemdin suddenly got nervous. "I do not understand what you mean. What planning? It was a fact. That guy wanted to kill me!" Although he denied this so-called assassination attempt, I already knew that Şemdin and Cihangir were close friends, even before they were imprisoned. Cihangir would never attempt to kill him.

The thing that was called a bomb by the press was nothing but a small quantity of match dust, and the Turkish press liked to exaggerate those kinds of incidents. Cihangir acquired a small amount of "gunpowder" from several boxes of matches, and then placed this explosive substance inside the bulb sockets in the model ship. Supposedly, Şemdin would plug the model ship in, to turn on the lights, and the electricity would contact with the gunpowder and the resulting explosion would kill him. This was a fabrication! You cannot kill anyone with a small quantity of gunpowder acquired from matches. At the most, that kind of explosion would only result in a loud noise. If Cihangir really wanted to kill Şemdin, there were many other methods, and, as I said, this incident was a scam. But it had worked. Thanks to this so-called killing attempt, Şemdin became the topic of conversation for both the press and the security forces for months. The repenter convict, Cihangir, made himself accepted within the political PKK prisoners by declaring, "Hey, even though I could not, I tried to kill this traitor of our organization." It was that simple.

There has been a rumor going around, in recent years, stating that Apo established the PKK, but did not leave anyone alive who could potentially replace him or oppose his leadership. There was much information pollution, regarding this propaganda.

If someone deserts the organization, particularly, someone from the command echelon, then he or she is immediately declared a traitor by the organization, as I was declared a traitor. Shamefully, that had put so much pressure on my parents.

In 2011, the prison administration placed a repenter comrade, who surrendered himself to the Turkish security forces, in the same cell as me. While together, I asked him how the organization was now viewing me. "You are being pictured as a bad example, in nearly all of our political and organizational trainings. Deniz's approach was this. His style was that. He was so into women. He would not conduct any missions against the enemy, and so on. The trainers were doing everything they could to defame you, Deniz." I replied to him that this was all normal, because I had quit the organization by fleeing. No one in the organization would think about, or remember, the heroic missions I had achieved in the past. However, if I had been captured by the enemy during a clash, then they would have declared me to be a great hero, by telling victory stories about me, that I did not even achieve. Since I fled the organization, people there would now do anything to blemish my past reputation. In their opinion, I am someone who surrendered himself to the enemy. To prevent other guerillas from deserting the organization, they had to slander anyone who had surrendered themselves.

I do not know if I am on the execution list, but the organization does not let high-ranking deserted guerillas, who collaborate with the security forces and who give secret details about the organization, live very long. On the other hand, they do not care about, or spend time and effort to find a foot guerilla, who served the organization for a couple months and then deserted.

Again, if the person who has left was from the command echelon, and if that person provided the security forces with some secret details that could potentially harm the organization, then he or she would definitely be put on the execution list. Şemdin Sakık is on the list, but Selim Çürükkaya is not. Selim wrote many humiliating things about the organization, but he did not participate in the missions with the Turkish security forces against the guerillas or in annihilating some of his own comrades. On the other hand, if they really wanted, the organization has the capability to kill both Osman Öcalan and Nizamettin Taş in Iraq in 24 hours.

The bond of companionship is very important in the organization. So, anyone who betrays this bond, would definitely pay in the end. In 2003, a guerilla killed his comrade and fled to Barzani, the Peshmerga force in northern Iraq. The organization did not go looking for him, but, when the Peshmerga forces would not deliver him, they were given a large amount of money, which convinced them to turn him over to the organization. That guerilla was taken to the camp and executed in front of three battalions of guerillas. Normally, the organization would never carry out executions in front of the guerillas, but as a lesson to everyone, the management made that decision. The guerillas were given a message. "If you betray your friend, you will ultimately pay for it."

If someone wanted to leave the organization voluntarily, and if he or she had not harmed his or her comrades or the organization, then they were free to go, and the organization would not hurt them or their family members. The organization would never forcibly make guerillas stay. A guerilla can leave whenever he or she wants, and that system has been the same ever since PKK was established.

Helin

One thing I cannot abide is when people casually slander someone without having any actual knowledge of what really happened. There is this issue of the former guerilla Helin. She was interviewed by an American journalist for a book which criticized the PKK. In that book, she said, "We live hand-to-mouth in the mountains, sometimes we suffer terrible hunger, sometimes we are forced to walk barefoot, and all the while Apo lives the life of comfort in luxury homes." She also claimed that everything done by the organization was in adulation of Apo. That when Apo spoke, everyone would stay silent. No one would dare raise any objections against him…

What she said is partially right, partially wrong. She is right about the life of luxury he enjoys. The organization had five villas in Syria in those days. Mostly female militants stay in these villas. They would be trained in these houses for future political functions in Turkey, Iran, Iraq, and Syria. Helin was one of them. I stayed in one of those villas, too. Living there was completely different than the standard of living in the countryside, specifically in the mountainous areas. Guerillas in the countryside cannot eat the same quality of food that the inhabitants of these houses eat every day. However, this is due to the challenging conditions they live in, in the countryside. Do guerrillas in Damascus have to live in poverty just because their fellow comrades are living in hardship in the mountains? You cannot use this logic. Let's imagine you live in the countryside of Garzan or Diyarbakır. Sometimes you cannot find bread and sometimes you run out of tea. So, should people in Damascus not eat anything, although they have plenty of food? Also, the people coming to Damascus are there to learn ideological training. Again, you are making them ready for a new future process. These people could not be made ready for the future under conditions such as the regular guerilla usually endures. After all, in that case, would they be able to give their attention to the tough conditions or to the ideological training?

Helin's statements were also inconsistent. If someone objects to a lifestyle, it is hypocritical if they do the thing that they so vocally objected to. Ask Helin how many years she had lived the pampered life in these houses, before her hypocritical complaints began. I stayed there together with Cemil Bayık, Duran Kalkan, or Murat Karayılan at various times throughout my career with the organization. I never witnessed a bodyguard or lower-ranking guerrilla wash these high-ranking officials' clothes. Put that "luxurious" label aside. These men washed their own clothes. Well, with one exception. Once, Cemil Bayık became so incapacitated because of a slipped disc in his back that we guerrillas washed his clothes for him during his recovery.

Helin, herself, was not a member of the presidency council, nor was she a member of the council of command. She was just an ordinary central committee member. Maybe you will not believe this, but even Helin's socks were being washed by her bodyguards. Everyone in the organization knows it. But let's say everything was just like she had claimed. Let's say that Apo and Cemil Bayık were dictators. These men had served the organization for as long as Helin had been alive, without shouldering nearly the same weight of responsibility. Helin was, nonetheless, quick to accept all the same privileges that they had earned, though in all ways, she was not even close to their level.

So, it was no surprise that no one in the organization liked Helin. She was also jailed by us, not once, but twice. Why did not she mention those things? When Apo was in Italy in 1999, Helin was in prison during the Second Extraordinary Congress of the PKK. She was thrown into jail along with Dr. Süleyman. They were in a relationship. From this date to 2003, she remained imprisoned. Did Helin mention any of this in her speeches? Of course not! While Helin was staying in the "luxurious" villas in Damascus for years, did she object to this lifestyle even once? From the inside, did she make any suggestion for change? Did she write any reports about how unfair her privileges were? On the contrary, she always wanted more and more.

I did not want to interfere in these incidents, so I did not say anything at the time. But they were ridiculous. For instance, on May 14, 1997, there was a vast military operation to the south: the Sandwich operation. Helin was the headquarters commander of the female force back then. She had had a swimming pool built at the academy and was giving the young women swimming lessons. In August, 1997, before this protracted strike against us, Helin had gathered 50 young women between the ages of 13 and 18 for a swimming lesson. Many comrades in the headquarters, both male and female, objected to this. We were in the middle of a battle, and she was teaching them how to swim! The men especially got so angry they said, "If the Turkish military brings their attack here, we swear we will not lift a finger to save you."

And indeed, the attack came to that pool. Helin did not know what to do with all these young, defenseless women. At the sound of gunfire, she suddenly decided to move them all to Gari Compound from Zap, under the command of a central committee member. Well, they got caught up in a tank ambush en route, in Amediye (which is connected to Dohuk) while crossing to Gari, and 17 of these young women were killed. Now, this same woman was up giving speeches, slandering people. But why did Helin not talk about her own failings; her own stupidity as a part of all of this?

Naturally, while I have been talking to you, I have not spoken about the bad sides of our members or revealed the deficits of the organization. This was because, if one thing was done by anyone in the organization, anyone could say it was the style of the entire organization. Yes, there had been individual conspiracies, extra-judicial killings, and conniving in the organization. Dozens of high-ranking commanders and other important names in the organization were eliminated by extra-judicial killings. However, I know for sure that those murders were not committed by order of the management of the organization. Rather, powerful individuals performed these executions in order to protect or advance their own interests. I cannot blame the organization for these incidents, because I know for a fact that the organization did not promote such a culture as this.

There was much other incorrect information in that book written by an American journalist—for instance, that no one was allowed to watch TV when Apo was arrested, since seeing him with handcuffs, under the Turkish flag would have caused all the comrades to quit their duties. This is simply not true. When there were such news reports on the TV, the organization would turn off the TV then but for a very different reason.

It was because these images caused such a serious hatred in the organization against the government. For example, one company commander who had watched these images went to the ammunition warehouse and collected as much cyanide as possible. He wanted to kill the Turkish soldiers with it... all the Turkish soldiers! And this was not just an ordinary guerrilla, either. He was a mature commander, who had been trained on self-discipline for a long time, who could control his feelings. He was somebody who would never normally act on emotion alone. But, if this event of watching our leader get imprisoned could cause even a high-ranking guerrilla to be overpowered by his feelings, how could we expect self-control from the ordinary guerrillas? Every member of the organization, from the lowest foot guerillas to Apo's cabinet, became so angry that we had to turn off the TVs in order to prevent these guerillas from performing any mission against the Turkish public in revenge. If the organization allowed the whole complex to continue to watch these insulting images, the camp location would have become a ticking bomb. Then, if the result were dozens of self-sacrifice missions and hundreds of Turkish casualties, would the Turkish state ever enter a peace process with the PKK again? No!

So, the main reason to shut off the TVs was not the advertised worry about an exodus of guerillas from the organization, as it was claimed. The reason was to prevent the guerilla from losing his self-discipline and performing individual missions that ultimately would harm our collective reputation. There were people who had given all their years to the organization. They were sincerely committed to Apo, personally. They had devoted their entire lives to him. When these people watched images of Apo's capture, would they have left his the organization? No. On the contrary, they would fight to the death for revenge.

Why doesn't anyone mention the fact that the organization forbade the use of the word "War" from 1999 to 2002? Apo deliberately would not allow anyone to use insulting or offensive language like "Fascist Turkish Government", when referring to the state. At one point, Nizamettin Taş even met with us. "Old comrades," he warned us, "you will either honestly change your outlook, or at the very least, you will adapt yourself to this new, political way of continuing our cause. By this I mean, that one way or another you will support the organization's efforts to achieve peace through political discourse, instead of fighting. Otherwise, we will open a prison camp just for you, like Mahmur camp in Iraq." For three years, this was how strongly they emphasized the concept of peace through peaceful means. On the other hand, this was how forceful they had to be in order to overwrite us guerillas' inclination towards war and revenge.

During this time, the dominant approach was that we were going to settle our disputes with Turkey through politics. All of us underwent training in this direction. I was one of the first ones who objected to the peace process then. I asserted, "Comrade! You were the very one who instructed me for years on the tactics of war! Now, how can you be the one to ask me to change completely, all of a sudden? I cannot shuck my armor and wear the necktie of politics instead, in such a short time."

Drug Commerce, Turkish State, and the PKK

Another issue, which had frequently been used to slander the PKK, was our so-called drug production. But in actuality it was not the PKK which produced all the drugs but the state itself. The military's own helicopters would take heroin from Gabar and transfer it to other locations. Hakkari had been the center of drug trade until 1995. Hakkari was the initial storage stop for all heroin arriving from Iran or Afghanistan. From Hakkari, it was then distributed to the west of Turkey and from there to Europe. The PKK was not responsible for this. We just were not powerful enough to disrupt this entrenched process. So, all we did was institute a tax on everyone else who was participating in this business. This dirty drug business still continues, although it is not done as vastly as it once was.

Again, the PKK never messed with this drug business. Most of the news in the media was wrong. Among our own, the PKK even gave harsh punishments to those who got involved in this business. If the state had just said the word, it would have taken the PKK such a short period of time to destroy the entire system of drug production and shipping in this region. We could have dismantled it in six months! But would the state allow this? No, because the state, itself, was in the drug business.

In the organization, only three crimes were never forgiven. The first crime was intentionally to kill your comrade. The second one was to harm the organization financially. The last one was to get into the drug business. If you had been issued a sentence for one of these crimes, the organization would definitely take its revenge once it found you, no matter how many years had passed.

In 2006, the organization detected that a comrade who was in charge of the guerilla arsenal in our camps in Iraq had sold some of our ammo to the drug smugglers. This man had served the organization for a very long time. The organization always sought to prevent rumors whenever possible, so when it had decided to perform an execution they would inform the family of the offender ahead of time. The organization called this man's family directly. The crimes of this keeper of the arsenal were read aloud in front of his family and an audience of other guerillas. Then, his family was asked if they approved of the execution of their son. All the members of the family approved the execution. Listen carefully. This person was executed with the full approval of his entire family.

I witnessed punishments for these drug-trade issues in person. For instance, a Kurdish farmer in a region in Çukurca planted marijuana, in an area connected to the city of Hakkari, which was close to the Turkey-Iraq border. Our comrades, there on foot patrol, discovered this field and informed our headquarters. We went there as a unit and destroyed the field. Then, we found out that that farmer was the father of a guerilla. No tolerance was shown to him. He was warned very harshly regardless of his affiliation with us. We let him know in no uncertain terms that we would execute him if he tried something like this again. The man must have had direct contact with the security forces and some other groups in the marijuana business. This drug was not grown in the mountainous regions. It required a flat valley. Therefore, marijuana was planted on the same areas tactically ideal for the military, so these fields were always grown close to military stations.

The organization thought that the Turkish state was deliberately and intentionally allowing drug-related activities in this region, where we Kurds also lived. This was because a drug-addicted Kurd would be no good for the organization. Even if those addicted Kurds did manage to join the organization, the harm they would cause would far outweigh any benefit they would provide. Therefore, some state men planned to get a majority of the Kurdish youth in the region addicted and tried to eliminate the PKK this way. But their plan did not work, because the organization destroyed those fields wherever they saw one. Far from engaging in the drug business, the organization did not even let any of its members drink alcohol. You never saw any guerilla with so much as a beer bottle in the organization.

Despite promoting the drug trade, the security forces in Turkey do sometimes conduct operations against drug farmers just for show. For example, in 2014, they staged some operations on those fields of cannabis. On both sides of the road, going to the military station in Lice, there are cannabis fields. Ever since I could remember, cannabis has been planted in these fields. Now, I am asking you, why did the Turkish state not touch those fields for all those years? After protecting them for so long, then why did they stage an operation there all of a sudden? Because they did not know about it? No. Everyone knew it very well. Just to sweeten their image and deceive the Turkish public, they performed this 2014 operation. Combat aircrafts and armed vehicles destroyed those fields, one by one. Why? What changed their thinking after years?

There were some certain Kurds in the east, who had been planting marijuana for a very long time. One man had always grown it in his field of 92,000 m^2. The security officials had been allowing it, in order to get their own share in this business. The only work of the marijuana farmers was to grow it and store it. They had no other source of income, so they absolutely had to contact the security forces if they wanted to transport the dried marijuana in July and August, without having it confiscated by the military. During the transfer, one third of the income from the dried marijuana was given to the senior military authorities and police officials to prevent the shipment from being captured by the state authorities. Maybe even half of the income. The amount of the protection payout could change, depending on the local conditions.

11

THE CHAOTIC SITUATION AT CENTRAL HEADQUARTERS COMMAND

We had been in the camp for two months when the traitors' court started. In front of an assemblage of 180 people, a three-person tribunal—comprised of Cemil Bayık, Halil Ataç and a female guerilla—conducted their investigation. The hearing of Şemdin, alone, lasted almost three days. First, Şemdin read his own defense. Then, the audiences, as a unit, uttered their criticism of him. Almost every single person stood up and evaluated him. I asked for permission to speak, and demanded to know, "How could you talk to a province commander as you did on the radio and use such insulting words?" Although Şemdin denied it at first, Cemil Bayık would have none of it. "Do not lie," he warned. "We have the recorded tapes of that conversation. We went back and heard what you said."

After Cemil said that, I asked another question. "Do you accept the legality of this investigation commission?" Şemdin asked me why I would ask him such a question. I told him that he once had said that no one in this organization was fit to judge him. He looked at me and, smiling, he said, "Comrade, you ask a very good question. I am a direct man. You're right. If Cuma were not here, I would not suffer either of those two tribunal members to sit in judgment of me. Cuma has always been honest. That's why I respect him a great deal. I do not take anyone in this organization seriously, besides Cuma," he said. While Şemdin was continuing his speech, Cemil Bayık cut him off. "You are lying in front of these 200 guerillas. Was it not you who took my weapon back the first chance you got? Were you not the one who put me in prison, Şemdin?" he demanded. Şemdin replied, "Back then there was a standing order, and I had to obey it." Cemil was enraged. "You knew that the order was wrong, and you knew how everything had developed to that point. If you had really wanted, you could have canceled the order. But you did not do it!"

The incident Cemil Bayık was talking about happened in 1986. After Mahsun Korkmaz died, someone called Kör Cemal was appointed as the leader of the Botan province. Although Kör Cemal was very good militarily, he did not have the capacity to understand the ideology and policy of the organization, but he was being mentored by someone intelligent—a comrade named Şahin Baliç. They were planning to overthrow the organization by eliminating Cemil Bayık in the field, and Apo in Damascus. Şahin Baliç assured Kör Cemal, "Leave Apo to me, I will take care of him. You deal with Cemil Bayık." Of course the team assisting him was the same: Sarı Baran, Kör Cemal, Hogir (Cemil Işık), Mehmet Şener, Şahin Baliç.

Kör Cemal had thought that if he could disarm Cemil Bayık, he could find some way to execute him while he was defenseless. By giving false information to Şemdin Sakık, he had actually managed to disarm Cemil Bayık with unfounded accusations. Meantime, with Cemil Bayık in jail, Şahin Baliç went to Damascus to assassinate Apo. He was thinking that he could execute Apo there at training camp. But, in 1987, the organization had Kör Cemal killed by Ebubekir (Halil Ataç) as soon as they learned of this plan. Metin (Şahin Baliç) was obliged to postpone his mission as the result of the sudden death of his accomplice. Şahin Baliç kept silent for a while after Kör Cemal was executed. But, two years later in 1989, he again approached Apo in an assassination attempt. His team acted more cleverly this time. Now, their strategy was to eliminate those around Apo and then Apo himself, after he was unprotected. They figured that the organization would maintain its integrity from the force of Apo's personality, even though each of his officers would die one by one. They planned to kill Apo last and then take control of the organization.

It was in support of this plan that Hasan Bindal, Apo's best friend since childhood, was shot and killed in 1990, while Şahin Baliç was delivering guerilla training in the Damascus School. Şahin Baliç himself shot Hasan Bindal with his M-16 "by mistake." Şahin Baliç's inner circle was quick to close around him and calm the environment by claiming that this was a normal training accident and such things were bound to happen.

However, Apo and the other senior executives were well aware that the killing of Hasan Bindal was not anything normal. The organization had already figured out that Sarı Baran, Cemil Işık, and Şahin Baliç had something to do with Kör Cemal's plan. But as they had no proof, they could not do anything. However, after the death of Hasan Bindal, it became obvious that this team clearly was a threat to be taken seriously. So, Şahin Baliç was immediately sentenced with the death penalty. Then, Şemdin Sakık was imprisoned. Because of all his previous atrocities, Hogir (Cemil Işık) fled the area. Mehmet Şener and Sarı Baran also ran away so as to avoid execution.

The result of this current investigation was a unanimous vote in favor of executing Şemdin. All the other officers, who had been arrested along with him, were ordered to be excommunicated from the organization. Apo came to the Turkish school, while they were imprisoned, and met with the guerillas who had decided on this sentence and, to their surprise, he told them he was against their decision, because of their own incompetence. "You were not principled as a command echelon. If you had put your shoulders to the wheel, if you had done everything you could have done to protect the organization from the beginning, this man would not have harmed the organization that much. Şemdin has had a free hand until now, because up until now, all of you simply have done nothing. Some of you were scared of Şemdin and some of you just turned your backs and pretended you did not see what was going on. As a result, the damages to our organization have already occurred. What sense does it make to execute Şemdin at this late date? Where were the region commanders during all of this? Where were the province commanders while he was acting like a traitor? It is easy to punish him with execution now. You act from the poor logic that Apo will approve the death sentence no matter what and he will bear all the responsibility. Well, I refuse to do your work for you now, since you failed to do your own before! I do not approve this death penalty!" he said. Everyone was shocked. No one was expecting such a harsh reaction from Apo. He even said, while looking directly at Cemil Bayık, "You haven't even performed some of the executions I have already approved." (You'll remember that Apo had wanted his brother to be executed before, and Cemil Bayık had canceled this decision.)

"This is why I do not approve this man's execution now. Take all of these men out of the prison now. They will join the training cohort again, from day one. If they get their acts together, if they recover their former utility, by undergoing all the training again, then I have no problem with them. We shall forgive them and reincorporate them. At that point, it will be just to give their duties back; they will have earned the right. But if they go back to acting from the same twisted logic, then we will not have any mercy. They will all be executed without further trial. This is my suggestion about those people. I am leaving now. You had better talk and discuss among yourselves and evaluate my suggestion. Then, tell me what you have decided regarding my decision."

Although the command structure and foot soldier level guerillas definitely did not want this, they accepted Apo's suggestion. All those arrested, including Şemdin, were taken out of the jail and began training again. Şemdin Sakık was even tapped, by the direct request of Apo, to teach the class on "War and the Army," and Ali Haydar Kaytan took over teaching "The History of the Party." The guerillas were still a bit disappointed by the fact that these people were lecturing them. Some guerillas even filed formal complaints, to the effect that, "These people were imprisoned up until yesterday and now they are lecturing us?" Şemdin was then even appointed as the commander general of Amanoses Field. That is to say, Apo not only spared Şemdin's life, but, in his mercy he also appointed him to an important post.

After Şemdin was arrested, Murat Karayılan and Duran Kalkan were appointed to Botan command, with Duran selected as commander. Unfortunately, Duran Kalkan could not cope with the problems with which he was confronted at headquarters. While Şemdin had been in charge, control and discipline at headquarters had largely deteriorated. It was such a chaotic environment that it was nearly impossible to reestablish order quickly. Also, because Duran had been given such a lofty position, some commanders of rank felt there may be favoritism within the organization. The officials at Damascus were not properly assigning people of merit to these critical positions, but were instead empowering those people they liked. Rumors began to spread. For example: "If this is how the party is going to act, then they cannot be trusted anymore."

Beyond that, there were even more issues. Some of these handpicked commanders withdrew from their regular duties. The organization, thinking their preferred commanders were going to do what they were supposed to do, assigned them with important missions. However, these belligerent commanders rejected their orders and did not complete their duties. Even more than that, they began to treat the southern Kurds in Iraq in a callous manner. Many of the Kurdish villagers were executed when they were falsely accused of being members of the KDP.

Because of the chaos found at headquarters, Apo decided to appoint Cemil Bayık as headquarters commander. This allowed Cemil to pick up the pieces and iron out the chaos, as soon as Şemdin Sakık's trial was complete. Many reports, written directly to Apo, concerning those problems began to arrive while I was training in Damascus. They said the leadership at headquarters could not control the situation, and the officials in Damascus must step in before disaster struck.

Apo, who was very ill back then, had kept Cemil Bayık at his side. Cemil had undergone two different ineffective operations to repair a slipped disc, and had yet to recover. However, even with his condition, there was no one else who could be trusted to put an end to the chaotic situation and restore order at headquarters. Although the guerillas suggested that either Murat Karayılan or Ebubekir should have gotten the command and fixed the ongoing problems, Apo did not accept these suggestions. Apo argued that neither man possessed the capability or the experience to do the job. In a speech to all those assembled in Damascus at the time, Apo addressed Cemil Bayık, "Cemil, I do not necessarily want you to go, since you have ongoing health issues, but you know the situation as well as I, and there is not another viable solution. I give you all the authority necessary to do what you must, so as to ensure the dominance and policies of the organization there." After this speech, Cemil Bayık was promoted and sent to headquarters. This was in December of 1996.

When Cemil Bayık finally arrived at headquarters, he first discharged everyone within the management structure. Realizing that simply releasing some officers from duty was not effective enough, Cemil decided to teach them a harsh lesson. He executed 17 ranked guerillas, whom he deemed to be part of the root of the problem. It is important to note that these executions were performed without the approval of Apo, but Bayık was quick to find the corruption within the command structure, and once he found the perpetrators, he executed them on the spot.

After the executions, many guerillas sent complaint reports to Damascus, stating that Cemil Bayık was executing high-ranking commanders without the approval of President Apo. When the correspondence arrived, there was a day I remember quite well. Apo came to school to give a lecture about party history, but he canceled it. Instead, he talked to those within the academy about what had transpired at headquarters. "You've all witnessed it," he said. "When I sent Cuma there, did I not tell him that he had my full authority to organize the party by whatever means necessary? What can you glean from that?"

At the time, there were 11 people from the PKK's central committee assembly at the academy. Turning to them, Apo repeated the question. Two of them stood and said, "Yes, you gave Cuma the authority to do anything in order to bring order to headquarters." So Apo replied, "Then why is there any criticism? I said to everyone at headquarters that Cemil Bayık will not ask for my approval for any of his decisions or actions. This allowed him to do what must be done. Why are they sending these reports to me? One of you should stand up and explain it! If Cuma had to execute 17 people, it shows that our organization was in great danger. I have known Cuma for many years and he never executed as many people as I wanted. These 17 executions show that there are not many people who properly follow the policies within our organization." Finishing with this pronouncement, he left the room. After this incident with the executions, order was slowly restored to central headquarters. There was now a fear amongst the guerillas, because they saw that executions could be carried out, without Apo's direct approval.

After completing his training, Şemdin was sent to Amanoses to be commander, but he continued to make mistake after mistake. Before he even reached his new post, he was giving speeches to the media. He said things such as: "My forces will turn Amanoses into Vietnam, and the Turkish security forces will not even dare enter the city." Naturally, this drew the attention of all the Turkish military, and they headed for that region. Şemdin's forces became targets and were subjected to repeated operations from the security forces. They were getting hit so hard that Şemdin had to relocate the province headquarters from Amanoses to Syria. During this period, the organization suffered many grave losses, all because of Şemdin's poor decisions.

This was the last straw. Apo did not want to give Şemdin another chance. "I do not want to see him anymore. Take him to headquarters and sit in judgment of him there. I will not object to any decisions you make." But, before Apo even gave those instructions, Şemdin had already been arrested and taken to Zap headquarters in the south. After the trial, Şemdin, commander of Amanoses, was lowered to the rank of a regular guerilla. But, there was a problem. Neither the headquarters officials nor members of the military council wanted Şemdin to join them. It was not until later that we heard Cemil Bayık had been kind enough to accept him.

During this time, I had been training in the camp at Damascus for almost nine months. We knew that training would soon be over, and we would all be assigned to different Zones. At the beginning of

April, 1997, we received intelligence that there was going to be a huge military operation against our camps located in the south (Iraq and Syria). Barzani and Talabani, the Kurdish leaders in northern Iraq, were going to ally with the Turkish soldiers in this operation against us.

Because of this unexpected attack, the officials at the training camp started to assign everyone to their new locations, even before training was complete. A group of 27 or 28 people, including myself, were the first to be organized, so that we could quickly make our way south. Before we left for Turkey, Apo spoke face to face with each commander. He asked each person to stand up, one after another, and tell him into which field they would like to go. His final decision would only be made after receiving the opinions of the others who were present at the meeting. Out of respect, not a one of us volunteered to be appointed to a specific field. We said that we would go anywhere the organization wanted us to go. When it came my turn, I answered the same as everyone else.

Once he heard my response, he asked the commanders in the committee where I should be assigned. Halil Ataç (Ebubekir) said, "He can go to Botan!" Dr. Ali said, "He should go to Amed!" There were two women on the committee, and they both replied, "Deniz came here from Garzan so he should be assigned to Garzan." After listening to each of them, Apo said, "I also want you to go to Garzan. However, Cemil Bayık will make the final decision. Now, go down south and meet with Comrade Cemil and you will report to the place that he deems most appropriate for you."

So it was that we set off in a group of 28 people. From Damascus, we first went to the city of Halep and then traveled from Halep to the region of Zap. Cuma said, "I want you all to stay with me for now. I will transfer you later to Garzan, with a battalion of guerillas." It was while we were there, that I was given command of a squad that used heavy weapons. In May of 1997, the field commanders and head-quarters leadership decided to send Cemil Bayık (Cuma) out of the Zap camp to a safer place, because the main part of the operation was going to take place in the Zap region. This made it too risky for a senior officer to stay there. He accepted their judgment, and went to Gari region in northern Iraq.

The media and press used their influence to create a fallacious atmosphere among the Turkish public. This made people begin to think that when the security forces went into Zap, the organization would be completely destroyed.

The operation began on May 14, 1997. It was vast, extending all the way into the Haftanin region in Iraq. According to the plan, Turkish security forces were going to bomb us from the air with fighter jets, and the Peshmerga forces of Barzani were going to attack on the ground. If the plan worked accordingly, our forces would be crushed between them. This is why the assault was named "Sandwich operation." For the first five or six days, there were fights on both fronts. We were stuck in the middle, just as planned, but the Turkish soldiers and the Peshmerga, under the control of Barzani, never left their positions to move toward us.

On the sixth day of the assault, Apo contacted us, via radio, and criticized our frontal defense tactics. He gave us instructions. "Our guerillas cannot endure very long in a fight such as this. The Turkish security forces have come in such large numbers that they are able to use more extensive military techniques. If you continue to stay positioned, as you have been, then you will lose many in this battle, because you are crowded together. Rather than staying bunched up like that, leave a few troops there, then have the rest of your forces go to Gari or Hakurki!"

The Turkish soldiers and Peshmerga saw our comrades leave their position and thought that we guerillas must be running away. It was under this pretense that they foolhardily came forward, thinking it was now safe to do so. I was part of a force of 200 to 300 people that were left scattered around the field. We did not fire at the security forces while they were coming towards us. Instead, we silently waited for them to come close to where we were hiding. As soon as they were close enough, a platoon of guerillas circled behind them and they found themselves completely surrounded by our forces. With this final tactic, we attacked the Peshmerga and Turkish soldiers, killing most of them.

During this battle, we were able to shoot down a Turkish attack helicopter using Russian missiles—a first in the history of our struggle against the Turkish security forces. In fact, the operation was temporarily ceased after the helicopter was shot down. With the Turkish soldiers not able to attack us using helicopters anymore, we had the advantage and were able to start a true offense against the enemy lines.

I remember quite well a hill in the Zap region. When the Turkish security forces captured it, they planted their flag as a sign of victory. They acted as if the Zap region was actually under their control, and that all of the guerillas had been killed. They even invited the Turkish TV channels there to do a live broadcast. Apo was furious and immediately made a counter statement to a news outlet in the Middle East, saying, "Okay, I accept that you were able to enter into our liberated zone within the Zap region. However, I wonder if your soldiers will be alive when they leave Zap."

Only one day after this live broadcast, the superior officers that provided the Turkish troops' command and control procedures were killed. All of these high-ranking generals boarded a Skorsky type helicopter and flew over the area of the clash to inspect the casualties that had been inflicted on their enemy. For security reasons, the Skorsky was accompanied by four Cobra-type attack helicopters. While they were surveying the battlefield, a squadron of guerillas was getting ready to ambush the security forces with missiles. They hid in an area that was close to the Turkish border. When they heard the helicopters, they checked the area with binoculars and saw the Skorsky and the four Cobra attack helicopters.

With this new knowledge, the guerillas immediately informed their senior leadership and were instructed: "Use all of your missiles to destroy that Skorsky, and do not target the Cobras." Because of their experience, the senior management immediately realized that the Skorsky was carrying some important commanders and the Cobras must be accompanying it for security. As instructed, our comrades targeted the Skorsky and were able to destroy it.

The destruction of the Skorsky put an immediate halt to the operation and a hush fell over the battlefield. It was as if there were no battle or soldiers on the field. We found out later, from listening to their radio communications, that the low-ranking commanders had panicked when all of the high-ranking commanders had been killed, and the Turkish soldiers were all asking one another whether they should continue to attack or just withdraw from the area.

Since there was no high-ranked commander left to lead the operation, the Turkish troops withdrew. With this turn of events, our guerillas headed in full force toward Barzani and his Peshmerga. Barzani, himself, led his troops onto the battlefield. Apo had given us strict orders to kill every single Peshmerga soldier who participated in this operation; therefore, Barzani was immediately taken out of the fight, because we guerillas were heading toward them with might and main.

Almost all the Peshmerga we had encircled were killed. We only spared the lives of the ones who directly surrendered themselves to us. Of course, it was very hard for us to slow down, because of our hatred for these Kurdish people who would fight against us. Many of these same Peshmerga soldiers had hidden in military posts within the cities under Barzani's control. Meanwhile, the YNK, led by Talabani, were fighting with us against the Barzani forces. In 1996, Barzani had made an agreement with the Iraqi regime of Saddam Hussein. Using the tanks of the Iraqi military, they invaded Erbil and defeated the YNK forces there. Talabani's wife was taken captive during the invasion. Apo intervened, and said to Barzani, "You will either set the woman free, or we will fight against you," and with this threat, he was able to save Talabani's wife. The YNK were very grateful for the help and supported us guerillas in the fight of 1997, by engaging the KDP forces. We guerillas laid siege to all the cities and military posts that belonged to Barzani. As we were destroying his forces, Barzani sent someone called Davud Bağistani to the senior management of the PKK as a mediator. He said that he would accept all of our conditions, if the PKK would declare a ceasefire.

The organization was much more cautious about a proposal of peace this time. Senior PKK officials told Barzani as much when they responded to his mediator. "Barzani, last year you accepted all of our peace terms and conditions, but then at the very first opportunity you broke our agreement." Barzani replied back: "I accept anything you include within the agreement, no strings attached. Do not give me even one more chance, if I violate it again." However, while Barzani was making these peace talks with us, he also communicated with the Turkish officials. "Help me as soon as possible. My forces and I will have to surrender to the PKK if you are too slow to aid us. There will be nothing left of what once was called Barzani's regional government."

With this call for help from Barzani, the Turkish military forces entered northern Iraq with nearly 100 tanks. Some of these tanks were placed between Zaho and Dohuk, on the border. Others were placed in several towns, and in the city of Dohuk itself. Basically, this meant there were two or three Turkish military tanks positioned in almost every town in northern Iraq. In addition to that, ten more Turkish tanks were delivered to the areas that had been invaded by the YNK forces. These extra tanks were added because five of the towns that were originally controlled by Barzani had been invaded by the combined force of the PKK and the YNK during the battle, and were now under our control. In a very short time, the organization had appointed all of the mayors, the district governors, and all other administrators to various public institutions. We were just about to invade Erbil when these Turkish tanks arrived to help Barzani and his forces. This unexpected aid completely changed the course of the battle. Besides the tanks, the Turkish military helped the Barzani forces with fighter jets and the Cobra-style attack helicopters from the air.

One of our original goals during this battle was to imprison Barzani when operations ceased, but these sudden developments prevented this from happening. Barzani's position at the negotiation table had strengthened, and he quickly dismissed all of his previous promises to the organization made before the Turkish aid. We ended up having to return control of all the military posts and districts we had taken. In return for those areas, we were officially handed control of the fields of Gari, Hakurki, Kandil, and Hiraniye (all in northern Iraq). Today there are still more than 400 villages in the region of Kandil that are governed by the organization. All of these municipalities belong to the organization.

The ceasefire agreement was reached, but it did not last long. Many of the tribal leaders, that had previously lived under the Barzani regime, objected to the transfer of their administration to the PKK. Therefore, fights began again.

Ten guerillas, including myself, headed up to the region of Gari for reconnaissance, so that we could begin planning a mission to annihilate the tribal leaders. During the night, we surveyed and explored the area where they were staying, and then rested under a tree when morning came. I do not like to rest or sleep in a group because there were always those people who disturb others by talking. That was why I moved 10 meters away from the rest of the group and laid under another large tree. I had a small Walkman cassette player on me, and I fell asleep while listening to it.

It was not very long before my comrades quietly called out my name. I initially thought that the Peshmerga forces had surrounded us while I slept, but I realized that there was a heaviness on my chest. I opened my eyes and looked towards my comrades. They were all giving me signals to stay still, and that is when I turned my eyes to the heaviness I had felt on my chest. There was a huge black snake stretched out from one end of my chest to the other and I could feel its head brushing against my head. I had never before been so terrified in my life and I felt that my heart would fail me, because it was such a frightening situation. One of my comrades quietly called out to me, "Deniz, switch off the Walkman if you can." I had to move one of my arms to switch it off and I was worried that if I did, the snake may bite me. I waited, immobilized for almost ten minutes. While I remained still, one side of the cassette in the player finished and the Walkman stopped by itself. As soon as it stopped playing music, the snake crawled down my chest and slithered into the bushes. I had witnessed many terrifying things in my life, including the risk of death, but I had never been so frightened as that before.

Defeating the Turkish Tanks

As I said, the Turkish tanks reached Barzani in no time, completely changing the course of the fight. To win, we were going to have to destroy those tanks, one way or another. For the first time in the history of the struggle of our organization, our comrades who had been trained in explosives were able to destroy three Turkish tanks with bombs they had buried underground. It was also during this time that the organization began to use remote controlled explosives. We activated these explosives using signals from our radios. At that time, we were not yet aware of the more advanced techniques of activating bombs, such as using vehicle remote controllers or other kinds of technical equipment. We simply used our hand radios to activate our bombs.

We became so good at using explosives that no matter which of our bombing tactics were countered by the Turkish security forces, the organization was able to acquire new techniques, using its advanced explosive development laboratories and bomb experts. Day and night, this group of experts manufactured advanced explosives in our laboratories, thus negating the preventive steps taken by the Turkish security forces. There was a group of almost 25 dedicated people working in these laboratories, with each one specialized in a specific field. There were some who worked on the construction of circuits for the bombs; some developed remote control; some supplied the explosives. Others trained the guerillas on the use of the bombs. Every three months, a new group of eager guerillas would be sent to the laboratories to be trained in the proper use of explosives.

The use of remote controlled bombs opened a way for the organization to utilize new tactics in its future attacks. After the introduction of this new, effective technique, the organization would not base its missions merely on raids and attacks against Turkish military posts as it once had. Suicide and bombing missions conducted by remote controlled explosives were not only more effective but also less risky for the guerillas in comparison to missions carried out through raids and attacks.

At this time, the Turkish security forces began to lose their bearings and were unable to figure out how we were destroying their tanks, one by one. When they realized we were blowing up their tanks with signals from radio activated explosives, they would not even patrol those areas for a while. This was because they did not know what kind of precautions to take against our new destructive technique. There's a device called a jammer, which was invented for jamming radars and for signal deception, but it had not yet been acquired by the Turkish military. Once the security forces acquired these things from the United States, we were not able to conduct bombing missions again for a long while.

The organization established a special group at headquarters that trained guerillas on the proper use of explosive goods. Special explosive production laboratories were established within Syria and Iraq. Hundreds of experiments were conducted by our bomb experts in order to develop new explosives and to stop the effects of jammers. By getting in touch with the explosive manufacturers in Europe and Russia, higher quality substances were obtained to produce bombs that were even more destructive. Although these high-quality explosive substances were expensive, they were not affected by jammers.

The War at the Musul-Duhok Line

After the breach of the ceasefire between the PKK and Barzani, I was placed among four battalions, who were assigned to the area where Barzani's family lived. Our goal was to drive Barzani's family and relatives out, so that he would be forced to sit at the negotiation table yet again. We executed attacks on the areas where they lived until the end of July. At the beginning of August, I was called back to headquarters in the Zap region. When I arrived, I found that the leadership at headquarters had established two mobile battalions. One of the commanders of these battalions approached me with a proposition: "Deniz, I want you to be a company commander within my battalion. Will you accept such a duty?" I decided to do so.

After I was assigned, we left the headquarters in Zap and traveled to where Cemil Bayık was staying at the field of Gari, within Iraq. Because there were already three battalion forces with Bayık, there was no need for our battalion to be stationed there. Despite the fact that negotiations had begun with Barzani once again, Bayık told us, "We are seriously at a stalemate with this man. He has another opportunity to stab us in the back yet again, because he can get help from the tank forces that have been deployed by Turkey. With this in mind, I want you to take two of these battalion forces along with you to the Soran line, so you can cut off any reinforcements from Barzani."

We knew that everything would be much easier if we could rid ourselves of the Peshmerga forces first. Many of the villages within the Soran district contained Peshmerga military posts, so we decided to raid each village as we passed. During this process, we almost completely destroyed five of these military posts. Rather than fight back against us, many of the Peshmerga forces ran away. With these victories, the Gari area was brought under the control of the organization. We actually had had an unofficial dominance in this area before, but the Peshmerga always caused us trouble. Whenever we ran across them, they would say, "What are you doing here? You can stay in Haftanin, Metina, Zap, and Zagros, but you should know that Gari is our land. The PKK cannot conduct any political or military activity here."

Even with their exasperation, the new agreement with Barzani officially delivered control of the Gari region to the organization. It was very important that we had this area, because it was in a strategic location. The cities of Zaho, Erbil, and Suleimaniye were located right in the middle of Gari, and it was also very close to the city of Mosul. Besides the importance of its location, the Turkish security forces had no right to fly over or attack the Gari region, since there were thousands of local peasants living there. On top of that, any kind of Turkish attack in Gari would be considered hostile by the Iraqi government.

I had had a bad experience while fighting to capture and control Gari that would have potentially affected my future commanding career. The Peshmerga had completely emptied a village of its inhabitants and were using it as military base. With that knowledge, we decided to raid this village and either kill or push back the Peshmerga forces. Before we began our mission, we received an order from the headquarters leadership. "If the Peshmerga forces are willing to surrender, do not kill them but take them all captive!"

Two weeks before our mission, I participated in a reconnaissance of the village to make sure it was full of Peshmerga forces. Our scouting showed that there were no civilians left inside the village. This would make our raid much easier, because we would not have to worry about the tactics or techniques that we would use during the attack. Even more important was the fact that we would not have to worry about the risk of killing civilians by mistake. As soon as our mission began, I heard the screams of women coming from one of the houses in the village. I immediately contacted the other guerillas on the radio and said, "Do not attack this house, there are probably civilians hiding inside." After we killed all the Peshmerga who were holed up in the other houses in the village, we encircled that one remaining home. Six women and six Peshmerga soldiers came out and surrendered. We found, to our surprise that these women served the Peshmerga soldiers by cooking meals and washing dishes and clothes.

When our commander had instructed us to bring back whomever we took captive, I do not think he thought there may be a possibility of civilian women in the village. In fact, we could not have guessed we would encounter such a complicated situation. So, because of our original instructions, we took the six women, with the captured soldiers, to our camp. When he saw the captive women, the company commander got angry. "Who the hell are they, Deniz? Why did you bring these women here?" I replied, "Comrade, they were hiding in the same village as the Peshmerga forces and they surrendered. You ordered me to bring all the captives, and I have done so."

He did not like my answer and said, "Comrade, have you lost your mind? Why did you not contact me over the radio and tell me about these women? The entire world will be against us now. All of the TV channels that speak for Barzani will say, 'The PKK have kidnapped our women, our wives.'" Honestly, it had not occurred to me that this could be a problem for the organization. Unfortunately, the exact thing that the commander feared came to pass. Almost all of the local television channels produced segments with false information, saying the PKK had killed all of the male soldiers and then had kidnapped and raped the women in the village. Of course, these channels did not mention that this village was being used as a base for Peshmerga forces. This incident was broadcast as if the PKK had purposefully attacked a village that had nothing but civilians inside.

Because of the media and the psychological pressure put on us, we had to set our captives free. We also had to prove that the women we captured had not been raped, and that we had let them go. If we had not released them, the Kurdish people under Barzani would have begun to think badly about our organization (i.e., that we were rapists). Also, any sympathy the Kurdish people might have had for the organization would suddenly vanish. In fact, the only real reason for the organization to keep captives was to have them used as a bargaining chip to swap for captured PKK members. We might have been able to trade up to 20 PKK captives for those six Peshmerga soldiers, but it did not work out, because we released them all.

Despite all we did to alleviate the situation, that village continued to nurse a deep hatred for the organization. They took very strict defensive measures that would not even allow our guerillas get within a single kilometer of the village. Since the village was located on the route leading to Mosul, we had to destroy it somehow, and, if we were successful, many areas would automatically come under our control.

Barzani's forces had placed Dochkas on top of almost all of the houses in the village and howitzers all around as well. This made it almost impossible to make raids. With that weaponry they had the advantage and could easily destroy us as soon as they knew we'd arrived. As a final solution, we decided to block all the roads into the village. If we did not let any vehicle go in that direction, they would eventually have to abandon the village when their supplies ran out.

Our plan began with one squad of guerillas laying an ambush on the road between the city of Dohuk and the village. A defense team that was composed of a squad of guerillas was also placed in a nearby area during the darkness of the night. After the ambush team raided the cars coming out, the defense team would shoot the target from a distance so that the ambush team could withdraw and escape. While we were waiting in the ambush area, I saw two trucks begin to drive out of the village. At first I thought that we would not be able to destroy them with only a single squad because there were only eight of us at the ambush site. It was very risky, but I changed my mind and told the guerilla next to me: "No matter what happens, we will shoot these cars. There is no other way out!" We were very lucky and were able to kill all 13 Peshmerga in the trucks before they were able to make a counterattack.

When our comrades went up to the trucks to take weapons and important documents, they found Russian-made Dragunov SVD assassination weapons on the Peshmerga. After taking all of these trophies, we returned to our camp. Seeing all of the Dragunovs made me think the people we just killed could not be regular Peshmerga soldiers, because these types of weapons are only carried by high-ranking commanders. One day later, while we were waiting in the camp, the hillers came to us and said, "Comrades, the village that you attacked yesterday is being evacuated. About twenty trucks arrived and are taking the villagers away." I responded, "Comrade, are you completely sure? That was not a village to give up a fight so easily!"

A few days later we got good news: those people who were traveling in the two trucks had been the senior Peshmerga commanders in that village. They left only the platoon commanders there and were driving to the city of Erbil for a meeting at Peshmerga headquarters. Since there was no senior commander left alive, the rest of the villagers had given up and abandoned the place. We were fortunate because we had been trying to empty that village for years, but had never been able to. It came down to one simple and easy ambush in a single day to do what could not be done before. With this obstacle out of the way, the roads from Mosul to Dohuk were open for the organization.

Saddam Hussein, the President of Iraq, did not intervene when our organization settled in the area that had been previously controlled by Barzani, because he was using a balanced policy between the forces that were present in the region. The PKK was a threat to the YNK and KDP in the region. But on the other hand, the YNK was allied with Iran. So, perhaps Saddam Hussein believed that the PKK could be used against both the YNK and the KDP whenever necessary.

After these challenging battles and struggles, the organization was able to establish its full authority within the Gari region. Soon after we had taken control, the organization relocated all of its critical institutions like the media, healthcare, ammunition warehouses, etc. into the region.

Experience with Treatments on the Battlefield

It is probably quite obvious, but we did struggle a lot. We were not always lucky and many of our comrades became disabled or martyred. For instance, on November 27, 1997 we created a plan to destroy a Peshmerga village which had been causing us trouble for many years. In fact, Duran Kalkan personally joined the coordination of the mission because he wanted to be present, as it got underway. It was the first time we had ever tried to raid this particular village, and we wanted it to be successful since it would also be carried out on the anniversary of the organization.

The Peshmerga forces had settled in this village, and they never left it unprotected. This circumstance made it very hard for us to attack because of the risk of killing civilians. If the Peshmerga forces left the village from time to time, then there was a possibility that we could lay down an ambush and kill them all outside of the village. But the opportunity never presented itself, and instead we had to sneak into the village after dark. On the night of November 27, we were able to approach very close to the village. We were just about to lay siege when suddenly the sound of explosions crashed through the darkness. This was the unfortunate way that we found out that mines had been set around the perimeter. Five of our comrades had their legs, ankles, and feet injured from the explosions and pieces of shell fragments. We were completely demoralized by the serious injuries that befell them. The mission was automatically canceled because of this unexpected failure.

An even worse circumstance was that there was only one doctor present in our battalion. He was also a newbie and had only recently graduated from a medical school in Turkey. He appeared to be both scared of the situation and inexperienced with these types of major injuries. He had an assistant with him who seemed to be just as inexperienced as the doctor was because he was not able to treat the wounded parts of the legs and feet. Our comrades were all groaning out in pain and the assistant was actually instructing the doctor how and where to fix the wounds, but the doctor could not dare to try. It was a chaotic environment as everyone in our battalion was suffering from the shock of the incident.

Mine explosions are probably the most common threat we guerillas experience in our lives. I had gotten quite familiar with amputations for wounds to the extremities, because I had witnessed so many of them throughout my time as a guerilla. There was one particular time back in 1995 that I remember just like it was yesterday. The Turkish security forces had handed us a huge loss in one of the battles, and we had to retreat from the area. When we came back to that same area after a couple of months, we found out the hard way that the area was littered with land mines. Many comrades lost their lives by stepping on those mines. The expert doctor in the battalion had introduced us to how to cut feet after a mine explosion, and I participated in an operation. The doctor said, "Comrades, watch me very carefully. You might need to use this procedure in the future, because there may not be doctors around." Step by step, he showed us how and where to cut the feet, how to stitch wounds, and other things that we needed to be aware of for these kind of incidents. Thanks to what I had learned by watching this doctor, I was able successfully to treat the wounded feet of a comrade.

During the aftermath of the explosion in 1997, neither the doctor nor his assistant was correctly treating our wounded comrades, so I intervened. "Move aside and just assist me!" I said. "Look doctor, you cannot treat feet in that way. Before you amputate, you need to find the main arteries that go through the inside and tie them off with medical cords. If you do not tie off these veins they will pull themselves further inside and you will not be able to find them again."

I went to the comrade whose condition was the worst and began helping the doctors with him. Using a knife, I first pulled up the flesh near the exposed part of the foot that needed to be amputated so I could find the main arteries. I was able to find them and tie them off. As I mentioned before, when the foot is amputated, those veins automatically pull themselves inside if you do not tie them off. If that happens, the chance of finding those veins is low. This means that the blood will continue to drain from the body and the patient will die.

There is also an important detail that the person performing the operation must take into account: if the wounded person is young then the bones of the foot should be cut a little above where the same cut would be made for an older wounded person. This is simply because the leg bones of a younger person will still grow until around the age of thirty. If you cut the bone to the proper length, there is a possibility that you may see the tibia and fibula emerge a couple of centimeters out of the flesh later on. You must cut the bone a couple centimeters into the inner part of the flesh, so even if the bone increases in length it will still stay inside.

There was no need to use anesthetic on our comrades, because the mines had already ruptured their legs and they were already in an extreme amount of pain. They would not even know that they were going through an amputation. We used Swiss-made saw blades to conduct these operations. When I was working on my comrades, I first revealed the three main arteries under the flesh and then tied them off. It is not possible to tie off the capillaries one by one, but it is essential that you tie off the crucial ones.

I had not noticed, but Duran Kalkan had been watching over my shoulder while I was giving instructions to the doctor on how to operate properly on our wounded. He said, "Comrade, just a word of advice to you. If you are already an expert on this, why are you wasting time instructing him? Start doing it yourself and none of our wounded will die."

Following his advice, I started to amputate the legs of our comrades one by one. I would first cut the flesh horizontally up to a point and then open the flesh on the sides to find the main arteries inside. After tying off the veins with a cord, I cut the flap 3 centimeters below the level of the tied veins and threw it away. After this procedure, the bone and the flesh surrounding it was left behind. Using one of our Swiss-made saw blades, I was able to cut the bones in the leg in only about 15 minutes.

You learn a lot of things through experiencing them. With what I learned from that doctor in 1995, I saved the lives of five comrades in 1997. In 2002, I came across some of those friends in an Iraqi camp and they were all doing well. They never had to go through any other surgeries. After the treatment I gave them, they had been sent to hospitals in Damascus and Iraq. However, the professional doctors did not have to do anything further.

I frequently encountered these kinds of incidents in my time with the organization and thus became more experienced on the various kinds of treatments and operations that we had to do. I learned how to treat a bullet wound, how to do first aid on deadly injuries, how to remove a bullet from the body, etc. Having learned these things, I was able to use my experience to support our doctors and other health professionals when they were either inexperienced or there were not enough of them when needed.

This mission was heavily criticized by our headquarters leadership. Aside from being unsuccessful in its purpose, the organization also criticized us for not conducting enough reconnaissance before the mission. In addition to our five comrades being seriously wounded before the mission began, the incident also left much of the group demoralized to an extent. It is upsetting to see your formerly healthy comrades become amputees, and one begins to wonder if the same thing might happen to you one day. Our disabled comrades were also unable to fight as guerillas anymore. Their options were either to be employed behind the front lines in passive work within the camps or to be transferred to European countries and employed to our political organizations to handle relations with the European states.

Slander

Winter camp preparations in the south were never as tough as our preparations in the north had to be. Because we were already in a safe region, we did not need to bother ourselves with building hidden underground bunkers. We also were able to carry the food we bought from Iraqi villagers to our camp, using vehicles and mules. On top of that, we were able to organize festivals during the winter camp period. Bands would come and play music which increased our morale. For example, a band named Koma Berxedan had once come from Europe to our camp in Iraq. Groups like this would visit all of the guerilla camps in the region.

In February 1998, I came across a big problem while staying in the winter camp. A female guerilla reported to one of our company commanders that: "Deniz and I love each other." I did not even know that this woman was staying in our camp. Our battalion commander had been temporarily assigned to Zap back then, and so he was not in the camp, but there was another company commander present. They listened to the slander from the female guerilla and then met with the other company commander, telling him everything.

One morning, I was having breakfast when a guerilla came and informed me that there was a meeting. This made me angry, and I responded as such: "If there was a meeting arranged for now then why am I just being informed of it? What in the hell is this?" Anyway, I went and sat down in the meeting room. The company commander who was temporarily assigned to be our battalion commander asked me, "Deniz, do not you know that a relationship with a female guerilla is forbidden in our organization?" I was shocked and replied, "What relationship are you talking about?" He said, "I heard that you were in a relationship with a woman in the organization!" Still angry I said, "You are full of shit. I am not in a relationship with anyone here." He said the name of this woman and asked if we loved each other. The woman guerilla replied, "Yes sir, I love Deniz." Then he asked her again if she loved me. This time she bent her head down as if shamed and stayed silent. I was surprised, because clearly someone was trying to cook my goose, and yet I could not figure out why they would do this.

It did not take me long to figure it out. Our normal battalion commander was also the commander of the mobile battalion at Zap field. That meant that he was superior to the temporarily assigned battalion commander in terms of both power and initiative. This man was planning to sweep aside and eliminate the powerful commanders who supported our battalion commander while he was absent and he had decided to start with me. Once he was rid of me, this despicable man would be able to spread rumors like: "You see? Our battalion commander let immoral incidents happen even though it is forbidden by our organization." This would weaken our commander and allow this dishonest one to take his place.

They asked: "Deniz, do you plead guilty?" I was given the right to answer, but I was also angry and said, "I neither accept the existence of this so-called relationship nor the legitimacy of this meeting!" And then I left the meeting room. In my absence, the committee sentenced me to jail time. One of the platoon commanders came to me and said, "They have reached a verdict about your guilt. You will be incarcerated, hand me your weapons." I said, "Okay, you can incarcerate me. However, I will not prepare my written defense until the battalion commander returns."

This company commander was devious. He did not keep me in the camp near my own guerilla force but instead extradited me to another region. Apo's nephew was the company commander in the region where I was transferred. I was good friends with him, and when he first saw me, he thought that I was there for a visit. While we were chatting, the temporarily assigned battalion commander told him via radio: "Put Deniz in jail immediately. I will provide you with the background information later."

I had been incarcerated for nearly a week when, on the seventh day, two guerillas came to me with a draft of 15 questions related to my prosecution. There were questions in the draft that had nothing to do with me. I said, "Leave me alone now. I will give you my responses when I finish writing them." I was trying to delay things so I could gain time. While I was putting things off, I noticed one particular night that everyone was in a hurry as if getting ready for something. This gave me the sense there must be something going on within the region. I found out, to my surprise, that our battalion commander and Cemil Bayık were visiting the camp in which I was incarcerated. The region commander informed our battalion commander about what happened with me: "The temporary battalion commander jailed Deniz." Our battalion commander got angry when he heard this and was even angrier when the region commander told him that Deniz supposedly had a relationship with a woman. Cemil

Bayık was listening and his curiosity was piqued, and he asked our battalion commander: "Comrade, what is going on here?" The battalion commander said, "We will need to visit the battalion in which Deniz is jailed to find out the truth."

Two days after they arrived at the camp where I was jailed, I was finally instructed to meet the battalion commander. When I left my cell the guerillas tried to return my weapons, but I told them, "I am not taking them back because I am still under arrest. You are going to have to carry them." Immediately we entered the battalion headquarters, we went to where Comrade Cuma was staying. I was embarrassed of course, because he already knew that I loved someone else. "Deniz, what the hell is this? Why has such a bad thing happened?" he asked.

"Comrade, I honestly did not even know that this woman was staying in our winter camp. I think that there is some kind of scam going on, but I do not know why." Our battalion commander was present during this talk as well, and he said, "I am the target Deniz. That devious commander is planning to pull me down by first targeting my closest friends. When you are prosecuted, I will be put under investigation for allowing such a relationship to go on inside my battalion. Even though this is a scam built upon lies, it will taint both of our reputations."

"How are you two going to handle this situation?" Comrade Cuma asked. The battalion commander said, "Deniz will go in front of the organization for prosecution, and I will take care of the rest." At that time, Şemdin was still hanging around Cuma because of the disaster at Amanoses and, since we knew each other from before, Şemdin approached me and asked, "Why did you place yourself in such a bad situation, Deniz?" And I replied: "It's not a big deal, Şemdin. Tomorrow, the truth will shed light on the situation, and all the lies will be made known."

The battalion commander summoned me around seven in the morning before the prosecution was set to begin. He said, "Deniz, when you go in there I want you to be in front of the organization while holding your weapon." I replied, "Comrade, I am already considered guilty as it is. I do not know that it would be wise to push the issue." He said, "If you seriously respect my authority, please take your weapon with you. Do you still not understand what the real problem is? This is a sneaky game being played against me, not you. Comrade Cuma and I are going to be present at the prosecution process to show support for you. We feel that it is important that you face your accusers with your weapon with you. Please take it back." His insistence worked on me, and I decided to take my weapon back.

The prosecution began at around 8:00 a.m. I made a statement: "I do not know this woman and I have not had a relationship with her. If I had, I would not withhold the truth from you, but instead I would accept any kind of punishment honestly and with no argument. However, I do not even know this woman, yet she says she loves me. This so-called love is unrequited because there are not any feelings between us. How can there be a love if only one member of a couple knows about it? Here you are, just now prosecuting me for this situation, yet you already had reached a decision and jailed me before even listening to my defense. Even if I am acquitted at the end of this trial, I will not serve this battalion any longer. You now know the truth, now reach a verdict!"

When the guerillas listened to my side of the story, they made a suggestion to discharge the temporary battalion commander who had wrongfully accused me. The request went through, and he was discharged for falsely representing the facts and was exiled to Zagros. This ended the trial, and I was reassigned to my company as a commander. Yet even with this promotion, the incident had hurt my pride. "I will not work in this battalion anymore. I will do whatever the organization asks me to do, but I will not do it here!" I said. Cemil Bayık said, "Okay Deniz, I understand. But, let's stay here and celebrate March 8, Women's Day, and then we will transfer you to another location."

The Resignation of Cemil Bayık

On the afternoon of March 13, one of the men who guarded Cemil Bayık came rushing to me and asked whether I had seen Şemdin. He had not been seen in the last three hours. The guards thought that perhaps he had been with me since Şemdin would sometimes visit me to have a chat. I had not seen him, but not a half hour later, I visited the guards and asked whether they had found Şemdin yet or not. No one had seen him, and Cemil Bayık did not even know about his disappearance.

The battalion commander and I finally visited Cuma to inform him of what was going on. Cemil Bayık seemed to be very sad when he heard the news and said, "Do not bother yourself and just let him escape! No one will go after him. He should stew in his own juices for now." In truth, it would have been easy to catch Şemdin because there was only one escape route from our camp area to the other regions. We could have had these places guarded before Şemdin reached them, but no matter how we insisted, Cemil Bayık did not want anyone to go and catch him.

A few days passed and the organization had not yet informed the press about Şemdin's escape. We learned that Şemdin had headed to the KDP and was under the protection of Barzani. As soon as Cemil Bayık learned about this, he gave a speech to BBC radio saying that Şemdin had no relationship with the PKK anymore. In response, Şemdin delivered a short speech with the BBC saying that he had quit the PKK. He even said, "I left the PKK, but I am still loyal to the values of Kurdish patriotism".

Şemdin's escape put Comrade Cuma in a tight spot. This was not the first escape to happen while Cuma was in charge. Three other senior executives had run away while they were in jail under Cemil Bayık's watch. For example, the brother of one of our founders, Baki Kara, had run away while being held by Cemil Bayık. Being held by Cemil Bayık was a great opportunity for the prisoners. If either Baki Kara or Şemdin had been imprisoned under some other senior commander, they would have either been executed or imprisoned without a means of escape. The only thing that Cemil Bayık would do is appropriate their weapons, after that they could walk freely around the place where Cemil Bayık stayed.

On top of that, these prisoners knew Cemil Bayık would not harm them. So, many prisoners abused the freedom they were given by him and ran away. Because of these escapes, people in the organization started to criticize Cemil Bayık saying, "Enough is enough. Why do these people always escape while they are under the watch of Cemil Bayık? Why does he treat them with such a soft attitude even though they are our prisoners?" Cuma was already depressed because of the executions he had to perform at headquarters between the years of 1996 and 1997. When Şemdin ran away, Cemil Bayık resigned from his duty as headquarters commander. Can you believe that? The most significant person in the organization next to President Apo himself had resigned.

In April 1998, we guerillas heard an instruction on the radio that came straight from Damascus: "Comrade Cuma, turn on your satellite phone on this specific day, at this specific time so that our leader, Apo, can address to you!" Cemil Bayık turned on his satellite phone at the appropriate time and Apo began talking to him in an angry manner without letting him get a word in edgewise. He even said some things that disturbed us all: "Are you selling out our organization, Cuma? If you are, then to whom? What did I instruct you before I made you headquarters commander? You had the full authority to do anything. I transferred my own authority to you. Now there have been some incidents, and you are resigning without even letting me know first. I entrusted much to you and now you are giving up on it just because of some criticism. There are many traitors who already want you to quit the organization, and now you are making them happy by acting upon their wishes. I reject your decision to resign. Return to headquarters in Zap immediately and establish your authority once again. Do whatever it takes, appoint whomever to wherever you need them and do not ever attempt to resign again as long as I am alive!" After he said these things, he abruptly hung up.

After he had been admonished, Cuma returned to Zap. Before he left, he told us, "When the guerilla council meeting is held in May, I want you to send two people." Normally, our battalion commander was the one who was supposed to participate in that meeting, but because of the unfortunate incidents we had just experienced, he did not want to leave the battalion. He wanted me to go in his stead.

I went to the guerilla council meeting in May, and Comrade Cuma was not there. At the time, I did not know why. Instead, Ebubekir came from Damascus to lead the meeting. Later, we heard that Cemil Bayık had been sent to Iran; however, we did not know the reason for his visit. We guessed that it might have something to do with tensions in our diplomatic relations with Iran, and since Cemil Bayık had been the one controlling the organization's relations there, it made sense that he would need to go to fix any problem that arose. He would never have to leave headquarters to go there unless there was a serious problem. We actually were told later that Cemil Bayık's slipped disc in his lower back had deteriorated and he had to be taken to Tehran for surgery. That was why he had delegated his duty to Ebubekir. After that we did not see Cuma for quite some time.

The Children of the Organization

In the spring of 1998, the members of the organization that were in command were going to travel to Zagros from Metina for a military meeting. We set off for the meeting in the night and had a lot of ground to cover before sunrise. During our trip, I noticed two of our female guerillas falling behind all the time. Because they were dropping back, the rest of the group had to stop until they caught up. Since the group had to stop frequently because of these two women, I told the other commander: "Comrade, you can lead the rest of the group. I am going to go and talk to these stragglers."

When I got to them, I saw that one of them was unable to walk without the help of the other. I first thought that she must be sick. I said, "Comrade is there a problem? Why are you falling behind repeatedly?" They replied, "No, there is nothing is wrong. We will catch up with you." They reached the rest of the group again, and even before ten minutes had passed, I realized that they had fallen behind yet again. I told the group: "You all continue on. I will stay with the stragglers and meet you at our destination."

I went to those two again and said, "Comrade, what is your problem? Are you sick? Or is your load too heavy? If you hand your bag over to me, I can carry it. You are disturbing the rest of the group." No matter how much I insisted, she would not give me her bag. The other woman finally whispered in my ear: "Deniz, I will tell you something but mum is the word. This comrade is pregnant, and that is why she is having such a hard time walking."

I was very surprised because that was the first time I had heard something like that in my entire time with the organization. "Do any of the commanders know about this?" I asked. "No, only a few other female guerillas know, that is all," she replied. I insisted further and took her rucksack, weapon, and other things she had been carrying and carried them myself.

Until the PKK's fifth congress, which was held in 1994, the standard punishment in the organization for having sexual intercourse was execution. However, this rule had been abolished by a direct order from Apo during the fifth congress. This woman had been impregnated by Dr. Süleyman, the brother of Selim Çürükkaya. Back then, Dr. Süleyman was a member of the PKK central committee. Because of the sexual intercourse, he was arrested when the Zagros meeting was over. We were all very curious because we did not know how he was going to be punished.

The pregnant guerilla was immediately transferred to the Maxmur camp within Iraq. In 2000, two years after the incident, I saw a little girl in a village that was 30 minutes from the Şehit Harun camp. The village was under the control of the YNK, Talabani. The girl was around two years old and was crying while holding one of her feet at the entrance to the village. I figured that she must be the daughter of a peasant or something. I decided to approach her and asked, "Why are you crying sweet girl? What is wrong?" She was young and so could not speak properly yet, but she was pointing at her foot. I saw there were nutlets from a plant known as devil's thorn stuck into the bottom of her foot. I had her lay down so I could carefully take the nutlets out. She finally stopped crying when the nutlets were removed. I held her hand and asked her, "Sweetie, can you show me where your house is?" I realized that she was pointing to the camp of my comrades. There were Kurdish peasants staying in that camp who used to live in Turkey, but they had run away from the oppression they faced from the Turkish security forces. I thought that she could be the daughter of one of those villagers.

I picked her up and carried her on my shoulders toward the camp. When we arrived at the entrance, someone asked, "Comrade, where did you find her? We have been searching for her since this morning." I told him the story, and then asked, "She is so cute. Whose child is she?" "She is our child, comrade, not the villagers'," he answered. To my surprise, she turned out to be Dr. Süleyman's daughter.

I was curious and so asked, "Comrade, why did you call her our child, then?" He said, "That is on the order of the organization. She is no longer Dr. Süleyman's daughter, but the organization's. The organization has assumed full responsibility of raising her." She was such a lovely child. I took her to the grocery store in the village and told her she could buy whatever she wants. She took whatever she saw: chocolate, biscuits, etc. It ended up costing me quite a bit. When we returned to the camp, I asked the guards where her mother was, and they told me that her mother was staying in the Maxmur camp. I asked them why the child was staying here if her mother was not here. "Comrade, the child is under our protection. We take care of her needs," they responded. That seemed strange to me, and I said to myself, "Life is full of surprises! I had carried her mother's rucksack when she was pregnant and here I was now carrying that baby on my shoulders."

There is an important fact about the organization, which I have said repeatedly: they cannot follow everyone around all the time. These forbidden love affairs can sometimes result in the impregnation of female guerillas. Later on in my time with the organization, I came across many other children like her. If necessary, the organization will raise and take care of them. There were children in Damascus whose parents were murdered by security forces and Apo was taking care of them personally. He would also visit orphan asylums at least three or four times a week and would play with the children for hours.

When I once visited an orphanage, I found that there were about 15 children there. Even though the organization no longer executed those who had sexual intercourse, they were not allowed to raise their children. They were all considered to be children of the organization, and the parents were allowed to see them from time to time.

12

THE WOMEN GUERILLAS OF THE ORGANIZATION

There used to be a more male-dominated family structure in the Kurdish communities, where the men were always superior to the women. The organization had a difficult time in its struggle to increase the social status of Kurdish women, but they finally achieved it, and it was difficult for Kurdish men to accept women being equal. This was mostly due to the fact that they had not seen anything like that from their parents as they grew up in their households. Similarly, women had difficulty adapting to their new status as well. And there were fewer of them in the organization—at most only one or two female guerillas per squad.

All of the easiest tasks would be given to women. For example, there were items like pans, glasses, spoons, teapots, forks, knifes, pots, etc. in each squad. In the beginning of the organization, only the female guerillas were responsible for the transportation of those things, but that changed as the years went on. Also, the male guerillas used to have a much different standpoint, regarding women. They felt that the women could not fight like them, could not endure the hardships of mountain life, and did not have the same stamina as the men. Those opinions changed dramatically after the year 1996.

Zeynep Kınacı's suicide mission changed men's opinion of female guerillas, because it was the first time in its history that someone had sacrificed themselves for the organization. Until then, no male guerilla ever dared strap explosives on themselves in order to perform such a mission. Since a woman was the first to carry out this act, the male guerillas naturally changed their stance and had more respect for the women. After her bravery, women began to participate in important missions, like raids, attacks, and ambushes. Nowadays, if an attack team consists of ten guerillas, at least four of them are chosen from among the female guerillas.

The women seemed to think they had to try harder in order to prove themselves. They would sometimes throw themselves into deadly situations before the men did. I witnessed this many times. Mostly, men would carry a load of about 25 kilograms in their rucksacks, but some women would carry close to 50 kilograms, just to stop the stereotype that they were weak, fragile, and useless.

Apo gave a lot of effort to achieving equality among men and women in Kurdish society, because he truly cared about women. For instance, in every single letter that he sent from prison, he would always say, "Send my greetings and respect to the women guerilla forces." He did not always mention the same thing for the men, but he never forgot the women. When he was first captured by security forces, the women guerillas became quite anxious for him. They would say, "We had a great protector, but now he has been arrested. What will happen to us? Will the new executives of the organization treat us with the same respect and care as Apo?" But, since Apo had laid such a strong foundation of equality, embraced by every member, the women continued to be treated with the same degree of respect and care as they always had.

Whether man or woman, though, criminals would still suffer the same consequences. No one had any special privilege when it came to those matters. I mentioned before that around 1999 or 2000, soon after Apo had been arrested, a female force traveled to Tehran to meet with Iranian officials, and 17 of the women were arrested when they returned. The organization never tolerated or ignored such treachery.

Despite all of the facts, most of the propaganda created about the PKK had to do with women. Our enemies always claimed that Kurdish peasant girls were being abducted by the organization and forced to have sexual intercourse with the guerillas. This was all slander and lies. There had definitely never been anything like that in the culture of our organization. How could we rape Kurdish peasants, if we could not even have intercourse with the one we love? Neither female nor male guerillas could bear the consequences of such a thing. Not a chance. If something like that had happened in the organization, the perpetrator would not only have been executed, but afterwards they would have been smashed into pieces.

The rules of the organization even forbade the kissing of the woman you loved. Sometimes, women made appearances on TV and in the newspapers, claiming they were rape victims who had been able to escape the organization. These accusations were all unsubstantiated. The organization had accused me of being in relationships with seven different women, never mind sexual intercourse. I swear to God that I only kissed one of them. Of course, there are always exceptions to the rule, and some guerillas do have voluntary sexual intercourse. Those relationships could result in situations like Dr. Süleyman's, whose child was being raised by the organization.

The organization was very strict on its ban of sexual relationships. Had they been allowed, many female guerillas would have become pregnant, and how could they raise their children while living a guerilla lifestyle in the wilderness and in the mountains? If you did end up having a child, then you would be separated from them. You, your wife, and your child would all be transferred to different regions. If everyone had the freedom of having intercourse with women everywhere they were deployed, then no one would ever know whose child was whose, causing degeneracy and immorality to flourish throughout the organization.

The libel and slander on this subject was the biggest reason for my anger toward the police and military forces in Turkey. They reported that we raped women and abducted girls. Those were all fabricated lies, created to defame the organization. The Turkish people came to regard the PKK, and its guerillas, as violent cannibals who even rape their own girls.

Had these slanders been true, the organization would not have the large support and participation that it has today. Also, there would not be nearly as many Kurdish people trying to join the organization. I swear, I once witnessed a peasant deliver his own daughter to the organization.

We would sometimes stay in the villages while we patrolled the countryside, and we were trusted so much that often the peasants would leave their houses and provide security for us, just so we might sleep more comfortably. If we were to lose that trust and confidence, it would be impossible to stay with those peasants anymore. If the public did not support us, the organization would have eventually burned out, but security and honor were two of the key things that the Kurdish public expected from the organization. We occasionally stayed in their mountain homes, and there were even times when a peasant would need to go to the city and he left without worry, because he could trust his daughter and wife with us. The people openly said, "I do not need to worry about my family, because they are in good hands."

The Turkish press would report that Cemil Bayık had six female guards whom he kept like a harem, and that he slept with those women every night. They had a photograph that supposedly proved this and showed it when they slandered him. But, actually, Mehmet Şener was the first one in the organization to have female guards, and later there were two other commanders that had them as well. One of them was Şemdin Sakık, and the other one was Osman Öcalan. Other than those two, no one else had female guards.

Actually, Cemil Bayık had two different types of guards—one being a platoon of guerillas that consisted of only men. They were all experienced and were often members from the beginning of the organization. In addition to this, he had a team of special forces that provided his close protection, and it, too, consisted of only male guerillas. Beyond never having female guards, he would not even talk to a woman alone. A regular male battalion commander or a male member from PKK headquarters could summon a female guerilla and speak with her alone, but I have personally seen Cemil go out of his way only to speak to women when someone else was present.

No one, especially anyone from the top of the organization, would dare engage in that kind of relationship, because if the senior members did, it would automatically trickle down until everyone else was doing it as well. This was the main reason I abstained from higher levels of appointment. The higher your rank, the less interaction you have with the women in the organization. At those levels, you could not chat with them for socialization or play sports with them in your free time. But as a regular guerilla, you had more opportunities to be around them and were able to play volleyball and soccer together, as well as join in other social activities.

There was not any sexuality, but rather, a sincere friendship in these men's and women's mixed activities. We males would sometimes even sleep in the same room with the females for a couple of nights. Believe me, neither the women nor the men would even think about engaging in sexual intercourse during those times. I explained this to both the police and senior military commanders. "You make fools of yourselves by listening to those unfounded claims. None of the Kurds in the east would believe in those lies. Only Turks in the western parts of the country would fall for such fiction." Turkish officials had used the media to present the organization to the Turkish public in such a bad light that now many Turks think the PKK guerillas live a degenerate life, though none of those things reflect the truth.

On the subject of Cemil Bayık's alleged infidelities, let's say a woman had some sort of problem and needed to talk with Comrade Cuma regarding it. Again, he would never meet with this woman alone. A couple of other male and female guerillas would accompany the woman when she visited with him. I am quite confident that the picture of Cuma surrounded by seven or eight girls, shown in the Turkish media, is just him with a women's youth group. It is the type of photo that might be taken at the end of those meetings. The girls thought of Cemil Bayık as a father.

Even a battalion commander had many opportunities to be around women if he wanted. He could be alone with a woman, chat with her, and could also have sexual intercourse, but only if that woman desired to as well. Even with those possibilities, something like that would never happen in the organization. No one would risk their position on the possibility of such rumors.

There was also the fact that the organization had thousands of members in the south, within Iran, Syria, and Iraq, and also the north, in Turkey. These thousands of guerillas could not be watched at all times, so there will, of course, be some outliers. However, those exceptions did not mean that the rules did not matter; these kinds of relationships were strictly prohibited. You cannot blame the whole organization for mistakes made by individuals. Take the Turkish state, as an example. Can we, as an organization, blame every single Turk for mistakes made by only one or two members of their security forces?

The women in the organization have always been a step ahead of the men. Many of the rights given to women, have not yet been granted to men. Sometimes, male comrade guerillas joke with one another saying, "I wish I had been born a woman." Let's say there were a bunch of men watching TV in the quarters, and later a woman joined them. Believe me, none of the men could watch TV in a relaxed position by stretching their legs or getting comfortable when a woman was present, even if they were a superior of that woman. We were more relaxed toward one another when there was not a woman among us. The same thing also went for the women. They were more comfortable in how they acted when they were together. Also, you could make jokes to a man, but never to a woman!

No matter what is said, Kurdish women are more free and autonomous today, because of the initiatives that Apo and the PKK created and enforced. The organization attached a great importance to women. They had private schools that were completely separate from the men's. One of those schools was located in the Kandil region of Iraq, and they got special training while they were there. While the women were being trained at those schools, the men undertook all the chores, such as cooking, washing, and cleaning. There was such great responsibility given to women guerillas within the organization.

The Betrayal of Şemdin Sakık

Now, back to where I left off. As I mentioned previously, we were going to begin our military council meeting without Comrade Cuma, because he was in Iran. Unfortunately, the Turkish military started a land operation against us even before we began the meeting. This campaign was similar to the one in 1997. The Turkish army would bombard us from the north, while the Peshmerga did the same from the south. They believed they would inflict a heavy blow to the PKK with this tactic, but luck was with us. The Peshmerga had learned its lesson from the recent defeat we had handed them and had not dared to join this military operation with the Turkish army. At the same time, the Turkish security forces had received a major blow from us in the Zagros and Metina Fields. When they reached Metina, they realized that the Peshmerga forces were not positioned to fight, but they had withdrawn instead. The only Peshmerga forces in the area had been positioned on the tops of hills nearby. Barzani had done this, so as not to offend Turkey. They did not even fight against us. As soon as the Turkish military realized how the situation was, they also withdrew. The organization's military council had been scattered to different regions before this operation was started, because of how risky it was to keep them all in the same place during battle. Around the beginning of June, the operation had failed, the troops were withdrawn, and our council members were able to come together again in Metina.

The meetings normally lasted around 15 days, but this time it was longer. They started in the mornings every day, and lasted until the evening. However, that year our meeting times coincided with the FIFA World Cup, and the guerillas wanted to watch the games. Because many of the games were played both during the morning and the afternoon, no one was able to concentrate on the issues that were being discussed. As a result, the senior officials postponed the meeting for 15 days. They said, "Okay, watch the games, but you will be staying here longer than expected." Everyone agreed with the schedule change. Once the games and meetings were over, I was assigned to a region located between the Haftanin region and Cudi Mountain.

As I stated before, Barzani first promised to side with Turkey against the PKK in the operation that took place in 1998, but later did not keep that promise. Due to this betrayal, Turkey had an issue of trust with Barzani's management in Iraq. To fix the trust issues, Barzani handed Şemdin Sakık over to the Turkish security forces. His actions were smart, since by handing over Şemdin to Turkey, he fixed both his relations with the country and rescued himself from the pressure that was coming from the organization concerning Şemdin's extradition. The Turkish media outlets broadcasted this as "Şemdin Sakık was captured by the Turkish security forces." They even said, "Special forces caught Şemdin after tracking him by helicopters, while he was traveling from one region to another." There was not an iota of truth to that story.

Şemdin had revealed many secret details about the organization. He told them where Apo was hiding, how the camp field was being protected, etc. His statements to the security forces were not only limited to that information, he also provided the details about the number of camps the organization had, where they were located, how many guerillas were staying in those camps, and which paths the guerillas were using to cross the border from Iraq to Turkey. These were not just speculation. His official statements were delivered to the organization, but I do not know by what means they were delivered. However, this often happened. About a week after a runaway was captured by security forces, the organization would obtain the statements they had given. I cannot say for sure whether the informant was a police officer, prosecutor, or judge, but we definitely obtained these statements somehow. Turkish security forces were able to force Apo to leave Syria, after the statements Şemdin Sakık had provided.

In his statement to security forces, Sakik said, "Even if you were able to destroy every single guerilla in Turkey, Apo will recruit new ones. This will continue as long he stays in his safe haven at Damascus." He had even used such a phrase as, "Apo is so good at persuading and influencing that he could make guerillas out of stone if you killed all of his fighters. Therefore, your main target needs to be where he stays in Damascus. Once you clear him from there, you should target Botan, because the inner circle of the organization stays there. Although the military headquarters is located in Zap, the Administration of the guerillas in the northern provinces are controlled from Botan, which can be compared to a power distribution unit. If you want to dismantle the organization, head toward those two areas with both barrels."

It was not long after Semdin's statements that the Turkish military began focusing on our units at Botan. This was proof that Şemdin had given up many secret details about the organization. When this was realized, Comrade Cemal (Murat Karayılan) was transferred to another region and Bahoz Erdal was assigned to Botan, to lead the organization's fight against the Turkish military instead. I was in the Haftanin region back then.

As soon as Apo was forced out of Damascus, the Turkish military started massive land and air attacks against our forces at Botan, just as Şemdin had suggested. This was no ordinary military operation. Most of these operations would last ten to 15 days, but this time, they did indeed come to destroy us. The campaign lasted for 50 days and they used heavy operational tactics; simultaneously attacking from the air and the land with frequent bombardments.

It was very obvious that Şemdin had provided them with the coordinates of strategic locations, because their fighter jets were bombing locations where our commanders were hiding. For example, the place where Comrade Cemal was staying was hit first by fighter jets, and then sieged by Turkish land forces. The soldiers would never be able to conduct such pinpoint attacks, if the details had not been provided by the traitor Şemdin.

During this battle, we lost 17 comrades, but the Turkish security forces had also suffered heavy losses. Our comrades had managed to gather some cryptographic radios from the Turkish soldiers we had killed. Using these radios, they were able to listen to the conversations of the enemy commanders, and learn their tactics and plans about the operation. During these talks, some of the Turkish generals even suggested using chemical weapons to kill Murat Karayılan and his guerillas. The generals were arguing about using chemical bombs, because the person who would determine the fate of the organization, after Apo, was Murat Karayılan, and he was trapped there. After a long discussion, they ended up not carrying out this plan, because some of the generals objected due to the risks associated with chemical warfare.

Retrieving the radios from the soldiers' bodies had been a real boon. We now knew most every single detail about their tactics; where the Turkish army would be attacking; which areas did not have many soldiers, etc. Once the risks were weighed, the guerillas found a possible escape route from the hill where the Turkish commanders had positioned themselves. Indeed, using this route, Murat Karayılan and the guerillas were able to make their escape. When the security forces figured out that our forces had gotten passed them, they began to track them with helicopters and picked up their trail in the foothills near Herekol Mountain.

Knowing that Murat and his guerillas were in the area, they deployed all their soldiers and rangers. During this clash, five personal bodyguards of Murat Karayılan were martyred. Because he had lost his guards, Murat Karayılan began to fight directly with the enemy himself. During the fight, two rangers shot and severely wounded him. As soon as the other guerillas noticed that Murat had been wounded, they positioned themselves around him and used their own bodies to guard him from the bullets coming from the rangers. In the end, Murat Karayılan was taken out of the area of battle, but was badly wounded.

Murat's guerillas immediately informed the other units in the region that Cemal was seriously wounded, and must be taken out of the area at all costs. One platoon of guerillas then engaged in a self-sacrifice mission. They had attacked the perimeter of the siege by directly going over the soldiers and rangers, and some of them were able to reach our force inside, but most of them lost their lives. Nearly 90 percent of our comrades lost their lives during this mission. But they were able to demoralize the Turkish soldiers who had become anxious because of the self-sacrifice mission, and so lifted the siege. In the end, our brave comrades were able to rescue Karayılan from the enemy, and from death.

Apo Leaves Syria

It was either September or October of 1998 when Apo delivered a speech over the radio. "My comrades, be prepared against our enemies. There are tough and stressful days ahead of us." Back then, we listened to the cryptographic radio broadcasts of the Turkish security forces and found they had deployed thousands of Turkish soldiers to the Turkey-Syria border. These Turkish soldiers were positioned within the cities of Hatay, Antep, and Mardin. In addition to that, Ankara was conducting intense diplomatic negotiations with the authorities of many foreign countries. So, both the warning given by Apo over the radio and the deployment of Turkish soldiers along the Syrian border caused us to acknowledge that trouble was soon coming. But we were never certain whether or not Turkey would run the risk of attacking Bashar Assad in Syria.

However, Syria could not handle the pressure for very long, because Turkey had the backing of international powers, and Syria did not have the strength to counteract the international consortium alone. Russia and Iran were the only two countries that supported Syria back then, and Russia was in a chaotic situation because of its economic crisis. So, Russia was not even in a position to raise its voice against the international consortium and, in fact, ended up turning a blind eye to Syria, for its own sake.

While we prepared ourselves for the worst possible outcome, we heard that Apo left Damascus on October 8. This was the first time we had encountered such a problem. Of course, Apo had left Damascus many times to visit several European countries to establish diplomatic relationships. During 1987 and 1988, he began a tour in Greece and traveled from there to many other European countries in order to conduct interviews with senior officials. However, this time, on October 8, 1998, we all knew that he was leaving Syria for good. The guerillas in the region were notified by the senior officials that, "We will prepare ourselves for war against those enemies!"

Because the Greek Parliament had officially invited Apo to stay in Greece, it was the first place he went after Syria. As soon as word got out that Apo was in Greece, the United States began to put pressure on the Greeks to extradite him to the Turks. The Greeks could not take the pressure for long. In the meantime, the Russian Duma Assembly made a decision to harbor Apo inside Russia, so he was transferred there by Greek intelligence.

Now, the U.S. put pressure on Russia to extradite Apo. Madeleine Albright was the head of the State Department back then. In 1998, Russia was suffering from a serious economic problem. The United States, taking advantage of the situation Russia found itself in, made an agreement (most probably economic) with Russia in return for Apo's deportation. Russia cracked under the pressure, and he was transferred to Italy. After that, Germany asked to have Apo transferred from Italy, because there was a warrant for him issued by the German courts. The Italians had actually asked the Germans to take Apo, but the German government was not interested in him at all. Because of this, Apo was stuck in Italy for a long while and applied for political asylum there. Even though he remained in Italy, he was still in contact with other governments. On top of that, our administration in Iraq, and representatives in Europe, were visiting Apo regularly. The Italians allocated a house for Apo in Rome and personally provided his security.

During that time, Apo declared a ceasefire. He addressed both the Europeans and the Turks. "You have always asked for a solution through negotiation and dialogue. Now, here I am in Europe. Our organization is ready for a solution through negotiation. We are ready to lay down our weapons. Let's solve this problem around the table." No one had taken Apo's efforts for peace seriously, at that time, but meanwhile, the senior executives of the organization were preparing our upper-level commanders for the worst-case scenario. They informed us that, by the end of the process, Apo was going to be extradited to the Turks. Unsurprisingly, that was exactly what happened. After staying in Italy for a while, he was sent to the Netherlands. Dutch officials sent him back to Greece from there. In Greece, Apo was not even allowed to leave the plane at first, because the Greeks were fearful of the pressure that would come from the United States. So, he was forced to go to yet another country. After spending a couple of days in Athens, Apo was sent to Kenya and was housed in the Greek Embassy in Nairobi. From there, the next step of the plan was for him to be transferred to Nelson Mandela's country, South Africa. In the end, though, he was arrested in Kenya and delivered to Turkey.

As soon as they heard Apo had been arrested, the senior officials, Murat Karayılan, Duran Kalkan, and Osman Öcalan, went to Cemil Bayık and said, "Comrade, the management of our organization should not be handed over to new comrades. Our situation is too dire!" They wanted Cemil to take control of the organization in Apo's absence. It was for this reason that Cemil Bayık was appointed president of the council of the 6th congress.

The 6th congress placed the blame for Apo's arrest on the European representatives of the PKK, because they had mapped out the plans before he had even left Damascus. Supposedly, our representatives had met with European officials and arranged political asylum for Apo. Through their agreement, Apo would supposedly be able to stay in Europe without any problems. When Apo did encounter problems in Europe, we soon realized that nothing had been arranged properly. Therefore, the congress decided to arrest the European management of the organization. New members of a European management team were quickly appointed. Murat Karayılan even traveled to Europe to meet with these newly appointed officials and even conducted parleys with state authorities in Germany, England, France, Italy, and the Netherlands. He also visited other extensions of the PKK in Europe. The political structure of the organization was not at all like that of the guerillas. They were seriously demoralized and despaired over Apo's arrest. They did not have the proper mentality but bemoaned, "Apo has been arrested. Our struggle is over, and now the organization will soon fall apart." While Murat Karayılan was visiting in Europe, he was able to motivate these brokenhearted, patriotic Kurds.

Iran was the first foreign power that tried to take advantage of the chaos within the organization. Iran had connections and political relations with the senior management until that time, and the organization was in regular contact with Iranian officials. But when Apo was arrested, those officials communicated directly with the commander of the female forces of the organization, without the permission of headquarters. Iran was a sneaky and dangerous state. They knew the structure and hierarchy of the organization, even better than Turkey did, and they prepared quite an intelligent plan. By infiltrating the commanders of the female forces, they were trying to capture the attention of one of the controlling structures in the organization. The female force was the most important force in the PKK, and that is why Iran wanted to contact them directly. They were going to try and take control of the organization by buying off the senior members of the female force.

Unfortunately, some senior officials of the female force accepted their heinous invitation, and traveled to Tehran to meet with those people. In the meeting that took place before they went on the trip to Iran, the female guerillas argued, "We are only committed to Apo. No one except him can tell us what to do, and with whom to speak." Somehow, the information regarding the Iranian invitation was leaked to Cemil Bayık, and he became frustrated when he was told that Iran wanted to get in contact with our female force, without first letting the organization know about it. He immediately sent a representative to Iran to deliver a harsh response. "This organization has senior management. If you want to ask something of the PKK, you can only ask us. Do not ask the members in the lower echelons of the organization!" Because our organization was struggling back then, the female guerillas who visited Iran were not punished. Nevertheless, we knew that at the first opportunity, Cuma would make them pay for what they had done.

Some people argued that the fight between the Turks and the Kurds would have ended after Apo's arrest, if he had broadcast a message through the media saying, "Our armed struggle is at an end, and from now on, we will only continue to defend the rights of Kurdish people through political means." As I mentioned before, once Apo was incarcerated, he continued to deliver instructions to our senior officials through the connection that was provided by the Americans. All of his instructions were implemented, word for word, even though a few were not welcomed by some of the guerillas. For example, during this term, nearly 80 percent of the PKK guerillas were withdrawn from Turkish territories, because Apo had ordered it. I remember his orders very well. It was August 2, 1999 and the guerilla forces in Turkey were ordered to leave their positions and retreat to the camps inside Iraq and Syria. The dialogue between Turkey and the PKK had begun the previous June. I do not know what kind of assurances were given to the PKK. All I knew was that our forces were supposed to leave the Turkish territories immediately.

Once these instructions were received, some of the guerillas raised their voices against the senior management of the organization. "If we are withdrawing from Turkey, have any of you heard what kind of assurances we will get in return for what we are doing?" They were right for worrying, because it is very difficult to recapture areas, once you withdraw.

Although there was some discontentment with this order, almost all of the provinces and regions obeyed it, and withdrew their forces to the south. The organization and Turkey had signed some sort of pact. According to this pact, the Turkish security forces would not attack the PKK forces as they withdrew from Turkey. The organization implemented this decision, despite resistance from some groups within the guerillas. The Turkish security forces ended up not even complying with the rules of the ceasefire to which they had agreed. While the guerilla forces were withdrawing from Turkey, they were trapped in tank ambushes, and almost four hundred militants were martyred. Even with this atrocity, the organization did not allow any missions to be conducted against the military forces in retaliation.

The forces in the north were directed to the southern line in Iraq. There was another problem in the south, awaiting the guerillas. An intensive force had been amassed there. After Apo had been arrested, hundreds of Syrian Kurds, Iranian Kurds, and our forces from Turkey had come to this spot. The camp capacity was not sufficient for such a large amount of people, and we had to spread into the fields of Barzani and the YNK, who, at first, said nothing against us being there. There was a place called Karadağ between the YNK and Iran, and we set up new camps there as well.

The Emergence of Self-Sacrifice (Suicide) Teams

The commander of Botan Field, Bahoz Erdal, visited our region of Haftanin in February of 1999. Apo had not yet been arrested at that time, but the senior officials of the organization were expecting it to happen soon. Bahoz was meeting with the guerillas and providing political and ideological training. We left our winter camps in March, because spring comes earlier to the south than it does to the north.

One day, a comrade was watching the news around 4:30 a.m. and saw that Apo had been arrested and was being flown to Turkey. He came directly to my room and informed me of what he had heard. I asked him, "Comrade, did you hear correctly?" He said all the TV channels were broadcasting the story. I began to watch the news, and around 8:00 a.m., Prime Minister Bulent Ecevit arranged a press briefing and declared to the world that Apo had, in fact, been arrested.

When the rest of the guerillas saw the news story, the camp became chaotic. The senior members, including myself, were not able to calm everyone down. It made the regular guerillas wonder about the future of the organization but panic did not spread to the members of the higher leadership. They remained calm because even though Apo was incarcerated, there was a Presidency Council that would take over decision-making.

The Presidency Council had been put into place before Apo left Damascus. It was created to lead the organization in his absence. It appeared that he had thought about all the possible probabilities, including his own arrest. The council was composed of Cemil Bayık, Duran Kalkan, Murat Karayılan, Nizamettin Taş, and a few female guerillas.

Although the commanders had prepared themselves for the possibility of Apo's extradition to Turkey, the regular guerillas were completely blindsided by the news. Mid-level commanders, like myself, had been told regularly, "Our leader could be caught at any time, so be prepared for such a situation!" None of these possibilities were reflected to the ground guerillas, which was a mistake, because they were so upset when they heard that he'd been arrested.

Bahoz Erdal was staying in our company during that period, and he played an active role in pacifying the disgruntled guerillas. He organized three to four different meetings daily to meet and talk with them about the situation. The ground guerillas were not very convinced, though, no matter what he said or did. Most of them openly indicated that they wanted to conduct self-sacrifice missions. Almost everyone was writing reports, trying to prove why he or she was the best to engage in a self-sacrifice mission. The atmosphere was very tense. Two guerillas from my battalion even set themselves on fire by pouring oil over their bodies. They did this simply because I would not allow them to cross into Turkey for a self-sacrifice mission. They gave the commanders a serious message. "If you do not let us engage in self-sacrifice missions, we will all burn ourselves alive." First aid was provided immediately, and, thankfully, they did not die but had serious burns all over their bodies.

We were expecting to receive a message from leadership regarding what to do about the out of control guerillas. As I said before, neither the ideology nor the policies of the organization encouraged us to target Turkish civilians. We had one target at which to discriminately aim, which was the system and the management within the security forces. With Apo's incarceration, the guerillas began to criticize the PKK's peaceful policies toward the Turkish public. They began openly saying, "We should kill every single Turk we see, whether civilian or not. We Kurds cannot dream of living under one state as the brothers of Turks any longer." The situation became very severe, and the Presidency Council members at headquarters were delivering speeches, via radio, to two or three regions a day just to try and calm down the guerillas. "No one should act on their own! Control your emotions and dull your hunger for vengeance until we instruct you on what to do!"

I remember Cemil Bayık telling the press, "The whole world should know that we will not act according to the normal rules of war anymore. We no longer recognize any of the world's rules on the matter." The reason for our distrust for the world came from the fact that many countries were involved in Apo's arrest, including Israel, Russia, Greece, Kenya, and the United States, all playing a part in it. Only the Prime Minister of Italy, Massimo D'Alema, tried to protect Apo. When the request was made to hand over Apo, Massimo tried to resist, but over time he had no strength left to resist. Even Russia and Germany would not dare keep Apo in their countries. That is why Cuma made the statement, "Now that you all have stabbed us in the back, do not complain about us applying terrorists' tactics. Sooner or later, whatever country had something to do with Apo's arrest will suffer the consequences."

After this press release, the professional self-sacrifice (suicide) units were established for the first time in the history of the organization. Many comrades voluntarily submitted applications to be part of these missions. The organization only accepted three hundred applicants out of thousands of applications. These soon-to-be self-sacrifice mission members were all from the higher ranks, and experienced guerillas. Although the selections were complete, the organization did not want to carry out these missions but rather wanted to continue planning and carefully preparing.

Meanwhile, the Kurds living in Europe and Turkey were protesting Apo's incarceration. There were those who set themselves on fire; who set the institutions of the state on fire, and who damaged public property. These civilian Kurds were acting on their own without any kind of guidance or instruction from the organization, which did not react through emotion. Our senior management cold-bloodedly drafted several plans to carry out against Turkey. The organization was doing two things at once: training new self-sacrifice mission candidates, and deploying the guerilla squads who were already prepared to perform missions against the security forces within Turkey.

There were forces ready to conduct missions in the Dersim and Amed regions. These forces were instructed not to start their missions until the self-sacrifice teams were trained. Soon, many guerilla missions began to occur across Turkey again. The organization's first self-sacrifice attack, against the senior executives of the KDP in Dohuk, Iraq, was performed during this period, because the KDP also took part in the consortium that aided in the arrest of Apo.

In March of 1999, another force of 300 guerillas gathered in central headquarters for training to perform missions in foreign countries. Around the middle of April, the groups began to be transferred to their final destinations. The plan called for them to be spread through several countries. There would be a group traveling to Kenya, a group sent to Israel, one sent to Greece, one to Russia, and another group sent to the United States. These guerillas were instructed to conduct missions against the elected officials, rather than the police or the military, within their destination countries. Moreover, they were specifically instructed to target the heads of state and the heads of state departments as much as possible. It was still not clear what sort of mission was to be carried out against Turkey, since Ankara had not yet declared how to approach the situation with Apo. We were not yet sure if the death penalty or a life sentence was going to be given to Apo.

Many of the self-sacrifice squad members arrived at their final destinations within Greece, Russia, and several European countries and waited for orders that told them to carry out their missions. There were three countries that were top priority targets: Israel, Greece, and Kenya. Israel was our first target since MOSSAD had provided the instant intelligence about Apo's location. They knew even before the CIA. Greece was high on the list because they had promised the organization to grant political asylum to Apo but did not keep their promise. Even worse, they forcefully sent Apo to Kenya. These things made Greece our second priority target. Kenya had used its SWAT team to conduct a raid at the Greek Embassy, while Apo was staying there, and their goal was to kill Apo during the clash. They knew that the people who were protecting Apo were armed, and that a firefight could result in his death.

The Kenyans' main plan was to break into the embassy, agitate the people with their weapons, and then kill Apo and his bodyguards, during the ensuing argument. Apo had foreseen this, and ordered his bodyguards and the Greek intelligence service officers not to fire when the SWAT teams entered the embassy building. He said, "They have something else on their minds. Do not be provoked by whatever it is that they say." Because of Kenya's heinous plot, they were our third target.

Even though we were going to get even with those three countries first, the United States was still a primary target. America had not backstabbed us quite like Israel had. Rather than providing intelligence information to the Turkish security forces, the United States put political pressure on the countries that were harboring Apo. Some European states also had a part in this scheme, and the organization had not forgotten this, but our priorities were already determined.

Meanwhile, a radical perspective began to develop with some members of the organization. There were many senior executives that began to say things like, "If Turkey set its mind on the complete destruction of our organization, then we should use whatever means necessary and available to counteract them." Even the idea of using chemical weapons against military posts and civilian crowds within big metropolises began to be heard regularly. There were also plans to poison the drinking water of military posts located in the countryside by putting poison into the pipelines. The senior leadership of the organization rejected these ideas. "Comrades! We told you that we would not obey the rules of war from now on. The situation is not that far out of control yet, but if the Turks go further and show a willingness to annihilate us, we may have to look at those sorts of tactics."

While Apo was in prison, he contacted the organization around the end of May, and ordered, "Do not execute any of the missions that you have been planning so far!" Once again the Americans provided the means of communication. This news reached us when there were many suicide attacks occurring within Turkey. On top of that, the Iranian Kurds had rebelled and were sending messages to us. "If the organization gives us the green light, we will cross the Turkish border and occupy the city of Van!" Apo's incarceration had also angered the Syrian Kurds, and they, too, began rebelling. Under Apo's instructions, the organization suspended all of its planned missions, including the ones that were supposed to be carried out by the self-sacrifice teams sent to foreign countries.

Many of the self-sacrifice units had already carefully chosen who their target would be: president, prime minister, deputies, etc. They were only waiting for the final approval of the organization. Also, many groups of guerillas had been placed within Turkey to carry out other missions. While we formerly had to be discriminate about our targets—being allowed to target only security forces—we were finally granted the right to kill anyone working within any kind of state institution. Basically, we were able to kill anyone working for the Turkish state but no civilians. It could be a teacher, bank accountant, deputy, or mayor. In the end, it did not matter, because we had to cancel the operations and planned attacks, according to Apo's instructions.

Some of the self-sacrifice units, who had been sent abroad, were arrested on their way back to Iraq. In fact, some of the groups that were returning from Russia are still incarcerated within Armenian prisons. Because of these arrests, the management of the organization informed the other units positioned inside Europe and in the United States, not to return, but live normal lives as sleeper cells. These guerillas were not going to engage in any kind of armed action but instead would live like normal citizens until they received new orders from the organization.

Because of the new contact with Apo, the organizational leadership and guerillas finally calmed down a bit. Turkey's approach with Apo had become quite clear. They were going to keep him, but they were not going to apply capital punishment. The Americans had guaranteed Apo's safety to the organization.

The Turks thought an internal struggle for power would ensue upon Apo's arrest. They felt that many senior commanders would race for leadership and would end up fighting each other. In the end, they thought the organization would be vanquished by its own internal clashes. When the Turkish officials decided to keep Apo, they had not considered the level of outcry and protests that came from the Kurds in Turkey and abroad. In fact, even the head of the State Department of the United States made a statement that said, "We were not expecting this much reaction to Apo's arrest." This suggests that even the Americans had not considered the potential "fall out." According to their way of thinking, the Kurds had already been divided into four different sections—Iran, Turkey, Iraq, and Syria—and thought of these four parts as having their own leaders.

What they had not expected was the power of Apo and the organization within those four areas. The Kurds in Iran were initially under the control of the KDP; however, the KDP began to lose its power over the Iranian Kurds in the middle of the 1980s. The Kurds in Iran embraced the control and authority of the PKK as a whole. Similarly, the KDP also had controlled the Kurds inside Syria. This situation changed over time, until the organization's status had grown to the point that the Syrian Kurds showed more commitment to Apo and the PKK than even the Kurds in Turkey.

After Apo was arrested, hundreds of Syrian and Iranian Kurds rushed to our camps in Iraq to volunteer for the self-sacrifice missions. Turkey and America were surprised at the support but no more than the organization, which had no idea that the Kurds would show such a reaction against Apo's incarceration.

Topal Nasır was the commander of the self-sacrifice teams. Under Nasır's command, these teams performed many missions within Turkey and inside territories controlled by the KDP. Apo was informed about the existence of these units while he was in prison and became extremely angry, saying, "These missions do not align with the policies of our organization. Why was such a force created?" Topal Nasır lashed out against Apo's criticism, and during one of the Presidency Council meetings he had said, "You tricked me into doing this, so as to get rid of me. You established this unit yourselves, and then appointed me as commander. You even made use of me and my men for the missions that were to be conducted against Turkey and north Iraq, and now you want to get rid of me! The only reason you have for arresting me is because of Apo's criticism against the creation of the unit!" After this speech, Topal Nasır was incarcerated.

The Case of Slav and Rubar

I was still staying in the Haftanin camp when all of these things happened. A month and a half before Apo was arrested, two incarcerated guerillas, a man and a woman, escaped from a Turkish prison and reached our camp's location…with a baby! The female guerilla said the baby was hers, and she had given birth while she was in prison. I did not know her real name, but her nickname was Slav. She had joined the organization in 1989. The nickname of the male guerilla was Rubar.

Since they were experienced comrades, we were happy to see them among us again. But, even though we were pleased that they were able to escape, we put them under preliminary investigation, to find out the truth of the matter, and make certain that they really had escaped from prison and were not simply released by security agents to work as informants. No matter how many investigations they were subjected to, they did not appear to be hiding anything, and this led us all to believe they really were prison escapees.

They told us that they had gotten married while in the prison. We asked them, "How did you make this child? The male and female cells were located in different places." They replied, "Comrades, we accompanied the security forces for months and were always out in the field to assist them in finding guerilla routes into Turkey, the locations of our ammunition dumps, and other similar topics. Sometimes, they left the two of us alone, and that is how we managed to have the child."

Because Apo's incarceration had taken such high priority, the investigation into Slav and Rubar was completed earlier than it normally would have been. We believed that what they told us was the truth. Also, Turkey seemed to act more professionally back then. There was news being broadcast that two PKK prisoners had escaped from Şırnak Prison, and the military were searching for them everywhere. However, these news stories were part of the game being played by the Turkish intelligence agencies.

After the investigation, Slav and Rubar were assigned to two different regions. Long after this incident, I visited Slav's company, I believe, in the month of March. The baby she claimed was hers was constantly crying. The noise bothered me, and I was unable to get any work done, so I asked one of the female guerillas to take the baby to her mother to be breastfed. Slav took the baby about 20 meters away and began breastfeeding her, but the baby continued to cry. This constant distraction made me angry, and I said, "Why is she still crying even though she's being breastfed?" It was about this time that I began to be suspicious about their story. I seriously wondered whether the baby really was hers or not. Also, another thought struck me while I was at that camp. The baby seemed calmer when she was around the other women guerillas, more so than when she was around her supposed mother. The baby actually cried when she was being held by Slav, and I could not make sense of this strange occurrence.

In April of 1999, the Turkish military raided our camp's location in the Haftanin region, while we were still there. Before they attacked us, these soldiers had attacked our camps in the Cudi region. I did not know it back then, but Slav's husband, Rubar, martyred two of our comrades and ran away before this operation even started. He went to the security forces and informed them about the other camp locations within the region.

I confronted Slav as soon as the news of her husband's betrayal reached us. We asked her, "Comrade, your husband surrendered himself to the security forces. Were you ever suspicious of his behaviors while the two of you were in prison?" She responded, "No, I was not, comrade. I do not understand why he would do something like that!" At this point, we were yet to be suspicious of Slav.

The soldiers reached the place where our female comrades were staying, but there was not a serious threat yet. It was then that Slav took the baby that she claimed was her own and strangled it to death. When the other female guerillas noticed what she had done, they asked her why she did it. She said, "The soldiers will be here soon. If she cries, they will easily find our location. I sacrificed my own flesh just to protect you, comrades! I could not take the risk of you all being killed because of my baby."

The female guerillas were gullible and believed what Slav said. In fact, they all hugged and told her, "Comrade! What a devoted guerilla you are! You killed your baby with your own hand just to protect the organization. Not every one of us could do that!" I was in the male guerilla campground when this happened, and my suspicion of Slav grew as soon as I heard of this incident. I met with the battalion commander and requested that there be an immediate investigation of the incident. The battalion commander rejected my request, because Slav was being hailed a great hero by just about everyone, for what she had done. "What's going on, Deniz? Are you aware of something that we are not?" I insisted and barely convinced him. "Comrade, create an investigation committee, and it will find the truth of the matter!"

Two female guerillas and I were appointed as members of the investigation committee. In fact, one of the females was Sözdar Avesta, who is currently the president of the KCK Executive Council. We had Slav transferred from her company to ours and placed her in jail. I immediately cut to the chase, saying, "Slav, you and your husband did not escape from the prison. Admit it! Do not waste our time!" We were in quite a stressful dilemma during our investigation. Slav was from Şırnak, Uludere, and there were probably dozens of her family and relatives serving the organization, and now we were accusing her of a serious crime.

No matter how hard I tried, she would not admit to anything. I went to the female company and asked their commander if there were any female guerillas that had raised children before joining the organization. We checked all the CVs and found that there were two. I called both of them, saying, "I want to ask you something personal, but please do not get the wrong idea! You were both married and had children before joining our struggle, right?" One of them said that she had two children. I said perfect! "Comrade, let's say there is a mom that breastfeeds her baby and the baby dies. Would the milk in the breasts bother the woman because it is not being used?" She replied, "There is not a woman who would be able to endure such pain. The milk has to be removed from the breasts." I thanked them and immediately headed back to the investigation room.

When I arrived back where the investigation was going on I said, "Slav, I am going to ask you something, and you must tell the truth this time. How many days has it been since you sacrificed your baby?" She replied, "It has been six days, comrade." I again asked, "Slav, except for the emotional trauma of killing your own baby, did you have any physical problems?" She said, "Comrade, I have been emotionally devastated, but I do not have any sickness, I am fine!" I said, "Slav, you are lying to us." I then asked one of the female commission members to take Slav into one of the empty rooms and check if she had milk in her breasts. Sozdar was moon-eyed from shock and asked me: "What kind of question is this, Deniz? What does it have to do with the investigation?" I told her just to be patient.

The female guerilla checked Slav's breasts and returned to the investigation area. She told us, "Comrade, there is nothing coming out of her breasts and, in fact, her body does not even have signs that she gave birth." Sozdar looked at me and started to laugh. "How do you know such things about women?" she asked. I replied, "I did what you were supposed to. I consulted the female comrades, and they told me to check the breasts to verify what she was saying."

In my life, I had never raised my hands against a woman before, but when the truth was revealed, I beat Slav badly. "You will either tell us the truth or I will beat you until you are dead. Whose child was she? Are you an informant? Who sent you here? What is your duty among us? You will tell us everything, Slav!" I said. Of course, she was very scared. She had never thought we would suspect her, especially after she sacrificed the baby.

After my severe beatings, she confessed that the baby actually belonged to a peasant family in one of the villages outside the city of Şırnak. The father was not at home when they had kidnapped the baby. Slav, Rubar, and a couple of Turkish agents broke into the house, killed the mother and the grandfather, and then left the house with the child. After that, they created the story of being married and running away from the prison. The security forces mentally prepared Rubar and Slav before their release. They prepared a list of answers to investigation questions that they may face when they reached our camps. They were professionally trained before they came back to us, and that is why we could not discover anything from the initial investigations.

"Slav, so you are an agent working for the security forces, and you were able to infiltrate us, but why did you kill that innocent baby?" Sick from fear, she replied, "Rubar ran away much earlier than planned. Some of my comrades began to think that I would run away like he had by killing a couple of them so I had to gain their trust back somehow. I thought killing the baby would help me do that."

I said, "What was your duty? Why did the military send you here? Give me a concrete answer and do not tell me that you are just here to collect information about the organization. With such professional planning, you must have been tasked with something quite important."

She gave me the names of two senior PKK members. One of them was her own uncle, an experienced comrade with the rank of commander. The other one was a deputy of the PKK Assembly who was later martyred in a clash in Gabar in 2008, by the name of Serif. Both of them were staying in Botan, and they were weak in an ideological sense, but they were good fighters. Slav said, "My duty was to kill them." I was surprised and asked her: "Why did they want you to kill these two people, since there are many other senior officials and battalion commanders present in this region? Did they explain why they chose those two?" She told me, "Comrade, I honestly do not know the reason. The Turks gave us two small tubes of cyanide to poison the company with whom we were staying, if those two could not be killed. They told us to mix the cyanide with the company's food, and then to run away." I asked, "Where is the poison now?" "Comrade, Rubar had it with him. He was going to give one of them to me, but we did not have an opportunity to meet after we were assigned to different regions."

"Slav, the security forces must have given you a few other targets to destroy. Tell me what the others were." She said, "Comrade, there was also the peasant Kurds at the Maxmur camp. Our last resort was to go to that camp with the baby and settle there. Once we were accepted by the group, we were going to convince them to return to Turkey."

This made everything crystal clear, and the organization was probably going to execute Slav. I thought a quick death would be too good for her. In my mind she needed to suffer for a long time, because of what she had done. I was still tearing my hair over the fact that she had strangled the baby, so I asked her again, "Tell me Slav, how did you kill the baby?" "Comrade, I strangled her with a scarf," she replied, crying. "Which of your hands did you use to kill her?" I asked. She indicated her right hand and said, "I pressed the scarf on her mouth with this hand." "Slav, stop crying and put your right hand on that rock!" I said. The female comrades that were part of the investigation council panicked, and asked me: "Comrade, what are you going to do?" I replied, "Just be patient."

I always carried a walking stick with me back then and on the bottom edge of the stick there was sharp piece of iron. We called this stick a "seke." As soon as Slav laid her hand on the rock, I hit her hand with that sharp piece of iron with all my strength. I think that a few of the metacarpals were broken by my swing, and she began to weep. "Do not be upset about your broken hand, Slav. You'll be dead in a few days anyway. Even though it's bad, I can understand how you could kill the mother and grandfather, but how could you kill that little baby? I wish you had killed one of us, instead of her. How could you be that cruel? Do you not have a conscience?" I asked while she cried in pain. The baby was so sweet. She had just started to stand up, and the first word she had learned was "Comrade," not even "mama" or "papa." I was so saddened by the tragedy of the situation, that I beat Slav a lot that day.

We prepared a written report of the trial and sent it to the headquarters. She was sentenced to death, and all our comrades were expecting her to be executed quite quickly. But not even a month had passed when headquarters informed us that Slav had been forgiven! I was completely shocked when I heard that.

The last time I saw Slav was either in 2004 or 2005. She was participating in an HPG Conference. Can you imagine that? She was there as a squad commander. I argued with myself that the organization had handled her too gently. She had infiltrated our organization as an agent for the Turks and committed many atrocities while doing their bidding. After all that, she was forgiven and raised to commander! "What's going on, Slav? What are you doing at this Conference?" I asked. "Hello, comrade Deniz! I came here to see my uncle," she said. I was even more shocked by this. Her uncle was the one that the security forces had sent her to kill.

As this is being written, it is 2015, and ten years have passed. Slav could possibly be a member of the PKK leadership. Can you imagine that? One of us runs away from the organization and surrenders to the security forces, and then is sent back to us as an insider. She does unimaginable things; causes a lot of damage, and then is forgiven by the organization. This is someone whose own family would have wanted her executed, because of what she had done.

Her parents and family immigrated to the Maxmur Camp between the years of 1993 and 1994 to escape the oppression of the Turkish security forces. That family had at least ten members who had been martyred since the organization had begun. They had informed headquarters that they wanted to see their daughter dead, as soon as they heard about what she had done. "Execute her immediately! She is not our daughter anymore." Up until this point, the organization had a more professional policy than what the Turkish officials followed. By pardoning Slav, they inadvertently promoted a message of hope to old dissenters. "The organization will always welcome you back as long as you're honest."

The Radical Change in Organizational Policy

On August 17, 1999, a catastrophic earthquake occurred in Turkey. Thousands of people lost their lives while they were sleeping in their beds, and the survivors were under extreme hardship. When this happened, the organization made both a verbal and written statement, announcing a ceasefire so that we could help the people in the area of the earthquake. Unfortunately, the Turkish officials rejected our offer. I mentioned before that the organization never considered the civilian Turkish public as enemies. In fact, helping each other after the earthquake would have been a great opportunity, for both the organization and the Turks, to put away their long-standing hatred toward one another. We were even ready to transfer thousands of our people to take part in search and rescue activities.

During this time, we were evacuating our camps in the south, along the Turkey/Iraq border, to make space for groups that would arrive from the north, because winter was on the way. There was no possibility that the guerillas of Amed would be able to travel all the way down to our camps at Kandil and Hakurki in the inner parts of Iraq, so the organization decided to relocate the forces that were already settled at the border to the camps located in Kandil. This would allow the forces coming from Turkey to settle in the emptied camps easily. It was during this time that my company was also relocated to Kandil.

Near the end of 1999, the organization called for an extraordinary congress. We heard that there was going to be a radical change in the strategy we used in our struggle. The guerilla forces were going to be abolished and the armed struggle was going to stop. This also, initially, called for us to retreat from regions we controlled within Turkey. Some of the comrades seriously objected to this withdrawal order. They wanted to know what was promised by Turkey in exchange for this retreat. They also had a legitimate worry about how to recapture the emptied territories, if the Turks, as they had in the past, did not keep their promises. However, that was not all. Apart from these two risks, there was also the potential that the regions the guerillas left could come under the influence of different political and ideological organizations. For example, a Dersim Field commander rejected the order of withdrawal by arguing that, "If my forces retreat now, the TIKKO or other similar Leftist organizations would capture these places." He was correct in his worries. If the PKK left the region, then TIKKO and others would gain the sympathy of the local public there, saying, "Look, the PKK has left you alone, but we are still here to protect you against oppressors." These reasons were why the Dersim Field commander and the Erzurum State commander refused to withdraw their forces. While the rest of our forces in Turkey retreated, these two commanders stubbornly stayed where they were and ignored all the warnings that came from headquarters.

The attitudes of both commanders in Dersim and Erzurum had a negative effect on some senior executives in the south. Guerillas from our leadership gathered and declared that Apo had handed the organization over to the Turks, so they were going to establish a separate organization to continue the fight for Kurdish rights. "Now that our organization has stopped its armed struggle, we will break away and continue the fight!" they said.

It was impossible for this group to establish an organization that was as professional as the PKK, and they knew it. However, there were people aligned with that group that could make the separation from the PKK more significant. Dr. Süleyman, Küçük Zeki, and Yılmaz were several well-known members who joined the separatists. These people had also been members of the committee at the organization's headquarters. They had a lot of control over the guerillas in the north, since they had worked there before. They were also loved and respected by many within the organization.

There was already a competitive division between the northern forces and the southern forces. Those in the north (the guerillas who were fighting inside the borders of Turkey) were supporting each other, while those in the south (those that were fighting in Iran, Syria, and Iraq) were taking sides with one another. The three commanders that I mentioned were planning to join up with the forces in the north and then establish a new organization under a different name.

While this was happening, the organization prepared a camp in Zagros and two other camps in Hinere, for the guerillas that were retreating back south. Many of the forces in the south had already been relocated to different camps before the arrival of the northern force. The organization did not want these two forces to meet, because the southern troops had already adapted to the new process through countless meetings and ideological trainings. The northern forces were not aware of the changes yet and were just following an order. Chances were good that they would cause trouble when they learned about the radical changes in the organization's policies. So, rather than have the southern forces be influenced by the northern ones, they had to be relocated to other camps.

My company was sent, by the organization, to the Kandil region before the northern forces arrived, because of the same reasoning. We set off from Haftanin as a whole company. However, even before we arrived at Metina, we were caught up in a tank ambush. Those were the same tanks that were placed in northern Iraq by the Turkish military in 1997. They also had built up military bases in the fields of Kanimasi, Bamerne, and Batufa. Their base in Bamerne was larger when compared to other places. There were around 45 tanks there. The Turks placed their tanks in a line extending between Zaho, Dohuk and Erbil. It was in this very line of tanks that we were caught up in an ambush. Eight comrades were martyred, and 13 were heavily injured. We were able to carry out all of our injured comrades, but we had to leave the martyred comrades there due to the frequent bombings by the tanks. The local guerilla forces in that region told us to continue on our trip, because they would bury our fallen comrades, when they were able.

It was a long journey, and we continued moving forward. A young man, probably in his late twenties, came up to our company as we were about to pass a point close to the Çukurca province of Hakkari. "Who are you, and where are you going?" I asked him. "Northward, to Turkey," he replied. "Then you are going the wrong way, and mustn't continue on this route!" I said.

We set off down the road again, and after about three hours of walking, we had a cigarette break somewhere in Iraq. I noticed that same young man had been following us all this time. I took my assistants with me, and told the rest of the company to continue walking. When he reached us, where we had waited for him, I asked, "You told us that you were going to Turkey. Why are you following us?" He replied, "I changed my mind and want to join your group instead." I replied, "If that is true, then go find our comrades located in your region, and they will tell you how to join us." He insisted on joining up with us. I told him flatly, "Look, we still have a long way ahead of us. We're going to Iran, and cannot take you with us." This did not deter him a bit, and he continued arguing with me. Since it appeared impossible to convince him to go back, I told him that I would shoot him if he did not leave. My goal was to scare him into leaving us alone, but he suddenly turned belligerent, and told me, "Who the hell are you? Do you have the heart to shoot a man?" I replied, "Do you have a death wish? Get out of here and do not ever follow us again!" I then turned and walked back to the rest of the company.

When I looked again, I saw that this crazy person was still following us, and hollered back to him, "Look, I am going to close my eyes and count to ten, and you are to get out of my sight. If you are still there when I open my eyes, I will shoot you." I closed my eyes and started to count. I was holding an M-16, but that must not have bothered him, because when I opened my eyes, he was still looking at us from the same spot. "Didn't I just tell you that I would kill you?" I angrily yelled. He replied dryly, "Who the hell are you? No one can kill me!" I was angry, and looked at the squad commander next to me. He said, "Comrade Deniz, let me kill him." I answered, "Comrade, do not let this crazy man get to you!" After that, we set off once again.

We began moving ahead, while he laughed out loudly, saying, "If you are not a real man, then why are you carrying that gun with you?" When I heard this, I got crazy, and thought, this is the last straw. In a quick instant, I turned back and shot him in the head. He fell to the ground, and I told those around me to go check to see if he were still alive. They went up to him and told me that yes, he was still alive. I said, "Raise him up, and each of you hold one of his arms!" When they had him held up, I shot him in the head one more time, and said, "Search his clothes well, and take whatever he has on him." Following this incident, we continued our trip.

It was nearly December when we finally reached Zagros. There were two different routes that go to Kandil from Zagros. One of them went over the Zagros Mountains, and the other went through Desta Hayati (Hayat Valley), a region that was under the control of the KDP. Since it was risky to use a road that was under Barzani's control, we decided to use the route that went through the Zagros Mountains. Unfortunately, by the time we got to the foothills near the mountains, it was snowing heavily. The snow reached 1-meter-high in a very short time, and it would no doubt have taken us forever to travel over the mountain, with the storm and heavy snow. To make matters worse, the organization had already banned the use of this route when it was snowing—a ban of which I was unaware at that time.

When we finally made it up the mountain, four of our comrades had frostbite on their feet. We wore thick socks and boots, but if you walk in the snow for a long time you have to be very careful, for, if moisture gets into your footwear, you must change it immediately. If you do not change into dry shoes, but continue to walk in the snow, your feet will get frostbitten. It is a very insidious injury. Unless you check your feet regularly during your travels, sometimes, you do not even know you have it until you reach a warmer spot. If you have frostbite, you might even be able to walk for nine hours, or even an entire day and not feel any pain, because of the numbness in your feet. But you will find out as soon as you enter a warmer environment, because of the pain and discomfort in your feet.

We set off at 7:00 a.m. that day, with two local pathfinder comrades, and walked until sunset. The two pathfinders were very familiar with the area, but it did not help, because of how much snow was falling. As the sun set, it became apparent that we had been traveling in a circle since morning. About that time was when our four comrades informed us of their frostbite. None of them realized that water had slowly seeped into their shoes.

We headed directly toward the guerilla company that was located in Hinere, in the Zagros Mountain, so that our comrades could be treated as quickly as possible. Unfortunately, all of them had to have their feet amputated at the ankles. To these comrades, and the ones who had been wounded in the tank ambush, I ordered, "Stay in the Hinere camp until spring. You will all join us when you have been properly treated, and your wounds have healed." Interestingly, even though they had good reason to remain with this local group, because of their wounds, none of them wanted to do that. Since we got lost in the Zagros Mountain, our only option was to go to Kandil through Iran. This meant we had a much longer distance to travel and carrying the wounded comrades would have slowed down the rest of the group.

While our company was still at the Hinere camp, some senior officials visited. One of them was Nizamettin Taş, nicknamed Botan. I do not know the real names of the others, but their nicknames were Serhat, Küçük Zeki, and Ekrem. (Ekrem had been the person who killed the well-known torturer and Turkish military captain, Esat Okay, on a bus in Istanbul in 1988.) Botan got angry with me because we were in the Zagros Mountains during the snowy season. "Have you lost your mind, Deniz? How could you drag such a large company through the Zagros mountains during a snowstorm?" he asked. I replied, "We had two options: climb up the Zagros Mountains or go through the Hayat Plain. Not only were our pathfinders not familiar with the road that goes through the Hayat Plain, but we also did not want to encounter Barzani's forces there. Besides that, we had a strict order to get to Kandil some-how, because there were forces coming from the north to stay where we had been located. If we stayed in our camp until winter was over, the northerners would have been left out in the cold."

Botan ordered me, "We are traveling to Kandil now. I want you and your company to be there in a week at the most by using the path that goes beside the river." These orders meant that they still expected us to travel on foot, despite the fact that we had so many injured comrades, and it was still snowing. I asked the guerillas in Hınere how many days it should take us to reach Kandil. They informed me that it would take at least four or five days. When I accounted for all the disadvantages we had; the injured, the weather conditions, and the length of the way, I realized that it would be impossible to take the company to Kandil on foot and, therefore, took that option off the table. Once I had settled that in my mind, I found the person who dealt with purchasing in the Hinere camp. This comrade lived somewhere between Iran and Iraq, where most smugglers lived, and he was responsible for providing the physical needs of the camp.

I went to him and asked if he could arrange for us to have vehicles. He asked me, "What are you going to do with vehicles here?" "We need to drive to Kandil Mountain as fast as we can," I replied. He was surprised. "Well, comrade, the organization banned the use of vehicles for transportation of guerillas! Didn't you know that?" I responded with, "Never mind the ban. Just tell me whether or not you can arrange it." When he answered that he could, I told him, "Get me fifteen trucks, and I will pay you cash now!" He got confused when he heard the number, and asked what was I going to do with that many vehicles. I explained, "I have a company with me, and we need at least fifteen trucks." He apologized, "Comrade, if you were two or three people, then perhaps it could be arranged; I could get you a car. However, if the organization heard that I arranged fifteen trucks for you, they would most likely execute me. You'd also have to drive through Iran. If you got noticed, and then arrested by the Iranian security forces, that would cause a huge crisis for the organization." I pleaded, "You just have to arrange the vehicles. Do not bother yourself with the risk." He did not appear convinced at first, but after a time of thinking he said, "Okay, but I have one condition. If you get caught, or if somebody complains, you will never say I was involved!" I assured him with, "I promise!" and then gave him ten thousand dollars to arrange for the vehicles.

I do not remember the exact number, but I think he arranged for 14 cars and two small trucks. I had all of our troops get into the vehicles at 10:00 p.m., during the darkness of night. We hired three Iranian guides, because we did not know which roads to drive inside Iran. We needed to go through two big Iranian cities, Pirançehir and Urmiye, before we reached our final destination in Kandil.

All 16 vehicles were driving as a convoy. Even though we sometimes passed by Iranian military posts, none of them stopped us. Nevertheless, there was an Iranian border control post, just before reaching Kandil. As we passed by this station, the Iranian soldiers stopped the first car in the convoy, so, we all had to stop while they inquired as to who we were. The Iranian guides were our means of communication in this situation, and I told them to tell the soldiers, openly, that we were PKK guerillas and we were heading to Kandil. The Iranian soldiers harshly told them that we could not use the road, since it was forbidden. I looked at our Iranian guide and asked him at most how many Iranian soldiers would be present at the station. "Well comrade, at most there would be 25 soldiers," he answered. I then said, "Tell this dump that they will either let us go, or we will take them all to Kandil as our captives."

I do not know exactly how my words were translated by our guide, but the Iranian soldiers could not even raise their voice to my threat. Once it was settled, all of our vehicles set off again. Before we reached Kandil, there was yet another guerilla camp on our route. When we approached this small camp, we got out of the vehicles and continued the rest of the journey on foot. It was around 5:00 a.m. when we arrived there. When the commander of the camp asked from where we were coming, I said, "Hınere!" He responded with, "If you had truly come from Hınere, then you would have entered the camp from the other side. I wonder, did you all use vehicles to get here?" I replied, "Yes, we did." He was moon-eyed and asked, "Didn't you have problems with the Iranians?" I told him, "Comrade, we traveled carefully." But I did not mention the stop at the Iranian border post, of course.

I was planning to reach Kandil after letting my company have a rest for a few days. However, on the morning of the second day, the commander came to me and said, "I have received word that you and your guerillas must make your way immediately to Kandil. You must set off as soon as possible." Hearing this, we left immediately and walked all day with almost no rest.

Our quarters had been prepared before we even arrived in Kandil. The camp was organized professionally, with everything clearly determined in advance, including who was going to stay where and with whom. There was a huge training academy right in the middle of the camp. Nizamettin Taş and Topal Nasır arrived in Kandil three days after we did. They were surprised to see us. "You set off one day later than we did, so how could you arrive here earlier, with all the injured and wounded guerillas?" they asked. I had warned the others to remain silent, so that I could explain. "Comrade, we traveled here by cars through Iran." Nizamettin got irritated with my answer. "How could you take such a risk?" I replied, "Well, comrade, I thought going through Iran was less risky than the road you asked us to use. I already had many comrades with frostbite, and I could not risk others getting frostbite also." He admonished, "As an organization, we have banned the use of cars. If we absolutely must use them, then we use only two cars at the most, at the same time. We never use that many vehicles with such a crowded group. What will happen if Iran makes trouble because of what you did?" I did not answer. Nizamettin Taş harshly said, "You will immediately give a defense in writing; not only for going through Iran with vehicles, but also for the comrades who lost their lives during the tank ambush."

As I went under investigation, I hid the fact that I was sent as a regional representative for the congress. I was just about to leave the meeting room when Botan asked, "Has anyone been sent from your region as a representative for the congress?" I replied, "No!" Botan got even angrier. "Why has no one been sent? We asked every region to send someone to represent them in the congress."

Botan went to the area where the congress was going to take place. The camp was very crowded, although it had not yet begun, since all the groups had not arrived. As I said, some commanders in the north had objected to the changes in the organization's Policy for Battle. The people in Kandil were divided into different groups of thought, regarding the change in party policy. Each group held secret meetings with the people who followed their ideals. Most of them, especially the representatives of the northern provinces, were planning to establish a new organization with the goal of continuing the armed fight against the Turks. Some people even claimed that the approach Apo had insisted upon, was nothing but surrender to the Turkish republic, and he should not be regarded as the leader of the organization any longer.

One day after our arrival, I went to the congressional area to see my old comrades, including Cuma, who had come from other regions. He called out to me as soon as he recognized who I was. We greeted each other and began talking as we drank our tea. "Comrade Deniz, I want to ask you something, and you must tell me the truth. Did you kill a peasant in between Haftanin and Kandil?" I told him that I had, and he asked how many. I said only one and he asked again, "Are you sure that you killed only one?" I responded rather harshly, "Comrade, I killed only one person. If I had killed three, I would say so, but I killed only one." He then asked me where I had killed him, and I responded, "Just across from the town of Metina, in the Kaşura region, near the border of Çukurca," He asked me why had I killed him, and I explained to him exactly what happened.

Cemil Bayık paused for a while, and I thought he looked confused, but then he said, "Comrade Deniz, I have different information regarding what you just told me, and it indicates that you killed four peasants before you crossed over the border. The local force of that region informed headquarters of the killings." I was shocked. "Comrade, I would definitely know if something like that happened, but I am telling you, only one person was killed, and I am the one that killed him, not the guerillas in my company. I am ready to be punished for it, if you think I am guilty. But, if the guerilla force of that region executed those peasants and are trying to place the blame on us, then you need to conduct a more comprehensive investigation." Cemil Bayık replied, "Comrade Deniz, you did yourself a disfavor. I wish you had not killed anyone."

I told him about the incident again: "The man was from the south and he first told us that he was travelling to the north. I showed him the way, but he did not go and began following us, saying that he wanted join our force. No matter how hard I tried, I could not convince him to leave us alone. He continued to provoke us and make jokes, until I shot him. My comrades searched his body and found a paper full of numbers belonging to Erbil and Suleimaniye. None of these numbers belonged where we were in the Dohuk or Zaho areas. What was he doing there with these numbers from Erbil and Suleimaniye on him? I do not know what his task was, or with whom he was working, but he did not appear to be an innocent person, comrade."

Cemil Bayık then asked again, why did we not have anyone representing the congress for our region. "Comrade, I was actually the representative sent from our region. However, when I was put under investigation by Botan, I thought that it would not be ethical to take part in the congress since I was facing imprisonment. If I were to get incarcerated at the end of this trial, some guerillas might complain about how a guilty person participated in the congress as a representative," I explained. He insisted that I participate as a representative, and said, "We will define the borders of the organization's new strategy during this congress, and you should represent your region. The trial is not a concern for now, it can be handled later." This congress was extremely important, because Apo's verbal instructions were going to be written down as official rules.

I prepared my written defense statements for both of the incidents and presented them to the officials before the congress in Kandil was over. The trial commission acquitted me on both incidents. Because of all this going on, I became worn out physically and emotionally. Also, the guerillas that came from Syria, Turkey, Iraq, and Iran had to be given political training, regarding the operation of the new policy. As a result, almost all of the ranked guerillas had to serve on the political training commissions. I had no knowledge of politics and was not good at ideological issues. It definitely would not look good if someone asked a question during a training session that I was leading, and I could not provide a satisfactory answer. It was for that main reason that 15 days after reaching Kandil, I resigned from my position as company commander. Although my resignation was initially rejected by management, they eventually accepted it.

As I mentioned before, there were diverse groups among the senior officials during this congress. Some of them wanted to establish a new party; some others insisted on not leaving the north and establishing a new party with the goal of armed struggle. Then, there were those who wanted to arrest the current commanders and elect a new president.

Meanwhile, Jalal Talabani was pressuring the organization to elect a new president in place of Apo. The organization was aware that this request was actually coming from foreign forces and that Talabani was only a puppet in this scheme. Cemil Bayık was put under great stress during these talks and said, "Apo has been arrested and can no longer physically serve as president. Unfortunately, it is time to forget about him and elect a new president for the future of the organization." And some others in leadership roles began to support those ungrateful views. They believed that Apo's leadership was physically over, and that the organization needed to continue its fights with a new leader. Cuma resisted those vicious tendencies, as strongly as he could, and explicitly stated that no one else should lead the organization as long as Apo was alive.

When Cemil Bayık became tough on the subject, people who had openly spoken against Apo withdrew themselves. After all, even though Apo was not among us, the organization was still regularly receiving notes from him. The interviews Apo had with his lawyers were being delivered to the guerillas as brochures and booklets. Everyone was reading them, and discussing his writings during the training. Apo often sent notes regarding the new policy of the organization, and according to this new restructuring plan, the name of the guerilla force would be changed to the HPG (Public Defense Forces). On the administrative side, a new political party named Public Movement would be established, and this party was going to represent our organization in Ankara.

When these radical changes were implemented, some in the party began to say, "We want big changes in our party's policy, so why do not we also change the name of the organization?" Cemil Bayık, Duran Kalkan, and Murat Karayılan harshly objected to the suggestion of a name change. They said that the PKK was not going to be abolished, even though they were implementing radical changes. At the end of this congress, the guerilla force and the political structure were now completely separate from one another, in terms of management. Back then, we did not have political parties in Iran, Iraq, and Syria. However, there were separate committees in the Kandil camp, representing the organization's political relations with these three countries. One committee represented us in Iran, another in Syria, and also another in Iraq. Serhat (aka Osman Öcalan) was the leader of these three political committees. The guerilla force also underwent a radical change with the decisions made during this congress. Our fight was going to be conducted by small, professional units, rather than large, crowded groups of guerillas. This new guerilla force was to be put under the command of Nizamettin Taş.

The organization managed to get all of the guerillas to embrace and adopt this new strategy by January of 2000. The guerilla commander of Erzurum province, who rejected the order to withdraw, was killed in a clash by Turkish security forces. The organization sent a guerilla force from the south to arrest the Dersim province commander, Hamili Yıldırım. When Hamili Yıldırım found out how serious the situation was, he gave up his stubborn attitudes and retreated with his forces to Iraq. The organization finally established its old dominance on its members again. The middle echelon of command—which was made up mostly of battalion, company, platoon, and squad commanders—began to side with Apo and his new strategy. This change in attitude strengthened the hands of senior executives like Cemil Bayık and Murat Karayılan, because they had always followed Apo's reasoning.

Before the congress ended, 17 of the senior female commanders who had met with Iranian officials, without permission from headquarters, were arrested. As I said, the organization never forgets about being double-crossed. The punishment was only delayed during extreme situations. In addition to these women, the people who had adopted an attitude against Apo were arrested at this same congress. Not one of these separatists thought that Cemil Bayık would be able to establish his authority in the absence of Apo. Seeing how people were being arrested, including senior members, made those who had wanted to establish a new organization suddenly shut their mouths.

In Pursuit of the Separatists

After the congress ended, a group of 23 people who had wanted to establish a new organization fled from the Kandil Camp, and set up a new camp within Iran, in order to lay down the fundamentals of their formation. I was a regular guerilla in a battalion back then, and before the group fled, their attitudes and behaviors set off red flags with the senior executives. There was thinking among the group that perhaps they were up to something, but no one knew exactly what it was. While this was going on, our camp was being led by Ebubekir (Halil Ataç). One day, he told me that he was assigning me to a special task. When I asked about the details of this task, Ebubekir said, "Deniz, you are close friends with most of the people within that group, correct?" I replied, "Yes!" and he said, "Okay! Get even closer to those people. Hang out with them. They must be up to something, but we just do not know what it is. Learn as many details as you can! Who is their leader, what do they want to do, and what is their purpose?"

With all that in mind, I began to spend time with the group more frequently. I joined in their meetings and chats, so I would be considered one of them. While I was with them, they would consult a senior executive, but I could not figure out who he was. One evening, while we three comrades were chatting, one of them turned to me and said, "We are going somewhere outside the camp tonight, and you are coming too!" When I asked where we were going, they said, "To Dole Koke [the congress area in Kandil]. Be ready at around 10:00 p.m."

We arrived at the congress field around that time. I came across a bout of good luck. There was a female comrade there whom I knew very well. The comrades with whom I had come left us, and I chatted with this woman for a while. She said, "Sevin is here as well. I can go and let her know you're here, if you want me to!" I replied, "No, I have a meeting now and will see her later." After our conversation, I realized that I had lost the other comrades. I searched inside some of the tents, but I could not find any of them, so I sat on a stone in an open field and waited for them. They finally found me at around 2:00 a.m. I asked, "Where the hell were you? I lost you!" They replied, "We were meeting with some comrades and it was too risky to leave the meeting and bring you inside. Next time!" I asked again, "With whom did you meet?" They said, "Selim Çürükkaya's brother Dr. Süleyman, Küçük Zeki, and Yılmaz." All of the men they named were members of the PKK's executive council. I thought those seniors must be the leaders of these separatists.

The following day, I met directly with Ebubekir when we returned to camp. There were a total of four training schools in the camp—three of them taught in Turkish, and one of them in Kurdish. These schools were located far from each another. Ebubekir was lecturing the students in one of the Turkish schools. As soon as I met with him, I said, "Comrade, there are three seniors from our organization leading these separatists!" Ebubekir was pleased that I had been able to uncover the names of the leaders. He said, "Good! Continue infiltrating their camp. Let us know immediately if you learn something new!" I said, "Comrade, I cannot often come visit you, it will begin to look too suspicious." He responded, "Then, we will give you a radio and you'll be able to communicate with me that way." I said, "Comrade, you cannot do that! I am not a commander anymore. Why would a regular guerilla carry a radio? Those who see it would want to know why I have a radio." He got angry when I replied and said, "You carry a bag. Can't you just hide a small radio in it? Whenever you need to, just leave the camp field, contact us, and hide it again." I could not really say anything against his harsh response, so I just took the radio.

I remember quite well that it had not been a week after that conversation when on the night of May 19, I was lying in my bed, and the duty officer came to see whether I was in the quarters or not. I learned that the nine separatists had fled the camp that very night. Since I was frequently with them, the battalion commander had told him: "Go and check if Deniz is still here, or if he has fled with them." As soon as I heard about this, I took my radio and left the camp to try and contact Ebubekir. His assistant, who knew of the situation, answered my call. I told him that the separatists had fled the camp area, and that they must take the necessary precautions.

In the time it took for our commanders to decide what to do, this separatist group had already reached a safe location between Iran and Iraq. The organization deployed many small, three-man units to detect the separatists' exact location. I was with one of these small groups. We searched for a few days in the countryside and were able to detect their exact location after following their traces and consulting with local peasants. They had stopped by a village on their way to Iran and asked for supplies, including oil, sugar, a pickaxe, a shovel, and some nylon. This made it clear to us that they were setting up a camp up in a nearby area. Duran Kalkan was immediately notified of the situation, and said, "Do not harm the regular guerilla runaways, but kill the three members of the headquarters committee wherever you find them."

We fought the separatists with a force of three battalions. Since we were ordered not to harm the majority of the group, we first asked them to surrender peacefully. But, rather than doing so, they used the negotiations of their surrender as a way to stall us until the darkness of night. They were the guerillas who had fought in the north for years and were able to flee the battle by taking advantage of the cover of darkness. They did leave two representatives behind to talk to us. I spoke with these two in order to understand the goals of the separatists. They said, "We're not giving up the fight for the Kurdish struggle. We will continue the armed struggle that the PKK has decided to forget."

The organization tasked me and another comrade with the duty of finding the locations of these runaways, within the cities of Iraq. We dressed as casual citizens and took only one small gun, one hand grenade, and the radio. We heard that the group was heading toward the city of Suleimaniye. On our way there, we stopped in a village to refill our supplies. The villagers treated us extraordinarily well and offered us food and tea. In the evening, just as we were getting ready to leave, they said, "Comrades, what is your hurry? Stay and rest. You can leave later," and kept us waiting there. Whenever we suggested leaving, they told us to wait a little bit longer. This made me realize that something was amiss. We stood up to head toward an exit, and the peasants made a circle around us. One of the elder peasants said, "We are not going to let you leave, because we do not know whether you are enemies or friends. The Peshmerga is on the way. You will have to wait until they arrive!"

We had no option but to wait. The two of us had no chance against 20 people. The Peshmerga arrived in two cars at around 2:00 a.m. I told them, "We are your comrades heading to the city Suleimaniye." Of course, they did not believe us. Back then, the relationship between the YNK and the PKK was negative. The YNK brought its forces and positioned them in a camp just across from our area. This behavior made the organization very uncomfortable.

While we were traveling with the YNK forces, I tried to contact our camp in Kandil via radio. I could not establish a connection, because the distance between Suleimaniye and Kandil was too great. "Take us to Suleimaniye. There are PKK members there to whom you can deliver us," I said. Back then, the organization had offices, representatives, and hospitals in some of the districts that were under the control of the YNK. I was unable to understand what they said to each other, since they spoke Sorani Kurdish. There was a translator with us, so that the conversation between us and their forces could be understood. Luckily, the other comrade knew how to speak Sorani. I warned him immediately, "Do not let them figure out that you know Sorani. Pretend that you do not understand what they're saying. If they figure out that you know the language, they will not talk in front of us."

The commander of the YNK forces was sitting on my right in the car. When we first set out, they asked us to surrender our weapons, but we had resisted. They also never searched us, so still did not know that we had hand grenades. At one point, the driver and the YNK commander were having a conversation and I asked my comrade to translate what they were saying. "They are planning on putting us in jail. They aren't taking us to our comrades in the YNK provinces," he said. I asked if he were sure, and he confirmed what he was. As soon as we arrived in Suleimaniye, I told the YNK translator to tell them to take us to our organization's hospital. They answered that they were already taking us there. Of course, I knew that the commander was actually telling the driver, "We are going directly to the military post, not to the hospital."

I turned to my comrade and said, "It is time to teach them a lesson they will never forget." I took my tobacco box from my pocket, rolled a cigarette, and offered it to the YNK commander sitting next to me. He waved his hand in a dismissive gesture, indicating that he did not want it. I pretended to take the lighter from my pocket, but pulled the hand grenade from where it was tied at my waist, and said, "Here is a kumbara for you!" (In the Sorani language, kumbara means bomb.) As soon as he saw the hand grenade in his face, he started to scream. Two other Peshmerga that had been riding in the back were trying to open the back door of the jeep so they could jump out; however, they could not even find the door handle in their panic and horror. I began to speak to them with my comrade simultaneously translating my speech into Sorani. "Everybody, calm down and stay quiet. Now, close the door. The car is already going 80 kilometers an hour. If you jump out of the car at that speed, you will die anyway. There is no need for me to activate the grenade."

I turned to the commander and said, "Look, I know you have been lying to us from the very beginning. We told you to take us to the PKK hospital. However, you are taking us to a military post. Now, you will take us to the hospital immediately." He was still shaking from fear and replied, "Comrade, we will take you wherever you want." Despite this, they took us to a place that looked like military barracks. I knew that the hospital's security was provided by PKK guerillas, and yet there were Peshmerga soldiers waiting at the gates into this place. I turned to the commander and asked, "Is this our hospital?" He said, "Yes it is, comrade! This is the main entrance; the hospital is in there." I asked them to call the director of the hospital outside. An overweight man in his 60s, wearing casual clothing came out. He definitely did not seem to be one of us. When he started toward the driver's side, I called him to come to where I was sitting in the vehicle instead. He was just about to look inside the car when the man next to me said, "Do not come in! There is a kumbara." When he was about to run back, I targeted him with my weapon and forced him to get in the car. To our surprise, he was the director of the prison, not a hospital. Because of his fear of my grenade, he told us certain facts. We had been brought to a military post and prison, located in the province of Qela Dize in the city of Suleimaniye.

During my exchange with the prison director, the Peshmerga soldiers had pointed the muzzles of their weapons at us and were waiting for an order to begin shooting. They thought that the pin of the hand grenade had already been pulled, and so they were afraid to shoot. When the commander ordered them to put their weapons down, they obeyed.

After that incident, we finally headed to what was, in fact, the hospital. I wanted to be sure, so I asked them to call a doctor outside before I released the captives in our vehicle. A doctor came out and welcomed us with polite Turkish. I asked him who he was and he told us that he was a doctor from Dersim. I said, "Do not take this the wrong way, but you do not look like one of us. Is there anyone else inside?" He appeared disappointed, but asked, "Who do you want me to call out?" I said, "Tell me the names of those inside, and I will tell you which to call on." While listing to the names, he said the name Medea. I recognized the name as a German national who could speak Turkish and Kurdish fluently, and had joined the organization back in 1992. Because I had met her once, I chose her to be called out, so I could make sure.

Soon Medea and the director of the hospital came out, and I recognized her, so we all got out of the car. The hospital director was surprised when he saw the commander of the YNK post. He asked what the commander was doing with us, and so I told him exactly what had happened. He got angry with me. "Comrade, why did you do this? This captive of yours is not an ordinary person. You can believe that he is going to cause us trouble as soon as he is freed." I replied, "Well, I do not care if he were the Assistant of Talabani. He lied to us several times, and I decided to punish him!" The director of the hospital had no response to what I said. "Okay, let them go now," he said.

We were saying goodbye to our captives by shaking their hands, when my comrade said, "I will play a trick on our captives, Deniz." The commander was standing at the end of the line wearing a loose, white shirt. My comrade dropped his grenade into the man's shirt, when he was leaving. The commander jumped about 2 meters high in fear and fell down unconscious. I was afraid that something serious might have happened to him, because of the stupid joke. I got angry with my comrade and severely criticized his behavior.

We stayed in the hospital that night. Initially, the hospital staff treated us well, since we were guests. However, without letting us know, the director of the hospital had informed the commander of a camp in the countryside, telling him, "There are two guerillas that were brought here by Peshmerga forces." The commander of the camp, Kani Yılmaz, thought that we were from the separatists who had fled from Kandil, and he had told the director, "Let them stay there tonight, and I will have our forces bring them here tomorrow morning."

After breakfast the next morning, the director of the hospital asked us where we were headed next. I said, "We are going to Suleimaniye. Could you arrange a car for us?" He asked, "Why are the two of you going to Suleimaniye?" I got a little upset with him. "Arrange the car, and do not bother yourself with the rest. It's none of your business!"

When we left the hospital, four guerillas approached, holding their weapons on us, forcing us into a car. They did not respond when I asked them who they were. I kept insisting they tell us who they were, as they drove us into the countryside. At last, one of them said that we were being taken to the Şehit Harun camp. While we were still on the way, I took out my radio on a high hill and instructed the communication officers to connect me with Ebubekir, who got quite angry, when he learned that we had been arrested and were being forcefully taken to the Kani Yılmaz camp. He flew into a rage and immediately began addressing him on the radio. "Who the hell are you Kani? How can you behave in such a disrespectful manner? How can you arrest members of the organization, without letting us know first?" Everyone in the car was listening to this conversation. Ebubekir spoke directly to me again and said, "Tell the driver to take you wherever you want to go!"

We drove back to Suleimaniye, and while back in the city, we got some intelligence that Dr. Süleyman and his supporters were hiding in a camp under control of Talabani in Iraq. I contacted Ebubekir immediately, and told him that in order for us to arrest the separatists, we were first going to have to kill the Peshmerga forces in the camp. I said, "Comrade, if you can afford a war with the YNK, send me only a single company of guerillas, and I will destroy this camp, with everyone hiding inside." After thoroughly discussing the issue with his assistant, Celal, Ebubekir ordered me to destroy the YNK camp. (As I've mentioned before, there is a tradition in the organization, that, if someone says, "I cannot do it. I cannot live the life of a guerilla," no one will oppose their decision and you'll be let go. On the other hand, if someone leaves the organization, taking some supporters for an ill reason, like separation, then no one would allow or approve of such a thing.)

Dr. Süleyman had gone too far. He was making insulting propaganda saying, "Apo had surrendered himself to the Turkish security forces, and now he is forcing the organization to surrender itself, as a whole." Because of these derogatory statements, Cemal said, "We will do whatever is necessary to kill these separatists. We will even run the risk of waging a war against Talabani, if we must."

After the decision was made, it did not take us long to begin forming our attack plans. Headquarters sent me a force of 80 people to command. They were well armed, with howitzers, anti-aircraft weapons, bazookas, bixi, and other heavy weapons. Negotiation was not an option at this point; we were going to destroy the camp.

While we were planning to annihilate the YNK camp, our enemy, Jalal Talabani, was planning to deal a major blow to the organization, with the help of the separatists, Dr. Süleyman, Küçük Zeki, and Yılmaz. Dr. Süleyman told Talabani, "The organization isn't ready for a fight. The guerillas are still in shock over the incarceration of Apo. Besides that, the guerilla forces in Turkey had been required to withdraw from their positions, and many of them were not happy with that. These things had caused conflict amongst them, and so they are not in a position to win a battle against your army. If you attack them now, I am certain many of them will just surrender."

Beyond that, Iranian officials were encouraging Talabani by saying, "You attack them from there, and we will close the border with thousands of Iranian soldiers over here. Our two forces will squeeze the PKK guerillas in the steep areas of Kandil Mountain and then destroy them by bombing them on both sides. Not to mention, it is winter and many of them may die from the cold and snowstorms if we can sweep them up toward the top of Kandil Mountain." Finally, Turkey also wanted to take part in this war. Turkish officials informed Talabani that, "You start the fight, and we will drop bombs on the PKK camps with our fighter jets." Turkey even sent many high-ranking military officers to Iraq to assist Talabani in the coordination of this final blow against the PKK. Talabani had established some YNK camps right across from our PKK camps and his troops began causing trouble for our guerillas that were staying in those camps. "You cannot go down to the city center, and you cannot pass from this area to another area. This is your border and you are all going to have to stay there." All of these things combined, turning into a problem that was even bigger than we thought, and it was not about to get any better.

13

THE WAR AGAINST THE YNK

Before we performed a raid on the YNK camp in Iraq, Murat Karayılan returned from his trip in Europe, and Comrade Cuma was in Syria at this point. Murat Karayılan became so angry when he saw the Peshmerga had taken position just across from the PKK camps. "How could you put yourself in such a ridiculous position, and let these men set up a military camp in front of you? Has the world ever witnessed two enemy troops drinking water from the same fountain? How did it come to be that our guerilla forces and the Peshmerga are staying in the same area?" The questions came like gunfire! "We will send them packing!" He declared.

The guerillas were surprised to hear this from Murat Karayılan, because since Apo had been arrested, they had been trained in negotiation and dialogue rather than combat. Karayılan deployed all the guerillas that were gathered in the camps into the fields of their previous duties and reordered them back into military units of companies, battalions, and platoons. Easy camp living was suddenly at an end, and we began to take positions along the border that belonged to the YNK forces. Once they realized that we were getting ready to attack their border units, they executed a raid on one of our camps and killed 12 of our comrades. Even worse, the comrades that fled from this raid were taken captive by Iranian authorities. Iran handed all of them over to Talabani for execution, causing more tension in the organization.

The changes in the YNK's attitude toward the guerillas confused them greatly. They began asking Duran Kalkan questions. "Why has the YNK changed their attitude toward us now and begun placing forces at our positions? Why is Iran dispatching weapons and soldiers towards the border, and we are remaining silent with all of this?" Duran Kalkan responded by saying, "We were curious as to how you would react in this situation and that's why we gave some concessions to the YNK and Iranian forces. Otherwise, the YNK would position itself just across from our forces and we would turn a blind eye to it. That would be an impossible situation! We could not let their approach against us make us crazy, but we had to let them do it so we understood your attitudes!"

Most of the people in the meeting were of the ranks of team, company, battalion, or headquarters commander. At that very meeting, by unanimous vote, the organization decided to wage war against the YNK. One of the commanders even stated, "Although we had diverse opinions about some issues within the organization, in such a situation as this, we must not turn against one another, and we need to forget our diversities. Go and get an official declaration of war. We will prepare and motivate our guerillas for battle. How dare Talabani's YNK rise against us? In the old days, Turkey, the KDP, and the YNK would unite their forces against us, but not be able to stand against the organization. If they now have the courage to fight us, then it clearly shows that we are in a miserable situation." I remember this important meeting very well with Duran Kalkan leaving the meeting hall laughing loudly. When one of the comrades asked him where he was going, he replied, "To start a war!"

During Murat Karayılan's leadership of the presidency council, the organization declared war against Talabani. Cemil Bayık approved this decision as well. Now the only problem in front of us was Iran. We were going to fight against the YNK, but we did not know whether Iran would join the fight or not, and without that knowledge we had to take extra precautions. Murat Karayılan stated, "If we want to keep Iran out of the war, our first act against the YNK must be very devastating. Iranian officials are smart and would never intervene in a war if they witness the YNK getting badly beaten. On the contrary, if they see us weakened by Talabani, they would fight alongside him with all of their forces." In order to ensure that we would cause a serious blow to Talabani, Murat Karayılan visited each company and battalion to arrange meetings with the guerillas to increase their motivation.

The Dilemma of Adopting the New or the Old Policy

After our forces withdrew from Turkey in 1999, many guerillas that had gone from the north to the south resigned their positions. Some of them started gardening within the battalion; growing tomatoes, peppers, and other vegetables. A comrade was in charge of the field in Amanoses, and when he went south, he became the logistician of a battalion. He was in charge of supplying the needs of the battalions, such as food, clothing, etc. Imagine! The commander, who led our fights in Amanoses just a short time ago was now dealing with camp logistics. There were some rumors, which ran rampant within the organization, reporting that the old leadership could not adapt to this new period within the organization. Many people argued that a guerilla that had long been a true fighter would not be able to engage in politics and dialogue. According to these people, even if he did acclimate, he would never truly be successful.

One evening, Nizamettin Taş visited us and led a meeting. He used this exact statement as he addressed us: "You will either adapt to this political process, the process of peace, or we will establish a prison camp like Maxmur and lock up all of you there. Your actions are demoralizing the newbies among you. Leave them alone, so that they aren't spoiled by your stories." While the new cadre was getting prepared for the new process, the old cadre began to criticize the attitude of the organization, saying, "Why is the organization now treating us like this?" They even explicitly said, "We have fought for the organization for years, and it is for this reason that the necessity of armed struggle occupies our minds. You cannot simply discard us because the strategy has changed." Also, during this period of change, many commanders from the old cadre, including myself, resigned from duty.

It was during one of these meetings that I stood up and criticized Nizamettin Taş. "Are the changes you are trying to impose upon us, the policy of the organization, or are they your personal views? You cannot impose these ideas on us, because you and the organization have trained us for violence, all these years. You trained us to understand that a good guerilla must have certain qualifications, of strong discipline, etc. You trained us how to fight. Now, because the strategy has changed, you cannot expect us easily to adapt in just a month. It's not as simple as changing clothes. We've been trained for years to become warriors and killers and now we are just supposed to forget about everything that belongs to the old ways? You need to be a bit rational about this and give us time, if you want us to undertake such a change. If the organization is serious about this new approach, it will only happen with the help and support of the old members. You're making distinctions between the two groups by claiming the old cadre is more prone to fighting, and the new one, to dialogue—it is a poor tactic to use on us. If peace is to be with the Turks, and the new strategy is to be successful, you can only make it happen with the help of the old cadre! If you disregard their efforts and experience, your chances of being successful are very small."

When Murat Karayılan arrived from Europe, the attitude toward the older commanders changed completely. Karayılan gathered the management together, and said, "How could you push aside these experienced people, who have devoted their years to the organization? It is thanks to them that the organization is where it is now. We cannot turn a blind eye to these people, just because we have changed our strategy. That's a bad approach, for even if we are turning a new page, we must do so including the old cadre!" I'll never forget the sentence that Murat Karayılan used at the end of his speech. "No one should fool themselves. The logic that the political process is different from the military process is very wrong. The main factor that provides and sustains peace is the existence of guerillas. A person who has never been in a fight, nor has any experience in killing, cannot be successful in politics and thus cannot pursue what is best for the organization, politically. Whoever pushed out the old guerillas will certainly pay for it one day."

These changes happened during Nizamettin Taş's (Botan's) period. After these meetings, Botan was already discharged, and Murat Karayılan was appointed to take his position. Botan was assigned as the head of a passive new institution, which was named the political public movement. He was told by senior commanders that, "Since you are so strong for politics, resign from your duties in the guerilla forces, and lead this political institution." After that, all of the old commanders were reappointed to their old duties before we waged war against the YNK.

Ape Hus Warrior teams

Initially, the organization plotted revenge against the YNK posted near our camp located at Karadağ. We were offended that the YNK would raid this particular camp. It would have been part of battle if they had attacked a normal guerilla camp. But at the camp in Karadağ, the organization was hosting newbies before they were sent to other camps, as well as people who had tasks of a more neutral nature, like tailoring, healthcare, and media. Ape Hus (Kadri Çelik) was arranging guerilla squads to be the instruments of our revenge. Ape Hus had served the Turkish army as a lieutenant in the past and was one of our best guerilla trainers. He arranged four squads, each consisting of 12 people. I was assigned as assistant to a squad commander of one of those squads. Each group was assigned to fight in a specific area. The purpose of these special squads was to assist local guerilla forces in the regions to which they were assigned. There were some military posts and heavy weapon positions on the hills, which would be difficult for the local guerillas to defeat. This meant that our task was to destroy those outposts so that the local forces could advance within the inner parts of the enemy lines.

These squads were chosen purely from specially trained guerillas, so we were extra careful about not incurring any losses. It would have been considered normal if five or six of our comrades from a regular local force were martyred during a clash. Guerillas often said, "We are at war, so of course we will occasionally lose our comrades." However, if three or four of our comrades from these specially selected squads were martyred, it would be considered equal to losing a whole battalion of regular guerilla forces. Because of this, we were ordered to retreat after the destruction of the YNK positions. The local forces would finish the job by going behind enemy lines.

Before starting our mission, the squad would prepare a fight schedule within the group. On the first night, the plan in my group was: six of us were going out to attack, while the rest of the group, six other guerillas, would stay behind and only fight if reinforcements were needed. The next night, we would stay behind, and those who remained behind the night before would attack the hills. As I had mentioned, our squad was responsible for destroying the Peshmerga fronts located on strategic hills.

One night, we had approximately 2,000 guerillas placed in positions at specific intervals across the 150 kilometer border with Talabani's area of control. Just before 11:00 p.m., my squad took advantage of the cover of darkness and managed to sneak as close as 50 meters to the YNK position on a nearby hill. After we moved into position, the large group of guerillas on the border began their missions simultaneously. One way or another, we were going to have to kill the Peshmerga positioned on that hill, and, if not, we would be killed when the YNK noticed our presence there.

We attacked in unison with the main force. The YNK was caught off guard, and it certainly did not expect such a large group of guerillas to attack. My team was able to capture the hill and began shooting the Peshmerga located on other hills and on the front lines with their own Soviet-made DShK 1938 heavy machine guns. When they realized that we had overrun one of their own strategic locations, the Peshmerga forces, on top of other hills, left their positions and ran away. They suffered many losses as they fled, and on that specific hill, my team killed 18 Peshmerga, and took three of them captive.

The next morning, we collected all the weapons and ammunition from the positions vacated by the Talabani forces and began planning the details of the new attack, which we would carry out later that night. Murat Karayılan ordered, "We will carry out raids again tonight, and strike another blow before they recover from the shock of last night's attack!"

That night, it was our team commander's turn to raid the Peshmerga positions with his five guerillas. The target was yet another strategic hill that was being held by Talabani forces. I communicated with the local guerilla forces and told them, "A squad of special guerilla forces will raid that hill. So, do not shoot at that location with heavy weapons!" The attack that night was going to begin at the same time as the previous night, and all the guerilla units had taken their positions as scheduled, except for our team commander and his troop who had not yet made it to the hill. We all waited, since the mission could not begin until that group snuck onto the hill.

I communicated to them over the radio. "Tell me your exact position!" The team commander replied, "Comrade, it is so dark, and I think we are lost. We are crossing a flat field, and we see no hill around us." I said, "Do not panic, you're on the right path. You will reach the edge of the hill if you walk another 300 meters." I contacted him again 15 minutes later, and he informed me that the squad was still positioned in the same place. This upset me. I was not aware that Duran Kalkan had been listening to our conversation and heard me give the squad commander a very hard time, with comments such as, "What kind of commander are you? There are 2,000 guerillas waiting for you. Either you get to the hill, or you return here immediately!" This time he replied, "We cannot go back, the Peshmerga are in the field with us." At this point, I realized he was frightened and was not about to come back to us or move forward to the hill. Since he was obviously incompetent, I asked him to give the radio to someone else in the squad, and he gave it to a female guerilla. As soon as I heard a female's voice on the other end of the radio, I said, "I do not want you, give the radio to one of your male comrades."

She became angry and harshly responded, "You want to speak to a male guerilla, but if we had a proper male leading us, all of these things would not have occurred." I did not want to talk with her, because she was as bold as brass and would no doubt risk death to climb up to the hill directly. That is why I had to speak with someone who was better at careful planning. I knew there was someone named Mahir in the squad, and I asked the female guerilla to hand the radio to him. I told Mahir how they could reach the hill by providing him with more details and also told him, "Comrade, all the other guerillas are waiting for you, climb up the hill as soon as possible!"

With Mahir's leadership, the squad were not only able to destroy the targets on that hill but were also able to capture the YNK headquarters commander's assistant. Later, I heard that the squad commander whom I had scolded fought bravely in the front and even broke his arm in the clash. That night, after the mission was over, I contacted him. "You were not like that before the attack, and we both know you did not get lost. Why did you not take the squad to the hill?" He said, "Comrade, I could not take responsibility of so many specially trained guerillas. It was a risky task. If you had sent me to the hill alone, I would have run up there in the front, but I could not take responsibility for all of those comrades." Angrily, I replied, "Are you an idiot? Was the organization not aware there could potentially be some losses during such a risky task?"

During my upbraiding of the commander, Duran Kalkan heard what I said and asked me to communicate with him via another channel on the radio. "Stop being so hard on him: it is obvious that he could not have taken the risk." I answered, "What else could I do? I guess I will discharge him." He said, "All right, discharge him, but do not drive him into a corner where he may harm himself."

The amount of losses for the YNK during the two nights of attacks were large. They lost hundreds of Peshmerga, and since the organization had to fight in such a vast area, we lost 105 comrades. On the third day of our attacks, Murat Karayılan ordered, "Rather than attacking the Peshmerga from the front, beginning today, we will directly target and kill the commanders that are positioned behind the line." That day, he personally led three battalions of guerillas in an invasion of their military headquarters, where the coordination of the war took place. We captured vehicles, bombs, weapons, and some DShK 1938s. In short, we gained a lot of ammo that could sustain us for a couple of years. To top it off, we captured 50 high-ranking YNK commanders.

By the time we caused Talabani such a great defeat, it was nearly winter. During that time of the year, Kandil is very cold and snowy. We were just about to close ourselves off within our winter camps, when the YNK began an attack. Once again, it was Peshmerga forces, but this time they were being coordinated by Turkish lieutenants. They attacked our camps with heavy weapons and howitzers. We lost almost 100 comrades during this unexpected attack. As I said, it was very cold and we were unable to complete a counterattack. Instead, we withdrew our forces from the Kandil Mountains to a much more secure area within Iraq.

During these skirmishes, Comrade Cuma had been staying in Syria. Cuma was going to travel through Iranian territories and visit our forces there, because we thought that the war in Kandil had ended, and it was safe for him to do so. During that time, there was news on Turkish media that claimed that Cemil Bayık and Halil Ataç were arrested in Iran. Because of our position within the organization, we knew that Cemil Bayık was still staying in Syria. Hearing the lies that were being broadcast by Turkey made us anxious. There was definitely something behind this deceptive news.

Two or three days later, four attack helicopters approached the area where we were hiding in Kandil. The helicopters all landed somewhere close to the border. Shortly after that, a convoy of vehicles entered our camp. We were informed later that these helicopters were Iranian Air Force helicopters that had transported Cemil Bayık from Syria to Kandil. Iranian officials made plans and said, "Turkey had Apo in its hands. If we somehow gain the trust of Cemil Bayık and ally with him, then we can increase our control on the organization." As I mentioned before, Iranian officials always carried out two-faced policies. Although they entered the war on the side of the YNK, they immediately switched sides to try and collaborate with the organization since the YNK had experienced such a serious blow from us. Even with this, they continued to be seen as supporting Talabani, but in fact started to support the organization in many ways behind the scenes. Welcome to the Middle East…It has always been like this.

For two months, YNK forces continued to attack the inner parts of the plains where we were located. During this two-month period, 210 guerillas were martyred. I was injured myself during the fighting in this period, being shot in my left hand. Two of my fingers are still dysfunctional because of that injury. I was actually advised to cross into Iran, to be treated by professional doctors, and decided I should go. I was first transported to a small healthcare facility that was operated by the organization at the Iran-Iraq border. The guides were to pick me up there and take me into Iran.

It was at this facility that I encountered a close friend of mine who had also been sent to Iran for treatment. He was a platoon commander, fighting on the same front as my squad during our fight against the YNK. The Iranian doctors had to amputate one of his legs. Unfortunately, amputation had not originally been necessary, since there was only a piece of shrapnel stuck under his patella that needed removing. The Iranian doctors initially removed the shrapnel but did not use proper disinfectant, and the wound became infected. It was then his leg had to be amputated because of the spread of infection in his body. This friend of mine had warned me not to travel to Iran when he heard that I was going there for treatment and had already informed the organization that he suspected the Iranian doctors were working with the Iranian intelligence service and deliberately disabling high-ranking guerillas. In fact, this problem had previously been noted by others. It could not be a coincidence that regular guerillas were being properly treated, but the ranked ones had often experienced disability after being treated there. So, after speaking with my friend, I decided not to go to Iran.

Our war with the YNK stopped completely around February of 2001. Iran and the YNK sent a group of five people for negotiations. The spokesperson for this group was someone in charge of the Iranian Intelligence Service and was assigned as commander of the Revolutionary Guard in Iran. Osman Öcalan joined the meeting as our representative of the organization. We did not know it at the time, but the organization told Osman, "Accept whatever they say, because it is winter now, and we have no chance to win a fight." The YNK were in a similar situation themselves, after suffering many losses. As a precondition of peace, they asked the organization once again to withdraw its forces from the inner parts of Iraq, to the outskirts of the Kandil Mountains. We returned control of the areas to the YNK and positioned ourselves in the Kandil Mountains, just as they asked. Our goal was to spend the winter uneventfully, and let the already exhausted guerillas rest until spring.

Break-Up with Sevin

While we were fighting the YNK, someone brought me a note from Sevin, the woman with whom I was in love. It was a short letter, reading, "Do whatever is necessary to stay alive until I see you again. I just need to talk with you one more time, and after that, I do not care what happens to you." I figured that something was not right. It seemed that she had heard about the bogus love affair, an incident which had occurred in Gari back in 1997. Even though it was a setup, Sevin may have believed it had been real, and as soon as the war with the YNK ended, she visited our camp. Before we even greeted each other, she asked me directly, "What did I tell you when we left each other in Damascus?" I replied, "You told me many things, can you be more specific?" She was mad as hell. "How many times have

I told you that I never wanted to hear your name mentioned with another woman, Deniz?" I replied, "I have always been committed to my promise to you. What have you heard?"

She went directly to the point. My guess had been correct, and she had heard about the incident that took place in 1997. I said, "Sevin, if that so-called love affair was real, do you think the organization would assign me as a commander again?" No matter what I said, she was not convinced. "If it were not real, it would not still be talked about among the guerillas. You are lying to me, Deniz. This is your last chance. I will kill you if I hear something like this again." I replied, "Do you think the organization will spare your life, if you kill me?" She answered, "I'm not stupid. I would tell everyone that it was an accident," and she was serious. "Okay, I will be more careful, but what if a woman guerilla claims she had a relationship with me, just like the previous incident that occurred in 1997. In such a situation, you will kill me directly, so I am no longer safe," I reasoned. I was frightened, because she was like a devil and had an authoritarian personality and would do most anything, based only on a whim.

"Do you really love me, Deniz?" She asked. I said, "I do. I would sacrifice myself for you, Sevin. But, if it costs me our struggle for Kurdish rights, then I would even sacrifice our love." She started laughing loudly. "I like your answer, Deniz." In this way I was able to mend fences with Sevin, but at the end of 2000, we were once again assigned to different fields, and I did not see her again until 2003. We would, occasionally, send letters to one another. I sent mine with groups that traveled from our region to Syria, while she sent hers with groups who were traveling back to Iraq.

I did not realize just how many letters she was writing, since I was always traveling from one field to another, and did not receive many of the letters she had written. One day, I got one from her, and she was very angry. "I have sent you many letters, but you are not even writing me a reply." At the end of 2002, a female force came to the officers' school in Damascus from the female headquarters. They had a separate congress that was independent from the men's. It was evening, and I saw Sevin among them. The next day, she visited me in my quarters. I had not known at the time, but she had become a member of the congress and thus had a female guard with her. She came into the ward and said, "Comrades, sorry, but could you please excuse Deniz and myself for a few minutes?" After everyone left, we started to argue, as we had previously, and by the end of it, she was very irate. "You are now free of me. Do whatever you want!" she said, and we broke up. I never saw her again, but I received a few letters asking how I was.

The Negotiations with Iran at Karadağ Camp

Beginning in March of 2001, our forces began marching again toward the inner parts of the territories controlled by the YNK. We once again took control of the places we had given back to Talabani after our signed agreement. When the YNK realized what was happening, they immediately notified Iran. In May, the same peace committee that had been sent to our camp, returned. This time, the organization sent Murat Karayılan as our spokesperson. During the negotiations, I was responsible for the meeting room security in Kandil and was able to hear everything they discussed.

One thing that astounded me during this meeting was that the Iranian intelligence officials were speaking fluent Turkish. When the meeting began, Murat Karayılan immediately said, "What the hell is this? We are fighting against the YNK, but we are negotiating with Iran? This does not make any sense to me!" Of course, the Iranians were not expecting a reaction quite like that, and one of them said, "You did not care when there were Iranian officials at the first meeting, so why do you care now? Nevertheless, it is not a problem. We will go and bring back a YNK representative." Murat

Karayılan then said, "Actually, we do not need a representative from the YNK here. Our organization fought against Iran in that battle as well. It's just that those YNK idiots let themselves be used by you Iranians!"

The spokesperson of the Iranian committee replied, "I admit, we had not expected such resistance from you during those battles. Also, for the first time in their history, the Turks retreated from the area without fighting, and this unfortunate development spoiled our plans. Now, it is your time to answer my questions. Why did you break the peace agreement that was signed before winter?" Murat Karayılan replied, "We did not recognize the legitimacy of that agreement!" The spokesman replied in surprise, "How could you not recognize it? The PKK legitimately signed it! Here are the signatures by both parties!" When he heard this Murat Karayılan calmly said, "Well, I do not recognize it. Go and discuss that matter with whomever signed it. I do not give a shit about it, because my guerillas and I fought against you there. You should have discussed the conditions of peace with me! My force will stay where they are positioned now. Go and tell Talabani and the YNK that we will continue to stay there. If they are not happy with this decision, then we will fight with them again!"

The Iranian official was really pissed off. "What kind of man are you? You do not even use a proper tone to discuss official matters!" Karayılan laughed and said, "Who told you that I'm a diplomat? I'm a guerilla, not a politician. I cannot speak as well as they. I speak directly and openly! Now listen to me carefully! I am going to tell you of our new conditions. Go and tell the YNK that if they accept these conditions, it will be well. If they do not, then they better prepare their forces for a new fight."

At his words, the Iranians went off the deep end. "This is not the style of the PKK that I know. If the PKK promises something, it is known that they keep their promise forever. That's what I know about your organization!" Karayılan answered, "You will either accept our conditions or pay the price! The Karadağ camp will be immediately emptied and controlled by the PKK. Our forces will continue to patrol in the buffer zone in the plains of northern Iraq, and the YNK forces will not enter this buffer zone, without first notifying us. Also, the PKK will control all of the districts and villages that are located within that area. The YNK will never again appoint mayors or district governors within this zone. And finally, you, the state of Iran, will vacate the stations that were previously empty."

When the Iranian commander heard the last condition, he said, "There is a possibility that the YNK might accept these conditions. However, the state of Iran will never accept such insulting conditions." Karayılan replied, "I do not care. Your country was the brains behind the scheme that resulted in war against the YNK. Although it was the YNK that appeared to fight against us, it was you who mentored them. You will pay the price for what you did, so that you will not dare to play games against us. Ever again!"

On May 20, 2011, the organization was officially informed that both Iran and the YNK had accepted the conditions of peace without any strings attached. Iran had only a small caveat with the agreement, and the organization had no problem with accommodating them. Tehran just wanted to be notified when guerilla forces crossed into Iran. This is because senior members of the organization first travel to Tehran when they visit European countries for diplomatic reasons.

There was an unusual problem encountered during this period. When the YNK delivered control of the more than 300 villages that were part of the peace accord, the PKK had a hard time meeting the needs of the villagers. The biggest problem was the absence of power lines and electricity. One of the first things the organization did, was allocate a large amount of money from its annual budget in order to build two dams in the region. Although in fact, the initial cost of the building was not as high as first thought, because many of the workers on the sites were guerillas.

The two dams would increase the quality of life for the people there, because they would have the capacity to meet the electricity needs of all the villages in the region. When they began operating, the organization not only provided electricity to the peasants, but also did not charge them for the use of the service. As a result, the peasants happily welcomed the other services offered by the organization. The second thing the organization accomplished was to establish committees within each village. The committees consisted of six or seven people to handle problems that would crop up among the peasants. These committees were authorized to make final decisions, regarding their conflicts and problems. Of course, if the peasants thought that the committee was unfair in its decisions, they were given the right to send an appeal to headquarters.

Once the potential threat of the YNK and Iran had been negated by the peace process, the organization was able to set its sights on peace with Turkey. Murat Karayılan was disappointed with Turkey's attitude toward the organization. On several occasions, he openly criticized Turkey, by saying, "We are trying to peacefully settle our differences with Turkey. Why then do they betray us by dispatching military officers to aid the YNK forces? Why are they still trying to stab us in the back?" This was still during the period when the organization was implementing Apo's orders for our troops. In fact, there were less than 500 guerillas left inside Turkey's borders. In some of the provinces, like Erzurum and Garzan, we did not leave a single guerilla behind. On top of that, the organization had sent nine of its senior members back to Turkey in order to show its sincerity for the peace process. This group surrendered themselves to the Turkish security forces in the Şemzinan (Şemdinli) District of the city of Hakkari. The organization sent them to Turkey as a goodwill gesture, and our trust was abused when our comrades were incarcerated. It has been 17 years, and these comrades are still in the Turkish prisons. One of them even died of a heart attack three months ago in the Diyarbakır E-Type prison.

At this juncture, the organization was wholeheartedly pursuing peace. As I mentioned before, the guerillas were only being trained in ways to promote the peace efforts. In fact, we guerillas were not given any battle training until the end of 2003. This was a difficult process for the organization. Iran was offering excessive incentives to continue fighting Turkey. "If you begin fighting against the Turks again, we will supply all your ammunitions and weapons free of charge! You will no longer have to worry yourselves over finding money for access to weapons!"

There was a very strange incident that developed between Iran and the organization in 1999 during our peace negotiations with Turkey. I am sure the Turkish intelligence officials might know of it. When Apo was first arrested, the organization prepared itself for a final conflict. This was going to be our life or death struggle in which we would attack with all our forces and weapons. For this last battle, we purchased expensive quality missiles from Europe. When they were on their way, they were first transported to Iran in carrier planes. Iran seized all of these missiles when Apo publicly declared that the organization was going to make peace with the state of Turkey. Iranian officials openly told senior members of our organization that, "You will either continue to fight against Turkey, or we will seize your missiles." On top of that, they made us an offer. "If you continue your armed struggle against Turkey, we will provide you with five times more of these weapons for free. Also, your guerillas will be allowed to use the Iranian side of the Turkish-Iranian border to conduct missions against Turkish military posts and then come into Iran to prevent potential losses from their retaliations."

Despite these incentives, the organization decided to continue its peace process with Turkey. It was not only Iran that was disturbed with this process but Syria as well. Syrian officials even arrested 50 mid-level organization members and handed them over to the Turkish security forces. It was very odd, since Syria had never handed over a single ground guerilla to Turkey before. It seemed as if Iraq were the only country that did not oppose the peace process, although there was also Barzani, who supported the peace process even though the organization had warred with him in the past.

The situation we were in at that point held many similarities to the guerilla struggles that had occurred in many other countries around the world. The guerilla force were disregarded if they waved the white flag of peace, and ignored the armed struggle. If this ambivalence lasted for a long period, the guerillas lost their motivation to fight, and this was a potential risk of which the organization was well aware. In that context, the war that we had with the YNK was almost like a treat for the guerillas. We had not fought against the Turkish security forces for almost three years and had been camping in Iraq and Syria during the peace process, which was making us sluggish. Everyone was occupied with mundane chores, like gardening, the raising of animals, and things of that nature. Our war with the YNK and Iran had served as a way for us to pull together.

We waited until the very end of 2004 for an answer from the Turkish officials. There were very few preconditions for which the organization had asked, so a final ceasefire was possible. For example, the organization did not ask for local PKK forces to be assigned to help with security in cities within Turkey that were mostly composed of Kurds. However, according to the current peace agreement between Turkey and the PKK, the establishment of local Kurdish security forces was an indispensable term of continued peace. At the time, Turkish officials were constantly putting pressure on the organization to lay down their arms and dissolve the guerilla forces. It is quite sad that the Turkish officials were not as familiar with the PKK as was Iran. Can you imagine that you would fight against a group for 40 years, and still not understand its goals and internal dynamics? Our organization was not only there to protect the welfare of the Kurds in Turkey, but also the Kurds in Iraq, Syria, and Iran.

Let's assume that we achieved peace with the state of Turkey. If that happened, who would defend the rights of the Kurds in those countries I just mentioned? Today, the Kurdish regimes, established in northern Iraq by Talabani (YNK) and Barzani (KDP), are not working for the welfare of the Kurds there. They are both extremely feudal at the management level. The PKK should be out there protecting the Kurds in the short term and changing the feudal systems into more socialist ones in the long-term. Also, the Turkish officials' insistence on the annihilation of the Guerrilla forces was pointless, because the organization had already brought its Armed forces out of Turkey into the camps in Iraq and Syria. The accuracy of this information could be checked from Turkish intelligence resources. The ARGK retreated completely, and in its stead the organization established the HPG (Kurdish Public Defense Force).

The Separation of the Guerilla Forces and Political Structure

The HPG organized its first conference in 2001. Until this conference, the guerilla force was above any other institution within the organization's leadership hierarchy. Every other institution acted in line with the prime authority of the headquarters commander. However, with the decisions that were made during the 7th congress, the guerilla forces and political forces were separated from one another and began acting as two independent institutions under the authority of the presidency council. One part of the change was that Duran Kalkan, Cemil Bayık, and Murat Karayılan served only with the guerilla forces. On the political side, Osman Öcalan and Nizamettin Taş were assigned to the top two positions. Nizamettin Taş and his team said to their supporters, "The war with the Turks is over, which now means the guerilla force is useless. The Kurdish Public Defense Forces have already replaced them in the major Kurdish cities in Turkey. A new era has begun, where situational control will be in the hands of the political elite. Comrades, if we secure our uniformity, then we will have more control over the organization as a whole."

Nizamettin Taş was supposed to be present during this first conference of the HPG, because he had to answer for the losses the guerillas had incurred when they withdrew from Turkey. As I mentioned before, the Turkish security forces laid ambushes at various locations and martyred many of our comrades, and Murat Karayılan was angry about this double cross. "If the Turks did not keep their promise, then why were our troops withdrawn from Turkey? Why did you not at least attack them in retaliation to this backstab?" Comrade Murat heavily criticized Nizamettin Taş in his absence.

After this congress, I was assigned commander to a company at headquarters. The group consisted of guerillas who were discharged for various reasons, or who recently joined the organization. It was September of 2001, and I was playing volleyball in the headquarters' backyard, when one of my comrades was running toward us shouting, "They hit America! Go and watch the news!" The attack was live on the TV, and we saw that the Twin Towers were in flames.

In the days after the attack, we talked a lot about the incident. We watched the news coming from the United States and were sure that the U.S. was going to attack Afghanistan, and then Iraq. Our organization was normally considered a terrorist group on the U.S. Department of State's terrorist organizations list. We wondered whether America would only target the radical Islamic groups in Iraq, or would they also target us. There were some among us who argued that if the U.S. was successful in its invasion of Iraq, the American forces would be able to harm organizations and groups within the cities but would not be able reach out and attack groups like the PKK that operate in the countryside, at steep elevations. Also, although American officials were part of the reason for Apo's incarceration, the American military had never targeted the organization directly. Likewise, the organization had never targeted an American citizen directly. The majority of us thought that the U.S. would never come after us, even though they invaded Iraq.

With the founding of the HPG (the Kurdish Public Defense Force), the guerillas' confusion, over lack of purpose, largely vanished. Everyone knew that there was nothing like the resolve of the guerilla forces, even though we were no longer fighting against Turkey. Also, the organization had made up its mind that if Ankara would take concrete steps toward peace, we would not leave a single guerilla in Turkey. Nevertheless, the guerilla force would still function until the welfare of the Kurds in Syria, Iraq, and Iran was assured.

Around the end of 2001, the organization began doubting Turkey's sincerity. In almost three years, Ankara had not taken a single step toward peace. There were no decrees or efforts to make necessary changes to the constitution, by the Turkish Parliament. Also, Turkish officials were still planning to marginalize the guerilla forces by wasting their time with lies, and then annihilating them when they were weakened. So when the organization realized their scheme, it began to pay more attention to guerilla training activities. The training was strict and continued day and night. Around this same time, the first book that Apo wrote in prison reached us in the camps. It was titled, *From the Sumerian Divine State to the Democratic Republic.* We began to use this book during the guerillas' political training. It generally consisted of information regarding the vital steps toward a peaceful solution between the Turks and Kurds.

The guerilla force's composition was completely restructured when the HPG was formed. The units were decreased in number, but the quality of the guerillas fighting in these small units increased dramatically. Our guerilla force consisted of only 3,000 quality soldiers, as opposed to the 7,000 or 8,000 it had once been. In addition, the trainers were hired from a more professional group. For example, when

I was staying at headquarters, the organization recruited a highly qualified trainer, who had learned professional military tactics in Russia, Armenia, and Greece, and knew many details about weapons and explosives. When he first visited my company for training, he said, "For this entire week I will train you on how to use a Dragunov sniper rifle." We criticized him saying, "We have been using this weapon for years now. What more can you teach us that we do not already know?" Even with our doubts, the man taught us things that we had never considered before; factors we should consider during shooting, such as how the wind, rain, and snow affect bullets. Also, how we could shoot a moving patrol car, or how we could shoot down a helicopter, as well as other advanced level training.

When we finished these weapons training sessions, we trained with poisons and chemical gasses. There were 63 mid-level commanders present at the training school back then, and this chemical gas training was given to only 13 of us, including myself. Before we were dispatched, the organization strictly warned each of us not to share our knowledge of poisons and chemical gasses with other guerillas. This meant the training stayed strictly with us. Where we would normally share our newfound knowledge with our comrades, this was one instance when we could not do so and were even required to swear that we would not use the skills acquired from that training without the knowledge of the organization. The punishment for breaking this oath was severe.

When we completed all that training, we were dispatched to other regions to train ground guerillas in everything except the poisons. The reason was because they were very risky to use but it was quite easy to obtain the substances needed to create them. Actually, some poisons were acquired from certain poisonous reptiles. First, you would kill them, and let them dry out under the sun, and when dry as paper, you pulverized them. Congratulations, you would now have poison strong enough to kill a human being.

The other method to create poison was just as simple. I do not remember exactly, but there were two main substances involved, one of which could be found in pharmacies and the other one in jewelry stores. When sulfuric acid or nitric acid was mixed with gold water, an extremely poisonous gas was formed. We were putting these two liquid substances into different cups, and then placing them in the space located at the front of the rockets. When those rockets hit the target and blew up, the two substances would interact with each other and kill every living thing around. Of course, the distance, speed, and direction of the wind were crucial when using such tactics. You would have to be at least 500 meters away from the target otherwise you would also be affected by the gas. Because of the ease of procurement, and the high rate of fatality, the organization did not want everyone trained in the use of poisons. That responsibility was given only to the people whom they deeply trusted.

While we were going through our intensive training, the former senior commanders and members of the Presidency Council gathered to create a new name for the organization. As I said, the organization underwent a wide scale structural change. The guerilla forces and the political groups were now completely independent from one another. This gathering resulted in a new name: KADEK (Kurdistan Peace and Democracy Congress). The guerilla forces rejected this change from the very beginning. Their commanders informed the Presidency Council that they did not recognize the name KADEK and would never use it. The guerillas said, "We were born with, grew up with, and will die with the PKK." The organization initially thought that only the military force objected to the title change, but it soon became apparent that even the Kurdish public were disappointed in it. At the beginning of 2003, the organization changed from KADEK to KONGRA-GEL (Public Congress). The guerillas also rejected this change. The senior executives tried convincing the guerilla force by saying, "This title change will be a fresh start for the image of the PKK in the world, since we are now considered a terrorist organization by some states. This way, we would turn the page, and start anew in our struggle." The senior officials figured that since we were at peace then, it would be better to get rid of the name PKK completely.

Also, Duran Kalkan visited the school back then, and said to us, "My comrades, to be honest, I also cannot get my head around this title change. However, as an organization, we are undergoing a huge structural and policy change. Look, I am one of those who laid out the foundations of the PKK, and we are not going change its name voluntarily, but we must do it to refresh our image with some countries."

Tragic Deaths

In 2002, when I was still in the guerilla officer training school, a shooting tournament was organized. A female guerilla and I made it to the finals, among 60 people. As finalists, we were first to shoot a cartridge case at 100 meters and then an empty tomato paste can at a distance of 300 meters. The winner would be determined after completion of the two shooting stages. That was the day I had ended my relationship with Sevin, and my mind was in a shambles, which made me unable to concentrate on the tournament. It is impossible to hit a bull's eye when your mind is busy elsewhere. On one occasion, I was able to pause my breathing, but I was not able to adjust the pressure on the trigger, which needed to be smooth and even. On another occasion, I was able to adjust the pressure correctly, but I was not able to control my breathing. It seemed impossible for me to do both of these essential things at the same time. Therefore, I asked the tournament committee to postpone the final for two days, and my request was accepted.

A shooter's psychological and emotional state is very important when shooting a gun, and if you are on an assassination mission, it is even more important. If you had had an argument or were upset before an assassination mission, the organization would never send you on the mission. As an assassin, you are monitored very closely by the organization. A team would examine you from all angles; your behavior, attitude, psychological state, etc. Only after you have been thoroughly vetted would they decide whether or not you were ready.

Three days later, I left early and went to where the tournament final was to be held. I visited the ammunition warehouse and carefully selected the bullets that I would use, because the quality of your bullets can change the outcome. Most of the time, they are made in the same factory and are the same type, but if you join a tournament it is wise to check the serial numbers on the bullets simply because bullet factories might change their type of gunpowder. This means that even though they can be the same type and size of bullet, they may not contain the same type of gunpowder. Using bullets with differing powders makes it harder to be accurate, so choosing bullets that had been made in the same batch ensures that problem is negated. And so, with that in mind, I chose five bullets with consecutive serial numbers.

Although I was now ready for the tournament, I still had some concerns that I could possibly lose to a newbie female guerilla, and that would be a disgrace. Being an older guerilla and having a chance of being beaten by a newcomer was upsetting to me. It could happen, because she was quite accurate at shooting targets. Because she had never smoked, she could easily control her breathing muscles and pause her breath properly. Whatever the consequences, I had to do something to limp this newbie out of the tournament.

One by one, I completed my shots. Four out of five hit their target. Since it was a tournament, we both had to use the same weapon. After I finished, I slightly displaced the scope of the rifle before giving her the weapon. She loaded her bullets into it and began shooting. She could not hit the target on her first or second try. The bullets were moving toward the same place, but not hitting the target. Because she had already missed two shots, she was automatically eliminated from the tournament. She seemed to dwell on it for a second but could not understand why she had missed. During all of this, I was watching quietly from a distance. The whole officer school was present at the competition field.

I was about to be announced as the winner of the competition but was struck with a guilty conscience. I went to the training commission and confessed to what I had done. The commission announced her name and informed her that she was the winner! "Deniz has just confessed that he played with the accuracy of the scope." They told her. She looked me in the eyes, and then turned to the commission, replying, "No, Deniz is the winner. It was my fault. I should have checked the accuracy of the scope before I attempted my shots. Despite the fact that Deniz played a trick on me, I am at fault since I ignored one of the essential rules of shooting. So, he is the winner."

She was right. Controlling your weapon was an essential rule that is strictly enforced by the organization. Even if you receive a weapon from someone whom you trust (even if this person is your father), you must check it before shooting. You can never say, "This gun is from someone I trust, and I do not need to check it."

In 2002, we actually experienced a very tragic incident related to this issue. Eight or nine new female guerillas joined our battalion. They had been trained before they were sent to us. However, their company commander wanted to give them one more drill to make sure they were ready.

It was raining heavily that day, and I was lecturing on theoretical issues to my guerillas in the company. Around 2:00 p.m., a guard headed toward me shouting, "The women's company commander is severely wounded! Hurry, she needs help!"

Upon hearing his cry, I immediately headed to where I knew she had been giving drills. When I arrived, she was still alive, but unfortunately the bullet had hit her carotid artery. An ice bag had been placed on the wound before we arrived. When I removed the bag, blood began gushing from the wounded artery. I replaced the bag to stop the bleeding and asked the commanders to send out all the newbies. When battalion commanders were all that were left in the room, I turned to them and said, "She's been shot in her carotid artery and only has a few minutes more to live."

She died from the loss of blood, and I left the scene to meet with the newbies that had been present and asked how it had happened. The youngest woman in the group was still weeping and inconsolable. Then, one of the others spoke up, "There were initially seven people present at the training, and another of our comrades joined us late. We were all holding weapons, but none of them were loaded. We knew they were not loaded, because the company commander had checked them, one by one, before giving them to us. Our comrade who arrived late asked our commander what she could do, and the commander told her to get a weapon and join the rest of the trainees. But the commander had not checked to see whether the weapon was loaded or not, like she had with the rest of us. We all lined up in front of her, and she ordered us to target her with our weapons. The training session was about learning how to pause our breath and have proper trigger control. She first lectured us on how to apply these two rules when shooting in theory. After that, she asked us to apply these techniques while holding our weapons toward her and then pulling the trigger. Apparently, the latecomer's gun was loaded, and when she pulled the trigger, she unknowingly hit our commander in the neck." She indicated that the girl who had been late was the 16-year-old who was crying.

It was a very tragic incident. In fact, after this incident, the organization banned company and battalion commanders from delivering weapon training like this. After 2002, professionally trained weapon instructors began to visit the battalions, one by one, to train the guerillas.

It was an awful time for the organization back then, experiencing tragic incidents one after another. Not even a week after the death of the female company commander, the weather was rainy again, and it was as if the heavens themselves had opened up. The rain gave me a very bad feeling, so I followed the instincts of my gut, radioed the battalion commander, and ordered him, "Take the hillers down. We will not have guards on that hill tonight." He asked why, and I replied, "The hill is high and they have radios. A lightning strike could hit them because of their radios."

(As an aside, that is a well-known historical hill. According to legend, even Alexander the Great could not get his troops over it.) Anyway, while I was still talking to the company commander on the radio, a lightning strike hit the top of that very hill. We immediately tried to contact the hiller, via the radio, but there was no answer. Even though it was the middle of the night, my assistant and I climbed up there in the heavy rain. When we arrived, the view we encountered was horrific. They had all been martyred. The death of those comrades and the female company commander within that very same week affected all of us psychologically.

In 2004, while I was staying in Hakurki, a note arrived indicating that the organization, after so many years of peace, was going to begin warring against Turkey again. The guerilla force staying in the south had to be trained immediately in guerilla war tactics, because many of them were newbies. My company was dispatched to Metina, the same year, for that very purpose. In only two months, I was to give accelerated guerilla training to these newbies.

I quickly prepared a list of supplies that were necessary to train them: 100,000 AK-47 bullets, 10,000 bixi bullets, 250 hand bombs, 100 rocket launchers, 50 kilograms TNT, 50 kilograms C4, etc. I listed every single item that was essential for their training and asked the Metina Field officials to get them for me.

It was a normal occurrence for our comrades to be accidentally wounded or even to die during this training. The organization considers a casualty rate of 3 percent (three deaths for 100 trainees) to be normal. During the training I gave in Metina, four guerillas in our battalion were wounded. There was an accidental detonation of a mine, and one of our comrades lost his eyes and another one's leg was torn apart. In one of the sabotage trainings the students were instructed to prepare their own mines. One of the comrades had been late for the training that day and so had not been present when the mine substances were distributed to other trainees. The trainer told him to go to the warehouse and get the proper substances himself. Normally, the trainer should have accompanied him and given him the substances by weighing them first. Since the trainee did not know how much he was supposed to take, he took five times more of the explosive than was required.

The training plan called for the mines that were prepared by the trainees to be buried underground in the training field. They would not kill anyone, even if someone stepped on them, because they did not contain enough of the explosive substance. At the most, there would only be a loud disturbing noise. Of course, the other comrades in the battalion were not aware of this. They were supposed to walk over them during the morning muster. The comrade who had been late to training that day, buried his mine at the spot where I usually greet my company in the morning. (Incidentally, I did not join in the morning muster that day, as I had watched a political show on TV late into the night and informed my guards not to wake me up in the morning.)

That morning, while I was sleeping, there was such a loud noise that I woke up and directly rushed to the assembly area. There were three comrades wounded, lying on the ground. A female guerilla had stepped on the mine while passing from our zone to hers. Every single area of her body was hit by shell fragments, from her head to her toes. She lost both eyes in this incident. As I applied first aid to her, and while cleaning the wounds on her head, I realized that one of her eye sockets was empty. The eye had probably been displaced by shell fragments. The other one was still in the eye socket but it had been hit by a fragment.

Everyone panicked wondering who may have planned such a plot. Everything was revealed once the investigation was complete. The trainee who was late for the training had in fact prepared a real mine. On top of that, the ground where he buried the mine was filled with pebbles. These small pieces of rock were propelled by the explosion like pieces of iron. I immediately called the instructor and asked him why he had given such an amount of explosive substance to that trainee. After thinking for a while, he remembered him and said that he had not given him the substances, but rather the trainee had gotten them himself. I could not put this trainer under investigation, since he was working as a part of the special forces. Despite this, I immediately had him arrested. He was sent back to special forces command after a few days of incarceration in my company.

After the incident, we delivered the seriously wounded comrades to a hospital in Dohuk, Iraq. One of them was treated there, but the comrade who lost her eyes was transferred from Iraq to a better treatment facility in Russia. Russia was quite professional in the realm of eye surgery, and in fact, the Russian doctors were able to treat the eye that was hit by a shrapnel fragment. We also transferred some our wounded comrades to Germany. German doctors were good at treatment as well.

14

INTERNAL CONFLICT WITHIN THE ORGANIZATION

In July of 2002, I was dispatched to Hakurki from the Kandil region. Hakurki is a guerilla camp located in the triangle of Iran, Iraq, and Turkey. When I arrived at the Hakurki camp, I found the organization had decided to relocate to our previously abandoned camps within the borders of Turkey. We were going to recapture the fronts we had deserted in 1999, because of the peace agreement. The organization was doing this simply because Ankara had not taken any concrete steps toward peace during this time frame. Some senior officials argued that the organization was going to be put into a state of war yet again. Apo harshly objected to this decision by sending a letter from his prison through his attorneys. "There has been a coalition government in Ankara, and they could not take the vital steps necessary for peace, because of their ideological fights. Nevertheless, the AKP (Justice and Development Party) has now come to power alone without the support of a coalition partner. We have to give it some time before we can say it has failed. Dispatch the guerillas to their old fronts within Turkey, but do not carry out any missions against the Turkish security forces. We should first wait and see whether there will be any progress toward the effort of peace."

In 2003, the United States invaded Iraq, and at the same time the organization had a split among the senior officials yet again. One faction argued the necessity of fighting against the American forces, while another faction defended the idea that it would be beneficial for the organization to ally with the American forces against Saddam Hussein and the Iraqi army. If we allied with them, we would be able to gain the trust of the U.S. government. In the long run, this partnership would help the organization in its fight against Turkey. During this period, the diplomatic relations between Ankara and Washington DC were already strained. Ankara, a strong ally of Washington, did not let the American forces use the military bases within Turkey during the war. It would be very advantageous for the organization to ally with the United States right away. I do not know if they actually signed an agreement with the U.S. government, but the American forces left us alone even though they destroyed many other organizations within Iraq.

We received intelligence that Nizamettin Taş and Osman Öcalan, the political elites of the organization, were secretly meeting with the American officials. Those two idiots were not aware that they were being used. It turned out that the Americans were aiming to attract them and then kill the rest of the seniors so they could take full control of the PKK. In 2003, when the danger became readily apparent, the organization gathered in a new congress. During that type of congress, a committee inspects the budget reports of both the guerilla forces and the political wings. A $30,000 deficit was found in the political wing's financial report. Cemil Bayık and Murat Karayılan made hay while the sun shone and gave a hard time to Nizamettin Taş. Although it was not a significant amount of deficit, it was a good opportunity to press Nizamettin Taş, since Bayık and Karayılan were seriously disturbed by his secret meetings with the U.S. officials.

Beyond this, the political side of the organization had gone too far in other matters, as well. I mentioned previously, that when Kongra-Gel was first formed, Nizamettin Taş and Osman Öcalan were planning to take control of the organization. In their minds, after they captured control during this congress, they were going to appoint their own men to leadership positions in the guerilla forces and get rid of both Murat Karayılan and Cemil Bayık. When the other senior officials noticed their plan, comrade Cuma made a smart offer to counteract their plans, declaring, "In this congress, the senior leadership should not volunteer for any position at the management level. We should rest for a while and let some new faces into the administration of our organization. Do you all agree with me?" In this way, Cuma and Karayılan sacrificed their positions at the administration level in order to prevent the potential harm that might be done by Nizamettin and Osman.

Osman Öcalan and Nizamettin Taş also developed their own plans before the start of this congress. Using their influence over the committee members, they made a pronouncement that everyone who had been invited to attend the congress must leave their weapons outside. This proclamation was all part of a bigger scam. If they were unable to win the coveted leadership roles through a legitimate election, then they were going to do it through a coup, and they knew it would be easier to arrest the guerillas if they were unarmed.

Murat Karayılan and Duran Kalkan were both surprised when asked to leave their arms at the main entrance of the congress hall. They said, "We are not leaving our weapons behind. We are guerillas, not political appointees like you. We will enter the hall with our guns, whether this is a congress or a conference." When their request was rejected, all the delegates of the military force withdrew from the congress. Cemil Bayık tried to ease the tension with Murat Karayılan by saying, "Hide an armed unit nearby, but make sure that the political wing does not know about it. If they try to stage a coup, the armed force will arrest every single one of them. After you arrange this, come back to the congress hall, hand over your weapons, and participate in the congress."

Cemil Bayık delivered the opening speech of the congress, informing the participants of the news that the senior officials were not going to be candidates for administrative level positions. Then, he let everyone know that he would not be volunteering for a position at the management level. Duran Kalkan and Murat Karayılan also said the same thing and reiterated that it was high time for the newbies to prove themselves. When the senior officials of the guerilla forces finished their speeches, the senior officials of the political wing began to speak. Nizamettin Taş went up to the podium first and caused eyebrows to rise when he declared that he was a candidate for the presidency of the congress. Similarly, Osman Öcalan also declared that he was a candidate.

When the congress took a recess, Cemil Bayık and Murat Karayılan went over to Botan and Osman Öcalan and asked them why they had not been loyal to their promises. Botan said, "Come on Cemal, we cannot give control over to the newbies. We, as an organization, cannot take such a large risk. There has to be at least a few of us among them, to guide them in their decisions. That is why we declared our candidacy." Cemil Bayık got annoyed with this reasoning, and asked, "Then, why the hell did you not inform us of this concern of yours?" Osman Öcalan and Botan stayed silent in response to his question.

The delegates in the congress were mostly from the political movement. The number of delegates from the guerilla force was not as large as it had previously been. Much of the decrease in numbers was a result of the fact that the guerilla women had their own distinct group and management, differing from the men's. Even their headquarters was located in a different place. Also, the female forces were subject to the control of the political wing for many concerns, except for issues involving battle. Osman and Botan were going to capture control of the organization by siding with the female force, and Cemil Bayık visited their leader and warned her not to be used by the political wing. She retorted to Cuma, "We will not take your side or theirs. We will use Apo's previous decisions for the basis of what we decide."

Since Cemil Bayık, Duran Kalkan, and Murat Karayılan had already gone in front of everyone and declared that they were not going to be candidates for any position, they would not now backtrack and announce that they would be candidates. That kind of reversal was unacceptable to the culture of the organization. With that option already crossed out, they sat together and argued the other potential options. "If Botan and Osman capture the congress, they would be powerless, without the control of the guerilla force. Therefore, one way or another, we have to prevent them from capturing the control of the guerillas, and there is only one way to achieve that. We will establish a new institution that will be a connection between the guerilla force and the Presidency Council. In terms of the hierarchal state, the new institution will be above the guerilla force but below the Presidency Council. If we can appoint our men to this new institution, then it would not be important whether or not they appoint their own men to the guerilla force leadership."

Zübeyir Aydar was elected president of the congress. Nizamettin Taş and Osman Öcalan were both elected as members of the congress, and when the congress members began arguing about the changes that needed to be made to the guerilla force, Cemil Bayık stood and suggested the establishment of a new institute, named the defense committee. The defense committee would more easily establish relations between the political wing and the guerilla forces. Of course, everyone accepted the proposal, since it came from Cuma. Just then, a comrade of ours stood up and said, "We should appoint Murat Karayılan as the leader of the defense committee. After all, he is the most experienced among us." What that man suggested came to pass. At the end of the voting process, Murat Karayılan was elected to lead the defense committee.

Once Karayılan was elected, he informed everyone that he was personally going to decide where anyone was assigned within the guerilla force. Because of this unexpected defeat, Botan and Öcalan were incapable of accomplishing their plan to capture control of the organization. Verbal threats began between the two sides, and Murat Karayılan sent word to the forces waiting outside to lay siege of the field of congress, and no one was to be allowed to leave. The weapons on Botan and Ferhat's guards were collected one by one. Botan and Ferhat then declared that they were sorry for what they had done, and they would respect the decisions made by the organization from then on. However, as soon as the organization lifted the ban on traveling outside the congressional field, Botan, Ferhat, and 15 other senior leaders fled and took refuge with Jalal Talabani. The organization asked Talabani to hand over the runaways, but he rejected their request, saying that he would not fulfill such a demand since American authorities were backing the group.

Assassination Attempt on Comrade Cemal

The first thing on Murat Karayılan's list, as head of the defense committee, was reorganizing the guerilla forces. Within this new structure, the HPG was not going to carry out attacks against the Turkish military posts as it had before. Instead, using small groups of men, it would predominantly perform assassinations and carry out sabotages. For example, the organization used to have 1,000 guerillas within the Amed region. With Comrade Cemal's changes, we would have at most 150 guerillas there. This number of guerillas was not going to be increased under any circumstance; however, the smaller unit of guerillas was expected to do the work that 1,000 guerillas had done in previous years. This was because the war technology that was being used by the Turks had greatly advanced. If we had continued to attack with large forces, we would lose many of our comrades, because of advanced war weaponry, such as fighter jets, attack helicopters, and tanks. Therefore, the organization decreased the number of guerillas fighting within Turkey, and began dispatching only the best ones there.

As a company commander in the Hakurki region, I was sent a battalion that was led by a particular female battalion commander with whom I was acquainted. Because of my prior knowledge, I knew that she was not qualified to lead the battalion, so I contacted headquarters and informed them, "You dispatched me here as a commander, but my superior officer is heavy-handed. Do not accuse me, if there is a crisis here in the near future." In fact, this woman was not trained well enough to properly lead three companies. After a short while, headquarters sent me a note that said, "Comrade Deniz, we assigned you there for the very reason you mentioned. You will help her in every aspect and guide her when necessary. Make her feel as if she is doing everything but go behind her and make sure that everything is in order." Even though I replied to them that I would do whatever I could, I was disturbed by this response. If it ever came out in the future, it might be said that I treated the battalion commander like dirt by seizing her initiative, and I could have been prosecuted for my actions.

In the beginning of 2004, while in Hakurki, I was first tasked with the responsibility of overseeing the construction of a monument for one of our fallen comrades, named Mahsun Korkmaz. His statue was to be placed in the park there. The United States had already invaded Iraq, which helped us a great deal. The organization had some construction vehicles before the invasion of Iraq, but their numbers were limited, since they were so expensive to keep. When the U.S. invaded, almost every battalion had passenger cars and heavy-duty machines. The company commanders had Hummers as staff cars. I do not know why, but at the time, Hummers were named Monica in Iraq, and we could easily buy a Monica for $5,000. In addition to that, there were also German-made Mercedes brand giant armored trucks, and we could buy one of those for $15,000. I do not know how accurate the information was, but it was said that those trucks had battle-tank engines. Apart from those, we could easily find crawler excavators, diggers, crawler dozers, and many other heavy-duty machines. Thanks to the coalition forces, almost every battalion had a few of those vehicles.

We needed many bricks and stones in order to build the park, and thanks to the machines, we were able to transport the necessary items to the park from hardware stores in Iraq easily. The construction was completed in two weeks. Normally, without the machines, it would have taken at least three months. The statue of Mahsun Korkmaz had to be built by a company located in Iran, and our comrades used one of the big trucks to bring the statue to Hakurki. The park was quite nice, and the organization would show it off to official committees from Europe when they visited. There was even a visitors' book they could sign. You would be amazed at the well-known local and foreign names who had written something in this book.

We had a magnificent opening ceremony planned for the park on August 15 when a tragic incident occurred in Kandil. The assistant to the headquarters commander was martyred. Our comrades had organized a theatre play for the opening, and during one of the rehearsals, the actors were given training bullets to make it more realistic and exciting. However, while Murat Karayılan and other senior members were watching the rehearsal, someone used a real bullet and shot the comrade sitting right next to Murat.

Since the shooting happened during rehearsal, at first no one noticed anything was wrong, but then this comrade fell lifelessly to the ground. Besides him, two other comrades were seriously wounded. Because of this incident, all celebrations that had been scheduled that year were canceled. The headquarters assistant, Erdal, was a deeply respected and loved person. In fact, the organization built a statue of him in the Pazarcık district of Elbistan, in Turkey.

The female guerilla that had used real bullets was detected by close inspection of video camera recordings. We initially thought that she had planned this heinous plot, but we were wrong. The female guerilla had not known that her gun was loaded with real bullets, and the real culprit had run away while we were interrogating her.

We figured out who it was and discovered that he had been incarcerated in Iraq for six years. The organization had tasked him with a very important job there in 1994, and he was cautioned that, "If you get caught, you should never tell them that you work for us!" The same thing was told to anyone who was sent out for an important mission. This person was supposed to kill someone with the nickname of Kemal, who was previously employed in the senior ranks of the organization. When the PYD was first established in Syria, Kemal had nominated himself as leader. As I mentioned before, this type of behavior does not go along with the organization's culture. One cannot just ask for a position. The organization rejected his nomination, and Kemal began working for the Iraqi intelligence service. His information and actions resulted in the incarceration of many guerillas in Iraq.

The man that killed the assistant of the headquarters commander had been commissioned to kill Kemal—as soon as it was found that he had been feeding information to Iraqi Intelligence—but he'd been caught before he was able to carry out his assassination mission. He had not been able to endure torture at the hands of Iraqi officials and confessed everything. In fact, when he confessed to the Iraqis that he was a member of the PKK, the organization's diplomatic relations with Iraq became tense. The senior members of the organization were disappointed by this, since he had been cautioned several times that, in case of his arrest, he was not to reveal his ties with the organization. Because of this betrayal, the organization had not helped him while he was incarcerated.

After six years of confinement, he was released. We were able to learn the details after the organization was able to capture him. He returned to the organization just to take revenge for the six years he had spent in jail. He rationalized his mission to kill Murat Karayılan by thinking, "In 1994 I volunteered to carry out that mission for the organization, but they threw me under the bus. I was going to take revenge for my lost time by killing an important person like Murat Karayılan." I do not know whether the organization executed him or not.

The Stolen Mule

Sometime in 2003 or 2004, while I was staying in a camp close to the park we had built, our comrades found a baby bear and a pig. Because they knew how much I loved animals, they brought them directly to me.

One day during their watch, the hillers noticed a big bear approaching the park area. They worried that it may attack our comrades and so killed it. Only after killing her had they noticed that it had been a mother bear and her cub. The pig, on the other hand, had been found during patrols. The baby bear was fine, but the pig turned out to be a troublemaker, and I was unable to cope with it.

In the end, I gave it to another guerilla force, who probably ate it. That pig would go everywhere, and traipse through the meeting and training zones; even entering the wards to hide in our sleeping bags. He was always able to find me in the darkness by checking every sleeping guerilla, one by one. I think he found me by smell, and he would touch my face with its nose to waken me, so that I could give him some space in my bed. He was a real devil. He also stole food from the bear. Their plates were normally in different places, but it did not matter. The pig would always swiftly finish his food and rush over to the bear's plate to eat again. The bear would usually protect her food with one of her paws, trying to keep the pig away by pushing him with her other paw. If the pig still insisted on eating from the bear's plate, then the bear would attack him with her claws, which convinced the pig to leave.

The baby bear was not nearly as naughty as the pig. I have never in my life seen another animal as smart as that bear. The first rule of looking after a bear is that you should not play around with it while it is hungry, because it could seriously harm you. However, after feeding it, you can play with it as you like. I fed milk to the bear for a while, and then she began to eat pure tomato sauce, which she loved. If you would let her, she would eat two cans of tomato sauce in one sitting. She was such an interesting creature; sometimes sitting in a chair just like a human being would do, and I would tickle her paws. If I tickled too hard, she would hold both of my hands very tightly and would sometimes even slap me in the face to stop the tickling. Other times, she would sit next to me and put her hand on my shoulder. She was such a cute animal.

One day, a comrade's father traveled all the way from Turkey, to our camp in Iraq, to visit his son. He wanted to take my bear back with him to Turkey. She was already grown up and, although I was sure she would never harm me, she might have harmed the other comrades. Also, I knew that I would soon be assigned to a new region, and it would be impossible to take her with me when I left. Therefore, I decided to give her to the comrade's father, but only after he promised me that he would never harm her.

Hakurki was where I reported for my next duty. In Hakurki there were no restrictions for ranked guerillas to have animals, so when I was dispatched there, the peasants gave me an almost two-year-old foal as a present, and he and I became very close. He loved to eat sugar cubes. Since he was old enough, I would sometimes take him with me when I visited other battalions. I could have ridden him during my journeys, but I did not have the heart for that, because he was more of a friend to me than an animal of burden. For example, let's say the distance to another battalion was four hours. I would ride him for 30 minutes at most and then walk the rest of the way. Some of my comrades would occasionally say in jest, "Comrade Deniz, you feed this horse every day. It's best to use him for riding, but you do not ride him or let us ride! Why then do you keep him with you all the time?"

While training in the winter camp of 2004, three teams from the southern province's logistics unit came along with 60 mules. Some of their loads had fallen into the water—some of their possessions had been damaged from the water, and two of their mules had drowned. We hosted them that night and saw them off the next day with their mules loaded again. I was not aware at the time, but someone from our battalion had shot and killed one of their mules, because it was making too much noise during the night. Mules are stubborn animals, whom you cannot force to move a single step once they have a fit of obstinacy.

It was not until later that the logisticians realized that one of their mules was missing. Of course, since they could not explain this loss to their superiors, they simply put the blame on us. "We stayed with Comrade Deniz's battalion last night, and someone from there most likely stole the mule from our herd." At the time of this incident, we had four mules of our own, which did not include the one for which they were looking.

In June of 2005, I was chatting with the comrades in the battalion, when three senior executives from the logisticians' battalion showed up unexpectedly—two women and a man. They told me, "Comrade Deniz, we want to tell you something, but we do not know exactly how to say it." I assured them they were free to tell me whatever it was they needed to express. "Comrade, we came here to put you under investigation on the charge of theft." Of course, I was surprised and asked them to give me more detail about this accusation. "While our caravan rested here, you and your region commander stole a mule that belonged to us." I was so surprised upon hearing this ridiculous accusation that I could not even reply for a while. The accusation was not yet finished. Not only had we stolen the mule, but also we had sent it to another region's commander, and that regional commander was going to be investigated next when they were through with the investigation against me and my battalion.

After finally taking all this in, I burst out in anger, "Are you out of your minds? You're saying that three highly ranked guerilla commanders would go and steal a mule, as if we did not have anything else to do? Do you even believe what you are accusing us of committing?" They replied in a kind tone, "Comrade, the Supreme Discipline Committee tasked us to investigate these claims. If you want to abject to the claims, then make an appeal to the High Guerilla Court." Our region commander then intervened, "Are you crazy? Who is making these claims about us? Do you have any solid proof in your hands? Are you aware of whom you are accusing with this bullshit?" No matter how angry we were, the committee began their formal investigation process.

They first checked out the mules in our battalion. I was making fun of the situation they had put themselves in, and asked, "Do you guys have a picture of the mule that was lost? How are you going to figure out that it's your mule, among ours?" They did not bother with a reply. The region commander and I were just about to give our official verbal statements regarding this incident when the guerilla that killed the mule, came to us and confessed his crime. "I killed that mule, and its carcass is lying behind those trees. You can go and check, if you do not believe me." The committee members did, in fact, go to the described location and inspected the carcass of the mule.

After we were cleared of any wrongdoing, I began to press the members of the investigation committee, one by one, and then sued them for mental anguish. I accused the members of the Supreme Discipline Committee of insulting senior commanders without further elaborating on details of the false claims. Because of this insult and mental anguish, I asked the judge to compensate my battalion with two new mules. The trial lasted for six months.

While the trial was ongoing, I visited the command ranks of the logisticians that had placed the blame on us and asked them, "What kind of people are you? Why didn't you come to us first, and talk about it before taking it to the Supreme Discipline Committee?" They all blushed. I added, "Do not ever come near our battalion again, not even to visit! We would not even help you if you were suffering at the hands of our enemies."

One day, central headquarters command sent me a note to withdraw my case. Initially I rejected it, but the senior members insisted, so finally I relinquished. "Okay, I will drop the case. However, those three members of the discipline committee will apologize to me in front of my guerillas. This ugly slander has not only defamed me, but also the reputation of my battalion. That's why these comrades will come here and abase themselves in front of everyone." They did in fact visit our battalion and did what I requested of them, and only then did I withdraw my lawsuit.

How to Destroy an Armored Military Vehicle

Before we began to fight against Turkey in 2004, the guerilla force was already trained on explosive substances. As I mentioned previously, to stay in line with new guerilla strategy, we were not going to carry out raids against military posts any longer. Instead, we would use more developed techniques, with reduced numbers of guerillas, and, therefore, advancing our knowledge on explosives was crucial. The training was constant and grueling. We had to invent new ways of activating bombs, since the Turkish security forces had figured out our tactics. For instance, we began using remote controlled explosives, and when the Turks took measures to disable them, we began using small hand radios to activate our bombs. You know those Motorola brand walkie-talkies that children use for fun? We used them to send activation signals to our bombs. Of course, the Turks soon figured out this tactic also and then imported devices called jammers.

The organization then began to use car remotes to counteract the influence of jammers. Many people do not know, but the remote that opens the trunk of a car sends a very powerful signal, and this signal can be effective for up to 6 kilometers. So, you can activate a bomb by hiding in a place that is 6 kilometers away from the detonation spot. The only thing that you should consider is that there should not be anything between you and the bomb that would potentially affect the signal, meaning that the bomb should be visual to the person who is detonating it. We used this method for a long time, because it made it nearly impossible to be caught. When the security forces found out we were using car remotes, they bought even more advanced jammers to deactivate them. Then, to counteract this, we had to buy more expensive and more effective gadgets from Europe. These new gadgets were effective even from longer distances. And since they were not using FM waves, we did not need to see the target to activate the bomb. These new tools were very expensive, but after a while the organization was able to manufacture them in its explosives development lab in Iraq.

We had a team of about 30 professionals in that lab, whose duty it was to develop those kinds of explosives to be used by the guerillas. The raw materials for the bombs were supplied from European countries. I remember one time the organization had a large shipment of electronic parts that were to be used in explosives. Unfortunately, our comrade transporting the items was caught in Germany, just before he headed into Iraq. Because of the money and work we had put into it, we lost almost $200,000. The German security officials interrogated our comrade in order to learn what he was planning to do with the electronic parts. He refused to answer any of the questions, so they seized the parts and let him go.

Those parts had been really important to us, because they were to be used for a small box-shaped device to disable the jammers. There were no circuits on these disablers. You simply buried one under the ground in the middle of the road. The most significant issue was identifying the vehicle in which the ranked soldiers were traveling, when a military convoy drove by. The soldiers of high rank usually traveled in armed vehicles called ZPTs. Then, while the convoy passed, we could easily destroy the armored military vehicles with our highly advanced box-shaped devices. This whole process was cyclical, since the guerillas and the soldiers were continuously counteracting one another's tactics.

There was a mission carried out by the organization in Lice-Diyarbakır in 2009. An armored vehicle, purchased for a million dollars by the Turkish military, was destroyed. The Chief of General Staff, Ilker Başbuğ, made a statement saying, "We could not quite figure out what kind of explosive the organization used in this mission." Actually, the organization had used propane gas tanks for that mission. Specifically, we used the empty propane tanks that were kept for our winter camps. We carefully cut the tanks into two equal parts along the welded line on their sides. Each tank was then filled with explosives and welded back together with the detonator cap on the outside. When those bombs exploded, they made such an unbelievable impact. The more pressure that was inside the bomb, the greater the explosion was going to be.

All these bombing tactics were developed in 2004. The Turkish security forces had been under the delusion that, "The organization had not been fighting for the last four to five years, and thus had probably fallen from power and been marginalized until now. They could not fight against us, even though they wanted." They were completely wrong in their thinking. Not only had we not weakened, but we actually progressed in many ways, including explosive manufacturing!

Ambush by Al-Qaeda Members

The Americans were going to elect a new president in the fall of 2004. One of my comrades asked whether I was supporting the Democrats or the Republican, Bush. I said that it would be better if Bush were elected as the president. This comrade got somewhat annoyed, and said, "You are a guerilla fighter, and you are supporting a Republican candidate? That is unbelievable!" I reminded him about the incident in 1999. "Was it not the U.S. that struck a major blow to our organization [C.I.A. handed over Apo to Turkey]?" He confirmed that it was, and I asked, "Was not this huge blow carried out during the tenure of a Democrat president?" With a red face, he answered, "Yes!" I said, "Comrade, look! The Republicans are at least frank about their intentions. If they are our enemies, they will say so openly. However, the Democrats are not like that. They pretend to be your ally when they hold a grudge against you, and they always use insidious politics. It is better for the organization if the Americans elect a Republican president. At least then we would know how they would approach us."

This is the same for the Democrats and Republicans within Turkey. You may find it strange, but no one in the organization would easily get annoyed with the supporters of the MHP (Nationalistic Movement Party) because they explicitly say what they think about people and organizations, such as, "I do not recognize the Kurds. I do not recognize the PKK, and the only potential solution is the complete surrender of the PKK." MHP supporters openly expose their feelings of hate. Then, there were the other groups. For example, there was the AKP. They pretended to be handling the peace process between Turkey and the Kurds, but at the same time, at every opportunity, they dispatched security forces to kill us. This was quite obviously an insidious policy to follow. MHP supporters explicitly say that they are nationalists and represent only the Turks. The Democrats claim that they represent every single ethnic and minority group within Turkey. They say they are the voices of the Lazes, the Kurds, the Alevis, the Cherkesses, the Arabs, the Sunnis, and the Shi'ites within Turkey. However, they do nothing when it comes to the basic rights of these groups. They are just crooks wearing the sympathetic mask of a friend.

Let's turn back to the Republicans and Democrats in the United States. George Bush was heavily criticized for things such as invading Afghanistan, invading Iraq, and putting the U.S. at war with the world. Obama, on the other hand, withdrew those American soldiers from Iraq and gained the love of many in the U.S. Now, go and look at the situation in Iraq. Who controls the state of Iraq today? Iran, a country which was the number one enemy of the United States. How many Sunnis are repressed and have suffered at the hands of Iranian-backed Shia Government in Iraq? Hundreds of thousands! When did Al-Qaeda manage to infiltrate into Iraq? When did ISIS appear on TV with the well-known beheadings? All of these things happened after Obama withdrew the American forces from Iraq. When one does not follow the politics of the world, one can be easily fooled. Many say that the Democrats act more humanely by recognizing and protecting universal human rights. That is nothing but a huge lie.

On November 27, 2004, we were preparing to celebrate the PKK's anniversary when disheartening news came from Iraq. Al-Qaeda, which is now operating under the name ISIS, martyred six of our comrades. Four of the six fallen comrades served in high positions at the management level. Since the incident took place in the KDP region, we first pressed the KDP forces on whether they had anything to do with what had happened. Barzani, himself, personally informed the organization that they had no prior knowledge regarding the plot. Later, the organization found out that the mission had been performed by one of the religious groups operating under Al-Qaeda. Our comrades were ambushed while they were traveling in a Toyota truck. The Al-Qaeda fighters broke the truck into pieces by shooting it with a long-barreled weapon. Afterward, the truck had been set on fire. The organization was bursting with anger because of this atrocity. It was hard to understand why Al-Qaeda had suddenly carried out such an attack against the organization, because we had never had a problem with them before.

It was learned later, that the ambush had been organized by someone who used to work for the organization. After discovering that, we knew that one way or another, we would take our revenge. A company commander, who had been acquainted with the man, was tasked with killing him. The defector had not only caused the death of our comrades but also leaked sensitive information to Al-Qaeda.

The company commander went to the territories controlled by Al-Qaeda, as if he had deserted the organization. Just to make his story look more realistic, the organization even disseminated an official order, saying that the company commander was a runaway, and was to be killed by guerillas, on sight. When he reached the Al-Qaeda camps under the guise of a PKK deserter, they introduced him directly to the former PKK member who had killed six of our comrades. Since they already knew each other, they were assigned to the same unit within Al-Qaeda. Our comrade worked with this defector for about a year and purposefully delayed his mission for revenge. He had remained there because he was not only able to gain the defector's trust but also was able to provide intelligence regarding Al-Qaeda's operations. Around the end of 2005, he placed the explosives acquired from the organization in the defector's vehicle. Before carrying out the mission, he notified guerilla headquarters, "We will travel to another Al-Qaeda camp in the morning. During the trip, I will stop the car at a gas station and get out of the car under the pretense of filling the tank. Then the vehicle will blow up and I will take our revenge!" Unfortunately, he had been unable to set the activation time of the explosive accurately. We heard later that the vehicle blew up before it reached the gas station. Everyone in the vehicle died including the company commander. We finally had our revenge but at the cost of another comrade's life.

Immediately after this dramatic event, Al-Qaeda communicated with the organization and, in a way, apologized to us, "Last year, we killed your comrades due to incorrect intelligence. We were told that those six PKK guerillas were traveling in our region for an assassination mission, and that's why we killed them." They apologized, but the explanations were not very convincing. So the organization criticized them saying, "If you were unsure about the accuracy of the intelligence, then why did you even carry out this atrocity?" After the argument, the relationship between Al-Qaeda and the PKK broke down completely. There had already been tension between the two groups. Al-Qaeda blamed the organization for creating an atheist group, and, besides that, they were displeased with the authority and dominance the PKK exerted on many of the other organizations operating in Iran, Iraq, Turkey, and Syria.

Let me give you an epiphany. In 2002, there appeared a very extreme and radical organization in Iran. It was a religious organization, working for Iran, which also had ties with Al-Qaeda in Iraq. In fact, it would be better to call it a gang, as it had no real command structure. It had close to 30 people in it. The members of the group would kidnap and rape women, especially from the areas where the Kurds lived and then would later leave these rape victims on the streets. These bandits were satisfying their sexual desires through "Muta marriage," a temporary form of marriage which is common in Iran, and then would abandon these poor girls. Hundreds of rape incidents like this occurred.

In the winter of 2002, the organization notified Iranian officials about these immoral incidents. We specifically asked them to arrest the members of this group, but the Iranian officials refuted the existence of rape cases by a gang within the Kurdish areas in Iran. They simply ignored our warnings. As a last resort, Murat Karayılan declared a harsh statement, "You will either extinguish this group or we will kill them all within Iran!" Iran still did not respond to our warnings. However, we had already finished our reconnaissance on this group within Iran. While they were in a meeting, we attacked the 30 Iranians that had been organizing this rape scheme in Iran and killed every single one of them. Both Iran and Al-Qaeda were very angry with our intervention against these so-called religious bandits within the territory of Iran. Nevertheless, after this mission, the Kurds in Iran declared their loyalty to the organization as a whole.

Living Just for Dying

At the beginning of February, sometime in that same period, my battalion commander asked me to dispatch my company to a place located close to the borders of Turkey, nine hours away from our camp. Snow covered everything, and, normally, a guerrilla force would not be allowed to travel during that time of the year. I suspected that something very important must have been going on and asked the battalion commander about the context of our task, but he refused to give me any details. Because we were again officially at war with Turkey, we were not allowed to travel by car. We had to walk all the way north, under the darkness of night during this cold season.

Three comrades from headquarters management welcomed us at our designated destination. There were many dilapidated dorms and a couple of meeting halls. It was very clear that the place had been deserted for a long period of time, and we were ordered to rebuild all of the structures. I was curious about the situation and asked, "Comrade, we will rebuild them all, but who will come here in the snowy season? Can you explain to me the reason that we are doing all of these preparations?" One of them whispered in my ear, "We will hold the guerilla forces' conference here on February 15. No one can know about it." That was strange, for the organization would never schedule a conference during the winter period. I later discovered that the goal was to throw the Turkish security forces off the scent, since they knew that we would normally never organize a conference in winter, and would not survey that region. Despite the fact we would not do winter reconnaissance there, we still took extra measures to ensure our safety. Everyone who participated in the conference was to turn their satellite phones off before they left their regions. Upon arrival, we collected everyone's satellite phones and sent them to a distant location.

The other reason for the organization to schedule a conference in winter was that the water level of the rivers in the region would get too high in the spring. You could not easily dispatch the Zagros guerilla force to headquarters in the spring, because the rivers in their region always overflowed. Of course, we normally had helper lines on most of the rivers, but security forces would destroy them as soon as they noticed them. So, scheduling the conference in February would also allow the representatives from Zagros to join us.

From those ruined buildings, we were able to build a dormitory, with a maximum occupancy of 230 guerillas, in just 20 days. The conference was larger than normal, because we expected representatives from Syria, Iran, Turkey, and Iraq. As soon as we were done with the construction work, I was assigned as a member of the conference preparation committee. The group was made up of seven guerillas, with the lowest rank being a headquarters committee member. Bahoz Erdal led the committee. We were going to examine all of the organization's regulations and discuss the points to be changed.

They had included me in the committee because of my experience in the field of guerilla life. They frequently consulted me on the evaluation of rules and regulations related to the daily lives of guerillas in the countryside. I remember it quite well. During one of those meetings, a headquarters committee member said, "Let's delete all the rules regarding the chain of command, and order from the regulations. We are an organization that consists of voluntary guerillas, and there cannot be a chain of command and order among voluntary fighters!" Bahoz Erdal and I strongly objected to this suggestion. I was given the floor and said, "This suggestion does not make any sense to me. If we do what you are suggesting, then we would have nothing but chaos. There will be a lot of confusion regarding what to do and when to do it. Guerillas will start to act on their own initiative, and no one would be held responsible for their mischief. Many different groups would emerge within the organization, and in the end we would perish." Bahoz Erdal agreed with me, saying, "It is not even appropriate to discuss such issues. We will highlight the points that need to be updated, however, what you are suggesting cannot even be discussed. Everything has a limit, and we have no authority to discuss such an issue."

When the conference began, the regulations we had worked on as a committee were up for a vote. Some rules that were not approved by the participants were crossed out, but most of them were accepted with only slight revisions. We also informed the participants of the issues that had been discussed but not included in the updated regulations. We even told them of the suggestion to abolish the chain of command, and every single one objected to the suggestion. Many guerillas even asked for the name of the person that had offered such a ridiculous suggestion.

Two of the people who offered the suggestion, one of whom was Dr. Ali, later left the organization. They had adopted a different fighting strategy within the organization and were saying, "Let's behave like the Tamil Tigers! It would be more than enough if we could carry out one or two large-scale missions every year, until we reached our goals. There is no need for the continuous planning of raids, sabotages, and ambushes." They were suggesting significant changes, not only to guerilla missions but also to the lifestyles of the guerillas. They adopted some dangerous ideas, such as the liberation of sexual intercourse among men and women guerillas and the abolishment of the hierarchy system. Changes at those levels would potentially destroy the order within the organization. Despite the fact that the guerrilla movement is completely voluntary, it requires some level of discipline and hierarchy among its members. The organization did not even allow those defectors to open those subjects up for discussion. In fact, Dr. Ali fled to Europe after this conference.

In May 2005, toward the end of the conference, the name Kongra-Gel was removed, and the organization again began using PKK. Another significant decision made during that conference was the ban on the use of mobile and satellite phones. On February 15, 2005 all of our computers, except the ones used by the HPG, were hacked by Turkish security forces, and had only black screens that displayed the date. Until this incident, we were allowed to use satellite phones and frequently surf the internet.

However, the organization's decision at this conference banned the use of the internet, satellite phones, and mobile phones. In retaliation, the organization paid a large sum of money to a hacker group in Europe to hack the computers of the Turkish General Staff and the Ministry of National Defense.

When the conference ended, the senior members came together to decide whom to assign and to where. One of them called me in and said, "Comrade, we have decided on the location of your new duty, and you will not reject it." When he said that, I realized that I was not being sent to the northern zone, to Turkey, although being dispatched to a field in Turkey was a great honor, no matter how high the risk of death. Not everyone was sent there, even though he or she may desire it. Only the best among us were sent. When I replied to this senior commander that I would not reject their decision, he said, "We heard that you rejected another assignment when you graduated from the guerilla officer's school, and that is why I wanted to warn you beforehand!"

The organization kept personal files on every single guerilla. These files contained information about their CV, reports, previous duty locations, achievements, failures, and disciplinary investigations. When he said what he did, I realized he had read my personal file. "You will go to Hakkari, Çukurca as a battalion commander." I responded, "All right, I will not object to it, but you will send me north at an appropriate time later." He asked, "Why are you so eager to be assigned to the north?" I replied, "I got tired of the ridiculous situation in the south, and there is a tight bond of friendship in the north. Many of the southern guerillas have yet to join a single clash, and so do not know the psychology of war. They often fight amongst themselves for mundane reasons. However, just to protect you, a comrade in the north would sacrifice himself without hesitation. You will not find friendship ties like that in the south, because guerillas here only think about their comfort, whereas there is loyalty, sincerity, and fellowship in the north, and that's why I want to go to there."

For many of us, even though life as a guerilla meant knowing that you would die sooner or later, you still want to go to the north. It was very difficult to establish discipline and order in a place that was so far from the war zone. In the north, if you ordered your guerillas to remain still all day long, all of them will do it without exception, and they would not even question why they were ordered to do so. However, you cannot achieve this discipline in the south, because the guerillas are too fond of their comfort there. You would be criticized for making them stand still and wait. The environment in the south simply is not suitable for guerilla training, even though the guerillas stationed there are trained throughout the year. The guerillas in the north are only trained in winter, when they stay in underground bunkers, but they have the opportunity to apply what they have learned during clashes that occur in the summer and spring months. In other words, a single clash against the Turks in the north was more instructive than a whole year of training in the south.

Manufacturing Mine Igniters with Animal Bones

When the guerilla conference ended, I went to Çukurca as I had been instructed. The region to which I was going was considered a large security risk, and we had a hard time patrolling the area because mines had been planted everywhere. Since it was located at the cross-section of the Turkish–Iraqi border, there were mines planted by Saddam Hussein, the Turkish security forces, and by us to protect ourselves from those two enemies. It seemed as if wherever we stepped, a mine explosion occurred. I immediately requested a mine detector from headquarters management. For approximately four months, we tried clearing the mines in an area between our battalion's campground and a nearby hill. It was crucial to detect and defuse the mines on the road that went to that hill for the safety of the entire battalion. Two of our comrades stepped on a mine and lost their legs, while we were building the underground bunkers for winter. We were able to properly treat them, but they would not be able to fight on the frontlines anymore.

We patrolled the area a couple of times in order to make sure that there was not a single mine left. I was told that the guerilla force that used to stay in that region had slightly modified the mines that were planted in the field for the safety of the campground. They replaced the metal mine igniters with sharp animal bones. With this innovation, the Turkish security forces would be unable to detect the mines since there were no metal parts, just TNT and a sharp bone. It ended up being just as bad for us, though! It was not Turkish soldiers, but our own comrades who had stepped on these hard to detect mines. At least four comrades lost their feet because of the mines' animal bone modification.

Furthermore, Turkish fighter jets had dropped barrel bombs on the surface of the field and many of them had never exploded. If you take a barrel bomb and hold it still, never turning it up or down, you can carry it for as long as you want. These bombs did not explode on contact, because they must roll for a couple meters for the igniter to activate. For example, there was a place in the south called Hell Hill. The Turkish security forces named it that because they could never take control of it. There were hundreds of barrel bombs that were dropped on that hill that dated back as far as 1992. Most of them were rusted, and you could not activate their igniters even if you kicked them. Nevertheless, you still had to be careful when messing with that kind of stuff. One of our comrades had been playing with one of those rusted barrel bombs, and it exploded, severing his hand at the wrist. He thought it would not explode, since it was so badly rusted.

Since our camp perimeter was surrounded by mines, our visitors had to wait at a far distance so a guide from the battalion could lead them safely across. If they came to us alone, they had a chance of stepping on a mine. In a strange way, the situation was advantageous because it increased our security. No one would dare come close to the camp area without first notifying us.

Peasants from Turkey would visit us every day to deliver newspapers. Since taxes were so high in Turkey, these peasants would also go into Iraq and acquire various kinds of products and then carry them back into Turkey to sell them in large cities, basically making a living on smuggling. Anyone who smuggled goods into Turkey from either Iran or Iraq was required to pay a tax to the organization. The amount of taxation was set according to the kind of items being smuggled. For example, taxation for weapon smuggling was very high. With the invasion of Iraq by the Americans, there was a great abundance of different kinds of weaponry in the region, because the Americans left a lot of them behind. There was a small town, located between Iraq and Iran, where these weapons had been left. They were being sold for $100 to $150. The weapons were so abundant, that the price of some guns was so low they were worthless. You could even buy a weapon for $20. The weapons left by the Iraqi army (Kalashnikovs) were especially worthless, because they were manufactured with old technology, and so, sometimes, were even cheaper than a toy gun.

There was an American company called Blackhawk, which played a large role in the marketing and selling of those weapons that were used during the invasion of Iraq. Blackhawk was a very brutal and inhumane force that I think was one of those special military units. At one stage during the Iraqi war, the media broadcasted news saying, "Iraqi soldiers killed civilians while deserting the Iraqi army." There was not a shred of truth to that report. It was not Iraqi soldiers but members of the Blackhawk Company who had killed those innocent Iraqi civilians. America conducted most of its dirty business in Iraq, through this company. I can confidently state that 90 percent of the civilian massacres in Iraq were conducted by Blackhawk. However, the cost was knocked back to the U.S. government. Those people who suffered at the hands of Blackhawk; who lost a loved one—a child, a wife, or a husband—will make the U.S. pay in the future.

As an organization, we decided to target Blackhawk members several times but were afraid the U.S. army would attack our bases and people in northern Iraq. Ultimately, Blackhawk was the mercenary for the United States. Those executions were not being performed without the knowledge of U.S. officials. The organization captured many images and videos, proving the atrocities that were committed by Blackhawk—murdered children, raped women, and tortured elderly people. I hope that the senior members of the organization will deliver the evidence to the Human Right Courts in Europe when the time is ripe. There were such terrifying tortures in those Iraqi prisons that one does not even dare talk about it, let alone watch it. Saddam's civilian supporters and army members were subject to unbelievable torture. After viewing the torture, we, as members of what had been labeled a terrorist group, were not even able to comprehend how a human being could be so cruel.

Although they did not conduct their business openly, the weapon market in Iraq was under the control of Blackhawk, and they sold thousands of weapons in the region via their local agents. In April 2005, I bought a weapon from them myself for only $1,100. The same weapon was normally sold for $7,000 in Turkey. Besides the price difference, the weapon also came with free extras, which included a scope, laser, and thermal camera. The organization bought such advanced weaponry from Blackhawk that I am sure even the Turkish security forces did not have them. One of our comrades bought a rifle from the Americans (I do not remember the brand) but this rifle was capable of shooting seven to eight full magazines without overheating. That was amazing!

It was not only the guerillas who needed those advanced weapons, but also the Turkish civilian public. Since my battalion was located at the border, we would witness smugglers crossing in and out of Iraq, with their mules, at least three times a week and would tax their loads, one by one. We really did not know how they were distributing those weapons within Turkey, or to whom they were selling these items. The only thing that was clear was the size of the demand for those killing machines. The Peshmerga forces were also aware of the weapon smuggling business. No peasant can smuggle even a single weapon from Iraq without bribing them first.

Those weapons were sometimes transported into Turkey directly from the Habur Border Checkpoint. I do not know if the Turkish customs officers were also bribed, but I know that sometimes several trucks loaded with weaponry would pass through these checkpoints without any trouble. For example, using the Habur Checkpoint just twice, the commander of our region was able to transport hundreds of weapons, 500 rockets, and 50,000 bullets into Turkey with a truck licensed in Turkey. On its third trip, from Iraq to Turkey, Turkish security forces confiscated 17 Dragunov assassination rifles from this same truck. They thought this was such a serious blow to the organization that the story of the confiscation was broadcast on the news—it was really quite funny. While the Turkish security forces were happy they had captured these 17 rifles, our comrades already had transported ammunition and weapons that we would use in our fights in Turkey for the next two years. On top of that, these weapons had been transported through Turkey's official checkpoint.

In spring of 2005, we reduced the three company guerilla forces down to two, because of the abundance of mines in the field. Meanwhile, the organization delivered to us 12 anti-aircraft guns and three missiles. We were going to use those weapons against the Turkish fighter jets if they flew toward organization headquarters in Iraq. Our camp's primary responsibility was to provide security against the Turks for guerilla headquarters in Iraq. We did not know how to use those missiles and anti-aircraft guns, so we were provided with professional technical support from Iraq. The fuses were highly sensitive and had to be kept immobile at all times, making maintenance and storage difficult. On the head of the missiles was an eye like a lens, and if it was subjected to vibration for a long period of time, it would lose its ability to properly hit a target.

Heading Right into Turkish Soldiers

In 2005, the organization was preparing a spectacular party for August 15. We were going to travel from Çukurca to Metina in Iraq to take part in this celebration as well. Even Duran Kalkan was to travel to Metina for it, on behalf of the defense committee. At the time of the party, the headquarters music group was staying in my battalion, and it was our responsibility to transport them and their musical instruments to Metina safely. Unfortunately, the group's load was huge, because of the speakers and many instruments, and we would not be able to reach Metina, even with two full nights of walking, because we had to carry all their equipment.

First, I sent a small group from our battalion on foot to Metina. Then, I took five guerillas, and the music group players with me, and we drove off to Iraq in trucks. On our route to Metina, there was a hill on the border of northern Iraq under the control of Turkish security forces. This road passed 20 meters downhill from where the Turkish soldiers were settled with eight tanks. In those days, the Turks had such freedom of control in northern Iraq. They were not subjected to any restrictions as far as patrolling in that area. They could send their military forces anywhere, at any time, without the permission of local Kurdish authorities, or the Iraqi Government. This situation changed when the U.S. invaded Iraq. Not only were they not able to patrol as they had previously, but the Turks also had to inform the local Kurdish authorities before they even left their military post on the hill. On top of that, whenever they had to leave the hill, the Turkish soldiers were escorted by Peshmerga forces. The Turks's old authority and supremacy in northern Iraq had ended with the invasion of Iraq.

While passing by the hill, we saw Turkish soldiers wandering around the road. They even walked around our trucks. The vehicles were moving slowly, because there was a car that had broken down directly in front of the hill, which slowed the traffic flow. We were all dressed in our guerilla uniforms and we were armed. One of the Turkish soldiers approached my side of the car and knocked on the window, to speak to me. The passenger windows of the truck were tinted so he could not see inside. I did not roll down the window so he walked to the driver's side. The driver opened the window halfway and began to talk with the soldier, and he informed the driver that the road was blocked, and that we needed to return and use one of the alternate routes to Metina.

Our driver said, "Okay!" and we left. There were two female guerillas in our vehicle who had never seen a Turkish soldier before. One of them asked, "Comrade Deniz, are those Turkish soldiers?" I said, "Yes!" She asked, "Won't there be a clash if they see us?" I answered, "No, comrade. This territory is under the control of Barzani, and they cannot directly fight against us as they did in the old days. Relax." Nevertheless, until we moved away from the hill, the women were still nervous, no matter what I told them. "Look, when we arrive in Metina, you will not tell anyone that we encountered Turkish soldiers on our route, understood?"

As soon as we reached Metina, we saw Duran Kalkan. Comrade Duran asked these two women, "How was your journey? Did you travel comfortably?" One of them said, "Comrade, a Turkish soldier stopped us." Duran Kalkan was confused, and asked "What soldiers? What are you talking about?" She then gave a more detailed answer: "Comrade, we were stopped by Turkish soldiers, and they even talked to our driver!" Duran Kalkan looked me directly in the eye and said, "Which route did you use? How did you encounter Turkish soldiers?" I replied, "Comrade, we were just passing by when a car broke down in front of the hill that the Turks use as a military post. They were wandering around the road to check what was going on. We encountered one of them, but they did not realize who we were."

Duran Kalkan got really angry with me, yelling, "Do not ever show such impudence again! This is northern Iraq, where we do not kill them, and they do not kill us. But if that soldier had acted indifferently to the rules—I mean if he had acted emotionally and had shot one of you—what would happen then, Deniz? Never take such a huge risk again!"

It was such a weird situation in northern Iraq, because while we were killing each other within Turkey, we did not interfere with each other in Iraq. We sometimes positioned ourselves right across the hill from where they were staying. They would have been able to kill all of us with a single artillery barrage, but really they could not because we had four battalions of guerillas in that region. If we had wanted, we could have destroyed that hill in a single night, and confiscated everything; tanks, howitzers, weapons, and ammunition. However, something on that scale would have spoiled our diplomatic relations with Barzani.

In fact, Turkey tried to trick the organization a few times, on that very issue. The purpose of the Turkish military posts in northern Iraq was to protect Barzani. In 2008, Yaşar Büyükanıt, the former Chief of General Staff of Turkey, wanted to use the units in the south against the PKK. In a district called Bamerli, in northern Iraq, there were 50 Turkish tanks. The tanks in that district were originally deployed there for Barzani's security but were going to be used to destroy the PKK camps in Iraq. It was unimaginable, but the Kurdish people in Bamerli actually laid down in front of the tanks and did not let them leave the district to destroy the PKK camps.

Dr. Ali and His Dangerous Ideas

I had many difficulties toward the end of 2005, because I had been promoted to the rank of battalion commander for the first time in my life. Serving as a battalion commander was completely different than serving as a company commander. Both have important responsibilities, but battalion commanders have even more. I was more relaxed when I was a company commander, because there was a superior above me. Even if I were to fail, he or she would fix any problems. However, at this point, I was the one who had to solve a problem when it emerged. As a company commander, I was responsible for only 40 to 50 guerillas, all of which were male. When I was promoted to battalion commander, not only did the number of guerillas under my responsibility increase, but I also had to deal with women guerillas from then on.

It was the first time I had ever had women in my force, and the responsibility associated with them was much greater than it was for the men. Females were very sensitive, emotional, and could be easily discouraged by a simple verbal warning, but the male guerillas were not like that. It was also really daunting when women guerillas had a problem, because they would never accept responsibility for their mistakes. Female guerillas also made me shy, and so I would not be as harsh with them about their faults. On the other hand, when a man committed a mistake, I could easily warn him or even harshly criticize him for that mistake. So, I had a real difficult time dealing with women and their problems. I asked headquarters for a change to my battalion, which may have been the first time anyone had requested that in the history organization. I said, "I do not want a female company in my battalion." Of course, the senior members rejected it. It was not possible and also not in line with the policy of the organization.

I would make no compromises when it came to discipline, but I was not nearly as jittery and harsh as the other commanders were. I would take part in social activities with the ground guerillas, talk to them, and get to know them by their names. However, I would also keep my distance from them when it was time for official works.

In November 2005, two comrades and I traveled to a place in Zagros, close to the Tigris River, to represent our region at a guerilla conference. It was an extraordinary conference, because it was the first time in the history of the Turkish Republic that someone at the highest level of the country was admitting that, "The Kurdish problem is our issue. We will end this problem. We put aside our guns and end this vicious cycle of violence, through dialogue and negotiation."

After this speech, given by Prime Minister Erdoğan, the organization wanted to schedule an extraordinary guerilla conference to discuss what kind of reaction we should give to Turkey. With the head of Turkey approaching the organization with peace messages, we thought we should act in accordance with their manner as well. On one hand, we were slowly getting ready to declare a ceasefire; on the other, we were worrying whether the government was sincere, determined, and serious in its desire to start such a peace initiative.

There were almost a hundred participants at the conference. Dr. Ali was there as the assistant to headquarters management. He still held the same old, ill thoughts. It was around that time that he had gathered enough support to raise his voice against the organization. He was all about there being more flexibility within the rigid lifestyle of the organization. He said, "We are so restrictive in terms of men and women's sexual lives. We should be more flexible on this now. Similarly, we expect the local peasants to be disciplined as much as the guerillas. This is wrong. It is also wrong that we constantly plan and carry out guerilla missions, but, rather, we should take the Tamil Tigers of Sri Lanka as an example and perform a mission once or twice a year at most. We should carry out war tactics only to open the path for political negotiations. The guerilla force should simply be symbolic and used only occasionally."

Dr. Ali and his friends not only opposed the lifestyles of the organization, but also rejected some of Apo's views. They were specifically against Apo's "Democratic republic thesis." In this thesis, Apo said, "In this republic, the Turks and Kurds will live together. The argument of separation from Turkey is beside the point. In return, the Turkish government will officially recognize the existence of Kurds within Turkey and also grant the Kurds their basic rights, including education in their mother tongue, and regional management." Apo had always been sincere in his views regarding the Turks. Nevertheless, Dr. Ali and his friends rejected this view. They argued that, "We have fought against the Turks for many years. Have we lost so many comrades only to make peace with the Turkish government?"

Nizamettin Taş and Osman Öcalan had the same opinion. They supported a separate Kurdish state that was totally independent of Turkey. The difference between Dr. Ali and his group from the entity that was established in 2003 by Nizamettin Taş and Osman Öcalan was that they held a greater dominance over the guerilla force. There were hundreds of mid-level commanders who were loyal to Dr. Ali, which is why this opposition posed such a serious danger to the unity of the organization. This large amount of support for Dr. Ali made him overconfident. They explicitly threatened the senior members of the organization, by saying, "Do not confuse us with Osman or Nizamettin. We have a lot of support within the guerilla force. You must pay attention to us and our views!"

The PKK central headquarters had to intervene at this conference, because of the split in opinion. We did not initially hear about those developments. Dr. Ali had planned everything in advance and was aiming to procure acceptance through members at the conference. However, he did not expect that the senior executives of the PKK would also attend the meeting. It seemed headquarters management had received many complaint reports from Dr. Ali's guerillas, regarding his behaviors and attitudes. Those letters had many details, such as how Dr. Ali carried himself as a guerilla, how he ignored Apo's views and opinions, and how he freed the men and women's relationships within his force. Dr. Ali was thinking that he would be too far from headquarters, and that the seniors of the PKK would not hear about his plans. But he had not realized they already found out everything through the information in the complaint reports.

Because the PKK's processes of communication are so strongly rooted, Dr. Ali's plan was easily exposed. I mentioned before that each guerilla has to write (at least) a report to central headquarters, once every six months, and to PKK central management, once every year, and there is no limitation on how many reports one can send. If necessary, you could even write 15 reports a year. Through these reports, the organization noticed the existence of the growing separation, before it grew too large.

In this conference, senior officials explained how those misguided thoughts would detrimentally affect the organization. In the end, everyone had to suffer through some self-criticism, since those thoughts were embraced by so many of the guerillas. In fact, Cemil Bayık said, "Even the ground guerillas have noticed the problem, because many of them reported it to us. How could you commanders be unaware of such a situation within your units? Each of you will make some self-criticism, and at the end of the meeting, you will pick a side!" Basically we were to either come to our senses, or the PKK was going to change the whole command structure that served across the region. There were hundreds of other people within the PKK that could be appointed in our places. We were not irreplaceable.

The issue was even larger than our leaders realized, since some of the senior members of the organization had adopted this new way of thinking. For instance, the headquarters management assistant and the commander of the Botan Field opposed the old rules engraved by Apo, and those commanders had a large area of influence. Unless the organization took precautions against this, those commanders could quickly influence the guerillas under their command. To help curb these problems, the organization discharged Dr. Ali from his duties at headquarters and appointed him as commander of the Botan Field. Rubar was removed from the Botan Field and assigned to Zagros. In short, both were removed from headquarters. The organization even appointed a very qualified and well-known female commander as Rubar's assistant. She was not there as an ordinary female guerilla, but her appointment as an assistant to Rubar was to pacify him.

There were many such qualified females in the organization, and when you looked at the positions that females held in other organizations around the world, you would see that not many of them were assigned to senior positions. However, there might be a couple exceptions. There were such talented female commanders in the PKK that they would have the men wrapped around their fingers. They were smart, had a good command of the situation, and were authoritative. These women in the PKK's higher ranks were so well regarded, that even the most rigid of men kept their mouths shut around them, let alone raised their voices against them.

When this female comrade was assigned as an assistant, Rubar directly resigned his position at Zagros, saying, "I want to resign from all my duties and rest for a couple of years." That was not the real reason behind the resignation, but he figured that he could not have free rein, while that female commander was his assistant. He could not command his forces as he wished anymore, because he would have to consult this woman on every single decision that he would make.

The Explosion at the Bookstore

An interesting decision was made at this guerilla force meeting in November 2005. For the first time in the history of the organization, electronic devices were not accepted in the meeting area for security reasons. As I previously mentioned, cell phones had already been banned. But from then on, there would not be any kind of electronic devices, such as TVs, microwaves, radios, or watches present in the meeting rooms. Murat Karayılan informed us that our meetings were going to be carried out through handwriting, and we would no longer be allowed to talk at the gatherings. To communicate, we had to write our comments on a piece of paper and hand it to others during the meetings. The idea behind this was generated because the organization had been warned that Turkish intelligence agencies eavesdropped on our meetings. I am not sure whether Turkey had technology that was capable of that, but we were warned to be more cautious about electronic gadgets. Also, from then on, all communication over the radio would be carried out using coded language, even in the south. Nothing was going to be said explicitly anymore.

After the Dr. Ali problem was settled, participants began to discuss the issue of the negotiations about peace with Turkey. While our discussions were going on, there was a bloody mission carried out in a town called Şemdinli in the city of Hakkari. Şemdinli was so small that there was only one open market. A vehicle was loaded with explosives, set there, and exploded, destroying the place. There had been a strict order from the organization since the year 2000 not to carry out any missions in Kurdistan cities. Therefore, we were all shocked. It definitely could not be one of our forces.

The region commander of Şemdinli had been present at this guerilla conference. He remarked, "The vehicle had been prepared to explode in the west, in one of the major Turkish cities. However, we canceled the mission, because the organization was going through the peace process again. I honestly have no idea who organized this explosion, and why it was carried out in Şemdinli." The militants, who were supposed to deliver this car to the Turkish city that was targeted, had disappeared. No one died in the explosion, but the financial costs were very high. Beyond that, the car exploded somewhere very close to where Turkish police officers were located.

Only a week later, while the organization was investigating the details of the incident, another explosion occurred in the same open market, but this time in front of a bookstore. Some local people, who were present near the explosion, caught two suspicious people, who had potentially organized the explosion. We learned from the news that these two people were, in fact, noncommissioned officers in the Turkish military. The local Kurds found many documents and weapons from the trunk of those officers' car. All of those documents were sent directly to the organization.

Now, because of the timeline, it was clear that both of the explosions had to be related to one another. The Chief of General staff, Yaşar Büyükanıt, went out of his way to protect those two officers. The public delivered them to the police, but at the time we did not know how the trial process went forward. In fact, the organization was later informed that the military officers had asked for help, directly from a specific person, who was neither a member of the police nor a military official. They had called Mehmet Ağar and said, "Boss, please help us as soon as possible! We are stuck in a very difficult situation." Mehmet Ağar was the person who was the mastermind behind both massacres conducted in the East against the Kurds, and the assassinations carried out against the rich Kurdish businessmen, between the years of 1992 and 1995. As an organization, we became very nervous about why those two officers did not seek help from the police or the head of General Staff, but instead, from Mehmet Ağar. At the time, he was only a deputy in the Turkish National Assembly. We began to think that he was planning something even bigger.

In fact, Mehmet Ağar's CV had a mile-long criminal record against the organization. He had engaged in monstrous crimes; while he served as a deputy, as a police chief, and while he worked with the Turkish Ministry of Interior Affairs. The organization figured out that dark plans were being mobilized to spoil the peace attempts, without the knowledge of the Turkish state officials. Those bombings were not propagated by the Turkish state. An unknown power was in action, trying to sow discontent between the Turks and the Kurds once again.

The AKP government is presently telling us they had gotten rid of all the Gulen movement supporters, within the ranks of the state. Well, they told us basically the same thing back then. They said they had gotten rid of the JITEM members; the people who had carried out extra-judicial killings in the old days, as well as the dark powers. There was an atmosphere created that seemed to indicate the AKP would not allow such dark days to return to Turkey.

Those explosions occurred while the AKP thought that everything was under their control, but this was proof that there were definitely some groups within Turkey, acting outside the AKP. You know how people occasionally argue the existence of a shadow government or a deep state within the state? I think that it is true. I mean, there was, in fact, such a power in Turkey. No matter what the state officials did, they could not get rid of this deep-rooted, shadowy structure within the state. The seniors within the organization would often say, "If Turkey really wants to get rid of those shadowy powers, and if the officials really want to figure out who is in control, then they have to interrogate Süleyman Demirel (a former president and prime minister), Mehmet Ağar (a former interior minister and police chief), Tansu Çiller (a former prime minister), Ünal Erkan (a former state of emergency governor in eastern Anatolia) and Hayri Kozakçıoğlu (a former governor and police chief). Those were the names that were at the center of the aforementioned shadowy incidents. They were the viruses that had infiltrated Turkey."

The drug trafficking from Gabar, via military helicopters, took place while Mehmet Ağar was in power. He was very much aware of this trafficking, and, in fact, high-ranking military officials, guerillas who deserted the organization, as well as special units (including JITEM) established by Mehmet Ağar, were all involved in this dark business. This team of crooks was involved in countless dirty dealings back then. Tansu Çiller, Doğan Güreş, Mehmet Ağar were all part of the same shadowy team.

Right after that explosion, Erdoğan visited the city of Hakkari, and gave a speech to the local Kurds, who were there to celebrate his visit. His speech made us both annoyed but also happy. Erdoğan said this, "You, the Kurds of Hakkari, will either love this country or you will walk away from these territories." In fact, after this threatening speech, the state of Turkey began to lose the hearts and minds of the people of Hakkari. The local Kurds stopped siding with the state and a majority of them began to take sides with the PKK. There were many village protection guards (rangers) working for the state security officials in the city of Hakkari, especially in the countryside. All of these rangers resigned from their duties upon hearing this speech delivered by Erdoğan. Of course, none of this was on paper. They contacted the PKK representatives in the region to inform them that they would work for the PKK from then on. Until that speech, the ANAP, the DYP, and almost all other political parties had some level of constituents in the city of Hakkari. But Erdoğan's threatening speech was the last straw for the people of Hakkari. In fact, it broke the Kurds' emotional ties with the state of Turkey.

With Erdoğan's speech, the organization negated the ceasefire. We even began carrying out more guerilla missions then we had originally planned. As I mentioned, we were using the smaller, more professional teams as opposed to larger groups as in the old days, and this tactic proved itself effective. The Chief of General Staff blamed the AKP government because of the organization's success. They blamed the government for not constructing asphalt roads in the towns and villages of eastern Anatolia, since it was easier for the organization (according to them) to plant mines under earth roads. After they blamed each other, we figured out that the soldiers were having a hard time taking precautions against our deadly missions. They were facing a new and unexpected tactic from us guerillas. While there used to be a guerilla force of 1,000 troops in a province, those numbers had dwindled to less than 70.

15

THAT'S ALL SHE WROTE!

When the training policy in the organization changed, you could no longer request to be assigned to a field in the north as you formerly could. First, each battalion would select the best candidates, with the potential to work in the north. Those people would then undergo a month of grueling physical and ideological training. During this second stage, the unqualified ones were eliminated. Guerillas had to pass a total of six training sessions, similar to the second one, to be eligible to fight in the north of Turkey.

In November 2005, during the guerilla conference at Zagros, I notified my superiors that I would like to fight as a ground guerilla within Turkey. I was, however, assigned to Çukurca, due to some health issues relating to shell fragments that were still in my knees from an explosion in 1994. Because of them, I was unable to walk smoothly, and even, occasionally, used a cane.

It was the summer of 1994 when seven guerillas and I were reconnoitering a military post between the towns of Sirvan and Hizan. The village from which we were collecting reconnaissance was within the area the rangers patrolled, so we had to be extra cautious. If we were noticed by either the peasants or the security forces, it was nearly impossible to flee and survive. Bahtiyar, one of my comrades, left his binoculars on a rock facing the sun after he completed his part of the reconnaissance. The lenses in the binoculars gave off a reflection, which allowed the soldiers, at their post, to notice us.

Of course, we were not initially aware of this situation. It was around 1:00 p.m. when I was checking the radio stations used by the soldiers in their military posts, close by. I noticed they were preparing for something and was sure that they had dispatched a force to the field—and were trying to sneak up on us. I finally realized that what I heard was coming from the military post that we had just surveyed, because we had a list indicating which military post was using what numerical code in their radio communications.

I told my comrades that we needed to leave the field immediately. I was just a squad commander back then, and the company commander asked, "Why are we leaving now? We have not even completed our reconnaissance." I replied, "Comrade, I believe the soldiers have seen us and are currently advancing in the field and, most likely, heading toward us." Upon hearing this, the company commander scanned the area with his binoculars and said to me, "Deniz, I do not see any movement around us. It looks safe. We should finish what we have started!" This time I replied, a bit angrily, "Listen to me! They are advancing with three squads and will lay siege somewhere." In the meantime, the soldiers on the radio were describing a strategic spot to one another, saying, "If we hold that area, they cannot run away. We will kill them all." I looked around and saw a high hill behind us. "Comrade, I am now certain that the soldiers are advancing to that hill over there, and will hold the hill in order to kill us all."

While I was still trying to convince my company commander, one of our comrades saw, with his binoculars, the soldiers in the field. They were still quite a distance from us, but there was something of which we were unaware: one of the military squads had already climbed up the hill! The soldiers began firing on us from above. I told the comrades, "Run to the other side of the hill, and I will stall them with cover fire." There was just one comrade and myself left behind, while the others climbed safely up the other side of the hill. Then, we heard gunshots coming from their position at the top. Bad luck! There were already two squads of enemy soldiers positioned on top, and now our comrades were in a gunfight. While that was going on, we also climbed the hill in order to support our comrades. The skirmish was within spitting distance of them. It was 2:00 p.m., and the weather was so hot that, because of the heat, we were not able to run even 100 meters.

Our company commander said we should position ourselves behind the rocks and fight the soldiers, but I objected. We were only eight guerillas, and we would not be able to protect ourselves for the five hours before darkness fell. I told him that we should leave that area as soon as possible, but he insisted, "No, there are good hiding spots on this hill. We can stay and fight them from here." No matter how hard I tried to convince him otherwise, he was the commander, and so his word was final. We stayed and continued to fight, positioning ourselves at 10-meter intervals. Approximately 30 minutes later, one of our fronts fell. The comrades fighting there had to flee their positions, because they came under intense fire from an M72 LAW (Light anti-tank weapon). One comrade and me were the only ones left at the position, fighting against the soldiers. I communicated, via radio, with the rest of team and said, "If you hurry as fast as you can, you'll be able to defend us from nearby, so that we can also retreat." And they answered, "Okay!"

In the meantime, we were not aware that the soldiers had gotten so close to us. There was only a distance of 6 meters between us. My comrade had a chance of running away, because there were large rocks that would hide him while running. However, I did not have the same terrain. I had only two large rocks behind which to hide, on a flat field. I thought about running over to my comrade, but it was too risky. I would no doubt have gotten shot. But what other option did I have? The answer was, none. I had to run to where he was; otherwise, the soldiers were going to kill me. I told my comrade, "You move further away, and I will take your place." He moved to where there was now almost 20 meters between us. I was just about to run to where he had been when the soldiers showed up right at that spot, at which point, I was just waiting between those two rocks. There appeared to be nothing left that I could do to save my life. In that moment, for the first time in my life, I told myself that I was at the end of the road. It was going to be impossible for me to leave alive. I was going to die. I was then on the radio, talking with the company commander, and he asked, "What can we do for you, Comrade Deniz?" I said, "Comrade, there is nothing you can do to save me. You and the men run as far as you can to save your own lives. I will stall them until I am out of ammunition."

"Okay. But if you have any documents or other secretive information on you, destroy them immediately. Do not let the soldiers capture them," he said. That was already on my mind. In my pockets, I had the communication codes that we used on the radio, some money, and some crucial documents that belonged to the organization. I took all of them out and set them on fire. While I was doing this, I heard the sound of a hand grenade primer. I was very well acquainted with this sound, since I had used primers many times. The sound meant that a bomb had been thrown, but I did not know which way it was coming from. I was still covered on both sides by the large rocks. As soon as I heard the sound of the primer, I knelt down and covered my head and eyes with both of my arms. The grenade fell 5 meters in front of me. Believe me, in that moment, my life passed before my eye, like a movie. I told myself, "Deniz, that's all she wrote!"

When you hear the sound of the primer you know the bomb will explode in five or six seconds. The duration is not standard, because Russian-made and NATO standard bombs differ from each other. When the bomb exploded, the shell fragments hit my knees, elbows, and cheeks. I still have shell fragments in my cheeks. I did not want them to be removed, because the doctors would have had to cut through my cheeks to get them. I was told that three points on my face would need to be cut to remove the pieces, but I did not want to have scars on my face. To this day, when I shave, it hurts me when the razor touches those fragments. My knees were badly wounded.

The soldiers began to chase my comrades and so did not even come close to check on whether I was dead or alive. I guess they thought that I was already dead.

There was no one left on the hill. I was in extreme pain, and my knees were bleeding. I wrapped them each with a piece of cloth, took my weapon, and started to crawl slowly. The trouble was that I had broken my radio, and I had set the codes and money on fire. I had nothing left on me with which to communicate with my comrades. I was there all alone.

A positive thing was I knew where the guerillas would normally hang out. As soon as I reached a wooded area, I laid down among the bushes. I wanted to rest until it was dark. Since I no longer had a radio, I really could not walk in daylight. It would be too risky, since I could not track the location of the soldiers.

During the darkness of night, I once again began to walk. All of my comrades probably thought I had been martyred. The closest comrade, who had been 20 meters away, would have known what that sound from the hand grenade meant and would have told the others that I had died. With that news, they would not have come back to search for me.

I had been brought this close to death, because of the negligence of one of my comrades, Bahtiyar. In the later years, I had to fire Bahtiyar from the organization. Both the guerillas and the senior executives were highly disturbed by his irresponsible behaviors. Near the winter of 1997, we had to relocate to another area to dig out our underground bunkers. Everyone carried something, and we set off for camp. Bahtiyar was also with us. He weighed around 80 to 90 kilograms and was almost 2 meters tall. When it came to eating, he could eat as much as six normal people would eat. However, when it came to work, he would always have an excuse of being ill, too tired, or busy working on something else. It became such a common pitch from him that everyone began to hate him for it. I just did not know what to do with him.

We were advancing toward our new field one night. Since my knees had been wounded, I was carrying the least heavy load. It was an oil can, which weighed about 18 kilograms. In the meantime, Bahtiyar was walking freely. He had neither been wounded in battle nor had a physical handicap. The company commander called me in the middle of the night, "Deniz, neither the management nor I want to see Bahtiyar any longer. Do whatever is necessary to get rid of him. Everyone is complaining about him." That let me know that the situation was more serious than I thought.

A female platoon commander and I headed toward the very end of the line to talk with Bahtiyar. It was 3:00 a.m. This comrade asked me what I was planning to do with him, and I replied that I was going to send him away. She asked me, to where specifically, and I said he could go wherever he wanted—even go to hell!

When we got to Bahtiyar, I spoke to him, saying, "Put down your weapons!" At that moment, we were walking close to the Silk Road, and I pointed out two clusters of lights—one on the right being a military post, and the other a village. "You can see both of them, right? Now, get out of here, Bahtiyar. No one wants to see you around here any longer. It's your call. You can go either to the military post or to the village. Do whatever you want, but never come back to us!" He suddenly began to cry, and I could not calm him. "Look Bahtiyar, I am trying to help you. The company commander may even kill you if he sees you around tomorrow. I'm saving your life! If you have half a brain, you will leave now!"

In the morning, the company commander said, "I have not seen Bahtiyar so far today. Where is he?" I replied, "You will not see him anymore, comrade. I sent him away!" He appeared annoyed, "What? Are you out of your mind? I told you that I did not want to see him. Why did you send him away?" I calmly replied again, "He has been demoralizing to the rest of the force, and he was not able to get accustomed to life in the mountains. The best option for him was to go away. I offered him two choices. He could either surrender to the security forces, or he could go to the village we passed by last night and continue his life as a normal Kurdish peasant!" The company commander remained silent for a while and finally said, "Indeed, you did well Deniz. No one will complain about him again!"

With his body structure, Bahtiyar was capable of carrying me if he had wanted. However, like a parasite living on animals, he had gotten used to living off the backs of other guerillas. Our region commander became very angry when he heard about what had happened, and said, "Who the hell do you think you are, firing someone from the organization? Is Bahtiyar your commodity? How dare you fire him?" He was specifically shouting at the company commander and myself. Finally, I could not take the scolding any longer, and replied, to him, "I am okay with whatever punishment you would impose. But just so you know, I do not take your criticism of me, regarding Bahtiyar, seriously!" Upon hearing this, the region commander lost his cool. "How dare you ignore my warnings? Who the hell do you think you are?" I replied again, "Go and ask the guerillas in the battalion. Find out if even one of them was content with Bahtiyar's presence!" Not a single guerilla, out of 60 that were asked, said that Bahtiyar was a good comrade. On top of that, a couple of them reiterated the necessity of Bahtiyar's dismissal from the battalion. The region commander could no longer complain to me upon hearing these confirmations.

Because of Bahtiyar's negligence in 1994, I occasionally had to use a cane. Before I left, there were hundreds of comrades in the organization who walked with the help of a cane. There were also some who used a cane, even though they had never been wounded. It is strange, but when you get used to the comfort of a cane, you feel as if you cannot walk without one. If you have never used one before, you do not know how comfortable it is. At night in the mountains, while resting, comrades would leave their canes and weapons on the ground. When they awoke and began traveling once again, many of them would take up their cane, but forgot their weapon on the ground, and would not realize they had left it behind until they had been walking for some time. They then would have to go back and retrieve it. The cane was like that. When you become used to it, it is like a natural part of your body. You might forget your weapon, but never the cane!

I only fully understood the damage which had been inflicted on my body through all the battles when I asked to be reassigned in the north. In 1993, I was wounded in an ambush in the Siirt Valley. A hand grenade had exploded in front of me in 1994, and, in 1996, I nearly died from a bullet that had stripped my skull. Since these injuries occurred one after another and had done such damage to my body, the headquarters commander told me, "Go see a doctor and provide us with a medical report that gives a detailed examination of your condition. After examining the report, I will decide whether you are eligible to fight in the north again or not."

I visited a hospital in Zaho, Iraq, to obtain my medical report. The doctor there told me, "I am not licensed to provide you with such a report. However, I can refer you to a doctor in Dohuk, Iraq who can give you that report." So, I went to Dohuk. We had some guides in Iraqi cities that would help us with these kinds of things. They would drive us to the hospitals and be our means of communication with the Arab doctors. The organization even had lodging facilities in these cities in case a guerilla had to stay for an extended period of time.

I was acquainted with a young man in his mid-twenties from Barzani's family in Dohuk. Before I visited the doctor, I made a call to him. "I must go to the hospital to get a medical report. Can you come with me? I do not want the doctor to make trouble." He said he would. At one time, he had wanted to join the organization, and I had been his intermediary. Headquarters management did not approve his request to join, because Barzani did not want his family members joining the organization. He had once written a letter to the PKK which said, "True, there are many PKK participants from my region, but do not ever allow my family members and relatives to join you." This young man was Barzani's nephew. It would look bad to Barzani if we enrolled him in the organization, and it may have even caused diplomatic tension with Barzani. Therefore, the organization said, "Tell him that there are other opportunities to serve the PKK. He does not need to be with the guerilla forces. He can better serve our struggle in the political arena."

I visited the hospital with the man, and the doctor examined me several times, causing me to remain in Dohuk for three days. In the hospital, the doctor ordered x-rays of my head and knees and, after checking the results, told me, "In order for us to remove those shell fragments, you'll need to undergo a risky surgery that carries a 60 percent chance of paralysis. If you doubt me, take these x-rays to the best physicians in Europe. You'll find that no one would easily take the risk of performing such a surgery." In fact, the physicians in Syria I visited in 1996 told me the same thing. It was then that I knew for sure that it would be impossible to gain a complete recovery.

I brought the reports directly to central headquarters, and gave them to Bahoz Erdal. He was the commander and also a doctor. He read them carefully, looked me in the eye, and said, "Comrade Deniz, you cannot even cross the Turkish border with these legs, let alone be assigned to the north." I was very upset when I heard those words. I could not stay in other fields anymore, and I missed life in the north so much! For instance, in 2005, the organization tried to assign me to a political position in Germany. I told them that I would never go there. How could I? I had fought as a guerilla for years. I did not even want to stay in the southern guerilla forces, let alone in Germany. The north was different. I knew I would be closer to death there but living there was so exciting!

I also stayed in Damascus, Syria for six months, which felt like six years to me. I could not get used to life there. It seemed impossible for me to leave the lifestyle I was used to in the mountains. Can you believe that in 16 days, it will be six years that I have been in this prison? You know, even though it has been six years, I still cannot sleep on a mattress. Because I was so used to sleeping on the bare ground outdoors, I could not get used to sleeping on those beds. I removed the mattress, set it aside, and slept on the hard wood. It was the same when we visited the city centers in Iraq or Syria for various reasons. The families who hosted us would prepare very comfortable beds, but no matter how hard I tried, I could not sleep on them. I would often roll up the woolen beds and just sleep on the bare ground. Over time, the hardships you encounter in guerilla life penetrate your personality, and that's why I did not want to stay in the south.

There was a constant risk of death, so people in the north were not troubled by small things, as was the case in the south. And as I mentioned several times before, the ties of fellowship were amazingly tight in the north, with large differences between the north and south in terms of comradeship and cohesion, because in the north you had no family or relatives other than your commander and guerilla comrades! Everything you had, as far as your brothers, sisters, fathers, mothers, and friends, were your guerilla comrades! You had no one else than them. It was not like that in the south, where they were so into their own conveniences. For example, in the south, if you were not content with your commander, you just wrote a report asking to be assigned to another company. Similarly, let's say you are in the south and become angry with the comrades in your company. You did not have to reconcile with them, because there were thousands of comrades in the south. You could simply go and make new friends. This was not the case for guerillas in the north. There, the guerilla units were small in numbers and, at most, would have five guerillas together. That was it. If two out of five got angry with the others, the situation would demoralize everyone within the unit as well. So, no one allowed such things to occur in the north. This helps to explain the gap between the south and north.

After seeing those x-rays, Bahoz Erdal ended up rejecting my request for a northern assignment. He explicitly said, "You will never go north, Deniz." But I had already set my mind on fighting in the north, no matter what he decided. Bahoz Erdal was severally criticized during that guerilla conference and was still down in the dumps, so I did not want to cause more angst. If I had pushed him a bit harder, he may have permanently destroyed my hopes. Besides, my continued insistence regarding the north could make him suspicious. Suspicions were sometimes raised within the organization if you insisted on being transferred to a particular place. The organization would get concerned about it, so I stopped bothering him at that time. Nevertheless, it was etched in my mind that I was going to make the same suggestion again at a more convenient time.

Talking to My Parents After Fourteen Years

The years of 2005 to 2007 were the beginning of a troubling time for us. We were forbidden to watch TV, use mobile phones, or any other electronic device, because they could potentially transmit unwanted signals. Radios were the only exception to this ban. We would often establish connections with headquarters through radio channels. The organization owned a radio channel that operated from Sweden into the rest of the world. If we wanted to send important news to headquarters, we would use our satellite phones to call the channel in Sweden. When our call was received there, we would tell them we needed to speak with someone from technical services. This was the code phrase to speak with someone who could deliver our message to headquarters in Iraq. Once it was clear that we were speaking with the right person, we would tell them our unit's numerical code, and then give them the message we wanted to send. If the message we were sending contained time-sensitive information on an emerging situation, the radio would do a live broadcast using a predetermined statement when it aired. There was a team of guerillas who were tasked with listening to this Swiss radio channel day and night, 24/7. As soon as the guerillas heard the predetermined message, they would call Sweden to learn the deeper details of what was going on. Everything aired on that channel was recorded, so the guerillas would never miss a message.

Turkish security forces had the ability to listen to our conversations and track our locations through phones. This forced us to take these sorts of precautions when communicating with headquarters.

While we used to call headquarters with our cell phones, the sudden raids by security forces on our highly secretive posts—and the speech of Abdulkadir Aksu, the Interior Minister of Turkey, on a live TV broadcast—forced us to use alternative methods. Part of his speech went, "If we do not listen to the guerillas in Gabar on a regular basis, the metropolitan cities in Turkey would run red with blood." Each region had at least one satellite and mobile phone, but they almost never used them to communicate with one another. We would always take the batteries and the SIM cards out of the phones when we were not using them to prevent our locations from being tracked.

It was in 2005 that I saw a comrade using a satellite phone to talk to his family in Turkey. A communication officer approached me and asked, "Comrade Deniz, do you not have any family still alive back in Turkey? I have never seen you call anyone." I said, "Comrade, it has been almost 14 years since I last spoke with my family. I'm sure they think that I am dead. Even if I call them now, what can I say to them? I do not even remember my siblings' faces."

Between the years of 1992 and 2005, I had never spoken to my family. Not face to face or on the phone. I had no idea what they had been doing for those 13 years, and I was not even curious. I had too much responsibility within the organization to have time for them. In fact, most of the time, I did not even have the necessary devices to reach them. Besides, I had a new and larger family within the organization. I viewed my superiors as my father and mother. The guerillas that fought in my battalion were also part of my family, and I viewed them as my blood brothers and sisters. Similarly, they also viewed me as their elder brother or even a father, in some cases. I was all they had. They would come to see me if they were hungry or in need of new uniforms, if they were sick, or if they were stressed, and I would take care of all their worries. Thus, I had become part of a larger family. I just did not have the time to think of my birth family.

On the other hand, one part of the culture of the organization was such that if a guerilla said that he or she wanted to talk to their family, the commander usually let them talk on the phone. However, it was totally not acceptable for a commander to talk to his or her parents on a regular basis. This was because, then every single guerrilla would want to communicate with their parents if their commanders did so. Frequent contact with parents could have the potential to spoil the discipline in the guerilla force, because the guerillas would not be able to concentrate on their training. Once a year, some parents would even come to the guerilla campground in the south and spend one or two weeks with their children—no matter how much we commanders disapproved of it.

Anyway, this communication officer insisted that I should call my parents. I said, "Comrade, I do not even know any of their phone numbers. What number would I call, even if I wanted to?" He replied, "That's not a big deal. Just tell me their names and surnames." I gave him my father's first and last name. There was a service in Turkey to find registered phone users by dialing 118. He did so and found three different telephone numbers registered to my father's name in the city of Batman, Turkey.

We dialed the first number and a female answered. I soon learned that she was my elder brother's wife. I told her my father's name and asked if I could talk to him, but, when I would not tell her who I was, she hung up on me.

We then called the second number. This time I recognized the voice as belonging to my uncle's wife. As had been the case with my brother's wife, she was about to hang up, when I said, "Do not hang up, aunt. I want to talk to my uncle." She handed the phone to him. "Uncle, how are you? Do you remember me? I am Deniz." He kept silent for a while, and then said, "Impossible. Who are you, my son? Tell me the truth! It has been years since Deniz died." I said, "Uncle, believe me. I'm Deniz!" He was not yet convinced, so I asked him to tell me my father's phone number, because I realized he was not going to believe me. He provided me with a mobile number saying, "My son, please do not lie to us. Do not joke with us! We are all old people."

To my surprise, my parents had moved to Istanbul. We called this third number, provided by my uncle, and my father picked up the phone. I suddenly remembered his voice. In Kurdish, he asked, "Who are you? What do you want?" I said, "Dad, it is I, Deniz, your son." I think he was shocked, because he could not speak for two minutes. It had been 14 years since they had last seen me. In that time, they had not even heard from me, so he did not initially accept that I was his son. "You are not my son. Please, do not make fun of us," he said, and I replied, "How can I convince you, father?" He said, "I do not know who you are, but you cannot convince me. Deniz died many years ago. We heard it from his friends." He was just about to hang up on me when I said, "Daddy, please do not hang up. Ask me something from my childhood. Ask me a question about a memory, an incident when we were together. Then, hang up if I cannot tell you the correct answer!" He kept silent for a while and finally asked, "Do you smoke?" I said, "Yes, I do." Then he asked me how I started smoking. I said, "You taught me how to smoke. You would always ask me to roll a cigarette when I was young. I would roll it, light it, and hand it over to you. I got used to it, since I took a drag each time I lit one." He suddenly began to sob and through his tears said, "My dear son, where have you been for so long? Please tell me where you are and I will come and get you right away." I replied, "Dad, do not worry about where I am. Where is my mother? I would like to talk to her, too."

My mother was just as shocked and cried so much. She said, "Son, it has been many years. Why did not you call us? Where are you? Tell us where you are! We will come and get you now!" I said, "Mom, do not worry. I am okay. Now, stop asking questions and tell me how you are. Is everything all right with the family?" She was stubborn, still trying to learn where I was. "Son, please tell me where you are. I will come right away," she said, and for the first time, I felt very sad.

After that, I talked to my siblings, one by one. The youngest of them was only a year old when I deserted my parents, and I did not witness her growing up. When my mother handed the phone to her, she did not want to talk to me at first. I heard her saying, "I do not have such a brother. I do not even know him. Why do you want me to talk with him now?" I did not cry while talking to my parents and other siblings, but I was moved to tears when I heard her reject me. My mother forcefully gave the phone to her. I was just about in tears.

My male siblings begged me to come back home. "Brother, please come back home. We are up against a wall because of you. We had to relocate to Istanbul!" When a family member joined the organization, the security forces would put leverage on the rest of the family, as punishment. Local Kurds were scared by security forces, the police, and the military. Unaccounted murders by the security forces were common. My parents were also subjected to this same cruel treatment. They left everything behind in Batman and began a new life from scratch in the city of Istanbul, because of the pressure from the security forces. Istanbul was a large city, and they had never been there before. They had no jobs or skills to obtain a job. On top of that, they had no money left in their pockets. They had lived in extreme poverty for a long time. My youngest sibling even said, "Brother, we have been through this pain because of you. Leave the organization and come back to us!"

My poor mother said, "Who do you have there, son? Who takes care of you there? Who cooks for you?" Of course, she did not know the internal dynamics of the organization. I said, "Mom, do not worry about me. I have 80 children here who take care of me so well." I, of course, was referring to the guerillas in the battalion. My mother got confused at first, but later laughed a lot when she figured out my humor.

I talked to my father again before ending the phone call and said, "Father, can you give me my uncle's phone number?" I had an uncle who was very keen and clever. Of course, I had told my father to call my uncle before I called him, so I would not have to convince him that I was, in fact, Deniz. When I did call, I said, "Uncle, I will tell you where I am staying but you must never tell my parents, okay?" He said, "Okay!" I said, "Look, I am staying 'here.' Visit me at your earliest convenience." My parents would definitely want to visit me if they heard that my uncle was going to visit. If I allowed my parents to visit, then the foot guerillas would want the same from their parents. At that point, it would have become a tradition, which would make it difficult to prevent in the future. The guerillas would begin to see it as a given right, and would want their parents to visit them each year. I told my uncle, "Go to this hotel in Zaho, within Iraq, and tell the front desk assistant that you want to see me. They will drive you to our camp field."

The organization would actually get angry if a guerilla did not speak to his or her parents for an extended period of time. Indeed, if the seniors recognized such a situation, they would even force those guerillas to contact their parents immediately and keep them posted about where they were staying, and how they were doing.

That night, one of the region commanders heavily criticized me. "Comrade Deniz, what kind of human being are you? How could someone keep himself from his family for 14 years?" I could not answer him. That night, in a haphazard manner and through the insistence of that communication officer, I spoke with my parents for the first time in 14 years. After that incident, I thought of a comrade whom I knew that had not spoken to his parents for close to ten years. He had no heart to call them, but I forced him to do so. His parents were not as far from the culture of the organization as my parents were. In fact, to some degree, they were acquainted with the goals of our struggle. His father even told him, "Son, whenever the organization needs us, we are ready to serve. Just let us know! Your mother, siblings, and I are ready to serve your guerillas there! Just let us know. It does not matter if we have to relocate to Iraq, Syria, or even somewhere within Turkey." We were deeply affected when we heard this conversation between a father and son. Not all Kurds, including my parents, were so devoted to the organization's struggle.

I have a very funny memory regarding the patriotic attitudes of a Kurdish parent. We had a comrade who acted in a movie that was produced by the organization, between the years of 2005 and 2006. He had a role as one of the leading actors. This comrade's father got very angry when he saw his son in that movie and contacted headquarters saying, "I sent this crook to you in order to become a guerilla, but you guys are using him as an actor in a movie! I cannot accept this! Send him to the mountains as soon as possible to fight as a guerilla!" We laughed a lot when we heard this.

The next day, I received a call on my radio from Zaho. "Deniz, you have a guest and he says that he is your uncle. Do you know him?" I said, "That is true, comrade. Keep him there for a while, and I will come and talk to him soon." I was caught totally unprepared and had not thought that my uncle would come to visit me only one day after I asked him. It was ill luck, because that day I had four guests from PKK headquarters in my battalion. I was in a meeting with them when I got another call from Zaho. It had not even been two hours since their first call. "Comrade, your guest is very angry and is asking us why you cannot see him now." Then, my uncle grabbed the radio and spoke to me directly, "My nephew, I came here to see you, but you are ignoring me!" I said, "Uncle, I will see you, but I have to see my guests off first." My uncle was not familiar with the culture of the organization. He responded harshly, "Buster, I came this far to see you, but look at you! You are not coming because you have other guests. I am your uncle. Why the hell are you not listening to me? You will come here right away!"

I had to explain the situation to my guests and ask for their forgiveness. I arranged a car to pick up my uncle from Zaho and bring him to Çukurca. As soon as he arrived, I introduced him to my comrades and invited him to my tent. He told me that he was hurrying because he was only excused from work for one day. We took pictures together, so that he could take them to my parents. My uncle told me that many of my friends from the neighborhood where I grew up had joined the organization. That was something of which I was unaware until then. Moreover, many of them who had joined after me had been martyred. My mother and father were very sad when their remains arrived back in the neighborhood. They figured I had died, since the new comrades had so quickly died. That was why they thought hope was lost of my return.

"Please do not ever tell my parents where I am staying, Uncle. I would be stuck in a difficult situation if they were to visit me here," He said, "Okay, but let us know how you are doing and where you are. Call us from time to time. My nephew, look! We had not heard from you for almost 14 years. Your parents were both sick over losing you."

When I was on the phone with my uncle I told him, "When you come visit me in Iraq, bring any young women or men that you know from the families where you are." I wanted to make them all PKK members, but, although there were many people that he could bring, he did not bring even a single one. The range from 15 to 20 years old is perfect in terms of our recruitment activities. I can say that people between the ages of 20 to 25 are also okay, but not as good as 15 to 20. Anyone over 25 just requires too much work in terms of recruiting. Indeed, the organization does not even want to recruit anyone over 25 to join the organization, because it is harder for them to adopt the lifestyles of the organization. We have wasted a lot of time trying to get people beyond that age to accept the organization's culture, lifestyle, traditions, and hardships.

Youths between the ages of 15 and 20 are not like that. They do not have prejudices regarding the organization or life in general. Let me explain it a better way using an example. We had a Kurdish patriot who joined the organization in his thirties. This man was fulfilling all of his religious obligations. He would pray five times a day, fast during Ramadan, and stay away from things banned by his religion. There were many people like him with us, and the organization never caused trouble for them regarding fulfillment of their religious activities. It even encouraged and provided an atmosphere in which everyone was free to believe in whatever they wanted. Despite that, people over the age of 30 never seemed to tolerate other religious beliefs in any way. They would openly criticize others as infidels, if they did not believe in God or did not fulfill their religious obligations. We repeatedly warned them saying, "Comrades! Let everyone be himself. Do not interfere in other religious beliefs or lifestyles. We are all free here!" No matter what we said, we often failed to persuade them to change their attitudes or behaviors toward others.

Turkish Intelligence Agents in Iraq

In the spring of 2006, one of the region commanders became very disabled, because of his back. The doctors in the camp were not able to treat him, so he was transferred to a professional medical facility as quickly as possible. Similar to many other comrades, he had a disc displaced at his waist, and we could see that he was in extreme pain. He could not sit or stand and was not able to endure the pain much longer.

I told him, "Comrade, I have connections in Iraq. Would you like to be treated there?" He gladly accepted my offer. So, we first notified headquarters about his transfer to Iraq. Bahoz Erdal was still the headquarters commander at the time, and he told me, "Deniz, only send him there if you really trust your connections. However, if there is even a tiny risk that he could be captured, then do not send him to Iraq. He is a senior commander, and it would be a serious problem for the organization if he were caught!"

I asked a close friend of mine, who was a battalion commander in the KPD Peshmerga forces, to help our region commander get proper treatment in Iraq. This was during a period of time when we did not have any problems with Barzani and the KDP. However, Turkish intelligence units would hang around the cities of Dohuk and Zaho in Iraq and would occasionally arrest our members who lived there. The organization inspected the locations of those Turkish intelligence agents in Iraq. We knew everything about their work there—where they were staying, whom they were seeing, etc. The organization actually had sent me to those Iraqi cities in 2005 for reconnaissance. I was tasked with finding PKK deserters and also identifying the lodging facilities and private houses where Turkish intelligence units were staying. As was the case in Turkey, the organization already had militants living in cities within Iraq, Syria, and Iran. These civilian militants collected information for the organization and would immediately contact us if they acquired sensitive information regarding our enemies. These civilian organization members helped me a lot when I was searching for the housing locations of these Turkish agents.

Although we knew all their addresses, we could do nothing, because they were staying in a region under Barzani's control. If we killed those agents, Turkey would make Barzani pay for their deaths and ask him why he had not protected them. Barzani had large-scale trade agreements with Turkey. The oil produced in northern Iraq is sold to the rest of the world through Turkey. Therefore, a scenario where the organization killed Turkish agents would seriously risk the agreements between Barzani and Turkey.

We saw the region commander off to Iraq as soon as the arrangements were made. Before he left, I asked him to communicate with us at least three times a day via his satellite phone, preferably in the morning, noon, and at night. For the first two days, we communicated with each other as planned. On the night of the third day, I was watching the news on a Turkish TV channel, ATV, when I heard that a senior PKK commander had been caught in Iraq. I began to panic and wondered if it were our region commander.

Of course, the people at central headquarters were also watching the news. They called me right afterwards, and asked if it were our region commander who had been caught. I said, "I'm not sure, since we haven't spoken since the afternoon. However, he is supposed to call me sometime around midnight." Bahoz Erdal got angry at this, and asked, "How could you not have an instantaneous source of communication with a region commander?" I said, "I will provide you with detailed information later." Then, I turned off the phone. It was around 11:00 p.m. I called the region commander perhaps ten times, but he never picked up his satellite phone. I thought it was highly likely that the news, broadcast by the Turkish TV channels, had been referring to him. If this was so, then the wheels would come off the bus! Barzani would be so angry with the Peshmerga if he discovered that some of his soldiers were assisting us in Iraq. I would also be in serious trouble if the region commander had been caught by Turkish agents and was at a complete loss at what to do.

I immediately called Barzani's nephew, the young man who had helped me during my hospital visits in Iraq. "Comrade, can you search to see if a senior PKK member had been caught by the Turks in Iraq today? Please pay extra attention to the cities of Dohuk and Zaho." He called me back, approximately two hours later, and said, "No, no members of the PKK were caught today." I replied, "Are you sure? Turkish TV channels were broadcasting that a senior PKK executive was arrested in Iraq." He said, "Comrade Deniz! That is impossible. The Turkish agents would definitely inform the KPD intelligence units if they had caught a PKK member in our territories." I was a bit relieved with his reply, but I was still nervous since the region commander had not yet contacted me.

It was around midnight, and my satellite phone rang. It was the region commander. I immediately asked, "Where have you been, comrade? I have been trying to communicate with you for hours! Why have you not answered my calls?" I told him that he was to return to the camp that same night, but he replied, "Comrade, I moved into a deep conversation with friends from the KDP and forgot to call you. The doctor has scheduled my treatment for tomorrow morning. I cannot return tonight!" I responded, "Comrade you have to return tonight. It is an order from headquarters management!"

We figured out that the news about a captured comrade was a scam. The Turkish intelligence units had probably gotten a bit of loose information about a senior PKK member visiting Iraq. They most probably knew that someone was coming but did not know to which city in Iraq he or she was going. Since the information was not fully accurate they used Turkish TV channels to broadcast false news, in order to create a panicked atmosphere within the organization. Indeed, they had been successful in making us nervous.

My close friend, who arranged the hospital visits, took the phone from the region commander and began to talk to me, "Comrade, why are you calling him back to Çukurca now? His treatment will start tomorrow." I explained to him what had happened that night. "The Turkish intelligence probably knows that he is in Iraq. We cannot take such a risk. Send him back tonight!" He replied, "Do you not trust me? This area is under Peshmerga's control. I have a battalion of Peshmerga forces under my authority. If the Turks find where this comrade is staying, they would have to kill each one of us to take him." This friend of mine was also a son of a well-known Kurdish tribe in northern Iraq. "Deniz, there is no need to be nervous. It would not just be the battalion. The Turks would have to kill every single member of my tribe if they tried to take our guest! Whatever happens, I will not surrender him to the Turks! Let him see the doctor tomorrow, and I will personally bring him back to your area!"

Traitors Among Us

I worked as a battalion commander in the Çukurca camp until the end of 2006. During that time, in April of the same year, selections were being made for new guerillas to be dispatched north. The selection process happened every year during the month of April. The new, dynamic guerrilla forces from the south were sent north while the worn out and fatigued guerillas, who had been fighting up there, would come south to rest. I went to Iraq to talk with the senior leadership as the new forces gathered there. I told them once again that I wanted to go north, but my suggestion was rejected, as it had been before.

There was a tragic incident that happened in July of 2006 that reminded me yet again that I needed to leave the crooked south and fight in the north with real comrades. A PKK committee member, with whom I was closely acquainted, was killed by an agent who infiltrated the organization. Sarı İbo, my dear friend, was murdered by this traitor. After the assassination, I knew there was no way I was going to stay in the south.

Sarı İbo was one of the oldest members of the organization. He had been around so long, that he was one of the few original members who came up with the idea to fight in the guerilla style against Turkey. He personally organized the first guerilla units and began the first battles against the Turkish security forces in Amed, Garzan, and even in Amanoses. He was a very important figure to the organization.

When I found out about his death, my entire world came crashing down around me. I could not stay in the south any longer.

The suspect was put through a deep and thorough investigation. He initially said that it had just been an accident, but, after interrogation, he confessed he had been working for a Turkish intelligence unit. He had been in close contact with the security forces since the first day he had infiltrated us. He also confessed that he was not alone, and provided us with the names of four other guerillas who were working for the Turks.

In 2004, the organization established a new unit within Turkey called "self-defense." Sarı İbo was the commander of this unit. Under normal conditions, it was difficult for our enemies to place their agents among us, because living in the mountains was quite strenuous, and it was not hard to figure out who was a real patriot and who was an agent. However, the living conditions of the self-defense committee members were not like that. They lived in the cities, as civilians. These five Kurdish traitors were placed in the self-defense committee by Turkish agents. The organization would initially send these people to either Iraq or Syria for a training session, which lasted only 45 days. The new self-defense committee members would be trained on basic military and ideological issues, and the agents had come to the south for that purpose. One of them figured out that Sarı İbo was an important person within the PKK and thought he would be in the Turks' good graces if he could kill him. He was going to make it appear as an accident, so no one would suspect his real identity. He was a fool that underestimated the organization.

The other four guerillas, disclosed by the killer, were pardoned, but the traitor who was responsible for Sarı's death was executed soon after the investigation. As I mentioned previously, the PKK banned capital punishment for all crimes except the crime of infiltrating the organization. Working for the enemy was unforgivable. Above all else, if you killed one of your comrades, without pity, there was zero chance you would be forgiven. Even if you deserted, the organization would never give up trying to find and execute you. Something similar to that happened in 2004. One of the guerillas killed a comrade and took refuge with Barzani. The organization offered the KDP a large sum of money to extradite him, and they took the offer. Once he was delivered to us, he was executed.

Sarı İbo's death affected me deeply. The day before it happened, we were together eating dinner and chatting happily about general things, and then, the next day he was gone. I was in a tough, unbearable emotional state. It was even more unbearable when you lost someone you loved, and Sarı İbo was loved by me. The PKK is what it is today because of people like him. He was a humble person, who never asked to be promoted, and would always volunteer for the unglorified jobs no one else wanted.

We had grown accustomed to losing ground guerillas in a clash. It was a part of life and did not affect our emotions as much. However, when your commander dies, you feel as if you have lost every member of your family. A commander becomes everything you have. They are irreplaceable.

The North and Bahoz Erdal

In August of 2006, I visited the commander of my region and said, "Comrade, I want to ask you to write a report saying I am able to fight in the north. Headquarters is unwilling to employ me there, but I know you can convince them. Do not take this the wrong way, but if you do not write such a letter, I will not help with anything here. I will even leave for Amed by myself!" There were other ranked comrades, who desired to be dispatched north, but headquarters would not allow them to go either. Because of that, I said to our region commander, "You can send me there or not, but I will form a group with them, and we will go anyway!" At this, the region commander became very angry, "If it were anyone other than I that you spoke to in this way, you'd be arrested. Do not ever abuse our friendship again, Deniz! How would you go to Amed without getting permission from the organization first?" He had gotten angry at my tone, but still wrote the letter that I needed.

Even with the letter from the region commander, I was rejected by headquarters yet again. The commander who wrote the letter for me, contacted them via radio and said, "Deniz insists that he must go. Can't we do something for him?" They answered, "Tell him to come down here, and we will talk to him face to face." I arrived at Zap headquarters after one day's journey on foot, and I was welcomed by Muşlu Kadri Çelik. Before joining us, Kadri had been a senior military officer in the Turkish army but resigned to join our struggle in Iraq. If I am not mistaken, his daughter was a politician in the HDP. He was one of the oldest members of the PKK, having joined in the 1980s. Everyone would call him Ape Hus, which meant Uncle Hüseyin. I asked Ape Hus to convince Bahoz Erdal to send me north. He said, "Deniz, why do you insist on this so much? You are not eligible to serve in the north because of the condition of your health."

I told him all of the reasons why I wanted to go to the north so badly. "I cannot take the lifestyle in the south anymore! Look, if you guys force me to stay here, I will not work. I will resign from my duties, and be a regular guerrilla again." Bahoz Erdal arrived at headquarters in the evening. Bahoz, a senior woman named Zaho, and Ape Hus called me to the meeting hall. Bahoz Erdal asked me why I wanted to go to the north so badly. Just as with Ape Hus, I explained everything to him. Of course, he was not satisfied with my reasoning and got upset. He said, "Be honest with us. You are simply running away from the problems, Deniz! You know there are structural difficulties in the south, and the guerillas are not disciplined well enough, which means you know that you have to work harder here. You simply want to run away because you do not want to help us fix the problems." I was not expecting such harsh criticism, and I responded, "You are partly correct, comrade. The problems you listed are deeply rooted in the south, but you will not change them no matter what you do here. So, just let me go back north!" He asked again, "How will you go with those legs?" His comment humiliated me, and I replied, "These legs were wounded in 1994, and yet I have been fighting as a guerilla ever since. Did I not have these same injured legs when I took part in the YNK war as a commander of the special teams? Why did no one question them then? When I was needed, you never considered the condition of my legs. But when the conditions were suitable, you always created an excuse that I was not well enough, my health situation was not good, or I could not go because my legs would be a problem. Comrade, you will either give me permission or you will not, but I will go there!"

When I finished saying all of this, Bahoz Erdal was really pissed off. "Okay, if you are not going to listen to our advice, go wherever you want to go and do whatever you want to do, Deniz! However, be aware that we do not approve of it. I cannot forcefully hold you here, so I do not care if you go on your own." After delivering this message, he angrily left the room. I felt relieved when he said that I could go on my own. I asked Zaho and Ape Hus to notify PKK headquarters so there would not be a problem when I reached the forces in the north. Zaho also became angry. "You do not obey our orders, and to top it off, you dare ask us to explain the situation to headquarters? Hell no, I am not doing what you ask! Tomorrow, Comrade Abbas (Duran Kalkan) will be here. Talk to him, and if he agrees with your reasoning, you can go north. If you go there against our orders, I will ask all the guerillas in the region to incarcerate you as soon as they see you!" I then uttered my final words, "I will not stay here if you threaten me with death, let alone incarceration! You need to understand me. I cannot stay here anymore, but I also do not want to leave you like this! Make an exception for me!" Ape Hus and Zaho began to talk between themselves. "Okay, we will explain your unique situation to Comrade Abbas tomorrow. If he approves, then it is okay with us too." I told them, "Look, I can convince Comrade Abbas, as long as you do not tell him that you do not approve of my dispatch to the north."

Duran Kalkan and Ali Haydar, who were working for the defense committee, arrived at headquarters. Surprisingly, they both approved of my assignment to the north. Now, there was only one problem left to solve. I had to travel with a guerilla unit. Bahoz Erdal said, "There is a unit which is leaving for the north soon. The only way you can travel with them is if they accept you among them. You will not be able to go if they do not! Are you okay with this? You will stay here if they do not want you to travel with them?" I said, "It's a deal!" Bahoz Erdal said, "Perfect. You may return to your battalion in Çukurca and prepare for the trip. Join us at our meeting next week, and you can go with them if they accept you."

I took my dispatch to the north as a certainty. I said goodbye to the guerilas in my battalion and visited the other nearby battalions, to say goodbye, as well. I went back to headquarters a week later, but before I went to see Bahoz Erdal, I went directly to the group of 25 guerilas with whom I would be traveling, and said, "Comrades, some senior members are going to ask you if you'll accept me traveling with you. My assignment in the north depends on what you say! I expect you'll help me on this issue," and with a single voice, they accepted me. It was almost evening when Bahoz Erdal entered the meeting hall. He was still angry with my insistence on leaving. I knew this from the way he looked at me. He then eyed the comrades, one by one, and said, "There is a runaway among you. Do you know who it is?" Everyone began to look at me and laugh.

The company commander raised his hand to get the floor. "Comrade, we are all okay with taking the runaway with us. We have no problem with it!" Bahoz Erdal said, "Think twice! His legs make him weak, and there are times when he cannot even walk. You all know that sometimes he can only walk with the help of a cane. On top of that, he might not even be able to carry his own load." Bahoz Erdal was correct. I was not able to carry more than two cartridge clips on my waist, while most guerilas carried six. The company commander said, "Comrade, we accept him, even knowing all that you just mentioned. If necessary, we will carry him on our shoulders the whole way there." Bahoz Erdal replied, "Okay, since you want him so much, then you can take him with you. It will not be I whom he'll be bothering on the way up north!"

Before I could finally leave, Bahoz Erdal put one more condition in front of me. "Deniz, I am now okay with you leaving, but I am assigning you to work for the executive committee of the state of Amed." Each state had an executive council consisting of three senior PKK members. One of them was the state commander, and the other two were his or her assistants. I accepted this condition without a problem, just so long as I could go north!

There was one other thing I had to do before leaving. Each guerilla was required to explain their reason for going and to record their plans, projects, and goals for when they arrived in the north. You would basically stand in front of a camera and tell what benefit you would provide the organization on the Northern Front. All these speeches were recorded and then archived in your personal files. The organization could then bring charges against you if you did not follow through on your videotaped goals and projects. Everyone in the company with whom I was traveling had already given their speeches, but I still needed to do mine so I could finally leave.

Traveling to the North

It was August 2006 when we set off north. Bahoz Erdal asked if we had any money, and I said, "I left my money with someone in the battalion, because it was allocated for their expenses." He asked, "How much money will you need until you reach the northern front?" I said, "Well, we will be traveling from one region to another. Our needs can be met by the guerilla forces on our way, so I do not think we'll need very much." He handed me 6,000 Euros.

We set off in the evening after a farewell party. We said goodbye to the administrators and guerillas at the guerilla officers' school, then went to the PKK headquarters to say goodbye to the people there. While we were there, I heard that Cemal (Murat Karayılan) was arriving there soon, and it made me nervous. Comrade Cemal would never send me if he learned that I was going north, so we finished our goodbyes and left immediately.

To our surprise, the commanders to the regions of Haftanin and Metina had met and were heading toward headquarters to welcome Comrade Cemal. We encountered them as we made our way and spoke with them for half an hour before continuing on our journey. There was one comrade among them, with whom I did not get along. We did not have a big problem between us, but we differed on some ideological issues. There were also seven female guerillas. Four of them were from our group, and the other three were from a nearby guerilla force, which had come to say goodbye to their friends. One of these females, whom I had known since 1996, was ranked as a battalion commander. The organization had produced a movie called "Beritan," and she was the lead actress in it.

The comrade with whom I had the problem, filed an official complaint against me with headquarters management, as soon as he arrived there. In his report, he said, "Deniz and Beritan were talking a distance away from the group and must be having a romantic relationship." Management discussed whether something on that level could be true. Much of the reason for this accusation came from the fact that I had worked in the same unit as Beritan, for a long time. Besides that, my past records, involving women, were not so good.

The headquarters commander of the female force said, "Stop that talking now. What would we do if we call Deniz back here and put him under investigation only to find out there was nothing? He could potentially kill someone out of anger. We all know how sensitive he is on these issues." On some matters, I was indeed extremely patient. Yet, on others, I would not listen to the organization or even a loved one. I would especially become angry if someone cast aspersions upon me. On the other hand, if I had done something wrong, I would inform my superiors before they found out. Since she knew me so well, the commander also said, "Deniz had a relationship before, but he did not hide it from us. Everyone knew about it. Why would he hide it now? We should call Beritan here first and investigate her. She will tell us the truth. We will call Deniz back only if Beritan accepts the existence of such a love affair!"

After the decision, Beritan was invited to headquarters management for a preliminary hearing and became irritated as soon as she heard the false claims. "How could you think of something like that between Deniz and me? I have always regarded him as a comrade and as a friend. You are saying these things to me, but if you ask the same questions of Deniz, he will become angry." Duran Kalkan also heard about it and became upset. "What you people have been discussing is disgusting. Deniz is on his way north now. Everything that you're saying about Deniz having a romantic affair, is built on assumptions. What if you are mistaken? If this claim is a lie, then Deniz will fight neither in the north nor in the south. So, shut your mouths now! Also, despite the fact that Deniz's past relationships with women looks bad, I deeply trust Beritan. She would never lie."

Certainly, I was not aware of this claim and the subsequent hearings with me at their center. We were heading north in a group of 20 guerillas along with a special force consisting of five people. This special force was traveling there to manufacture explosives that could be used in our sabotage missions. Our first destination was the headquarters of this special guerilla force. Our group was intentionally traveling slowly, because we had heard that there were five other groups in Haftanin waiting to cross into Turkish territories. Groups were only allowed to cross into Turkey at certain intervals of time, because of security concerns. That is to say, we would have to wait in Haftanin, even if we arrived in a timely manner.

From Haftanin, you can cross into Turkey utilizing two different routes. The first one was through Botan, and the second one went through Iran. Our group was planning to use the road that went through Botan. When we finally reached Haftanin, it was the beginning of September. The senior who was responsible for our passage into Turkey informed us, "Your group is too large. I cannot allow you to cross into Turkey together. We'll have to divide you into two small groups for security reasons. It would be preferable if one group had 12 guerillas and the other, 13." So, according to this new plan, one of the groups will move first and wait for the second group in the Garzan district within Turkey. We were introduced to our local guides, once the planning was complete. The guides informed us that the first group would set off that night. We were told to walk on foot until the Turkish-Iraqi border and then get on trucks to cross into Turkey.

Our guides were all peasants who were registered in the village protection system. As I mentioned before, the organization had not carried out any missions against the rangers since 1996. The organization had established close contact with each village that was registered in the protection system. Those Kurdish rangers were still serving the Turkish security forces but only on paper. Their weapons were from the Turks, but they were not using the weapons to raid us as they did in the old days and, in fact, had secretly begun working for the organization. Those rangers would inform us when the Turkish security forces were planning to carry out missions against us. The peasants would notify us about which regions would be affected by the mission, how many soldiers would take part, what kind of weapons would be used, and how long the operation would last. They would tell us every single detail. Thus, the organization no longer forced the ranger villages to stop what they were doing. In previous years, peasants who enrolled in this system would be considered traitors by the organization. This invaluable information would have been impossible to get without the help of the rangers. It was especially crucial for me and the guerillas that the border villages were enrolled in the ranger system. They provided a great advantage on a regular basis and were a huge relief for the times we needed to cross into Turkey.

The first group was to cross into Turkey from Hakkari, on the Iranian side, and my group was to cross from Şırnak, on the Botan side. After the first group left, my group stayed in Haftanin for an entire week. The other groups that had been waiting in Haftanin, before our arrival, had been recently sent. As I said, there had to be a certain interval of time between the groups leaving for Turkey. More specifically, until the group that left from Haftanin reached Botan, the group waiting at Haftanin was not allowed to cross into Turkey. Similarly, when the group in Botan reached Gabar, another group waiting in Botan was allowed to move toward Gabar. The movement of the guerillas within Turkey followed this strict, systematic guideline.

While my group was waiting in Haftanin, Comrade Abbas (Duran Kalkan) informed us, "Deniz, your group might not be able to make it north in time. Winter is coming shortly, and you must prepare yourself for this scenario!" I was disappointed and told them that something like that was unacceptable. I would go north whatever it took. As soon as Duran Kalkan left Haftanin, I contacted the guides and told them that they would immediately guide us north. "Comrade, the other group hasn't yet arrived in Botan. What you are asking us to do is against the rules of the organization. It is not only a risk but can also leave us in the lurch," they said. I strongly insisted, and they were finally convinced. We all set off under the cover of darkness, without notifying the regional command.

I got a strange feeling while crossing the Turkish border. Because I had stayed in the south for a long time, my knowledge on how the security forces were positioned, which roads they were using, and where the road control posts were located was all outdated. The three local guides were with us to show us through these unfamiliar areas. It is hard to understand what I am trying to say unless you have been to the Iraqi-Turkish border. The mountains are high and intertwined, and there is not even a single road. You can easily get lost if you are not careful. There were also some specific places, located near the cross-sections of Iran, Iraq, and Turkey, where you could be in the three different countries within a matter of steps. There were some territories where no one was sure whether they were a part of Turkey, Iraq, or Iran. The comrades would sometimes make jokes. "I stood guard in the lands of three different states today."

In addition to the difficulties of the terrain, there were many military posts across the border. We sometimes had to walk very close to these posts, since there was no alternative route. We were so close to them that the distance between the Turkish soldiers and ourselves would sometimes be less than 200 meters. Also, it was no longer like the old days. The soldiers now had projectors that would light everything up as bright as day, so we had to cross into Turkey before the soldiers turned them on, or we would have been easily noticed.

The Kurdish guides traveling with us were highly experienced, since they also worked with the Turkish soldiers as rangers. They knew what time the projectors were turned on, how many thermal cameras the military posts had, which direction the cameras would survey, and many other details. One of the guides was extremely knowledgeable on these issues. He had worked alongside the Turkish soldiers for quite some time, and even protected them from us at one time! Yet, here he was leading our group on this trip.

If I was not mistaken, we were just about to cross into Turkey at a point close to the Gülyazı Turkish military battalion (Roboski in Kurdish). Suddenly, it became very bright all around us. I turned to the experienced ranger and said, "Comrade, what are we going to do now? The soldiers will definitely notice us if we continue to walk under this light." He replied, "Do not worry, comrade. I will take care of it now." He talked with the other rangers and then left me alone with the remaining 12 guerillas. We had a smoke break and before we even finished our second cigarette, all the projectors were turned off and it was again pitch black. The two remaining guides said, "Hurry up, we need to pass the military post as quickly as possible!" We walked right under the Gülyazı Military Post, and, since it was dark, none of the soldiers noticed us. We had not walked 500 meters from the place, when the projectors were turned on again.

To our luck, other local rangers were guarding those projectors. Our guide, who had left us during the cigarette break, visited those rangers and asked them to turn off the lights for ten minutes, so that we could pass unnoticed. The local ranger guards told the soldiers, "There was an electrical short on the electricity unit. Some of the breakers may have gone bad, and we will fix it soon."

This is my personal view, meaning that I do not have concrete evidence to support what I am about to say from this specific incident, but I have heard similar things from other ranked comrades. The Turkish soldiers probably noticed we were passing through that area even with the lights off. However, they did not want to mess with us. Even if they did not notice us in the dark, they surely must have in the morning. We were walking on an earthen path when we passed under the military post, so our shoe prints must have been visible. Whether they noticed them or not, they never sent a team to track us down. I not only experienced this first hand, but also have heard it from many other comrades; it is probably not a coincidence. The fighting near the border posts was really just a sham. We had scratched the soldiers' back, and they had scratched ours. This still goes on in the region.

In fact, turning a blind eye to one another was quite common between the years of 1994 and 1996. Each military post had a certain perimeter that was a border for their safety. It was usually a circle with a 300-meter radius around the post, and we were fine as long as we did not cross into that circle. The soldiers would see us traveling with 100 guerillas, and they did nothing, as long as we kept outside of their perimeter. As a result, we were very cautious about it. There was a lie that the soldiers and guerillas fought with each other all the time. Not so. Both groups were sick of fighting, and that is why we tried to avoid contact, as much as possible.

Here is a story that I personally witnessed. While we were patrolling within our territory in Bitlis, in 1994, a Turkish military post commander from the Mutki district contacted us via radio. "Fellas, do not cross into my area, and I promise I will not carry out missions against you in the countryside. Do whatever you want in other areas. I do not care! But do not carry out any attack within the area under my responsibility." One of our guerilla commanders replied to him, "Okay, we will not! However, you will withdraw your ambush teams back to your military post. We will never lay siege to your post, no matter how many soldiers you have there, as long as you do not carry out any mission against us!" The military commander accepted our terms. "It's a deal! You scratch my back, and I'll scratch yours!" Even back then, the soldiers were sick of fighting and losing their friends, just as we guerillas were. We also encountered a similar situation in Lice, Diyarbakır. The military squadron leader in Lice informed us, "I do not care what you do in other districts, but I will not touch you as long as you cause no trouble to me here!" The psychology has always been like that, and it will continue to stay the same.

Another thing that caught my attention was that we could not see a single Turkish soldier outside when the Turkish Supreme Military Council meetings were to take place. None of the military commanders would plan or carry out missions close to the months of August and December. The meetings were held twice a year to hand out new promotions and assignments. The guerillas would be greatly relaxed and free in the months of June, July, October, and November because of those meetings. Military commanders were all aware that the smallest mistake during a mission carried out close to those months could affect their promotions and assignments to the higher positions. For example, let's assume that a commander carried out a mission against us in September 2015 and lost five soldiers in the battle. Since the Supreme Military Council would have already been held in August 2015, those losses would fall off the agenda until the next meeting. Nevertheless, if the same losses occurred in July 2015, that commander would be the main topic of discussion at the Supreme Military Council meeting, since it would be held shortly after the incident. The organization was well aware of this situation. We knew we would have a free hand prior to these meetings. The military posts would not intervene during those months, even if they captured our image and found our location through their advanced techniques. The military commanders would never allow even the smallest risk, that could potentially spoil their career goals.

Interestingly, we had a similar situation within the organization. None of the guerilla commanders wanted to carry out missions close to when the Supreme Guerilla Conference was going to take place for the same reason as the Turkish military commanders. No one wanted to be the main topic of discussion at the meeting. If your failure became part of the agenda, the seniors would mark your copybook, and your future would be finished. You could even be taken out of the guerilla force and reassigned to mundane activities carried out by civilians. This was one of the heaviest punishments a guerilla could be sentenced. It would have been considered even worse than death.

As I said, the travel from the south to the north was very stressful for me. After we passed by Gülyazı military post, we continued on our walk until morning. Just before sunrise, we decided to rest at a place in the slopes of the Kel Mehmet Mountains. Since we had walked all through the night, everyone fell asleep in the first spot they found. It was around nine in the morning when I heard the sounds of a helicopter and immediately switched on my radio. I wondered if the soldiers were out in the field for a mission. There was not a single conversation to be heard on the channels used by the Turkish military. We certainly could not listen to the talks on the radio anymore, because of encryption, but there was a signal-level indicator on the screen that indicated whether there were any communications going on around you. Therefore, even though we could not listen to their conversations, we could look at the changes of the signal levels and figure out whether they were communicating with each other and whether they were close to us.

The noise was coming from far away, but I was still nervous. I was certain that it was a Skorsky, and not an attack helicopter, and after a while, I was finally able to see it with my binoculars. It was flying a very particular path, which made it seem as if it were looking for something specific. At this point, it was 1:00 p.m. and we were just about to have lunch when I noticed another helicopter. This time, it was a Cobra-type attack helicopter. This made me even more nervous, and I began to think that the Turks had probably noticed us sneak across the border and were trying to locate our position from the air. I went over to one of the guides and asked if they could find out what was going on. "Comrade, there is a road there that goes from the district of Uludere to Beytüşşebap. There is probably a military convoy passing by, and those helicopters are flying over it to provide security." I was incredibly relieved by this explanation. However, I also felt angry with the guide. "You idiot. Why have you not said something about this before when you knew that there was a road over there? I thought they were carrying out an operation."

If I had been familiar with that area, I would not have worried so much about it, because if you have stayed in a place for any length of time, you know every single detail about it—where the military posts are located, where the roads lead, and where you can safely hide. I had never been to the area between Uludere and Beytüşşebap before. I had only seen it on the videotapes that we were required to watch before setting off from headquarters on our journey. The organization had a tradition where each region in Turkey had a civilian camera crew that consisted of five people: a head cinematographer and his or her assistants. Disguised as tourists, these teams would go around their assigned regions to videotape and photograph the terrain—mountains, military posts, police districts, villages, lodging places, caves, and other places, in detail. This was really grueling work. It would take at least four to five months to videotape an entire region within Turkey. The crew had to be extra careful not to be noticed by the security forces, let alone doing the work for which they were there. All of these videotapes and photographs would be delivered to headquarters management to be used for training purposes. For example, let's say that a guerilla force of 50 was to be dispatched to Amed in Turkey in 2006. Every single member of this force must watch the tapes that pertain to the main routes of travel, alternative routes, and important points in the state where they were to be sent. Sometimes, it would take days to record notes and finish watching the tapes. As a guerilla, you had to learn everything about the area of your assignment before you were dispatched there. It was like a pre-reconnaissance.

16

THE TRIP TO AMED

The organization and Turkey came to an agreement on the terms of a ceasefire on the day we reached the Botan Field. Winter was coming, and it rained every day. Dr. Ali was the Botan Field commander, and he wanted to see me personally. "Comrade Deniz, I would like you and your team to stay here for a couple of days. There are things I want to discuss with you," he said. I figured out that he wanted to learn what was going on at headquarters. More specifically, he wanted to know whether the seniors at headquarters were still complaining about him.

I explicitly said to him, "Comrade, as long as you do not revise or change your perspective on the essential points of the organization, you have no chance to survive among us. You will either desert us or change your own lifestyle." He asked me to be more specific. I said, "For instance, issues regarding women." (Dr. Ali was not a person of pure, genuine love. He would use a false love to satisfy his sexual desires. This was clear because he would find a new person to "love" wherever he was assigned. Real lovers cannot forget each other even though years pass. Beyond just himself, he was trying to impose these immoral ideals on everyone. He wanted everyone to have the freedom of sexual intercourse with any woman as long as both sides agreed.)

If a field commander, such as Dr. Ali, were having a sexual relationship with anyone at any time, what would you do if you were a guerilla under his command? Would you not want the same freedom and not be called to account for it since your commander was doing the exact same thing? A guerilla always mimics his or her commander. In fact, Dr. Ali was having his explicit affairs on purpose in order to try and normalize this behavior among his guerillas. For this reason and others I told him that he was way off base. He asked, "Do they criticize me for this at headquarters?" I said, "Comrade, to tell you the truth, you will be put under investigation either this year or next for this immoral behavior! If I were you, I would be more careful and stop that behavior altogether!"

Beyond his forbidden affairs with women, Dr. Ali's skills as a commander were very poor. There had been heavy losses while he was commanding in the field of Botan. In 2006, a company commander was martyred along with his 25 guerillas. Besides that, he had not carried out a successful mission in Botan since he had been assigned there. In the north, all of the states (Erzurum, Garzan, Dersim, Amed, Serhad, and Amanoses) had been actively completing guerilla missions, while there had not even been a single mission carried out against the Turkish security forces in Botan, even though Botan had a guerilla force numbering 400, while the other states had forces numbering somewhere between 80 to 90 people. Additionally, all of the guerillas in Botan were from specially trained forces. There was a noticeable difference in the number of guerillas between the old times and after 2002. We used to have at least 4,000 guerillas in Botan between the years of 1992 and 1993. In line with that policy I mentioned before, the numbers were seriously decreased.

Dr. Ali also had a ridiculous notion that the organization did not need to carry out missions in order to achieve its goals. He thought we should only carry out missions when needed, similar to the Tamil Tigers in Sri Lanka. This was a faulty approach, because the guerillas would weaken as fighters if they did not carry out missions over an extended period of time. They would get used to comfort and quickly forget about the hardships of the guerilla lifestyle. Once they became soft, they would surely begin to argue with each other over silly, mundane things.

I told all of these concerns of mine to Dr. Ali. "Be prepared, comrade! The organization will hold you accountable for incapacitating such a special force." He replied, "I have a response for headquarters." I said, "Comrade Ali, it is your call. I am warning you as a friend. You asked me, and I explained the concerns about you. This is how you are perceived at headquarters. I would be especially careful regarding your approach to women guerillas. Many of your guerillas have already sent complaint reports about your attitude toward women!"

While we were still waiting in Botan, Amed guerilla state management informed us that, "No more guerilla forces should come here this year! We cannot arrange lodging for any newcomers, and the guerilla groups are about to go into their bunkers." It was disheartening news. I did not complain to them because they were right; it was just about to snow. We would leave traces in the snow as we traveled. Even though there was enough lodging capacity, we could not travel to those bunkers because security forces would find us by following our traces on the snow. We would have caused all of the guerillas in the Amed region to be discovered.

With this new development, we continued to stay at the Botan Field. Until new orders arrived, we did not know what to do. Then, when we began our extended stay, we heard that a mid-field commander, Nurettin Sofi, was being called back from the north to the south. Nurettin Sofi once served as headquarters commander, after Bahoz Erdal had been assigned to another duty. Later, we also heard that the Dersim Field commander, Sabri Tendürek, was also summoned back south. A guerilla conference had been scheduled. On their way back, the two high-ranking commanders were instructed to use different routes to increase their safety, even though they were setting off from relatively close locations. If something were to happen to one, the other should at least be saved. The organization had a strict rule: field commanders had to travel alone while they were in the north.

Despite this rule, those two commanders met in a rural area located in Amed. While they were there, they decided to travel together for the rest of the trip. They rationalized their behavior by arguing that they had enough guards around them in case something happened. I encountered them when they stopped in Botan to rest. Nurettin Sofi asked where I was going. "I was supposed to be assigned to Amed, but you said you did not want anyone else there," I answered. He no doubt noticed from the tone of my voice that I was not happy with his decision. He said, "Comrade, we can make an exception for you!" Filled with excitement, I asked how he could make this happen. "You were told that we did not want a group there. Take two guerillas with you, for security purposes, and head there. We desperately need commander-level guerillas in Amed," he said.

That same day, I chose two comrades and set off for Amed through Siirt. I mentioned earlier in my life story that there was a corridor on the Eruh-Pervari line which we opened by allying with Botan forces 12 years ago. It was still open and safe to travel for guerilla forces. It was so strange that the Turkish security forces had not yet returned to the military posts they deserted after our heavy bombardments. We were going to use this corridor first to travel to Garzan and then to Amed. When the three of us reached a point close to the city of Siirt, we got an order via radio to travel somewhere else, to a location in Garzan, where I had previously stayed, more than four years ago. Since it was fall, we traveled during the day, because it was mostly rainy and foggy, and there was no need to travel in the dark of night. It was highly unlikely that we would be noticed by the security forces.

Toward the end of October, we arrived in Şirvan. Nurettin Sofi delivered another order to us, via radio. "Deniz, you should stay where you are for now, because it is almost winter. Also, the command leadership of the Sirvan region is relatively new; all of them having been assigned there in the middle of 2006. They do not know the area well, so you should stay and assist them whenever necessary, since you are familiar with that terrain. I promise that you will pass into Amed in the spring of 2007." I said, "Okay. If I am going to stay here just for the winter, then there is no problem." I was, in fact, very familiar with the area since I had previously worked for a long time there. The guerilla forces of Sirvan had been raided twice by the Turkish security forces during their last two winter camps. Since they had not dug their underground bunkers in safe locations, they left their camps and ran away in the middle of the cold winter season. This is why Nurettin Sofi asked me to stay there and train them to find a secure bunker location.

Life in an Underground Bunker

The Sirvan region force consisted of 22 guerillas, and with the addition of the three of us, the number increased to 25. The north had sensitive rules regarding the structure and composition of underground winter camps. There could be a maximum of 12 guerillas living in a single underground bunker. Normally, eight is the ideal number, but no one would hold you accountable if you placed 12 guerillas in one. Due to this rule, I divided the group in half—one with 12 and the other with 13. Based on my past experiences regarding the Sirvan region, I decided on two locations for the bunkers. One was close to Bitlis, and the other was close to the city of Siirt. It was about a four or five-day walk between the two locations.

Once my planned areas were laid out, a guerilla from the Sirvan force objected, saying, "Comrade Deniz, both of these locations are extremely dangerous and have potential risks. We cannot set up our winter camps there!" I asked, "Why do you think they are risky?" He replied, "The soldiers frequently carry out operations in those areas, making them not secure!" I laughed at him and said, "That is why I am lodging you guys at those two spots. Have an open mind! Would a fighter, whether they are a soldier or guerilla, carefully patrol their immediate surroundings that they see every day? No! What do we guerillas do when we first climb a hill? Do we not carefully reconnoiter the distant location? The soldiers fight using the same mentality we do. Most of the time, they would never check their immediate surroundings, expecting it always to be secure. They automatically assume that the guerillas are not stupid enough to dig underground bunkers under a military post. That is why we will lodge at those two locations, which are in close proximity to the military posts. It does not matter if they carry out missions, while we hide right next to them. We will sit quietly in our bunkers. Our goal is to survive the winter, not fight with them! We will keep our mouths shut and wait still!"

Soldiers often carried out missions trying to detect our bunkers and even sometimes walked just above us. We could easily hear their voices, but they were unaware of our presence. The underground bunkers were 2.5 meters under ground level. We dug that deep for our own safety. After that, we would cover the top of the dug-out area with thick woodpiles. After that, we stretched a thick nylon canvas on top of the parallel wooden sticks to prevent water and snow from leaking into the bunker. This nylon canvas would then be covered with dirt and earth. After that we would put one layer of pebbles on top of the earth and one more layer of dirt and earth on the pebbles. All of those steps made it impossible to detect whether or not there was a bunker under that area. If you stepped on top of the bunker, and jumped as much as you wanted, you would not even feel a bit of movement. It just felt like normal terrain. That's why our bunkers were safe throughout the winter season. The artificial structure looked so natural that no one could figure out if there were a bunker there.

If the number of guerillas was at the maximum of 12, then we built two sleeping quarters in the bunker. The 12 would be split between them. Say we built one of the sleeping quarters in a particular spot. We would then dig a tunnel 5 meters away from that quarter and build the second one in that spot. This allowed there be a tunnel between the two quarters. The sleeping quarters would also be used as classrooms. At the center of the first tunnel, we would dig yet another tunnel, but this one would be 20 meters long. The restroom and bathrooms would be built at the end of this longer tunnel. There would also be a secret exit door next to the restrooms. From one of the two sleeping quarters, we would dig another tunnel of 20 meters near the main entrance of the underground bunker, giving us at least two exit points per bunker.

Finally, from the other sleeping quarters, we would dig a tunnel of 6 meters, ending at our kitchen. There were two wood stoves in the kitchen. We would cook our meals and bake our bread using those stoves. The meals would only be cooked at night since the burning wood would produce smoke. The use of the stove was twofold. It spread warmth in the bunker, and we could cook our meals for the next day. Lunch for the following day would be cooked just before sunrise, and kept for that afternoon. During the daylight hours, we would heat our meals with propane gas powered burner stoves.

Life was hard underground. We were definitely not allowed to use the wood stove to heat the bunkers unless there was rain, snow, or fog, because the security forces could detect our location from the smoke. During the 1990s, the number of guerilla forces in the north was quite large and they would not always stay in the bunkers throughout the entire winter. Every once in a while, we would go outside and train in the open air. Since our numbers were large, we would be able to fight the security forces if they detected us while we were outside. But, as I mentioned several times before, the number of guerillas in the north was dramatically reduced after the year 2000. There were only ten to 12 guerillas per bunker. We would not dare leave the bunkers, since we could not fight against the security forces with only 12 guerillas. All of the organization's privacy rules had to be obeyed because of this lack of numbers, or we would have been sitting ducks for the Turks. Several times, we would see large numbers of Turkish security forces pass close to our bunker. If we had wanted to, we could abruptly kill them all without losing a single guerilla. However, our actions would reveal our bunker location to the security forces, so, no matter what happened, we would do nothing but wait quietly until winter was over.

Constructing an underground bunker was an artful work. If you were not experienced in understanding the essentials of building a bunker with things like ventilation, you would have a hard time living in that bunker during the winter. For instance, if the restrooms were built at the same level or lower than the sleeping quarters, then you could not sleep because of the stinking odor. The restrooms had to be built higher than the other rooms, so the smell would rise away from our quarters. Besides that, the long tunnel of 20 meters that led to the restrooms should not be dug in a straight line. If you dug it in a zigzag pattern, then you would have neither the stinking odor nor any other discomfort. As

I said, the inexperienced guerillas would often build their bunkers but disregard this small, but important detail. If they did build it incorrectly, they would sometimes have to build a new, higher restroom in the middle of the winter season.

Another significant detail that we had to take into account while constructing bunkers was the need for fresh water for the entire winter. There must be a fountain or fresh water source, no further than within a 300-meter perimeter of the underground bunker. We would supply our water needs from these water resources though pipes buried under the ground. The militants would supply the pipes from local cities and installing them underground benefited us in two ways. The security forces would not notice them nor would the water freeze from the cold temperatures. If we had no choice but to build our bunkers in an area with no fresh water resource, then we had to supply our water needs by melting snow.

There were also two other stoves in each sleeping quarter in order to heat the rooms. Additionally, there was a TV in one of the quarters for training purposes. We used a Honda brand power generator for the TV, which was really useful, because it was fairly quiet and could easily supply our electricity needs throughout winter. Similar to the tunnel we built for the restrooms, we would build another tunnel of similar length for our power generator room. The only difference between a restroom and a power-generator room was the tiny window for air ventilation. The gas that came out of the generator was highly poisonous. If you forgot to leave an open space in the walls of the generator room, the gas could potentially leak into the sleeping quarters and perhaps kill the guerillas. We generally used the generators during the night. We did not need to use lights in the bunker during the day, since we had small windows the size of a coin, in the ceiling of each room, and the daylight would leak into our rooms through those tiny windows. When we noticed movement through the signal changes on our radio, one of us would immediately go out and close all those tiny windows, including the space left for power generator ventilation, with dirt and bushes.

A year later, during the 2007 to 2008 winter camp, we encountered a life-threatening situation regarding power generator use. One night, I was feeling very tired after training and told my comrades that I was going to bed early. They said, "Okay comrade, have a good rest. We are going to watch a movie tonight." The women guerillas also came to the men's sleeping quarters to watch the movie with them. Everyone was gathered in one quarter, and it was so loud that I could not sleep. I decided to rest in the women's quarters until the movie was finished. I guess it was 7:00 or 8:00 p.m. when I left the men's quarters.

Before I left, I told the male comrades, "I'm going to sleep in the women's quarters until you're finished with the movie. Come and wake me so that the women can sleep in their quarters." The ventilation was good where the women stayed, and the water supply was right there as well. I woke up by myself around 11:30 p.m. and thought the movie was still playing, since no one had come to waken me yet. I stood and became dizzy. To my chagrin, the running generator had caused poisonous gas to spread throughout the bunker, and every room was filled with gas, because the generator's ventilation had been blocked by heavy snow.

After thoroughly washing my face, I went to the men's quarters to check on my comrades. All of them were lying quietly in front of the TV. I immediately turned off the power generator and cleared the snow that was piled in front of the ventilation areas. After that, I went to the kitchen and filled a large cup with water. Using a piece of cloth, I wiped all their faces. Two of them awoke and said that they were going outside to breathe fresh air. I said, "Don't you dare!" They were clearly novices and had never dealt with gas poisoning before. "If you go out now and expose yourself to fresh air, you will lose consciousness again, and this time it will last even longer! Just wait for a while. You will need to go out slowly."

While I was still taking care of the other comrades, one of them ignored my warnings and rushed outside the bunker through the emergency exit located at the restroom. He fainted as soon as went through the door and lay unconscious until morning. The next day, we did not carry out any training sessions. As you can see, those power generators could pose more of a risk to us than even the security forces, because gas poisoning was a very sneaky death! You would not even feel it. Fortunately, I was experienced with these issues, since I had encountered similar incidents a couple of times before.

Back during the 2006 to 2007 winter period, we built two bunkers at those strategic locations I mentioned earlier. The camp where I was staying was in the foothills. The Turkish security forces regularly carried out land operations in the months of December, January, February, March, and April. During these operations, they would regularly search the field to destroy underground bunkers. They had walked right above our bunker many times. I sometimes was even able to hear their conversations by turning my ear toward the ceiling. They would check everywhere during those search operations, but none of the soldiers thought to check under the very ground where they walked. As I said, even the soldiers did not suspect that we would have bunkers so close to their military posts. It made no sense to them that the guerillas would come and build bunkers right in the foothills, close to a military post. I am sure the soldiers would even deny that claim today, but it was true. As the well-known Chinese philosopher Sun Tzu once said, "Pretend inferiority and encourage your enemy's arrogance."

Now, you might wonder how we were able to build such complicated bunkers right under the foothills of a military post in the woods. You might ask, "Did anyone notice you?" No one noticed us because we only worked on the bunkers at night, and we were extremely quiet. We did not even use axes to cut the big trees for the roof of the bunkers but used handsaws instead. Besides that, the season to construct a bunker was extremely important. It had to be before the leaves fell from the trees, since we needed cover.

Toward the middle of November, 2006, we finished building our winter camp and carrying all of our things into the bunker. After that, we retreated to the mountainous areas, since it was still too early to stay there. We entered the bunker in the beginning of December, 2006, just before it began snowing. Everything from shoes to clothes, and food to beverages was available in the bunker. There was rice, beans, wheat, cheeses, olives, tomato paste, oil, flour, honey, fried meat, various kinds of canned food, and even treats, such as chocolates, to supply us until spring. Each camp had one person who was in charge of provisions supply. He or she would prepare a list of supplies, before we entered into our winter camp. They would estimate the quantity of supplies according to the number of guerillas. After that, the provisions would be supplied by the civilian militants who lived nearby in the cities. We would pay special attention to the storage of two things in particular: sugar and salt. They were special because they could easily get spoiled by moisture. We kept them in large metal bowls to try and prevent that from happening. In some of the bunkers, we would also have a tailor. The tailor would sew two pairs of guerilla uniforms for each of our comrades throughout the winter season.

Supply of Explosive Substances

During 2006 and 2007, when we arrived in the Sirvan region, I encountered a serious problem before we even entered our bunkers. The local guerilla forces of Sirvan had set land mines along every possible route that the Turkish security forces might use. They even insisted on planting mines around our underground bunker locations, but, no matter how hard they tried, I would not let them. If a mine exploded near our bunker, the security forces would easily figure out we were hiding close by.

I asked these local guerilla forces what kind of mines they used and where exactly they had planted them. They told me they acquired a type of fertilizer from a company. I was informed that this fertilizer was also used in the production of explosives, so TNT was no longer needed. This fertilizer was given to some construction companies with special permission from the state for the purpose of preparing explosives. More specifically, the construction companies used this fertilizer to blow up rocks while building roads or tunnels in the area. It was red in color. According to the label on the packages, it stayed fresh for six months. If it were not used within six months, it would lose its explosive effect. Because of this time constraint, it was not as useful as TNT for the guerillas. I asked the Sirvan forces if they could figure out a method to solve the six-month expiration problem. They said, "Comrade, we can indeed fix the problem. It is simple! We just melt the fertilizer to keep the explosive substance active for more than six months. It actually lasts for years if you melt it and keep it in that form!" I asked them if they had tested that method or if they were just guessing. They said, "Yes, we have tested it before." They even showed it to me. One of them started a fire in the woods, placed a metal sheet on top of the fire, and then a can on the sheet. Before the can was heated, one of the guerillas poured the fertilizer into it, so that the fertilizer was never in direct contact with the fire. In less than ten minutes, the fertilizer completely melted and turned into a liquid form. The guerillas told me that they would either pour the liquid substance into a tomato sauce can or into a large oil can, depending on the size of the target they wanted to blow up.

During the demonstration, they poured it into a small can. In less than five minutes, the liquid turned into a solid that was as hard as concrete. During the hardening process, the guerillas placed a stick in the middle of the can to prepare a spot for the detonator igniter. One of the guerillas stirred the liquid continuously to prevent it from sticking in the middle of the hard mass. When the fertilizer finished solidifying, he pulled the stick out and placed a detonator igniter in the open spot. There you go! You now have an explosive as strong as TNT. I had never witnessed an explosive being made from fertilizer before. Of course, we had used another kind of fertilizer, ammonium nitrate, but it was not as powerful as TNT. I asked these guerillas how many kilograms of that fertilizer they had in their capacity. They said, "We have around 300 kilograms." I asked, "Why did you not acquire even more of it? We could have shipped it to other guerilla forces!" They replied, "Comrade, this company was not able to supply us with more, without the risk of being recognized by the security forces. It is a difficult to acquire substance, and is only sold with special permission. Besides, the security forces have to be present during its use to make sure that it is not being used for anything other than construction."

The comrades had acquired the fertilizer from a construction company owned by a former mayor of the city of Siirt. I believe that back in 2003, he had even been a deputy but had resigned later. Because of his resignation, the general elections in the city of Siirt had to be repeated, and current President Erdoğan joined the Turkish General National Assembly as a deputy instead of him. If I am not mistaken, his name was Mervan Gül.

There was a high-quality, fresh-water resource in the city of Bitlis. Mervan Gül's construction company had won the bidding, and they were going to use pipelines to transfer this water from Bitlis to the small district of Tillo, in Siirt. This district was the home of President Erdoğan's wife, Emine Erdoğan. All of those pipes were laid down in a district that had less than a couple thousand people, just for the relatives of Emine Erdoğan. The company knew very well that they had to pay taxes to the organization for this construction work. If they did not pay, we would not let them do the job. Before we went into our winter camp, I traveled to the construction site to see what was going on. There were concrete pipes that had a radius of at least 2 meters. I wanted to talk to someone in charge to figure out whether we could get more fertilizer from them. The son of Mervan Gül met me, and I asked, "Comrade, how and where can we get this fertilizer?"

"Comrade, I cannot really help you get more of it. Let's say we bought a 100 kilograms of the fertilizer. We have to use that exact amount in the place that was indicated on the sales agreement. The security forces and the soldiers come and check the quantity before we use it. Also, we use the explosives under their control, and only after they make sure that it is used on its predetermined area." I could not push him further on the issue. I said, "Okay, I understand. If you do come across some extra let us know. We will buy it from you!" The organization was supposed to receive taxes totaling $150,000 from the construction work. I thought that we could reduce the amount if we could receive some fertilizer in return. It would be very profitable for us, because a single kilogram of TNT was ten times more expensive than the same amount of this fertilizer, even though they had the same explosive impact.

Before we arrived, the Sirvan guerilla forces had planted mines, using this fertilizer, at almost every point in the region. I wanted to see the exact locations of the mines before we entered our bunkers, and noticed that they had acted stupidly. They had planted mines on the road that had been built for the water pipeline project. I said, "Comrades, I can see the reason for planting mines on the routes that the soldiers use, but why did you put mines on the road used by the construction company?" One of them replied, "Comrade Deniz, we noticed that the soldiers accompany the workers when they use those explosives. We thought that we could carry out a mission against those soldiers in the future." I replied, "Are you nuts? That will mean blowing up soldiers close to where you're hiding! Will they not figure out that you are camping nearby? Go and remove the electric circuits from those mines immediately," and they did as I ordered.

I was curious as to how much fertilizer they had used in the mines. They told me that they'd placed four large cans of mines, which equated to almost 80 kilograms. I grew angry when I heard that they had planted four cans at the same spot. "Are you idiots? Why did you plant so much explosive for a single Ford Transit military vehicle? You will go out and remove those mines from the place where you put them. We can use them more efficiently in more than one mission! Do not waste them all for a single mission!" With such a large quantity of explosives, we could easily destroy two fully armored vehicles. The soldiers would actually often use a Ford Transit truck to travel from one spot to another, and that was not even an armored vehicle. We could easily destroy a Ford minibus with only 7 kilograms of explosives. If the soldiers were traveling by car, then 3 kilograms of explosives would be more than enough. For a tank, a single anti-tank mine would be enough to kill the passengers. With a single large can containing 20 kilograms of fertilizer, we could easily prepare three anti-tank mines. So, the local forces of Sirvan had acted foolishly by planting 80 kilograms of mines at a single spot, despite the fact that the organization provided clear guidelines as to what kind of vehicle required how much explosive.

At this point, it was nearly the winter of 2006, and we entered our bunkers a couple days before it began snowing. We wanted to watch TV on the first night, but it had somehow gotten damaged. It seemed like some moisture had gotten to it under the ground. It was an old one with cathode ray tubes, and the screen went black as soon as we switched it on. It would be a terrible winter camp without a working TV. As I mentioned earlier, we camped close to the company that was building the water pipelines. It would take two hours on foot at most to reach their worksite. I asked the comrades, "Was there a TV at that worksite?" They said, "Yes. It was even bigger than ours!" Ours was a small one, of only 37 inches.

I said to three comrades, "Take this money with you and tell the company that they could either sell their TV to us or buy a new one from the city and give it to us." The comrades talked to the manager of the company, and he said, "The workers here watch TV at night. If I take this TV from their rest area and give it to you, some of the workers will wonder what is going on. Not all of the workers are aware that we are in contact with guerillas. But I understand that you are also in need of a TV. What do you suggest we do?" Our comrades told him directly, "Go and buy a new one from the city!" So, the manager went to Bitlis and bought a brand new TV. Early morning of the next day, those three comrades returned to our bunker with a brand new TV.

Besides entertainment, we also needed a TV in the bunker in order to watch the CDs and tapes we received from headquarters. In the old days, we were also allowed to watch TV channels, but that changed after a tragic incident that occurred in 2006. A strict order was given about not watching any live TV channels in the bunkers, throughout the winter period. In 2006, 14 comrades had been martyred in a bunker located between the Kulp district of Diyarbakır and the city of Muş. After this incident, watching live TV channels was banned all over the northern states. Those comrades had hidden two satellite dishes, just outside their underground bunkers, to watch live TV channels during the camp period. One was a TURKSAT, which they needed to watch the Turkish TV channels, and the other was a HOTBIRD, which they needed so they could watch the organization's media outlets all over the world. Their bunker was located on the top of a hill just outside of the city of Muş. One night before the 2006 Nowruz celebrations, one of them walked outside the bunker to adjust the satellite dish positions, so they could acquire a better signal. When the guerilla did that, the soldiers noticed movement up on the hill. They carried out a mission the very same night and killed all of our comrades hiding in the bunker.

Similarly, although much more limited, mobile phones could be used in the northern provinces until the year 2006 when the guerillas were warned not to carry their own mobile phones anymore. The organization even issued a notice stating that those who were seen using a mobile phone or a laptop were going to be prosecuted for being an agent of the enemy. We guerillas were certainly aware that the Turkish security forces could listen to our conversations and detect our location by tracking our smart phone. Indeed, the Interior Minister, during that time, made a public statement. His name was Abdulkadir Aksu, if I am not mistaken. He said during a live TV program, "If we did not listen to the guerillas in Gabar for a full day, the metropolitan cities in Turkey would turn into a pool of human blood." After that live TV broadcast, the organization figured out that the security forces were, in fact, listening to our conversations via smart phones and other electronic devices. Aksu had not used the name of Gabar randomly. Gabar was very important for the organization, since the deployment of the entire special guerrilla forces would be done through Gabar. Also, the guerillas that would be sent to the city centers would be dispatched from Gabar.

Our Bunker Location Revealed

During the winter periods, we placed an antenna on the top of a nearby tree before we entered our bunkers. It was not a huge antenna but just a thin silver colored cable. We had very heavy radios, which weighed close to 10 kilograms. Thanks to those radios and antennae, we were able to learn what was going on outside. During my spare daytimes, and especially at night, I would listen to the radio channels used by the Turkish soldiers. It was either the first or the second day of January, 2007, between 1:30 and 2:00 a.m., when I heard constant noise coming from a radio channel used by the Turks. Since the small radios had better signal coverage in the open air, I grabbed one and headed outside the bunker to figure out what was going on. Because of our experience from years of fighting, we guerillas knew that specific channels would be used by soldiers only when they were carrying out operations in the field. At that time, I noticed that busy communication was happening across almost all of these operation channels. So, I was sure that the soldiers were somewhere close to us.

Even though we were unable to listen to the soldiers because they used encrypted radios, their commanders sometimes communicated with the local Kurdish rangers without encryption—so then, we were able to listen to them. Also, not every single member of a military squad had an encrypted radio, which was a huge advantage to us, because we were able to figure out the positions and plans of the soldiers when a communication was going on between a commander and ranger or a ground guerilla.

I was certain the soldiers were carrying out an operation. Many of the comrades staying with me were unfamiliar with the terrain of the Sirvan region, since they had only been dispatched here since the middle of 2006. Everyone abruptly became nervous. The guerillas were in a panic, discussing among themselves whether or not we should leave the shelter. I told them that we were all going to remain in the bunker and wait for the sunrise. Once the sun was up, I half-opened the emergency exit door and checked our surroundings with binoculars. Soldiers were everywhere, looking high and low for something. While I was watching, one of the mines planted by the Sirvan local guerilla forces exploded. This made me very angry, because it was an extremely foolish idea to plant mines near the winter camp area. Luckily, the soldiers withdrew before finding our bunker location. It was a very stressful day for all of us.

At the beginning of February, 2006, the Turkish military carried out another land operation. Our fears had become real, and, this time, we might really have to leave our bunker. The soldiers were probably sure that there was an underground bunker close by, because of the mine detonation.

I was even more stressed because of some other information that had been delivered to me. I mentioned earlier that I had encountered Nurettin Sofi when I was waiting in the Botan region. There was a guerilla, a squad commander from Pervari, in Comrade Sufi's team of bodyguards. He was present wherever Nurettin Sofi went. When I was just about to leave from Sirvan for Amed, Nurettin Sofi communicated to me via radio, "Deniz, you should stay with the Sirvan force this winter. They are all newbies to the area, and you should help them whenever necessary!" During this conversation, Nurettin Sofi also asked me where I was going to build the underground bunkers for winter. I told him about the two places I already mentioned. I was later informed that only 20 days after this conversation, the close bodyguard of Comrade Sufi, the squad commander from Pervari, surrendered to the Turkish security forces. He had informed the security forces of many secretive details, including our camp locations.

We were told about this leak of information very late. The information obtained from the bodyguard was the reason why Turkish security forces were carrying out a land operation in that area in January. I was confused, because the security forces that I knew carried out operations only twice a year at most—once in the fall just after the leaves fell and in the spring just before the trees sprouted new growth.

Considering all of those problems, I decided it was in our best interest to leave our winter camp. It was a troublesome time for us. How could we safely relocate to another region, without leaving footprints on the snow? Anyway, we left the bunker and I asked everyone to take off their shoes leaving only their socks on. There was a stream 200 meters from our bunker. Stepping on rocks, we walked toward the stream without stepping on the snow or the mud. Since we were not wearing shoes, we did not leave any traces of our passing on the rocks. When we reached the stream, we put our shoes on again and continued our walk in the water. It was icy cold, so it was easier said than done!

We did not get frostbite, because it would occur only if we had walked in snow first. If we entered the water after a long walk on snow, or if we stepped on snow after a long walk in water, then we would get frostbite. Also, not all types of snow would cause frostbite. There was a light, tiny snow that was as shiny as crystal, which would usually fall near the end of February and the beginning of March. This was the most dangerous type of snow for us. It would quickly burn the feet of guerillas, when there had been only a slight contact with water. The snow that fell during the months of December and January would not easily burn our feet.

We walked in the water until we came across a road with which I was familiar. At this point, I divided our group of 13 into two. I remembered from being there, in 1992 and 1993, that there was a cave under the road where we were. Not everyone knew that this cave existed. I am sure that even the security forces are still not aware of the existence of such a hideout. It was just across the Bitlis stream, close to the road. I left seven comrades inside the cave, and said to them, "I want you to hide inside here until further notice. You can do anything other than start a fire for either cooking or heating!" No one could hear them from outside but starting a fire would be very risky. The problem was not the visible smoke, since it would spread and dissipate in the cave, but actually the odor of the fire. It could be easily noticed by search dogs used by the soldiers.

I took the rest of the group with me and climbed to higher terrain to check how the soldiers were positioned around the field. I wanted to figure out what kind of an operation it was. Was it a simple routine search or a planned operation based on intelligence? We watched them for several hours until it got dark. At the end of the day, I was 100 percent sure that it was not a routine military operation. The soldiers were certainly looking for something, and it was probably us. The soldiers camped in the field for approximately two days and then retreated to their headquarters.

Since the soldiers never found our bunker, we went back to it. We would focus heavily on ideological training during our winter camps. I said to my comrades, "We have to speed up the training, since the soldiers will probably carry out another operation to find us. We should complete everything before they arrive so that the winter camp will achieve its purpose." Just as I had guessed, the soldiers returned to the field on February 26, 2006. I said, "We have to desert this bunker permanently. We cannot return here again, as we did before. I do not think the soldiers will stop until they find us." Everybody agreed with me, but there was a problem. It was freezing outside. We had no problem when it came to our food supply, for we could carry the food that we stocked in the bunker, or we could use the secret food storages buried under the ground at several points out in the field. But how could we tackle the cold?

Back in the 90s I had the privilege of being introduced to some caves in the region, but I had not visited them for a long time, and I did not know if they were still a secure place to hide. On the other hand, I also did not want to share their location with these comrades, whom I had met only two or three months ago. Those caves were all perfectly hidden, and their entrances were so small that we had to crawl to get inside. However, once you entered, you would be amazed by their size. Some of them were even as large as a soccer stadium. Approximately 200 guerillas could easily stay inside these caves. Some of them had rooms carved out of the rock. I guess those caves had been used by people as homes in some ancient time. We also would not have to consider heat during the winter, because not only would those caves be warm during the cold season but also cool in the hot summer season. Only mid-level commanders had the privilege to be shown these places. They were kept secret to be used only during a dire situation. If their location was made public to all the guerillas, the organization would not be able to use them again in case one of the guerillas surrendered to the security forces.

On February 26, 2006, the military carried out a land operation, even larger than the previous two. We could see hundreds of soldiers patrolling the field. Some of the comrades became angry with me, saying, "Comrade Deniz, why on earth are we not killing those soldiers while they walk right across from us like sitting ducks?" From this reaction, you could see that they were clearly inexperienced. They did not consider the possible consequences of such an abrupt attack on the soldiers. In a sense, they were right; occasionally, large groups of soldiers would travel right across us comfortably not on guard. I still do not know why those soldiers were so confident of their safety. They walked one behind the other, just like sitting ducks, without leaving any space for security. Just three of us could easily have killed them all with Kalashnikovs. However, it would be dangerous for us later, because there were hundreds of other soldiers in the field, and eventually they would kill us.

If they had noticed us, the soldiers would lay siege to the area and destroy us with cobra attack helicopters, heavy rocket bombardments, and LAW flamethrowers. They would not even try to capture us alive. In the end, even if we had killed 50 soldiers, all 13 of us would be dead as well. Since the guerilla forces of Sirvan were composed of relative newbies, they were inexperienced on these issues. No matter how far they pushed me to begin a mission to kill those sitting ducks, I rejected their offer. "You will take revenge for the hardships, cold, and pain to which you are exposed when you have more opportunity to disguise yourself and burst out of the trees—when you have the upper hand in the battle! But not now... You must learn to be patient!"

Mereto Massacre

The last operation went on for nearly a week. If I remember correctly, it was in the month of March when we abandoned our underground bunker permanently. We received news that Apo had been poisoned in prison. Once my comrades heard this, they boiled with vengeance. Some of them said, "How can the government kill our leader in a time of peace and negotiation?" I was not able to share their feelings for vengeance any longer. They were pushing me to organize a mission against the Turkish soldiers in retaliation. On March 4, as soon as the security forces withdrew from the region, we returned to our bunker but not to stay. It had been 15 days since we had last taken a shower. Everyone showered, packed their stuff, and we left the bunker on March 6.

The first thing I did when we left was hand over our heavy radio to the region commander, since we had to walk on foot from one region to another until the end of fall. It weighed nearly 10 kilograms, and we only used it to listen to instructions that were delivered by headquarters management, while we camped for the winter. The communication time was pre-determined: every day from 11:00 to 11:30 a.m.

Since I was scheduled to pass into the state of Amed in the spring of 2007, I decided to teach the guerilla force of Sirvan about the details of the area. Around that time, we heard from the radio news that security forces had killed seven guerillas and captured one in the Kulp district of Diyarbakır. A day later, headquarters sent a message, via radio, to the groups of guerillas within Turkey: "A group of comrades has been martyred in Kulp. Someone tell us which state has authority over this group!" Kulp is a region located in a buffer zone. If the news were accurate, this guerilla force could be under the authority of either the state of Amed or the State of Garzan.

No one responded to headquarters management that day, but three days later, Bahoz Erdal sent a new message over the radio. "We were able to acquire more detail regarding the incident. It occurred in the state of Garzan. In fact, one of our own people martyred those seven comrades. Afterward, he surrendered himself to the security forces!" Apparently, the Turkish media outlets consciously misled the public just to get credit for those seven deaths, but there was something still wrong. There were supposed to be nine guerillas in Garzan, not eight. Seven of them had been martyred and one of them had surrendered, so there was still one unaccounted for. Where was the last one? The Garzan state commander said via radio, "We have verified that those seven comrades were from our Dorşin region. One of our comrades probably managed to run away from this massacre. However, we still do not know where he might be."

Since the terrain was still covered in snow, none of the guerilla forces would leave their bunkers to search for Hayri, the lost comrade. We still did not know for sure if he was alive. The headquarters management in Zaho delivered another message, "None of the forces should act on their own to find Hayri. We will try to find him through our civilian comrades in the region." The headquarters had two civilian comrades travel and search the villages around Dorşin. Hayri was found hiding in a small village. Out of curiosity, the comrades asked him, "How could one person kill seven guerillas by himself?" Hayri then told them everything:

"The code name of the person who was responsible for the massacre and who had surrendered himself to the security forces was Mereto. His real name was Galip. I was on guard the night it happened, and Mereto was going to guard after me. Because we were hiding in a three-story cave with one entrance, one person was more than enough to stand guard. The opening was located at the top of the cave. One person would guard the entrance, while the remaining guerillas rested in an area located on the second floor. We would not use the third floor, under normal circumstances. After my guard shift was over, I woke Mereto and lay down next to the other comrades. After laying there a short time, I realized morning was approaching and knew that our comrades would awaken, make a lot of noise, and keep me from sleeping. With this in mind, I decided to go to the third floor to sleep.

I was nearly asleep when I heard gunshots. I turned the torch on but could not see anything. Mereto had gone around and collected the comrades' weapons while they slept. I was the only one who was awake during this, because I had just finished my guard duty. There was a hidden exit on the bottom floor of the cave where I was staying of which Mereto was not aware. Even before we camped for the winter, we were suspicious of Mereto, because of his strange behavior and attitude. We even thought that he might be an agent working for the enemy. Indeed, we even had a meeting to discuss whether we should arrest him or not. Nevertheless, our squad commander told us, 'The region commander isn't here, and it would be rude for us to arrest Mereto without the commander knowing. Besides that, we were already low in number. If we arrest him now, then we will need to watch him nonstop for the rest of the winter season. Let's wait for spring.' The commander had shown everyone except Mereto the hidden exit location in case he was untrustworthy and tried something. This exit was located at the end of a tunnel that was nearly 200 meters in length.

When I heard the gunshots that night, I wanted to get my weapon from the second floor before I left through the secret exit on the bottom floor. I was sure that the security forces had nothing to do with the shooting, because it was the middle of night. It would be unusual for security forces to lay a siege in the middle of the night, in the winter. I came down to the second floor and noticed that all of the comrades were shot. There was blood everywhere. A comrade named Behzat, the group commander in charge of us, was lying there heavily wounded but still able to talk. 'Hayri, Mereto shot us all. Take all of the secret documents and radio codes that I have. Flee through the tunnel I showed you and inform our leaders that Mereto committed this heinous act.' I said, 'Comrade, I can carry you out. I do not think you are seriously wounded. Let's go together.' He replied, 'Do not push me, Hayri. Take the documents and get out of here.' It was then that I noticed he was covered in blood from the waist down. When I was just about to leave, Mereto started shooting down from the third floor. He probably wanted to make sure that everyone was dead. During that barrage, I was shot in the leg. I was able to reach this village with my wounded leg and was waiting for the organization to find me."

An Uncertain Journey

On May 19, 2007, I set off from the Sex Cuma district of Bitlis to the state of Amed. Once you pass through the city of Batman, there is a rest area about 10 kilometers from the city of Bitlis. I was acquainted with the owner of a restaurant there, so after sunset, I sent two of my comrades there to tell him, "Send my regards to the owner. Ask him to send enough food for our group." The comrades returned with their arms full of bags that contained kebabs and other types of food that we had not eaten in a long time. We stayed there that night and set off the next day.

I was traveling with a guerilla force from Mutki. My bodyguard and I were going to separate from them after we reached Mutki. Once in the city, I hired two local guides that were familiar with the terrain of the region and set off for Muş on May 24, 2007. The last time I had been in that area was in 1994 and 1995, 12 years previously. I hired the two guides because I did not know what kind of precautions the security forces were taking; which roads they used, or where they were hiding. At that time, I had a long beard and shaved head, and I walked slowly with the help of a cane. We traveled day and night walking next to the road. It was May 27 at around 6:00 p.m. when we reached a certain point. (It usually became dark around 8:00 p.m. during that season.) The ground where we were standing was covered in footprints of soldiers. From the looks of them, the footprints were new, probably only a day old.

I told the guides, "Look, we are going in the direction that the security forces went before us. Those footprints are new." After I said that, I began to smell the odor of smoke which made me even more nervous. I asked the guides if shepherds stayed in the area during this season. One of the guides sniffed the air and said, "Comrade, I do not smell smoke." I replied, "You may not, but there is a smoke odor in the air. We need to be extra careful. It's either the peasants burning wood or the soldiers."

When we continued on we left 15 meters between each of us as a security measure. On the way, I stopped and drank from a small pond that had formed from melting snow. While I drank, the guides continued walking. The distance increased to more than 40 meters between us. Suddenly, I noticed what looked to be three people on the side of the road. I wondered if I were imagining them, so I looked more closely and carefully again. I was right. Not only were there three people there, but they had weapons in their hands and were targeting our guides. I immediately began firing on them, and they returned fire in my direction. It seemed we were stuck in the middle of an ambush and had not been aware of it.

We later learned that the ambush was carried out by Turkish soldiers and the rangers of the Has village of Muş. We started retreating. The soldiers probably thought I was an old guerilla because of my long beard and cane. I also was not as fast as the other comrades. At some point, I had to stop and rest for a second, and I thought I had lost the soldiers. The two guides were looking toward us at a distance of about 50 meters. One of them suddenly shouted, "Lay down immediately!" When I stopped to rest, I had laid my back on the ground. When I raised my head to look back, I saw a soldier targeting us with a flamethrower. I did not even have time to fire at him with my weapon. Luckily, the soldier could not hit us because our guides began to shoot at him. My bodyguard and I stood up and again began running.

We ran for half an hour until we reached a valley. The terrain was open, without a single tree or rock behind which to hide. It was clear that we could not flee the soldiers by running, so I decided to stop the guides and the guard, and said, "Our only chance of survival is to run toward the soldiers. One way or another, we have to pass into the wooded area behind them. We can conceal ourselves there. If we do not do that, we will all die here!"

My plan ended up working. We ran into the woods and waited, completely still, until it got dark. It was pitch black at around 8:30 p.m. On one side of us, there were soldiers still searching. On the other, there was a military battalion post. Additionally, a military aircraft was dispatching even more soldiers into the field for the search operation. We were stuck. We could not wait where we were any longer, so we began walking again not knowing where we were headed. We walked until sunrise. We had probably avoided the soldiers, but we were also exhausted, and I said to my comrades, "We are all tired, so we should find a safe place and rest for now. Once we figure out where we are, we will continue traveling in the afternoon."

It was around five in the morning. I checked the terrain, and saw a field with long grasses in it, but the grass was very thin. The security forces would easily detect that someone had hidden in the grasses if we slept there. So, I told my comrades to sleep on the side of the field. At around 10:00 a.m. I woke up to the sound of shouting. There was a village 200 meters from where we were resting. Someone from the village was shouting, but we could not understand him because he was speaking in Arabic. We could not figure out if the villager had seen us and was telling the peasants something about us. It was in our best interest to wait until there was movement toward us from the village. We waited, hiding inside the tall, thin grass until sunset. We would not have been so badly frightened if we had known whether or not we were to die soon. The uncertainty was more stressful. We waited for hours without knowing what was going on around us.

We set off again when it got dark. We were still walking without knowing where we were going. We began following a path in the woods. There were so many trees that it was very hard to walk without hitting them in the darkness. I turned to my comrades and said, "Let's rest here for the night. We will check our surroundings and continue traveling when the sun rises." Everyone agreed with me. We thought we could have a good rest where we were, without being noticed. We had been walking for the last four days and our feet were in extreme pain because we had not had time to wash our socks. We all took off our socks and washed our feet and the socks with soap and water. Everyone slept well that night. Around one in the afternoon, we heard gunshots that sounded like a Kalashnikov-brand weapon. The noise came from nearby, but we could not see anything because of the thick woods. Again, we stayed where we were and waited for the sun to set. Near midnight we set off again.

Establishing Peace with the Village Protection Guards

There was a military post called Üçevler in a district of the city of Muş. We passed near it and reached the guerilla forces of Muş where the Garzan state guerilla commander was waiting. He was still discouraged because of the incident in that cave in Dorşin and asked me, "Comrade Deniz, would it not be better if you stayed here in Garzan?" I replied, "Comrade, you are correct, but I have been assigned to work in Amed. I have to go there as soon as possible." I stayed there for a few more days and while I was there, I received a message from central headquarters that Commander Bahoz Erdal wanted to talk to me. I figured out that the state commander and guerilla forces of Garzan had spoken with Bahoz Erdal to convince me to stay in their region. I could easily reject the offer from the state commander, but it was much more difficult for me to convince the ground guerillas, who were aware of this weakness of mine and thus knew that I would not ignore their offer. So, I accepted and stayed in Garzan, even though I wanted to be in Amed.

Although I agreed to stay, there was still a problem. The administrative level of Garzan had no open positions. How could I be assigned a position when there was no place for me to be? When they said they would relocate someone else to open a space for me, I said to them, "Assign me under one of those comrades as a consultant. I will do whatever the organization asks me to do, but do not relocate anyone because of me!" They rejected my offer and a comrade named Azad was dismissed from his duty, so that I could be assigned to his position. Azad was highly disappointed because of this. The fighting season of spring had just begun and nothing serious had happened yet. There was nothing on his record indicating he should be dismissed. As soon as I heard what happened, I spoke with Azad. He was from the city of Van in Turkey. I said, "Comrade, my authority is yours. We will act as co-leaders if necessary. You keep the money and codes, because we will govern this region together." When commanders handed their positions over to their successors, they would give them all their money, codes, and secret documents regarding the organization. I did not take any of them, because that would have demoralized Azad even more.

In fact, if I had no choice but to stay somewhere in the state of Garzan, Bitlis was the most appropriate place for me, since I had been there on duty in the past. I knew next to nothing about Muş. When I informed Garzan state management about this, they told me to wait for a while, because they were going to task me with a different type of guerilla work. Before too much time had passed, I was notified that I would be in charge of handling the organization's relations with the rangers in Muş. There were too many villages registered in the village protection system in Muş. I was charged with opening intimate dialogue with the rangers to convince them to stop attacking the guerilla forces in the region. The organization was willing to accept any terms offered by the rangers for peace to be established. Our orders stated that we were not to attack them even if they refused to quit the village protection system. But those terms only held as long as they did not fight against us or help the Turkish security forces fight against us. The state commander of Garzan said to me, "Deniz, your task of convincing the rangers to accept our peace terms is even more important for us than ten successful guerilla missions that you might achieve in the region."

The bilateral relations of the organization with the rangers were getting better each year throughout the Turkish territories. The organization had not carried out any armed missions against the rangers since 1996, unless, of course, we were provoked. After the year 2000, the organization was in a very close relationship with many of the ranger villages in Turkey. We would meet regularly with these rangers and perform lots of give and take. We had gotten so close to each other that some ranger villages were even willing to quit the village protection system and hand their guns back over to the Turkish state. The organization asked them to continue what they had been doing. We would speak to them and say, "Do not quit the village protection system. If you do, you cannot graze your animals on the summer ranges or, easily travel in the region. You will have to leave and immigrate to the big cities. For now, you are at least being paid on a regular basis and you have no restrictions on using the summer ranges. You will lose all of those privileges if you quit."

Each year, from the beginning of spring until the end of fall, the Turkish Gendarme forces, or rural police, would apply a grazing ban in eastern Anatolia. This ban would especially hit the regions of Şırnak, Bingöl, Erzurum, and Garzan. The ban prevented Kurdish farmers from letting their animals graze in the pastures. Of course, the villages that were registered in the protection system were exempt from this restriction. The ranger villages would freely graze their animals on those pastures, while their fellow Kurds would be banned because they were unwilling to cooperate with the state against the organization.

Since I was now going to work in Muş, the senior commanders and I had to plan administrative changes in order to control the area more effectively. The first thing we did was to divide the Garzan province into two parts, east and west, as far as administrative control was concerned. I was assigned as commander of the east. According to this new planning, Muş, Kulp, Sason, Batman, and Mutki were assigned under the control of the commander of the west. Tatvan, Bitlis city center, and Siirt were to be under my control in the east. This was the area with which I was tasked to establish better relations with the rangers. There were too many villages registered in the village protection system in the east. The interior parts of Muş, Kulp, Sason, and some districts of Kozluk were all ranger villagers.

I officially started my duty as commander of the east on June 1, 2007. I still did not know which tribes in the region were part of the ranger system, nor which tribes did not side with either us or the state. One day, I saw my comrade, Azad, using binoculars to look out at the plains. I asked him what he was doing. He answered, "Comrade Deniz, there are some nomads on the plains, and I think they are the same nomads we have spoken with before. They are one of the friendly groups." "Okay then," I replied, "Why are you waiting? Send a couple of comrades there to welcome those friends! In the meantime, you can give me a small tour of the field!"

We were chatting at our campground around 9:30 p.m. when we heard gunshots from the area where the nomads were settling. I immediately climbed up to a high spot, so I could listen to the radio channels used by the soldiers. I heard the ranger nomads talking to the soldiers. Azad had been mistaken. Those nomads were not friendly to the organization. From listening to their conversations over the radio, I learned what had happened down there. One of our squad commanders and two other guerillas had visited the nomads' tent to greet them, as we had asked them to do. Initially, they had not noticed these nomads were not patriots. While they were all drinking tea, other nomads surrounded the tent. Their plan had been to catch our comrades alive and deliver them to the soldiers. However, one of our comrades had pulled the primer on a hand grenade and threw it at the rangers coming towards him. He and one of the rangers had died in the explosion, while the other two comrades had been captured alive.

As soon as the rangers finished talking with the soldiers, I contacted them from another radio channel. "Set our comrades free! Do not deliver them to the security forces! I promise we will not come down to take revenge for our fallen comrade if you let those two comrades go!" The chief ranger began to swear at me over the radio. Thirty minutes had not even passed when the security forces came by, in panzers, to get the comrades.

I conducted a detailed search on this tribe after this incident. They were of the Badikan tribe from the Kulp district of Diyarbakır. A few weeks after the incident, I contacted that chief ranger again. His name was Abdülhamit. I asked him, "Abdülhamit, why did you commit such a dishonorable act?" He replied, "Your men came down here to kill me!" I said, "Comrade, are you out of your mind? Would a person who wanted to kill you sit and drink tea in the tent with you?" The Kurds have a tradition that when an enemy comes and sits in your home, you cannot do anything to him, even though he or she is your enemy." I told him again, "You could even say to our comrades, 'Look, we are enemies, but you are in my home now and you are my guest. Have a cup of tea and then get out of here.' Do you Kurds not have this tradition, too, Abdülhamit?"

There were around 60 tents on the plains. After this incident, the Turkish security forces regularly patrolled the nomads, with those large panzers, since they knew that sooner or later we would seek revenge for what the rangers had done. I said on the radio to Abdülhamit, "Thirteen tanks could not discourage us against revenge, let alone those three panzers! In fact, we can kill you right in front of your house, in the city when you return at the end of the summer. Neither the soldiers nor the police can protect you from us! If you had any brains, you would come and apologize to us."

Despite all of these warnings, Abdülhamit not only continued to reject us but continued to swear at me on the radio. On top of that, he was patrolling the area to find and kill us with his ranger team. I could take it no more. This man needed to be punished. I notified organization management about the issue. According to organizational policy, it was forbidden to carry out a mission against the rangers, but this was an exceptional situation. The organization gave us permission to kill three people, one of which was Abdülhamit. "Comrades, you can kill Abdülhamit, his brother, and his cousin. But do not harm anyone else in the tribe."

As soon as we received approval from the organization, our comrades planted mines at four different locations on the road that the rangers used daily. I was strict in my warning to the region commander. I said, "Be careful not to kill anyone else. The organization has allowed us to kill three specific people. We would be in trouble if we, even accidentally, kill the other rangers."

Because I was the commander of the whole eastern front in Garzan, I had to visit the three regions under my control regularly—Dorşin, Sason, and Mutki—to supervise their activities. In June 2008, I visited the guerilla force located in Dorşin for this reason. The commander of the Dorşin region said to me, "Comrade Deniz, we have successfully carried out a mission in the city of Muş." They planted mines on the railway and detonated them while a train was passing by. I asked whether it was a passenger train or a freight train. "It was a freight train with no civilians inside. There were only some guards on it," he said. Their goal was to cause financial damage by destroying the goods that were loaded on the freight cars. I said, "Comrade, why did you carry out such a mission? Was it really necessary? Besides, why did you not inform me about your plan before carrying it out?" He was disheartened when I criticized him. I returned to Muş after a couple of days in Dorşin.

As I mentioned earlier, the guerrilla force in Muş planted mines at four different points on the same road. I was critical of their actions and said, "Why are you wasting so many mines to kill just three rangers?" One of them replied, "Comrade, we thought that if we missed them on our first attempt, we would definitely kill them on the second or next attempts. That's why we planted so many mines on the same road." They had gathered a lot of information about this ranger: the color and brand of his car, what days and times he would leave the summer range, and what time he would return.

Before we actually carried out our mission, the rangers contacted me. They wanted to meet and talk to us about what had happened. I notified headquarters about their request. Once they heard the request, headquarters ordered me to talk to them before killing the three.

Over the radio, I said to the rangers, "Tell your chief that he should meet us on Wednesday at 1:00 p.m. in the foothills of the mountains across from your summer range." Interestingly, it was not the chief ranger that had come to the meeting place but a woman and a different man. This woman was a Kurd living in Germany. I do not remember exactly, but she was either the aunt or sister of the chief ranger. The rangers had used this woman to contact headquarters through our political extensions in Europe. Before meeting with us, she explained the situation to our political outlet in Germany and apologized on behalf of her brother. Hearing her words made me realize that Abdülhamit was aware we were going to take revenge on him and that was why he had used his relative to apologize to us.

This woman introduced herself to us first and then asked us to forgive Abdülhamit's past mistake. I told her how the incident occurred, "One of our comrades had gone to welcome them and they killed him. On top of that, they delivered two others to security forces, even though I had cautioned them not to do so. What would you do if you were in my shoes?" She did not expect such a harsh question from me. After staying silent for a moment, she said, "I would probably kill them, too. But please do not retaliate. Forgive them for this." I replied to her plea, "Honestly, it is not in my hands to forgive them. I will ask headquarters. Also, I must inform you that Abdülhamit and all the other rangers will have to abandon the plains, even if we agree to forgive them. The problem is not just with us but also with the local Kurds. Your relatives are inflicting cruelty on the villagers by abusing the power that arises from the village protection system. They do not let the Kurds that are not in the system graze their animals on those summer ranges. Also, they confiscated the lands of those same Kurds. Therefore, as a precondition of our peace agreement, your relatives will leave the plains and hand those lands back over to their legitimate owners, until I hear from the organization."

After our conversation, I had to cancel the mission we had already planned. It would be extremely dishonest to carry out an assassination attempt while negotiating with the enemy. I gave orders to my comrades, "You can leave the mines wherever you planted them, but take all the igniters out of them now. We might need to use them again if we cannot reach an agreement with the rangers." They did exactly as I asked them.

Later, however, one of the mines accidently exploded. It rains a lot on the plains of Muş, even during the summer season. In a stroke of bad luck, lightning hit the mine during a bout of heavy rainfall. There was a very loud explosion. When the rangers realized their road to the summer range was planted with mines, they immediately notified the soldiers.

We were using binoculars, from quite a distance, to follow what was going on down on the plains. Two squads of soldiers came from the Üçevler military post. The soldiers used mine detectors and found the remaining three mines.

The rangers became nervous when they found that the road was full of mines. I contacted the chief ranger via radio to explain why the mines were there. Even before I finished my explanation, he began swearing at me. I said, "Look, your manner of speech is unseemly. You are an old man and the chief of the rangers. You should know how to speak to a person properly. If we had really wanted to, we could have already killed you, even without the mines. How many times have you driven on that road during the last two months? Did we ever blow any of those mines?"

Living in fear for one's life is not an easy thing. We guerillas were used to it, but not Abdülhamit, which is why he was so frightened when he found out about the mines. He replied to me helplessly, "What do you guys want from me? Just tell me and I will accept all your terms without negotiation!" I said, "Turn off your radio for now, the security forces may be listening to our conversation. I will contact you later."

Two days after this conversation, the same woman and man that we had met before, came to our campground. I explained to them why the road was planted with mines. "Look, I am going to be honest with you. If you had not come and spoken with us, we were going to kill Abdülhamit and two other men. When you visited us for forgiveness, we delayed our mission. Not a single one of those mines had an igniter on it. We deactivated them, since we were going through the process of negotiation with you, but lightning struck one, and it went off. It was an unfortunate incident that was outside of our control! Now, go and tell Abdülhamit that we will kill him and two others if he ignores our previously stated terms." The woman said, "Okay, all of your terms will be fulfilled without negotiation. I am the one who is in charge of this issue from now on. If a problem emerges, you must contact me first!"

Of course, in the meantime, I visited other rangers in the region and signed peace agreements with most of them. Toward the end of 2008, there were no rangers left to fight the organization. The official records still had them registered as part of the village protection system, yet the agreement meant they would not carry out missions against us any longer. They all accepted the terms set by the organization and declared their loyalty to us.

The main reason the organization chose me to broker for peace, was because I was the most familiar with the people of that region. I was never alone when I met the rangers at these meetings. The organization had a strict rule stating that at least three guerillas must be present to represent the organization. I was able to convince the rangers by telling them, "Brothers! We have been fighting each other for many years now, and yet none of us has had a conclusive victory. In fact, both sides have had heavy losses during those battles. It is now time to forgive each other's past mistakes."

Before meeting with the chief of a ranger village, we would do detailed research on the families that lived in that specific village. We would find out whether the families living there had been exposed to an injustice through us, whether someone had been recklessly killed by us, or whether any civilians in that village had been exposed to cruelty by the organization in the past. Only after that would we meet with the villagers and apologize to them for the mistakes we had made, and would explicitly ask for their forgiveness.

Many of the ranger villagers responded to our call for peace. Our reasonable approach had worked. I told those villagers, "We are not asking you to lay down your weapons or quit the village protection system. We understand that you had to register with the system to earn your keep, or you'd have to relocate to the big cities on the west end of Turkey. Instead, you chose to stay in the region and be rangers. Again, we are not blaming you for this. You can continue being a ranger as long as you do not carry out missions against the organization, or mistreat the local Kurds, who are not registered in the ranger system. Keep your weapons and continue to get a monthly salary from the Turks, but do not lead military operations by fighting on the front lines. Use your ranger title just to earn your keep! Additionally, if you can, inform us beforehand about military operations, so that we may prepare ourselves."

As I mentioned before, there were two groups of people that posed a major threat to us. First, there were the organization members who deserted us and aligned themselves with the Turkish soldiers. Second, were the Kurdish peasants who registered in the village protection system. Both of those groups were closely familiar with our fighting strategy. For example, in the winter of 2003 to 2004, the Turkish security forces were able to kill 13 of our comrades, with the help of PKK members who had deserted. That was a tragedy for us. Without the help and guidance of those traitors, the Turks would not have been able to hand us such a huge defeat, though our comrades were able to wound a Turkish squadron commander in that clash. One of those traitors had carried that squadron commander on his back away from where the battle was taking place. You can find more details if you search the archives of the security forces.

On the other hand, there were some special combat groups within the rangers. For example, if there were 80 to 90 rangers in a village, 20 of them would be assigned to that special group. The soldiers would give highly advanced weapons to that group. The Turks would task this special team to patrol in the mountainous areas and dry gulches to search for us. Indeed, many of our comrades lost their lives during those ambushes. I would tell the peasants, "You will not take part in any of these special combat groups anymore. You can stay in the village protection system, but you will not have these special groups!" During one of those meetings, one of the rangers stood up and said, "How are we going to explain this to the soldiers? They will think that we are helping the organization, as soon as they hear that we have stopped using those special groups!" I replied, "Go and talk to the commanders of the soldiers. Tell them that your families are being targeted because of the special combat groups. Tell them that you can continue to work as normal village protection guards, but you cannot take part in those special teams!"

These special combat teams were posing not only a threat to us but also to the local public, since they were given extreme authority within the Turkish state. They sometimes carried out raids on non-ranger households, and would torture the inhabitants, blaming them for supplying the guerillas with provisions. They acted like the police or soldiers, even though they were not given such authority. They would detain whomever they wanted and then beat the tar out of them. I specifically cautioned the rangers not to carry out those kinds of malpractices anymore.

My other request for the rangers was for them to supply us with the ammunition they received from the Turkish state at no cost. The soldiers distributed ammunition and weapons to the rangers on a regular basis in return for their service to the state, but the ammo and weapons were under the strict control of the soldiers. For example, let's say that a village was given 100 cartridge clips full of bullets, 40 hand grenades, and ten LAW flamethrowers. The villagers were required to tell the soldiers where, how, and why they used the ammo in those weapons. The villagers were also required to hand back their used cartridges to the soldiers. I told the villagers some things they could do if the soldiers asked for used cartridges, saying, "You will go up to a distant field, from your village, and use only a couple of cartridges, as if you were in a real battle, or were victims of an ambush. But really, you will be giving us a portion of your ammunition and weapons and then return back to your village. You will then contact the soldiers and inform them that you had been abruptly attacked by a large guerilla group and that you were able to resist us for some time but had to flee without being able to collect the used cartridges." This was just one tactic I shared with them, explaining that, by this method, each village protection guard would be able to supply us with 100 cartridges each month. The chief rangers did not object to our request. After all, they would be able to resupply their own ammo needs, through the soldiers, at no cost.

And, finally, I asked the rangers to supply our provision needs, whenever necessary. I told them, "We will occasionally send you a list of provisions we need. You share our needs with each other, so that one place will provide us with sugar, another with flour, and another with oil." When we were supplied by the normal Kurdish peasants, we would pay them fairly. We were not going to pay anything to the rangers for supplying us, since they already had a good salary that was paid by the state.

Almost all of the villages registered in the village protection system had accepted our terms of peace, except the ones located in Sason, Muş, Kulp, and Mutki. We could not get along with the ones who refused, no matter how hard we tried. For example, the rangers in Mutki were not Kurds but Arabs. I did not know Arabic, and even the comrades who did speak Arabic could not communicate with them, because of the difference in dialects. Beyond the lack of communication, there was also another Arab village in the region that rejected our peace terms, saying that the organization had not helped them in the past, during a time when they had rioted against the state.

17

RECRUITING NEW GUERILLAS

When I was assigned to work in the Garzan province, I was also tasked with recruiting new guerillas from the city centers there. I did this while simultaneously handling the peace negotiations with the rangers. I had to establish recruitment committees in all the cities under my jurisdiction, within Kurdistan. We needed active intermediaries, who would guide the younger generation of Kurds when they wanted to join the organization. These committee members would visit coffee shops, shopping centers, mosques, and even the schools in Turkey to come across the willing Kurdish youth and then would direct them to our camps in Iraq and Syria. For this job, I sought help from the civilian organization members of the self-defense units who were already covertly organized within the cities.

I traveled to Bitlis to establish the committees. I do not recall the exact date, but on the day I arrived in downtown Bitlis, the nephew of Ali Babacan, who was the Economy Minister back then, had been killed in a guerilla mission carried out against the Gülyazı Military Post. I gave some advice to the guerilla forces before I left Bitlis. "If you want to carry out successful missions, do not waste your time seeking opportunities in the countryside. Instead, plan your missions in downtown Bitlis. The security forces are already searching for you in the countryside. All of their plans and operations are directed at ending you outside of the city. You cannot be successful there. Sneak into downtown and hit them at their heart, where they feel they are most secure."

There was only one way to achieve this goal. Small guerilla teams had to sneak into the downtown area by carefully passing the military posts located at the perimeters of the city. Security measures used in the cities were much weaker than the ones used in the countryside. The soldiers were ten times more careful and prepared against a potential attack in the countryside than the police officers in the cities were. The soldiers would guard a military post with at least four or five guards. The police officers were often negligent, and we had witnessed this fact on many reconnaissance missions. The police officers were extremely inattentive and like sitting ducks for us. We knew what kind of vehicles they were using, where they hung out in their spare time, where they shopped, and at what time they started and ended their work at the police station.

I think the main reason for their negligence originated from their exaggerated trust in the presence of military posts around the perimeter of the city. The police officers probably thought that a guerilla mission would most likely be carried out against a military post, so they never considered themselves a target of the organization. They were clearly mistaken. It was for this reason that I told the Bitlis guerilla forces to sneak into Bitlis and carry out simultaneous missions at several police stations. They even blew a police panzer sky high on Sirvan-Siirt state road, after I left Bitlis. The security forces lost seven police officers during that mission.

The roads in the region were all paved and sealed, and no longer earthen roads, as they had been in the old days. This made planting mines on those roads and highways a more difficult job, but it was not impossible. There were two basic methods for planting a mine under a paved road. First, with the help of a drill, we would cut a large circle in the road. Then we would pry up that circle-shaped piece out of the road, using a lever. Once that piece was extracted, we would dig to a depth of approximately 1 meter. Then, would carefully place the mine and igniter into the hole. The mine had an antenna with a strong signal connected to it. Finally, we would fill the hole with the dirt we'd taken out and place the circle-shaped piece back into place. Once completed, all we had to do was find a secure place to wait for a vehicle belonging to the security forces to pass. This method was very hard to achieve and highly time consuming. It took at least three days to cut the circle out of the road. Then, [we had a second method] we could dig a tunnel from the side of the road to the middle of the road, usually around 2 meters long. A squad of guerillas would open this tunnel in just a single night of work. In rare instances, as when the soil under the paved road was rocky, it would take three to four days. In those situations, we would hide the entrance of the tunnel with bushes during the day and continue to work after the sun went down.

The guerilla group in Bitlis carried out their mission using this second method. They began waiting 20 meters from the road, after they planted the mine in the center using their tunnel. They used a cable to activate the bomb instead of an antenna. On one side of the cable an igniter was connected to the mine, and on the other side there was a 12-volt battery. Our comrades sat on the side, waiting, with the battery. They buried the cable a bit underground, so no one would notice it, because earlier, while they waited for a panzer to pass by, a young shepherd girl noticed the cable, and pulled it up as she followed where it led, and saw our comrades when she reached the end. To their surprise, she was a patriotic Kurd, and said, "Comrades, you haven't hidden the cable well enough. I can hide it for you, if you'd like."

Our comrades accepted her offer. Fifteen minutes later, a panzer passed by, and they were able to destroy it by activating the mine. We even heard later that the shepherd girl had been taken in for interrogation, by the security forces. They asked her, "You have been strolling around here. Have you seen anyone?"

The soldiers still thought the peasants would inform the security forces as soon as they saw us, but, once again, they were highly mistaken. While those greedy Turkish politicians were occupied with their comfort in Ankara and wasting our time with the so-called peace process, we had already won the loyalty of the rangers and the Kurdish peasants within the region. The Kurdish public began directly helping the organization, with no fear of retaliation from the security forces. They would even go out of their way to bury that cable in order to protect our comrades.

Hakkı Gabar

In August, 2007, a new state commander, named Hakkı Gabar, was assigned to Garzan in Nurettin Sofis stead. I had written and sent an official complaint report regarding Hakkı to headquarters concerning a deadly mistake he had committed in the past. Now, here he was assigned to be my superior. Such bad luck! There was a secret path used by the guerillas for years when they traveled from the south to the north. The security forces discovered it, and Hakkı's guerilla group was using the path, when they were raided by Turkish soldiers using howitzers. Under normal conditions, a commander would have to notify headquarters when encountering a situation such as this, because the groups traveling behind do not yet know about the danger. Hakkı and his group did not inform headquarters, even though they were attacked by the Turkish soldiers while traveling on that path. The guerilla group traveling behind them (a group that had set out for our region), used the same path since they had not been warned the path was discovered by the soldiers. Eleven guerillas from that group were martyred—for nothing—on the exact same spot where Hakkı's group had been attacked.

Initially, I did not know that Hakkı's group had also been attacked. I learned all the facts while Hakkı's group was resting in our campground in Muş. I immediately went to Hakkı and asked him why he had not notified headquarters that the path had been discovered by the enemy. Even though Hakkı's own guerillas were telling me that they had been exposed to fire from panzers and howitzers, Hakkı was telling me that he was not aware of the existence of such an attack. How could that be? It was a total dilemma.

In the meantime, headquarters leadership was communicating with the states over the radio to figure out how the tragic incident had occurred. The state commanders of Haftanin, Botan, and Garzan were all discussing, between themselves, about when the path was discovered by the security forces. I walked in on the conversation and announced that Hakkı Gabar was the only person responsible for those 11 losses, and then I told them the whole story. After my report, Hakkı was put under investigation and began to view me as an enemy.

As luck would have it, this man I complained about years ago was now my superior. As soon as Hakkı was appointed to Garzan, he visited my jurisdiction on the eastern front. He criticized me over absurd things. "How can you continue to be comfortable when one of your comrades died and the other two were captured alive and delivered to security forces by the rangers? Why have you been waiting for so long to get vengeance?" I responded, "We will take our revenge if necessary! However, the organization gave me an order on this matter. We cannot just randomly fire at and kill all of those rangers as we would have in the old days, Hakkı! The organization tasked us to kill specific people, and we will kill them when the time comes!" Hakkı did not have a ready reply to my answer.

As I mentioned, 11 of our comrades had been martyred by the security forces, while traveling from the south to the north. Headquarters demanded that Garzan forces must carry out a mission of revenge for our martyred comrades. Hakkı was the state commander and was still staying in my field at that point. While we were deciding what kind of mission we should carry out, a comrade suggested planting mines on the intercity roads, between the city of Diyarbakır and Muş.

We planted the mines in four different spots on that road. The comrades blocked the passage of vehicles from both sides of the road around 8:30 p.m., and we did not allow any vehicle to continue their trip until 4:00 a.m. the next morning. First, we collected the keys of the cars and then searched inside each of them. Then, we checked the identification cards of the passengers and drivers to figure out whether there were any civilian security forces traveling in any of those vehicles. We expected some of the vehicle owners to notify the security forces about our road blockade, so we did not collect the cell phones. We also figured that the security forces would arrive at our mine trap location soon, since the line of vehicles extended at least a kilometer down the road. They had to be suspicious about why all those cars were stopped. Yet, they did not come. We also could not find any state-owned car (it did not need to be a security force vehicle) at our blockade that we could damage for revenge. There was clearly no gain in continuing to operate the blockade, so we reopened the road back to traffic and left the area.

Before we left, some comrades insisted that we at least set a car on fire to show that we had been on that road. I was highly disappointed by this suggestion. I said, "Whose car are we going to set on fire and on what grounds?" One of them gave me a stupid response. "Let's ask them one by one and find someone who did not vote for the HDP [A Kurdish political party operating in Turkey] during the elections, then set his car on fire!" I angrily responded to him, "What?! In the end, all of these people are Kurds! What kind of suggestion was that? Everybody is free to vote for any party they want."

It had not even been a week when the security forces found all but one of the mines buried under the road. That remaining mine is still buried under the Muş-Diyarbakır intercity road. It was quite a large mine, made from a propane gas tank and two 18-kilogram capacity oil cans filled with TNT. There was no battery attached to it, but it was still there under the road. After our comrades planted the mine, the state highway authority of Turkey sealed it with asphalt. After that, our comrades were able to find the cable connected to the mine. They extended the cable further from the road, so they could use it in a future mine explosion mission. All they needed to do was connect a 12-volt battery to the cable. It has been almost nine years, and that mine is still there. After I surrendered myself to the security forces, I notified them about the exact location of the mine, but they did not even give a shit about it.

Falling in Love Again

In 2007, we were not able to carry out any missions in the Muş region. We spent most of our time preparing for winter. As I mentioned, the guerilla force in Dorşin had been completely destroyed by a traitor in the cave where they were camping. It was vital that we reestablish our presence in that area, so I dispatched some guerillas from Muş to Dorşin. Nevertheless, our reinforcement force was annihilated by the Turkish security forces, because of the negligence of Hakkı Gabar.

Toward the beginning of fall, Hakkı, our state commander, informed me that he had dispatched some guerillas from his field to mine by using an encrypted radio message. Until that time, I was only being accompanied by eight guerillas. The group, sent by Hakkı, arrived in our region on the night of October 29. There were seven guerillas—three women and four men.

In 2006, while I traveled from the south to the north, I had a digital camera with me the entire time. When I visited a group while on the road back to Turkey, I would have pictures taken with them, to keep as a memory of my time spent there. I had a bodyguard with me, and he carried the camera and took pictures of me with the other guerillas, as well as the beautiful views of nature. In the winter of 2006 to 2007, while staying in a camp in Bitlis, Sex Cuma, I finally had an opportunity to see those pictures. While going through them, I found a picture with a woman in it. Something strange happened to me when I saw her. You know how people say, "Love at first sight"? After seeing that picture, I now think it is true, and she was constantly on my mind. I always wondered if I would ever see her again. I tried, several times, to find out with which force she was staying, but I could never find anything. I also was not able to ask anyone about her explicitly, since I felt shy when it came to these kinds of issues and I did not want anyone to learn about this platonic love.

On October 30, 2007, I awoke and met with a group of new arrivals, and would you believe that the woman with whom I had fallen in love from a single picture, was standing there in front of me! I was ecstatic, and my whole world changed in the blink of an eye. She and two other female guerillas were going to stay with us until the end of winter. I sent the remaining men to Dorşin. As I said before, the Dorşin guerilla force had been doomed by a traitor and these four men were going to reestablish our presence there. I took the rest of the group and decided to camp in an area where the borders of Bingöl, Muş, and Solhan met. Our winter season camp was in a buffer zone, and the soldiers would never carry out air or land operations within that area. Neither the Diyarbakır, Muş, Bitlis, nor Bingöl security forces staked a claim in this place, so none of them would enter the area. From their perspective, it would be extra work just to carry out an operation in this area, since there was uncertainty concerning the terms of jurisdiction of authority. That place was so secure for building a winter bunker that we stayed there for the three consecutive years of 2008, 2009, and 2010, without being noticed. The only problem was that the terrain was very rocky, so we literally had to carve out the rocks in order to build it.

During the winter of 2008, our supply of provisions had been used up earlier than expected, so we were forced to leave the bunker to resupply ourselves from the hidden food storages buried underground in the region. Everything was frozen outside, and some of the comrades were constantly falling down, because of the slippery ground. While walking on the hillside, we had to be extra careful, or we could fall down over the cliff. I ordered a comrade to walk at the front of the group and make indentions in the ice, with a digger, so that we could walk easier. The boots I was wearing were good on the ice. They were an American brand I had bought while staying in Iraq and had a good grip on both ice and snow, which allowed me to walk with confidence. After a while, because of my better traction, I wound up walking 50 meters ahead of the group, checking the ground before they stepped on it. I noticed there was a cliff up ahead. I immediately turned around and said, "Stop, wherever you are now! We have to find another path!" I noticed Asmin, the woman with whom I fell in love, and another guerilla were staying just behind me, 5 or 6 meters back. From where they were standing, I sensed that they might fall down the cliff side. I started walking toward them to help them walk by, letting them hold onto me, when Asmin suddenly slid down the side. I looked over and saw that she was holding onto a bush, 10 meters down, and screaming in fear. The cliff was nearly 60 meters high. If she fell, her chances of staying alive were almost zero.

I started to climb down through the bushes to the location where she was holding on desperately. When I got to a point that was close, I reached out to pull her up back onto the hill. I could not pull her up using one hand, because she was a little overweight, and we both began rolling down together. There was a spiky tree that the Kurds called "Guni." I was able to grab onto one of these trees, as I rolled. I held Asmin with one hand and the tree with the other. I realized that it was impossible for me to save her by myself. We waited, unmoving, so as not to lose energy until the comrades could reach us with help. I was exhausted, and my hand was bleeding from the spikes on the tree. It was also freezing cold. Luckily, the other comrades reached us and were able to pull Asmin and myself up the hill with the help of a rope.

When I climbed up, I saw that many of Asmin's fingernails were torn apart, as she had tried to hold onto something while falling. I was in a similar situation. My hands were in bad shape, because they had slid across the rocky surface. They were bleeding badly and the skin on my palm was torn apart. I did not immediately realize that I had also hurt my back. It made itself known when I tried to stand up and felt a huge pain in my lower back.

With the help of my comrades, I was able to return to our campground, and Asmin began hanging around with me after that incident. She witnessed that I had risked my own life in order to save hers. That night, with everyone present, she stated, "My life is not my own any longer. If you had not saved me, I would now be dead. Comrade Deniz! Wherever you go, I will follow as your servant from now on—because I owe my life to you."

She began feeling affection for me. We stayed in the same underground bunker throughout winter, and I was getting more nervous as time passed. Asmin and the other two women were temporarily assigned to my jurisdiction. I would have to dispatch them to their new fields of duty in April, at the latest. When I told Asmin what was going to happen in the near future, she became frustrated and said, "I am not going anywhere. I will stay wherever you are." I said, "No Asmin. You have to go or the other comrades will sense the relationship between us. It might cause us problems." She hastily responded, "Why did you risk your life for me then? You are not a regular ground guerilla, but are one of the three most authorized people in the state of Garzan. How could you risk your own life just to save an ordinary guerilla like me?"

I had to convince her to leave the region, one way or another. I would be in serious trouble if someone noticed how close we had become. (Asmin was only her nickname; her real name was Selma Doner.) I said, "Asmin, I have feelings toward you also, but it is risky for us both if you stay here with me. People might start gossiping that Comrade Deniz is keeping the woman he loves close to himself, and we could not explain that to headquarters!"

Since we had confessed our feelings to each other, I decided to tell Asmin about all my previous relationships with other women, including the ones that were slanderous. I did not want her to be confused by hearing them from other guerillas. "Asmin, I will be honest with you. I loved only one woman from 1992 to 2000. We broke up, but I still cannot forget her. Also, people said that I hung out with other women. These were all lies, but I was put under investigation for them, and there was found to be no truth to them. I am telling all of this to you, so that you do not blame me in the future if you hear about it from others. Now, if you really love me, just go wherever the organization wants you to go. Do not insist on staying close to me. Otherwise, we might both be in serious trouble!"

Finally, Asmin was convinced. She realized I was correct. Headquarters dispatched her to a field that was quite close to me, in Bitlis. Asmin and the other two women guerillas traveled to Bitlis in the middle of the April.

Unmanned Aircraft Systems

Toward the end of my career in the organization, the Turkish security forces began using unmanned aircraft systems, called Herons. The use of this technology became so popular that it was in the news. It was often reported that the PKK was beaten down by the use of this new technology. Nevertheless, these Herons were not as troublesome to the guerillas as was reflected in the media. Even before these high-tech reconnaissance-gathering machines began to be used by the Turkish military, we had already been provided with a brochure on how to prevent detection by them. The organizations that were fighting against Israel in Palestine sent us a brochure with information on what features the Herons had, how much area they could cover, how large their surveillance capacity was, and what precautions could be used against them.

Even though the PKK did not have any dialogue with Hamas and Hezbollah, it did have a close relationship with the Palestine National Salvation Front. This strong relationship was built years ago, in 1992, when the PKK began fighting against Israel with PNSF forces to help the assimilated and suppressed Palestinian people. In those clashes against Israeli soldiers, the organization had 17 martyred members. The fact that the Kurds sacrificed themselves for the Palestinian people during those years strengthened the relationship between the PKK and Palestine. The Palestinian organizations began to assist us on many fronts in return. I personally witnessed their help. I was even able to read three letters written to Apo by Yasser Arafat.

The head of general staff back then was Yaşar Büyükanıt. He delivered a fallacious public speech on TV, saying, "We are now able to watch the PKK camps located in Iraq and Syria 24/7 with the help of our Herons." That was nothing but a big lie. In fact, the security forces had carried out a large land and air operation in 2008, based on the reconnaissance data collected by those unmanned aircraft. In the middle of February, thousands of soldiers were dispatched to the south in Iraq. It was partially reflected in the media, but of course it contained misleading information. In that operation, the organization inflicted a heavy blow against the Turkish military. The Turkish soldiers were probably under the illusion that they would destroy the PKK camps in the south in the middle of winter based on what the Herons had seen.

Yes, it was true that the enemy was able to watch our camp locations, but the guerillas were highly mobile. We would always relocate to another place before an operation began against us. The Turkish jets would bomb those empty camps and then misinform the public, through false news. How many times have you witnessed on the media that the PKK camps were wiped off the map? I bet it has probably been more than a hundred times. I do not understand how the public buys those lies. If that news were true, would there even be a single PKK member alive today? No!

In the operation that was carried out in 2008, the organization had also been warned about the Turks' arrival. The invasion of Iraq by the Americans changed the rules of the game for the Turks. The Iraq of today is not the same as Saddam Hussein's Iraq. Today, if the Turks want to carry out a military operation within Iraq, they must go through three steps. First, they have to get permission from the United States. Then, they must get permission from the Iraqi Central Government, which is controlled by the Iranians. Finally, the Kurdistan regional government in the north of Iraq has to be notified. Now, do you think an operation, which is supposed to be carried out secretly, can stay secret while the Turks obtain permission from these three authorities? Worse than that, one of the authorities from whom you needed to get approval was your enemy, the Iranian-backed Shia government in Iraq. In fact, when the organization was forewarned about the Turkish security forces' mission in Iraq, we were also leaked information that Barzani was going to support the Turks during the operation. The organization put leverage on Barzani to withdraw his military support from the Turks, and Barzani did not dare join the operation.

Turkish fighter jets had crashed the empty campgrounds with their million-dollar bombs, as our comrades had been forewarned. But the Turkish army air corps had landed into an area circled by guerillas. Many of those soldiers lost their lives there. I do not know how it was reflected in the public records, but in that operation that took place in February of 2008, at least 120 Turkish soldiers lost their lives.

I was staying in Muş while this operation was being carried out. I had learned instantly what happened, by listening to our comrades' radio talks via those big radios. From Metina to Zagros, we had lost only 20 comrades in the air strikes, and that was only because of a mistake by a battalion commander. A group of guerillas had been mistakenly dispatched right into the field, where Turkish air corps had already landed, and they were all killed by the soldiers. There was a famous saying within the organization regarding that 2008 operation: "There were two losers in 2008; the one was the head of Turkish General Staff, and the other was Mazlum Bardakçı, the battalion commander." And, if I am not mistaken, Mazlum Bardakçı was martyred in 2012 in Amanoses.

In the end, that operation, which was carried out based on some reconnaissance data collected through Herons, ended with a large crash and burn for the Turks. In fact, the Turkish military would not dare to enter into Iraq for a long time after that defeat.

In the north, there were also many Herons flying above the countryside, where we guerillas usually stayed, and often they flew very high. Nevertheless, we were able to hear their presence. In the brochure that was delivered by the Palestinians, there was a note saying that Herons would not take images if they flew very high, which was true. If a Heron were flying high from the ground, then we could freely continue to carry out our activities. However, if it were flying at a low altitude, then we had to be extra careful. Otherwise, these unmanned aircraft systems could send our pictures and location coordinates directly to the nearest security forces. Additionally, if a Heron detected something on the ground, it would fly back and forth over that place a couple times, at which point we would have to remain completely still. It mattered not whether it was night or day. If there were movement, the Heron could easily detect us. But if we remained still, on the ground—whether in mountainous areas or on a wide open plain—the Herons were not able to detect us.

Also, we would be careful about setting a fire for heating or cooking if the weather were rainy. I do not know how, but the Herons were able to detect the heat easily during relatively rainy weather. Other than that, during the day times when the sky was clear, they could easily detect vivid colors, including green, blue, and red. The Herons had amazing capabilities in the most challenging conditions. Occasionally, we would set a fire during the evenings in order to sit around and socialize with each other. Some nights, though, we would hear the noise of Herons flying above us, and we would quickly kill the fire—first by spreading dirt on it and then water, trapping the heat under the dirt, since some of the Herons were heat-sensitive. Since the Turkish security forces began to use these aircraft, we guerillas began to be more sensitive on the issues, which clearly improved the situational awareness of the Turkish security forces, even without stepping into the field to do reconnaissance. We quickly adapted to the hardships posed by the Herons. For example, as soon as we started a fire in the wood burning stove during the winter camps, a couple of comrades would go outside the bunker and check to see whether there was any light leakage. If there were such a situation, our comrades would properly close those exposed areas with dirt and earth.

Headquarters also had taken some precautions against the risk of being detected by Herons. For example, after some information exchange with the Palestinians, the seniors instructed the guerilla forces, fighting in the north, to build half-open camouflage spots at certain locations in the shape of a coffer. While we guerillas were resting somewhere, we would hide in these coffers, our rucksacks, explosive materials, and the kitchen tools that we carried along with us. Then, one of the comrades would cover the open side of the coffer with his tent. After hiding the items, the Herons were not able to detect us, even if they flew over us all day as long as we remained still. But these unmanned aircraft systems seriously limited our freedom of mobility. However, we were still able to travel from one place to another as long as we abided by the precautions.

The Palestine National Salvation Front was very experienced on how to get these unmanned aircraft systems out of the way, since they were exposed to them for a longer period of time by the Israeli security forces. They had developed valuable tactics and combined them into a brochure. That brochure had really helped us to get over our novitiate period with almost no loss.

Besides Herons, the Turkish security forces used another type of unmanned aircraft system, which was small, and it could be launched quickly by projecting it through the air. The soldiers would use them to increase their situational awareness when they were out on the field. They were American made, if I remember correctly. The smaller ones would not pose a huge threat to us guerillas, since we were able to shoot them down, when they often flew at a low altitude.

One of the areas in which the organization was most successful was the importance given to continuing education among the guerillas. Whichever tactic or technology the security forces adopted, we immediately got trained in that direction. We would exchange ideas with the other groups around the world and then develop our own counter tactics. At least 70 percent of the activities of the organization depended on training in various areas. The remaining 30 percent consisted of all other works. That is why I still do not understand why there was always such fallacious propaganda after each air attack carried out in Iraq, stating that, "The PKK was doomed, their camp grounds were completely destroyed, and no one was left alive." If there were even a small amount of truth in those news items, the organization would have been destroyed at least 20 times by now!

Denigration of the Kurds

The training activities had always been crucial for the organization; especially the training of the ranked guerillas. In each guerilla camp, there was at least one ranked guerilla-training academy. I would argue that the training given in those camps was not even given at the universities in Turkey. In those camps, each guerilla would undergo a systematic and professional training. The basic philosophy of the organization was to raise awareness among the guerillas, because you can talk, discuss, and debate about anything with an informed person. On the other hand, even talking, let alone discussing, is difficult with an uninformed person. You cannot make them change their ideas, because of the deeply rooted prejudices. That is why 70 percent of all the activities of the organization is composed of training. We were trained in almost everything. Beginning with 2005, the organization even began to give training on quantum physics.

Newbies, who successfully completed the ideological training, would then be trained on guerilla-war tactics. The ideological training might become boring for some; however, the guerilla training was not like that. In fact, some training had to be taken maybe five times by each guerilla, but no one was offended by those repetitions, because every one of us was aware that it was in our best interest to advance ourselves on guerilla tactics. Indeed, some comrades among us were highly insensitive to the ideological training. Even though they were physically in the classroom, their minds would be somewhere else. Nevertheless, during the war-tactic classes, the guerillas began to act like different people, participating in discussions and asking multiple questions.

The training would change the way in which those guerillas saw the world and world incidents. The guerillas no longer went at one another, tooth and nail, for petty situations after completing this training. We witnessed this change, especially on the subject of religion. Since the organization was not against any religious view, it would not view any one religion above another. In other words, they would not say anything like "Qur'an is good, Torah and Bible are bad." It gave complete freedom on searching for, choosing, and living a religion of your choice. Additionally, it would not let any members of a specific religion tyrannize guerillas with different religious beliefs. The organization was open to every religion, and it was not an atheist organization, as continuously reflected in the Turkish press. We had comrades among us who were atheists, Marxists, Christians, and Muslims. For the most part, we respected each other's religious beliefs. You could worship whatever you wanted, as long as you respected your comrades' beliefs.

This was one of the basic reasons why so many civilian Kurds were eagerly joining the organization. The PKK provided great freedoms to the people, especially the women. Kurds in the east of Turkey were now free to believe whatever they wanted—and free to marry whomever they wished. Apo had a good comment that he used during the training: "A person can take the national test for a university enrollment after going through primary, secondary, and high schools. If he gets high scores on the test, he will have many opportunities in front of him, such as studying to be a doctor or an engineer. He can choose any of them and then professionalize in that field. Let society be free to choose whatever they wish, as long as they do not interfere with others' rights. There is to be no making everyone believe in the same God or same religion. Let them use their free will." The appeal of the PKK for Kurdish people originated from those basic rights granted to them.

If we were in fact an absolute atheist or Marxist organization—and forced people to be either atheist or Marxist as it has been depicted in the media—would those thousands of Kurds have continued to join us with their hearts and souls? I personally visited several Kurdish villages many times, and I organized meetings with thousands of Kurdish peasants. In those villages, we would often gather in mosques. If we imposed atheism on people, would they let us carry out our meetings in the mosques?

I even have a funny story about one of these mosque visits. In 1993, we had a meeting with the peasants in a village of Siirt, Kurtalan. After the evening prayer, before the community left, I went up to the stage. During the speech, we hung the flag of the PKK inside the mosque. The Turkish soldiers came to the village while I was still speaking to villagers. There were shelters in each village in which to hide that were arranged beforehand in case security forces raided the villages. We immediately hid in a shelter, but because of the hurry, we had forgotten the PKK flag inside the mosque.

The soldiers, of course, noticed that all the men peasants were leaving the mosque. The ranked Turkish commander was smart and had checked his watch and figured that the praying time was already over. He entered the mosque to check, and as he was thinking about what all those villagers were doing there, he asked the imam, "Where are your comrades, dear Imam?" The imam had replied, "Comrades? There is no one here, but those who came for the evening prayers." The commander replied, smiling, "Tell them not to leave their flag behind while fleeing next time, okay?" Then, the soldiers left the village, and we guerillas continued our recruitment meeting.

The PKK is an organization which respects the people and their ideas. The executives of the organization gave great importance to the guerillas' attitudes and behavior. Some basic principles were taught and practiced by everyone. For example, it would not matter whether it was your inferior or superior—no one would sit with legs crossed in front of others. When we were talking with people in the community, we kneeled. If you paid specific attention to the images of our seniors in the media, you would notice this. Cemil Bayık, Duran Kalkan, and Murat Karayılan participated in several press statements or interviews. You never saw those seniors of the organization sitting cross-legged in front of a journalist. Villagers respected and embraced this demeanor of the guerilla. Also, if we guerillas were staying near to their village, the peasants felt comfortable and secure, knowing that we would protect their families against a possible atrocity from the soldiers.

The biggest share in the growth of participation in the PKK, and its acceptance by the Kurdish civilians, arose from our demeanor. When the PKK was not present, there was the KDP, which was founded in Iraq between the years 1946 and 1947. Their influence now is somewhere close to the bottom, and the Kurds do not accept their authority. Many constituents of the KDP simply support it in order to receive a favor, such as a position, in return. Similarly, look at the other Kurdish organizations operating in Iraq, such as the YNG, which had also lost its authority and influence on the Kurds of the Middle East. None of the Kurdish organizations which were active during 1950s and 1960s before the PKK was established are still active. Why? Because these so-called Kurdish parties deceived the Kurds to get their votes, but they did not serve their interests. They did not strive to win the hearts and minds of the Kurdish peasants! What helped us to reach our popularity was simply our way of treating the people.

We could not explain this to the Turkish community in the western parts of the country, because we could not make our voices heard by them in a positive light. Through slanders and false information, we were not given the opportunity to let the Turks know why we were fighting, instead of living a comfortable life, having families, and raising children. A simple example: As you know, the HDP is a political party operating under the Turkish Grand National Assembly. Its goal is to reach the Turks in other parts of the country and inform them about the injustices to which the Kurds have been exposed since the establishment of the Turkish Republic. During the last three days, there have been at least ten attacks by the civilian Turks, against HDP buildings in the western cities. Shooting, breaking glass in the office buildings, plundering, and beatings; everything you can imagine! Why is this still occurring? Simply because many political parties in Turkey win the support of their constituents on this fascist polarization among the Kurds and the Turks. A permanent solution to this deep-rooted problem would not serve their agenda.

The basic factor in the continuance and growth of this problem is that Turks are still unaware of the goals and the *raison d'être* of this Kurdish organization, which has by now been fighting against them for more than 30 years. They have always denied our presence, never accepted the fact that Kurds have also lived in these territories for centuries, and disseminated sheer calumnies that the "PKK is not an organization representing the rights of Kurds but is composed of Armenians and Christians with a plot of foreign powers to destroy the unity of the Turkish Republic!" If they really wanted to end this problem, they would "know their enemy" first. If one takes a closer look into the history of the PKK, you will easily see that many of our founders were Turks, not Kurds. Apo, our president; his assistant Kemal Pir; Hakkı Kara; an important figure within the organization, were all Turks. Duran Kalkan, from Adana, Osmaniye, from where well-known Turkish nationalist and politician, Devlet Bahçeli, is also a Turk. There are many other senior comrades, who also have Turkish origins but now serve the PKK. Therefore, you cannot call the PKK a Kurdish movement. There are as many Turks in the organization as there are Kurds. Nevertheless, we were unable to explain this situation to the Turks living in the western parts of Turkey, because of the prejudice planted by the Turkish officials. Instead of trying to set the seal on this problem, the Turkish government has been creating polarization between the two public entities for years by using the propaganda that the PKK was composed of manslayers: Armenians, Jews, and even atheists, besides Kurds. In the near past, around 2012, did not Erdoğan say, "The PKK is composed of a bunch of Zoroaster"? Because of such long-established and media-backed prejudices, the organization had been unable to express its grievances to the civilian Turks. Besides, everyone should be counted as a human being, regardless of his or her race or religious beliefs.

In today's Turkey, almost everyone views the PKK as a plot against Turkey. Almost any government in Turkey has yet to take a concrete step towards peace and stability. Politicians, prime ministers, presidents or bureaucrats—all liars! They would occasionally indicate in the media that they strove to end the problem peacefully, but those public statements were nothing but attempts to save the day for their own greedy goals. These dishonest politicians ignored their fallen soldiers, as well as our guerillas, for the sake of their own benefits, because a soldier might be nothing but the son of a poor Anatolian peasant. Did not, in fact, one of the Turkish ministers say in a public statement, "Who cares if a few soldiers died in our fight against PKK?"

Shortly after the 2001 economic crash in Turkey, many foreign agents contacted the organization, stating, "Do not let this opportunity pass you by! Now is the right time to separate from Turkey and declare your independence!" Those agents, in fact, had also reached out to the ground guerillas. Affected by those agents' support, many guerillas were insisting they deal a deathblow to the Turks in 2001. Back then, the senior commanders at headquarters settled the ground guerillas' discussions by telling them, "This is a plot imposed upon us by some foreign powers, for their own benefits. We should never, ever achieve our goals in a dastardly way!"

During that economic crisis, Iran and Syria put a great pressure on the organization. They were so-called allies of Turkey at the same time. Nevertheless, if you ever have the opportunity to check the archives of the organization or speak to another senior from the organization, you would easily see how many times the state of Iran reached out to organization headquarters in order to convince them to "move in for the kill" while Turkey was experiencing turmoil due to that same economic crash. The organization rejected all of those encouragements and offers of help, even though we had the power to achieve just that. In fact, in 2012, the organization held a small-scale "rehearsal" as the AKP increased its push on the guerillas. Every single day for a month, there was news coming from eastern Anatolia of martyred Turkish soldiers. Apo ceased the guerillas' desire for revenge by sending an order from prison. Even the Kurdish public was armed at that time. If Apo had not interfered, a civil war would definitely have broken out in Turkey.

However, the organization never considered starting a civil war within Turkey by letting the Kurdish civilians fight against the Turkish civilians. Nevertheless, when the organization figured out that the Turkish government was not fulfilling the conditions of the peace negotiations, it gave a warning message to the government in 2011–2012. "You Turks will either fulfill your obligations or we will respond to your negligence, not only with guerilla missions but also with a civilian Kurdish revolt!" They had many losses in the border areas, especially in the towns of Hakkari and Şırnak. It was a huge blow to the Turks. Almost 80 percent of Beytüşşebap were registered in the village protection system. Despite that, the security forces even lost control of the town there. They were so desperate that they could not even relocate to a safer place but hid in their military post. The security forces completely lost control in the countryside and mountainous areas of the city of Hakkari. We had literally established our liberated zones within Turkey.

There occurred three so-called "peace agreements" between Turkey and the PKK. In each agreement, we were promised that the Turks were going to address our grievances arising from basic democratic rights. Nevertheless, nothing was changed or fulfilled. The guerillas, more specifically the mid-level guerillas, stomped with rage at these deceptions. Our trust of the Turkish government almost ran out.

For example, the government deliberately undermined the peace process of 1993. The Turks even annihilated all pro-peace Turkish people with unaccounted murders. Initially, a journalist who had sensitive information about the cause of PKK, Uğur Mumcu, was assassinated by an explosion. Then President Turgut Özal; a high-ranked General in the Turkish Gendarmerie, Eşref Bitlis; a regional commander in the Turkish military, Bahtiyar Aydın, and so many other pro-peace military officials and politicians, were annihilated, one by one.

The exact same thing happened during the peace process of 1996–1997. The deceased Prime Minister Erbakan had desired to solve this problem. And some generals in the army were also supporting him. However, a post-modern coup occurred in Turkey and Erbakan and all of his friends were eliminated from the politics.

When the peace negotiations began in 2013, the AKP also wanted to settle the Kurdish problem around the table. However, they were not sincere about the establishment of peace, even though they had come to power with a unified government. Those politicians at the AKP always had a second agenda, which they hid from us. In that period, even top Turkish generals, Yaşar Büyükanıt and İlker Başbuğ, supported the peace process. They both declared to the media that the Kurdish problem would not be fixed by solely relying on military power. İlker Başbuğ even declared that the politicians had some vital responsibilities to fulfill, which were even more important than the military operations. I still do not know who was behind the mentorship of the AKP politicians and Erdoğan, but the AKP was definitely not sincere with establishing the order, stabilizing the country, and winning the hearts and minds of Kurds in the east. Despite the fact that it was literally the only political power with such control on the government and bureaucracy, they always had something else in their mind.

Meeting with an Old Enemy

Until the end of 2008, I stayed in the eastern fronts of the state of Garzan, Dorşin, Sason, and Muş. I did not have the opportunity to visit the fronts in the west due to my workload. In the winter of 2008–2009, I heard that headquarters had assigned two women comrades to my field. I learned that Asmin asked headquarters to be assigned to my duty field in the east. Of course, I got very angry with her when she arrived at our campground, because there had already been some complaints filed by the guerillas concerning a possible relationship between Asmin and myself during the winter of 2007–2008. Because of the existence of such complaints, it was completely wrong for Asmin to make a request to be assigned to my field and for the regional commander to have approved such a request.

I did not want another investigation of me because of this. Therefore, I immediately communicated with the state commander via radio, saying, "Comrade, you more or less know the relationship between Asmin and me. We had complaints about it by some of our comrades and now, despite that, you assigned her to my field! What was your purpose?" He replied, "Deniz, I meant no offense! Asmin asked, and pretty much insisted on it, so I assigned her to your field!" I asked, "Have you notified headquarters of the women guerillas, before assigning Asmin close to me?" "Yes, I did," he said. "Okay, then, if you are all aware and okay with this, then I should not be bothered about it!" I replied.

That same winter, my superior, the field commander, sent some news, stating, "I will be staying in your region this winter, Deniz. Arrange a place for me. He was then in Erzurum, and was to visit all the regions in Garzan, one by one. Later, he again contacted me via the radio and asked where I was staying. I told him that I was going to stay in Muş that winter. He said, "Comrade Deniz, I do not want to stay in Muş. Ask your guerilla force to arrange a place for me in Dorşin." "Heval, where I am staying is much safer, compared to the campground in Dorşin. If the security forces hear that you are staying in Dorşin, you do not have a chance of escaping alive," I told him.

He still insisted, so I arranged a place for him in Dorşin, and he spent that winter there. At the beginning of spring, before the snow even began to melt, he contacted me via radio on April 6. "Deniz, come to the camp where I am staying in Dorşin. I need to talk to you as soon as possible!" he said. The area in which I was staying was still covered with snow of 2 meters' height. In that field in Muş, the guerillas would leave their winter bunkers either at the end of April, or in the middle of May. Nevertheless, I left the bunker and headed to Dorşin, because of the field commander's insistence. I did not know that the head of Sason force had also been called to Dorşin.

For a week, the field commander held separate meetings with the forces of Dorşin, Sason and Muş. In one of those meetings, the relationship between Asmin and me came up. The field commander asked me, "Deniz, what is this all about? The comrades have been criticizing you, and, if I am not mistaken, this relationship between you and Asmin became the agenda last year, too." I said,

"It is true comrade! It did become the topic of discussion last year, also. Despite that, the state commander assigned her to my field! If you already knew the existence of such a relationship, why did you assign her to me?" I asked.

"So, you do not deny it? There is indeed something between the two of you!" "Why should I deny it? I have feelings for her. If you asked me if my feelings toward her were affecting the quality of the work I am doing, I would adamantly say no, they do not," I replied. "Okay, we will close this issue here. I will explain to my superiors, so that no one will ever talk about it anymore," he said.

That discussion occurred on April 19, of 2009. I remember the date quite well, because it coincided with the date of the first KCK operations [Operations carried out by Turkish police against the political wing of the PKK] against the organization, which truly shocked us. The local elections had recently been held, and the BDP (Peace and Democracy Party) had achieved a great success and was able to win the majority of votes in more than 79 districts in Eastern Anatolia. We even knew that the seniors of the organization were regularly meeting with the Turkish government to negotiate the terms of peace. Despite these ongoing meetings, we could not attach any meaning to the KCK operations. A weird situation had developed. The Turkish government was meeting with the seniors of the guerilla force of the organization, but the Turkish security forces were carrying out operations against the political wing of the organization in order to incarcerate them. On the one hand, we were being told to lay down our arms and weapons and discuss the terms of peace around a table through politics. On the other hand, the state arrested the professional politicians.

In 2009, after that meeting, the field commander (Hakkı) told me that I was to travel with him to the town of Siirt. We left Dorşin on May 13. We had five other guerillas from the Sason guerilla force with us. We had two possible routes to use when traveling to Siirt—either through Mutki-Bitlis, or through Sason-Kozluk.

Since everywhere was covered in snow, the Sason-Kozluk path would be too risky to use. Comrades could become frostbitten. The Mutki-Bitlis path was also risky, because it passed through the plains. I informed the field commander, Hakkı, about both of these risks waiting in front of us. "Comrade Hakkı, we have two options. One is a mountainous road, but covered with snow; the other one is an open field, but has security risks. You make the choice, since I do not want top responsibility in case something happens," I said. He told me, "We will travel through the plains, in Sason!"

When we reached Sason, it was almost spring. The trees were coming into leaf, the snow had melted, and the weather was very nice. We rested in Sason for two days, with 11 people in total. Around evening, I climbed up to a high hill and reconnoitered the area before setting off again. I noticed that many of the passages were held by the security forces. As spring arrived, the security forces had positioned themselves in the field. I told Hakkı, "Comrade, all the passages are held by the soldiers! We cannot make it through that way." He asked me what other options we had. I replied, "Those soldiers are positioned there during the daytime. I think they only lay an ambush during the evenings. That leaves us only one option. We will pass through there during the daytime before sunset. The area is already wooded and we can travel, carefully hiding behind the trees." He accepted my plan.

The next day around 6:00 a.m., we set off as planned. I was correct. The soldiers were laying ambush only at night, not in the daytime. The terrain was empty. I suppose the security forces were thinking that no one would be brave enough to pass through that area during daylight.

When we reached Kozluk, we stepped onto a flat plain. There was neither a wooded area, nor a hill behind which we could hide. We were walking in wheat fields, but around 1:00 p.m., when the sun was shining directly above us, we started to walk the perimeter of the field, since the wheat was absorbing all the sun's heat and making it difficult for us to walk in the middle. We had a large obstacle waiting before us; the Kozluk Stream. None of us had ever passed over this stream before. We did not know at which points it was shallow or deep. At sunset, we tried to pass over it, four or five times, from several different spots. Nevertheless, we were not able to cross. Not only was it very deep, but also the current was very strong. We could not move into the water for even 10 meters. We had to find an alternate way.

I said, "Comrade Hakkı, we now have two options in front of us. We can either reach the Silk Road and board one of the international transportation trucks going to, or passing by Bitlis." The trucks were important for the organization, because cars, minibuses and cabs would be stopped at security checkpoints, in various cities. However, the international trucks were exempt from this stop and search procedure. Someone must make a specific complaint for a truck to be stopped by the security forces. Hakkı did not accept my first offer. "Then, there is one option left, comrade," I said. "We will go into one of the villages, find us a vehicle, and pass over the stream, under the guise of passengers."

In line with my second plan, we arrived at a village in the middle of the night. Since it was late, the lights were off in almost every single house. The peasants were probably already sleeping. Nevertheless, we noticed a torch light close by. Two peasants were talking and, at the same time, working on something. We headed towards the light and noticed that one of the peasants was digging a hole, while the other one was holding the torch. He had dug almost 1.5 meters deep. After our greeting with them, I asked why they were digging that hole in the middle of the night. One of them said, "Comrade, we are looking for a treasure." I again asked, "Why are you searching for it at this time of the night? Besides, who told you that there was a treasure buried here?" He replied, "It is taken for granted that there is a large amount of treasure here, comrade." I felt sorry for them. They were probably wasting their time, and responded, "We have something we need to do. We have to cross the Kozluk Stream. We've already tried, but were not able to manage to do it.

Could you please find a vehicle in the village and drive us to the other side of the stream!" He replied, "Comrade, why do you want to use the bridge? If we use the bridge, you will have to pass through the downtown. It is very risky. You will be easily noticed, if we are stopped by security officials, patrolling at night. Let me show you where to cross the river." "Are you sure you can cross the stream? We already tried it, and not only is the water deep but the current is also too strong," I said. They then left their treasure hunt behind and took us to a point along the stream. Unbelievable! The place where they brought us was only 10 meters down from the spot that we had tried all night to cross. This peasant got into the water and walked to other side of the stream in five minutes. We were all shocked, and, one by one, we crossed the stream.

It was 2:00 a.m., and we were not only soaked but also exhausted. We were all dying for a sleep; nevertheless, we were then very close to the town of Kozluk. The slightest sight of us that might be captured by the soldiers would cost us our lives. Since Kozluk was a flat plain, without a single wooded area, it would be enough for the soldiers to attack us with a single panzer. We were an open and easy target.

Leaving 15 meter intervals between each of us, we laid down in a lentil field to rest. The next day, we had to continue to hide in the field, until the sun set, so as not to be recognized by the peasants. This was easier said than done. Can you imagine what it actually means to lay still, without moving, from 2:00 a.m., until sunset, approximately 20 hours? Try to lay down in your living room, without moving, for a couple hours! You will understand what I mean.

When the sun finally set, we first headed to Siirt-Baykan and then to the city of Bitlis. Three days after we reached Bitlis, the state management gathered for another meeting. I threw heavy criticism toward the superiors regarding the martyrdom of the comrade who was taken from his position, so that I could be appointed as a commander to Garzan state. The state commander assumed the full responsibility for that incident and apologized to everyone. "We made a serious mistake. As soon as we dismissed that comrade, we should have sent him to another region—probably to the south," he said.

Before the meeting ended, Hakkı offered something weird. "I am alone when fulfilling my responsibilities. As you all know, I am in charge of three states. Because of my workload, I am occasionally unable to travel to each state and to each region within them. When I last visited the state of Garzan, I could only visit two regions to check on how the guerillas were doing. I need an assistant, at the level of a senior commander, so that I can properly carry out my supervisory responsibilities. This person could visit the places that I cannot," he said. Our state commander replied to Hakkı, "That is understandable. With whom do you want to work? Give me a name!" Hakkı gave my name.

I was so surprised. Hakkı and I never got along well. I had filed official complaints about Hakkı, not just one time but several times. I had even criticized him in the meeting when Hakkı was forcing us to carry out a mission against the rangers, without letting the organization first know about it. He was assuming full responsibility of potential losses that might result from that mission. Despite all my complaints about him, he was asking the state management to assign me as his assistant. He definitely had something else on his mind.

I rejected his offer. "There are other comrades in the field, especially in the state of Amed, and they are more experienced and capable than I. Take one of them as an assistant." He continued to insist on me. "I want Deniz as my assistant!" The state commander said, "Hakkı, this is not something I can decide by myself. Let me discuss this issue with the other states…"

Those kinds of appointments would be done through a consensus. No ranked guerilla could be appointed to a position at the request of a state or field commander. Our field commander informed the state commanders of Erzurum and Amed about this request. They both rejected it. Amed province commander even said, "This does not make any sense to me. Deniz was supposed to be here, in my state. You stole him from me, saying that you really needed him. Why are you now planning to assign him under the field commander as an assistant? If you do not need him in your state, simply send him to Amed, as soon as possible!"

In the meantime, I figured out that Hakkı's real purpose was to keep me under his close control. If I were away from him, I could easily talk about and criticize him. But, if I worked under his control, as an assistant, he was thinking that he could control my behavior. When he continued to insist, I said, "You know what? It is indeed okay for me to work as his assistant. Let's not waste each other's time anymore. I am willing to work as assistant to field commander Hakkı."

Hakkı was extremely intelligent but also a double dealer. If I had not accepted his offer, he would probably have gotten in touch with headquarters management and filed a complaint about me, saying that I was dodging my duty. He knew that I had rejected two assignments in my past. Headquarters might think that blowing off a position was getting to be a habit in my character. Therefore, after second thought, I offered myself to work under him.

This time, Hakkı could not make sense of seeing me suddenly accepting his offer, since I had initially harshly rejected it. He probably thought that I might do something to him, while working under him. Towards the end of the meeting, he hemmed and hawed around, and then said, "Deniz, I think it is good for the organization, if you continue to carry out your activities in Garzan."

Right then, I began to drive him further into the corner, as I saw him step back. "Comrades! Hakkı, the field commander, has been constantly pushing us to carry out even more missions against the security forces. He compares Garzan with the state of Amed, in terms of the number of missions carried out against the security forces. This comparison is misleading. Our state is relatively new, compared to other states in the region. We have not even transferred enough guerillas from the south to fill the duty positions in our state. How can we carry out missions against the security forces when we do not fully control the areas in which we stay? Most of the guerillas assigned here are not even familiar with the terrain. Give us some time before calling us to account. Stop pressuring us to carry out large missions, as the other states do. We are not able to achieve this due to the circumstances I have just outlined. I will continue to lead the eastern fronts in Garzan only if Hakkı stops blaming me for not being success-ful. However, if you continue to complain about my performance, discharge me now!" All but Hakkı agreed with my words.

After my harsh critique of Hakkı, he began to give me a hard time, "Deniz, you have always ignored the authority of headquarters and have not paid attention to the rules!" He began to talk about an incident of mine, which occurred in the past; in 2007. The supreme guerilla force commandment had gathered for a conference. This conference would periodically gather about every two years in order to discuss the issues related to the guerillas. That year, some decisions were made, regarding the internal workings of the guerillas in each state. I had strongly objected to two of the decisions that were dis-cussed in that meeting. I had not gossiped about them, as many others had done. I barged into the con-versation, in front of everyone, and then explained my concerns about those two decisions. I said, "You are disregarding the special circumstances of the states within Turkey when considering those changes and you are making a big mistake."

One of the decisions supported by the majority of the conference participants, was that each state was going to recruit its own guerillas from then on. The second decision related to each state being responsible for self-financing from then on. I had mentioned the tragic incident, which occurred in the 2006–2007 winter camp in Dorşin. One of our comrades had killed seven others, while they were asleep, and had then fled. This tragedy had, unavoidably, created an atmosphere of nervousness and dis-trust among the guerillas. Everybody knew that it could be a fatal decision to accept a new guerilla among us immediately. We would not know the newbie very well, and we would not even know if he or she had any connections to the security forces. Therefore, we would not be able to know how hon-est they were or what might be in their past, yet we were expected to accept them immediately. How could we know that this newbie would not do any harm to his or her comrades in the winter camp when they spent the winter in the bunker? That is why I raised my objection and suggested to them that guerillas who would fight in the north should be selected only from the experienced ones in the south (Syria and Iraq) with whom the organization had formed a trusting relationship. I suggested. "We can recruit newbies from our regions, but they should be first sent to the south to be trained and to fig-ure out their real intentions for joining us. Someone's real personality and character is only understood after a couple years living among us. After this period, we should let only the most trusted guerillas be assigned to north," I said.

It was also a faulty approach to hold each state responsible for suppling itself financially, because our state (Garzan) did not have the same opportunities that Amed or other states had at that time. For example, the state of Amed covers a very large area and almost all of Kurdistan's big cities fall within its borders. The guerilla management of Amed state was in a close relationship with the industrial establishments and rich merchants. They were able to collect large sums of money monthly. Now, Garzan has not a single economically wealthy city within its borders. There was nei-ther an industrial establishment, nor rich merchants who could support us financially. The Kurdish public, living in our cities, were also poor. They were not able to support their families, let alone help us financially.

If this decision had taken place in the old times, it would not be a problem for us guerillas, because, as a member of a guerilla force, we were given the right of collecting taxes from the factories and large construction companies, building roads, dams, and other facilities within our regions. However, all this had changed in 2003. The authority to collect taxes from those facilities had been taken from the guerilla forces and given to the KCK. Therefore, the taxes were then being collected by our civilian comrades, carrying out activities within the cities. The guerilla force was banned from collecting taxes anymore. All these taxes were to be spent by the self-defense units organized within the Kurdish cities. With those authority changes, the guerilla force had begun to experience financial difficulties, meaning we began to be unable to self-finance ourselves. It became so bad that we were sometimes unable to find money to buy ammunition and, therefore, unable to engage in reconnaissance activities within city centers before carrying out missions.

Headquarters had also stopped sending money to us. Now, when we were in trouble, we asked for help from the state of Amed. That was why I had objected to that issue when discussed at the meeting. I had told them that the financial opportunities were not equally distributed across each state, and only a few states were able to self-finance their activities. I had told them that the state of Garzan would not be able to fundraise money from the cities under its authority, due to their income circumstances. It was similar for Amanoses. What could the guerillas in Amanoses do to earn money? Were they supposed to collect money from the tourists? What would the guerillas in Garzan do? The people living there were already poor. Were we supposed to establish a mint and print our own bank notes?

Fortunately, it was not only I who opposed those decisions. In fact, the field commander of Dersim supported me by saying, "The Dersim Field is still borrowing money from the state of Amed, plus Amed is also sending uniforms to our guerillas, since we do not have money to buy fabrics. Under those circumstances, how could you expect us to fund ourselves?"

In May 2009, Hakkı again tried to defame me by using those objections I had raised in 2007. He said to me, "You always object the decisions of the organization! You are a rebel." He even went further and began to insult me by saying, "There were 300 other high-ranked commanders in that conference. Were they not as intelligent or capable as you were? Could they not consider those caveats? Why were you the only one objecting to those decisions? What was your real purpose? Are you against the policies of the organization?" Despite his accusations, the fact remained that there was nothing to show me as rebelling against the long-established rules and regulations of the party.

18

DECISION TO KEEP MY HANDS OFF

During the winter of 2008–2009, the Turkish security forces carried out several land operations on our field at the triangle cities of Muş, Bingöl, and Kulp. This field was previously convicted of a well-known incident, perpetrated by some dark forces within the PKK. Additionally, many of the guerilla missions which were carried out without the prior knowledge of headquarters, in 1992 and 1993, had also occurred in this same field. I mentioned before about the malicious boarding of unarmed Turkish soldiers into a civilian bus and them being sent off without protection or escorts. They became sitting ducks to Şemdin Sakık, and all those soldiers were killed by him in 1993 in this same field.

There was really something going on in this region, but neither the guerillas nor the seniors at headquarters were aware of what was happening. The incidents taking place were out of our control. For example, we were carrying out a simple mission against the security forces, simply to intimidate them—and we knew that it would not throw a deathblow to them. However, we would sometimes find that the mission was more successful than what we had originally thought would happen. This only occurred in that field and never in the others. It was as if some unseen forces were opening up space for us, so that we could establish our PKK authority there. We could not figure out whether there was a trap behind this, but we were freely moving and carrying out our activities there. Neither the security forces nor the rangers were interfering with us.

It was extremely unusual that the soldiers were carrying out operations in the Bingöl, Solhan, and Kulp triangle in the middle of winter under the snow cover. Even Apo was highly disturbed by those operations occurring in that area. I remember it very well. He had sent a note to us from prison via his lawyers. It said, "What is going on in that triangle again? Who is the guerilla commander there? How could the soldiers carry out a land sweep during this winter season?" I felt nervous when I read that note, since I had the sole responsibility if something bad were to happen. As you know, Şemdin Sakık was one of the previous guerilla commanders of this region, and I could experience what he experienced.

Apo had used the words, "What is going on in that triangle again?" for a reason. They were carefully structured words. It was not an ordinary sentence trying to understand what was going on there. Rather, Apo was implying something dangerous, which caused my nervousness. I had no connection with the Turkish security forces or the intelligence services and could not figure out why Apo implied that in his note. It was an area which was under the control of the Turkish national police and their intelligence units rather than the security forces, and their own intelligence. I was stuck with a difficult situation. Almost all the traitors within the PKK, who secretly worked for the Turkish intelligence units, had also worked in this field. For instance, we all knew that Mahmut Yildirim (Yeşil) [A Kurdish contract killer who worked for the Turkish National Intelligence Organization] was meeting with Şemdin Sakık in this area.

For days, reading that note several times, I thought carefully and finally came to the conclusion that Apo was trying to warn headquarters about the existence of a potential agent/traitor working for the Turks. He was warning them to be extra-careful about the guerilla commander of this triangle. Then, headquarters would focus on all the activities and guerilla missions going on in this region in order to discover the traitor. With a single mistake I could easily face a traitor charge. Due to this risk, I asked my superior, the state commander of Garzan, to assign me to a different position, during the meeting we held in May 2009.

The state commander asked why I was insisting on such a change now. I said, "I have been here for a few years and want to be assigned to a western front. The comrade who has been in charge there could now take my position." Unfortunately, I was not as familiar with the terrain of the western front, and the state commander rejected my proposal. He said, "Comrade Deniz, you have established such close relations with the rangers in the eastern front and you are acquainted with the Kurdish peasants living there. If you leave now, we will lose all our contacts and friends there. I cannot take such a huge risk!"

"Comrade! I understand your concerns. However, I will now ask you a question and you will be honest with me. After the arrival of that note from Apo, has anyone from the PKK administration asked you any question regarding me?" "Yes, they did. They asked me to provide the name of the person who was staying in that region. In fact, I asked them then if I could reassign you to another field if they had concerns about you, but, they did not answer me back," he replied. Headquarters and the defense committee would know which commander was assigned to which field. Nevertheless, the PKK administration could not know that, since they had no direct connection to the headquarters of the guerrilla force.

I knew for sure then that someone was testing me and looking for a possible mistake that I might have committed in the past. The words used by Apo had left question marks in the minds of many guerillas. Apo had not uttered those words for no reason. Someone had probably warned him beforehand. Those dark forces operating within the Turkish security forces or the organization were planning to carry out a mission, similar to the killing of 33 Turkish soldiers.

Considering all those risks, I again said to my state commander that I could not work in that region any longer. The organization had also forced the Turks to agree to the establishment of the "Parliamentary Commission Investigating Truths," in Oslo, as a precondition of the peace talks. This was supposed to be a double-headed commission, with both the Turks and the organization needing to explain, and give account, to the civilian Turks and Kurds, of all dark incidents which occurred throughout this war. As the Turkish security forces did, we, as an organization, had also committed some atrocities that we had to face. Several Kurdish rangers were killed, unarmed civilian villagers had pain inflicted upon them, and some of them were killed, simply because they were siding with the Turks. The organization was trying to wash its hands of those atrocities, as individual guerilla missions rather than the policy of headquarters. We were going to pay the price for all the atrocities we had committed up until that time by holding specific individuals responsible for them. For that job, the organization needed names.

In the past, we had carried out horrific atrocities against some villages. In those missions, children, women, and older people were all killed, along with the rangers, but, by 2009, most of the guerillas who had participated in those missions had already lost their lives during clashes with the security forces. There was only myself and a few other comrades left alive. So, who would be the best candidate to assume the responsibilities for all those missions carried out against the Kurdish villagers in the 1990s? It was going to be either me or one of the other two. Right then, I figured that I could be held responsible for everything, since I was assigned to this critical post—the triangle of Bitlis, Solhan, and Kulp.

As a matter of fact, I decided not to carry out any more missions and did not participate in a single one during the next three years. If I had made a mission and even achieved great results, I would be put under investigation for any small error. For example, in 2008, I sent one of our comrades to the downtown area of Muş to collect intelligence about critical infrastructure that we might attack. He had carried out an awesome reconnaissance. We bought a car for $4,000 and loaded it with explosive materials. There was a bus, which would be transporting 40 mid- to high-ranking soldiers every morning from the downtown of Muş to their duty posts at the airport. This bus would also bring them back to downtown at the end of the day. We were going to park our explosive-loaded vehicle on the bus route and detonate it when the bus drove by.

All those high-ranking soldiers were traveling within an unprotected bus. There was neither a panzer nor a security vehicle escorting them during their journey. Even if there were an armored panzer escorting them, we could still have blown it up, but there was the example of 33 soldiers, killed by Şemdin, facing us as a caution. We had to consider whether those soldiers were given purposefully to us as prey to serve some other force's larger objectives and goals. If so, we could find ourselves where Şemdin was after killing those 33 unarmed soldiers.

It could have been a blockbuster mission if we killed those 40 soldiers. Everything was planned and we could get them, without harming a single civilian. However, I did not allow my forces to carry out that mission. As I said, the organization would probably congratulate and reward us initially. Nevertheless, one week later, we could be put under investigation because of a small detail we had missed. You could be detained by a question like, "Why did you park the explosive-loaded vehicle here but not there?"

There were many other examples of these kinds of investigations. In 2009, an armored vehicle was blown up by guerilla forces, either in the town of Lice or in Genc. I do not remember exactly. That explosion hit all the news channels and attracted the attention of the public. The head of the Turkish General Staff even delivered a public speech saying, "We still do not know how this explosion was carried out or what kind of explosive was used; whether a missile, propane tank filled with explosives, or land mine." The comrade who planned and carried out this mission was initially thanked by headquarters for his success. I remember it very well. Everyone was talking about how successful he was. He had suddenly become a hero. But not a month passed and the same comrade was put under investigation because of the incident and was discharged from his position.

In fact, an order had arrived from headquarters to carry out a retaliatory mission against the security forces. That is why that comrade destroyed the armored vehicle. However, he was discharged from his position and told, "Why did you carry out such a big mission when we are negotiating the terms of peace with the Turks? Are you a traitor? Do you work for the Turkish security forces?"

Indeed, carrying out even a simple mission had become too risky for us guerillas after 2004, compared to earlier years. It was not because the security forces were better than we, or that they had more advanced war technology. The PKK had more than a thousand already planned missions in its pocket to carry out in Turkey when the time came. For all those future missions, the reconnaissance would be completed, and the explosives, mines and the weapons would already be arranged. The only drawback was to consider every possible aspect of any liability.

After 2004, as commanders, we were required to take into account all possible military and political consequences of a single guerilla mission before carrying it out. It had not been that way during the 1990s. Back then, the more Turkish security forces you killed, the more successful you would be considered by the organization. However, this was no longer the case. We were in close contact with the European Union, the United States, and many countries in the Middle East. In short, we were then connected to world politics. No matter what they said in the media, most of those powers had already accepted that the PKK was an organization defending the basic rights of the Kurds against the oppressive Turks, and we did not want to spoil our relations with these powers by carrying out attacks against the security forces with tragic consequences. Therefore, the guerillas were then required to limit their attacks to retaliatory purposes. We would engage in clashes as long as we could legitimize their consequences to the other world powers. Otherwise, we could run the risk of losing our legitimacy of defending Kurdish rights. Other than those concerns, as an organization, we had sat with the Turks at the negotiation table where we had to be extra careful. The Turks had strong tools in their hands in order to legitimize their military operations, including diplomats stationed around the world, legitimate information outlets, and media resources. They could use those resources to fabricate a story and make the world believe it, as the Americans had in the Iraqi war. We did not have many of those same resources. Therefore, even the smallest mistake we might make could change the point of view of those with whom the organization was in a close relationship. We did not now have a free hand, as we had in the old days.

I decided to keep myself free from any kind of guerilla missions between 2006 and 2009. However, it was not because of running the risk of spoiling the organization's bilateral relations with world powers. Rather, it was mainly because of the concerns I had. My remaining passive for three years aroused the attention of some of my ranked comrades. They began to ask me questions, such as, "Deniz, you have planned and carried out many successful guerilla missions in the past. Why this change now? You have not carried out any missions for three years. This could be a problem for your future career!" I would keep them at bay by replying, "Comrades, I decided not to kill as many people as I had in the old days. I will now only kill the enemy forces when it is necessary!" Of course, they were not satisfied with my answers.

Being Tested for Loyalty

The organization was probably suspicious of me, since I was not carrying out any kind of missions against the security forces. In September, 2009, I was sent to a mission planned by the region management. They were probably trying to test my loyalty to the party. There was a military control post right at the entrance of the town of Kulp, though it was not part of the military infrastructure. The security forces had placed a container at the entrance to the city and were randomly stopping and searching cars, driving through the city. I was asked to destroy this post, along with the soldiers (maybe it had been police officers). It was an easy job for me.

I was escorted by two local guides as I headed towards Kulp to reconnoiter. I told the region management, "I do not need those guides. I'm familiar with the area," but they insisted on me traveling with them. When we reached a point close to the town of Kulp, I noticed, via the radio, that the soldiers were in frequent communication with one another. I was sure that they were up to something. Most probably, they were sending squads to the field for an ambush, so we began to travel a different route. We were all able to reach our target without being ambushed.

Since I had safely reached my destination, the guides were to return to their homes. Before they left, I warned them, perhaps three times, not to use the path about which I was suspicious. There was another path, much longer but much safer. I described to both of them this second route back to Sason. Unfortunately, they ignored my warnings and used the other path, probably because it was much shorter compared to one I had described. I still do not know whether the Kurdish villagers or a traitor among us informed the security forces, but the soldiers had advance knowledge of an executive, from the Garzan state, passing through their region. That is why they had set ambushes everywhere. One of those two guides was martyred in that ambush on his way back home. He was the son of a well-known person in that region. If I am not mistaken, his name was Berxwedan. That comrade was carrying a camera and a couple memory cards with him. Unfortunately, all those things were captured by the soldiers. That military operation lasted a few days. The soldiers thought that I was still in that region, but I had already reached the town of Kulp.

When I arrived there, I asked three civilian comrades to go downtown and take pictures of everything. I then created a map, using those pictures, highlighting all police stations, the central police command, military posts, district Governorship Building, and everything else that might possibly retaliate against me after carrying out my mission on that control post at the exit of town. Some of the military posts and police stations were very close to my target. I might be caught, so I had to be extra careful. After the reconnaissance, I decided that I needed at least four others to carry out this mission.

A vehicle full of explosives was going to drive close to the search and control area, and the driver was going to blow up the vehicle when the soldiers were close to him. Of course, I needed a volunteer to carry out this first part of the plan, because it was a self-sacrificing mission. After the explosion, the guerillas, driving in another vehicle, were going to kill all the remaining soldiers with hackbut fires. No one was going to be left alive. After the reconnaissance and planning, I returned to Sason. I told the regional management that everything was planned, but I had delayed the mission to find a suitable guerilla for the self-sacrificing mission. In fact, my goal was to delay the mission as much as possible for the reasons I outlined before.

Around that time, my superior, the Garzan State guerilla commander, was assigned to another post in the south. I was very well acquainted with the new person replacing him. The old state commander was very talented. However, similar to me, he was not getting along well with his superior, Hakkı, the region commander. He objected to all of Hakkı's nonsense orders. Hakkı did not want him under his command, so he had asked headquarters to relocate him to another position.

Since I was able to postpone the mission at Kulp, by the excuse of finding a voluntary self-sacrificing guerilla, Hakkı assigned me to another mission. A thermal power plant was being built somewhere close to the town of Kulp. He asked me to go there and collect the building taxes. Normally, the Kurdish self-defense teams, our civilian comrades, were supposed to collect that tax. However, the owner of the company that was to build the plant had refused to pay them. In such situations, we armed guerillas would pay a visit to them and collect the taxes.

The amount of tax was calculated according to the scale of the job done by the company. In most situations, it would be 10 percent of the amount the contractor was paid by the state. According to the research conducted by our self-defense teams, this contractor was paid $145,000,000 to build that plant. After our visit, he agreed to pay the tax. Nevertheless, this man had many friends who were able to negotiate the tax amount with us. By contacting some important names from the organization's European representatives, seniors from Kandil, and even some Kurdish politicians from Turkey, he was able to reduce the tax amount to $5,000,000. He informed us that, "I'm not able to drive to Kulp to give you the money, so let's decide on a meeting point, somewhere in Amed. It can be Hazro, Lice, Genc, or any other town of your choice. If you cannot meet me there, connect me with someone from those places, so that I can pay my taxes." There was no problem left to solve. He was willing to pay it. I communicated with the state guerilla commander of Amed to have him collect the taxes. I later confirmed that the owner had paid all $5,000,000 in three monthly installments.

Despite this, the field commander, Hakkı, had ordered a squad from the Dorşin guerilla force to burn all the construction vehicles belonging to this company. While I was planning activities to be carried out in my new post in Muş, the Amed guerilla commander contacted me via radio. He asked me, in an angry tone, "Comrade Deniz, why did you set this man's vehicles on fire? He had paid all his taxes." I replied, "Comrade, I did not know that the company vehicles had been burned. I am in Muş now. I do not even work there anymore."

This was very strange, because I was supposed to be informed before this mission was carried out since I was the contact person between the owner and the organization. Now, I could be held responsible for whatever happened there. Headquarters would contact me and ask, "What was your purpose? Are you trying to spoil our relations with the Kurdish businessmen? Do you work for the government?" It was just a matter of time before I might be put under investigation because of it.

Toward the end of 2009, before headquarters heard about this incident, I reached out to them to let them know the truth. Hakkı was always doing something destructive behind my back. I contacted headquarters and told them that the unjust mission had been carried out by Dorşin guerilla forces, with the order of field commander Hakkı. In this way, I was able to save myself from the trap planned by Hakkı.

Winter, Fallen Comrades, and Traitors

I spent the winter of 2009 to 2010 in a camp near the city of Muş. That winter season, I had decided to gather all female guerillas and have them stay in a single underground bunker, instead of scattering them in different locations. All the women guerillas in my region, nine in total, and seven men guerillas were arranged to stay there. I stayed in another bunker with 13 other guerillas.

The remaining nine guerillas in our region stayed in another camp near to the town of Sason. Before it started to snow, I checked all the underground bunkers to make sure they were safe enough. During these visits, I also shared the encrypted communication codes with the commander of each of the bunkers. I told them, "Keep those codes to yourself and let me know immediately if something happens!"

It was January 22, 2010. I received a radio communication from the Dorşin guerilla commander. He informed me that one of the women guerillas had fled the camp and surrendered to the Turkish security forces. Normally, in the case of a deserting guerilla, the winter underground bunker had to be evacuated, since that traitor would possibly inform the security forces about its location. After a long discussion in our bunker in Muş, we decided, as a group, to travel to Dorşin and bring all those comrades back to our bunker.

According to the plan, four of our comrades and the Muş region commander would set off for Dorşin to bring those comrades back to our area. In the meantime, we were to stay in the camp and prepare sleeping quarters for the newcomers. It was morning, and the comrades were just about to set out, when the Muş region commander came up to me and said, "Comrade Deniz, I cannot bear this cold weather and snow. I do not think I will be able to travel such a distance in these conditions." There was another region commander staying with us, who could potentially lead the other four comrades. However, he was our guest and not a member of our team. He was to go to Dersim Field in the spring of 2010. It would be rude to assign a guest with a duty related to our field.

That left only one option. I was to lead the four guerillas to Dorşin. We set off on January 23 at 8:00 a.m. It was so snowy outside, and, in some places, the snow had piled up to more than 2 meters. It was freezing cold and also snowing non-stop. Normally, it would take only three hours of walking, between our camp in Muş and Dorşin camp, but, that day, we walked from 8:00 a.m. until 4:00 p.m. and could still see our camp field in Muş. In eight hours, we had only been able to cover a distance of less than 2 kilometers.

Around 5:00 p.m., we stopped and started a fire, since we were all exhausted. We sat around the fire to warm our bodies. While sitting, one of the comrades began to talk weirdly. He was speaking nonsensical words. His name was Xelil, and he was originally a Syrian Kurd. Then, he also began to act strangely. Not only his speaking, but also his gestures had changed, as if he were a drunken person. Poor comrade, he had lost one of his shoes while walking in the snow and had not stopped us to go back and find it, because it would delay our trip. As soon as I noticed his situation, I told the other comrades that he would no doubt soon die, so that they would not be too shocked. The heat of a fire could kill a person, who had been subjected to severe cold for a long time, and I told them to move him away from fire. I had had a lot of experience of those situations. If any of your body parts are subjected to direct contact with the snow, you should never get close to a fire's heat, because you could lose your life!

Three meters away from the fire, we laid down two sleeping bags and put Xelil on them. He was now unconscious. The four of us began to rub his hands and feet to increase the blood circulation in his body, but then his speech became completely unrecognizable. He was like a toddler who was just learning to talk. He passed away before 7:00 p.m.

We were all demoralized, and I told the remaining three comrades, "We will stay awake, close to each other, around this fire. It is too risky to travel at night in this cold. We will keep the fire alive; however, nobody is going to sleep!" Because we were sitting on the snowy ground and the temperatures were so extremely cold, we would not make it to the morning if we fell asleep next to that fire.

It was −22 degrees Fahrenheit, and we had to move our bodies regularly, even though they were warmed up from the heat of the fire. Otherwise, the blood in your body would stop flowing. In order to stay awake, we chatted with each other until sunrise. I was hitting my comrades' heads with my cane when they closed their eyes.

As soon as the sun rose, we placed Xelil's corpse into a sleeping bag and then buried him under the snow. Nothing would happen to the corpse at that time of year. It would not decompose until spring. On the other hand, there were also no wild beasts living in that region. We could return to this place, just before the spring, and then bury him.

After we buried Xelil's body in the snow, we had not even walked 15 meters when a comrade shouted at me, "Comrade Deniz, I am exhausted and I cannot even move my legs. You go on. I will stay here." His name was Hebun. The three of us spent quite a bit of time convincing him to continue with us. We rubbed his hands and feet but nothing worked. He insisted on staying there. Since we were all waiting in the snow, the other two comrades told me, "Comrade Deniz, if we keep waiting here, we will all die. We should continue on, whether Hebun comes with us or not."

I had to make a choice. We were either going to leave Hebun there alone and continue on our journey, or we all were going to stay there with him and die. It would have been unjust of me if I let the others die because of one comrade. Therefore, I decided to leave Hebun to save the lives of others. We set up a tent and left a lot of firewood in front of it. We started a fire and left his share of food in the tent and then set off. Hebun had to survive for at least two days, until we could return from the Dorşin camp. If luck were with him, we would then carry him with us on our way back to the camp field in Muş.

If it had been my decision only, I would never have left Hebun alone there. However, the other two comrades were also beginning to feel exhausted because of the cold. As I said, we were either going to all die together, or we were going to continue our trip and leave him behind. I later learned that Hebun committed suicide in the tent. He shot himself in the head. Hebun knew that he would die if he stayed in that tent, and I also knew that. If he had forced himself to come with us, he might have been alive today. The chance of survival was very small if he remained there.

As the remaining members of our group, we continued our trip to Dorşin, under a heavy blizzard. Shortly before sunset, we started a fire and gathered around it once again to warm our bodies. We were using green wood for our fire, because it would not produce as much smoke as dead wood. The next morning, I experienced one of the scariest things in my life. I was not able to see! Two things might have potentially affected my eyesight: the exposure to the fire's smoke or the white colored snow that covered everything. My two comrades did not know the route to Dorşin, and, though I was not able to see anything, I trying to describe the way to them, as well as I could.

One comrade started to cry when he saw me like that. "Comrade Deniz, if you die, then we will die as well. We do not know the route, nor do we have any experience with these winter conditions. If you wish, I will carry you on my shoulders and you can just describe the way to Dorşin. Please, do not give up! Do not leave us alone!" The comrades began to describe to me things in the terrain, such as the trees, streams, rocks, and hills, and I gave them instructions to follow, as much as I could remember from the 1990s.

I did not let them carry me on their shoulders. Instead, they held my hands and we walked together. We reached a village on the evening of the fourth day. I asked them to go to the third house, after passing over the bridge. I was acquainted with the people living there. The family was shocked to see us in that season. It was highly unusual, since all the guerillas were hiding in their bunkers. I was still unable to see. While sitting there, I heard the sound of an old woman, with whom I was familiar. I asked her if she would sit next to me. I quietly informed her about the condition of my eyes, and asked her, "Ma, I cannot see. Do you think this is something permanent? If not, what should I do to recover my eyesight?" She asked me how many days I had been suffering from this. "We haven't slept for four days ma, and my eyes have been like this for the past two days," "Son, do not worry, there is a remedy to fix it," she said.

"I will check on you tomorrow," she said. Before I even asked, she told me the reason for the temporary blindness in my eyes. "Son, you probably were exposed to smoke in the snow. Your eyes are infected. These potato and onion slices will kill all the germs piled up in your eyes. Do not worry! You will be fine!" she said.

We stayed in that village until I recovered from my temporary blindness and then set off again to reach our comrades at Dorşin. When we met them, they appeared very nervous. They had left their underground bunker due to the potential risk of a military siege.

They had been in a mobile position, changing their location weekly. I found the commander of the Dorşin force and asked him to give me all the details regarding this desertion incident and was angry with what I heard. This woman had, in fact, deserted the camp on January 2. However, we were not informed about the incident until January 22—20 days after the incident! Even though the Dorşin force did not feel the need to seek help from us, they should have informed all the bunkers immediately, because this woman, that surrendered to the security forces, might have informed them about the locations of all bunkers in the region. I could not understand how they could act in such an irresponsible manner. They could have caused the whole region to be doomed by the security forces, because of their negligence.

The region commander of Kulp (the comrade who was responsible for the winter camp in Dorşin) and the field commander, Hakkı, were getting along pretty well. Hakkı had directly appointed this comrade as the region commander, without consulting the other seniors in the Garzan State. Despite the fact that this new region commander was an older and experienced person, it was not appropriate for Hakkı to have appointed someone on his own. Consequently, I raised my objections to this assignment, told them that this region commander should not be staying in our region for two reasons. First, Hakkı had appointed him without complying with the long-established organization rules. Second, I knew this comrade from the south, and even though he was experienced and excellent in ideological training, he was not good at planning guerilla missions. Despite my objections, the field commander brushed off my words, saying that this new fellow was going to work as a region commander. Normally, Hakkı was required to schedule a meeting to discuss this appointment with the seniors of the state administration.

I later learned that the field commander had told the new region commander, "Deniz has a soft spot for women, and he may be in relationship with someone in Muş. Let me know if you hear anything about it!"

As I mentioned, I stayed in Kulp (Dorşin) from January 29 to March 19 in order to learn the details of the desertion incident. I noticed that, during my stay there, the region commander was giving me the cold shoulder. He looked at me with suspicious eyes. Since he was an inferior to me, in no way should he have treated me like that. Besides, he was primarily liable for all the negative things happening then. The woman deserted the camp while under his command. My two comrades had lost their lives just because he was not able to control one woman under his authority.

With whomever I talked, at Dorşin, I was informed that the deserter was not someone who would normally desert us and surrender to Turkish security forces. Therefore, I gave this region commander a very hard time. "Why did not you pay attention to the problems of this women guerilla? She was not someone who would readily desert us, and even though she deserted, she would not surrender herself to the security forces. Her father was killed by the security forces in 1993! There is something else going on, of which we are not aware." Her father's homicide was recorded as an "unsolved murder," which was very common during 1990s.

We carried out more detailed research and found out that the deserter had not surrendered herself to the Turkish security forces. She was caught by them in the city of Batman. Later, findings indicated that, in fact, the region commander had a part in her desertion. That is why he was cold towards me. He was trying to create a different agenda to make others forget about his own mistake in the desertion incident.

In Dorşin camp, two other senior commanders were present when this incident occurred—a woman PKK Headquarters Committee member and a woman who was state guerilla commander of the women in Garzan. When I talked with them, I discovered that everyone was annoyed with the state guerilla commander. The guerillas were not satisfied with his style, attitude, behavior, or his approach to them. This made me angry. "If you people already knew that this person was incapable of being a leader, why did you not inform headquarters so that he could have been discharged from his duty?" The women's state commander replied, "Comrade Deniz, we thought we could discharge him after consulting with all the seniors in the state, during the spring. We simply wanted to wait until we met with you!" I got even more furious and turned on the headquarters committee member, replying, "It is true, that she was not authorized to discharge someone without consulting the rest of the state administration! Nevertheless, you were accorded such authority! You are a member of the headquarters executive council and could have discharged the region commander with a few words!" She said again, that she had decided to wait until I reached Dorşin. Nonsense!

Back to Home

We stayed in Dorşin until the snow melted, but it was still cold. We could have lost other comrades if we had traveled in that weather. I had also decided that there was no need to bring the Dorşin force back to Muş, since the security forces had not carried out any operation in such a long time. It appeared clear that the deserter had not provided them with any information regarding the camp locations. I think it was March 19, when I departed for Muş. I left behind those two comrades, who traveled with me to Dorşin, in case the Dorşin force needed extra manpower against a potential military attack.

When I reached the camp in Muş, I was told that the comrades had executed one of the guerillas among them. The region commander had decided to execute him without notifying anyone. Since they had made such a decision without first informing me, I asked the region commander to give me a written report explaining his reasoning. I said to him, "How could you decide such a decision by yourself? You could have waited for my return or reached out to the field commander, before carrying out that execution! You are, no doubt, in trouble!"

He said to me, "Comrade Deniz! It was the middle of winter, and you were not here. We were not able to use the radio to inform you, since we could have been detected by the security forces. I could not keep him in prison until the end of winter, because he would have needed constant guarding by the comrades. He might even have harmed one of us. I could not take the risk, so I decided to execute him right away!" I asked, "Did you have any solid evidence that he was an agent working for the security forces? On what grounds did you decide to execute him?" In response, he showed me letters that the prisoner had signed. During the investigation, he had admitted everything.

Others had suspected him of being an infiltrated agent because of his weird behaviors. I was told that he had been engaging in activities during the evenings that could compromise the safety of the camp. For example, we never went out with a torch at night. Nevertheless, he had been going out of the bunker with a torch in his hand, despite all the warnings given by his comrades. Also, he had been staying awake nights and frequently checking the sleeping quarters, as if he were doing reconnaissance for a mission. He often had given excuses to skip the training sessions. But, when he did attend the training, he had asked questions that did not fit the agenda and had put his comrades on guard. For all those reasons, the comrades had naturally been suspicious of him. So, after a short meeting, all of them decided to put him under immediate investigation. They turned on the heat until the truth came out. He had confessed that he was an agent working for the security forces, not the military, but with the police force. He had been tasked with killing a high-ranked guerilla and capturing all the codes on him or her and then delivering them to the police.

This man was from Diyarbakır–Baglar, and, according to his written report, the police had threatened him into doing what he had planned. He had been mixed up in illegal business; probably drug dealing or smuggling. The police had caught him and kept him in jail for a few days until he was exhausted. Then they threatened him. "You will either help us or spend the rest of your life in prison." He had confessed everything in his signed report: "The security forces threatened me and my family members, because of the illegal business I carried out in the past. I had no other option but to go along with their request."

The comrades asked him why he had specifically chosen our camp field in which to carry out his plans. They asked why he had not gone to another region, instead of ours. He replied, "I was initially staying near the state guerilla commander of Garzan, and he was seriously injured in one of the clashes with the security forces. I was then assigned to two other posts. During my assignments there, I frequently heard the name of Comrade Deniz. Therefore, I figured that he must be someone of importance in the organization. That is why I chose to kill him. If I killed such an important figure within the party, I thought I could get in good graces with the police department and could pay my debt to them, and they would probably let me alone."

He had even planned on how to kill me. He said that he was going to be my close protection guard and then shoot me as we traveled, for a meeting, from our region to another. I still find it hard to believe. I had stayed with this man for a month. He was highly sincere and sympathetic. I never thought that he could have been an agent.

Towards the End

When I was headed for Muş, on March 19, this region commander had talked on the radio to the state commander. Since I was traveling by myself, I gave all my attention to security and was not closely following the radio talks. Some comrades later informed me about this conversation. The region commander had told the state commander that I was in love with a woman, but the woman he had in mind wasn't Asmin. The state commander told the region commander, "It's impossible! As far as I know, Deniz is in love with Asmin. Besides, the woman of whom you speak, is a very close associate of Asmin. You must be mistaken! How could Deniz fall in love with that girl when he is in love with Asmin?"

Since the state commander did not believe those accusations, the region commander directly communicated with Hakkı, a close friend of his. In response, Hakkı, my old enemy, ordered the state commander to put me under investigation.

I still was not aware of those developments. However, the cold attitude of the region commander was a bee in my bonnet, and I sensed that something was not normal at Dorşin. The region commander's behavior towards me was extremely weird. He did not even answer my questions, and not only that, the other guerillas had put up a social barrier between themselves and me. It was as if I were carrying a contagious and fatal disease. There was definitely something going on, of which I was not yet aware.

While I was still in Muş, I requested the female PKK headquarters member in Dorşin to visit me. When she arrived, I asked her, "Comrade, I felt that something was not normal there? Do you have any advance knowledge of anything of which I am not aware?" This woman began talking and told me the entire story. The region commander had told everyone some false things, regarding me. "Comrade, there is a situation, and the field commander ordered them to put you under an investigation," she said, shocking me. I replied, "Comrade, it is totally disgusting to suggest that I am in such a relationship! I am in love with Asmin and most everyone knows about it. If the region commander had charged me with being love with Asmin, I would accept all charges. Even though they know the truth, why are they using this other woman's name (Şilan) in this false rumor? I just do not understand this!"

In response to my question, the headquarters member said to me, "Deniz, I am not 100 percent sure. However, my guess would be that you are the butt of something! My best advice to you is to watch extra carefully your every single movement!" I thought she was right and asked, "Comrade, whom do you think is behind all these claims?" She said, "It certainly cannot be the region commander. He has neither the power nor the courage to challenge you. You, yourself, have the authority to discharge him or even to incarcerate him, without consulting the state commander. I think that idiot is just a tool in this scheme. Nevertheless, I do not know from whom he takes his orders to treat you in such a disrespectful manner."

I was sure, then, that Hakkı was going to arrest me. However, I was confident that, in the end, they could not charge me with anything, since, in fact, I did not have any relations with Şilan. So, I was feeling rather comfortable about it. Even if they might have incarcerated me for a while, they would eventually have had to drop all the charges against me, since the relationship they claimed was not true. I was even pleased that Hakkı and his puppets would have to act the guilty goat, when the truth was known to everyone.

After breakfast, on the morning of April 7, 2010, the region commander of Muş, along with Hakkı's tool in this scheme, the Dorşin region commander, came up to me. The Muş region commander was a decent person and a very committed and respectful comrade to me. I was listening to a music channel when they arrived. My close protection guard was with me. The Muş region commander asked, "Comrade Deniz, can we have a talk with you, privately?" I said "Of course," and asked my guard to step outside the room. The sneaky Dorşin region commander did not want to talk with me. He was just waiting for the Muş region commander to speak.

"Comrade, there is an issue that we need to discuss with you, but I honestly do not know how to begin," he said. He was clearly having a difficult time in repeating those slanders to my face. I said, "Comrade! Do not feel guilty or disrespectful towards me. I already know everything. You will probably tell me that I am having a relationship with a woman, and so you will have to incarcerate me until the investigation committee reveals the truth." They were both shocked that I was aware of what was going on. Without hesitation, I handed over to the Muş region commander my Glock brand gun, my money, and all the documents and codes that belonged to the organization. Then, I requested permission to speak to the woman who was the member of PKK Headquarters Committee. They agreed. She arrived within two hours. I asked the region commanders to leave, so that I could speak to her privately. When they left, I asked her, "Comrade, who requested or approved this arrest warrant? You can freely speak, since I have already been informed that I will be incarcerated. Please do not hide anything from me!"

She began to tell me everything that I did not know. "The field commander, Hakkı, is behind this scheme. Honestly, I do not know what happened between you two, but he is obsessed with you. He is full of hate against you, and he openly expresses his grudge at every opportunity. In one way or another, he will defame you!" I answered, "Comrade. I want to thank you for being honest with me. I have one last request of you. As you know, Hakkı is now going to gather an investigation committee in order to seek the truth. Those two region commanders are not authorized to be part of this committee, since their ranks are lower than mine. And they cannot be appointed as the head of the committee, because the head of the committee has to be a superior of mine. That leaves only one option. Since Hakkı cannot be on the committee, you are the only one who can possibly lead the investigation. If you are asked, please accept this duty and reveal the truths, fairly and squarely." She accepted my request.

Being Incarcerated

An investigation committee was established within two days. I was incarcerated on the grounds that I was having a love affair with this girl named Şilan. I was put into jail on April 7, 2010, and no one visited me for the first two days. I was all alone. On the third day, the members of the investigation committee, two region commanders, and the PKK headquarters member came into my cell. They did not bring an official hearing question draft, but the headquarters member verbally asked me to write down everything I knew about the claims against myself. She asked, "Did you, in fact, have such a relationship with Şilan? If yes, how long have you been together? If not, then why do you think you are being accused of it? Please thoroughly explain anything you know." I responded that I understood and would write everything explicitly.

A few days into my incarceration, the women I loved, Asmin, gave me a visit. Under normal circumstances, guerillas were not allowed to speak to incarcerated guerillas. Normally, if someone noticed a guerilla visiting an incarcerated comrade, that person would also be jailed for some time for acting against the rules of the organization. However, the guards that were on duty that night were all my old guerilla friends, who had worked under my authority for years. The night shift guard asked me what to do about Asmin, and I told him to let her in. Asmin came inside and said, "Deniz, tell me the truth. Is there a relationship between you and Şilan?" I answered, "I swear on my honor and on my life that it is all just a lie! The reason I am being incarcerated, has nothing to do with Şilan. I am stuck in the middle of a bigger scheme. Someone is trying to end my career in the organization. It is mainly because I fearlessly criticized many of the misdemeanors committed by the seniors here, and they know very well that I will file charges with headquarters against them. That is why they want to defame me, before I complain about them. You know me, Asmin! I cannot turn my back to injustices, as the other commanders do, in order to protect their positions. I have always criticized even the smallest mistake, regardless of whether it was perpetrated by my superior or inferior. I have always warned the person ahead of time, no matter who he or she was. I think that is why I am being punished now. They want to teach me a lesson by incarcerating me. Do not worry. In one way or another, the truth will be known by everyone!" Asmin left, feeling relieved, after my talk to her.

I was kept in the jail longer than I thought. It had been almost six days, and the committee was meeting regularly and asking me to talk about past incidents, which were not even related to my present incarceration. I was now in serious danger since I was being tried and accused for different occurrences—such as Deniz, who had not killed the rangers who martyred our comrades, or, Deniz did not kill the man who stole the tax revenues of the organization. The committee began to ask me questions on incidents that had occurred in the past.

The guerillas in the campground were also misinformed about me. I had been introduced to everyone as a traitor—as an agent of the government. Everyone was gossiping about me and field commander Hakkı was joining the trials, via radio, and made false statements about me, such as, "Deniz is weak in terms of guerilla fighting. He always objected to decisions made at the Supreme Guerilla Conference meetings, and he even occasionally objected to the decisions made by headquarters." Hakkı openly accused me of being an agent in front of everyone.

Suicide

It was April 13, 2010 when I heard a gunshot while in my cell. Asmin had been furious when she heard the claims made about me. During one of the meetings, which had gathered to discuss the issues related to my trial, she had told everyone, "You should have, at least, some moral values. This commander was one of the seniors, in one of the top administrative positions of the Garzan State, until yesterday. We've gathered, perhaps a hundred times before to discuss the issues in our units. I do not remember anyone criticizing Comrade Deniz about the issues for which we are criticizing him now. What in the world were you thinking back then? Why did not raise those concerns before? Now, you've incarcerated him claiming that he is in a love affair with Şilan. Let's assume that it is true. Why do you not try him on that accusation? Why do you bring up all those past incidents that he had never been accused of before? Be decent and try him on the charge for which you incarcerated him! If you were concerned about those past incidents, why didn't anyone say something about them until now?" She had gotten right in everyone's face, as she yelled.

After Asmin had finished, one of the women guerillas irritated her by saying, "Are you stupid, Asmin? Do not you see what he has done to you? This man has been cheating on you, with your best friend Şilan! One of the comrades even saw them while they were kissing. I do not understand why you are defending him!" Just then, Şilan had intervened and told Asmin that it was all nothing but lies.

Asmin had been so upset with the words she had heard, that she stood up and said, "Whatever you are saying is just a lie! The truth will be revealed eventually. I do not understand what kind of degenerates you are, and I cannot stay in the same place with you, even for one more day." She then left the meeting hall, and as soon as she left the field, she put her gun under her chin, and pulled the trigger. That had been the gunshot sound I heard. She died immediately.

Since I was still in my cell, I did not know what had happened. I only heard the gunshot. I immediately asked the guerilla guarding my cell, "Comrade, what happened? From where did that gunshot come?" I did not know why, but my heart had filled with horror, and I felt that something very bad had happened. The guerilla told me that he did not know what had happened, either. Then I heard lamenting and crying. Believe me, right then I felt that something had happened to Asmin, but I was helpless. In the meantime, one of the women guerillas came to my cell and began to scream at us, "It all happened because of you, Deniz!"

A chill ran down on my back, and I lost my bearings. I pleaded with the guard to let me out immediately, and, when he did, I started to shout, "What did you do to Asmin? Why did she commit suicide?" She was not someone to commit suicide easily. She had a strong character. In addition to many of her relatives, Asmin's sister was also fighting as a guerilla in the organization. Asmin was not someone to give up on life so easily. Then, one of my older guerillas told me what had happened in that meeting. Despite the fact that I was incarcerated, guerillas from my unit would visit me daily and inform me about all that was discussed, regarding my situation.

Asmin had written a note before she committed suicide, but I was not allowed to read it. No matter how much I requested, I was not given permission to read that note. I asked to read it just once, but they would not let me. To this day, I wonder what was written in that note. It was probably something about me. Emotionally, I was devastated. In fact, if I had had a weapon in my hand, I would also have committed suicide. Life was meaningless to me right then. One of the guards told me that they had wrapped Asmin's body in a blanket and buried her in a place on the west side of the camp. It was very tough to lose someone you loved.

The state commander had contacted the comrades, via the radio, and said, "If Asmin committed suicide, then Deniz might also want to kill himself. They deeply loved each other, so be cautions." Upon this order, beginning on April 14, I was incarcerated with both hands and ankles secured during the nights and hands tied during the daytime. Prior to that day, I was allowed to use my personal items in my cell; however, now everything was taken away.

It was tough for me. After a few days, some of the guerillas (but not those from Garzan) started beating me regularly. I remember their faces well. Guerillas from Dersim, Cudi, and Erbil forces beat me several times in my cell, while my hands and ankles were tied. Three of my teeth were broken during those beatings. There was a guerilla, who had worked under me for a long time, by the name of Baran. One night, while I was being beaten by those bastards, he showed up in the cell and said to them, "You're not even from the Garzan State. Who the hell do you think you are, to have the right to beat him?" Baran then pulled out his gun and pointed it towards one of the guys beating me when he replied in a sarcastic manner. He then said, "I swear to God, I will kill you all if you ever come to this cell again."

On the afternoon of May 1, I was informed that the field commander of the Amed State women's guerilla force would be the head of the investigation committee from then on in place of the PKK headquarters member. Similar to the Dorşin region commander, she was a close associate of Hakkı, the field commander. She would do whatever Hakkı told her to do.

Hakkı had sent out a bunch of questions, drafted by him, to the investigation committee. As soon as the PKK headquarters member read the questions, she had said, "I cannot let you try Deniz on these questions. You incarcerated him, arguing that he was having an affair with Şilan. However, many of the questions in this draft have nothing to do with that. I do not think we can find justice here. I am resigning my duty in this commission."

These two region commanders brought me the draft, prepared by Hakkı. There were 22 questions in the draft and only three of them were related to my so-called affair with Şilan. The remaining questions were about me and our leader, Apo. They had gone too far. I was being accused of being disrespectful to our leader. As soon as I saw the draft, I figured out that Hakkı was not trying to discharge me from my position. It was even worse. He was trying to sentence me with capital punishment. Besides, I did not know how they convinced Şilan, but she had admitted that she, in fact, had an affair with me. She was probably forced, by some means, to make that false statement.

On May 2, 2010, my trial was scheduled to begin, with the new committee head from Amed. I knew the rules of the organization very well. I would not be sentenced to death unless they could provide solid evidence that I was an agent, as they claimed. However, there was one other thing with which I needed to be extra careful. Hakkı and his supporters would try to get on my nerves, by beatings and lying, so that I would attempt to run away. They would have the right to kill me if I fled. I knew that a couple comrades had been killed in the past, using this tactic.

For example, Topal Nasır (Faruk Bozkurt) was executed in that way. He was not getting along well with Osman Öcalan. He was a decent and hardworking guerilla, similar to myself. He would explicitly criticize the mistakes made by others during the meetings and conferences. I remember him saying, "I do not have any problem with the organization. If my seniors ordered me, I would wait at the entrance of this meeting hall, like a dog, for ten years. However, I do not accept the authority of Ferhat (Osman Öcalan). I cannot be in the same place with him; even for two days. I do not recognize him as my superior." Because of being honest and blunt, Topal Nasır was put into a scheme, very similar to the one I was experiencing. While he was incarcerated, the guerillas were cautioned with the false information that the security forces would come and rescue him from us. He was executed in 1999 on the grounds that he was against the rules established by Apo, who would never have approved such an execution if he were not incarcerated at that time.

Similar to Topal Nasır, I would have been pushed to flee, because of the beatings, and then they would kill me while running away. No one could be held responsible for killing a deserter, especially if the deserter were a commander. Headquarters would be informed that, "Deniz was fleeing, and we killed him to prevent him from surrendering to security forces to share our top-secret information with them." In this way, Hakkı and his supporters would evade responsibility. Because of this knowledge, I had to be extra careful and I did not cry out, no matter what they did to me.

The Trial

They fiddled with my comfort a lot during my incarceration. Under normal conditions, an incarcerated or jailed commander would be dealt with by someone of the same level. But Hakkı even sent newbie guerillas, who had joined us toward the end of 2009, to tie my hands and feet. Can you imagine how I was insulted? I had served the organization longer than the age of the guerillas who were now beating me and tying me up. That was extremely humiliating for someone of my rank. Despite all these cruel attacks on me, I kept myself calm. I knew that Hakkı and his supporters' real intent was to provoke me to do something stupid, so that they could kill me before the trial.

Believe me, I would have run away from the prison, from the first day of my incarceration. However, all I wanted was to wait for the trail to start. I wanted to know everything. What was their purpose? Why were they pushing me so strongly? Who were they blaming? Headquarters, Hakkı, or me? I had already prepared my written report for the questions I was given before.

I was set in front of everyone at the investigation on May 2, 2010. I was to read my answers loudly and then the committee was going to decide whether I would be acquitted or found guilty. I was just about to read my defense when this new committee head stopped me and said, "Your report will not be read. There is no need for that. We all know what happened. We, the investigation committee members will inform the attendants about your case and they will then offer their thoughts, to help us reach a verdict." Can you believe that? I was being tried and not even given the right for self-defense. I was shocked. I had never heard of something like that happening in the organization. I could not raise any objection. Therefore, I just kept quiet.

The head of the committee began to inform the attendants, using a microphone. She spoke for approximately an hour. I discovered that all she mentioned in her speech were the slanders made by Hakkı. "Why did you talk to the rangers? Why did you not kill that man? Do you want to take a revenge for Apo? Apo values women guerillas very much, but you used women for your sexual purposes. Do you work for the security forces? Why have not you carried out any missions during the past three years? Why do you not kill any police or soldiers?" I was asked to respond to these asinine questions. I could not believe what I was being told. According to their claims, I had had love affairs with seven different women guerillas.

As soon as she finished with her speech, she turned to the attendants and asked about their opinions of me. One of the comrades (an older one) stood up and said, "Comrade, you have read this and you have informed us, but let's give him a right to defend himself before we provide you with our opinions. Let's learn what he wants to say in response to your claims. Let us hear directly from Deniz whether those claims are true or false." Being encouraged by this comrade, two other comrades asked for the floor, and they both said, "This trial has seriously malfunctioned. You cannot ask us to make comments before hearing how the accused would respond to your claims. What you are doing is against the rules of the organization!" Being exposed to these pressures, the investigation committee allowed me to defend myself, though against their will.

I was honest in answering all the questions and claims made against me. I said to them all, "Comrades! I was in love with only two women in this organization. One of them was Sevin and the other one was Asmin. I loved those two women, and I do not deny it. Additionally, I never hid these relations from anyone. Even commanders from PKK headquarters knew about them." I turned and looked at the faces of the investigation committee and said to them, "My feelings towards Asmin were known, both by the field commander Hakkı, and the state commander, as well as the other region commanders. Despite this, none of you said that because we had such a relationship that we should not be assigned to work at the same field. If you were concerned about this relationship, you could easily have assigned one of us to Garzan and the other to Amed. However, you did not do that when I complained about Asmin's assignment to my region. By the way, where did you find the names of these other five women shown on the list? I do not even know them. Either they loved me unconditionally in a platonic way, or this is just another slander of yours! As a result, I do not accept any of the claims on your investigation files, regarding my relations with women!"

Then I began to talk about the other claims made on me. "You have just accused me of meeting with the village protection guards without the knowledge of headquarters. You cannot just make a claim and expect the people to believe it. If this claim of yours is, in fact, true, show proof to everyone here. Now, tell us the exact date and hour that I met with the rangers. I swear that I will accept all the charges if you can provide the attendants with even a small bit of proof. Look! I have worked for this organization for almost 20 years. I am not stupid! I can provide you with the exact days, hours, and locations on which I met with these rangers. On top of that, I can provide you with the names, from the organization, who were with me during those visits! I never met with these rangers alone. You are also accusing me of not executing those three rangers, even though they martyred one of our comrades. This claim, with which you are charging me, does not fit the culture and ethical values of our organization. On one hand, you start a peace negotiation with the rangers, and, on the other, you will kill their leaders. In fact, I was given an order from headquarters commander not to kill Abdülhamit, the head ranger. Until today, I have never acted according to my own decisions, for works to be carried out in the name of the organization. If I had acted in such a way, I never hid it from the organization."

As I mentioned earlier, the decision to execute these three rangers was canceled later by headquarters. Despite this, field commander Hakkı had ordered his own guerilla force to kill these rangers in order to seek revenge. I had said to him, "Comrade, listen to me carefully! You are not acting professionally! What you are doing is against the policies of the organization, and you will defame all of us. We are not backstabbers! We already discussed the peace terms with them! Call your guerillas back here and stop them before carrying out this mission."

While I was dealing with this problem back then, another shocking piece of news had reached me. It was in 2009. There was a thermal power plant in our region. We visited this plant each year and collected our taxes. In 2009, I was told that someone visited this plant and collected the taxes in the name of PKK, even though he was not one of us. Because of this, field commander Hakkı contacted me to arrest this man and then kill him.

I found out the name of this person and then contacted to him, using our civilian representatives working in the cities. Twice, I told this person to visit us at a location in the countryside, where we could save ourselves, if the security forces noticed our meeting. Nevertheless, this man was clever, and, on both visits, he came to the meeting point with a large group of his relatives. He never came alone, so that we could have him pay back what he had taken from us. I could not keep him and send the rest of the crowd away, because we were going to execute him if he were found guilty. Since he showed up with his relatives, we could not carry out our killing mission. During his second visit, I told him to go home and then return next week, alone! The man left and never came back. He fled when he understood that he was going to be put under investigation. The tax amount he had collected, using our names, was not very large. We, as an organization, would annually collect $5,000,000 from this group, whereas he had collected only 120,000 Turkish lira. Completely stupid!

Then I heard on the news that he had been incarcerated in January 2010 for being a member of the KCK. Since he was arrested by the police, there was no way I could carry out my assassination mission. Now, go tell this to Hakkı.

Since I did not kill the man who had collected our taxes and also not killed those three rangers who martyred one of our comrades, Hakkı had been very upset with me. During the trial, he brought up those two issues in front of everyone and said to me, "You ignore the orders of your superiors; you act like a rebel!"

Another question that I faced during the trial, was my objection to two decisions made at the Supreme Guerilla Conference. I had never worked behind the scenes as many of the seniors had. I had never provoked others against the party by meeting secretly with them. I had always openly stated my objections during the conference. In that specific case, my suggestions were denied by the majority. I had explained my concerns to them, but the majority disagreed with me. As a result, I respected their decisions.

During the trial, I turned to the guerillas who had worked with me in the past and asked them, "Comrades. Did I not tell you that, even though I disagreed, we had to act according to the decisions of the majority!" They all loudly replied that, "You are telling the truth Deniz! We all witnessed that!"

I answered all of their questions, one by one, but, they kept asking questions, looking to find something for which they could accuse me!

Finally, I was asked about something which occurred in 2009. I think I mentioned it before. During 2009, I was carrying a digital camera. We had heard on the news that Prime Minister Recep Tayyip Erdoğan (the current President of Turkey) was going to visit the city of Van to deliver a speech during an opening ceremony, so I gave my camera to one of the civilian PKK members and said to him, "Comrade, go to this ceremony and take as many pictures as you can. I especially want to see the people sitting in the VIP seats, so focus on that area. Take as many pictures as possible, regarding the protection detail." I was curious to learn how the prime minister was protected.

Similar to a journalist, this militant was able to take pictures of all the VIP guests from a very close distance. He took pictures of where the prime minister, ministers, governor and other people at the protocol stage sat, and how they were protected by the close protection guards. Studying these pictures, I was able to figure out how many guards were on duty, how they were positioned, the position of the civilian police officers, the locations and numbers of jammers, and all the other details regarding their security precautions. The organization has never targeted politicians or high-level bureaucrats such as governors. Nevertheless, it did not mean that the organization did not carry out any reconnaissance or intelligence activities concerning them. That kind of reconnaissance would be conducted on a regular basis and in a systematic manner, in case it became necessary to carry out a mission against those targets. However, the organization was very strict about not targeting the politicians.

I puzzled for hours over those pictures taken by my comrade, and reached a simple conclusion. If we really wanted, the prime minister and the other VIP guests could be easily killed in Turkey.

As luck would have it, those pictures I had collected as a part of reconnaissance activities put me into serious trouble during the trial. I was asked questions like, "Why did you take so many pictures of Erdoğan? Are you a fan of his? Do you work for the state? Are you an agent? Do you support the AKP? Why have you been keeping so many pictures of this man on your camera?" Those were such stupid questions!

I replied, "I carried out reconnaissance for a potential future mission that we could carry out against the elected officials. Tell me if you know for sure the AKP is going to keep its promises given at Oslo! What are we going to do if they do not? Nothing is certain, but the unforeseen! That is why I kept those pictures—in case we needed to plan a guerilla mission in the future." The investigation committee members were not satisfied with my answer.

That day, I successfully argued my way out of the falsehoods. Despite the fact that the committee members were prejudiced against me, the guerilla attendants of the trial took a stand with me, and when the committee noticed that, they began to repeat the questions, which I had already answered, "Why did not you execute the person who collected taxes on behalf of the organization from the thermal plant? Who was your contact from the Turkish security forces? Were there any other people, like yourself, who infiltrated us?"

At that moment, I knew that I was not going to find justice there. Regardless of my answers, the committee had already made their decision about me. No matter how strong was my defense, they were not going to release or acquit me. In fact, let alone releasing me, they were trying to find a way to execute me by repeatedly asking those questions regarding whether I was an agent for the Turkish government.

The trial lasted for two days. The committee informed everyone that they were able to reach a verdict on the evening of May 4. Before the decision was declared to me, I asked for the floor, in order to state my last words regarding my defense. As I said, this committee was composed of people appointed by Hakkı. No one could expect them to be objective in their decision. In front of all the attendants, I said, "I do not accept the legitimacy of this investigation committee. You were all appointed by the person who hates me. Therefore, I now request for you all to retry me with a new committee, composed of unbiased members. I personally believe that the state commanders of Amed and Garzan would be ideal candidates for this job. I would like them to examine all the lies said about me, my defense proposal, and also the opinions of the attendants of this trial and then reach a verdict."

Before I finished my words, I turned back and looked into the face of the president of the investigation committee, "I do not believe the verdict you reached is unbiased. You do not even have firsthand knowledge of all these incidents for which you tried me. When all those things happened, you were not even in Turkey. You were in the south, in Iraq. You are here simply to fulfill the wishes of Hakkı!" She suddenly blushed.

As I said, I would be immediately acquitted if either Amed or Garzan state commanders would serve on this committee, because they both had the knowledge of my activities in the region including where, when, and with whom I met with those rangers. I would be exculpated. The trial attendees were in full agreement with my suggestion, and because of the pressure coming from them, the committee had to adjourn in order to discuss my request in private.

During the break, one of my older guerillas visited me and said, "Comrade Deniz, this is between you and me but be very careful now. Hakkı has already sanctioned your execution. No matter what you do or whomever serves on your trial, you will be seriously harmed. Hakkı even ordered us to kill you if you attempt to flee. They will kill you even for a shadow of mistake!"

Why did this man hate me so strongly? Why did he want to annihilate me? I had filed complaints about him to headquarters, and we had been rude towards each other, but none of these incidents would seem enough to have created in him his desire to kill me. He could easily assign me to a different post, away from him.

Approximately an hour later, the investigation committee gathered again and informed everyone about that I was to retried, with a new committee, composed of new members. Apparently, they feared the potential pressure that might come from the attendees. Nevertheless, I was also informed that neither the Amed nor the Garzan state commander would be allowed to serve on my trial committee. Instead, three guerillas from the camp in which I was incarcerated, were going to serve on the committee. Everything was to begin again, and I was to remain arrested in the meantime.

I was pissed off with their verdict, because the current committee was going to decide who should serve on the new committee. Hakkı could easily assign another three of his supporters and obtain a guilty verdict. I knew for sure then that I was going to have to get myself away from there, one way or another. Before the attendants left, I asked for a stand and said, "I have a message for you committee members. First, as long as you three will decide who shall serve on the new committee, I will be found guilty no matter what I say. So, do not bother yourself with establishing a new committee. I know you will appoint prejudiced people like yourselves! Second, I want to inform all of you that I will hurt you when the time comes!" No one was expecting me to speak like that. The committee members were all dazed. One of them even asked me if I were threatening them. I said, "Take it as you like! I said what I said."

I had always been loyal to the organization's struggle for the well-being of the Kurds. Everyone who was acquainted with me knew that very well. I looked at the faces of the people on the committee and said, "I would even have sacrificed myself for Asmin. Nevertheless, since this organization caused her to take her own life unjustly, I can now stand against this organization and secure revenge for her! Whether you assign your own men or unbiased guerillas to my trial committee, you will shed light on Asmin's suicide incident! Those who played a part in it will suffer the consequences! I have fought among you for almost 20 years. I have fulfilled all the duties that I was assigned. However, if necessary, I will make no bones about fighting against you all to get revenge for Asmin! You already know whom I will kill for that!" I said, as I flung all these statements right in their faces!

The head of the investigation committee got really upset with my words. She ordered her close protection guards to tie my hands and feet. Four guerillas suddenly jumped on me. They dragged me to the cell where they were keeping me as their captive.

I was so confused. I would never harm the organization for which I had worked for so many years. Besides, how could I harm the guerillas that I trained and regarded as my brothers and sons? Nevertheless, I could not help myself from thinking about how to kill Hakkı. Three creeps were behind this entire scheme. Hakkı was leading the region commander of Dorşin and the field commander of Amed, who was in charge of the women guerillas. These three had to be killed as revenge for Asmin's death. Of course, there were some other ass kissers, but they were not as important as the first three.

Even if I was released after a second trial, I would not be able to stay in this region. The organization would probably assign me to a camp located in the south—in Iraq or in Syria. In that case, I would never be able to find those three bloody-minded creeps. Besides, I already had a bad reputation, even though all those claims were nothing but lies. I was tried in front of my own soldiers and I lost face because of those lies. Therefore, even though I would be assigned to the south, everyone was going to gossip about me. I had no option but to leave my beloved organization.

I had a strong character. When I said no to something, I would never do it. Similarly, when I promised to do something, I would do it even at the expense of my life. I would always stick to my guns. For the sake of the Kurds in Turkey and the Middle East, I had given my youth and sacrificed the years that I would have had the opportunity to raise a family, work in a stable job, and live in comfort. Nevertheless, I will never forget those two women, Asmin, who was pushed into suicide and Şilan, who fell in disrepute because of those three evil people. As I had fought for my people, the Kurds, for 18 years, without even blinking an eye, I would fight for the woman I loved for the rest of my life. That innocent Asmin committed suicide by shooting herself in the head only 30 meters away from me. Şilan, who was placed into this scheme, was kept in her tent, with both her hands and feet tied, even though she had nothing to do with anything! I was depressed, demoralized, and tired. I said to myself, "Fuck this shit!" Right then, I decided that I could not be part of this organization any longer, when people like Hakkı were highly valued and respected. I stomped with rage.

On the evening of May 4, only one guard was assigned to watch in front of my tent for the night shift of 7:00 p.m. to 9:00 p.m. He was one of the newbies. He asked me, "Comrade Deniz, how will this investigation end? When will they set you free so that you can be our commander again?" I looked in his eyes. He appeared to be a decent guy. I said, "You are oblivious of what is really happening here, young comrade. Nothing is really what it seems to be. In this scheme, I am just a tool to disguise the dirty businesses of some others. During this meeting, has anyone asked a question regarding the losses Hakkı caused during the past year? No! Has there been any discussion about who was supposed to be held responsible for the desertion incident and the subsequent losses occurred during that winter? No! If all those losses were questioned, wouldn't the region commander be in the prison now? Wouldn't all the guerillas under his authority be put under investigation? Can you now see the bigger picture? Thanks to the slander about me, all these incidents were deleted from discussion.

SECTION C

Prison and Beyond

19

LEAVING THE PKK

It was 8:55 that same night. The new night shift guard was supposed to take over his duty soon. I had already made up my mind. I would not stay among these people any longer. My hands and feet were still tied. The young guard with whom I had chatted earlier in the night left the tent to wake up the next guard. In the meantime, I was pretending to be asleep. I first got rid of the ropes on my feet. However, my hands were tied extremely tight. No matter how hard I tried, I could not untie my hands. It was pitch dark. No one could see beyond the end of his nose. It was also raining heavily—a perfect opportunity for me to flee the camp area. Then, something unimaginable came right on top the rain and the pitch dark. I was familiar with the new night shift guard. He had problems with his eyes. He was having a hard time seeing objects at night. I could not have arranged this scenario, even if I had tried.

The guard was walking back and forth around the tent. As soon as he walked by, I put on my shoes, stood up, and then started to run away in the opposite direction from him. As I mentioned, it was pitch black. I could not see anything. Besides, it was very hard to run without falling with my hands tied. While moving away from the campground, I stumbled on a small piece of rock and fell down. The guard heard the noise and began to shout, "Who is there?" I kept my silence. He shouted again, asking who was there. I immediately sat down where I fell. I knew how the guerillas were trained for these kinds of situations. The guard would start firing toward me, if there was no answer to his call after the third time. That was exactly what happened. He shouted for the third time and then started to rake the field with his gunfire.

Due to the noise of gunshots, everyone woke up. I was still hiding right next to the campground in the area where I had fallen down. I knew in which direction they would move to search for me. Therefore, I hid in a place where they would never look for me. All the guerillas in the camp were out searching for me. With torches in their hands, they were looking high and low to find me. Only a couple were left in the camp to protect the stuff left behind. In the meantime, I got rid of the ropes tied on my hands. I waited still at the same spot until 12:00 a.m. While they were searching for me all over, I was so close to them that I was even able to listen to their talking.

I was soaked to the skin from the rain. The guerillas returned to the campground around 12:30 a.m. and went back to their sleeping quarters. They thought that I was already too far away. Around 1:30 a.m.,

I stood up and started to walk away from the campground quietly and slowly. I decided to go to Amed, Kulp.

You may wonder if I was nervous while running away. Definitely not! I had been in this organization for years. I already knew how they would search and look for me. That is why I was extremely self-confident while fleeing. In a way, I followed a negative logic. I mean I did nothing that would normally be done while searching for someone who deserted us. I kept myself away from the places they might patrol and search for me.

Surrendering Myself to the Security Forces

I was heading towards the thermal power plant that I had mentioned earlier by following the vehicle road. It was a road full of hairpin turns. For a moment, I felt that someone was approaching towards me, from one of the hairpins. To my surprise, two guerillas had set an ambush at one of the turns in order to shoot anyone that might walk towards them. They were just leaving their positions. I was lucky. They probably wanted to be back in the camp before sunrise. I immediately threw myself to the other side of the road before they saw me. I waited there until those two comrades passed by me and disappeared. Then, I continued on my trip, but this time even more carefully.

I knew some workers at the plant were in close relationship with the security forces. Therefore, I needed to go there to find one who could possibly connect me with a soldier. However, there was a big problem. The perimeter of the plant was being guarded by village protection guards. They would immediately notify the organization as soon as they saw me surrendering myself to the security forces. Therefore, I decided to wait far away from the plant for a vehicle to pass by. I was fortunate. Soon, I saw a truck driving towards the plant. I stopped it. The driver was shocked to see a guerilla at that time of the day. He said, "Comrade, what are you doing here?" I said, "Take me inside the plant construction site. I cannot just walk in because there are rangers around." I was finally secure. He drove me inside the site. I asked the driver if he had any contact information from the military post close to the plant. He said, "Yes, I do!" I asked him whose phone number he had. He said, "Comrade, I have the mobile phone number of the company commander!" I said, "Great, please dial the number and hand the phone over to me." I then talked directly with the Turkish company commander and said to him, "Come to this place now. It has to be only you and your superior, the squadron leader. I do not want anyone else!"

The military commander initially accepted my offer but then began to ask me questions, such as who was I, and why did I want to talk to them. I guess he thought that it was an ambush trap. He was shocked when I said to him that I was Deniz, from the Garzan State. He said, "Are you being honest with me? Can I really believe what you said?" I answered, "Well, believe me or not, it is your call! I will be at the meeting point at the scheduled time." I had described a meeting spot, which was clearly a place too flat for me to lay an ambush, even I actually wanted. Besides, one could easily see the whole area, even from a 500 meter distance. Therefore, the military officials even had a chance to retreat if they suspected anything.

Indeed, they all came to the meeting point at the scheduled time. There were the three—the company commander, the squadron commander, and the driver. The presence of the driver was not a big deal. I just did not want any ranger, who could possibly be in connection with the organization, to be there. I surrendered myself to them right there. My career with the organization ended in that way.

I had better alternatives in front of me rather than surrendering myself. I could easily have gone to the south—to Iraq or Syria—and lived there until the end of my life. I also could have gone to Europe.

I had connections that could guide me until I reached Germany or France. However, I was blinded with the desire for Asmin's revenge.

We are in 2015. It has been almost six years, and I still could not forget Asmin. I always think of her before going to sleep at night. I had thought that, if I surrendered myself to the security forces, I could be saved from obsession with Hakkı, who not only pushed Asmin to kill herself but had also accused me of being an agent for the security force, despite my successful career in the organization.

I do not want to hold the organization responsible, as a whole, for whatever I was exposed to back then. In all my life, I have never dished on someone. If I told you that all those things occurred because of the general characteristics, culture, morals, and ethics of the organization, it would be a complete lie. It would not be right. Nevertheless, just as you have corrupt politicians in your government affairs, we also had corrupt guerillas who would do most anything for their own gain.

Conflicts Between the Soldiers and the Police

After surrendering myself to the security forces, I was transported to a gendarme military unit. Gendarme counterterrorism units from the cities of Batman, Siirt, Bitlis, Diyarbakır, and Muş soon came to see me, where I was being held. They were not allowed to talk to me as a group. Instead, the units from each of the cities visited my cell, one by one, and asked questions. In the meantime, the Turkish National Police terror teams also arrived to the gendarme post. It was very weird. The gendarme commander did not let the police officers talk with me, let alone ask questions of me. The police officers were not even allowed to listen to my conversations with the others. I told the gendarme commander, "Look, they came from Diyarbakır police department. They may have some questions, too. Give them some time so that they can talk with me, also." The gendarme commander rejected my offer. The police officers were really offended, as they were not allowed to talk or listen.

At that moment, I realized that, similar to the structural and hierarchical problems existent among the different units within the organization, the Turkish police and the gendarme units also had problems between one other. These security forces were not cooperating on such a sensitive subject as fighting against their common enemy. The gendarme did not let the police ask me even a single question, while I was held in the gendarme post. Some soldiers came to talk to me when I was later held at the police department. In a similar way, the police did not let the soldiers talk with me. Even more amazing was when I told them things at the gendarme post, the gendarme commanders asked me not to give that information to the police. Again, in a similar fashion, when I was interviewed at the police department, the police directors asked me not to share any of the information with the gendarme later. This was such an awkward situation for me.

Like the jealousy among the police and the gendarme, there was even a competition among the different gendarme units. The gendarme units that arrived from different cities were not allowed to listen to each other's interview sessions with me. Only the gendarme commander of Kulp and a senior commander from a Diyarbakır military unit were present in each of the sessions. Nevertheless, the counterterrorism teams from other areas visited me one by one. The Muş counterterrorism unit visited me, asked the questions they had for me and then left the post. After them, the Bitlis counterterrorism unit came into the room where I was being held.

Oddly enough, neither the police officers nor the gendarme counterterrorism teams asked me any clearly prepared question. They did not even know investigation techniques. I was shocked that people at those levels were employed in those units. They were clearly illiterate concerning the PKK. I am not even sure if they were properly trained to work at counterterrorism units. For example, none of them asked me one question about what the organization would do in the forthcoming period. Where would we attack next? What were our plans for the summer? Where did we acquire the weapons and ammos for the fight? How was this equipment being transported to the organization? Who were the intermediaries providing these things? What were the possible missions to be used in the future, or, what tactics would we mostly use when carrying out those missions? None of them, even nearly, put a finger on those issues. Actually, there was a fellow from the Sason gendarme counterterrorism unit that had asked a couple of questions about our potential future missions.

All they were interested in was to learn the details about incidents that had occurred in the past. They were consumed with the past! They often asked me who had planned and carried out a specific mission in their jurisdiction of authority. I was so pissed off with their mentality. Those missions were already planned and accomplished. What benefit would it provide to find out the persons who executed them? Move on! Focus on what could happen in the future. Without exception, both the police officers and the gendarme units were all the same. They all thought to get into their superiors' good graces by shedding light on the past missions carried out by the PKK. Interestingly, preventing missions from being carried out was not considered by them as a success. Why? Because it would not make the news. Their success would not be publicized. I even thought, in my mind, that if the members of the enemy forces were so unqualified, then we as an organization were also not so successful, since we had failed to beat such a group of people for so long.

I even had a quarrel with the squadron commander of Muş's counterterrorism team. I do not remember his name, but he was someone with grey hair. He opened a file in front of me. I saw the pictures of civilian Kurdish peasants. He started to show me the pictures one by one and asked, "Has this peasant ever helped you? Is this peasant in connection with the organization?" I looked at the pictures. They were peasants, generally around the age of 70 or 80 years. Never mind helping us, they were probably unable to walk without the help of a cane. I was confused and upset. I looked at the pictures several times to make sure that I was not mistaken, but it was true. They were all very old peasants. After I was sure, I looked this squadron commander in the eye and said, "Are you kidding me? Those people could not even help themselves. How could you expect them to help the organization? Let's assume that they, in fact, helped the organization. Would you go and arrest those people in their 80s? Your stupid attitudes and behaviors push peasants into the organization. You arrested innocent peasants, most particularly the old peasants, and then all their families and relatives came to us to get their revenge by killing soldiers. I am not telling you not to arrest anyone. Nevertheless, do not incarcerate a peasant simply because he or she may have helped us. If you get the intelligence that one of us is planning a mission and is working day and night to kill security forces, or is organizing missions to be carried out in cities, then go and arrest that person. Do not arrest people just because they aid and abet to us. You anger people by your own stupid acts. You push and prod people into the organization. After each of those unjust arrests, we would have at least five new participants, who were joining us looking for revenge."

After a small pause, I continued my speech. "Leave those innocent civilian peasants alone. Ask me questions that would directly give you answers. Take those pictures away from me. I do not want to see them anymore. Instead, ask me what kind of actions the organization plans to carry out in Muş in the future! Ask me proper questions." Of course, he and his assistants became angry when I spoke so bluntly. He asked, "How would you know when and how the organization would carry out its future missions?" I just laughed at him. How could a ranked person be so stupid? "I was the senior commander of Garzan State, until a couple hours ago. If you do not know, we commanders plan those missions carefully, and the ground guerillas carry them out! Who do you think will know those missions better than I? I'm telling you again, I was in charge of three regions and a front in Garzan. Do you think there could be someone better than I who would know all the reconnaissance activities and future missions that are to be carried out in the city of Muş?" Despite all my explanations, they insisted on me answering their stupid questions regarding the peasants.

They wasted all the time allocated for them by showing me the peasant pictures in that file. The squadron commander of Kulp said to him, "Time is up! You will now leave the room, so that the next group can come in!" The squadron commander of Muş said that he had some more questions to ask. The commander from Kulp replied to him, saying, "You wasted your time with bullshit. You should have come here better prepared, with carefully drafted questions!"

Being Fooled

I still get angry about how I was financially ripped off when I surrendered myself to the gendarme. Before I surrendered myself, I had 3,000 Euro on me. It was my own personal money that I was going to use in case I changed my mind and decided to go either to Europe or Iraq. I initially handed over the money to the truck driver I had stopped to take me into the thermal power plant construction site. I said to him, "Comrade, take this money and give it to my uncle. He lives at this address in the city of Batman. Tell my uncle to give it to my parents."

I then thought of the possibility that the driver would not give the money to my uncle and just pocket the cash. Therefore, I talked to the commander of the gendarme about my concerns regarding the money I had handed to the driver. I told him, "I've given the driver some money, but could you please take it back from him and give it over to my parents." The commander said, "Sure," and took it from the driver. In the meantime, the legal "detain period" (four days) at the gendarme post had ended. They could not keep me with them any longer. I was to be sent to prison. I did not have two pennies to rub together. Therefore, I said to gendarme commander, "Could you please give me some money from the amount you took from the driver? I will need some cash to meet my needs in prison, until my parents visit me." They gave me only 35 Turkish lira (less than 10 Euros), even though they had my 3,000 Euros.

I trusted that the gendarme commander would, in fact, give my money to my parents. I still remember his name: Mustafa Yaşar Yıldırım. I remember everything he said that day. "Are you out of mind? Why did you give the money to a peasant truck driver? You should have given it to us. Do not worry, we will take it back from him and deliver it to your parents."

My parents were notified about my surrender. My father, mother, and uncle showed up at the gendarme post on the second day of my detainment. After so many years of separation, I had a chance to talk to them, face to face, for a couple of hours. My mother began to cry as soon as she saw me. She could not say a single word, but cried for half an hour. Before she was asked to leave the post, she said to me, "Deniz, I am happy that I could see you alive one more time, before they kill you. That means everything in this life for me!" My father was the same. Poor man! He also cried a lot. Apparently, they had missed me very much, even though they had other children. I was so angry with the security forces present there. They had given my parents high hopes when the gendarme commander told my father, "Do not worry at all! Deniz will not even be incarcerated, because he is helping us. He might be held in prison, at most, for two months. After that, he will be free!"

I did not ask my parents whether they had received my money from the gendarme commander, because the gendarme officials were present throughout my whole visit with them. It would have been rude to ask whether the commander had given it to them, in front of his own soldiers. I honestly thought that such a senior ranked person would be honest with me! My father had even asked me if I needed money. My parents were already poor. How could I accept money from them? Therefore, I told him that I did not need anything.

Unfortunately, not even a penny of those 3,000 Euros was handed over to my parents. I was very disappointed when I learned about it. A friend called Atilla (I do not know whether it was his nickname or real name) from the Diyarbakır Police Department counterterrorism unit, with the help of the public prosecutor handling my files, wrote a petition to the court on my behalf. We filed it, but the court decided that the money belonged to the organization, so it was to be confiscated and then delivered to the state treasury. I got even angrier with the squadron commander when I read the court's decision. He had misused my trust. I wished I had not talked to the security forces to whom I gave the money. The peasant truck driver would have probably delivered it to my parents.

A relative of mine, along with my parents, visited me on the night of the third day. He was a well-known village protection guard. He was the commander of the special ranger forces of the Kulp district of Diyarbakır. He was one of those who had left the organization and begun to work for the state security forces. I did not know that he was a relative of mine until I saw him with my parents. When I was still in the organization, I was getting many complaints about him, from the peasants, who were telling us that he was even more dangerous than the security forces, and that he often oppressed them. This man was leading the state security forces in carrying out ambushes and other missions against the guerillas. His name was Talat Eryılmaz, and he still visits me in prison, from time to time.

I mentioned before that one of our comrades was killed in an ambush, while travelling from Kulp to Sason, in 2009. This ranger was the very same one who had laid that ambush. Because of that, we had planned a mission to kill him for revenge. Our bomb units had prepared a timed explosive that would be attached to his vehicle. We had instructed one of our civilian employees, "Attach this explosive under the car of that ranger and then activate the timer, using the remote controller. Be careful! You need to carry out a perfect reconnaissance before activating it. Find out when this crook leaves home and on which day he uses his car. Do not waste our explosive!" I had surrendered myself to the security forces only five months after we had instructed this civilian organization member to carry out the mission. I thought he was already dead. Therefore, I was surprised when I saw that ranger sitting next to my parents.

Since he was still alive, the militant we had sent was clearly not successful with carrying out the mission. Still, no one knows what actually happened to that militant and the explosive. During our visit, I told Talat, "Comrade, we guerillas were going to annihilate you with a bomb attached to your car. Check your car carefully. Since you are still alive, either the explosive did not activate, or the militant we sent to kill you made a mistake!" You should have seen his face! He was so panicked and immediately asked me, "What bomb? Who is going to kill me? What the hell are you talking about?" I intentionally made him more nervous by saying, "The bomb must have been placed on your car, but, why are you still here? I wonder what could have happened to it?" He asked me how we knew which car he drove. I said, "Do not be dumb. You know very well that we guerillas always reconnoiter in the cities in order to prepare plans for our future attacks!" I heard that Talat sold his car soon after this talk.

I had only one request for the security forces, and said to them, "If you put me in jail, I will not be any good to you. You may perhaps visit me occasionally and ask questions, but I do not know if I will be willing to talk with you then. If you want to get the maximum benefit from me, let me work with you. Give me two squads, one composed of Kurdish rangers and the other one with soldiers. You can even give me the special ranger squad that is led by my relative, Talat. You all trust Talat. He has worked with you for years! Kill me, if I cannot annihilate the Garzan state in six months! I promise I will end the dominance of the organization in Garzan!" Again, all I wanted was to catch and kill those three bastards: Hakkı, the Kulp region commander, and the woman field guerilla commander of Amed.

Talat was present as I talked to the gendarme commander. He even supported me by saying, "You trust me deeply, and you are well aware that I have been fighting against the guerillas in places that you could not even walk. Look, I am literally nothing when compared to the experiences and knowledge that Deniz possesses! Assign a ranger team to him. Deniz and I will doom the guerilla presence there in that area!" The gendarme officials initially welcomed our offer. The commander even said, "Of course. That is what we have been considering." Nevertheless, nothing happened.

During my detainment at the gendarme post, I gave a lot of advice to the soldiers. "Your fight strategy against the organization is seriously flawed. As in the old days, it is almost impossible to get into close contact with the guerillas in the countryside. There are now only 15 guerillas, where there used to be 300. You have zero chance to encounter these 15 guerillas. On the other hand, if you continue to dispatch hundreds of soldiers into the open fields for operations, you will lose many of them. We do not need to carry out missions against you anymore by laying siege to the military posts or infiltrating the cities, because you come to us with hundreds of sitting ducks. If you want to gain control in the countryside again, you have to form small fighting squads. For example, if your squads are now composed of 18 soldiers, divide that into three equal, separate units; six, six, and six. The members of those teams must have strong self-control. They must be dispatched to the field and wait in an ambush position, for days, to get in close contact with the guerilla teams. You can only establish dominance in the countryside in this way. Those large participation land operations have literally no effect on us. You have to fight in smaller units to disguise yourself."

In return, the gendarme commander said to me, "Deniz, we do not have such qualified soldiers among us." I responded with, "That's fine. If you do not have such fighters, leave it to me!" I was very open with him, and said, "Look, you do no harm to us with only those two spring and fall land operations, but you deceive the Turkish public with exaggerated news. I have been fighting in your jurisdiction of authority since 2006. Haven't you carried out land operations both in the fall and in spring throughout those four years? You have! Have you ever had close contact with guerilla units during those operations? No! Never! Have you ever been able to capture images of guerillas traveling in the mountainous areas with your expensive unmanned flying vehicles? No! Do not you see that you did nothing but waste your resources! I can tell you about a single spot where you can direct your forces. Dispatch only one small unit there. Tell them to remain there quietly for a couple of days. I swear to you that they will get into a hot encounter with guerilla units, in no longer than three days. How do the guerilla units travel from Botan Field to Amed State? Dersim, Erzurum, Bingöl, Bitlis; all these groups reach their final destinations using that spot that passes inside the territories of Garzan. If your soldiers can hold that passage spot, and if the states within Turkey are not supplied with new guerillas for a year, then none of those guerilla forces who are already positioned within Turkey, would dare to carry out missions against the security forces."

Again, my suggestions were initially welcomed with excitement. The soldiers even verbally supported and encouraged me. Later, I figured out that they were reluctant to do what I suggested. I do not know if the commanders did not trust me or they did not have the guts to do what I told them.

Nevertheless, if they had held that passage, they would have had worry-free years ahead of them. I would then, in return, ask them to let me go and kill Hakkı and his team.

Sentencing

I was taken to the courthouse in the city of Diyarbakır on Saturday, May 8. As it was the weekend, the courthouse was extremely quiet. Even the prosecutor and the judge, who were supposed to handle the incidents of that weekend, were not there. After a phone talk with the prosecutor, the soldiers took me to the prosecutor's house. He had read all the files that required his signatures. After that, I was transported to the prison.

I was handed over to the prison administrators at 12:30 p.m. By this time, I had been in this prison for six years, three hours and 30 minutes. [It was May 8, 2015, 4:00 p.m.] I still remember which guards and prison directors were on duty that day. As soon as I stepped into the facility, I was taken in front of the second director, Tahsin Muş. He talked to me for almost two hours and asked me whether I wanted to stay alone for a couple days or be assigned to a repentant cell immediately. I preferred staying alone, until I got over the shock I was experiencing. Additionally, I did not know who was staying in which cell.

On Monday morning, the head guardian called me into his room and showed me pictures from two separate files. They were the photos of the comrades staying in the repentant cells; one file for each cell. The head guardian said, "Look at the pictures and decide in which cell you want to stay." I picked one of them and was taken directly there. Two comrades with whom I had been acquainted previously welcomed me as soon as I arrived. I knew both of them very well. I then greeted the rest of the comrades, one by one. Everyone was waiting to hear my story and my reason for quitting the organization. I told them everything that I had suffered. One of them said, "Comrade, I wish you had not surrendered yourself. It would have been better if you had traveled to Europe. You will probably be given a life sentence." Hearing that was demoralizing and I asked, "How can someone who surrendered himself be sentenced to life?" Time showed that I had been seriously mistaken.

My first hearing soon took place. I told the judge everything. A ranked soldier from the military accompanied me during all my trials. At the end of that first appearance in front of the judge, the soldier told me, "Do not worry Deniz! You will be free soon." Naturally, I was happy to hear that. My second trial was scheduled for December 30, 2010. I remember the date very well, because the former President of Turkey, Abdullah Gül, had visited Diyarbakır on the same day, which turned out to be one of the worst days of my life. I thought the judge would recall me for more trials, but, interestingly, he sentenced me to 51 years on that day. It should not be determined so quickly!

I looked at the judge and said, "I should not be given such a long sentence. You did not catch me, nor did you capture me wounded from a clash. I surrendered myself with my own free will. I do not understand how you can sentence me to 51 years, even though I had put my application in to benefit from the repentance law."

The ranked soldier accompanying me was also shocked. He even told the judge that there might have been a mistake and so checked everything again. The judge responded that there was no mistake on this sentencing decision. Then the soldier looked at me and asked, "Deniz, have you not applied for the repentance law?" I answered, "Of course, I did. Why would I be put in a repentant cell if I had not applied for it?" It never rains, but pours. Back then, I had no money with which to hire a lawyer, who would thoroughly go over my files, so the police department arranged someone for me. His name was

Mervan. I guess he was one of the legal aid lawyers. He said that he objected to the decision of the lower court, but had not heard anything from the higher court. I was not even called to a hearing, so, I guess he had lied to me. I could not believe anything that was happening at that time. Why had my trial been concluded in such a swift manner? I thought I would stay, at most, 10 years and then be released.

There was a comrade in my cell, who is still with us. His trial lasted for more than four years. I was brought to the prison on May 8 and the court sentenced me on December 30. Deniz Koçer, here you are, sentenced to three consecutive life sentences plus 15 years. It was a total of 51 years of incarceration. I was deeply depressed when I heard of that.

Two months later, officers from the Diyarbakır Police Department wanted to visit me in prison in order to get some information regarding the organization. I rejected this interview request. "I helped you a great deal, and what did you do for me in return? You let the judge's decision pass unchallenged!" They were all friendly and extremely nice when trying to get information from me. Nevertheless, I was left on my own on the date of the trial. There was no one there to raise objections to the judge or at least give solace to me.

I was housed at the Diyarbakır Police Department for a whole week before the judge gave his final sentencing decision. The prosecutor, who prepared my files for the court, was also present during those seven days. He interviewed me every day. He told me that I should not be worried, since he was going to help me to get a reduced sentence. The prosecutor, the head of counterterrorism unit, and I, were all sitting together, chatting for hours. We became like friends. The prosecutor asked me to explain the hierarchical command order within the organization. I drew it out for him in 15 minutes. They were all amazed with the extent of my knowledge regarding the organization. The prosecutor even said to me, "Deniz, God has sent such a talented person to us!" I swear, he used exactly these words. So, what happened next? Only a couple days after I was praised with such words, I was sentenced to 51 years. This is the judge's decision. The normal release date: 2061. The conditional release date: 2044. This is what I still do not understand. I was sitting with the prosecutor and the head of the counterterrorism unit on December 23. They promised me many things. Nevertheless, the same prosecutor clearly had asked the judge to punish me with three consecutive life sentences, plus 15 years. Can you see the confusion? It was also weird that, despite the fact that this prosecutor had prepared my files and charges, from the very beginning, he did not show up at the court on December 30. Instead, there was another prosecutor in the court on that day. He probably could not look at me after all those promises.

I could understand if I had not provided them with any information, but I told them everything, regarding Hakkı and me. They could have said, "That man is a double-crosser. Let him rot in the prison," if I had not told them anything, or if I had misinformed them. But I had helped them in many aspects, even preventing a couple of missions that were to be carried out. Of course, I do not know if they would have recognized my part in preventing those missions, but many lives were saved, after they took precautions, thanks to the intelligence I provided. For example, the police officers showed me a picture, and I told them, "This man is very dangerous. He has been preparing to carry out a mission in downtown Bingöl or Bitlis. Arrest him as soon as you see him."

The man was caught one week after my statement. He was driving a car that had a trunk loaded with explosive materials. As soon as he was caught, I was invited to the police department. I told the officers at the counterterrorism unit that, "Do not waste your time. He will never tell you anything. He will never speak, even if you beat him or let him starve." As I said, he did not utter a single word.

I even informed the police officers about a large explosive mission which was to be carried out by the organization in the future in Istanbul. A guerilla was sent by the organization to Istanbul in 2006.

He was an expert in preparing explosives and was given a large amount of money to start a business there. The organization said to him, "Settle into Istanbul and start a business. Live a normal life. Get married, have kids, visit the mosque. When the time comes, we will let you know, and you will carry out the mission." He was one of our sleeper cells in the city of Istanbul. After I surrendered myself, I notified the police and the gendarme units about him.

I did not personally know this person, even if shown a couple of pictures. However, I knew his parents very well. I told the officers, "He's the son of that family and is now in Istanbul. He was sent there from Iraq, in 2006. He must own a shop there by now." I knew him very well, because he contacted me in 2007 and said, "Comrade Deniz, I settled and started my business. Send me the explosive materials, as soon as possible. I am ready to carry out the mission." I did not allow this delivery to occur at that time, because it was still too early. He was new in his neighborhood. He had to stay there at least for three or more years to be acquainted with the people and to gain their trust. If he had performed his mission only after one year, he would easily be on the list of potential suspects. Otherwise, if he stayed there for a couple of years, got acquainted with his neighbors, and visited the mosque regularly, no one would suspect him. I gave all this information to the security forces, but he has not yet been arrested. I guess they will arrest him after the bomb goes off.

Big Mistake

I think now that the idea of surrendering myself to the security forces was a huge and irreparable mistake, because nothing worked out as I planned. The investigation period lasted for four to five days and then I was directly sent to prison. Yet I had planned to kill Hakkı for revenge of Asmin's death. That had been the sole purpose of my surrender to the military.

If I had my choice, I would never stay even one day in prison. If I had not told them about the missions I carried out, or crimes I committed, the security forces could never have found out about them. I was just trying to be honest. I even gave them the exact dates and times of the missions. The security forces had initially not believed me. They thought I was taking a wild guess. Nevertheless, they were all amazed when they checked the accuracy of my statements against the incidents archived by the counterterrorism department. They also checked the statements of the guerillas who had surrendered themselves between the years 1994 and 1995. They saw that all the dates I had given them matched not only the archived information but also with the statements provided by the repenter former guerillas.

When I surrendered myself, I warned the commanders, "Do not ever inform the media and the press about my surrendering." I had experience in legal issues. The judiciary authorities would learn about my arrest, as soon as the information was given to the press. In that case, the security forces could keep me for only four days; the legal duration given to security forces by the law. I then had to be delivered to the prison. Therefore, as soon as I surrendered, I told the commanders, "Do not inform anyone about my surrender. I will give you some sensitive information and, in return, you will let me kill Hakkı. So, we will both win in the end."

20

THE PRISON AND THE GENERAL

Neither the police nor the gendarme visited me for a long time. How could they? They had promised me that I would soon be released. They were going to visit me after a couple of months, but I rejected their request to see me. I told the prison guards that I had no desire to sit and talk with deceivers!

As I said, the only reason for my surrender was to get my revenge on Hakkı, but after the incarceration, all my hopes disappeared. I told myself several times, "Deniz, you put yourself into this hot water and you will bear the losses."

Almost two months after my surrender, Şilan, the woman who was accused of having an affair with me, also fled the organization. I had already informed the police officers during my first questioning at the police department, "The woman, Şilan, will definitely also surrender herself," and as I prophesied, Şilan had, in fact, deserted the organization towards the end of May.

I was invited to the courthouse when she surrendered herself. The prosecutor asked me if I knew her. I replied, "Yes, I do. I know her very well." He asked me whether Şilan had carried out any missions. I said, "No, she has never participated in an action." Şilan was set free after the investigation period.

Later, a general who was on duty in the Eastern Anatolia region, asked a couple of times to see me in person. Each time, we met outside the prison environment. I was hosted at the military guesthouse, when I was not in prison. We would talk together for hours. After each of these talks, the general said, "Deniz, I wish we'd had the chance to meet before! I wish I'd met you before the judge sentenced you to such a long term!" He appeared to be furious with the length of my sentence. I told him everything about the trial process. "The security forces neither paid attention to the information I provided them nor did they help me at the court. Besides that, they also depicted my surrender in a misleading manner. The media was informed that I had been captured by the diligent works of the security forces. Liars!"

I believe no one wanted to take a risk, since I surrendered myself close to the date of Supreme Military Council meeting. As I mentioned before, the time before those meetings were great relaxation periods for the guerillas. None of the military commanders would easily carry out an operation against the guerillas during those times. They simply did not want to be the topic on the agenda. On the other hand, the military commanders were already viewing my surrender as a great success for themselves. They did not consider it necessary to carry out operations in the places I had told them.

This general, whom I had recently met, did not understand why I was sentenced to such a long term, despite all my helpful information. I was even later offered a way out of prison, but did not like it. I was told, "We can get you out of here in one of the two ways; either as an escape or by death." I replied, "I cannot accept such an offer, because I have no legal assurance in either situation. It was true that I would be free, but I would not have any life security. If someone got angry with me one day and shot me in the head, nothing would happen, because I would already be a person shown as dead, in the records."

They could, in fact, have easily closed my investigation file, if they had really wanted to set me free. I had trusted those officers and told them everything about myself. How could they know which missions I had carried out or planned, if I had not told them? They should have set me free, for the sake of the intelligence I provided them about Hakkı. Same for the prosecutor. He was not with me while I was carrying out those missions. The police could tell him that I joined the organization in 2009 and deserted it in 2010. Again, the only mistake I made was to be honest and overconfident with the police and the gendarme. There was no arrest or search warrant out for me until I surrendered myself. I had a clean record. That was why it would have been an easy job for the security forces. They could have said to the prosecutor, "Deniz joined the organization in 2009 and surrendered himself in 2010. He is applying for repentance law and should be set free, since he has no record."

This general that I mentioned earlier was much affected by the things I told him. Therefore, he asked to read the statement that I gave, soon after my surrender, to figure out what could have gone wrong during the trial process. He could not find a single statement, regarding me, from the gendarme. Right then, I figured out that the information I had provided had not been archived or had been intentionally deleted by someone to free themselves from a potential future responsibility.

The general was persistent and kept hard on the heels of those responsible. Every single archive that was held by the gendarme was searched, with no results. Nothing was left behind. Can you imagine? All that strategic information had not even been stored at the military archives. Even a person with the rank of general could not find out a single thing about my initial statements. Again, most probably, the gendarme commander had destroyed all that information in order to protect himself from a future investigation.

I even remembered the name of the person who was taking notes on a computer when I was giving my statement. The general spoke to him in my presence and asked where those statements were archived. He said, "General, those notes were all discarded, because the gendarme units were not ready to carry out a mission against the targets." The general went crazy as soon as he heard the explanation. "I need to see those files! Where did you archive them?" He could not give an answer. The general shouted again, "Where are the damn files?" The record keeper was frightened, and said, "General, the files might be stored at the headquarters of the intelligence gathering unit of the gendarme." All to no end! He could find nothing in Ankara, either.

The Reach of the Organization in the Prison

The organization has wide control within the prisons and has too many civilian supporters working as guards there. We repentants are sometimes amazed at how on earth the authorities allow so many people from the organization to work in prisons. Once, the soldiers took me out of the prison at 8:00 a.m. to take me to the office of this general I mentioned, without the guards even being informed. The general and I boarded a helicopter and flew to Muş region. It was a secret meeting, and we thought no one knew about it. The next day, we heard on the radio that a repentant convict from Diyarbakır E-Type Prison Facility had been taken outside the prison to join a reconnaissance activity with the soldiers. By this, you see just how strong a control they have in the prisons.

Using its supporters, the organization even reached out to me, while I was incarcerated. I was told, "Ask for a transfer to a political convicts' cell from the repentant convicts' cell. If you do so, we will do anything you wish for you and your parents."

Of course, I disregarded their offer. The organization was well aware of the danger waiting before them. They thought I would share their sensitive information with the security forces, such as the secret locations of ammunitions, the coded words we used for communication, the coordinates of the guerilla campgrounds, and our secret hideouts. I had surrendered myself on May 5, 2010. Look at the security forces' archives! The Garzan province could not carry out any missions during the year I surrendered myself. They thought I would talk to the security forces about all the plans we had made during the winter camp to be carried out in the spring of 2010. Therefore, they were occupied with defense preparations rather than carrying out those plans. Believe me, they were nervous about whether I had compromised those details of the Garzan state. It was simply because I knew the whole state intimately. I even knew where underground bunkers would be dug for the 2011 winter.

I was later informed by some guards in the prison that the organization had accepted that I had been right on many of the issues discussed during my trial at Garzan state. For example, the headquarters commander had said, "Deniz met with those rangers upon our instructions and orders. He never did anything without first confirming with us." One of the comrades even brought me the transcripts of the radio talks that were broadcast after my desertion. The state commander of Garzan had said, "How could something like that happen? Deniz would never desert us just because he had a relationship with a woman. There must definitely be something else." He was an old friend of mine. We had known each other for almost 15 years. He had asked the others, "What did you ask Deniz during the investigation? With what did you threaten him, so that he deserted us?" If Hakkı and his men had told the truth, everyone would have figured out the plot played against me. Therefore, no one could give a proper answer to the state commander's questions.

Nevertheless, Hakkı had continued telling lies about me on many issues. He had burst with anger, because I was able to escape before he killed me. Therefore, he had cast aspersions on me at every opportunity. I heard that he had told the Kurdish villagers, "Deniz gave to the security forces, the names of at least 60 to 70 patriot villagers who have been helping the organization. That bastard would have even given his father's name for his own benefit." In fact, many civilian villagers had panicked over whether their names had really been leaked to the security forces. Hundreds of them then decided to desert their homes, due to the risk of being arrested. They all returned only after a few months passed and they realized that they were not being searched for by the police or gendarme. Hakkı had also told headquarters that I was working as an informant for the security forces during my time in the organization. Some of my close comrades had even started to believe Hakkı, since I had stayed in Garzan for three years and had not carried out a single mission against the police or the military.

All this information was delivered to me while I was incarcerated. Headquarters asked me to give them a written response for all the claims of which I had been accused. However, I did not bother myself with that. I even told my parents not to be in touch with anyone coming from the organization, but they did not give up pressuring me. They goaded my parents in order to get to me. The civilian members of the organization even put leverage on my parents to try and convince me to leave the repentant convicts' cell. My elder brother once visited me in prison. Each convict is given 45 minutes to talk to his family member during the visit, but he did not even talk to me for one minute. He was very angry with me, since I was staying at the repentance convicts' cell, and told me, "What the hell are you doing with the repentant convicts? We can't take the pressure coming from the organization anymore. Should we move to Istanbul again, just because you won't change your mind?" I replied, "Brother, I surrendered myself, and I will continue to stay in the cell I am staying in now! I will never be a part of them again, even though they threaten to kill me!"

Believe me, I would be in a much better shape now if I had accepted the offer proposed by the organization and transferred to the cell of the comrades captured by the security forces. The organization would have taken very good care of my parents, if I had done that. Nevertheless, I did not change my mind. I always thought that the Turkish state would look after my parents and me. However, I was mistaken about that. They did not help me, and they did not even give a shit about the threats of the organization to my parents.

I sent several petitions to the Ministry of Justice. I sent petitions to various other institutions within Turkey. Nevertheless, not even one of them condescended to write me a response. Actually, the Ministry of Justice sent me a one paragraph note saying, "We are working on the issues you have outlined. We will let you know about the results in the future." It has been almost five years, and no one has responded to me yet, regarding my petition. Actually, none of my petitions involved personal requests. They were for the good of all the convicts.

My Testimonies

You would never believe what ridiculous things I went through after I surrendered myself to the security forces. After hearing what I had to say, you would definitely think the Turkish security forces had rocks in their heads. When I first surrendered to the gendarme units, I provided them with a name from the organization of someone who used to torture the local Kurdish peasants. He was also incarcerated in the same prison, and I really wanted him to pay the price for what he had done in the past, to innocent people. I told them that I would be happy to be a witness against him at the court. For that purpose, I was transported to the courthouse in Diyarbakır, to give my testimony. Do you know that the person against whom I was to give my testimony was put in the same vehicle as me on our way to the court? Even worse, my right hand and his left hand were handcuffed to each other with a single handcuff. Can you imagine that situation? I have never seen such gross stupidity in my life.

Naturally, this man threatened me all the way to the prosecutor's office. He asked me, "Why did you give my name to the gendarme? Why did you snitch on me? I will kill you at the very first opportunity I have. I will even contact the organization to kill your parents." I was really stressed, as I was supposed to have served as an anonymous witness. This was the first stupid act I encountered.

Now, the second one. Earlier, in one of the KCK trials, I was forcefully taken out of prison to give my testimony against one of the arrested suspects. There were more than ten suspects in that trial. The courtroom was jam packed with relatives of the suspects. There were close to 200 people. You know how I was asked to give my testimony about that suspect? I was put on the stand in front of those ten suspects and that large crowd, and then asked to start giving my testimony. This stupid incident took place in Diyarbakır 6th High Felony Court. Before I was put in front of that crowd, I had a chance to talk with the judge in his chambers, and he told me then that I had to give my testimony in front of everyone. I began to tell him off, "What kind of judge are you? How could you earn your law degree? Shame on you! You want me to help you by revealing my identity in front of everyone! Look! I do not care about my own life. I am willing to take the risk. I am not afraid of death! However, I have parents and they are out there, unprotected. You want to make them a target? Are you trying to kill them?" I was so furious.

When I was put on the stand, the court bailiff began to read aloud the note he was holding. "Deniz Koçer. His mother's name is blah, blah. His father's name is blah, blah. He is from the city of Batman. He used to reside at this address." He read everything aloud, in front of everyone. After that, he looked at me and asked me to verify the accuracy of all the information he had read. Did he really need to read all that private information, regarding me, in front of that large crowd? No! He had my ID card in his hand. He could have checked everything by looking at the card. Alternatively, he could have come close to me and verified everything quietly. The court bailiff did that on purpose! I was forced to keep my silence. The court secretary, the judge, and the attorney had all given me a message. Look, we made your information public. If you say something about the suspects, you and your family will be targeted by the organization.

When the judge asked me to start my testimony on the suspect, I said, "Your Honor, I do not even know this man! How could I give a testimony about him?" The chief of the court angrily asked, "How come you do not know him? We have a statement about him with your signature!" he replied. I was acting sarcastically because of the situation I was put in and replied, "Your honor, I do not remember giving such a statement. Call the officer who wrote it down and ask him to be your witness."

The officials in the Turkish justice system are such idiots. Even though I was closely acquainted with this man, I had told the judge that I did not know him. "Your honor, I have never seen this man before, I am not acquainted with him, and I do not know him." This man had, in fact, killed dozens of innocent villagers, bullied, and racketeered them. Can you see the irony? The security officers had revealed my real identity in front of such a man and his relatives, disclosed the address where my parents were staying, and then asked me to give a testimony against him! What stupidity!

The officials seriously risked the life of my parents and me, when they were, in fact, supposed to repay me for my willingness to provide testimony. That was a real life threat. If I had presented my testimony in the court, a relative of one of those suspects would not have hesitated to go and kill one of my parents as a warning. The justice system had, officially, forced me to get even in one of their own matters. I was given the message that not only I but also my parents would be a target if I helped the security forces. Such incidents took place many times during 2010 and 2011. Sometimes I do seriously wonder whether there is even a single smart person working for the Turkish state.

After my appearance in the court that day, the brother of the prisoner had called my parents' house and openly threatened them. Moreover, he sent a letter containing insults and threats to their house. The letter said, "Either you keep your son quiet or we will kill you all!" My parents still have a copy of that letter. The original is being kept by Batman Police Department, counterterrorism unit.

After those ridiculous incidents to which I was subjected, those cheeky officials continued to call me to the courthouse to give testimony against the people whom I mentioned in my initial statements with the gendarme and the police. I rejected all of them. I even denied the information that I had provided in all my previous statements. I openly said to the security officers, "You are traitors. I sincerely trusted you. Nevertheless, you wasted my trust. Since you have been acting treacherously, I will do the very same from now on!"

In my first statement, stored at Diyarbakır Police Department, my first sentence read, "I will do whatever you want, but I have one condition. You will help me get my revenge on Hakkı, and you will also fulfill the rules of secrecy and witness protection"—and the police officers told me that they surely would. They even told me that it was an insult to them that I was warning them about the rules of witness protection. Nevertheless, I was subjected to those incidents I just mentioned. It not only happened once, it happened maybe on three different occasions. Right then, I figured out that they were selfish and only concerned about their own successes, at the expense of another person or his parents' lives and that's why I began to reject all my initial statements, given at the police and gendarme departments. I said, "You can even go and sue me for giving you misleading information. I do not care! I will never ever provide a testimony for you again. Do not ever knock my door again!"

Put yourself into my shoes! Would you continue to help the security officials after all that insulting treatment? That KCK trial was the last straw for me. I called the police officers from Diyarbakır PD and said to them, "I provided you with all that information under one condition! I told you that I would provide testimony against some people in my statements, as long as you do not expose me to them. You accepted all my conditions. Why did you break your promise?" I received the same old lies. "It was a mistake, Deniz. We do not even know how the judge made such a huge mistake." I was so disgusted with all of them. After that court appearance, the security officials attempted to visit me several times to apologize, but I rejected them at each visit.

The Prison Environment

Initially, I struggled a great deal to get used to prison conditions. I encountered an atmosphere worse than I could have imagined. For instance, the physical conditions of the quarters. It is a two-story cell. The bedroom is located at upstairs. The kitchen and the living room are downstairs. There is only one heater in this two-story cell. The windows are from the 1970s, and the cold weather comes directly into our cell during the cold days. It is usually 17 degrees Fahrenheit (−8 degrees Celsius) in the winter. It gets so cold that we are usually not able to leave our beds. It is just the opposite in the summer. It starts getting hot in June, and we experience exhaustion from the heat, until the end of September. There is only one ceiling fan and it is downstairs, not upstairs where we sleep. It becomes impossible to sleep at nights in the summer season. We spend all night awake, tossing and turning in our beds. We usually fall asleep, from exhaustion, just before the sunrise.

We have a television, a kitchen, and a dinner table near the entrance at the first floor. There is also a small area, surrounded by high walls, right by the shower area on this floor. It is a place where we have fresh air daily. We have access to this place from the morning until 6:30 p.m. We are not allowed to use it during the night. Therefore, our life is basically confined to this two-story cell and its small fresh air area.

We have bunk beds in the upstairs. In some cells, these bunks have three beds, since there are so many people incarcerated. We hear that some cells are so crowded that people are even sleeping on the floors. In our cell no one uses a mattress, except for two. This is because of the lifestyle to which we became accustomed in the mountains. It has been almost six years, and I still cannot sleep on a mattress. We mostly sleep on a solid wood platform. We might, at times, place a thin blanket on the wood, when it is very cold outside.

There is a shower and a restroom on the first floor of the cell. We are fortunate that there are only seven people living in our cell. However, this number ranges from 25 to 30 in other cells in the prison. We are provided with hot water twice a day, for 15 minutes, at 2:00 p.m. and 6:00 p.m. Therefore, we all have to take a shower within those 15 minutes, meaning, we have approximately two minutes each.

Since two minutes is really too short of a time, we created a routine among ourselves. Three of us use the allocated hot water time at 2:00 p.m., and the remaining four shower at 6:00 p.m. That way, each of us has more time to wash. These 15 minutes are the same for all the cells, regardless of their size. As I said, there are cells in this prison with over 30 convicts. I cannot even imagine how they handle the shower time.

Within our cell, we have a weekly schedule for cleaning. We wash the floors, both upstairs and downstairs, with soap and water every Saturday. Apart from that, every day, we have one person responsible for the kitchen works and dishwashing. We prisoners pay out of our own pockets for the cleaning materials—detergent, soap, bleach and other things. The prison administration do not have a budget for that.

We even pay for the electricity and water we use within the cells. Each cell has its own electric and water meter box. We pay approximately 20–25 Turkisk Lira during the winters, and 50–60 Turkish lira during the summers. We have to pay these bills as a cell unit, and it is very serious. If we do not pay on time, our water and electricity is shut off immediately and we would literally then be in the dark. Once Şemdin Sakık did not pay his bill, saying that he did not have the money for it and was left in the dark for days. Do you see how the Turkish state protected the repenters? In fact, the state security forces were able to deal their biggest blow to the organization with the help of Şemdin. He provided the state with such sensitive information about our structure that the organization did not recover from the damages he caused, for approximately three years. What did Şemdin get in return for his help? He also received a life sentence. He is going to die in this prison. He was thrown away like a piece of old clothing, after being used by the security forces.

There are two "counting sessions" carried out every day by the prison guards; one at 7:00 a.m., and the other one at 8:00 p.m. The guards also occasionally search our personal items. Our cell does not have anyone who would be considered a troublemaker, and none of us are on drugs or marijuana.

I generally wake up at 7:30 a.m. We have our breakfast around 8:30 a.m. There is a handcraft workshop that opens at 9:00 a.m., and I usually go there every day to build model ships for sale. We are allowed to work there until 11:00 a.m., but we have to be back in our cells between 11:00 a.m. and 1:00 p.m. I go back to my cell and have lunch with my comrades during that time. After lunch, we make tea and watch the news on the TV. At 1:00 p.m., I go back to the handcraft workshop and continue to work on the model I am building until 4:00 p.m. We have to return to our cells around 4:15 p.m. I usually hang out in the small fresh air area until dinner.

I take a shower before eating dinner. Then, I either read the newspaper or watch TV. We also need to pay for the newspapers. It is good that we are allowed to read any newspaper we want. As a group, we generally buy *Milliyet* or *Hürriyet*. We also enjoy watching political talk shows during the evenings. Unfortunately, those shows are only available on certain nights. The prisoners are allowed to watch the following 13 channels; ATV, Kanal D, Star TV, Show, CNN Türk, NTV, Kanal 7, IMC, TRT 1, TRT Kürdi, TRT Spor, Meclis TV and Kral TV. However, we often only watch two channels: NTV and CNN Türk.

We have three meals a day. For that, each convict has to pay a monthly fee of 150 Turkish lira. Meals are generally pretty standard. For breakfast, we are given a small pot of chocolate spread, honey, eggs, and sometimes milk or a piece of cake, but not all together in one meal. One day, we get the chocolate spread and the egg. Another day, it is honey and a piece of cake. We have our own tea to fix. In addition to that, sometimes milk is served with the breakfast. Each person is given two breads each day. For dinner, we mostly have either pasta or brown beans. No one likes to eat the dinner in our cell. However, lunch is always good. On Tuesdays and Fridays, we have chicken or boiled beef. On Thursdays, each of us is given four burgers.

The worst thing about being in the prison is that we prisoners do not have any social activity in which we can actively participate. We spend most of our time in the cells. There are neither educational nor social activities in which we can engage. When I was first incarcerated, the prison administration offered some courses and training on computer use, football, volleyball, and handball. Participating in these made the time pass very quickly. Leaving our cell to engage in those activities provided a great deal of relief for us. There is not a single course or any training being offered now. The new director of the prison canceled all the previously provided activities. We are stuck in this cell 24/7. This is not something that will last for a day, for a month, or for a year. We will be here until we die…

We questioned the prosecutor about this, when he visited our cell during one of those routine controls. I told him that, since we were repentant, at least one privilege should be given to the convicts staying in our cell. "We left the organization and surrendered ourselves to the state security forces. To some extent, we helped those officials in their fight against the organization, so our sentences should not be the same the other prisoners that are held here," I said. He replied with the classic response, which they use all the time. "There are only seven of you in your cell and you know the rules. We, as the prison administration, need at least ten signatures to start a social activity. Additionally, it is not possible to mingle you with the others, because you are repentants! Your lives would be under a serious threat, if we joined you with them." Each time we ask for something, we are given that same response, so we remain deprived of everything. It is true that the rule states there must be at least ten signatures for a course, training, or a social activity to be opened. However, there are only seven people in this goddamn cell, and so we are stuck here. One might argue that we at least have the opportunity to join the model shipbuilding in the handcrafts workroom, but that is not actually a social activity for us. It is the only way we can earn some money while we are incarcerated. It is true that we are stepping outside the cell to go there, but it is not really a social activity. Several times, I have asked the prosecutors and prison administrators to give us freedom from this strict rule, but each time they ignore my requests.

The prison director even considers the repentant convicts' situation equal to the people who are convicted for petty things, such as theft. He told us, "The other prisoners are in a similar situation. They also are not able to participate in social activities, since they do not have enough signatures." In response, I said, "The convicts that you are talking about are here for only a month or two and then freed. They are not as deeply affected as we repentants, by not being able to join social activities. However, we will be incarcerated here forever." The director was very stubborn. No matter what I asked him, he told me that he could not make an exception due to the military type structure of the prison. I have been here for almost six years. During this period, I have witnessed a petty criminal being arrested and then set free four times! Each time, he has been released, with parole, has committed another petty crime, and then been incarcerated again. It is not ethical to compare those people with us. The prison administrators should make a concession for us, so that we can benefit from some social activities.

We are allowed to do sports once a week, for 30–45 minutes. There are two sports fields. One is an outdoor field, and the other is indoors. Each week, we are allowed to use only one of those fields. Again, since we are less in numbers, we are unable to play any games. What can seven people do on a soccer field? During the administration of the former director, we were allowed to play soccer with the other prisoners, but, as I said, the new director is strictly against that. He always says that it is dangerous to mix different types of convicts, though there has not been a single incident so far.

Another strange thing here is that we are not allowed to see the doctors whenever we need them. Each cell has a specific day on which to visit the doctor's office. For instance, our cell is allowed to visit the infirmary on Wednesdays only. Let's say one of us gets sick on Thursday. If it is not a life threatening issue, that person literally has to wait until the following Wednesday to see the doctor and get medications. In such cases, somebody from the infirmary visits the cell and checks the sick person from behind the bars. He does not even touch your body, but figures out your condition by simply looking at you. If he decides that there is no urgency, then you have to wait until the next week and no one can change that decision. You can see the bullshit going on here.

Moreover, even though you can visit the doctor on the day you are allowed, you do not expect to get a proper diagnosis and treatment. The doctor just talks with you and then prescribes you a bunch of medicines. All diagnoses are based on your talk with the doctor. He does not even bother himself with the basics, such as checking heartbeats and pulse.

I have a serious problem with both of my knees. I was taken to a university hospital at least four times because of that problem. The doctors at the hospital examined my MRI and X-ray images and then informed me that I needed to have surgery as soon as possible. You know what the doctor at the prison told me? He said to me that there was no need for surgery, as long as I did not play soccer, run, or even walk. He told me that I would be fine, if I no longer did any of those things, including the walking. I still do not know if he was making fun of me, or he was, in fact, serious, but, I have not yet been allowed to have that surgery.

The problem with my knees progressed so badly, that one of my legs had to be put into a cast, and it remained in that cast for ten days. I removed it myself, when I could no longer endure lying still in the bed. I knew there would be calcification in my knees without some mobility.

Honestly, I do not even feel like visiting the infirmary when I really need it. There used to be only male staff working there. Later, three female doctors and a nurse. These women are very well-behaved and decent. Over time, the male doctors became very lax in their conversations. I am amazed at how freely and easily they speak about immoral things, even when patients are present in the infirmary. One day, I could not take it anymore, and I yelled at the male doctors, "You cannot speak like that when there are women around. You must pay attention to the tone of your conversation!" They all resented my words, but I did not care.

You know, I think the public is morally corrupted. It was not like that when I left my parents years ago. People would care about their language. I sometimes asked myself why I wasted those best years of my life for those morally corrupt people!

Political Guerilla Prisoners Versus Repenters

There are two different types of cells in the prisons where the incarcerated guerillas are kept. Within the first type, the prison administration keep the PKK members, who have been caught by the Turkish security forces. This type of cell is called political prisoners' cell. The guerillas who surrender themselves to the security forces are kept in the second type, which is known as the repenter captives' cell. And since I had voluntarily surrendered myself, this is where I stayed.

The number of repenters staying in the prisons is decreasing as the days pass. As people witness the intolerance of the state towards them, they decide to side with the organization again by requesting their transfer to the political prisoners' cells. When I was first brought in, there were two women repenter guerilla cells in the prison. Unbelievable, but the political guerilla prisoners rioted against the administration to have those two repenter cells closed down and they were successful. The administration closed those two cells and transferred the women repenter guerillas to other prisons in Turkey. The Turkish politicians always say that they have established their full authority over all of Turkey and even some regions of the Middle East, but that is not accurate. It is actually funny that they claim such control when they are not even able to establish their authority in their own prisons.

The Ministry of Justice operates prisons on a simple rule: to fulfill all the demands of the political guerilla prisoner, even at the expense of the repenters so that there is no trouble. The Turkish officials are even willing to sacrifice the repenter, who sided with them, just to prevent potential chaos in the prisons. Would you call that full dominance and authority?

When those two women's repenter cells were closed down, I asked the guards to let me talk to the director of the prison. There were even two police officers accompanying me, when I visited the director. I said to him, "Look! Your solution of pleasing the political guerilla prisoners is seriously mistaken. You are losing the hearts of those repentant people, just to make the political ones happy. By closing down those two cells, you were officially serving the goals of the organization, which encourages its political prisoners to riot in the prisons, simply to force the repenters to change their minds, and turn back to the organization. You should leave at least one of those women repenter cells open, so that those women guerillas would not return their loyalty to the organization, just to be able to stay in this prison."

As a result, even though those repenter women did not really want it, many of them asked for their transfer to the political prisoners' cells, just to be able to stay close to their families that live in the surrounding cities. They had no other feasible options. If they resisted moving to a political prisoners' cell, they would take the risk of being transferred to other prisons that were located in the western parts of Turkey, when almost all of those prisoners' parents and families live in this region, and if they were sent to the west, they would have no one visiting them, including their own parents. You do not understand the reality that those people come from mostly poor parents, and those Kurdish parents are not even able to earn enough money to supply their basic needs. Because of this, those prisoners simply submit their request to be transferred to a political prisoners' cell. Do you see the irony here? Your own state pushes those repenters back into the arms of the organization.

The male political prisoners and some of the prison staff attempted to put similar pressure on the repenter men's cell, also. They threatened the prison administration to be either sent to their side, or sent to prisons in the western parts of Turkey. There was even a head guardian working in the prison and he tried everything possible to close our cells. He was a pure organization member and did not hide it, even from the prison administration. Many times, he visited our cells and openly threatened us to return to the organization's side. We officially complained about him to the administration, but each time we went away empty handed. At some point, I could not take those pressures anymore, so I visited the prison prosecutor and the director and said to them, "Look, your own staff member is forcing us to return to the organization, and regularly threatening us. I do not understand how you can allow such a follower of the organization to work as the head guardian in this prison. I am telling you! He works for the organization. Do you not see what is happening here? We were 19 people just a year ago and are now only seven. Why do you think those people left us? They got sick of hearing threats. They got sick of your negligence towards them and they got sick of being treated in such a derogatory manner in a Turkish prison, which is apparently controlled by the organization. I am warning you. You are helping the organization by allowing those people to put pressure on us." Thank God, I had those two police officers accompany me during that visit, because the director had already made his mind up that he was going to close down our cells.

Other than those unacceptable treatments, the prison administration also once worked on a very stupid idea concerning the repenters. They decided to gather all repenter guerilla prisoners in a single prison located in the western part of Turkey, in order to get rid of the pressures applied by the political guerilla prisoners. Something like that would be a disaster for all the repenters, as I have already mentioned. We were all Kurds. Our parents, families and relatives all lived in this area. Here in this prison, my parents are at least able to visit and see me once every three weeks. If I were transferred to a prison in the west, they would hardly be able to visit me once every six months due to the financial concerns. Challenging it, we repenters were able to suspend that project temporarily, and I hope the administrators will not think about carrying out such a plan in the future.

Because of such uncertainties, we have at least one comrade leaving us each year. It is sad to see that people are giving up. They pack up their stuff, say goodbye to each of us, and then leave. They just do not want to tolerate such injustices any longer. They have too many things to think about. Their parents and families are living in desperate conditions outside. They are subject to continuous pressure inside the prison. On top of that, the Turkish state is ignorant of all of those things, and so, finally, they just give up. They do not want the load of so many problems. Therefore, they just transfer to the political guerilla prisoners' cell. They go to that cell even though they know that they will be ignored for at least six months or more. The problems do not end because you join them. The political prisoners punish them by not talking to them for almost a year. Only after that time are they allowed to make friends; allowed to chat with the other prisoners and to sit and eat with them. Our repenter comrades go there, even though they knew those problems. They do that just because they care about their parents, families and loved ones. They say, "I'm willing to suffer the consequences as long as the organization leaves my family alone!"

The repenter friends who leave us are actually right. They make the right choice. We do not even know how the Turkish state will treat us in the future. Everything is uncertain, including the state. We are being treated differently from one director to another. There simply is no standard. By changing their support to the organization, people at least have a stability to their life in prison. They know what they will encounter and do not expect too many surprises. I do not think there is another country in the world as undisciplined, disorganized, and without standard rules and politics as Turkey.

It is an extremely stressful environment here, and so complex that sometimes we repenters do not get along with each other due to circumstances out of our control. In the prison's view, we are all the same; nevertheless, it is not actually like that. For instance, many of the siblings of the repenters are also incarcerated but among the political guerilla convicts. One sibling is in the cell for repenters, and the other one is in the cell of political convicts. Worse than that, another sibling might still have not been caught or killed by the security forces, and he or she is fighting in the countryside, while a sibling is locked up in the repenter convicts' cell. We are in such a confusing and frustrating situation.

That problem, in fact, poses a life-threatening situation for us. The Ministry of Justice officials are largely negligent regarding which convict stays in which cell. For example, I gave a testimony to the security forces about the sibling of one of the repenter comrades, who used to stay in our cell. Think what would happen if that repenter comrade heard about it? Would he not try to kill me? Would I be safe? Such a big risk! However, no one cared about it.

The brother, sister, or a relative of someone who deserted the organization might still be fighting for them. In other words, one might have deserted the organization, but his or her loved ones could still be part of it, and this is actually very common. So, due to my testimony, I asked the prison administration to transfer the comrade staying in my cell to another prison, explaining to them my concerns for safety.

"Look, I gave a testimony about the brother of this repentant comrade. If he hears about it, I could be in a serious trouble." You know what happened? The prison administration decided to transfer me, not him, to another prison! They were going to send me away, instead of him. Thank God, a gendarme commander intervened and canceled that bullshit. That repenter comrade was transferred to Mardin/Midyat Prison Facility.

The Ministry of Justice generally fouls up on these transfer issues. They need to be in close contact with the police and the gendarme forces when they make decisions on those issues. Those two security agencies should direct the Ministry of Justice, according to the information provided by the repenters, and should inform the Ministry of Justice about the information and testimonies given by the repenters—and then require the prison administrators to assign convicts into cells, considering that information. As those security agencies do not direct the Ministry of Justice, the officials who work at the prisons have their freedom, in regard to cell arrangements. We know of many convicts who lost their lives, because of such negligence.

Prison Staff and Corruption

I do not think that the prison administrators or the guards are properly trained on correctional issues. They all work on one principle: punishment. They do not view us as human beings who need treatment. Rather, in their eyes, we are guilty animals who need nothing but the severest punishment. There is no program or policy, such as listening to the problems of the convicts and treating or educating them.

For instance, we convicts are only able see the prison administrators in two situations. On the day of your trial, they came to your cell and took you to the court. That was, literally, the only time you could guarantee to see the directors of the prison. Second, on very rare occasions, they visit your cell if a fight has occurred between the convicts. In that situation, the directors visit your cell not to talk to you but to threaten you. Would it not be better if the prosecutor, the director, or even a regular guard came to visit us in our cell, and then chatted with us on general topics? We really need them to spend some time with us. We are bored there and are all about to burnout.

I can understand that how they treat us is because of the prejudices drilled into their brains. But what about the general prisoners, who have had nothing to do with terrorism? The administrators, at least, should try to help these petty criminals get out of their cycle of crime. You are doing no constructive good to them by simply putting them into a locked cell. They should try to understand why these people commit these crimes. Everyone here needs treatment. For example, there are many people incarcerated because of theft. I do not think the prison administrators talk to them in order to try and figure out why those people fell into a life of crime. Not all prisoners are the same. There may be some among them who have committed theft, because they had no other option. There are many here who have committed a homicide, and I wonder if some of them were given proper treatment, whether they might be able to change their lives for the better. Locking them up and leaving them alone is not the solution. I can tell you, that we are desperately in need of psychological support. We feel as if we need someone to come and talk to us. However, the prison administration think we have to be left alone.

This prison mentality in Turkey needs urgent revision. Prisons should be viewed as rehabilitation or educational centers, which work with incarcerated people to help them successfully reenter society.

Look at the room in which you are interviewing me now, Murat. There are 30 computers donated by the European Union to be used for the social activities of the convicts. Why were they given? Why did the European Union pay so much money and buy those computers? They donated them for the incarcerated people's educational activities. In ten more days, I will have lived in this prison for six years, and I have been allowed to use those computers only once throughout those six years. All those computers will be left to fall apart. [In fact, all of them were covered with a thick layer of dust. It was clear that they had not been used for a long time.]

If they trained us with various courses, the prison facility could also make money out of it. There used to be a textile workshop, a football pitch, and a volleyball court here when I first arrived. They are all closed down now. There was even a carpentry workshop, but the prison administrators closed it down. Why? Because many administrators are engaged in fraud and corruption. For example, the official who was the director of that carpentry workshop bought the wood for 100 Turkish lira from the store and then sold it to us for 200 Turkish lira. He and a couple of other administrators shared the profit among themselves. In the end, all the courses were closed down because of that.

In fact, the same thing continues now. As I mentioned, we are allowed to work at the handcrafts workshop every day. The convicts are allowed to draw pictures, build ships, or make sculptures of various things to be sold outside the prison facility. The administrators increase the price of materials each month. For example, let's say I bought a bundle of rope for 100 Turkish lira one month. There is no way I can buy the same thing for the same price when I need it again. I paid 150 Turkish lira for the same bundle of rope in the following month. I was told that the prices changed due to inflation. How could a material's price increase by 50 percent in a month?

I once informed the prison prosecutor about this fraud. However, the director of the prison was getting his share from this corrupt business, too. He sabotaged my talk with the prosecutor with answers that made no sense. The prosecutor could not even understand what was going on, because of the director's interference in the conversation. I could not inform the official authorities, since we were sold those materials without receipts. So, we cannot even prove this injustice. The prison administrators would say that we were lying. We are already known as terrorists by many of them. So, who do you think the officials in Ankara would believe?

Never mind all those corrupt businesses. The cell, in which we stay, has not been given any maintenance for the past six years. They should at least have painted the walls. They are filthy and it bothers us. We convicts know that the Ministry of Justice allocates an annual budget for keeping up the maintenance in the prison. They buy a few cans of paint and then paint the areas seen by everyone, and that's it. Where does the rest of the money go? No one knows. The walls are like rubbish. Even an animal would not want to stay in those cells.

They say that a controller from Ankara visits the prison to make sure that everything is on the right track. Trust me, I have never seen anyone checking our cell during the last six years. No one cares what the prisoners are doing—how they are treated, how their life standards are, what the physical condition of their cell is. No one gives a shit about any of those things. We hear from the guards that the controller tours around the facility, has a lunch or dinner at an expensive restaurant in the city of Diyarbakır and then returns to Ankara. They just aren't doing what they are supposed to do and they are not doing their jobs well. Those controllers should check on where the annual budget money, provided by the Ministry of Justice, is being spent. They should check on whether the money is being used for its intended purpose. Everyone, from the prisoners, to the officers working here, knows that the budget allocated for those types of repairs is shared between the director and his assistant.

For example, the prison administration had a greenhouse facility built in the backyard of the prison area. Rumors spread that the cost of construction was billed for four times more than what it actually cost. As you can guess, the money was shared among our corrupt administrators. Worse than that, the administration has not yet allowed anyone to raise vegetables in that greenhouse. It just sits there. Forgetting about all the corruption, they should at least let us use that field to plant vegetables.

You know, if those guys found out that I had complained about their corrupt businesses, they would not hesitate to give me a really hard time. They would even try to transfer me to another prison. Most of the convicts are aware of this corruption in the prison. However, no one wants to fight against it in fear of being transferred to another facility. The parents of most of the prisoners incarcerated here live in the city of Diyarbakır, so, in order to stay close to their parents, all those convicts endure the pressure and maltreatment.

The corruption pretty much started after the new director was appointed. No one dared to confront him, because he has close political connections. I had wanted to report these happenings by writing petitions to the Ministry of Justice. Unfortunately, we would not have been able to follow the movement of where the petition went. The guards might read it and tear it up. As I mentioned before, I am personally not afraid of anything. The worst they can do to me is to transfer me to another facility, and I could accept that. But, shame on the Ministry of Justice officials and the prison prosecutor if they would allow my transfer simply because I told the truth.

The Duped Repenters

I am not sure whether the petitions I sent to the Minister of the Interior, Beşir Atalay, regarding the situation of the repenters in the prison, reached him, but I also sent the same messages to the Minister of Justice. I wrote to both of them: "We repenters voluntarily surrendered to the government. We were not arrested in a clash or operation. We personally gave ourselves to you. Now, look at us! Without exception, we have all been sentenced to life!"

You talked about a repentance law from the government, but you have sentenced those who surrendered themselves to 50 years in prison! As I mentioned, I am staying in the repenter convicts' cell, and all of us were sentenced to life, even though we had expected to benefit from the repentance law. We will all die here in this prison. What I do not understand is whether that repentance law has actually ever been applied to any convict.

For example, there are two comrades here, who used to be active within the organization years ago and left to live in major Iraqi cities. They are both married and have children. The Turkish security forces, and the MIT (Turkish National Intelligence Agency) contacted them in order to persuade them to return to Turkey. They were both told, "Return to Turkey, and after a short trial period, we will set both of you free with the repentance law." The MIT managed to convince them to return to Turkey, and then both of them were given a life sentence.

An intelligence officer, from the gendarme, had promised them this freedom. As I said, both of those comrades were living comfortably as regular Iraqi citizens. They accepted this offer because they both wanted to be able to visit their parents who lived within the borders of Turkey. The gendarme intelligence officer had told them, "Return, let your trial begin, and I promise that you will not be punished. If you accept my offer, you will have no problem going back and forth between Turkey and Iraq." Both of the comrades came here in order to take advantage of that offer. But, to their surprise, when they surrendered themselves to the security officers, they were unable to see the intelligence officer who had promised to help them. They asked where they could find him, but the other officials told them, "You cannot see him again. He was assigned to another post in Ankara." No one cared about the promises, since the man who had promised all those things was no longer there. In short, they were both duped into returning. They both were sentenced to life.

One of these comrades was able to bring his wife and child to the city of Uşak. The woman and the child now live there all alone. Was this justice? Do you security officers call this a successful career? That comrade, who was able to bring his family to Turkey, was fortunate. The other comrade's wife is still in Iraq, living alone with a two-year-old baby. Can you imagine what kind of psychological stress that comrade is under? He's not able to see his child, and does not even now know if they are getting along. At least I have my parents visiting, and letting me know how everyone is doing, as do other inmates, but this poor comrade has no way of hearing news. I get very angry about these stupid schemes, whenever I talk about them. The security officers ruined the unity of two families, just to show themselves successful in the media. Of course, there may have been others who were affected in this way.

That particular intelligence officer actually contacted 15 former guerilla comrades in Iraq. The remaining 13 were astute enough not to accept the offer. They had said to the two comrades, who were willing to surrender themselves, "Comrades, we will not accept this offer. If you are so willing to do that, you go and see what will happen. If they really keep their promises, then we will also travel to Turkey and surrender ourselves." When the ones who had remained in Iraq heard that those two had not only been arrested but also been sentenced to life, they all immediately gave up the idea of returning to Turkey.

I have told my concerns about those policies to the security forces many times. "You are using a strategy that will do serious harm to your cause in the long run! By incarcerating those who voluntarily surrendered themselves and giving them a life sentence, you close the doors for the ones, within the organization, who want to desert it. If those who voluntarily surrendered were set free, after a few years of incarceration, believe me many others would follow them. If this former guerilla was released back into society, he would be seen by his neighbors, relatives, or someone from the neighborhood. I told you, every single family has a member fighting for the organization. Those mothers and fathers would say, 'Hey, that family's son has returned and he was not punished so severely, so why should our son continue to fight in the mountains? He should return to us, too.' Believe me, those mothers who see other mothers rejoined with their sons and daughters, will try to encourage their sons and daughters to come back to them. Life out there is not easy, and no mother in the world, including Kurdish mothers, would want their child to live such a life. However, when these mothers see that the Turkish state punishes the guerillas who surrender themselves with a life sentence, they will warn their sons not to return to Turkey. They will say, 'Oh my son, please stay where you are, and do not ever come back here. It is better to live in mountains than to be locked up for the rest of your life!'"

The Turkish governments have been unsuccessful in terms of benefitting from the repenters. You do not have to look too far to see what Barzani had been doing. He had a special force, other than his Peshmerga soldiers, which consisted of approximately 1,500 guerillas, who used to fight for the PKK. The chief commander of this force was a person named Aziz Veysi, a former PKK guerilla commander. Although Barzani was not experienced in politics, he was very good at taking advantage of every opportunity. Such a professional group of fighters was not easy to obtain. Many governments spend a lot of money to train their soldiers to be professional.

Barzani was clever, because he knew how to recruit those former PKK guerillas. During the Iraqi war, when the United States invaded Iraq, the most effective force fighting in the coalition forces was Barzani's special forces, which consisted of former PKK members. This situation was even reflected in the media, when the Turkish press informed the public that, "A former ranked PKK commander was assigned to the head of general staff position in the territory controlled by Barzani within Iraq." If the guerillas in the countryside had doubts, and were sick of fighting for years, would they surrender themselves to Turkish security forces and receive a life sentence, or would they go and enroll in this special force, get a monthly salary, and live a regular life? Which one would you do?

Have you ever thought why those repentant former guerillas asked for their transfer to a D-Type prison facility (the facility in which only political guerillas were incarcerated) when they saw that the Turkish government did not protect them? Believe it or not, many of the local institutions, municipalities, health and even education departments are under the direct control of the organization in this region. This includes the prison guards who work at the prisons in that area. The officers in the prison are included in this. The Turkish government can either take it or leave it. This is the reality and everyone here knows it. When a guerilla deserts the organization and prefers to stay in the repenter convicts' cell, the organization asks the local agencies (municipalities and other places under its control) to fire their parents, family members, relatives, and even their friends. I mean they push you into the corner by pressuring the individuals that you love. The repenters here are in such a difficult situation. You have no idea what the hell we repenters go through. Our loved ones are all fired from their jobs, just because we prefer to stay in the repenter convicts' cell. Who will take care of our parents? Who will give them jobs? That is why many of our repenter comrades ask for a transfer to the political guerilla prisoners' cell.

If you stay among the political prisoners, the organization meets all your needs in the prison. You receive a monthly salary from the organization, in a Turkish state controlled prison! Moreover, since you are now a hero, one of your parents or family members is immediately given a good paying job in one of the institutions in the region, and you decide who will get that job! Can you see the irony here? The organization is, in fact, doing what the Turkish state should be doing for the repenter guerillas. The organization convinces the repenter guerilla convicts to move into D-Type Facilities with those great incentives, and then looks after them, whereas, the Turkish state should actually be doing the same thing.

A comrade, who had been incarcerated in a repenter convicts' cell for almost 15 years when I was first brought here, left us five days ago, and joined the ones at the D-Type. He said that he could not take it anymore. He had joined the military operations, helped the security forces in the field, but in return, was not rewarded with any kind of reduction in his life sentence. Even worse, his family has been subjected to community pressure, since their son was viewed as a traitor by many Kurds. The prison guards sometimes visit our cells in the middle of the night and swear at us. They blame us for being traitors to the Kurdish cause in their government's prison, because we deserted the organization, sided with the state, and chose to stay in the repenter convicts' cell. In their eyes, we are nothing but servants of the enemy!

I do not think the person who sits at the top of the Ministry of Justice is aware of this situation. My family lived in the city of Batman. They had to leave it temporarily and move to Istanbul when I joined the organization. However, they returned to Batman after I surrendered myself just to be able to be close to me. Since I am staying at the repenter convicts' cell, no one from my family or from my relatives is allowed to have a job at the municipalities or other local institutions. I have six siblings. They all work in daily, temporary jobs, in order to earn their livelihood. It is only because I sided with the Turkish state as a repenter, against the organization, which has been carrying out its intimidation procedures in this clever way. They do not punish us, but the ones we love. Once, my father visited the Batman City Municipality, and asked for a worker's position for one of my brothers. He was insulted in front of everyone and told, "How do you dare to come here and ask for a job for your son? Go back now and take care of your repenter bastard first!"

Because of all these things occurring outside, it is desperately hard to wait in here. Moreover, most of our repenter friends, who could not take those pressures any more, began to switch to D-Type Facilities, one by one. The comrades who left us, often said, "Why should I side with the Turkish state if we repenters and the political guerilla convicts are sentenced to the same punishment? At least my family and parents will be okay, if I transfer to the political convicts. They will be given a job, with a monthly salary, and will also be welcomed with respect in the neighborhood."

In 2010, when I was first incarcerated, there were 19 comrades in repenter convicts' cell. There are now only seven left. Before those comrades left, they all explained their reasoning to us. For instance, the one that left us last week said, "I surrendered myself because I trusted the Turkish government. However, so far, they have neither protected nor helped us. I was tried, as a repenter, in the same trial as a political guerilla suspect, in front of the same judge. I told the judge, in a polite manner, that I wanted to benefit from the repentance law. I even told him that I wanted to work for the Turkish government. The political prisoner, on the other hand, swore at the judge and mocked him in front of the crowd. In the end, we both received the same punishment. So, why should I continue to remain on the side of the government, if it does not bring me any benefit?" Unfortunately, those comrades are right in their reasoning.

I do not know if the people who worked at the judiciary and security agencies in Turkey are dumb, or if they knew something of which we are not aware. They could benefit from the people who voluntarily surrender themselves, if they would conduct a deep investigation into finding out why a former guerilla now wanted to side with the government and, only after that, use the ones that they felt were fully trustworthy. If we really wanted, we could easily go to Iraq or one of the European countries. I could even stay in Turkey, with a fake ID. But, despite all those opportunities, I surrendered myself to the security forces.

There were even frequent skirmishes between the Turkish security forces and the organization in 2011. I wrote a letter to the commander back then, asking, "Why do you make those repenters wait in their cells? You have been giving statements to the media, saying that you have been establishing a special troop and that you are recruiting people for a professional army, similar to the one in the United States. You cannot find more professional soldiers than these repenters incarcerated in prisons. I argue that your 20-year-trained marron berets cannot fight as effectively as a three-year-trained guerila. It's because those repenters are former guerillas! They know the fighting strategy of the organization, from ambushes to explosives. They've spent their life in the mountains, during the hot weather in the summer and cold in the winter. They've lived on the edge and know how to struggle against the hardships of the life."

The officials assume that the organization will change the tactics, locations of arms and provisions, codes, and other things after each repenter surrenders himself or herself to the security forces. This is partly true. Yes, the organization has to take some measures when a guerilla deserts from a specific region. However, even though the locations might change, the former guerillas can still correctly guess the potential future locations and hideouts of the organization in the region from which they came. Therefore, those repenters should not be a burden on the shoulders of the state, but should be employed in the areas for which they are best suited.

For example, on the evening of the day that I surrendered myself to the gendarme, the thermal cameras, used by the security forces, captured an image of a group of guerillas from Garzan State. They showed me the pictures. I asked them at what time the thermal cameras recorded those images, and they said they were recorded at 12:30 a.m. I checked the time, and found it to be 3:00 a.m. It had been two and a half hours since they were taken. I thought for a while and then said, "That guerilla group must be at the foothills of this mountain by now. They will walk only until 4:00 a.m., and then they will find a place to hide and rest before sunrise." Of course, the soldiers did not trust me, but I insisted, "Look! Carry out a land operation to those two spots and you can arrest them all without any killing." I heard that some of the gendarme officials said that they could not trust me at this point. I responded, "I really do not care whatever you do! But, the group is there."

The gendarme ignored what I said. In fact, the gendarme forces are regarded, within the organization, as the most awkward and least dangerous security force in Turkey. The police are the most dangerous enemy for the guerillas. In fact, the police never encounter the guerilla in the countryside. The Turkish police has established a kind of special operation team in recent years, but I never encountered those teams in the areas in which I fought. The reason why the police are regarded as more dangerous for the organization is the cruelty and pressure they apply to local civilian Kurds living in cities. If you went to Iraq and picked a random guerilla and asked him or her if they wanted to kill five soldiers or two police officers, without exception, all of them would say that they were obsessed with killing police officers. The only reason for this is the injustice and inhumane attitude of the police officers towards the civilian Kurds. The soldiers carry out operations to engage in skirmishes with us and face us directly. In these skirmishes, either they kill us, or we kill them. It is the rule of the game! However, the police do not play the game according to its rules. They treacherously push the civilian Kurds into a corner, in order to hurt us.

The public, especially the youth in the southeastern cities of Turkey, occasionally organize a peaceful demonstration march. We watch those mass movements on the TV, and sometimes the police are so cruel towards the civilians that we, who are thought to be terrorists, cannot even bring ourselves to watch them. The police are indiscriminately beating up women, children, and elderly people. All the guerilla units in the training camps are required to watch videos of the demonstration marches. I once received a DVD of police cruelty from 2006. The funerals of 13 organization members, who were martyred in the countryside, had been brought to the city of Diyarbakır in March (I think on March 26). Six of those comrades were going to be buried in a graveyard in Diyarbakır. If I am not mistaken, eight civilian Kurdish people were killed by the security forces during the funeral ceremony. Believe me, when a guerilla watches those videos, he or she wants to tear apart the first police officer they see—so eager are they to seek revenge.

There was another video from the city of Van. The police had caught a nine- or ten-year-old child and intentionally broke his arm by twisting it. I still cannot forget the screaming of that poor Kurdish child. I cannot understand how a human being could be so cruel towards a child. We would explode with anger when we watched those types of videos, and that was the reason that we hated the police more than any other security forces in Turkey. I think it was in 2006 that Cemil Bayık officially ordered all the guerillas, operating within the borders of Turkey, to make their priority target the police, not the soldiers.

When I was being questioned at the police department, I explained all those misapplications of duty, to the directors of the police. "You are following a mistaken policy. You will lose the hearts and minds of the public, if you continue to behave in that way. Try to cause the Kurdish youth to admire you, when they are around! Approach them while they still live in the cities, otherwise, you will encounter them fighting against you in five to ten years, in the countryside." This would not have been something difficult to achieve. Two or three official committees could have been formed, and one of those committees could engage the Kurdish youth living in the cities, while the other one could visit their parents on a regular basis. In this way, they would become acquainted with the Kurds more closely. Then, they could have established one other committee to take care of religious affairs; having them visit the mosques and religious organizations, and talking regularly with them. This would have created an atmosphere in which those three committees could work efficiently together. Also, they should have stopped marginalizing the Kurds. Stopped seeing every single Kurd as a potential enemy. Stopped disseminating propaganda on the TV by continuously saying, "Those are not Kurds but are Armenians, or Zoroaster, or atheists." Those types of derogatory statements, in fact, made the public even angrier. And they still did not see the fact, that every single Kurdish household had at least one member fighting for the organization.

Almost 90 percent of the people living in that region are Muslims! Who cared what they believed before? If they are now called infidels, Armenians, or atheists, the love of those people is lost, and those insulting words push the Kurds of the region into the arms of the organization. For example, not too long ago, in 2005, after the statement of Prime Minister Erdoğan towards the people of Hakkari directing them, "You people either will love this country, or leave this country," the applications from Hakkari to join the organization tripled. I can even say that the city of Hakkari, as a whole, joined the organization. They should have stopped bitching with words such as, "The people who support PKK are not Muslim Kurds, but Armenians." Instead, they should have organized teams who could communicate, who could understand the grievances of the Kurds in the east, and employed equal numbers of men and women in those teams, letting them engage with the public. Let them show their love and respect to the Kurds. Let them socialize with the Kurds. Stop seeing them as your enemies. If you really want to gain the hearts and minds of these people, you have no other option but getting close to them!" I explained this on several occasions. It only passed over their heads. It has been almost six years since I was incarcerated. The officials have neither established a committee nor developed any projects to socialize with the public.

Members of the Turkish government do not fulfill their obligations but then question why the Kurdish people feel such a profound sympathy towards the organization and why the peasants aid and abet the guerillas. So, what have they done so far for the Kurds that they feel as if they have the right to call the Kurds into account for supporting the organization? When they see a Kurdish child on the street, do they caress his head, ask if he needs anything, or give him a piece of candy? Do they meet with his parents, talk and socialize with them, and let them see their sincerity and love? If they would do what I told them, that family would never forget their favor, and they would not encourage their children to go up to the mountains and kill security officers.

Ruining the Life of the Loved Ones

We repenters not only ruin our own lives but also the lives of our families. Consider the comrade who came here from Iraq and surrendered himself to the security forces on the promise that he would soon be freed. His brother used to work for the city of Batman Municipality. When he decided to stay in the repenter convicts' cell, his brother was fired from his job. His brother's whole family, including his wife and children, were put into a very difficult situation. Since all the doors were closed to them, the whole family had to immigrate to the west, to the city of Izmir. They had to leave the place where they were born and had lived for so many years, just because one of the siblings took the side of the security forces. We learned later that his brother now works there as a painter.

My situation is the same. None of my brothers are eligible to apply for a job at the municipality, just because I sided with the Turkish government. Moreover, my poor father became ill because of me. I caused him to have many psychological illnesses. He is always thinking and worrying about me while I am in prison. I am also a financial burden for them. They feel as if they need to send me money all the time.

No matter whether it is accepted or not, the organization has full control on local matters. It has the power to put pressure on any family it wants, whenever it wants. Consider the prisons. Many of the employers are closely associated with the organization. For example, on February 19, 2009, my region commander was arrested. Only six days later, on February 25, I was able to read all the statements he gave to the police and the gendarme. I was able to obtain all that information, taken during the questioning stage at the security forces, despite the fact that I was incarcerated in the repenter convicts' cell. As his lawyer was not present, that left only three options for any leakage—someone from the police, the gendarme, or the prosecutor's office.

If the government claims that it has full authority all over of Turkey, then it should at least control who is assigned to work in its prisons, but, at least 70 percent of the prison staff work for the organization. Those prison guards do whatever they are told by the organization. Let me give you an example that occurred recently. A new repenter comrade was brought to our cell three days ago. He had been in the snow for a prolonged period of time, while he was fleeing away from the organization. His toes were all frozen and he was in very bad straits. The doctors had to cut off all the toes on one of his feet, and two toes on the other one. Only one day after that operation, he was discharged from the hospital, and immediately transferred to the prison, and put in a bed in the prison infirmary. A clown, who had been arrested on a criminal case, kept calling him, "The repentant asshole," and no one, from the doctors to the prison guards, even attempted to stop him from throwing those cusswords. The patient was also subjected to similar cusswords, all during his stay in that infirmary. I still find it hard to accept those situations. Something on that level would not even occur in Kandil camp, a place that is under the full control of the PKK. However, it is occurring in a prison, which is officially under the control of the Turkish Republic.

On the third day of his arrival to the infirmary, that comrade was brought to our cell in order to prevent potential quarrels between him and the other convicts. We were all shocked at how the Turkish state could incarcerate a person in such a bad shape, before properly treating him in a hospital. He was not even able to go to the restroom by himself, he was in such miserable condition. Yesterday, we took him to the open area, attached to our cell; first shaving him, and then giving him a bath.

Believe me, if he were among the political prisoners, he would be taken care of so well. The prison administration would probably even bring a special physician from outside, to treat him properly. He would even stay in the infirmary until he was fully recovered. They would take good care of him.

Now, look how he has been treated, just because he surrendered himself. His feet are still bleeding. The administration should have at least asked him if he were able to stay in a cell. We current residents of our cell forced the administration to accept him back into the infirmary, and he stayed there for two more nights. Again, one of the clowns there swore at him for being a repenter. Therefore, he sent us a message please to carry him back to the cell, despite the fact that he needed infirmary care. If you remember, all the beds are located on the second floor. This boy could not even go to the restroom by himself, let alone climb up the stairs. He is still sleeping on the first floor in the kitchen area.

We take to heart those kinds of insulting actions even though we experience them all the time, when we visit the infirmary or go to the sports hall. Everyone looks at us as the enemy. Not only the guards but also the criminal Kurdish convicts treat us as if they would kill us at the very first opportunity. Everyone here has a connection with the organization—some having their siblings, relatives, parents, or friends fighting in the mountains for the organization. The same goes for both the prison staff and the other convicts. We repenters are stuck among all those organization supporters. They sometimes smile to our faces, but we know that they want to kill us, because we are repenters in their eyes.

We feel devastated because the Turkish state does not protect us in its own prison. Many of our friends have requested their transfer to organization supporters' cells just because they could not take the Turks' negligence. Many of us transferred there, despite the risk of being mocked for years.

When a repenter is transferred to a political guerilla prisoners' cell, he or she is left isolated for at least for six to ten months as a kind of punishment. The political prisoners will always wonder, "What did this repenter do with the Turkish government? What kind of information did he leak to the security forces? Has he ever lead military operations, by showing them the secret hideouts? Which militants were arrested because of the information he provided to the Turks?" They will look at you as a traitor for a very long time. Therefore, the problems do not end, even when we change sides. But, despite all this isolation and prejudice, many of the repenters switch to the political prisoners' cell.

I have heard from the old repenters, that it was not like that in the old days. Until the year of 2000, no one would dare to say something bad to the repenters, because the security forces needed their help and experience. Back then, they were taken out to the countryside to fight alongside the security forces. Now, the security forces do not need them anymore, so they are no longer valuable to them.

I told the prosecutors all those problems, especially during the initial years of my incarceration. I talked with them for hours. Two guerillas are put on trial. The same prosecutor prepares both files. One of the guerillas says, "I quit the organization and I am sorry about whatever happened in the past, but I am now siding with the Turkish state." On the other hand, the second guerilla says, "Down with the Turks!" He openly declares that he is still in the organization. The prosecutor asks for the same punishment for those two. It has always happened this way.

Is it right to give both of them the same punishment? Where is the justice! We often got angry with ourselves for having surrendered to the security forces. We think again and again about the circumstances we suffer, the life conditions to which we are subjected, and the punishments we endure. This upsets us all. Everyone in the cell gets especially angry with me, since I did not go to Iraq or Europe and live a free life, even though I had that opportunity. I respond to them, admitting that I was a fool. Two other comrades, Engin Papatya and Şükrü Arslan, who were deceived by the MIT [Turkish National Intelligence Agency] and brought from Iraq, said the same thing. They both left the organization in 1987 and had been living a regular civilian life in Iraq, for almost 13 years. They were employed as workers at construction sites. They had not committed any crimes or carried out any missions while they were in the organization. The lying state knocked on their doors, and told them, "Come back to Turkey. We will try you both, and then set you free!" However, they were both sentenced to life in prison. Their wives and children were left high and dry. What kind of justice is this? If you were the son of that man, would you not take revenge on the Turkish state? Would you not want to kill the intelligence officer who deceived your father? Would you not want to annihilate the chief Justice of Diyarbakır 7th court, who ruined his life in 2000 despite the fact that he knew the truth?

Consider the most recent repentance law that was put into effect by the Turkish Grand National Assembly. The politicians are saying that they will not punish the organization members who have not participated in any guerilla missions. I do not understand this mentality. What good is it for the state to convince guerillas that have not carried out any missions to lay down their arms? I am sure that 90 percent of the organization members have participated in at least one mission. As a state, you are putting into force a bullshit repentance law, which targets the inexperienced newbies, who literally know nothing about the organization. And since your target group is very specific, you achieve nothing by that law.

There has been no repentance law designed, so far, that targeted the commander cadre of the organization. Convincing one commander to surrender himself, is equal to defusing at least 30 guerillas. Because, if you can achieve that, the state in which that commander used to work cannot carry out any missions for at least a year. However, the organization does not care whether ground guerillas, most particularly the newbies, desert the organization, because there is no information that can be leaked by a newbie. Those types of issues should be carefully examined, when designing the repentance laws.

The officials must do something so that the repenters do not feel so alone. I have already mentioned that there are so many things that could be done. Nevertheless, if a general amnesty law is put into effect that frees all the repenters and political guerilla prisoners at the same time, you will lose the hearts and minds of the repenter convicts and their families, simply because the organization will argue that the general amnesty was granted because of its negotiations with the state. They would say that such an amnesty would not have been granted, if it were not for the organization. Our problems would not vanish, even if we were set free. The political guerilla prisoners would be welcomed as heroes, when released. We, on the other hand, would be regarded as traitors in the community.

The organization is also against the word "amnesty." For example, if the Turkish government today declared that it was forgiving all the political guerilla prisoners, the organization would harshly object, because no one who served the organization, including myself, would think that they had committed a crime. Amnesty is granted for criminals. We are not criminals. We simply defended our rights against a racist and oppressive regime. Thus, the government should also be careful in selecting appropriate language before carrying out its plans. For example, officials could say that they are freeing all the convicts because of a mutual agreement they had signed with the organization.

On the other hand, even if the state is unable to free all those repenters, who were sentenced to life, they should at least release the ones who have served ten to 15 years. The officials should consider applying a positive discrimination towards the people who deserted the organization and sided with them. For instance, there is a former militant, named Faruk, in our cell. He never went to the mountains, and he had stayed with the political guerilla prisoners during the first eight years of his incarceration. He later switched to the repentant cells. He is now 60 years old, and has been here for almost 23 years. He has never been given a reduction in his sentence due to good conduct. I do not understand why the officials are keeping him incarcerated. Let him go! Let him live out the last days of his life with his parents.

I explained all those situations to many senior officials, but no one paid any attention to me. I think they thought that I was asking for those changes for myself. If they implemented what I told them, they would have already weakened the organization. They would have had high dropout numbers from the mid-level members of the organization.

As a state, if you do not offer a way out for the guerillas who have already engaged in an armed conflict, you can never end this problem within Turkey. No one will give up on fighting, if the state continues to sentence guerillas to life whether or not they voluntarily surrendered themselves. In each of the prisons, especially the ones located in the east, there are staff members who work for the organization under the guise of state employees, and those prison employees are in close daily contact with headquarters. They inform the outside guerillas about how badly the repenters are treated by the state, and how they are discarded by the security forces. Do you think that someone who wanted to desert the organization would leave it, upon hearing of this negligence?

Forget the arguments about providing reduced sentences for the repenters and even about providing financial help to the repenter convicts, but at least have visits to the cells of repenter convicts, just to show them that they are not alone. The organization, morally and financially, supports the political guerilla prisoners. Many of the prison guards also support the political prisoners. However, the repenters are all by themselves. No one is expecting anything financial but just showing your love and interest in those people would mean so much. But everything is denied to the repenters, and all is left to the control of a corrupt prison administration. If they were allowed, the prison administration would even disarray our cells.

I wish it were only us getting affected by those mistreatments, but our parents also go through many hardships, because we sided with the Turkish state. A while ago, my parents would not even dare to visit me in this prison, because the visitors are first required to wait outside the facility, until their paperwork is done. Each week, hundreds of people come here to visit their loved ones; most being relatives of the political guerilla prisoners. I do not know whether the prison guards or the organization instructed them to do so, but the visitors of the political guerilla convicts always threaten our parents when they encounter them. For a long time, my parents could not come here to visit me because they were so frightened by those threats.

Another comrade's family came here three times and left without having a chance to talk with him. The visitors of the political guerilla prisoners threatened his wife and small children. They frightened the wife saying, "Are you here to visit your repenter dog?" The Turkish soldiers guarding the main entrance of the prison never intervened, so the wife and children had to leave the area, even though guarded by Turkish soldiers. That repenter friend could not take that treatment of his wife and children anymore, so he requested his transfer to the political prisoners' cell.

We repenter convicts can endure many difficulties, but our parents are not like us. They are more vulnerable than we. They are in the public's eye 24/7. They have to go to the grocery stores, coffee shops, schools, and other places, and are constantly being denigrated at these places, when they come across any of the organization supporters. Remember that many Kurds supported the organization, so they faced problems daily, and life was very hard for them. We are even lucky compared to our families. We are locked up in a cell every day, and only leave when we visit the infirmary. We do not have to come in contact with anyone, but our parents do.

The father of one of our comrades has not visited his son in prison for the last 15 years. The old man could not take the pressure of being insulted at the coffee shops, grocery stores, parks, and other social places. People had said to him, "What kind of bastard did you bring up? He's a traitor to the Kurdish cause!" That poor man has had serious psychological problems because of that abuse and is still refusing to see his son.

Finally, the psychology of prison is very difficult, and you cannot understand what I mean, unless you are incarcerated. We always think and worry about our parents and family members. Some comrades here are married and have children. Their situation is even worse compared to mine. They always think about their sons and daughters and have missed all those beautiful years with their children.

Once a month, we are allowed to have conjugal visits with our wives. Since I am not married, I meet with my parents during those days. Occasionally, my parents miss that day, and it is really tough when they do not come. If my parents, or another comrade's wife doesn't visit, we wonder, over and over, if something bad has happened to them, and lose our sleep until we hear from them. In the best-case scenario, it takes weeks to learn whether they are okay or not. During that time, our attitude, behavior, and even appetite changes, including our tone of voice!

21
PENITENCE (SECOND THOUGHTS)

I do not regret anything I have done, except for two incidents. I fought against the Turkish state for legitimate reasons. We, as the organization, have never demanded anything illogical. We initially set out to achieve a free Kurdish state, but after 1993, we changed our minds. We decided that an autonomous region in the Turkish Republic would be best for the interest of the Kurds.

The first incident, for which I am still deeply regretful, is the one I had with the Kurdish village protection guards, during the initial years of my career in the organization, and it still psychologically disturbs me. I feel extremely sad, whenever I remember what happened on that day.

I still do not understand how we carried out that massacre. I just do not get it! It haunts my sleep. It was normal to have a fight with a soldier, village protection guard, or a police officer. Either you killed them or they killed you. It was completely normal—the rules of the fight. However, we should never have killed those civilian Kurdish peasants. Those people should not have been harmed. The very reason for starting this fight against the Turkish state was to protect the rights of these poor Kurdish peasants. If we, as the organization, harmed the people that we were, in fact, supposed to protect, then we had a serious problem.

The second thing that I still regret is the assassination that I committed in the city of Siirt, in 1993. I felt very guilty about that assassination, because I did not know the man I killed. Who he was, or what he was doing there. He died for nothing. His only fault was to be at the wrong place at the wrong time.

After that sad incident, I always raised my objections to the missions to be carried out in city centers. I never approved of carrying out bombing or assassination missions within them. But I accepted the fact that those types of missions strengthened the hands of the organization, because whenever a bomb went off in a city center, the organization had more power with which to negotiate with the government. It was easy to kill by hiding inside of a crowd. However, there was always the risk of killing civilians by mistake. Many innocent civilians, in fact, lost their lives during our city missions. Furthermore, it was not just about the people who lost their lives. Think about the psychological effects on the people on the city. Do you think people can continue to behave normally, after a bomb goes off in a familiar place? The fear of uncertainty is really difficult.

After such an incident, the public would be nervous for a long time, wondering when it might happen again. Once that psychological fear dominates a society, it affects everything from the social life to the economy. In the past, there occurred a bombing mission in Diyarbakır, in the district of Baglar, in which a couple adults and three children lost their lives. We were getting news from our civilian organization members that the psychological damage was serious. Parents would not let their children play outside very often. And when they did, the mothers ran out to check on their children whenever they heard a loud noise in the neighborhood, on the assumption that another bomb had exploded. Society is unable to live a normal life under that uncertainty. After anything unusual happens in that neighborhood, mothers will worry about whether their child has been killed or whether something has happened to another of their loved ones. Several times, I faced this situation with the seniors of the organization. I said to them, "If we really need to carry out a mission in a city, the target must be clear and only the target should be killed. We should stop using explosives, since innocent civilians and children also die. If necessary, we should train more assassins for those kinds of mission so that we do not kill anyone mistakenly."

Other than those two incidents, I feel absolutely no regret about anything I did before. I have a clear conscience about my missions in the organization. I am aware of what I did and why I did it. All my fight was for the righteous struggle of the Kurdish cause. Twenty years of experience within the organization taught me many things. I had a close brush with death many times and was seriously wounded at least six or seven times. I never had a guarantee to live one more day when I was in the organization. We were, in fact, aware that we could lose our lives at any moment.

Just before graduating from the ranked guerilla school in the organization, each cadet was given a document with close to 100 questions in it. There were every kind of question you could imagine. For example, have you ever had a guilty conscience regarding what you have done so far? That question is specifically asked of the guerillas in the commander echelon on many occasions. Ranked guerillas were required to provide a detailed written response to that question. There were other similar questions in that document, such as, "Which guerilla mission have you enjoyed the most? What kind of missions were you planning to carry out in the future? In which regions did you want to fight and why?" All your answers were recorded in your electronic file and kept at the organization's archives. Let's say you were going to be assigned to a position, the seniors would check your answers to those questions to determine whether you would be qualified for that future position, figuring out your personality, through inspection of your files.

Headquarters did not send me to another mission in the Turkish state-sided Kurdish villages, because of the report I wrote after completing that mission. I was not sent on any other mission, even though I was a good fighter. It was simply because the seniors knew that I could not take such another horror. I would have gone crazy, if I were forced to engage in another civilian massacre. In that bloody mission that we carried out in a village between the towns of Şirwan and Hizan in 1993, I had harshly argued with the platoon commander, even though I was just a squad leader at that time. The argument became so serious that we were just about to kill each other.

The mission we carried out was successful. All of the village protection guards that worked for the Turkish state were killed. Only the women, children, and elderly people were left in the village. The platoon commander ordered our comrades to put the rest of the people into a line to be executed by firing squad. There were six children between the ages of four to five in that line. After the quarrel I had with the platoon commander, I headed towards the line and took out all the little children. At that moment, I realized that there was also an old man, probably at his 60s. I remember it like it was yesterday. He said to me, "My son, I have one last request before your friends kill us." I said, "Please tell me." He asked me to give him a cigarette. I took out my tobacco box and rolled up a cigarette for him.

In the meantime, the platoon commander began yelling at me, "Deniz, what the hell do you think you are doing? Leave the group! We will start shooting them now!" I was already upset with him about this whole execution thing. It was completely unnecessary. Angrily, I said to him, "We are not going to kill this old man!" I held his hand and took him out of the group. I said to him, "Please take these children with you and go away from here as soon as possible!" You should have seen how happy that old man was. He tried to kiss my hand to show his respect for me, but I did not allow him to do such a thing, and said to him, "Grandfather, take the children and leave now. There is nothing more I can do for you."

I headed back to the platoon commander and continued to quarrel with him. I still had hopes that I could also save the rest of the group. I said, "Look at me! You cannot kill innocent women and elderly like this. It would be justifiable to kill them if they had fought against us! But, they did not! What good does it do to kill these people now? They've surrendered to us, so what is the rationale to kill them? Please, let them go with their children!"

The platoon commander burst with anger. He would have even shot me if he had had that authority. I had chastened him in front of the other guerillas. However, those 24 innocent civilians were all executed by the firing squad. I still feel guilty about that incident. If I had tried harder, I might have been able to convince the platoon commander to leave the village without killing those women and elderly. Nevertheless, I was young; only 21 years old, and arguing with a 40-year-old platoon commander. I am still unable to remember that civilian massacre without remorse. There has been a pain in my heart because of that day and it will remain until the day I die.

Back then, I had notified headquarters about that incident, with a written complaint. Later, even Apo harshly criticized me, as I was being trained at the guerilla-training academy in Syria. I was the only one left alive from that mission that was carried out in 1993. Many of those comrades had died before 1996. Apo did not know all the details of that mission—that I had argued with the platoon commander not to kill those civilians. How could he? Since I was the only survivor of that massacre, he had called me on the carpet. "How could you be that brutal and unmerciful? How could you kill those civilians without feeling any remorse?" He gave me a roasting for more than an hour for that massacre.

I could have said to Apo that I had taken no part in that massacre. I mean, I could easily blame the fallen comrades, who carried out the execution. However, that would have been unethical. Therefore, I kept quiet and did not let him know about what had actually happened there. Apo was a smart person and he remembered me at the graduation ceremony of the academy, and said, "Deniz, you will not kill civilians anymore. I do not want to ever hear of something like that." I said, "I promise, leader Apo! I will never ever do anything like that again."

Even though I promised him, it was sometimes difficult to fight in the countryside without killing innocent people, for reasons that were out of our control. For example, we would sometimes be put under heavy fire from a house in a village. Someone would be shooting at us from the door or the windows of the house. We would not know who else might be inside the house, but in order to protect ourselves in those situations, we would use a rocket-propelled grenade to destroy the house. However, we never had a clear conscience about whoever else might have been in that building. There was no way of finding out if there had been women, children, or elderly people hiding in there, therefore, it was morally difficult for us to attack an enclosed target.

Other than that, we would sometimes kill innocent people out of revenge. The passion for revenge was something that we guerillas had to be extremely careful of. In some missions, we lost comrades we had known for years, with whom we had eaten our meals, and with whom we shared memories. In such circumstances, our eyes would be completely blinded, and we desired to kill anyone related to the enemy, regardless of their gender or age. Those were the times we lost our rational thinking and sought nothing but revenge.

As I mentioned, in general, I do not have feelings of guilt for anything I did, except for those couple of incidents. I had legitimate grievances for which to fight. Moreover, even though I deserted the organization, I am still a Kurd. I will continue to fight for those rights until they are granted to my people by the Turkish state. I am telling you—even if I am released at the age of 70, I will again fight for the right to speak in my mother tongue.

For years, we Kurdish people asked for two simple things: the recognition of the Kurdish identity by the Turkish Constitutional Law, and the use of the Kurdish language, for public services in the cities that are dominated by large Kurdish populations. Were we requesting things that were really too difficult for the Turks to provide? We only wanted to protect our basic rights. We did not ask to be provided with any extra rights that would compromise those of Turks—but simply to be able to freely speak in our own language and to have our separate identity recognized. I wanted this stupid denial thing to end.

This is why I do not feel any regret and said, when I surrendered to the Turkish security forces, "I left the organization on my own, but that does not mean that I have stopped being a Kurd. I am a Kurd and I want my right to speak Kurdish. I want my identity to be recognized. I am demanding those rights as a citizen of the Turkish Republic."

Tell me if there is any other country in the world like Turkey, which treats its own citizens in this restrictive manner? At the time I was incarcerated, in 2010, it was legally forbidden to speak Kurdish in public institutions. My mother would come to the prison to visit me, and we could only communicate through hand gestures behind the glass. She could not say anything, because she did not know Turkish. The prison guards would mute the microphone if my mother accidently spoke something in Kurdish. In all of those visits, we would mostly spend the time looking at one another.

I witnessed the same thing when I surrendered to security forces. My mother, father, uncle, and a relative ranger came to visit me. I told the ranked gendarme officers there, "Look! My mother does not know Turkish, so I will have to speak Kurdish." At first, they agreed. Nevertheless, after only two or three minutes, they openly showed their discontent with my speaking Kurdish to my mother, and I had to ask her to stop talking. You can imagine how hurtful was that for my mother.

Look! We are now in 2015. There has been no improvement of the circumstances. When my mother goes to the hospital, in an emergency, she is unable to explain anything, because she is unable to communicate with the doctor or the nurses. She must have one of my siblings accompany her whenever she visits a public institution, including the hospital, because she is unable to describe her discomfort to them. That is what many other Kurds in Turkey daily experience in their lives. Would it really be too difficult for the Turks to assign doctors, police officers, teachers, and other public servants who can speak Kurdish to the eastern cities where the majority of the population is Kurd? Is it really a matter of honor for the Turks? The society in this region is unable to associate itself with the state, because they do not speak the same language, nor do they understand Turkish, and it is the same for every single public service, including the courts. Kurdish peasants are appealing to your courts to fix their legal issues. However, in most cases, they are unable to state their problems, because they are unable to communicate with the judges, the prosecutors, or even with the attorneys. So, they do not bother themselves anymore to apply to the courts of the Turkish Republic. Instead, they submit their legal matters to the mobile courts, established by the organization, in the mountainous areas, because the PKK officials, who work at those mobile courts, speak the same language as the Kurdish peasants. They should not be blamed for doing that!

I wish all of those basic rights had been safeguarded, within the constitution, during the initial years of the young Turkish Republic, as it had been promised, before the War of Liberation. We would not have had that bloody war if it had been written in the constitution, that all societies that live in Turkey, are the citizens of the Turkish Republic. (The present constitution states, "All the people who live in Turkey are Turks!") Whether or not the Turks accept it, there are hundreds of thousands of other nationalities in this country, including, but not limited to, Armenians, Christians, Lazzas, Alewis, Arabs, Circassians, and, of course, the Kurds. What good was it to deny the identity of those groups? Why have they been alienated, by using such fascist statements in the constitution?

If it were written, that anyone living within the borders of Turkey was a citizen of the Turkish Republic, no one would be offended, because people could have freely stated, "I am a Kurd, Armenian, Laz, or whatever, but I am a citizen of the Turkish Republic."

Another irritating thing was that for tens of years, the mandatory daily utterance of the Turkish Vow at primary schools was ordered. Thank God, the former government rescinded its use. Before that, every morning, the primary school aged children, began their first lesson reciting the vow, saying, "How happy is the one who says he or she is a Turk!" As a state, they had thousands of schools teaching this to the children in the eastern parts of the country, where the majority of the population is Kurd. Those kids did not even know how to speak Turkish but you forced them to say that they were happy to be a Turk when in fact they are Kurdish. Why were they made to say that for so many years? Was it to satisfy the state's fascist sentiments? It is time to realize that not only Turks live in this country. In fact, since these Kurdish children could not speak Turkish, they got nothing from the schools until the third grade. There was even a movie produced, in which an inspector, sent by Ankara, Ministry of Education, was asking Kurdish children what they had learned before the start of third grade. One of the children gave an exemplary answer, saying, "I learned nothing, because I spent the first three years simply looking at the teacher." Unfortunately, this was the case in many Kurdish villages across the eastern parts of Turkey. When those youngsters returned home, their parents and the people around them continued to speak Kurdish, and they were called a Kurd at home. But then the state forced them to say in school, "How happy is the one who says he or she is a Turk!" Imagine the psychological dilemma imposed upon those children.

Furthermore, there is a highly erroneous assumption, frequently used among Turkish society and the media, stating, "If we legally accept the Kurd's cultural and linguistic rights, then they would demand endless requests, including independence." People who say things like that are not thinking rationally. Was there any obstacle in front of the PKK to fight for independence? Could the organization not apply its old fight strategy if it really wanted that? What could the Turkish government do if the organization returned to its previous strategy?

If the government were thinking like the Sri Lankan government, which killed all the members of the Tamil Tigers, they would be seriously mistaken. We were in no way similar to the fight that occurred in Sri Lanka. Turks and Kurds had intermingled with each other through marriage bonds. Moreover, there were Kurds now living in every single city of Turkey. Turkey cannot say that it could destroy the whole of eastern Anatolia, even using a hundred fighter jets, or hundreds of thousands of troops. Listen to me carefully. Those two societies are highly intertwined. If they carried out such an annihilation mission, the whole country would be in a worse condition than what Syria is now. A civil war would break out, and the Kurds and Turks would kill one another, until one day you would look outside and see the United Nations' troops building a green line between the two communities, and on that day, it would be the end of the emotional ties between the Kurds and the Turks.

The PKK has reached a position today where they have hundreds of contact offices all around the world, let alone having institutions within Turkey. Accept it or not, the organization acts like a government in the eastern parts of Turkey. Do you know how many television channels the PKK have airing in the east? At least five, and they all broadcast over satellite. These TV outlets have viewers, not only from Turkey but all over the world. The organization spends terrific amounts of money to keep those TV channels operating, though they do not have any advertisement revenue as do the Turkish TV channels. Furthermore, the organization has dozens of radio channels. Wherever you are in the world, you can listen to their radio channels, which broadcast in Kurdish.

Let me mention you about the institutions. Is there an alternative religious leaders union in the eastern cities in which the Kurds form the majority? Yes, there is. The members of this union are assigned and paid by the organization. If you travel in those cities, look to see whether the Kurdish people are praying at the mosques operated by the Turkish government or the ones operated by the organization.

Check the courthouses. Other than some serious murder cases, the number of cases the Turkish Republic courts look at each year, in the eastern parts of the country, is very low. The Kurdish people take their cases to the courts of the organization, since the Turks do not offer judiciary services in Kurdish.

This has been the situation since 2006 in the eastern cities of Turkey. The Turks do not see their own mistakes but always complain that, "The PKK has established tax collection tents, and received taxes from the public, and they have established mobile courts in which to try the public." The Turks should understand that no one is being tried forcefully. The Kurdish public appreciates those services from the organization. The people would come to us and say, "I have an issue with that man. I would like you to establish a court and try us." Therefore, the Turkish government is losing their influence in the east. Why? Because the PKK offers services that are not offered by the state. Everyone in the region is happy about the existence of those services, except for the government. However, be honest. Who would not want to be judged in a court that offers services in his or her native tongue?

Again, other than serious criminal cases, none of the Kurds would choose to go to the courts of the Turkish state in the east. Can you give me at least one example of the Turkish state resolving a conflict between two Kurdish tribes? You cannot, because there are none. The most tragic cases in the east are the tribal fights, and there was recently one between two tribes. Fifty people from both sides lost their lives. The security forces had to apply a three-day curfew. Who do you think resolved that conflict? Not the government! The PKK intervened. They established a court, appointed an attorney and a judge, and brought peace between those two tribes.

In return for providing those services, the organization would collect taxes from the big companies, such as the water dam construction companies, and other facilities in the region. Moreover, those tax revenues were not shared among a few influential and rich elites, as happens in Turkey. The money generated from the taxes would be shared among the poor Kurdish people and the incarcerated guerillas, who fought for the organization.

The PKK not only provided social justice in the east, but it also ended many of the old traditions. For instance, it was the PKK who ended the tradition of polygamy in the region. A man, who was married to two or more women, could not benefit from from the public services provided by the PKK nor was he allowed to be hired by any employer in the region. When the people saw those examples, they figured out that the PKK was harshly against polygamy, and they stopped the practice. Has the state ever done anything like that?

Consider the old days. There was a male-dominated society here in the east. The women were considered as something to be bought and sold. They were beaten without the worry of criminal sanctions. They were killed because of honor issues and even forced to commit suicide, because of some simple mistake they had committed! The PKK, not the Turkish government, put an end to those practices.

Today, if a man beats his wife in the territories that are unofficially controlled by the PKK, that man will be kept away from his house and his salary will be stopped by the organization, and his whole salary given to his wife. The husband is only able to return to the house whenever his wife agrees to it.

Do you think the state would provide that same protection to Turkish women? The PKK has also been providing help to tortured, beaten, and raped Kurdish women. How many times have you witnessed, on the news, that women under the protection of the Turkish government have been killed by their disgruntled husbands?

Today, PKK has even established some small-sized urgent care facilities in the region within the borders of Turkey. The Kurdish soldiers, who fought against ISIS in Syria and Iraq, were even treated at those facilities, but the Turkish police once raided one of those hospitals, and detained eight injured Kurds, just because they fought against ISIS.

Why do I tell you all about this now? I mentioned those things to you, because the Turks' claim of, "If we give them what they want, they will ask for even more," is nothing but bullshit, and headquarters repeats, "We want independence as it was in the old days, not an autonomy."

The Turkish government should provide the Kurds, in Turkey, with their basic human rights, without imposing upon the organization the precondition of laying down arms. Turkey knows very well that "laying down arms" is the very last condition of peace with terrorist organizations, around the world. The President has been reiterating that Ankara has been applying the model of peace that was previously adopted between England and Ireland. Erdoğan, himself, knows that the laying down of arms was the last phase of the peace agreement in Ireland. In that case, the Irish people were first given their cultural and political rights, and only then did they lay down their arms.

But the state will not even change its constitution, by accepting the fact that there are people living in Turkey, other than Turks. They do not allow the others the right to education in their mother tongue and are constantly looking for excuses to end the peace process. And now, they ask the organization to put down their arms! For example, in 2013, three private schools that taught in Kurdish were opened in the cities of Diyarbakır, Hakkari, and Cizre. All of those schools were closed down with lame conditions and were only opened again after those ridiculous conditions were met. Have any of those schools caused any segregation between the Turks and the Kurds? No! Give those rights to the Kurds, protect them with a new constitution, and then the organization will lay down their arms. You would not even have to ask them to do it, because if they did not, their reputation would be blackened in eyes of the world powers. Even worse, after all those amendments, if the organization still resisted stopping the armed struggle, Turkey would have a legitimate right to use force against the Kurds, and none of the world powers would criticize the Turks for killing organization members.

Nevertheless, if the Turks insist on the PKK's laying down arms as the precondition of peace, the organization would not consider sitting at the negotiation table, let alone the Kurds who live in Turkey. Nothing is really certain about the Kurds of Syria, Iraq, and Iran. The organization needs some safeguards for the well-being of the Kurds in other countries. Let's just say that the PKK laid down their arms now. Who is going to stop the ISIS barbarity in the Middle East? Who is going to defend the innocent Kurds, who otherwise might be killed by ISIS terrorists? Furthermore, the Middle East is a complex place. Take Iran, for instance. I heard from the news that Iran bombed the PKK camps in Kandil. If the PKK had no guerillas now, who would call Iran to account for that bombing? Would Turkey protect the Kurds in those three areas (Iran, Syria, and Iraq) as a state?

I wish the bureaucrats and the politicians in Turkey would at least exercise half of a brain. They are not aware of the opportunity they have in front of them—if they, as a state, established peace with the PKK now and told the organization, "Do not lay down your arms. We, as the Turkish Republic, will provide you with official uniforms and monthly payments, if you act as our military post in the Middle East. We'd like to see you working officially for the Turkish Republic, in which Turks and Kurds live in peace." If you Turks could achieve something like that, then Iran, Iraq, and Syria would not stand against Turkey, and Turkey would be the leader of the Middle East.

There are many governments in Europe, which want to put the guerilla forces of the PKK under their control. Hasn't the United States government just declared that their strongest allies in the fight against ISIS are the PYD guerilla forces? Hasn't the president of France hosted PYD representatives in his official office? For God's sake! Is it that difficult to understand? If you assure the Kurds that you would provide them with basic human rights and if you aimed to use the PKK as an armed force rather than planning to annihilate it, believe me, the Turkish Republic would be in a much more stable position than it is now. However, the Turkish politicians are not that smart, because the Turkish state knows very well that if the PKK gives a promise on anything, it would assuredly keep it. It would never turn back on them.

It is now your government's call. As I said, the PKK is an excellent opportunity for the Turks. Just like America, which has military posts in Germany, Saudi Arabia, and Japan, the PKK can become the military post of Turkey in the Middle East.

I do not remember exactly, but eight or nine years ago, there were again discussions about laying down arms. It was either Apo or Cemil Bayık that said, "The guerillas' presence throughout the borders of Turkey, is an assurance of safety for Turkey, because we control and protect the borders of Turkey." Has not this statement proven itself this year? Has a single bullet ever reached into Turkey, from the field where the PYD is positioned against ISIS? Just ask the military generals. They will all tell you that Turkey feels the most secure on its Syrian border. They all know that a potential danger coming from there would be blocked by PYD guerillas, even though the PYD is regarded as a terrorist organization.

The Turks might not like some of the demands proposed by the organization, but most of those demands are related to basic human rights. Such rights should never have been a subject of bargaining, but the government has wasted a lot of our time discussing them. In 2013, the organization set free 15 of its captives, including district governors, police officers, and state employees, when the peace process began. It asked for only one favor in return for this gesture. There were some incarcerated political guerillas with terminal illnesses, and it asked the Turkish government to set them free during the last days of their lives, so that they could spend that time with their parents and families. It is now April, 2015, and the Turkish government has not freed any of those prisoners with terminal illnesses.

Maybe you do not see it, but this situation breeds hatred among Kurdish people against the Turks. As a state, which claims to be the future leading actor of the Middle East, would they not at least bargain for the release of prisoners with terminal illnesses? Most of them have cancers in their last stages.

These kinds of amnesties were occasionally granted in the past. For example, during the years of 1992 and 1993, not only were terminally ill prisoners released, the state even swapped incarcerated high-ranked guerilla commanders for captive Turkish soldiers. Rıza Altun, who was recently arrested for being a KCK member, was also released at that time, along with other important figures, such as Mustafa Karasu and Hamili Yıldırım. All those people were released by the Turkish government. Did they not hold top positions in the organization, when they were arrested? Were they not the founding members of the organization, who attended the initial meetings of the organization, which were held at Ankara-Dikmen in 1976? All of those high-ranked guerillas were arrested in the 1980s and then were set free in 1992 after bargaining processes.

As a human being, I am running into some confliction in this matter. You set the high-ranked commanders of the organization free, after bargaining, but now insist on incarcerating regular guerillas with terminal illnesses. Do you know how many Palestinian soldiers were released by Israel in return for one low-profile Israeli soldier? The government of Israel set 1,000 incarcerated Palestinian soldiers free in return for a single Israeli soldier.

Contrary to that example, a human being has zero value in this country. In 2008, the organization took eight soldiers as captives in Hakkari, Çukurca. The organization then set them free, without bargaining with the Turkish government. The Minister of Justice at the time, Mehmet Ali Şahin, said, "I wish we had received their corpses rather than getting them alive." We guerillas were all shocked by this statement, coming from a senior Turkish politician. Mehmet Ali Şahin later explained that the Turkish state was highly humiliated when those captives were released by the organization. That is the value of a human being in Turkey. The Vice President at the time, Hüseyin Çelik, made a similar statement, saying, "We will not gather the deputies of the Turkish Grand National Assembly simply because a few Turkish soldiers died."

The Peace Process and Dersim (Alevi) Kurds

One of those who deserted the PKK wrote a newspaper article stating, "The guerillas from Dersim are being targeted by the headquarters management of the organization!" I personally witnessed that the guerillas from Dersim often had a complicated mindset. Most of the people from Dersim still vote for the Republican Public Party, a party who killed and tortured thousands of people from Dersim during the initial years of the Turkish Republic. Moreover, whenever the organization would begin a peace negotiation with Ankara, Dersim Kurds would harshly object. Those were the things that always confused my thoughts towards Dersim Kurds. On one hand, they would support democracy and liberalism, but, on the other, they would be against the peace process.

Consider the history of the Turkish Republic. All of the cruelties, tortures, and assimilation programs against the Kurds began with the government of the Republican Public Party. So, how could they still vote for the same party? Look at the recent news regarding the Dersim massacres. New excavations are being carried out, and despite this, those people continue to vote for their own murderers. The AKP still cannot find a constituency there. The HDP (People's Democracy Party) won the local elections for the mayoral position but was unsuccessful in the general elections. Therefore, the Alevi Kurds, especially those from Dersim, do not provide much trust in the organization. We never knew what their real agenda was.

In fact, the organization would take into account how Dersim Alevi Kurds would react before carrying out any of its strategic movements. The headquarters would definitely consider the reaction that would come from the Alevi Kurd guerillas. Of course, there were a couple of exceptions. Mustafa Karasu was an Alevi Kurd. Everyone liked and respected him. Similarly, Ali Haydar Kaytan was also a respected Alevi Kurd, with the rank of commander. Nevertheless, Alevi commanders, like Hamili

Yildirim, and a few others from the HPG commanders, would be considered as unreliable in the organization. We could never fully trust them.

I would find it very strange that whenever the organization would attempt to enter into a dialogue process with Ankara, the guerilla cadre from Dersim would fiercely stand against it. The organization had that type of obstacle in front of it, when it came to peace negotiations. Nevertheless, those problems were so large, that they could not be resolved by the seniors.

The Alevi Kurds (also some of the rank-and-file from the general population), would also not want to enter into a peace process, because the seniors did want it. They explicitly stated that, "If we were going to make peace with the Turks—if we were going to give up our independence, after securing our cultural rights, and the rights of education in our mother tongue—then why the hell have we lost so many of our comrades to this fight for so many years! The fight we had pursued until now had fallen on stony ground. By sitting at the table with the Turks, we were betraying our martyred comrades of this war. They gave their lives for nothing!"

The seniors from the organization responded to those pro-fight guerillas, with, "Comrades, those deaths were necessary, because initially our presence was being denied. We had to pay the price to make ourselves recognized by the Turkish officials. Today, it has paid off. We are on a different level from yesterday, and we cannot continue in our present fight strategy. We have to move on. Now is the time for securing peace. Before, the Turkish governments denied our existence, by saying that there was no such place as a nation of Kurds. We were called Armenians, Jews, mountain Turks, or even the agents of foreign powers. The Turks officially denied our presence back then. However, we Kurds are sitting at the negotiation table with those who doubted our existence. The Turks now say, "We have Kurdish citizens. They have their own rights and they will receive all those rights as the conditions improve. That is why we should move on! We cannot continue fighting forever!" I remember that day of discussion and the middle echelon was somewhat calmed down, by being told those things.

In a similar way to the Alevi Kurds, I still do not understand the mentality of the Turkish people. They interpret the incidents occurring around them in a very emotional way, not thinking rationally. I think it is mostly because of the media's reporting. What the Turks and Kurds have gone through during the last 40 or so years has damaged both sides, which have suffered thousands of martyrs. The PKK that was once underestimated is not a simple ordinary organization today. The United States officials met several times with PKK seniors before they invaded Iraq. The Germans, French, Brits, and many others visited PKK headquarters regularly to exchange opinions on several matters and held meetings with the seniors. Iran, Syria, Iraq, and Barzani's regional administration were all intimidated by the guerilla forces of the PKK, and the Turks have not yet seen the bigger picture. The PKK is, in fact, a unique force, which could contribute to the military power of Turkey and could potentially side with the Turkish government against all their enemies. If they would just establish the Goddamn, long-delayed peace treaty, and use this ready-trained power for much bigger goals in the Middle East. I cannot readily believe that the Turks have not had one single politician who had an idea like this.

The members of the Turkish society have all put on blinders caused by the greedy politicians and their corrupt media outlets. They still think that peace between the two communities is not possible, since so many innocent people, rangers, and soldiers have lost their lives during the past 40 years. Similar to mid-level guerillas, the Turkish politicians frequently claim that establishing peace would be a betrayal to the ones who lost their lives in this fight. Therefore, they support the continuance of military struggle against the Kurds. Such lame excuses!

If the Turkish government really wanted to end this fight, it could double, even triple the number of Turks who would also want peace, if the politicians were sincere and demonstrated a desire to end this bloody fight. There would then be no legitimate reason to continue the fighting.

The parents, families, and children of the martyred soldiers should be approached first and consulted about a peace process, so that they would not feel as if they had lost their sons and fathers to a hopeless cause. The government officials should say to them, "My dear brothers and sisters! The Kurds are a distinct society from us Turks, and they had some requests for us, such as education in their mother tongue and the recognition of their distinct identity, which was formed even before the foundation of the Turkish Republic. We have neglected those demands for years and rejected their very presence, referring to them as the pioneers of the foreign powers. Our politicians were not mature, and the bureaucrats were illiterate. At this point, we understand that we are unable to solve this problem by fighting and killing each other. Yesterday, your sons, brothers, uncles, and fathers died. Tomorrow, you, your sons, your brothers, or uncles will die if we insist on continuing this war. It would benefit both Turks and Kurds, to end this fight."

The Right Way to Establish the Peace

The Turkish society is not knowledgeable enough to see what is going on behind the scenes in the political arena. Rather than reading and thinking over the issues, they unconditionally accept what the media imposes upon them and this is not beneficial. However, this situation could be used for a good purpose if the harsh opinions of the Turkish public regarding a peace process could be changed by their respected journalists, writing articles with a more soothing language. This would help ease that process rather than fueling the atmosphere of differences and polarizing the conflict between the Kurds and Turks. The TV commentators could actually explain why the society desperately needs peace.

Of course, there would still be people who would want to sabotage the peace process and support the continuance of the fight, thinking, "My son, or my husband, died in this war, and the fight should not stop until we defeat all the Kurds. So, for that purpose, more sons and fathers should also die, if it is necessary." That is a seriously mistaken rationale.

The good thing is that aside from this group of people who do not think rationally, there are also many people who do support the peace process. For example, when the peace negotiations first started, a group of intellectuals were tasked by the Turkish government to organize meetings in 20 different locations with the families of Turks who had lost their loved ones in this fight. Except for one or two, none of the families raised objections to the establishment of peace through dialogue. Many of the families explicitly stated, "Stop this war. My son died for it, but I do not want others to experience the same pain!" We witnessed it on the news. The society was eager to see peace. However, the politicians slowed down the process by making excuses as to how they were to persuade the people.

The AKP government should have established a special ministry to handle the works related to the peace process, by employing highly intelligent people from the areas of politics, international relations, psychology, and sociology. This ministry should have oversight of the media and press and not allow broadcasts that would further polarize the Kurds and Turks. Instead, it would encourage them, as well as talk shows, to publish and broadcast news that would contribute to the peace.

This is the right time for it, because there have been no soldiers' funerals in the past two years, from west to east. People are happy about that, and the public should be informed about those positive sides to the negotiations. The officials should report, "If this war ends, both sides will win and our economy will grow stronger. The money that is currently spent on arms, weapons, and security forces, would be spent for health, education, and many other beneficial programs." Who could be disturbed by those things as long as they thought rationally? The Kurdish society, in the east, is already fed up, living under war conditions for so long. The people there ask for nothing, but to live a normal life without the threat and oppression of the security forces. They simply want to live without the worry of losing their children to the war. The tradesmen there also want this fight to end. They want an end to their store windows being broken every day. They want the end of Molotov bombs burning their work places. They want to live just like normal human beings. Therefore, a ministry, which should have been established years ago, would not only prevent polarizing ideas but would also help to inform both Turks and Kurds about the potential positive gains of peace.

Some sectors of the Turkish public have consistently used the media and press for discrimination against and polarization towards the Kurds. For example, the Turkish society has suggested for years that Apo, the leader of the organization, was a monster, a bloodthirsty baby killer, and even a sex addict. Sadly, the public has believed whatever the media spewed out to them, and never searched for the truth. If Apo were really a dictator, do you think those millions of Kurds would have followed him to their death? Cannot the Turks see this? At least? In actuality, this person they slandered as a baby killer has never even touched a gun in his life. I had been personally responsible for Apo's protection while he was still in Syria. When Apo took a walk, there would be one comrade in front of him, and two behind, for security reasons, and he would get really upset if one of those "close protection guards" passed by him, with their gun showing. He would quiver with rage. He hated any type of arms or weapons. Therefore, we even disguised our guns while protecting him. When he was asked the reason for starting an armed rebellion against the Turks, despite the fact that he hated the use of guns, he would say, "The Turks gave us no other option but the armed struggle." If you read the recent history of Turkey, you would understand that our political parties shut down, one by one, and so the organization gravitated towards an armed struggle, but only after all the political channels disappeared.

I wish the Turkish media had been more objective, specifically about Apo. I wish they had reported Apo's unifying and integrative statements regarding the Turkish and Kurdish societies. Then, you would understand whether Apo was, in fact, a terrorist, or an opportunity to establish unity between the Turks and the Kurds within Turkey.

The peace will only come if the media stops reporting the news given to them by greedy people, who benefit from this fight, politically and economically. We repenters watched the news a few days ago, and could not help laughing. Six different TV channels broadcasted a specific news item with the exact same words. The only difference was the tone of the speakers. It was about the clash that occurred between the PKK guerillas and security forces in the city of Agri. Not only did the Turkish state not allow the full details of the incident to be heard by the public, it was also apparent that it had ordered the TV channels to present the news in the way in which it had been ordered. In fact, a publication ban was applied, shortly after this initial news. It was a shame, since the organization news reaches us here, even though we are incarcerated. But remember the connections the organization had with the prison guards. We learned about the details of this incident through a document sent by headquarters to prisons.

Mr. President Erdoğan had stated in his public speech that, "Our soldiers have been fighting against the terrorists in order to rescue our captured soldiers." He further claimed that 15 Turkish soldiers were left unattended, by the Kurdish public, until they died.

Actually, those 15 soldiers had been intentionally sent close to a group of guerillas, during the darkness of night, and the guerillas had been shocked to see these "sitting ducks" in front of them. It was a highly unusual situation, and they figured out that there was something fishy going on, since the organization and the Turkish state were in a peace process negotiation back then. They just could not understand the reason why those soldiers were sent to die. So, before carrying out an attack against them, the guerillas had responded in an intelligent way and contacted headquarters to inform them of this weird situation. Headquarters replied, telling them not to carry out an attack to annihilate the soldiers but only to defend themselves.

You know how this incident was reflected to the public? Erdoğan appeared on TV and said that 40 terrorists had encircled Turkish soldiers in order to put an end to the peace process. Let's imagine, for a moment, that the guerillas had, in fact, laid an ambush on the Turkish soldiers. Even if it were true, would you report it to the public as if you were giving happy news? It seemed, from Erdoğan's speech, that the Turkish public was looking forward to hearing of the soldiers' funerals. Those 15 soldiers were intentionally sent there to be martyred by the guerillas. The incident took place just before the national parliamentary elections, and the goal was to gain the votes of nationalist Turks by provoking their fascist sentiments. Thank God, the PKK was not taken in by that scheme. Those soldiers, mostly the sons of low-income Turkish citizens from different parts of Anatolia, were of no importance to the government. That's why they had been sent in as sitting ducks. The guerillas could have easily annihilated them, if they had acted irrationally.

As these types of clashes began to occur, the organization disseminated a public statement. "We are about to run out of patience. The Turkish government will either keep its promise or pay the price for betrayal." Believe me, we Kurds are fed up with their deceitful tricks.

In this context, it is essential to have an impartial watch committee. The government kept posting public statements that the organization did not fulfill its promises, attacked their soldiers, and ambushed security forces. If they were openly honest, they would not object to the forming of a watch committee, which would examine all the incidents that occurred during the peace negotiations. If we had had something like that, the Turkish officials would not have been able to apply a media blackout in order to disguise their dirty schemes after each of the sensational martyr news reports.

The committee did not need to include only the Kurds. It would have been acceptable for others to be included, as long as they were reasonable and objective people. Other governments which had terrorism in their countries established such committees. In some countries, those committees were formed with the participation of objective third party states, while in others they were formed with the participation of objective, intellectual people from both sides of the conflict.

Before the last peace process began between Turkey and the PKK, the seniors at the PKK asked the Turks to accept the mediatory role of the U.S. officials, or, as an alternative, the seniors also agreed that it would be acceptable to have unbiased, academic and intellectual people present during the peace talks. Turkish officials rejected both of these offers.

It was very important to establish this peace watch committee as soon as possible, so that this committee could examine all the incidents which might occur during the peace process and inform the public which side had not fulfilled its promises. In this way, the Turkish government could not blame the PKK for every single incident using its huge media and press outlets. With the establishment of such a committee, both the Kurds and the Turks would have an opportunity to learn the facts about any incidents that might be carried out in an attempt to deter the peace process.

Let me explain this through an incident that occurred in the city of Agri. If there had been a peace watch committee, the public would have instantly learned the truth, and the government would not have been able to apply a broadcast ban in order to disguise its guilt in the incident. The governor of Agri delivered this absurd statement after the incident. "The security forces were informed that a large group of terrorists would be visiting the festival area to carry out an attack against civilians, and that is why we dispatched those 15 soldiers, in order to ensure the protection of the festival ground." There were way too many contradictions in that explanation. I have never heard such an ignorant public statement before. If the security forces heard that a large group of terrorists were coming, then why the hell did the officials dispatch only 15 soldiers? Moreover, it was the middle of the night. They knew that a group of 40 guerillas were coming, but they sent only 15 soldiers to fight against them. This is bullshit. Anyone with a half a brain knows that 15 soldiers cannot stop 40 guerillas. The security officials knew this better than anyone.

After that incident, non-governmental organizations met with the guerillas who had taken part in that clash. The guerillas explicitly stated, "We figured out that the Turkish soldiers were sent there to be martyred, and since we knew it was a scheme, we shot them in non-lethal parts of their bodies, just to protect ourselves."

The organization lost two guerillas in that fight and if I am not mistaken there were five wounded Turkish soldiers. Believe me, if the guerillas had, in fact, wanted to annihilate them, they would have. It was flat terrain and under the darkness of the night; those 15 soldiers would have been easily killed by 40 guerillas. The Turkish press later disseminated inaccurate information about the incident. The guerillas were said to have used 10,000 bullets, which was impossible. Forty guerillas cannot even carry such a large amount of ammunition. Moreover, the empty shells that were shown on the news were the types that could only be used on G-3 NATO standard rifles and Turkish-made rifles by MKE. Everyone knows that the organization uses Russian made Dragunovs.

It was nothing but a scheme, planned and carried out by some deep, dark powers rooted in the bureaucratic and political institutions of Turkey. If you remember, the AKP government even attempted to blame the head of general staff for the failure. The Chief General acted very cleverly and said to the media, "We Turkish soldiers had nothing to do with this operation. The operation was carried out with the direct orders of the governor of Agri, without notifying us."

It was risky business for anyone to dare to spoil the peace process. Turkey gave large promises to the organization in the presence of the United Kingdom in the Oslo peace talks. Therefore, whoever dishonored its words would pay the price. Hence, the schemes against the organization had to be carried out in such a manner that no one would suspect that it was, in fact, planned by the government.

The governors in Turkey worked under the authority of the government. If the news of the funerals of those 15 soldiers was disseminated to the cities in Anatolia, who would benefit the most from it? The government! Thanks to this incident, which happened just before the elections, the AKP would get the votes of the MHP. Unfortunately, the Turkish public was once again fueled with hatred, and since there was a publication ban, no one learned what did actually happen there.

Potential Threats

A fight, which lasted more than 40 years, cannot end without a price being paid for it. If the officials are, in fact, sincere on ending this fight, the Turkish government should take any precautions it can and prevent provocative actions that would potentially damage the peace process. For example, Tony Blair started the peace process with the IRA and during the initial years of the talks, the IRA would occasionally carry out missions against British targets. However, in the sixth year of the process, after the demands of the Irish people were acceded to, allegedly some pro-fight guerillas within the IRA carried out a mission in London. It was later discovered that the mission was not carried out by the IRA but by a group of Brits who were highly discontent with the peace process.

I tell you this, because similar incidents are highly likely to occur in Turkey, as well, and the Turkish public should be ready for that. Elites, who would be economically affected by the peace process, will definitely encourage sabotage missions. The government officials would be hesitant to disappoint those rich elites and would worry that the constituency support for the AKP would decrease if they pissed off the economic elites by establishing peace. Actually, I think it would be just the reverse. The government, which could end this long-lasting fight, would make history in Middle East. The people, both Kurds and Turks, would never forget the leader who established partnership between the two groups. But the politicians are unable to risk losing their economic resources. They do not understand that peace is a kind of war, without guns. Just as you paid the price with your soldiers in war, you would also pay a price for the peace but not with martyrs.

Unfortunately, there is no other option left between the two societies. This peace process will either be concluded with the establishment of peace, or there will be the continued division of borders between the Turks and Kurds. If the Turkish government does not keep its promises that were given in Oslo, this fight will begin again, and this time, it is not going to be out in the countryside. It will be right in the heart of cities. The country will experience a situation very similar to what is now happening in Syria. The YDGH, the city branch of the PKK, has been arming itself for the last two years. The missions that were previously carried out in the countryside would be carried out by the YDGH in city centers. I am not sure whether the AKP government would take such a risk just to keep its economic elites happy.

Therefore, if this peace process does not end in success, the YDGH is the group of which people should be afraid. The members of the YDGH are highly trained in city fights. They know the location of every district, street, apartment, building, and hideout in the cities. I am sure that the security forces are aware of the situation, since they witnessed it in the town of Cizre. The security forces could not get into the town, because of the armed siege carried out by the YDGH members. In those clashes, heavy artillery weapons were used against the Turkish security forces. No one wondered, then, how that artillery had gotten into a town controlled by Turks. Those weapons had already been in Cizre for years. The organization followed the same strategy in most of the towns and cities in the east, and they were to be used when the time came and it was high time for Cizre. That is why the guerillas used bazookas, Russian made PKs, missiles, and other things, because you can destroy both armored vehicles and helicopters using that type of weaponry.

No one should fool themselves. There would be no stopping us if we really wanted to take it back. The town of Cizre is no longer under the control of Turkey, but is a liberated zone. The government could only recapture it by targeting everyone living in that town; however, the cost would be very heavy. Turkey would have a hard time to rationalize the civilian killings in the international arena.

22

THE TURKS, THE KURDS, AND THE LAST CHANCE

The incarcerated leader, Apo, still had an influence and control over the members of the organization, but his authority had been diminishing, because he had stayed away from the headquarters for more than ten years. If Ankara cannot secure the peace within the next two or so years, Apo will no longer have control over the guerillas.

Apo's recent prison speeches even indicated this. In his last statement, Apo said, via his lawyers, "If Ankara fails to take concrete steps towards the peace soon, the Turkish officials should stop visiting me here." He told the same thing to the Kurdish peace committees, visiting him at the prison. "Do not bother yourself with visiting me here, until the AKP government does something toward the peace."

I know the internal workings of the organization very well, and if Apo delivers similar public statements a few more times, the organization will get the message that Apo has lost hope in the peace talks, so they should plan new fight strategies in order to forcefully bring the Turks back to the negotiation table. Kandil, the headquarters of the organization, would immediately declare war on Turkey, and after Turkey was brought back to the negotiation table, the demands of the organization would be completely different. I do not think that the organization would continue to follow a policy based on the fellowship of Turks and Kurds after so many betrayals.

The organization does not have a secret agenda concerning this peace process. The seniors are all very sincere, and the guerillas in the camps have been trained in what they were going to do after the peace with Turkey. The seniors believed Erdoğan and his cabinet, and I hope Erdoğan does not fail them for some other goals. Otherwise, the results will be disastrous.

The guerillas have been used as a scapegoat, through the peace process of the last three years. What do you think would happen if the seniors abruptly told them that the peace process was over, and they were returning to the fight strategy? The guerillas would definitely go crazy and not listen to the seniors any longer. There was a large middle-class echelon in the organization with a considerable amount of influence, and if this group adopted a particular attitude, the senior management could have a hard time to do what they wanted. The middle class would criticize the fight strategy (assuming that Turkey fulfilled all of the promises given at Oslo) by saying, "You, seniors have trained us for peace for the last three years and have talked about living together with the Turks. You asked for education in the mother tongue and for the recognition of the Kurdish nationality as a distinct group. Turkey has fulfilled all these demands, so why are we now returning to the fight strategy again?" Guerillas were sick of fighting and they wanted this fight to end, as soon as possible.

Besides, there is no other option left between the two communities. Of course, that would be a whole other story, if Turkey should risk division of its territories, chaos in the country, or a turmoil similar to that which erupted in Syria and Iraq. Kurdish scholars and politicians, Şerafettin Elçi and Leyla Zana, have repeatedly said during the last two years that they both believe that this peace process is the last chance for Turkey to secure a permanent peace within the country, remarking, "If Ankara cannot settle this problem with this generation of Kurds, they will be unlikely to make peace with the next generation." This is very true, and this is why I have said several times that this peace process is the last opportunity for Turkey.

With more than 20 years of experience within the organization, I know something of the oppressions and tortures to which the Kurds were subjected in the old days. I very well remember the pressures that took place during the 80s and 90s, but I do not know what happened before then. Nevertheless, the Kurdish youth living in the region experienced violence on a daily basis. They all sacrificed their fathers, brothers, sisters, or uncles to this fight. They were in clashes with the police every day. Their psychology and way of thinking was very different from us, old guerillas.

If Ankara continues to delay the establishment of a permanent peace, while the wise seniors of the organization, such as Cemil Bayık and Murat Karayılan, are still alive, their chances of making peace with the new radicalized Kurdish generation is extremely low. The new generation considers Turkey an enemy because of the losses they have suffered so far and they are unable to think rationally. They do not want to live within the borders of Turkey, as the seniors of the organization would have them do. Rather, they want to establish a Free Kurdistan by carving territories out of Turkey. If these highly radicalized and politicized Kurdish youth have a voice in those matters in the future, their demands will be different than the demands of the current seniors of the organization. They will say, "We are a distinct society, and each society has the right of governing itself, and determining its own fate. Since we are a society of 40 million, including the Kurds in Syria, Iran, and Iraq, we can also have our own state." The new generation thinks like that!

The Kurdish youth, in this region, follow world and Turkish politics more than the Turkish youth in the west. Moreover, the organization, the PKK, intentionally tries to put those young people into the middle of ideological and political issues. There are always guidance and inducements towards certain subjects. If Turkey does not keep its promise in the peace negotiations, this radicalized Kurdish youth will carry out large missions in the metropolises of Turkey. The PKK has already thought about every possibility, and if the negotiations end with peace, then the seniors will convert the energy of this Kurdish youth into socio-economic activities. But, if they once again end with disagreement, then this radicalized youth will be motivated to start turmoil and chaos in the big cities of Turkey.

The stupidity of the Turkish police officers and military personnel also contributes to the radicalization of that youth. Those government officials have always approached the Kurdish youth with hatred and have punished them with severe beatings. The police officers working in the region had to be specifically warned and then trained about those issues. If there is a demonstration march, let the youth spend their energy by walking peacefully and do not block them! Do not irritate them. If this Kurdish youth has no encounters with the police when they march, they will give up carrying out marches after a couple of trials, and they will not take part in protest activities any longer. However, if the police directors continue to assign 1,000 police officers for only 100 young protesters, these youth will become further radicalized, and, in the end, you will not be able to control them. Unfortunately, the directors of the police and gendarme forces are both inexperienced and uneducated in these issues. They place the police officers among the Kurdish youth and that creates an atmosphere of stress. For this reason, if the peace process fails again, the organization will spread the war out to cities and metropolises through these youth. Remember the Kobane incidents, which occurred in 2014. Throughout those two days, life was paralyzed in Diyarbakır, Turkey. Both the police and other security forces were up against the wall. Except for the periods of the military coups, tanks went down the city roads for the first time in the history of Turkey. The organization had that ready potential. It could easily cause similar turmoil and chaos in the metropolises of both the east and the west of Turkey, by using these youth as it did in Diyarbakır.

Final Thoughts

Sometimes, I very much miss the life in the countryside; the fresh air, the silence of the mountains, peace and the atmosphere of true friendship. But, here I am, always stuck among four walls. Even worse, I know that I am going to end my life here.

Sometimes you see the sun, and sometimes you cannot. I have never cried until recently, but I came very close to it several times. I drew this destiny with my own hands. I am totally responsible for the incidents that took place after I deserted the organization, and I sometimes feel very angry with myself: I was not such an idiot once. I was blind not to see ahead of me. I do not understand how I put myself into such a situation.

I think about my parents a lot. I am so embarrassed for them. After I was incarcerated, my parents struggled much because of me. They relocated from Istanbul to Batman. They have been subjected to many pressures and threats in their neighborhood there. They have been insulted in front of my siblings, and, besides that, they now have to look after me as well. They are already poor, but they still try to send me some money each month, as if it were not enough for them to have moved to Batman just to be close to me. They also visit me every week, and that is an extra financial burden for them.

I cannot take this situation anymore. I not only destroyed my own life, but I also put my family in a difficult situation. I blame myself continually for this. Because I have never contributed financially to my family, and now I have become a financial burden on them.

I know my parents, but I do not even know my siblings. When my father first visited me in prison, he brought pictures of my siblings. That was such a weird feeling. I could not recognize some of them. I asked my father to write their names on the pictures, so that I could memorize them.

On the second visit, there was a girl about 18 or 19 standing just behind my mother. I asked my mother who she was. "She is your sister, my son. You have never seen her before," she said. I felt so strange. My sister took the handset, on the other side of the glass, and said, "I want to call you my brother, but I do not know you at all," and then put the handset on the table. She started to cry. I have been emotionally affected by such things. It has been almost six years, and I have just started to get acquainted with my sister.

Despite all of these things, I never lost my hope. In fact, my hopes are the only thing that keeps me going in here. One cannot live here without hopes and dreams. I always dream of leaving here one day. The thing that I want the most is to spend time with my nephews and nieces, for at least a few days before I die.

PART III
Conclusion

23

LESSONS FROM A TERRORIST'S OWN STORY

Turkey was in an ongoing peace process with the PKK when Deniz was incarcerated. Nevertheless, there is now a renewed conflict which is very similar to what occurred in the 1990s—unaccounted murders, repression, denial of identity, declaration of state of emergency, curfews, and forced migration.

Between 2005 and 2016, the state and the organization has undergone three failed peace attempts. Beginning with 2015, Turkish security forces started to carry out operations against the PKK militants and arrested hundreds of Kurdish civilians for their alleged ties to the PKK. In the meantime, young Kurdish militants who were clandestinely positioned in the city centers started to take control of the some Kurdish towns and the neighborhoods and declared war against the Turkish government. During these clashes, hundreds of people, including Turkish security officers, Kurdish civilians, and PKK members lost their lives (Baser & Ozturk, 2015; Cagaptay, 2015; Srivastava, 2016; Uras, 2015).

The fights lasted for months and many town centers in southeastern Anatolia were completely destroyed. More than 200,000 Kurdish civilians were forced to leave their homes and relocate to other parts of the country (Srivastava, 2016). On the other hand, as the corpses of the Turkish security officers were delivered to their home towns in the western parts of the country, the ethnic tensions have risen, and several arson attacks took place against Kurdish-owned property and many HDP offices. As such, the insights offered by Deniz are likely to continue to be relevant for some time (Marcus, 2015; Yeginsu, 2015).

Of course, the generalizability of Deniz's insights is a relevant issue. Those who are recruited to relay a life history tend to be special and talented; thus their perceptions and views may be unique. The insights provided by a single person might not reflect the ideas and opinions of the others from the same group. Accordingly, there are always issues of generalizability with a life history.

Still, although this study employed the story of only one subject, Deniz was a "freedom fighter" for nearly 20 years and rose to a position of leadership. He was ideally situated to share insights based on years of experience and on access to meetings and relationships that few would have. He was able to provide a rich, textured look into what a life of a terrorist is like and into the inner workings of a terrorist organization. Thus, he offered us lessons that can be tested with other life histories of PKK freedom fighters and of those drawn from other terrorist insurgencies.

In this regard, this final chapter will focus on—and draw lessons about—the nature of terrorism, especially for those who continue to join the PKK. Building on the work of life-course scholars, Deniz's experiences will be assessed through the lens of a life-course perspective. The discussion thus will focus on the onset, persistence, and desistance of his career as a "freedom fighter." The book will conclude by drawing lessons about the future of the terrorist conflict in Turkey. Deniz's insights will be used to address the key issue between the PKK and Turkey: Is peace possible? Or what would it take for freedom fighters such as Deniz—and he represents the steady flow of Kurdish young adults into the PKK—to stop fighting Turkey and become peaceful?

As a prelude to this discussion, the recent development regarding the conflict between the PKK and the Turkish government will be examined. Again, this sets the context for why more Kurdish "freedom fighters" will be recruited and engage in terrorist acts—and why the insights from Deniz's life history will continue to be of special value.

The Current State of the Conflict Between the PKK and Turkey

When Deniz turned himself in in 2010, Turkey was in a peace process with the PKK. People, especially the Kurds of Turkey, were hopeful that the peace process would work this time, since unlike the former governments of Turkey, the AKP (the Justice and Development Party) government came to power with strong and functional influence on major state institutions (Dalay, 2015). Neither the opposition parties had enough seats in the parliament to block the progression of the peace, nor the military structure was strong enough (as in the old days) to undermine the wishes of the political structures. There was basically no obstacle in front of the AKP for not ending this long-term conflict. However, there is now a renewed bloody conflict between both the parties.

The most serious damage to the AKP government occurred on September 13, 2011 when sound recordings were leaked to the internet of one of the secret meetings between the head of the Turkish National Intelligence Agency, Hakan Fidan, and the senior PKK administrators of Mustafa Karasu, Zübeyir Aydar, and Sabri Ok. The peace process was sabotaged again, and this time the damage proved fatal. The recordings indicated that the negotiations between the government and senior PKK members had begun even before 2009 and the meetings had been secretly held in Oslo, Norway (Hurriyet, 2011; Milliyet, 2011; NTV, 2011). On February 7, 2012, the Turkish police attempted to arrest the head of the National Intelligence Agency on the accusation of engaging in talks with terrorist group members on the grounds that directly engaging with a "terrorist" organization was a constitutional crime (TRT, 2012).

Holding direct talks with the PKK could actually be a milestone of this peace initiative. These meetings were the first time in history that a Turkish government had sat at the negotiation table to learn the exact demands of the PKK without using intermediaries. Fearing a potential negative reaction from the Turkish public, the meetings had been held secretly. Nevertheless, this initiative also failed due to the leakages about the talks to the media.

The Wise People Commission

After these successive sabotage attempts, the peace talks restarted again in 2013. The AKP allowed the Peace and Democracy Party members to meet with their incarcerated leader Abdullah Öcalan in Imrali on a regular basis to discuss peace terms. After months of negotiations with the Turkish government,

Abdullah Öcalan issued a historic letter on March 21, 2013 to be read during the Nowruz celebrations in the city of Diyarbakır (Akyol, 2015; Ensaroglu, 2013).

> We have now reached a point where guns must go silent and ideas and politics must speak. We will unite in the face of those who try to split us. From now on, a new period begins when politics, not guns, will come to the fore. It is now time for armed elements to withdraw outside the country. (Abdullah Öcalan, 2013)

Thus, in return for political reforms to be carried out by the AKP government, Öcalan openly instructed Kandil to abandon its armed struggle against Turkey and called for the withdrawal of PKK insurgents outside the Turkish territories (Akyol, 2015). Only four days after the delivery of this speech in Diyarbakır, the PKK management in Iraq declared a ceasefire and reaffirmed their loyalty to their leader, Abdullah Öcalan.

On April 3, 2013, the AKP government started the initiative to establish an independent third-party committee that would help the government to persuade the society about the benefits of the peaceful resolution of the Kurdish issue. As a result, a committee under the name of the "Wise People Commission" was established in 2013. The committee consisted of 63 people drawn from varied backgrounds, including academics, intellectuals, NGO representatives, and even well-known movie actors. To help shape the public opinion on the peaceful resolution of the conflict, the committee held several meetings with the public in seven different regions of Turkey (Gursel, 2013). Erdoğan also ordered the establishment of a parliamentary commission that would assess the progress of the peace process under the Turkish Grand National Assembly. Nevertheless, the main opposition parties—the Republican People's Party (CHP) and the Nationalist Movement Party (MHP)—declared that they would not participate in this parliamentary commission (Akyol, 2015; Gursel, 2013; Marcus, 2015).

In the meantime, the withdrawal of Kurdish guerilla forces from Turkey started in May, 2013. Nevertheless, the PKK administrators halted this process as soon as it was determined that the Turkish soldiers were taking over the Kurds' abandoned positions and building new, fortified mountain outposts (Albayrak & Parkinson, 2013; Marcus, 2015; Miller, 2013). In response, the PKK administrators in Kandil ordered the establishment of political dominance over the southeastern Anatolia region through the use of pro-PKK institutions (Marcus, 2015). Because the Turkish government wanted to avoid any conflict that might potentially spoil the peace process, PKK guerillas were given a free hand to carry out many activities, including setting up checkpoints and disseminating propaganda material within the areas largely dominated by the Kurds (Akyol, 2015).

The Civil War in Syria

The civil war that erupted in Syria worsened the situation in Turkey. Suddenly, the Syrian wing of the PKK, the Democratic Union Party (PYD), became the hero of the West as it fought against the ISIS threat. The U.S. military began to carry out joint operations with the YPG guerillas in Syria. YPG guerillas were armed by the United States and acquired a significant amount of territory across the border of Turkey by taking advantage of the failed Assad regime. The growing power of the PKK through its Syrian wing—the YPG—made Ankara highly nervous (Anna, Gordon, & Smith, 2015; Akyol, 2015; Jones, 2016; Marcus, 2015).

Toward the end of September 2014, the Kurdish YPG militants fighting against ISIS—mainly in Rojava, the Kurdish part of Syria—ran out of ammunition and other supplies. Large demonstrations occurred in various cities of Turkey, because the Turkish government refused to open the nation's borders so that military and economic aid could reach Syria from Northern Iraq. Seeing the AKP government's unwillingness to allow the transfer of Northern Iraqi forces into Syria through Turkish territories, the Kurds of Diyarbakır organized one of the largest protests against the AKP government; this lasted from October 6 to 9 in 2014 (Radikal, 2014). During the heavy clashes between the demonstrators and the police, more than 50 civilian Kurds lost their lives (Barnard & Gordon, 2015; Marcus, 2015; Nissenbaum, 2015). Thus, the insensitivity of Turkish officials to the sufferings of the Kurds at the hand of ISIS, as well as media depictions of alleged aid given by the Turkish government to some Islamic groups in Syria, seriously damaged the peace process (Dalay, 2015).

The Defeat of the AKP in the June 7 Elections

On June 7, 2015, even though it acquired the largest percentage of the votes, the AKP experienced a serious defeat in the general elections since it was no longer eligible to govern Turkey as a unified government, as had been the case since 2002. By surpassing the 10 percent threshold that was needed to enter the Turkish Parliament, the pro-Kurdish political party, the Peoples' Democratic Party, secured 80 seats and the AKP, for the first time in its history, could not secure an outright majority in parliament.

Being denied the parliamentary majority needed to make constitutional changes, Erdoğan was upset with this major victory of the HDP (Akyol, 2015; Basar, 2015; Baser & Ozturk, 2015; Dalay, 2015; Imogen, 2015; Marcus, 2015). No one was expecting the HDP to surpass the election threshold. In fact, the HDP was the first pro-Kurdish political party to achieve this level of success in the history of the Turkish Republic. This defeat denied Erdoğan the ability to alter the constitution to strengthen his power and autocratic control in the country. According to some commentators, Erdoğan reacted by intentionally undermining the peace process, as AKP had lost its majority in the parliament as a result of the HDP's success (Akyol, 2015; Basar, 2015; Imogen, 2015; Marcus, 2015).

The Renewed Conflict

First, the AKP intentionally failed to form a coalition government with the other political parties in order to push the country towards snap elections scheduled for November 1, 2015. Later, the verbal fight among Erdoğan and the pro-Kurdish politicians began to occur as a result of the Syrian war, which resulted in the increased national sentiments among the Kurds. In June 2015, Erdoğan announced that Ankara would never allow anyone to establish a state—namely a Kurdish state—across its borders (Barnard & Gordon, 2015; Dalay, 2015; Marcus, 2015; Nissenbaum, 2015).

On July 20, 2015, an ISIS suicide bomber carried out an attack during a press briefing in a Kurdish city and killed 32 pro-Kurdish activists who were just about to set off for Kobane to fight against ISIS. The same day, the KCK President Cemil Bayık ended the peace process and encouraged the Kurds within Turkey to prepare for a civilian outbreak against the Turkish government (Marszal & Akkoc, 2015). The PKK central command claimed that even though the attack was carried out by ISIS, it was aided by the Turkish government. Hostilities began between both sides again. The PKK openly accused the Turkish government and then ended the two-year-old peace process by killing more than 60 police officers and soldiers within a month (Akyol, 2015; Dalay, 2015; Marcus, 2015).

As a result, beginning with July 2015, the peace process that started early in 2013 had broken down again. Turkish security forces started to carry out operations against the PKK militants and arrested hundreds of Kurdish civilians for their alleged ties to the PKK. In the meantime, following the orders of the KCK, young Kurdish militants who were clandestinely positioned in the city centers started to take control of some Kurdish towns and neighborhoods, and they declared war against the Turkish government. The street fighting among the police and the militants was so intense that, after a period, the AKP government decided to hand over control of some Kurdish cities to military officials (Basar, 2015; Marcus, 2015).

The militants dug trenches and placed bombs in the streets under their control so that security forces could not enter into their zone. The fight among the military and the Kurdish youths lasted for months, and in the end town centers were completely destroyed. Extreme violence was applied by both sides. Hundreds of people, Turkish security officers, Kurdish civilians, and PKK members lost their lives during these fights. Approximately 200,000 Kurdish civilians evacuated their homes and relocated to different cities as a direct result of this conflict (Marcus, 2015; Yeginsu, 2015). As the corpses of the Turkish security officers were delivered to their home towns in the western parts of the country, the ethnic tensions have risen. Several arson attacks took place against Kurdish-owned property and many HDP offices.

On October 10, 2015, a suicide attack was carried out in Ankara by an ISIS member in a peace rally—Labor, Peace, and Democracy Rally—organized by the major leftist groups in Turkey, including the pro-Kurdish political party, the HDP. This attack resulted in the death of more than 100 activists. Reports indicated that another 500 people were seriously wounded (Letsch & Shaheen, 2015). Since the bombing events occurred only 21 days before the snap elections of November 1, 2015, some claimed that this increasing level of terrorist threat was planned by the AKP government to undercut the HDP's electoral appeal in the forthcoming elections (Baser & Ozturk, 2015; Don, 2015; Johnson, 2015; Lizzie, 2015).

Indeed, the AKP was able to obtain the majority of the seats in the parliament in the November 1, 2015 elections. During the five-month period prior to the elections, the country had experienced substantial economic and political instability due to the dramatic ISIS attacks in Ankara and Suruç, the increased violence among the security forces and PKK militants, and the economic slowdown and decreasing value of the Turkish lira against foreign currencies (Imogen, 2015). People experiencing this insecurity and economic instability voted for the AKP, believing that a strong, unified government could return Turkey to its previous period of security and wealth (Baser & Ozturk, 2015; Cagaptay, 2015; Srivastava, 2016; Uras, 2015).

For some, the strategy devised by President Erdoğan actually worked. The AKP secured 319 seats in the parliament by winning constituencies from two different groups: Turkish nationalists who wanted to get revenge from the PKK militants, and the Kurdish voters who were tired of the repressive measures applied by the Turkish security forces. In fact, many Kurds blamed the PKK for the escalation of violence in Kurdish cities and, as a result, voted for the AKP in the snap elections (Cagaptay, 2015).

Holding the AKP government responsible for failing to provide the security for the October 10 peace rally, the PKK carried out a suicide mission against a military convoy carrying both civilian and military personnel in the city of Ankara on February 17, 2016 and killed 30 people and injured 60 (Srivastava, 2016). Following this incident, the security forces increased their crackdowns against PKK militants who positioned themselves in the city centers in southeastern Anatolia. Harsh military measures were applied. Civilian casualties increased, and curfews paralyzed the social and economic activities in those cities. The AKP government blamed the HDP for carrying out the terrorist activities of the PKK in the cities. Tens of HDP leaders across Turkey were arrested and then charged on the grounds of promoting a culture of violence and terrorism (Jones, 2016).

In retaliation, two months after the first suicide mission, on March 13, 2016, the PKK carried out another suicide attack by targeting a bus carrying civilian commuters in Ankara. This attack killed another 37 civilians and injured 125 people (Osborne, 2016). In response, Erdoğan publicly announced that there would be no more effort to return to the peace process with the PKK. For him, the time for negotiation had passed; the only remaining option was the complete liquidation of the PKK and its extensions from the region (Jones, 2016). Today, many Kurds and pro-peace groups have lost all hope that the peace process will resume. Accordingly, the conflict between the Turkish government and the PKK will continue unabated. More "freedom fighters" similar to Deniz will be recruited and engage in terrorist attacks. In this context, Deniz's insight about his joining, being a part of, and leaving the PKK will retain much salience.

Terrorism across the Life-Course

As Sampson and Laub (1993) note, the life courses of individuals consist of pathways and turning points. For Kurdish young adults such as Deniz, the decision to change the trajectory of their lives and pursue terrorism—freedom fighting in their eyes—represented a remarkable turning point. Using a life-course framework, this section attempts to discuss the key factors that led Deniz—and likely others like him—to experience a turning point that led to the onset of their becoming a terrorist. A life-course perspective also sensitizes us to the importance of explaining persistence or stability—in this case, why Deniz remained as a terrorist for nearly two decades. This issue is thus addressed. Finally, a life-course perspective leads us to ask why individuals desist from a given activity. Why did Deniz decide to leave the PKK and no longer pursue fighting for the freedom of the Kurdish people?

Onset: Becoming a Terrorist as a Turning Point

The radicalization experience of Deniz that resulted in terrorist action also developed as a result of a number of life course events that occurred mostly during the childhood and early adolescence of the subject. This complex set of factors—turning points—that combined to entrench Deniz on a terrorism pathway can be grouped under four categories: (1) a sense of injustice, (2) personality traits, (3) opportunity structures to recruit, and (4) sense of duty and honor.

The events that occurred under these four main categories of turning points explain how grievances and vulnerabilities were transformed into hatred of the Turks and how hatred was transformed into a justification of violence for Deniz.

Sense of Injustice. The key factor that led Deniz—and likely other Kurds—to join the PKK was the feeling of injustice and resentment caused by the agents of the Turkish state. In fact, Deniz and his siblings became exposed to the feelings of discrimination and alienation beginning with their early childhood. Since the use of the Kurdish language was forbidden by the Turkish state, Deniz's parents had been using a radio to listen secretly to the news related to the Kurds from a radio channel—The Voice of Erivan—that broadcasted from Armenia. As he noted in his life history, "We listened to this channel religiously". (p. 47)

Additionally, his cousin, who lived at that time in the city of Diyarbakır, would visit the family from time to time and give them cassettes to play that would teach them about the history of the Kurds and the Kurdish culture. This cousin would caution Deniz and the other siblings to be very careful when listening to these tapes. "Listen to them" he cautioned. "Hide them well. Don't ever let the soldiers see them, or they will set your house on fire." (p. 47)

Because Deniz was only a child at that time, he was unable to grasp why they had to be extra careful when listening to a tape that told stories about the history and the culture of the Kurds. Nevertheless, these verbal warnings that he received from his parents and his cousin—and the beatings applied by the agents of Turkey—slowly created an "us-versus-them" paradigm in his mind. Thus, cognitive individual experiences of Deniz—his knowledge and thoughts—slowly shaped the way he should think about the Turks. As Deniz noted in his life history:

> Since I was young, I couldn't understand very well what it all meant. The only concept which I think I understood, was that the Turkish soldiers didn't like anything Kurdish. (p. 47)
>
> I was young and the truth was new for me, so I was very curious about what I was learning. (p. 47)
>
> …we were very careful to hide the tapes. When the soldiers performed raids, they would sometimes find these tapes, and then beat everyone in the entire household, breaking all the tapes. (p. 47)

As the years passed, Deniz experienced an enabling environment for radicalization, which was essentially characterized by a widely shared sense of grievances and injustice among the Kurdish villagers.

His eldest brother secretly dropped out of primary school because of the abuse that he suffered while attending. There were two main reasons for this mistreatment. First, even though he was a Kurd and only spoke Kurdish, the education was only provided in Turkish. Due to the mandatory use of Turkish language at the schools, thousands of Kurds in fact had little choice but to leave and forgo formal education. Worse still, even though the local Kurdish population had to pay an education tax, their children could not benefit from the education service. This situation caused deep resentment among the Kurds. Those Kurds who continued their education experienced considerable stress at the school because they were unable to communicate with the teachers. In Deniz's words:

> …my brother complained that he didn't understand the language spoken there, saying, "I don't understand any Turkish. I speak Kurdish at home, at work, and in the marketplace through the evenings. I understand nothing in that school." (p. 47)

Second, the teachers, who were appointed by Turkish officials in Ankara, were cruel in their attitudes toward the Kurdish children who were unable to speak Turkish.

> They beat the children in the school. They make us stand on one foot for minutes at a time, and they rap us on our knuckles until I can't even feel my fingers. (p. 47)

In fact, the harshness of the Turkish teachers encouraged many of the Kurdish youth to drop out of school—often without their families' knowledge. They would wander around in the countryside until the school was finished for the day. The Kurdish families learned about this fact only when they received the school report at the end of the year.

As a direct result of this mistreatment, neither Deniz nor any of his siblings finished even their primary school education when they lived in the village. Listening to the injustices applied to his eldest brothers, Deniz had no desire to start a formal training at the school.

> I never went to school. I never liked school. It had no charm for me, and I had been affected by my brothers' experiences as well. (p. 47)

Worse still, many families were pessimistic about the future of the Kurds because of the longstanding historical injustices and concrete grievances endured by the Kurdish people over the course of the previous century. Deniz's father had witnessed some of these incidents with the Turks, and he had reached the conclusion that the Kurds had no prospects for a good future. Their identity was so suppressed that he did not even object to Deniz's rejection of education, arguing that, "We are Kurds, and would never be rewarded by the unyielding state, no matter how hard we might study in school." (p. 48)

The life history of Deniz also indicates that the excessive repression applied by Turkish state authorities contributed to a climate of mutual distrust among the Kurds and Turks, which caused Kurdish antagonism to grow:

> Every two days, those soldiers would gather up all the males in the village, into the village square, except for the very young boys. We had no idea what they were planning. Even as children, the one thing we understood clearly, was that whenever soldiers arrived, they brought beatings along with them. First, they would force all the men they had gathered into the square, to lie down on the ground. Then they would beat them with rifle butts or their boots, smashing their heads until they lost consciousness. The women and the children weren't subjected to such treatment, but they were forced to watch this cruelty, screaming out at what they witnessed. No matter what happened, no one was allowed to leave the scene until the Turkish military commander allowed them to leave. (p. 49)
> …the beatings were extreme. True beatings! (p. 50)

As a child, Deniz was forced to watch while his father and the other adult males in the village were beaten by the Turkish soldiers. Without doubt, these excessive measures applied by the Turkish military fueled the feelings of rejection among the Kurds, including Deniz, and over time turned some of them into bitter enemies of the Turkish society to which they no longer experienced any meaningful form of bond.

> By that time, I had not personally been beaten by the Turkish soldiers. But the soldiers' treatment of the other members of our village was more than enough to spark my desire for revenge, and this spark grew rapidly. (p. 51)

Over time, these beatings became a routine that was carried out once every two nights. The men in the village became so sick of the beatings that they started to develop tactics to evade the oppression.

> Since the soldiers' arrival was always unpredictable, and usually at night while everyone was asleep, the men in the village had no time to hide. Eventually, the male elders became so fed up with beatings that they would sleep in the barns, hidden inside the straw, to avoid the assaults. (p. 50)

Even though Deniz was not directly subjected to this physical abuse, these practices were experienced by his elder brothers and parents. The subsequent feelings of injustice, exclusion, and humiliation have been powerful forces in Deniz's mind and shaped his attitudes toward the Turks. Thus, his radicalization process was advanced by how he framed as unjust the unsatisfying events and grievances that occurred early in the life of his brothers.

Over time, Deniz became more and more prone to radicalization—and the possibility of becoming a terrorist—as he grew increasingly resentful of the injustice practices of the agents of the Turkish state. The feelings of discontent and perceived adversity formed the foundation for stepping onto the path to extremism. Eventually, he developed the "us-versus-them" paradigm.

> The language they spoke in the school wasn't the same language we spoke at home or in the village. That language was only spoken by soldiers or teachers, who treated people badly. Both groups were cruel. (p. 47)

Initially, the Kurdish villagers did not even know why they were being subjected to such harsh and cruel treatments at the hands of the Turks. They were being arrested, subjected to torture, and then released on a regular basis. Many of them experienced stress and mental confusion in response to these practices.

> It was a confusing situation in the village, and although our people hadn't done anything wrong, we hid to avoid these attacks. (p. 50)
>
> Although they hadn't committed any crime, they ran away simply to avoid getting beaten. Their wives and children got left behind. (p. 50)

Over time, the villagers figured out that there was a group called "Apocular" and the Turkish soldiers were raiding their village to punish the sympathizers of this group.

> When Turkish soldiers arrived in the village, they would ask, "Have you seen the Apo Sympathizers? Have you fed any of those men? Have they passed by the village?" At that time, we didn't know what the term even meant. We first learned of the existence of Apo, and his group of Kurdish Freedom Fighters, from the Turkish soldiers trying to eradicate them. (p. 50)

So, in a way, the oppression carried out by the Turks not only informed the Kurdish villagers about the existence of the PKK but also pushed them toward this organization who fought for them. As the Kurds—who were not sympathizers or part of this subversive activity—were targeted by the state and labeled as the enemy, they reasoned that they might as well support the Kurdish movement if they were going to face repression in any case. Thus, many repressed and tortured people later joined to the PKK or other groups who opposed the regime in Turkey.

> We had no concept of a Kurdistan, or even that we were Kurdish, and certainly no idea about any "Apo Sympathizers," until the soldiers came to our village and told us. (p. 51)
>
> So by beating all the men in the village over and over, simply on the suspicion of sympathizing with this "Apo," the Turkish soldiers, themselves, educated us about this group that stood in defense of villagers like ourselves. (p. 51)
>
> Because of their inhumane and unjustified attacks, the Turkish military had spontaneously caused neutral villagers, such as ourselves, actively to seek to find and join this group of rebels, whose name we had never heard, except from Turkish soldiers. (p. 51)

Not surprisingly, therefore, as a child of a father who was constantly beaten by Turkish security forces, Deniz grew up to oppose and mistrust his perceived oppressor, the Turks, violently. At the cognitive level, what Deniz knew and believed about the Turks affected how he perceived them.

> These were really bad days. Being forced to watch my father, my elder brothers, and the other respected men of the village getting severely beaten, broke my heart as well as the hearts of all the other boys in the village. But, being just a few, and young, there was nothing we could do. We could only stay silent or weep in despair. If there were a hundred people in the village, there were two thousand soldiers. We were helpless. And that helpless suffering planted the seeds of hatred in our hearts. We had begun to learn to hate. We hated not only the soldiers, but our hate grew to include the Turkish people, and even the Turkish language. (p. 51)

Accordingly, the personal experiences and the major life events that occurred during Deniz's childhood created a fertile ground for his radicalization. That is, the oppression provoked political violence (Fanon, 1965; Schmid, 1983). Deniz often cited as a prime motive for the joining the PKK the injustice of their treatment by a Turkish government that wished to rob them of identity, dignity, security, and freedom.

Further, the existence of shadowy forces used by the Turkish security forces against the Kurds was another factor that contributed to Deniz's radicalization. Hezbollah (different from the worldwide known Lebanon Shia group) is an ethnic Islamic movement that mostly fought against the leftist-based PKK in Turkey between 1980s and mid-1990s. Although the Turkish Hezbollah did not directly attack the secular Turkish state, many members and sympathizers of the PKK were killed by this conservative religious group (McDowall, 2000, p. 434). The Kurds soon figured out that the Turkish security forces were using Hezbollah against the nationalist Kurds, mainly the PKK members. On any given day during the 1990s, it was common for Hezbollah to kill a PKK member or a sympathizer in broad daylight (McKiernan, 2006). Nevertheless, no suspects were arrested for the commission of these crimes, even though perpetrators were known Hezbollah members.

This practice of turning a blind eye to those atrocities committed by Hezbollah further antagonized the feelings of Kurds against the Turkish security forces.

> During this period, there were so many "unsolved" murders that everyone knew it was Hezbollah, if the manner of death were a cleaver or a beheading. (p. 58)
>
> …while the Patriotic Youth were subject to such oppression and torture, the members of Hezbollah could go around freely carrying anything they liked—knives, cleavers, or guns. The police did nothing to Hezbollah members, even if they were found with these weapons. (p. 57)

During that time, Hezbollah had killed many of our friends. They practiced many kinds of nastiness then, from unidentified murders and kidnapping to literal back-stabbing. The fact that Hezbollah committed those murders with the support of the state was yet another factor that pushed us into the arms of the PKK. We had started to think that we could cope with these horrors, only if we joined the PKK. (p. 57)

In summary, it is clear that Deniz's radicalization was enabled by an environment that was characterized by a deep sense of injustice tied to the oppression, exclusion, cruelty, and humiliation that the Kurdish people suffered at the hands of the Turkish security forces. These sentiments played a significant role in shaping Deniz's attitudes toward the Turkish state. As a direct result of these sentiments, he became more and more prone to radicalization and to becoming a "freedom fighter."

Personality Traits. It is important to note that the subject of this life story, Deniz, was neither an offender with a varied criminal background nor drawn from the social or economic margins of Kurdish society. Instead, he was a person with strong ethical values. For the most part, his family background was not problematic. Deniz did not come from a broken family and did not suffer parental abuse or the use of violence as a means of discipline and communication within the family. During the interview he noted about his family:

My father has always been so sensitive. He never physically abused any of his children, through his entire life. In the culture of our family, children should never be beaten; neither girls nor boys. Discipline in the family was maintained through discussion. Our elders would always caution us, saying "Do this like that, or don't do that. That's bad, or, don't let anyone talk poorly about us. Don't tarnish the name of the family!"

Additionally, Deniz's parents were highly strict on ethical values. They always cautioned their children specifically about two moral values; (1) always telling the truth no matter what the consequences would be, and (2) not stealing from the others. His parents' teachings of ethical values clearly shaped Deniz's character. Even when he experienced serious events that had the potential to cause him trouble and bring punishment, Deniz refused to lie to disguise his responsibility.

My family was very sensitive about lies and theft. (p. 46)

Throughout my childhood, I had never lied. I had always been honest. Even if I made a mistake, I always confessed it. (p. 48)

Aside from being frank and straightforward all the time, Deniz was highly disturbed when others around him lied. Whenever such an incident occurred, he would openly warn the person by publicly criticizing him or her.

Since I never lied, I could not stand hearing others telling lies. Once, when my elder brother was telling a huge lie, I was so upset by it that I told my father everything that had really happened. (p. 49)

Other than these personal qualities, Deniz's childhood has no sign of him being action-oriented or manifesting a proclivity for aggression of violence. He was a person who kept himself away from problematic situations. He knew how to act properly and behave amongst other people. Even when he was confronted with tense and problematic situations, he would act calmly.

> I never caused any neighbors to talk badly about me—in any of the places we lived. I never had a fight with my siblings, or with the neighbors' children. I always kept myself away from such problematic situations. When someone swore at me or humiliated me, I would never retaliate at that time. I would leave the scene and look for something to occupy my mind, and although I was furious, I would hold my tongue, bottle my anger and try to keep command of myself. I would make peace, leaving no ill-will behind. (p. 48).

Moreover, Deniz did not suffer from any psychological problems. On the contrary, he was smart and quick to grasp the things occurring around him. He knew how to learn from the past mistakes. Even though he had no actual school experience, he learned how to read and write by himself.

It is important to note that feuds between rival groups were common among the Kurdish communities during the 1970s and 1980s. In fact, Deniz's tribe was a part of feud that took many lives on both sides of the fight. In fact, his family had to abandon their village when Deniz was only six years old due to fear of retaliation from the other side.

> …the other side attacked my family and killed three people. Then we attacked, and killed seven of them. Every day, the fighting was ferocious, and gunfire was so loud and frequent, that we couldn't even leave the house. (p. 51)
>
> As a result of this feud, many people from the opposing families were killed. Therefore, on the night of the incident, we fled the village. We left behind every animal, and all of our belongings. We ran to a different village, very far away, and settled there for our safety. (p. 51)

As a result of these fights between the families, violence had become an everyday element in handling conflicts in Deniz's community. During these continuous battles among the two tribes, Deniz became familiar with the use of guns, fights, and the killing of other people.

> Over time, my personality began to be altered by the repetition of incidents such as this. Although I did not yet participate in the violence myself, the beatings, blood, and gun battles had become an ordinary part of my environment. Gunshots no longer caused me panic. Everyone in the village used guns. It became so common, that it no longer seemed to be a crime, but just a fact of life. So, then, even if a gunshot were heard right in the center of the town square, nobody would investigate. (p. 51)

Not only did he come to see such acts (the use of guns and applying violence to resolve conflicts) as normal but he also learned the value of courage through the incidents that occurred during those battles.

> During one battle, a wounded neighbor was carried into our place. A group of women gathered and began to clean his wound. When they extracted a bullet from his chest, they realized he had been shot in the back, and so must have been running away. The women instantly stopped taking

care of him. One of them even said, "This coward has sold out his friends, he was shot while leaving them, let's just let him die." I remember this very, very well. (p. 51)

The fact that the women in the village had refused to treat that wounded neighbor, once they decided he was a coward, inspired Deniz to act bravely in every situation in the future—including in situations that might cost him his life. Thus, courage became one of the most important virtues in the eyes of Deniz.

Due to the abundance of these deadly encounters among the Kurdish tribes, the use of firearms was common not only among the males but also among the females of the Kurdish community of that time. Deniz also stated that he loved to learn how to use guns. He found it exciting and thrilling to use such weapons:

I was always shocked and amazed at the weapons I saw on him during those short visits! The fugitives sometimes had weapons that we didn't even have in the village. I loved weapons, and I envied the people who used them. In my father's absence, my uncle had taught me how to use an AK-47. I had learned everything about it; how it worked, how many bullets could be loaded into it, and how it was cleaned. Everything. (p. 52)

In summary, Deniz did not suffer from any psychological, mental, or personality disorders that would predispose him towards the use of violence. On the contrary, he had high moral values and empathy for the others around him. Not only was he a strong person with high personal qualities such as being straightforward, courageous, and rational, but also he was a valued member of his family and community. He thus chose to become a "freedom fighter" not due to an underlying pathology but because he possessed the positive traits of moral conviction, attachment to others, and physical courage, including a willingness to use firearms if necessary.

Opportunity Structures to Recruit. Even though Deniz's family members were able to protect themselves from retaliation by relocating to another village, the family could not provide sufficient livelihood because they had left all their belongings in the first village. As a result, the family had to move to the city of Batman to have access to more job opportunities that would help them recover financially.

Deniz had difficulty adapting to city life initially. He literally had no social life for the first couple of years. He would go to work early in the morning and only return to home late at night.

Our social life was nonexistent. Even family members had no time to visit each other, since it was such tiresome work. We would hit the pillow as soon as we had finished dinner. Then, the next morning, we would arise early, have a quick breakfast, and set off back to work. (p. 54)

One inadvertent consequence of moving to the city was that Deniz encountered increased opportunities to become familiar with the group he had only heard about until then, the PKK.

The only thing I liked about the urban period was that, as my awareness of this group who protected us Kurds grew, living in the city gave me opportunities to meet some sympathizers of this group in person. Thanks to demonstrations held in the city, and the television and radio programs broadcasting the speeches given in the tea houses, I had the chance to be better acquainted with the PKK. (p. 55)

Various ideological activists played leading roles in the radicalization of Deniz in the city life. Thus, Deniz began to join the mass protests and meetings organized by Kurdish activists in Batman. The speeches delivered by some of the influential Kurdish politicians of that time—including Leyla Zana and Nizamettin Tonguç—played a significant role in his radicalization.

Social identification with these groups in the city life inarguably influenced Deniz's decision to join the organization. Seeing that these politicians were resourceful, educated, and well-integrated—and even considered as role models in the context of the Kurdish community—Deniz began to identify with the organization. Through participation of these meetings and protests, he reinforced his previous experiences of the sense of injustice.

From these social events held in the city, Deniz surmised that the Kurds were systematically deprived of their rights to equal opportunity, that they were obstructed from expressing their cultural identities, that they were excluded from political participation through legitimate channels, and that they were even forbidden to use their language.

> I remember, in those city days, the demonstrations held before the 1991 elections. Big Kurdish names, such as Leyla Zana and Nizamettin Tonguç, would gather the masses and deliver power-fully influential speeches. People from every neighborhood and district would join these demonstrations and listen very carefully to what was being said. We came to understand from the speeches that there was an ethnic minority population in Turkey called the Kurdish, and that we, ourselves, were members of this population. We learned that this minority population had been consistently oppressed. Only Turks had had the right to speak on the record at the highest levels of Turkish Parliament. These speeches declared that we Kurds also needed access to the parliament, and from now on, we wanted to be there, to be heard, and to be given the right to affect decisions that influenced our own region. (p. 54)

Thus, even though Deniz was spending most of his time working long hours at the factory, he attended these gatherings at every opportunity available to him. Deniz indicated that the propaganda delivered by these politicians played a key role in his radicalization process. Indeed, the incidents he had experienced previously in the village seemed to lend credence to the claims made by the Kurdish politicians during demonstrations.

> The way the teacher had beaten up my elder brothers because they didn't speak Turkish; the oppression and torture against our male villagers, after the military coup, and even in the present day. (p. 54)

In Deniz's eyes, these politicians were charismatic and motivated by idealism and a strong sense of justice, responding to the real suffering of others. They shaped his thinking:

> Soon, I was going to the demonstrations whenever I had an opportunity. I was very young, so I was easily influenced by what was said. (p. 54)

These speeches offered doctrinal arguments that served to legitimize extremist positions for Deniz. They disseminated propaganda supported by real grievances. These Kurdish ideological leaders were thus able to transform the widespread grievances of the Kurds into an agenda for violent struggle.

These politicians specifically highlighted the fact that Turks and Kurds were two different groups, and, as a group, the Kurds had been unsuccessful in obtaining a desired place in the society because of the discriminatory policies applied by the Turks. This situation of goal blockage had created frustration for many of the Kurds. There was, they claimed, only one option: it was crucial for every Kurdish youth to join the PKK, given the current authoritarian Turkish regime and the absence of alternative methods of political participation.

> Every individual who gave us beatings, who oppressed us, who tortured us—from police offic-ers to teachers to soldiers—all spoke Turkish. Suddenly, we clearly understood the differences between us. Turks were not Kurdish, and they did not like us. We became more aware of our isolation. We, as the Kurdish populace, had been alienated, and I began to absorb the meaning of my identity as a Kurd. (p. 54)

In short, these politicians were able to mobilize hundreds of young Kurds to join the PKK by mixing together emotional and rational considerations and by highlighting that there was only one solution to ending the Kurdish subjugation—participation in an organization that offered the only effective means and thus hope of Kurdish liberation.

In addition to these ideological activists, Deniz's cousin, who had a university education, played a large role in his and his friends' decision to join the PKK. Deniz showed great respect to his cousin because it was extremely rare for a Kurdish youth to have a university education under the circum-stances of that time. According to Deniz, his cousin was a charismatic person motivated by idealism and a strong sense of justice.

> He was once thrown into jail because he joined a demonstration. He was placed in Diyarbakır Penitentiary and was constantly tortured while there. All his teeth were removed with a pair of pliers! He didn't have a single tooth left inside his mouth. Yet no amount of torture had made him change his beliefs. One day he gave my friends and me a very effective speech: "We are Kurdish, and we own our Kurdish lands, so why don't we have someone from our people representing us in the decision making levels of state affairs? Why can't those officials who are obliged to serve us Kurds actually speak any Kurdish themselves? Why do they always treat us so poorly? Why can five or six soldiers gather all our villagers and beat up all the men in front of their wives and children?" (p. 56)

Moving to the city, Deniz also acquired more access to broadcast news outlets. The systematic anti-Kurd slandering campaign presented by these sources deepened his antagonism toward the Turks. Without exception, the news related to the Kurds was humiliating and provocative in nature, and incited the need for revenge or action.

> If a few of our people disappeared in a neighborhood, it would hit the news with a deliberate spin against us. "Those who have gone up to the mountains are either the Armenians' unacknowl-edged children or bandits. They are irredeemable. They are traitors." (p. 56–57)

Moreover, through his participation in demonstrations, Deniz met and developed close relation-ships with new friends who shared similar opinions and beliefs. Soon, he felt a part of this small group of like-minded individuals. The similarity of ideas and the friendship bonds bred further a connection among the group members, which deepened as they experienced a series of events. They engaged in various activities, including field trips to learn more about the history of the Kurds and the solutions to overcome the current state of oppression and discrimination. By talking to each other and meeting with PKK ideologues at nearby locations, these friends reinforced each other by transmitting radical ideas and attitudes. Accordingly, the social network ties of Deniz fostered his radicalization as he increasingly adopted the attitudes and behaviors of other in the network.

> I soon developed a very close circle of friends in Batman; about six or seven people, and we were spending most of our time together. We were all smoking back then, but never used alcohol or drugs, and never committed even petty crimes, like theft. (p. 54)
>
> During this time, we began to gather into groups and listen for hours to Kurdish-language tapes. But all of this had to be in secret, because speaking Kurdish or even listening to something in Kurdish was forbidden. (p. 54)

Over time, in-group socialization occurred. The feelings of injustice and aggression were displaced onto a causal agent, the Turks. The Turkish security forces were vilified and began to be regarded as the enemy. As the anger towards the Turks built, Deniz and his friends became increasingly sympathetic towards extremist ideology.

In the meantime, a new phenomenon began to occur frequently in the neighborhood in which Deniz lived. The youths with whom Deniz played in the streets would disappear suddenly, and no one would hear from them again. Deniz and his friends later learned that these young Kurdish boys and girls were leaving their homes to serve in the PKK as guerillas in the mountains and countryside. Deniz and his friends were impressed as they saw how those young Kurds sacrificed the comfort of their homes and the best years of their life to serve their people's cause. Moreover, leaving home to join the fight was regarded as an essential element of being a good Kurd by the community.

> Meanwhile, a new phenomenon had begun. The neighborhood friends with whom we always met and played suddenly started to disappear, and we never saw them again. Gradually we understood that they had all joined the PKK. So, we then came to see the disappearance of our youth as ordinary. For most families, it became a point of pride in the fact that their children had joined the PKK. Sometimes a single person, or at times, a few people would disappear all at once. This impressed us a great deal, as we grew older. (p. 55)

Deniz and his close friends started to talk about this new phenomenon of disappearance, and they started to discuss the idea of making the same sacrifice for the sake of their community. Without informing their parents, they began to travel to nearby locations where participation in the PKK was high in the hope of gaining more information about why and how people were going up to the mountains.

> We started talking about these issues within our circle of friends, and began thinking and discussing together what we could do for the cause of helping secure the freedom of our Kurdish people. We knew that PKK participation was high in the regions of Silvan and Hasankeyf. We began exploring these regions, in our time off from work, in order to get more information about the PKK. We talked to people there, and tried to understand why they left daily life in favor of heading up into the mountains. (p. 55)

Through these field trips, they also acquired the contact information of local intermediaries who could help them to join the organization.

> Once our decision was made, I got in touch with the people who were going to take us to the mountains. I knew someone from another neighborhood who made these sorts of arrangements. (p. 58)

Because Deniz grew up in a village and spent most of his time as a shepherd grazing the animals over the mountains, his friends had confidence that he could enable them to reach the mountains. Deniz not only was familiar but also experienced with the hardships of life in the mountains. He knew requisite survival techniques. Thus, his past experience with countryside life actually further encouraged his friends' desire to join the movement.

> Though we didn't have a leader, I knew better than my friends what was involved. Not only did I know the intermediaries who would take us to the mountains, but also I had once lived in the villages. Since I had been a shepherd from when I was little, I knew the conditions in the mountains very well. The other members of the group had all grown up in the city, and had always enjoyed a comfortable environment. They knew nothing about roughing it, or had no idea where to take shelter; what to eat, or where to find clean water in the mountains. The fact that I was experienced gave my friends confidence. (p. 58)

Notably, even though Deniz's parents were familiar with and sympathetic to the struggle given by the PKK at that time, they never approved or encouraged their children to join the movement. Moreover, as the disappearance of youngsters became more frequent, Deniz's mother increased her warnings to her children, cautioning them not to leave the family to join the organization.

> She would say to us, "Now this family's son or daughter has gone missing. They have probably gone up into the mountains. I agree that there must be a separate Kurdish state, a new Kurdistan, and the oppression should decrease against us Kurds. But, rather than joining a rebellion, it is more important that we should stay together as a family. So, my sons, please do not ever go up to the mountains. Don't ever join the organization." (p. 55)

Nevertheless, for Deniz, belonging to a group and being accepted by peers overruled most other considerations, including the frequent warnings of his mother. By socializing with his friends, Deniz gradually adopted the idea of joining the PKK. He and his associates made the transformation from being PKK sympathizers to active supporters, ready the join the organization.

> My mother's constant warnings did not work on me. Within our friends' circle, we had already decided to go up to the mountains and join the organization. (p. 55)

In summary, as Cloward (1959; see also Cullen, 1984) has noted, criminal or deviant roles cannot be undertaken unless actors have access to the opportunity to learn the requisite values and skills and have access to the means to discharge the role. This is the case regardless of whether a person wishes to become a jack-roller (Shaw, 1930), professional thief (Sutherland, 1937), gang member (Cloward & Ohlin, 1960), or PKK "freedom fighter." In this regard, by moving to the city, Deniz was able to become a terrorist because he could learn the ideology, have the network support, and be sufficiently close to the "mountains" to join the PKK and be a terrorist.

A Sense of Duty. Although Deniz did not have a regular job, he was not a socially alienated individual who left society for this reason. He did not join the PKK because of the so-called economic opportunities provided by the organization or out of boredom and a desire to have an action-oriented adventure. He was not drawn into terrorism because he found it thrilling or because he was seduced by its excitement. He did not have fantasies about the heroism associated with being involved in the guerilla struggle. In fact, it was not a life that he wanted to pursue.

On the contrary, Deniz and his friends were pushed toward terrorism by ideological and related beliefs. He joined the PKK in pursuit of a cause he regarded as just. He had been forced to watch helplessly as his father and other adult men of the village were severely beaten. He had to see the Kurds regarded as second-class citizens of Turkey—their identity as Kurds rejected and their basic human rights denied by the Turkish state. These experiences upset him and the other young Kurdish boys in their village. As a result, Deniz and his associates felt obliged to participate in the organization because they would be disloyal to their Kurdish community if they did not do so.

> We all strongly believed that we had to do something for our oppressed people. We were all the right age, each between 17 and 19 years old. (p. 58)
>
> Our economic situation was bad. Our family was leading a poor life, but no one came to us to make any promises. We weren't offered money or authority in return for joining the organization. This is what I want the state and then the Turkish people to understand. What do they think someone would prefer; to leave the compassion of their parents and family, and all the comforts of home, in favor of a challenging life in difficult conditions? For people to choose this kind of life voluntarily, there must definitely be a strong reason behind it. I still don't understand how the people living in the other regions in Turkey could not grasp this. (p. 58–59)

The acts of the security forces had provoked these feelings of humiliation and revenge and had served to forge a bond between Deniz and the ideological preachers, catalyzing his acceptance of the radical narrative and its associated values. After a while, not only Deniz but also the other young Kurds began develop a sense that they had an ethical responsibility to defend the Kurdish nation against the suppressive regimes.

> When we looked around, we realized that those who were oppressed, beaten, and killed were always Kurdish. Kurds were the ones killed with chemical gases by Saddam in Iraq. Kurds were the ones tortured by soldiers in Turkey. Kurds were the ones who were suppressed by the regime in Iran. Kurds were the minority who lived in Syria, but did not even have their own ID cards—their own ethnic identity. (p. 56)

These statements clearly indicate that Deniz was attracted to the fight carried out by the organization because of the legitimate grievances disregarded by the Turkish state. His grievances were gradually transformed into hatred of the Turkish security forces, and this hatred was regarded as a legitimate justification for revenge through violence. That is, Deniz ultimately decided to engage in terrorism because he experienced a cognitive transformation in which a deep sense of honor and duty motivated his joining the PKK.

Indeed Deniz and the other Kurds who joined the organization regarded themselves as the "givers" of their community—they had more concern for their nation's well-being. These Kurdish youngsters believed that they had an obligation to fight on behalf of the Kurdish people's future—even though participating in the war against Turkey would likely cost them their lives.

> The indifference of the state towards the people of our region; our torture; the oppression and torture in the neighboring countries against Kurds—collectively created our natural desire for revenge. (p. 57)
>
> And that helpless suffering planted the seeds of hatred in our hearts. We had begun to learn to hate. We hated not only the soldiers, but our hate grew to include the Turkish people, and even the Turkish language. (p. 51)
>
> We agreed, saying, "Since the Turkish Government does not recognize our national identity, and since it either ignores us or oppresses us, then why shouldn't we join this organization which fights for us?" (p. 57)
>
> So, all of us got very clear on one point. We were going to get revenge for what the soldiers had done. And we were going to get it by joining with these Apo sympathizers who were such a threat that the Turkish soldiers felt compelled to hunt them down everywhere. (p. 51)

Therefore, many Kurdish youths joined the PKK not because of their violent propensity or to fulfill some social or psychological needs such as excitement or identity. Rather, they become terrorists because of the injustices and violence they were subjected to at the hands of Turkish security forces and the subsequent sense that they had an obligation to defend their people through armed insurrection.

Persistence: Being a Terrorist

This section will explore the factors that led Deniz to persist in his role as a "freedom fighter" in the PKK for approximately 20 years. The factors that led Deniz and potentially other PKK recruits to stay in the organization despite all the hardships of guerilla life can be grouped under six main categories: (1) a strong sense of purpose, (2) a belief that death was inevitable, (3) personal traits, (4) support from his "comrades", (5) military success, and (6) advancement in the PKK organization.

A Strong Sense of Purpose. Deniz believed that he was part of a legitimate fight for freedom that would be pursued according to high ethical standards. Accordingly, he viewed himself not as a murderer but as a soldier in a war to free his people. Thus, having a strong sense of purpose was a fundamental component of Deniz's life. When he woke up every day in the guerilla camps, he never wondered what he was going to do with himself. Rather, he took control of his own life and engaged with a meaningful goal: destroying the security forces to make the enemy sit at the negotiation table. Accordingly, he channeled his mental activities towards achieving this altruistic purpose—that of sacrificing his own life for the future generations of the Kurds.

> I have a clear conscience about my missions in the organization. I am aware of what I did and why I did it. All my fight was for the righteous struggle of the Kurdish cause. (p. 382)

On several occasions, Deniz indicated that the root cause of the guerillas' fight against the Turkish government arose from two main factors: the denial of the Kurdish identity by the fascist statement in the Turkish constitution, and the legal restriction that prohibited the use of Kurdish language. He expressed how Kurdish people were unable to communicate with the state when they needed to see a doctor, when they had a judicial problem, or when they were in need of other kinds of public services. He stated how Kurdish children were indirectly denied access to education because they were unable to speak Turkish. He cited how the names of the Kurdish towns were replaced, one by one, by Turkish names as a policy of cultural repression. By citing these legitimate grievances, Deniz fought for the organization for approximately two decades.

> We only wanted to protect our basic rights. We did not ask to be provided with any extra rights that would compromise those of Turks—but simply to be able to freely speak in our own language and to have our separate identity recognized. I wanted this stupid denial thing to end. (p. 384)
>
> At the time I was incarcerated, in 2010, it was legally forbidden to speak Kurdish in public institutions. My mother would come to the prison to visit me, and we could only communicate through hand gestures behind the glass. She could not say anything, because she did not know Turkish. The prison guards would mute the microphone if my mother accidently spoke something in Kurdish. In all of those visits, we would mostly spend the time looking at one another. (p. 384)
>
> Look! We are now in 2015. There has been no improvement of the circumstances. When my mother goes to the hospital, in an emergency, she is unable to explain anything, because she is unable to communicate with the doctor or the nurses. She must have one of my siblings accompany her whenever she visits a public institution, including the hospital, because she is unable to describe her discomfort to them. That is what many other Kurds in Turkey daily experience in their lives. Would it really be too difficult for the Turks to assign doctors, police officers, teachers, and other public servants who can speak Kurdish to the eastern cities where the majority of the population is Kurd? Is it really a matter of honor for the Turks? The society in this region is unable to associate itself with the state, because they do not speak the same language, nor do they understand Turkish. (p. 384)

Deniz truly believed in the legitimacy of his cause and continued to live his life accordingly. Despite the fact that he deserted the organization in 2010, on several occasions, he reiterated that he would continue to fight for these rights—if he were released from prison at some point in the future—until they are granted to the Kurds of Turkey.

> I am telling you—even if I am released at the age of 70, I will again fight for the right to speak in my mother tongue. (p. 384)

Beyond believing that the Kurdish cause was righteous, Deniz also felt that his "freedom fighting," was guided by high ethical standards. As he indicated in his life history, neither the Kurdish politicians who indoctrinated young Kurds in town centers nor the PKK ideologues who trained guerillas at the training camps used an ideological curriculum that aimed at the dehumanization of the Turks as a whole.

The organization leadership had very firm standing orders prohibiting missions against anyone but the security forces. (p. 98)

The problem for the organization was the system, not the people. In other words, the PKK's only issue was with the political authorities who didn't recognize the democratic rights of the Kurdish people. So, our training included absolutely nothing about seeing the civilian Turks as enemies. (p. 64)

Accordingly, Deniz and other recruits were continuously cautioned to kill or attack only specific targets, which was often the security forces. The PKK never allowed its members to carry out attacks against the Turkish civilians in the city centers. Therefore, even though de-humanization of "the enemy" as a whole has been the constant feature of the indoctrination process of almost all terrorist groups in the world, it was not the case for the PKK.

Instead, Deniz—and potentially other guerillas—had a clear sense of purpose in his mind: fighting ethically for the rights of Kurdish individuals. In fact, many incidents noted in his life history suggested the Kurdish guerillas rarely acted militarily in an opportunistic way even though doing so would bring them huge advantage over the enemy. For example, Deniz and his team did not even take advantage of the opportunities that arose when the enemy suffered natural catastrophes. Thus, on August 17, 1999, an earthquake killed approximately 20,000 people in Turkey. As noted in Deniz's account, the PKK announced that it was ready to declare a ceasefire and help in the search and rescue activities as soon as the news about the earthquake hit the media. Unfortunately, the Turkish officials rejected this offer. Notably, in the midst of the ensuing chaos from the earthquake, the PKK could easily have attacked from the southeastern borders of the country and have captured a sizeable territory.

I mentioned before that the organization never considered the civilian Turkish public as enemies. In fact, helping each other after the earthquake would have been a great opportunity, for both the organization and the Turks, to put away their long-standing hatred toward one another. We were even ready to transfer thousands of our people to take part in search and rescue activities. (p. 216)

In another incident, Deniz and his guerilla friends were informed by the villagers that a Turkish military outpost had been hit by an avalanche and the entire unit—approximately 40 Turkish soldiers—had been buried under the snow and killed. The villagers offered to go the military outpost and collect all weapons and ammunition as war booty. Nevertheless, the guerillas harshly objected to this offer by arguing that:

A natural disaster happened, and it would be against the morals of the organization to profit from the spoils in such a situation. (p. 63)

Finally, Deniz noted on various occasions how foreign governments' officials approached the PKK to use its force as leverage against Turkey. For example, whenever Ankara started peace negotiations with the PKK, Iranian officials would contact the organization's headquarters and offer incentives in return for the continuance of war against Turkey. Or, as depicted in the life history, foreign involvement was clearly evident in the 2001 economic crash that shook Turkey. As Ankara was crippled with chaos and facing the grave danger of a social outbreak, many nations—including Iraq, Iran, and Syria—had contacted PKK headquarters and encouraged them to deal the deathblow by declaring its independence. The seniors of the PKK regarded these kinds of acts as treacherous.

> …the organization was wholeheartedly pursuing peace…when Iran was offering excessive incentives to continue fighting Turkey. "If you begin fighting against the Turks again, we will supply all your ammunitions and weapons free of charge! You will no longer have to worry yourselves over finding money for access to weapons!" (p. 236)
>
> Shortly after the 2001 economic crash in Turkey, many foreign agents contacted the organization, stating, "Do not let this opportunity pass by you by! Now is the right time to separate from Turkey and declare your independence!" Those agents, in fact, had also reached out to the ground guerillas. Affected by those agents' support, many guerillas were insisting they deal a deathblow to the Turks in 2001. Back then, the senior commanders at headquarters settled the ground guerillas' discussions by telling them, "This is a plot imposed upon us by some foreign powers, for their own benefits. We should never, ever achieve our goals in a dastardly way!" (p. 317)

In short, Deniz was able to persist as a terrorist because he was motivated by a strong sense of purpose that he was carrying out a legitimate fight to free the Kurdish people according to strong ethical principles. He was thus engaged in a moral crusade that supplied motivation for him to carry on the fight over the course of nearly two decades.

> This is what I want the state and then the Turkish people to understand. What do they think someone would prefer; to leave the compassion of their parents and family, and all the comforts of home, in favor of a challenging life in difficult conditions? For people to choose this kind of life voluntarily, there must definitely be a strong reason behind it. I still don't understand how the people living in the other regions in Turkey could not grasp this. (p. 59)

A Belief That Death Was Inevitable. Deniz was well aware of the fact that death was, for most "freedom fighters," a near inevitable reality. By participating in the organization, he knew that he might be killed at any minute when deployed on a mission. Thus, the decision to remain in the PKK was a fate Deniz had intentionally chosen—and was thus not to be feared.

> As guerillas, we never dreamed of living a long life. We could be martyred any time, and we were very aware of this. Sometimes you would lose a friend who had stood by your side night and day. Therefore, death had become common for us. This outlook motivated us to do anything to fulfill our duties. (p. 102)

When Deniz joined the organization, he never thought about the possibility of ever returning to his old life, getting married, or raising children. He abandoned all these hopes so that he could carry out missions as bold as brass. He was not scared of death. Rather, he was willing to sacrifice himself if it would serve the interests of the Kurds.

> We had left our families in order to fight. Any militant who joined the organization had already abandoned all hope that he would ever go back home. That's why we were brave. We had already

given up everything. This was a big disadvantage for the military and a great advantage for the organization. (p. 78)

I had a close brush with death many times and was seriously wounded at least six or seven times. I never had a guarantee to live one more day when I was in the organization. We were, in fact, aware that we could lose our lives at any moment. (p. 382)

After all the repression, torture, and denial of identity experienced by his Kurdish people, nothing would scare Deniz and his friends. They were no longer afraid of the security forces. What more could the Turkish government do to them? The worst they could do was to kill innocent Kurds and they were already doing that anyway. So, these guerillas who went up to the mountains had nothing to lose. They gave all their free will to the organization. They became willing to carry out any mission they were assigned.

Remember when Apo was arrested by the CIA and then handed over to the Turkish officials in Africa. The guerillas in the camps located in Syria and Iraq had become frenzied as soon as the Turkish Prime Minister Bulent Ecevit declared to the world that Apo had, in fact, been arrested. As noted in the life history, the PKK's senior leaders had a difficult time trying to calm down the foot soldiers. Within hours, thousands of guerillas had submitted their letters volunteering to carry out suicide missions against the Turkish government. When their applications were rejected, some of the guerillas had even set themselves on fire to protest their leaders' decisions.

Many comrades voluntarily submitted applications to be part of these missions. The organization only accepted three hundred applicants out of thousands of applications. These soon-to-be self-sacrifice mission members were all from the higher ranks, and experienced guerillas. (p. 209)

Another sign that death did not scare Deniz was his eagerness to be assigned to a position in the north—in Turkey—even though the risk of losing his life was much higher in that sector because of its proximity to the enemy forces. In fact, Deniz had many opportunities to stay safely in the camps located in Iraq and to live a luxurious life for years to come. He was offered a position to serve in the close protection guard of the leader Apo. He was even offered a position in one of the European capitals to work as the political representative of the organization. Nevertheless, Deniz turned down these offers simply because he wanted to fight in the war zone in defiance of Turkish tyranny. Accordingly, he persisted in his military activities because death—the inevitable outcome for the PKK guerilla—was to be embraced, not feared.

Personal Traits. Deniz had the ability to endure not only the years of physical hardships of guerilla life but also the psychological and emotional consequences of killing enemy forces and of seeing his close friends being killed one after another. As depicted in his life history, the pursuit of a guerilla life was often characterized by total misery. Most of the time, the PKK guerillas had to travel during the darkness of the night so as to avoid being detected and risk being captured or killed. Sometimes, they had to travel in bitter cold weather when visibility was very low due to fog or rain. In the winter, their freedom of movement was severely restricted since walking on the snow left footprints for the security forces. In the summer season, it was challenging to travel on foot due to the extreme heat. When traveling, they could only rest when they could find a secure place. For that, they had to know where the Turkish troops were located, which paths through the mountain were reliable, whether the surrounding area was mined, and so on. Being unaware of the enemy's position or the use of high-tech devices by the enemy made them highly vulnerable.

> …I have said it before, that you can't force someone to stay in those conditions. Combat aside, sometimes people just couldn't handle the difficulty of our daily life and returned back home. Whomever wanted to leave, would just depart. (p. 88)
>
> We had to walk all the way north, under the darkness of night during this cold season. (p. 254)
>
> It was so snowy outside, and, in some places, the snow had piled up to more than 2 meters. It was freezing cold and also snowing non-stop. Normally, it would take only three hours of walking, between our camp in Muş and Dorşin camp, but, that day, we walked from 8:00 a.m. until 4:00 p.m. and could still see our camp field in Muş. In eight hours, we had only been able to cover a distance of less than 2 kilometers. (p. 331)
>
> It was −22 degrees Fahrenheit, and we had to move our bodies regularly, even though they were warmed up from the heat of the fire. Otherwise, the bloodstream in your body would stop flowing. In order to stay awake, we chatted with each other until sunrise. I was hitting my comrades' heads with my cane when they closed their eyes. (p. 331)

In the winters, they had to spend at least three to four months underground. They had to build bunkers that included rooms in which to live, a kitchen, and a bathroom. They also had to acquire supplies from the town centers and carry them to the countryside without being noticed by the security forces (including drones). Then, they had to spend the entire winter—approximately four months—in these small quarters.

> …we were all ensconced in camp, we all knew that, short of an emergency, nobody could leave. (p. 85)
>
> With the supplies purchased, now the most difficult part of the task had just begun. We had to carry all of these staples we had just secured into the countryside. (p. 136)
>
> We would travel each of these planned paths twice, without carrying anything, before loading and transporting the supplies by mule. (p. 136)

Once they settled in their camp, they were aware that none of them could leave until the winter was over. Thus, they had to be precisely accurate in predicting their needs including, food, clothes, fuel, ammo, training materials, weapons, and all other materials. They had to follow other strict precautions as well. For example, even though they had stoves, they were able to light them only when it was dark to prevent detection by the security forces—a hardship they had to endure no matter how cold it became during the daytime.

> Life was hard underground. We were definitely not allowed to use the wood stove to heat the bunkers unless there was rain, snow, or fog, because the security forces could detect our location from the smoke. (p. 289)

Beyond these physical hardships, there were always security concerns. For example, during some winter camps, Deniz and his friends had to depart their underground bunker before the spring came because they suspected that the soldiers might raid their location. Enduring freezing cold weather, they had to leave all the food and camp materials behind and exit the camp on barefoot by stepping on the rocks to avoid leaving any footprints.

Their troubles did not end with the conclusion of the winter season. At this juncture, they faced the challenging of finding food on which to survive, aside from planning missions against the enemy. Beginning with the mid-1990s, the PKK guerillas had difficulty meeting their basic needs because almost all villages were emptied by the Turkish government as a measure of counterterrorism policy.

> Also, our ability to meet our needs was diminishing, as more and more villages were abandoned. It began with simple shortages. For days, we'd be unable to drink tea, simply because we didn't have any. We would finally get tea, only to run out of sugar for it. Tea and sugar would finally present themselves in sufficient quantities, and that's when we'd run out of flour to make bread. But we survived all that. Things got hard, but we all did our best to meet every challenge with fortitude. (p. 102)

The possibility of being killed at any time was another burden the guerillas had to bear in their daily lives. As noted in the life history, Deniz witnessed the deaths and injuries of his comrades many times. On the second day after Deniz joined the organization, the place at which he was staying was razed to the ground, and several of his comrades were killed by Turkish fighter jets attacks. On the night he set off to reach his first assigned place, the group he was traveling with entered into a mine field and three mines exploded. Several of his comrades were seriously wounded, and some of them lost their lives. Even though he was just a new recruit, Deniz was able to cope with these extreme hardships that transpired in the first days of his life in the PKK.

> A huge noise woke us up on the second day. Of course, we didn't yet understand everything, since we were new, but, we were terrified. The experienced ones warned us, "Fighter jets! Air attack!" (p. 62)
>
> The campground was hit every half hour by six alternating attack aircraft. After the heavy sorties were over, we came under fire by Cobra style helicopters. (p. 87)
>
> Three mines exploded as soon as the front group passed the border. Nine people were seriously wounded, including the battalion commander. Someone barked, "Everyone stay in place! Don't move!" The commander in the back of the group marched to the front to help the injured and stepped on a mine before he got to them. We were new, and we had no idea what was happening. The casualties were heavy. The mine completely severed the feet from the nearest three people. Two more of our comrades lost their eyes from the shrapnel, and five people sustained serious wounds in various parts of their bodies. (p. 77)

Death was a natural part of the guerilla life, and it could come to anybody at any time from an endless list of possibilities: sometimes from the military operations carried out by the security forces, sometimes from the mines planted by the security forces, sometimes from natural disasters, sometimes from a traitor infiltrated into the organization by the enemy, or sometimes even from regular training activities as a result of a simple mistake.

Sari Ibo's death affected me deeply. The day before it happened, we were together eating dinner and chatting happily about general things, and then, the next day he was gone. I was in a tough, unbearable emotional state. It was even more unbearable when you lost someone you loved, and Sari Ibo was loved by me. (p. 278)

The operation against us had destroyed all our food and clothing. Our entire regional force was physically and emotionally drained. Can you imagine how it would feel to lose 60 comrades all at once? (p. 118)

We were just about to lay siege when suddenly the sound of explosions crashed through the darkness. Five of our comrades had their legs, ankles, and feet injured from the explosions and pieces of shell fragments. We were completely demoralized by the serious injuries that befell them. (p. 193)

…a lightning strike hit the top of that very hill…When we arrived, the view we encountered was horrific. They had all been martyred. The death of those comrades and the female company commander within that very same week affected all of us psychologically. (p. 242)

There was an accidental detonation of a mine, and one of our comrades lost his eyes and another one's leg was torn apart. (p. 242)

In fact, one of our own people martyred those seven comrades. Afterward, he surrendered himself to the security forces. (p. 297–298)

…the guerilla force in Dorşin had been completely destroyed by a traitor in the cave where they were camping. (p. 310)

One of our comrades had killed seven others, while they were asleep, and had then fled. This tragedy had, unavoidably, created an atmosphere of nervousness and distrust among the guerillas. (p. 323)

Indeed, Deniz came close to death several times in his PKK career, despite experiencing serious injuries, he never considered leaving his life as a guerilla. In 1993, he was ambushed and was shot in his lower abdomen. His friends thought he was dead so they left him behind. For more than 24 hours, he waited for someone to come and take him to a place where he could receive medical treatment. In 1994, a hand grenade exploded just in front of him, seriously damaging his face and knees. Because of the shell fragments that remained in his knees, he had to use a cane after that year. In 1996, a sniper bullet stripped his skull and broke the skull bone. Again, his friends thought he was dead. If Deniz did not have a strong personality, he would have given up fighting.

When the bomb exploded, the shell fragments hit my knees, elbows, and cheeks. I still have shell fragments in my cheeks. I did not want them to be removed, because the doctors would have had to cut through my cheeks to get them. I was told that three points on my face would need to be cut to take remove the pieces, but I did not want to have scars on my face. (p. 268)

My wounds were severe, and I was not able to stand and walk. I was losing a lot of blood and had fallen unconscious from time to time. (p. 95)

I suddenly felt a pain in my head [the bullet struck his skull]. It was as if I had been hit with a very solid object. I do not remember anything after that. (p. 143)

I only fully understood the damage which had been inflicted on my body through all the battles when I asked to be reassigned in the north. In 1993, I was wounded in an ambush in the Siirt

Valley [after he carried out the assassination mission]. A hand grenade had exploded in front of me in 1994, and, in 1996, I nearly died from a bullet that had stripped my skull. (p. 269)

After all these unfortunate injuries, PKK headquarters wanted to assign Deniz to Damascus—next to the President Apo—for advanced ideological training. It was a golden opportunity for him to rescue himself from the hardships of the guerilla life. To the surprise of everyone, Deniz refused this offer by arguing that he needed to gain more military experience in the field of war.

A couple of years following this invitation, Deniz was invited to Damascus for the second time. Again, he rejected the offer, arguing that his battalion had just suffered a serious defeat and lost 60 guerillas, including the battalion commander. Again, relocating to Damascus would have offered Deniz physical comfort, but he chose to stay in the north because he did not want to leave his fighters without an experienced commander.

> Then, through the radio, he told me, "You are wanted in Damascus. Prepare ASAP!" But I told him…one of our best platoon commanders just died. I'm the only leader left who really knows the area. Can we wait until spring?" Not that I did not want to go to Damascus by the personal invitation of our leader! I did. But it was even more important to me that I not abandon my responsibilities. (p. 138)

Therefore, the life of a guerilla is characterized by pain, suffering, desperate conditions, misery, deprivation, and the risk of death. Not all PKK guerillas had the physical and psychological capacity to endure such hardships—especially over a lengthy period of time. As Deniz noted in his life history, those who could not bear these difficulties would either be allowed to quit the organization or ask to be assigned to less overwhelming positions. Unlike many of his comrades, Deniz had the personality to endure years of physical and emotional hardship.

> After all, we had been well aware before even joining the PKK that life in the organization was not going to be easy. (p. 102)

Support from His Comrades. Another factor that led Deniz to stay in the PKK for approximately two decades was the existence of an environment that nourished friendships and social solidarity in the organization. The PKK leaders were committed to creating strong friendship ties among members. For example, the first day Deniz and the other new recruits arrived at the training camp area, they were instructed to call everyone "comrade" regardless of the rank or the status an individual might hold. In the eyes of the organization, friendship came before anything else, including hierarchy and authority.

> It was our first day in Gabar, when the senior militants first taught us to call each other "heval" (comrade). We were going to call everyone "comrade," no matter what authority or rank they had. (p. 61)

Thus, esprit de corps—a sense of friendship and unity—was a very important issue for everyone in the organization. The guerillas had to have rapport among each other.

For the organization to function, it was required for you to be close to everyone and never "on the out" with anyone. Because the advent of personal discrimination in the organization begins the dissolution of the sense of brotherhood, which leads to loss of confidence—then to loss of effectiveness, and then to failure. (p. 87)

Deniz stated that whenever PKK members faced stressful situations or difficult times, fellow "comrades"—especially senior ones—provided vital sources of support that helped them to cope with their feelings of depression or anxiety. These supportive interactions among the members strengthened social bonds.

They were also always helping us in many ways. There was a powerful atmosphere of friendship and brotherhood. Some of the newcomers frequently got tired and lost their motivation, but no one would yell at them. On the contrary, they would be approached in a friendly manner, and asked, "What's the matter? Is this too much of a load for you to carry? Are you ill? If you want, we can give your burden to someone else." (p. 61)

When Deniz personally experienced difficult times, there was always someone that he could talk to to receive advice or help. Seniors in the organization conveyed that they were always available when a member might be stressed. They welcomed talking about concerns and were willing to provide practical and emotional support. Thus, Deniz and the other guerillas knew that they were not on their own. There was always someone that they could count on.

…when we had a problem, we were to inform the person whom they appointed as the squad leader. If he wasn't available, we were told who to contact next. (p. 61)

This company commander had a big hand in shaping my personality and character…while he was my commander, I took all of his actions and demeanor to heart. I looked up to him as a role model, and I always tried to act as I imagined that he would. I so wanted to emulate him with his ability to fight; his character, and his behavior throughout daily life. He was one of the rare people in the organization who was loved by everyone. Whenever someone had a problem or had failed at something, he would talk to that person for hours. Every guerilla knew that commander Orhan was someone who would think rationally and take care of everyone. (p. 108)

The guerillas could ask for help even for mundane and simple things. Deniz, for example, noted in his life history that a senior and well-known PKK member—Sakine Cansız—helped him to write his report regarding the criticisms and opinions about the training that he had received before being transferred to his first duty area.

She was someone who valued the new young comrades and was constantly trying to help them. In particular, she would handle comrades plagued by psychological distresses and would try to solve their problems by talking with them. She had already told me that she would write the report for me. I gave her just a few main points. She was able to write a report which was about four pages in length, just using my brief information. (p. 76)

Seeing how his seniors listened to every word expressed by troubled guerillas, responded to every cry for help, and offered advice when needed, Deniz in turn learned to support the guerillas under his command when they needed him. Even though he was given an opportunity to settle in Syria for further ideological training, Deniz turned down this offer so as not to leave his comrades without an experienced commander in the middle of the winter.

> Torn as I was, my gut told me it would not be right for me to go to Damascus at that time. We had already lost 50 to 60 guerillas the previous spring. The entire executive board had been dismissed, and the membership of two region commanders had been suspended. Moreover, the platoon commander had just been martyred. If I had accepted Apo's invitation, despite such conditions, I would have left my company in a dire situation. If I thought about nothing but my own interests, of course I would have gone straight to Apo in Damascus! But I liked my men very much. They were very committed to me. If I left them alone in winter camp and something happened to them, I would regret it for the rest of my days. (p. 138)

This friendship atmosphere was so real that over time, Deniz and the other guerillas began to see their comrades as their own family members. For example, Deniz regarded some of his commanders as his parents and, as he rose to a leadership position himself, regarded the guerillas under his command as his own.

> As I was so young, commander Orhan would always advise me as if I were his own son. (p. 108)
> …when your commander dies, you feel as if you have lost every member of your family. A commander becomes everything you have. They are irreplaceable. (p. 278)
> I said, "Mom, do not worry about me. I have 80 children here who take care of me so well." I, of course, was referring to the guerillas in the battalion. (p. 273)
> Between the years of 1992 and 2005, I had never spoken to my family. Not face to face or on the phone…I had a new and larger family within the organization. I viewed my superiors as my father and mother. The guerillas that fought in my battalion were also part of my family, and I viewed them as my blood brothers and sisters. Similarly, they also viewed me as their elder brother or even a father, in some cases. I was all they had. They would come to see me if they were hungry or in need of new uniforms, if they were sick, or if they were stressed, and I would take care of all their worries. Thus, I had become part of a larger family. I just did not have the time to think of my birth family. (p. 272)

Deniz put in more than five requests to be reassigned to the north once he was forced to stay in the camps located in Iraq and Syria towards the end of his career due to his health conditions. He cited the existence of the high-quality friendship and support among the guerillas in the north when he was asked for the rationale behind his insistence to be transferred. When his commanders told him that his physical condition precluded an assignment to the north, he responded by arguing that he very much missed the true friendship environment among the guerillas in the north. The comrades in this network offered support, encouragement, and help—even though it was sometimes at the expense of their lives—and, as a result, he warned that he would travel to the north on his own if permission to do so was not granted.

"You can send me there or not, but I will form a group with them, and we will go [to north] anyway!" At this, the region commander became very angry, "If it were anyone other than I that you spoke to in this way, you'd be arrested. (p. 278–279)

…there is a tight bond of friendship in the north…just to protect you, a comrade in the north would sacrifice himself without hesitation. You will not find friendship ties like that in the south, because guerillas here only think about their comfort, whereas there is loyalty, sincerity, and fellowship in the north, and that's why I want to go to there." (p. 256)

Support from his comrades was thus one of the most significant factors that kept Deniz in the organization for so many years. These ties had an important place in his heart. In his final interview, he lamented the loss of the context of friendship provided by his former life.

Sometimes, I very much miss the life in the countryside; the fresh air, the silence of the mountains, peace and the atmosphere of true friendship. (p. 398)

Military Success. Another factor that helped to entrench Deniz in the PKK for nearly two decades was his belief that the organization's armed struggle against the enemy could in fact be effective. He was well aware that the guerilla fighters had superior qualities that would allow them to defeat the enemies' regular army. As he noted in his life history, guerillas joined the PKK to sacrifice their lives, whereas Turkish soldiers were counting the days before they could return to their homes after their compulsory military service. This level of commitment was a great advantage for the PKK because the guerrillas were fighting bravely without any concern for the future.

…the difference between our mentality and the soldiers' was our greatest advantage in battle. Mentally, the soldiers were family men. They wouldn't take any risks. They spent their downtime counting the days to return home. Even during a battle, they were inevitably thinking of their homes, families, and their children. We were exactly the opposite. We had left our families in order to fight. Any militant who joined the organization had already abandoned all hope that he would ever go back home. That's why we were brave. We had already given up everything. (p. 78)

On the other hand, the majority of the guerillas were already familiar with the hardships of the countryside life because they were often the children of Kurdish peasants who lived in the region. By contrast, the Turkish security forces—especially the military forces—were composed of young, inexperienced soldiers who joined the military only because it was a mandatory requirement for all Turkish citizens. They also often grew up in the city and were trained only for three months before being sent directly to the battlefield to fight against experienced guerillas.

Being accustomed to the terrain was also a plus for us. There was a big difference between a city-raised, briefly trained Turkish Soldier and the village-born guerilla, who had survived off the land and its harsh conditions for many years. (p. 78)

When we performed a mission in the summer, they would follow us just long enough to make a good showing. Then, they [the Turkish soldiers] returned. It was like a sport. They didn't risk going into the forest or steep areas. They were so predictable. (p. 111)

Moreover, the guerillas were much more nimble due to their command structure and the size of units. As Deniz stated in the life history, units consisting of a very small number of guerillas—usually 15 to 20 members—were operating across an entire region within Turkey, which made it extremely difficult for the Turkish soldiers to come into close contact with them. Additionally, the guerillas often were able to inflict damage on the enemy because the Turkish soldiers were dispatched to the countryside in large numbers.

> We do not need to carry out missions against you anymore by laying siege to the military posts or infiltrating the cities, because you come to us with hundreds of sitting ducks. (p. 353)
>
> I still do not know why those soldiers were so confident of their safety. They walked one behind the other, just like sitting ducks, without leaving any space for security. Just three of us could easily have killed them all with Kalashnikovs. (p. 297)

Further, the guerillas were trained to divide their units quickly into even smaller groups to maneuver and attack enemy forces without being noticed, whereas the security forces had to act with large forces and often depended on orders from the hierarchy that delayed their ability to counter guerilla threats. In fact, Deniz noted in his life history that the unwieldy decision chain of Turkish soldiers often spared the guerillas from heavy casualties because they were able to flee conflicts while soldiers were awaiting the order to attack.

> We are able to move in small groups; are highly maneuverable, and each squad commander is empowered to use his own initiative. (p. 86)
>
> Because, in a regular army no individual has the right to act based on their own initiative. All movements are connected to, and hindered by, the chain of command. So, all we had to do with a conventional army was to take our precautions until some soldier made a decision in the chain of command. (p. 82)
>
> In fact, they cannot act at all, without the approval of their superiors. This strategic bottleneck was a big advantage for us. The bureaucratic delay induced by the enemy's hierarchy, often postponed their utilization of long-range artillery or airstrikes, because they needed to get permission for everything. Their hierarchy was that strict. (p. 86)
>
> To thwart a blockade, for example, we divided ourselves into small contingents of just 15 to 20 people. This dramatically increased our ability to maneuver and attack. Had we attacked in a large group, it would have been impossible to go unnoticed. But, in small units, and in the darkness of night, we could all pass undetected through a narrow corridor. (p. 78)

Other than these qualities, the PKK guerillas had also the advantage of hiding among the civilian population, seeming to be normal Kurdish peasants. Deniz and his friends would carry out missions and then disguise themselves and blend into the large crowd. Even though the soldiers knew that they were hiding among the civilians, they were unable to counterattack due to the risk of causing collateral damage.

> …what could the military do to us? Their hands were tied. We were among the civilians so they couldn't risk attacking us from the air; they could only fly by with their combat helicopters and try to intimidate us. (p. 119)

The PKK had the further advantage of employing civilian Kurds to carry out its reconnaissance activities in urban areas. The organization relied on its civilian urban sympathizers to collect information about the enemy so that the guerillas could enter the cities and carry out missions. As noted by Deniz in the life history, the organization was even able to collect intelligence on the president of Turkey via a Kurdish civilian who disguised himself as a journalist. This gathering of intelligence was in preparation for a potential future mission that would be carried out if the AKP did not keep its promises regarding the peace process.

> The organization had a tradition where each region in Turkey had a civilian camera crew that consisted of five people: a head cinematographer and his or her assistants. Disguised as tourists, these teams would go around their assigned regions to videotape and photograph the terrain—mountains, military posts, police districts, villages, lodging places, caves, and other places, in detail. This was really grueling work. It would take at least four to five months to videotape an entire region within Turkey. All of these videotapes and photographs would be delivered to headquarters management to be used for training purposes. (p. 285)
>
> Studying these pictures, I was able to figure out how many guards were on duty, how they were positioned, the position of the civilian police officers, the locations and numbers of jammers, and all the other details regarding their security precautions. (p. 342)
>
> I puzzled for hours over those pictures taken by my comrade, and reached a simple conclusion. If we really wanted, the prime minister and the other VIP guests could be easily killed in Turkey. (p. 343)
>
> The police officers were often negligent, and we had witnessed this fact on many reconnaissance missions. The police officers were extremely inattentive and like sitting ducks for us. We knew what kind of vehicles they were using, where they hung out in their spare time, where they shopped, and at what time they started and ended their work at the police station. (p. 307)
>
> …in 2008, I sent one of our comrades to the downtown area of Muş to collect intelligence about critical infrastructure that we might attack. He had carried out an awesome reconnaissance. We bought a car for $4,000 and loaded it with explosive materials. There was a bus, which would be transporting 40 mid-to high-ranking soldiers every morning from the downtown of Muş to their duty posts at the airport. This bus would also bring them back to downtown at the end of the day. We were going to park our explosive-loaded vehicle on the bus route and detonate it when the bus drove by. (p. 327)
>
> The PKK had more than a thousand already planned missions in its pocket to carry out in Turkey when the time came. For all those future missions, the reconnaissance would be completed, and the explosives, mines and the weapons would already be arranged. (p. 328)

Due to these tactical advantages of guerilla warfare, the PKK was able to fight against thousands of soldiers using a relatively low number of guerillas. As Deniz noted in his life history:

> They [Turkish soldiers] use all kinds of advanced weapons. But personal resilience and strength of character are diminished. We knew this, and used it to our advantage. How else could we have ever engaged a regular army brigade of 2,000 to 3,000 soldiers in battle with just one platoon of about 50 to 60 guerrillas? We could defend ourselves against such a large force without any loss of efficacy, because guerrilla warfare is irregular warfare. (p. 86)

Even though Deniz lost many of his comrades during these encounters with the Turkish security forces, he knew that the enemy was suffering even worse casualties as a direct result of their guerilla missions. Thanks to their guerilla tactics, Deniz and his friends were able to capture military bases located in isolated areas in the mountainous terrain. As the organization wiped out the military posts one by one via its ambush, infiltration, and raid tactics, the rest of the Turkish posts were deserted by the soldiers due to an increased level of demoralization and the incoming threat that awaited them. Of course, leveling those military posts provided extra benefits for the PKK organization. As the soldiers fled to the posts located close to the city centers, they left behind virtually all their belongings. Seizing the enemies' technologically advanced weapons and ammunition not only increased the morale of the guerillas but also their combat effectiveness.

> …this mission had skyrocketed our troop morale, besides securing our revenge. (p. 84)
> …this battle had been a good morale booster for us since we had sustained only a few losses but had caused many causalties on the other side. (p. 109)
> ….the soldiers there knew we would be gunning for them next. So, in the summer of 1994, before we could attack the station, the military evacuated their post and withdrew to the city center. (p. 112)
> ….the military finally understood that we guerillas even had the power to capture their bases. That's why the bases in the unsafe regions were abandoned, one by one, and the military force was gathered in specific central locations. (p. 66)
> The security forces brought panzers against us that first day, but when our ambush groups destroyed the tanks, the rest of the soldiers withdrew… (p. 119)
> During this process, we almost completely destroyed five of these military posts. Rather than fight back against us, many of the Peshmerga forces ran away. (p. 190)
> We knew that after we destroyed one of the ranger teams, the rest would withdraw. (p. 135)

Beyond the effects of these carefully planned guerilla missions, the guerillas were able to intimidate the Turkish soldiers through simple land mining and assassination missions. As Deniz noted in the life history, assassinating one Turkish soldier while he was on guard was more than enough to cause panic among the entire military battalion. The uncertainty of when and where death would occur seriously limited the mobility of the Turkish security forces. Deniz recounted how the military would leave its positions after the PKK had carried out two or three successful assassination missions.

> The military now had no will to remain in their positions—not only because of the mines, but because of the snipers we sent to demoralize them. Our men were hiding in the steep and wooded field at a distance of 150 to 200 meters. When they found an opportunity, they would shoot a soldier with a Dragunov assassin weapon and then retreat. We caused the military to feel so frustrated and disheartened, because now they were the ones unable to move freely throughout the autumn. Finally, they left all three of the hills and withdrew to their headquarters. (p. 135)

These lethal missions not only defeated the enemy but also increased the Kurdish villagers' respect for the PKK. Over time, many of the villagers' opinions—not only the neutral ones but also the ones registered in the village protection system—changed, and they began supporting as the PKK proved itself against the Turkish security forces.

> We wanted our message to the public to be clear—that we could control any roads we wanted, wherever they were, for however long we wanted. This was not an easy feat to accomplish in 1995, and it made a strong impression on the populace. (p. 119)
>
> This mission made a great impact on the region. A ranger had bashed the dead body of a guerilla into pieces, and that ranger and his team were completely eliminated, before even a month had passed. All of the rangers in the region became afraid of us after this mission. They were now more careful. From their disrespect of our fallen comrade, we had taught them complete respect. (p. 111)
>
> They were no longer afraid of their government…the fact that our own Kurdish people were organizing these kinds of revolutionary activities in the city centers, and finding their courage to stand up against the cruel acts of the security forces, was a great morale booster for us guerrillas in the field. (p. 102)

Deniz also believed that the armed struggle against the enemy was effective not only in eliminating the enemy forces but also in forcing Turkish state officials to sit at the negotiation table. Deniz and the others in the organization were well aware that the years of repression, denial of the Kurdish identity, and the ban on the use of the Kurdish language was in fact halted by the Turkish officials only after successful guerilla missions that inflicted heavy casualties on their military forces. In fact, as noted in the life history, whenever a tension occurred between the guerilla wing and the political wing of the PKK, the ground guerillas would say; "Look my friend, if it were not for my hard scrabbling in the countryside, you wouldn't even be able to talk to the public now. You wouldn't have been granted the right to enter the Turkish Parliament and play the role you do in the mechanisms of decision" (p. 129).

> The seniors from the organization responded to those pro-fight guerillas, with, "Comrades, those deaths were necessary, because initially our presence was being denied. We had to pay the price to make ourselves recognized by the Turkish officials. Today, it has paid off. We have to move on. Now is the time for securing peace. Before, the Turkish governments denied our existence, by saying that there was no such place as a nation of Kurds. We were called Armenians, Jews, mountain Turks, or even the agents of foreign powers. The Turks officially denied our presence back then. However, we Kurds are sitting at the negotiation table with those who doubted our existence. The Turks now say, "We have Kurdish citizens. They have their own rights and they will receive all those rights as the conditions improve." That is why we should move on! We cannot continue fighting forever!" (p. 390)
>
> Our violent missions were only justified because that's what it took to bring the state to the negotiation table. (p. 65)

Deniz fought for the organization for approximately 20 years in large part because he witnessed that their successful guerilla missions had proved themselves effective in depleting and weakening the enemy forces, in changing the balance of forces between the enemy and the organization, and in forcing the state to consider settling this dispute through negotiation rather than fighting with arms. Various ingenious methods of fighting that were devised by the organization—including the use of civilian sympathizers to collect reconnaissance, land mining, assassinations, sabotage, ambushes, infiltrations, raids, and also suicide missions—not only paralyzed the normal functioning of the Turkish state but also annihilated its security forces.

Advancement in the PKK Organization. The final factor that kept Deniz and potentially other guerillas in the organization was the existence of opportunities the PKK provided to advance within it. As an organization, the PKK had various positions distributed across a hierarchy of ranks. Thus, the guerillas regarded membership in the PKK much like a military career rather than as a caste system where they had to be happy with their assigned low-level status for the rest of their lives. Anyone who started a career in the PKK could rise from being a ground guerilla to the ranks of squad, platoon, company, battalion, region, province, and field commander over the years. Doing so, of course, depended on their possessing the capabilities to fulfill positional duties and to satisfy specific criteria outlined by the PKK, such as esprit de corps, loyalty to the party, discipline, and being experienced in guerilla tactics.

> There were certain criteria that must be satisfied, in order to earn promotions in the guerilla force. A leading criterion was to have self-command of the standards of the party. You must be committed to your comrades, without any discrimination. You must protect your comrades under any circumstances and think of them before yourself. You should never relinquish your air of military discipline. You must be experienced in guerilla combat tactics and styles of action and even conduct missions yourself, when necessary. Insufficiencies were especially impossible to justify in someone appointed as a commander. Finally, no one could request a certain rank or position. You had to understand that duties were only appointed to you based on your own performance and the needs of the organization. (p. 107)

Thus, merit and qualifications were the main criteria when a member was appointed to a position as a commander. As Deniz noted in his life history: "We sometimes witnessed a newbie being appointed as a commander over those who had been in the organization for 15 years" (p. 87).

Deniz also revealed in his life history that, even though anyone who qualified for a ranked position was promoted without discrimination, the organization would take into account candidates' experience and skills when appointing them to specific zones. For example, Deniz indicated that only the best applicants would be sent to the posts located in Botan and the Middle Field due to the strategic importance of these two sectors for the organization.

> There was a hierarchy to the zones of responsibility, which was taken into account when guerillas were selected for promotion to the level of field commander. For us, Botan Field was the most important, both because of its proximity to the south, and because it had a force of 4,000 to 5,000 guerrillas, where most other zones only had a few hundred guerrillas…Equivalent in importance to Botan Field, our Middle Field was strategically crucial because all our forces used it to transfer from one field to another, such as the Northern Field and Amanoses. On the other hand, it was in the center of everything (hence its name), and the Middle Field was also our center of greatest contact with the public. All the city centers in the Middle Field were under the control of the PKK. Therefore, the most experienced and skilled commander would be appointed to this field. (p. 124)

As promotion was provided, so was demotion. It is important to note that no member's position was guaranteed forever. The organization would demote even a commander to ground guerilla if that person no longer possessed the characteristics of being a good commander. In fact, as Deniz noted in his life history, the PKK never refrained from discharging the entire command cadre of a region whenever it was deemed necessary.

> If a person was assigned as a commander and later couldn't fulfill all the regulations, he would be dismissed and someone else appointed in his place. (p. 87)
>
> Basically we were to either come to our senses, or the PKK was going to change the whole command structure that served across the region. There were hundreds of other people within the PKK that could be appointed in our places. We were not irreplaceable. (p. 262)
>
> He told me, "If the organization appoints you to a position, you don't have the luxury of refusal. They think you deserve this promotion and you will do your duty. Don't worry," he added dryly, "If you don't perform well, they won't hesitate to fire you." (p. 108)

There was no exception for anybody. Even the brother of Apo, Osman Öcalan, was expelled from his position at the PKK central command and demoted to a normal guerilla position when it was heard that he was secretly engaging in talks with foreign state agents.

> He was dismissed from his post in the PKK central command, and his membership to participate in decision-making and missions was suspended until the fifth congress (until 1995). This was the most severe punishment for him. During this time, he was assigned to the most basic labor forces. He dealt with kitchen chores, cooking, washing-up, baking bread, and keeping watch. He had no one's respect; neither did he have any friends. As I said before, whatever your rank or authority is, if you commit a crime, you get punished—even if you are Apo's own flesh and blood. (p. 106)

In summary, the final factor that led Deniz to persist in his career in the PKK was the existence of nondiscriminatory advancement opportunities. Beginning as a rank and file guerilla, Deniz quickly ascended the ladders of the PKK hierarchy due to his dedication and motivation in the ideology of the organization. He was very young when he was first appointed as the platoon commander.

> I was so young that I rejected the assignment at first. I told the leadership that the job would be too challenging for me, and that I simply couldn't accept it. (p. 108)
>
> A few days before leaving the winter camp of 1994, I was appointed as a platoon commander, even though I was quite young. Since I was pretty inexperienced, I had hard times adjusting to being in this position of authority. Almost everyone in my team was older than me, and it was very difficult for me to give orders to these people. Guerillas, who were almost the same age as my father, were under my command. (p. 107)

Nevertheless, his character, knowledge of the terrain, experience in combat, unique ability to guess the plans of the enemy by analyzing the existent information, and attitudes toward his comrades ensured his promotion to one of the leading positions in the PKK.

Desistance: Leaving the PKK and Giving Up Terrorism

The goal of this section is to explore the factors that lead to desistance among the PKK members. The life history of Deniz indicated that various factors contributed to why individuals left the PKK and desisted from terrorist activities. Thus, some guerillas quit terrorism simply by getting killed. Some left the PKK due to the rigors and hardships of life as a guerilla. Some left because they made a mistake and did not want to suffer the consequences. And some others left to surrender themselves to the security forces in the hope of seeking revenge for an injustice they attributed to the PKK. Therefore, the factors that led the guerillas to stop being a terrorist can be grouped under four main categories: (1) casualties of war, (2) challenges of life as a terrorist, (3) fear of accountability, (4) retaliation for unjust treatment.

Casualties of War. This category includes not only the guerillas who were killed in the course of the fight against the enemy, but also those who were wounded and suffered from debilitating physical conditions. These might be caused by stepping on mines or by being shot. At times, they involved serious illness or problems such as frostbite.

> When we finally made it up the mountain, four of our comrades had frostbite on their feet… Unfortunately, all of them had to have their feet amputated at the ankles. (p. 218)
>
> The casualties were heavy. The mine completely severed the feet from the nearest three people. Two more of our comrades lost their eyes from the shrapnel, and five people sustained serious wounds in various parts of their bodies. (p. 77)
>
> With the tanks not allowing us to move, the enemy executed an intense bombardment of the summit by combat helicopters. Since we had no reinforcement, we lost our positions at the top. At least ten guerillas lost their lives and 12 guerillas were seriously wounded, waiting for death. We took the wounded to the field doctor, where they were treated, but without any high hopes. (p. 115)
>
> Indeed, six of our comrades got wounded in that particular battle, and three of their conditions were serious. Each were shot in their chests. Without surgery, they would die, but there was no way to bring a doctor from a hospital to the countryside. Therefore, all these comrades did die. (p. 137)
>
> I started to amputate the legs of our comrades one by one. I would first cut the flesh horizontally up to a point and then open the flesh on the sides to find the main arteries inside. After tying off the veins with a cord, I cut the flap 3 centimeters below the level of the tied veins and threw it away. After this procedure, the bone and the flesh surrounding it was left behind. Using one of our Swiss-made saw blades, I was able to cut the bones in the leg in only about 15 minutes. (p. 194)

Thus, the people in this category desisted from the PKK because they had little choice after suffering from serious debilitating injuries—they stepped on mines, their legs were amputated, or they went blind. As noted in the life history, these debilitated guerillas either quit the life in the PKK fully or were transferred to non-war zones and carried out the more passive works of the organization.

> It is upsetting to see your formerly healthy comrades become amputees, and one begins to wonder if the same thing might happen to you one day. This also leaves our disabled comrades unable to fight as guerillas anymore. Their options are either to be employed behind the front lines in passive work within the camps or to be transferred to European countries and employed to our political organizations to handle relations with the European states. (p. 194)
>
> Meanwhile, those with the amputated feet were sent to Apo, in Damascus, to serve the organization from the background. (p. 77)

Challenges of Life as a Terrorist. This category includes the recruits who could not cope with the dangers and hardships inherent in life as a terrorist. As outlined previously, not everyone who joins to PKK is able to endure the physical and emotional hardships of the guerilla life. Therefore, these people would be given the opportunity of either quitting the organization or working behind the scenes in less grueling works.

> After all, we had been well aware before even joining the PKK that life in the organization was not going to be easy. While those who could endure all of these privations became guerillas, those who couldn't bear them worked instead to support our activities behind the scenes in the European countries and in southern Kurdistan, Iran, Iraq and Syria. (p. 102)

As noted by Deniz in the life history, the guerillas were free to leave the PKK as long as they did not harm the organization by helping the security forces. Thus, the PKK allowed the guerillas to depart without any fear of retaliation. In fact, Deniz conveyed that there were hundreds, sometimes thousands, of guerillas in each camp, and so it was impossible to watch every guerilla 24/7. Therefore, the PKK would simply let the guerillas quit their membership if they did not want to serve any longer.

> If someone wanted to leave the organization voluntarily, and if he or she had not harmed his or her comrades or the organization, then they were free to go, and the organization would not hurt them or their family members. The organization would never forcibly make guerillas stay. A guerilla can leave whenever he or she wants, and that system has been the same ever since PKK was established. (p. 177)
>
> You could never force someone to stay in the mountains. In some camps, there were hundreds of PKK members; in some of them, thousands. There were a great many chores and a lot of work to be shared. Now tell me, how would you force people to stay in a working camp like that? Would you follow them 24/7? It is impossible. (p. 58)
>
> Cemil Bayık seemed to be very sad when he heard the news and said, "Do not bother yourself and just let him escape! No one will go after him. He should stew in his own juices for now." In truth, it would have been easy to catch Şemdin because there was only one escape route from our camp area to the other regions. We could have had these places guarded before Şemdin reached them, but no matter how we insisted, Cemil Bayık did not want anyone to go and catch him. (p. xx)
>
> …they do not care about, or spend time and effort to find a foot guerilla, who served the organization for a couple months and then deserted. (p. 197)
>
> However, the organization does not care whether ground guerillas, most particularly the newbies, desert the organization, because there is no information that can be leaked by a newbie. (p. 378)

Notably, the life history of Deniz also indicated that some guerillas who were unable to cope with the hardships of the life would simply commit suicide to relieve themselves from the misery. Committing suicide as a way of desistence was especially common for those who were unable to endure the harsh winter conditions.

> After we buried Xelil's body in the snow, we had not even walked 15 meters away when a comrade shouted at me, "Comrade Deniz, I am exhausted and I cannot even move my legs. You go on.

I will stay here." His name was Hebun. The three of us spent quite a bit of time convincing him to continue with us. We rubbed his hands and feet but nothing worked. He insisted on staying there. Since we were all waiting in the snow, the other two comrades told me, "Comrade Deniz, if we keep waiting here, we will all die. We should continue on, whether Hebun comes with us or not." …We set up a tent and left a lot of firewood in front of it. We started a fire and left his share of food in the tent and then set off…Hebun had committed suicide in the tent. He shot himself in the head. (p. 332)

Thus, the people in this category usually leave the PKK early in their careers because they cannot take the rigors of the guerilla life or they miss their family. They do not have the ability to endure the hardships of life so they simply quit or in some cases commit suicide. The important thing is that the PKK allows them to leave on the promise that they will not damage the organization by leaking information to the security forces.

Fear of Accountability. This category includes the leaders and others who made mistakes or did something wrong that would subject them to prison or even execution. As noted in the life history of Deniz, many of the guerrillas, especially those holding senior positions, ended their career in the organization by fleeing so as to avoid capital punishment or imprisonment.

The company commander had been sentenced for a mission he had enacted. He ran away because he just could not bear his punishment. (p. 138)

Botan and Ferhat then declared that they were sorry for what they had done, and they would respect the decisions made by the organization from then on. However, as soon as the organization lifted the ban on traveling outside the congressional field, Botan, Ferhat, and 15 other senior leaders fled and took refuge with Jalal Talabani. The organization asked Talabani to hand over the runaways, but he rejected their request, saying that he would not fulfill such a demand since American authorities were backing the group. (p. 246)

As soon as Osman Öcalan heard that he was sentenced to death, he fled from the PUK and took shelter in Iran. Osman knew that the PUK's military force wasn't strong enough to protect him from the organization. (p. 105)

One of our comrades had killed seven others, while they were asleep, and had then fled. (p. 323)

…in 1989, he executed two entire villages, complete with women and children, for no reason…Directly after this incident, Cemil Işık was brought under internal investigation. While under inquiry for this, Işık ran away to save himself from the same fate befalling the rest of the cabal he had established. (p. 170)

Nevertheless, as Deniz reiterated several times, the PKK would never give up its pursuit of deserters who committed the crimes of treason and murder of another comrade. Therefore, even though guerillas who were sentenced to the death penalty often fled the organization to save their lives, the organization would usually find and then execute them.

[Apo is talking] This organization would never leave someone alive once we have issued a death penalty in his name. Tell Selim that we have issued no death penalty. If we had, he would already be dead. (p. 169)

As I mentioned previously, the PKK banned capital punishment for all crimes except the crime of infiltrating the organization. Working for the enemy was unforgivable. Above all else, if you killed one of your comrades, without pity, there was zero chance you would be forgiven. Even if you deserted, the organization would never give up trying to find and execute you. (p. 278)

In 2003, a guerilla killed his comrade and fled to Barzani, the Peshmerga force in northern Iraq. The organization did not go looking for him, but, when the Peshmerga forces would not deliver him, they were given a large amount of money, which convinced them to turn him over to the organization. That guerilla was taken to the camp and executed in front of three battalions of guerillas. (p. 176)

In summary, people in this category desisted from terrorism because they committed grave errors and physically attacked others. Understanding that they would be placed on trial, and harshly sanctioned, they fled to escape such accountability.

Retaliation for Unjust Treatment. The final category that led PKK members to desist from participation in the organization involved those who felt unfairly treated by the PKK and, in turn, took the side of the security forces. The main character of this life story, Deniz, falls into this category. Because his girlfriend was driven to suicide and he did not believe he could receive justice in a rigged trial against him, he left the PKK in hopes of killing the leader he held responsible.

In 2010, Deniz was incarcerated by the organization for a crime he allegedly had not committed. Despite the fact that he was ready to defend himself in front of a formal trial committee, he became highly suspicious of the situation when he was asked questions regarding past events that were unrelated to the current investigation. The investigation committee had brought up past incidents in front of Deniz for which he had not been previously accused. Some of these questions were phrased in a way that directly blamed Deniz for defying Apo. Thus, Deniz became convinced that he was not going to find justice in that forum.

I was kept in the jail longer than I thought. It had been almost six days, and the committee was meeting regularly and asking me to talk about past incidents, which were not even related to my present incarceration. I was now in serious danger since I was being tried and accused for different occurrences—such as Deniz, who had not killed the rangers who martyred our comrades, or, Deniz did not kill the man who stole the tax revenues of the organization. The committee began to ask me questions on incidents that had occurred in the past. (p. 337)

There were 22 questions in the draft and only three of them were related to my so-called affair with Şilan. The remaining questions were about me and our leader, Apo. They had gone too far. I was being accused of being disrespectful to our leader. As soon as I saw the draft, I figured out that Hakkı was not trying to discharge me from my position. It was even worse. He was trying to sentence me with capital punishment. (p. 339)

…one of my older guerillas visited me and said, "Comrade Deniz, this is between you and me but be very careful now. Hakkı has already sanctioned your execution. No matter what you do or whomever serves on your trial, you will be seriously harmed. Hakkı even ordered us to kill you if you attempt to flee. They will kill you even for a shadow of mistake!" (p. 344)

Even more dangerous than these accusations, rumors had spread in the camp that Deniz could in fact be an agent working for the Turkish security forces. Thus, he began to be subjected to extreme beatings while his ankles and hands were tied in his cell. Deniz noted in his life history that three of his teeth were broken during those beatings (p. 339). Moreover, before his trial had started, Deniz's girlfriend, Asmin, committed suicide as a protest to the slanderous accusations made about Deniz and the treatment to which Deniz was being subjected.

The suicide of his girlfriend was the final straw for Deniz. He had not thought about running away until Asmin was pushed into committing suicide. Deniz initially thought that he could acquit himself from all the other accusations because they were simply not true. Hakkı and the others did not have any solid evidence that could result in Deniz's conviction and receipt of capital punishment. Nevertheless, upon Asmin's death, Deniz changed his mind about defending himself. He decided to leave the PKK and then seek revenge against the people who caused Asmin's suicide.

> I looked at the faces of the people on the committee and said, "I would even have sacrificed myself for Asmin. Nevertheless, since this organization caused her to take her own life unjustly, I can now stand against this organization and secure revenge for her! Those who played a part in it will suffer the consequences! I have fought among you for almost 20 years. I have fulfilled all the duties that I was assigned. However, if necessary, I will make no bones about fighting against you all to get revenge for Asmin! (p. 344)
>
> I could not help myself from thinking about how to kill Hakkı. (p. 344)
>
> As I had fought for my people, the Kurds, for 18 years, without even blinking an eye, I would fight for the woman I loved for the rest of my life. That innocent Asmin committed suicide by shooting herself in the head only 30 meters away from me. I was depressed, demoralized, and tired. I said to myself, "Fuck this shit!" Right then, I decided that I could not be part of this organization any longer, when people like Hakkı were highly valued and respected. I stomped with rage. (p. 345)

Thus, Deniz had a unique set of reasons to desist from the PKK. He desisted in the hope of exacting revenge on those who had pushed his girlfriend to commit suicide. There was no way he could stay in the PKK. He was abandoned by his friends, subjected to harsh beatings, and he was accused for incidents that occurred years ago. As a direct result of these pressures, he felt a deep sense of injustice and a desire for revenge.

Thus, revenge for unjust treatment was the main reason for Deniz's desistance from the PKK. For that, Deniz planned to surrender himself to the security forces. He thought that he could convince them to give him the opportunity to kill Hakkı if he helped the security forces to prevent some already planned future missions of the PKK.

> I could easily have gone to the south—to Iraq or Syria—and live there until the end of my life. I also could have gone to Europe. I had connections that could guide me until I reached Germany or France. However, I was blinded with the desire for Asmin's revenge. (p. 348–349)
>
> I had thought that, if I surrendered myself to the security forces, I could be saved from obsession with Hakkı, who not only pushed Asmin to kill herself but had also accused me of being an agent for the security force, despite my successful career in the organization. (p. 349)

It is important to highlight that even though Deniz left the organization due to his desire for vengeance, he never defamed the PKK as a whole. Rather, he reiterated that he had a problem with a single individual, and, given the context, he concluded that he could not contact headquarters to make his voice heard. Further, he knew that he could be murdered by one of Hakkı's men if he had continued to stay in the camp until the end of his trial. That is why he chose to desert.

> I do not want to hold the organization responsible, as a whole, for whatever I was exposed to back then. In all my life, I have never dished on someone. If I told you that all those things occurred because of the general characteristics, culture, morals, and ethics of the organization, it would be a complete lie. It would not be right. Nevertheless, just as you have corrupt politicians in your government affairs, we also had corrupt guerillas who would do most anything for their own gain. (p. 349)

In summary, Deniz did not leave the PKK because of reasons often cited in the terrorism literature; apprehension by security forces, disillusionment with the reality of life in PKK, experiencing a sense of changing priorities, or the burden of his own internal moral limits. He never longed for the freedoms of a normal life; for being able to live a settled life, or for going about his own affairs without the fear of enemy threat. Rather, Deniz desisted from terrorism due to his growing desire to exact vengeance. A wide variety of triggers led to the desistance of Deniz; feelings of mistreatment, his comrades' hypocrisy, being undervalued, the dissemination of scandalous rumors, and finally the suicide of his girlfriend.

There were in fact too many factors that might potentially inhibit Deniz from disengaging from the PKK. Deniz made approximately a two-decade investment in terms of friendship and social support. The organization provided him a substitute "family" and identity, security against enemies, and the opportunity to pursue a righteous cause. As outlined in the previous section, one of his key motivations in his lengthy persistence as a "freedom fighter" was the sense of belonging to a group of like-minded individuals. By leaving the organization, Deniz sacrificed many of the advantages of being a member of the PKK—status, authority, respect from others, and a sense of self-importance.

By leaving the PKK, he also risked his life. He well understood that the organization would not allow someone at his rank to depart in this way without imposing a significant penalty. As he mentioned in the life history, only the new recruits, who had hard times getting used to the rigors of the guerilla life, could leave without any consequences. However, it was different for long-time guerillas who had been part of the core group and who knew sensitive information about the PKK that might cause serious problems if it were shared with the security forces.

> I do not know if I am on the execution list, but the organization does not let high-ranking deserted guerillas, who collaborate with the security forces and who give secret details about the organization, live very long. On the other hand, they do not care about, or spend time and effort to find a foot guerilla, who served the organization for a couple months and then deserted. (p. 176)

Even though he had many options in front of him, Deniz chose to surrender himself to the security forces in order to exact revenge on behalf of the women he loved. Nevertheless, without moral support and protection from the Turkish security forces, Deniz found himself in a social vacuum. Having broken away from an intense daily life and social group, he described his new life as being characterized by loneliness and social isolation. He even repented about his decision to surrender on various occasions. He explicitly stated that his career prospects were ruined.

I drew this destiny with my own hands. I am totally responsible for the incidents that took place after I deserted the organization, and I sometimes feel very angry with myself: I was not such an idiot once. I was blind not to see ahead of me. I do not understand how I put myself into such a situation [surrendering himself to the security forces]. (p. 398)

Conclusion: Is Peace Possible?

In this final section, the daunting issue of the possibility of peace is addressed. To be sure, this is a complex issue that involves political interests and forces that are not easily resolved. However, the purpose here is to approach this policy debate in a different way—by drawing in most respects from the insights offered by Deniz. Beyond the internal politics of Turkey, his views are particularly relevant in revealing why military repression is almost certainly to be a failed solution. Given the organizational strength of the PKK, the attempt to eradicate the PKK is likely to be ineffective or, if effective, to generate the use of more lethal methods of terrorism. In addition, it might ultimately prove useful to listen to Deniz, a PKK member and devoted Kurd, in terms of what he sees as the only pathway to piece.

The Futility of a Military Solution

Two important lessons can be drawn from the life history of Deniz on the issue of Turkey's military approach to the eradication of PKK terrorism. First, the PKK is a decades-old, very sophisticated military organization. Attempts to eradicate it through a concerted Turkish military campaign are unlikely to be effective. The PKK can replace its members through recruiting, knows how to adapt to Turkish attack strategies, can blend into the population, and is well-trained, well-armed, and well-financed.

The PKK has its own strengths that cannot be disrupted easily by the military efforts of Turkey. It has a strong code of ethics that governs personal conduct, military conduct (e.g., they do not go out and kill just anybody, all killings must be justifiable), and organizational conduct (how people are treated within the PKK). The organization has a merit and accountability system; all actions, especially in military operations, are reviewed and assessed. Members who are successful rise up its leadership hierarchy; those who prove incompetent get demoted downward in the organization. No one is immune to being reviewed and sanctioned. Even the leaders of the PKK are held accountable—and demoted or executed when their strategic failures or personal misdeeds call for such punishment. Promotions are held to be based on merit. There is no favoritism. Thus, promotion and demotion are standard practices.

The PKK is an organization that attaches high importance to equality and social integration. Everyone is seen as a comrade—including women—and gender equality is stressed. This facilitates social integration and provides high participation rates from the Kurdish women. The ideology of the PKK is based on Marxist theory, not on religion, which distinguishes it from other Islamic terrorist groups where there is no clear end goal beyond religious hegemony. The PKK guerillas are rational. They want their political freedom and the recognition of their ethnic identity. These people view themselves as moral crusaders. They have a strong ideological goal; they fight for justice. Even though the Turkish government has portrayed them as terrorists, separatists, or baby killers, these people are viewed by their community as "freedom fighters." As a result, the Kurdish public feels a duty of loyalty to the members of the PKK who have willingly given their lives for them.

The PKK embraces democratic socialism. Everyone shares the same food and same clothes. Everyone can speak up against wrongdoings. Everyone, including the seniors, can be criticized. There is a real sense of equality. Each individual is as valuable as everyone else. There is no place for favoritism in the PKK. These values and procedures not only tie Kurdish people into the organization but also make the PKK very effective.

The PKK has its own tactical expertise and ability to learn from its past mistakes. It is constantly evolving and developing military knowledge of effective planning. The organization's leaders regularly train their members. The PKK has support from the Kurds in the region, often including the village protection guards that are armed and salaried by the Turkish Republic. It is funded by different sources. It has huge financial support from Europe and other places. More importantly, the PKK has safe havens in the region. It can hide out in Iraq, in Iran, in Syria, and even in many European countries.

As well as having these strengths that make its military defeat unlikely, the PKK has weaknesses—as any organization would. For example, there are power struggles among the leaders in the PKK, which occur regularly (not just in times of succession). There is goal conflict, when the goal of the PKK is in dispute (e.g., war or peace—continuing armed conflict or entering negotiations?). There are leadership failures at all levels that can exact a high cost (e.g., when they occur, guerillas are martyred). There is the challenge of adapting to expensive high-tech military technology used by Turkey. Other challenges include the changing politics and the instability of the region—the Middle East.

Despite the existence of these challenges, it is almost impossible to eradicate the PKK, especially when people such as Deniz exist in large numbers and are willing to sacrifice themselves for the future of the Kurds. Today, approximately 28 million Kurds live in the region across Iraq, Iran, Syria, and Turkey. These people are not willing to abandon their sons, daughters, uncles, or fathers fighting at the mountains. This is the reason why the PKK is still thriving. It has unlimited recruitment resources. Even if the Turkish government murders hundreds of PKK members, the PKK has resources to resupply its guerilla force. As Seyit Riza stated in 1937 just before he was executed by Turkish officials:

> I am 75 years old, I am becoming a martyr, I am joining the Kurdistan martyrs. Kurdish youth will get revenge. Down with oppressors! (Dersimi, 1992, p. 229)

There will always be more Denizs who are willing to fight for the PKK. As Deniz noted in his life history, the PKK has thousands of volunteers who are ready to undertake suicide missions. Therefore, even if the PKK has organizational flaws, it also possesses positive attributes that will nourish its viability for the foreseeable future. Given what Deniz informed us about the nature of the PKK organization, the ability of Turkey to solve its Kurdish problem via military methods seems certain to fail. Thus, Ankara appears misguided in its message to the Turkish people that the PKK will be eradicated through military repression.

In fact, Turkey has been using the military and cultural repression measures—village evacuation, expropriation of Kurdish areas, mandatory deportation, a ban on the use of Kurdish language, destruction of the houses, murder of innocent Kurds, depopulation, unaccounted murders, degradation, violence, and torture—since the beginning of the 20th century, even before the PKK emerged as an organization. In these past times, tens of thousands of Kurds were killed, extreme human rights violations occurred, millions of Kurds were displaced, and the social and economic structure of the region was damaged. Notably, none of these measures proved effective.

[1920s] …the assimilation against the Kurdish identity started in the new republic. Many governmental positions in Kurdistan were filled by Turks. Ankara started a campaign to delete everything referring to the Kurdish language. In this context, Kurdish place names were all replaced by Turkish names (Lewis, 1968; McDowall, 2000).

[1924] …the law number 1505 allowed the state officials the expropriation of the Kurdish areas by the state and then the redistribution of these lands to Turkish speaking population (White, 2000, p. 72).

[1925] …The court of Tribunals of Independence moved from one city to another, thousands of Kurds were slaughtered without trials. (Romano, 2006, p. 35).

[1927] "Whole villages were burnt or razed to the ground, and men, women and children killed" (McDowall, 2000, p. 196).

[1932] Approximately 3,000 non-combatants were killed and their villages were burnt down (McDowall, 2000, p. 206).

[1932] …the Kurdish population was going to be dispersed to remote areas to extinguish their language and Kurdish identity. The records indicate that approximately one million Kurds were displaced until 1938 (O'Ballance, 1996, p. 16).

[1937]…The homes were destroyed, villages were burned down and depopulated, and the civilians who hid in the caves and animal barns were killed by poisonous gas and artillery. The Alevi Kurds committed collective suicides to escape from the brutality of the Turkish soldiers (Dersimi, 1992).

[1937] It was found out that 40,000 Dersim Kurds died during the military offensives (McDowall, 2000, p. 93; White, 2000, p. 83).

[1940]…After the rebellion was suppressed, a brutal campaign of repression started against the Kurds in the region. Hundreds of villages were destroyed, and thousands of innocent women, men, and children were killed (Romano, 2006, p. 35).

[1967]…in 1967, Ankara enacted a law forbidding the publication, taping, and recording of any kind of materials in Kurdish (Izady, 1992).

[1967]…a special commando unit was sent to the region, and a clearing operation was started. Tens of Kurds were killed, and thousands of them were tortured and severely beaten (White, 2000, p. 133).

[1980]…the law number 1587, prohibited naming Kurdish children with Kurdish names (McDowall, 2000).

[In 1983] Two-thirds of the whole Turkish army was deployed to Kurdistan to suppress the Kurdish national aspirations (McDowall, 2000).

[1986] In 1986 Ankara renamed 2,842 villages out of 3,524 in major Kurdish cities by Turkish names to erase the Kurdish identity in the region (McDowall, 2000).

[1989] …village (Badan) was blamed for providing new recruits for the PKK, and thus the entire population of the village (children, women, elderly people) was held for a day under the burning heat of the sun in the garrison compound (de Bellaigue, 2009, p. 228).

[1991] The tribes that did not want to join the village guard system were expelled from their lands, and military forces destroyed their houses (McDowall, 2000, p. 425).

[1992] The police and the military units were allowed to apply a special terror law according to which they could detain anybody for 45 days without any charge (McKiernan, 2006, p. 105).

[1993] Villages that supported the PKK were burnt, and the peasants were arrested and subjected to torture (de Bellaigue, 2009).

[1999] By 1999, it was reported that more than 3,500 villages and pastures were forcefully relocated to destroy the potential safe havens for PKK fighters. The witnesses of these relocations indicated that they were subjected to inhumane actions including; degrading behavior, arbitrary arrest, violence, torture, extra-judicial killings, sexual victimization, and the destruction of their livestock and food stocks (McDowall, 2000, p. 440).

[2010] A judicial inquiry, which occurred during the 2010s, later found that an execution squad was formed during [prime minister] Tansu Çiller's government that was responsible for the death of more than 5,000 Kurds between 1993 and 1996 (de Bellaigue, 2009, p. 224).

[2016] The fights lasted for months and many town centers in southeastern Anatolia were completely destroyed. More than 200,000 Kurdish civilians were forced to leave their homes and relocate to other parts of the country (Srivastava, 2016).

All these historical excerpts clearly indicate that attempting to solve the Kurdish problem within the context of security policies and through the application of military measures has been tried many times over. Again, no evidence exists that they have been effective in any enduring way that has brought peace to all parties involved. Unending violence and terrorist acts loom on the horizon. Many people, on both sides, are likely to perish.

In fact, the PKK emerged only after these years of military and cultural repression measures. That is, not only were these measures ineffective, but they also created resentment among the Kurds and led to the establishment of the PKK as a means of resisting inhumane policies and practices. Therefore, the PKK is not only part of the cause of this bloody fight, but also the direct result of the denial and annihilation measures applied by the former governments of Turkey.

Second, even if the Turkish military is successful in using its latest technology and fighter jets to inflict large casualties on the PKK, there are likely to be two unanticipated consequences—according to Deniz. One of these is that a concerted military campaign to eradicate the PKK will generate much violence and, in turn, foster deeper feelings of grievance and victimization—factors that only make the Kurds increasingly resistant. In turn, this growing sense of injustice will increase participation in the PKK. Thus, the more Ankara cracks down on the Kurd, the more people—especially youths—will be drawn to join the PKK as a matter of duty and patriotism. Thus, it is highly unlikely that the Turkish military is going to subjugate the PKK. Again, 28 million Kurds live in the area, with new children born every day. These people support the PKK from their hearts. There are hundreds of thousands of Kurdish mothers who have lost their sons—and daughters—to this fight. This means that thousands of other Denizs are available to be recruited. The more the Turkish state represses the Kurds, the more the Kurds will join the PKK. Therefore, military measures are limited in their effectiveness.

This assessment does not mean that Turkey cannot kill many PKK members. The Turkish military is skilled and technologically advanced. Thus, Ankara can degrade, hurt, or derail the PKK through military measures; it can inflict serious casualties on the PKK. What it will never be able to do, however, is to destroy the PKK completely as long as there are Kurdish people who are willing to die for the cause of freedom.

Moreover, beyond having unlimited human resources, the PKK also possesses decades of guerilla-fighting experience—knowing how to inflict pain and casualties on the enemy forces. As noted in the life history, Turkey should understand that it cannot stop the PKK from killing more police officers or military personnel. There are hundreds of isolated police stations, military posts, and government buildings across Turkey. The PKK can simply undertake hit-and-run attacks whenever it wishes to inflict damage. Further, one Kurd who is willing to sacrifice his or her life for the Kurdish cause can kill 50 police officers, including in the capital city of Ankara.

A second consideration is that the PKK can respond to eradication efforts by engaging in warfare that is even more asymmetrical. Rather than attack military and police outposts with guerillas, the PKK will start to use more bombings by suicide missions. This tactic is problematic for Turkey and its citizens because it is impossible to prevent such self-sacrifice in this kind of war. Still, the reality is that the more the Turkish government presses forward with a massive military campaign, the more likely it is that the PKK will see that their most effective counter-strategy is not direct military confrontation but to employ large numbers of suicide bombers. Notably, the PKK could even start to target the Turkish civilian population, something it has long resisted doing. But if given "no choice," attacking such targets would seem to be an inevitable outcome. And as Deniz noted in the life story, there are hundreds of thousands of Kurds living in each and every city of Turkey who deeply sympathize with the ideology of the PKK. Thus, it will not be difficult for the PKK to create chaos in the major Turkish cities using these Kurds.

> If the [Turkish] government were thinking like the Sri Lankan government, which killed all the members of the Tamil Tigers, they would be seriously mistaken. We were in no way similar to the fight that occurred in Sri Lanka. Turks and Kurds had intermingled with each other through marriage bonds. Moreover, there were Kurds now living in every single city of Turkey. Turkey cannot say that that it could destroy the whole of eastern Anatolia, even using a hundred fighter jets, or hundreds of thousands of troops. Listen to me carefully. Those two societies are highly intertwined. If they carried out such an annihilation mission, the whole country would be in worse condition than what Syria is now. A civil war would break out, and the Kurds and Turks would kill one another, until one day you would look outside and see the United Nations' troops building a green line between the two communities, and on that day, it would be the end of the emotional ties between the Kurds and the Turks. (p. 385)

Political Obstacles in Turkey

Among others, two important barriers will have to be surmounted if peace is to be achieved in Turkey. First, many victims and families of victims of PKK violence are opposed to rewarding the Kurdish organization with peace. They seek not reconciliation but revenge. Second, suspicion exists that Turkish President Erdoğan made the decision to use this conflict with the PKK to stay in power and deepen his authoritarian control—and that he will continue to do so.

One of the frequently asked questions during the peace negotiations with the PKK was the following: "How can we make peace when there are too many victims that suffered the worst consequences of this war?" It is true that families of police and military still want vengeance—not peace—and accordingly they protest peace negotiation efforts between the state and the PKK.

Indeed, Deniz noted in his life history that a fight that has lasted for more than 40 years cannot end without paying the price for it. He reiterated that the peace process will be sabotaged by several groups, not only by the primary victims of this bloody fight but also by the groups that would be affected by the end of the conflict.

Deniz's perception seems accurate. In fact, former leaders of Turkey—Özal, Erbakan, and Ecevit—who wanted to end this vicious cycle of violence through peaceful ways were all displaced. For example, in 1993, Prime Minister Özal had brought the issue of peace to the point of signing an agreement with the PKK, but he suddenly died of a heart attack (a forensic analysis of Özal's corpse, which was carried out in 2013, actually indicated that he was poisoned). A similar fate befell Prime Minister Erbakan. In 1996, he also came close to reaching an agreement with the PKK. The PKK was ready to lay down its arms, when Erbakan was suddenly overthrown by a post-modern military coup in 1997. In 2000, Prime Minister Ecevit was about to make a deal with the PKK, but the country was suddenly driven into a financial crisis. Similar to Özal, Ecevit was later poisoned by his doctors and left paralyzed. He was overthrown by the forces that were disturbed by the prospect of peace. Further, when the peace negotiation between the AKP government and the PKK restarted in 2011, Apo told the government officials the following:

> Now you are negotiating with me here, and a similar thing can also happen to you tomorrow. They can do to you what they did to Özal, Erbakan and Ecevit. There are many internal and external forces that want to or that may want to hinder the development of this process. This is called oversetting the car for the fourth time. (Çandar, 2012, p. 59)

Deniz argued that the groups who may want to hinder the peace process will most likely use the families of the martyred military personnel and police officers for their purposes. Thus, he cautioned that this group of family members should be approached first and informed about the root causes of the fight between the Kurds and the Turks. That is, they should be told that the Kurds resorted to violence only after all the other outlets—including the political ones—were closed to them. Therefore, the PKK is not the sole cause of the fight between the Kurds and the Turks today. Their insurgency is mainly the end result of years of repression, denial, humiliation, and annihilation of the Kurds in Turkey. That is, their very own government bears much of the responsibility for the death of thousands of Turkish security officers.

> The parents, families, and children of the martyred soldiers should be approached first and consulted about a peace process, so that they would not feel as if they had lost their sons and fathers to a hopeless cause. The government officials should say to them, "My dear brothers and sisters! The Kurds are a distinct society from us Turks, and they had some requests for us, such as education in their mother tongue and the recognition of their distinct identity, which was formed even before the foundation of the Turkish Republic. We have neglected those demands for years and rejected their very presence, referring to them as the pioneers of the foreign powers. Our politicians were not mature, and the bureaucrats were illiterate. At this point, we understand that we are unable to solve this problem by fighting and killing each other. Yesterday, your sons, brothers, uncles, and fathers died. Tomorrow, you, your sons, your brothers, or uncles will die if we insist on continuing this war. It would benefit both Turks and Kurds, to end this fight." (p. 391)

Therefore, this serious obstacle to the resolution of the problem—Turkish public opinion, especially that expressed by those who have lost loved ones in this fight—should be addressed through the media, and Turkish citizens prepared for a peaceful resolution of the conflict. They should be told that what the

Turks and Kurds have experienced during the last 40 years has damaged both sides. Not only Turkish mothers and wives, but also Kurdish mothers and wives have suffered the pain of losing a loved one in this war. There is no winner in this fight.

The Turkish public, especially the families of martyred security officers, should understand that there will be more bloodshed on both sides as long as this fight continues and is not resolved through democratic means. Military attacks aimed at eradicating the PKK may bring some solace, providing a sense of accomplishment and a measure of vengeance. But this approach ultimately cannot work. Therefore, the Turks should set aside their pride and honor and start to think this issue through from a rational perspective. For example, if the peace attempt that was started by Özal—when the guerrillas laid down their weapons and he was just about to sign the agreement—could have been secured with success, then today, more than 3,000 civilians and security officers would still be alive, thousands of wives and children would have had their fathers by their side, and thousands of parents would not be suffering from the pain of losing their sons in this fight. Moreover, the money that has been used to meet military expenditure could have been spent on other societal needs.

> If this war ends, both sides will win and our economy will grow stronger. The money that is currently spent on arms, weapons, and security forces, would be spent for health, education, and many other beneficial programs. Who could be disturbed by those things as long as they thought rationally? The Kurdish society, in the east, is already fed up, living under war conditions for so long. The people there ask for nothing, but to live a normal life without the threat and oppression of the security forces. (p. 392)

Second, the political parties in Turkey—especially the ones in power—have a tradition of using the conflict with the PKK as a means of gaining the votes of nationalist and Kemalist people in Turkey. Although this maneuver risks ongoing armed insurrection and needless deaths, it has thus far reaped benefits for Turkish politicians. Unfortunately, the AKP decided to follow this strategy during the last general elections in Turkey, held in 2015. Erdoğan allegedly sacrificed the peace attempts that were initiated in 2009 in order to stay in power and deepen his authoritarian control in the country. The resumption of violence in the last election ensured his victory when, until that point, it had looked unlikely.

Erdoğan controlled Turkey via the AKP as a unified government between 2002 and 2015, for approximately 13 years. Nevertheless, after the June 7, 2015 elections, the AKP was no longer eligible to stay in power by itself. For the first time in its history, the pro-Kurdish political party, the HDP, surpassed the 10 percent threshold that allowed them to hold seats in the Turkish parliament; they won 13 percent of the votes and thus secured 80 seats. The success of the HDP in the general election blocked the AKP from its outside majority (60 percent) in the parliament. This level of majority was needed by the AKP for it legally to pass the necessary constitutional changes that would permit Erdoğan to establish a presidential system. In such a system, he would enjoy expanded power and move closer to exercising autocratic control in the country (Akyol, 2015; Basar, 2015; Baser & Ozturk, 2015; Dalay, 2015; Imogen, 2015; Marcus, 2015).

At that time, the AKP politicians had two options available: form a coalition government with one of the opposition parties or drag the country into snap elections. Even though it was possible to establish a coalition government with one of the main opposition parties, Erdoğan and his cabinet intentionally failed to do so. They did not want to diminish their power and thus their control. Therefore, after failing to reach an agreement with the leaders of the opposition parties for a potential coalition government, the AKP announced to the public that a snap election would be held in six months—on November 1, 2015.

Within this six-month period, bombs exploded in major cities of Turkey, leaving tens dead and hundreds injured. The ceasefire between the PKK and the security forces ended. In the aftermath, more than 400 Turkish police officers and military personnel lost their lives, hundreds of civilian Kurds were arrested for their alleged ties to the PKK, the street fights began between the militants and the security officers, Kurdish town centers were completely destroyed during the clashes, military law was applied, and more than 200,000 Kurds evacuated their homes to protect their families.

The country turned back to the 1990s in just two months. Economic and political instability increased, and the Turkish lira lost a substantial value against the foreign currencies. The AKP politicians explicitly warned the Turkish public that to ensure national security, Turkey needed a strong, unified government. They claimed that if the public did not vote for them in the upcoming snap elections, this atmosphere of chaos and instability would continue. The citizens accepted this deceptive message. A majority of the public, including the Kurds, voted for the AKP, believing that a strong, unified government could return Turkey to its previous period of security and wealth (Baser & Ozturk, 2015; Cagaptay, 2015; Srivastava, 2016; Uras, 2015).

It thus appears that Erdoğan intentionally called off the peace process so that the AKP would regain its outright majority in the parliament. To achieve this goal, he did not hesitate to invoke the fight against terrorism and exploit the national sensitivities of the Turkish population. As Deniz noted:

> Those 15 soldiers were intentionally sent there to be martyred by the guerillas. The incident took place just before the national parliamentary elections, and the goal was to gain the votes of nationalist Turks by provoking their fascist sentiments. Thank God, the PKK was not taken in by that scheme. (p. 393)

Because the opposition parties did not support him for more executive power, Erdoğan first prevented the AKP from forming a coalition with the opposition parties and then allegedly started a small-scale civil war that resulted in the deaths of hundreds of security officers, Kurdish guerillas, and innocent civilians. Erdoğan was well aware that the HDP was able to pass the 10 percent threshold by winning the support of religiously conservative Kurds who had previously voted for the AKP since 2002. Therefore, he aimed to regain these conservative votes by attacking the HDP and associating it with the leftist Marxist organization, PKK. For that purpose, he publicly announced that it was impossible to continue a peace process with Kurdish militants and then urged the Turkish parliament to strip HDP politicians from their immunity of prosecution on the grounds that they had links with terrorist groups.

In the end, Erdoğan achieved his goals. He ordered the army to launch air strikes on PKK camps located in Iraq, revived the conflict with the Kurds, stoked Turkish nationalist sentiments, and undermined support for the HDP by luring away religiously conservative Kurds in the snap election. The increasing level of terrorist threat planned by the AKP government thus undercut the HDP's appeal in the November, 2015 elections. Again, however, this was accomplished at a heavy cost, including the loss of hundreds of innocent lives. Today, Turkey has a government that is increasingly authoritarian and now sits on the edge of civil war. The prospects for peace, which seemed so bright, now have dimmed just because Erdoğan used the conflict to fuel his ability to stay in power and have more control.

Listening to Deniz: A Pathway to Peace

Just as there are factions within the Turkish community that may oppose the government's sitting downs with PKK members to make peace, there are some factions within the PKK that do not want negotiations and peace because their only goal is to have a separate independent Kurdish state. As Deniz noted in his life history, differences of opinions have often surfaced inside the PKK cadre over the prospect of establishing peace with Turkey. Some militants who fought for the PKK not only harshly objected to negotiations with Ankara but also threatened to leave the organization if a peace were made with the Turks.

> I would find it very strange that whenever the organization would attempt to enter into a dialogue process with Ankara, the guerilla cadre from [the field of] Dersim would fiercely stand against it. (p. 390)
>
> They [Dersim Kurds] explicitly stated that, "If we were going to make peace with the Turks— if we were going to give up our independence, after securing our cultural rights, and the rights of education in our mother tongue—then why the hell have we lost so many of our comrades to this fight for so many years!" (p. 390)

Besides the Dersim Kurds, there are some other small factions within the PKK that emerged after the imprisonment of the leader of the party—Apo. In 1999, while incarcerated, Apo asked the PKK to withdraw its forces from Turkey as a precondition of the peace negotiations. A small group of PKK commanders had disregarded this order and argued that Apo had handed over the control of the party to the Turks and was acting according to their wishes—that is, surrendering and liquidating the PKK. As Deniz stated in his life history, according to these commanders, the era of the PKK was over, and it was high time for the guerillas to unite under a new organization that would continue to fight for the Kurds.

> Some of them wanted to establish a new party; some others insisted on not leaving the north and establishing a new party with the goal of armed struggle. Then, there were those who wanted to arrest the current commanders and elect a new president. (p. 221)

Therefore, the PKK is also not bereft of factions in which guerillas have different goals in their minds regarding the future of the Kurds. These factions within the party may act independently and undermine peace by undertaking terrorist actions on their own. As such, the seniors of the party will first have to overcome this potential resistance if they want to secure a permanent peace with Turkey.

Nevertheless, as Deniz stated in his life history, even though there may be a small group of factions resisting the peace process, they would be of little importance to the PKK as a whole. That is because the majority of the guerillas, as well as of the civilian Kurds living in Turkey, favor the peaceful resolution of the conflict. Like Deniz, they are weary of the years of repression, denial, relocation, and the killing of their loved ones. Accordingly, Deniz's words on what would it take for freedom fighters to stop fighting Turkey and become peaceful may offer a pathway to peace.

> The people there ask for nothing, but to live a normal life without the threat and oppression of the security forces. They simply want to live without the worry of losing their children to the war. (p. 392)

From his life history, it seems that Deniz desires two concessions from the Turkish community for peace to be achievable. First, he wants the people of Turkey to understand why the Kurdish people feel a deep resentment and grievance towards the Turks. Deniz wants the Turks to know how misunderstandings, false information, and propaganda manufactured by the Turkish government have fueled the conflict for the last four decades.

He would like it understood that the Kurdish issue is not a problem that began with the PKK but rather originated a century ago, as a direct result of the betrayal of the promises given to the Kurds: if they fought with the Turks against external enemies, they would live within the borders of the new state in autonomous regions and could protect their culture, language, and customs. Unfortunately, none of these promises were kept. In 1923, a nationalist state was created in which the Turks were the dominant ethnic group.

Since then, the Kurds have been massacred regularly, repressed, and denied a homeland. Most important, they have been humiliated by the Turkish state by denying them not just political freedom but also the right to their culture, language, and customs. They were not allowed to use their language—or even allowed to give their children Kurdish names. They have even been depicted as animals and lied about purposefully. For example, the Kurds who joined to the PKK to fight for their rights were often regarded as separatists, baby killers, murderers, and terrorists—but not as people who were seeking freedom and justice.

> Kurds do not have the faces of human beings; they should be migrated to Africa to join the half-human half-animals who lived there. We need a solution [to the Kurdish question] as sharp as a sword. (quoted in McDowall, 2000, p. 408)

According to Deniz, this lack of understanding of why the PKK exists is a main reason why the Kurdish problem continues to this day. The decades of slandering, denigration, and misinformation created such a sense of pride and honor in the Turkish public's minds that it does not allow them to show any sense of respect to the Kurdish cause.

> The basic factor in the continuance and growth of this problem is that Turks are still unaware of the goals and the *raison d'être* of this Kurdish organization, which has by now been fighting against them for more than 30 years. (p. 317)
>
> Instead of trying to set the seal on this problem, the Turkish government has been creating polarization between the two public entities for years by using the propaganda that the PKK was composed of manslayers, Armenians, Jews, and even atheists, besides Kurds. In the near past, around 2012, did not Erdoğan say, "The PKK is composed of a bunch of Zoroaster"? Because of such long-established and media-backed prejudices, the organization had been unable to express its grievances to the civilian Turks. (p. 317)

> The peace will only come if the media stops reporting the news given to them by greedy people, who benefit from this fight, politically and economically. (p. 392)

Therefore, there is an urgent need for an initiative that would provide a platform for the Turks and Kurds to achieve a genuine understanding of one another. As Deniz noted in the life history, the majority of the Kurds, including Deniz, have justified their participation in the PKK by citing these historical injustices and grievances—views given credence by their own personal experiences suffered at the hands of the Turkish security forces. Therefore, the Turkish civil society representatives, political parties, bureaucrats, journalists, and academics should come together and provide more insights into what Kurdish people—more specifically the PKK—actually want and why they want it.

> For years, we Kurdish people asked for two simple things: the recognition of the Kurdish identity by the Turkish Constitutional Law, and the use of the Kurdish language, for public services in the cities that are dominated by large Kurdish populations. Were these requests really too difficult for the Turks to provide? We only wanted to protect our basic rights. We did not ask to be provided with any extra rights that would compromise those of Turks—but simply to be able to freely speak in our own language and to have our separate identity recognized. (p. 384)
>
> The Turks might not like some of the demands proposed by the organization, but most of those demands are related to basic human rights. Such rights should never have been a subject of bargaining, but the government has wasted a lot of our time discussing them. (p. 388)

Additionally, and equally importantly, Turkish society should be provided with the truth that the Kurdish people do not view the PKK as a terrorist organization, and that they do not like their sons or daughters to be called as terrorists. In the eyes of the Kurdish community, those who went up to the mountains to join the struggle are viewed as heroes. A large proportion of the Kurds supports the PKK's cause. As a result, these kinds of derogatory statements further antagonize the Kurds and only serve to attenuate their emotional ties to the Turkish public. Therefore, the Turkish citizenry should be informed about the necessity of treating the PKK as the legitimate representative of the Kurds and accordingly recognize the PKK's leader, Apo, as a partner in the negotiated settlement of the conflict. As Deniz noted in the life story, Apo's inclusion into the negotiations is particularly important since he is the only person in the PKK that everybody would listen without objection.

> …the Turkish society has suggested for years that Apo, the leader of the organization, was a monster, a bloodthirsty baby killer, and even a sex addict. Sadly, the public has believed whatever the media spewed out to them, and never searched for the truth. If Apo were really a dictator, do you think those millions of Kurds would have followed him to their death? Cannot the Turks see this? At least? (p. 392)
>
> I wish the Turkish media had been more objective, specifically about Apo. I wish they had reported Apo's unifying and integrative statements regarding the Turkish and Kurdish societies. (p. 392)

As Deniz noted in the life history, today, the PKK is an essential part of the Kurdish community. Treating it as a terrorist organization will not help Ankara achieve the peaceful resolution of the conflict. Instead, it will leave only one option open for Turkey: the use of its security forces in a military operation, something that it has pursued unsuccessfully for the past four decades.

> The PKK has reached a position today where they have hundreds of contact offices all around the world, let alone having institutions within Turkey. Accept it or not, the organization acts like a government in the eastern parts of Turkey. (p. 386)
>
> Hasn't the United States government just declared that their strongest allies in the fight against ISIS are the PYD guerilla forces? Hasn't the president of France hosted PYD representatives in his official office? For God's sake! Is it that difficult to understand? If you assure the Kurds that you would provide them with basic human rights and if you aimed to use PKK as an armed force rather than planning to annihilate it, believe me, the Turkish Republic would be in a much more stable position than it is now. (p. 388)

In summary, Deniz wants the Turkish public to understand that historically the Turkish state has not supported true diversity but has engaged in cultural cleansing and annihilation that was very similar to what happened in Serbia, Croatia, and Bosnia. No people would accept this—certainly not the Turks if the situation were reversed. Peace is only possible if the Turkish public realizes what it means to be a Kurd within the Turkish Republic. Therefore, Deniz wants the Turkish authorities to stop portraying the PKK as a terrorist organization, to regard the guerillas as rational actors, and to try to integrate the Kurds into the broader Turkish community by granting them their basic rights. Not to do so is to consign Turkey to the fate suffered by Serbia, Bosnia, Iraq, and Syria.

> …in general, I do not have feelings of guilt for anything I did, except for those couple of incidents. I had legitimate grievances for which to fight. Moreover, even though I deserted the organization, I am still a Kurd. I will continue to fight for those rights until they are granted to my people by the Turkish state. I am telling you—even if I am released at the age of 70, I will again fight for the right to speak in my mother tongue. (p. 384)
>
> I left the organization [the PKK] on my own, but that does not mean that I have stopped being a Kurd. I am a Kurd and I want my right to speak Kurdish. I want my identity to be recognized. I am demanding those rights as a citizen of the Turkish Republic. (p. 384)

Second, Deniz wants the Turkish people to know that the Kurds do not hate them. They simply want to live together as peoples who are connected but diverse. As he noted in his life history, the PKK never inculcated feelings of hatred toward the Turks into the hearts of the guerillas. They did not do so even during the 1990s—a time when the sole goal of the organization was to establish an independent Kurdish state, and, more importantly, when thousands of Kurdish youths joined the PKK for the express purpose of seeking revenge against the repressive system that humiliated, tortured, and killed their parents.

> In 1992, the year I joined the organization, the main purpose of the PKK was to establish an independent Kurdish state. In other words, it was to set free the Kurdish areas in Turkey, Syria, Iran and Iraq. The guerilla was always motivated by this purpose. But, despite the strength of our mission to establish an independent Kurdish state, the senior PKK executives were always

emphasizing that we had no problems with Turkish people…The reason for our fight with Turkey was just the current fascist system. In other words, no matter what, we were going to stay friends with Turkish people forever. (p. 64)

In the period during which I joined the organization, most Kurdish patriots were joining because they had been subject to violence at the hands of the Turkish police or soldiers. We all had friends with the view that "Turkish soldiers tortured my innocent family, and my relatives. Why shouldn't I take my revenge on the innocent Turks?" These people were objecting to the doctrine that we must stay friends with Turks, as we were being told in the trainings. But the organization was strictly against such anti-Turk sentiments and would prevent them as much as possible. The senior executives were always calming down our friends who joined the organization for revenge. They told them, "We can't solve the problem by acting from the desire for revenge and killing innocent people. On the contrary, if we used such a method, we would lose the validity of our own struggle. So, although it is right that we fight for our own people, we should never include innocent people in this war. We must respect others." (p. 64–65)

This reluctance to vilify the Turkish people is evident when the history of the fight between the Turks and Kurds is examined. With one or two exceptions, the PKK has never carried out missions against the innocent civilian Turks. It has never turned the Turkish cities into blood baths and created an atmosphere of chaos, even though undertaking such a terrorist mission would have been very easy. The PKK has never seized movie theaters and killed hundreds of innocent civilians to force the government to withdraw its forces from Kurdistan—as the Chechen Islamic radicals did in Russia in 2002. The PKK has never hijacked planes and crashed them into the critical infrastructure, leaving thousands of dead—as the Al-Qaeda terrorists did in the United States. The PKK has never carried out bombing missions to commuter transportation systems and killed hundreds, injured thousands—as ETA did in Spain in 2004. The PKK has never shot innocent children and youths who are in summer camps—as a far right terrorist did in Norway in 2011. The PKK has never used its bombing abilities to kill spectators who stand by the finish line of a marathon—as occurred in Boston in 2013. The PKK has never carried out a series of attacks in a city center that would include suicide bombings, mass shootings at cafes, restaurants, football stadium, and entertainment avenues—as ISIS did in central Paris in 2015. And the PKK has never instructed its guerillas to drive a truck into a crowd celebrating a national day—as has just happened in Nice, France.

Rather, the PKK has so far followed a rational policy of discriminate war—targeting only members of the Turkish security forces as a means of retaliation. And they have done so only because all the other options for conflict resolution have been foreclosed to them. It is important to note that the leader of the PKK, Abdullah Öcalan, initially started his struggle for freedom and reform in the political arena. He turned to armed struggle only after he lost all hope that the elites in the Turkish political system would listen to the voices of the Kurds. Recall that Öcalan was incarcerated, and the group he was leading was depicted by Turkish authorities as nothing more than a bunch of bandits.

The PKK has engaged in a discriminate war because, as Deniz noted, his life's purpose, as well as that for his guerilla comrades, is not to fight forever. They have been engaged in armed conflict in hopes of securing a successful peace negotiation. They have been struggling to attain their basic human rights and freedoms—not to incite hatred and animosity against the Turkish civilians. Today, the Kurds—the

PKK—do not even ask for compensation for whatever injustices they have been subjected in the past. They want one simple thing—peace and freedom.

The PKK has several times indicated its sincere desire for peace by showing that they are willing to sit at the negotiation table and work out a reasonable agreement. Nevertheless, their patience is wearing thin because each of the former peace initiatives was undermined by the Turkish authorities. The PKK and the Kurds have grown weary of the deceitful tricks played by the Turkish governments. For example, in 1999, while guerilla forces were withdrawing from Turkish territories as a precondition of the peace negotiations, the Turkish military set up tank ambushes and treacherously killed hundreds of guerillas—despite the fact that the PKK was assured by Ankara that no one would be killed during the withdrawal. Or, recently, President Erdoğan spoiled the three-year-long peace process as a political means of increasing his authoritarian control in the country. As might be anticipated, these deceptions have created considerable mistrust of Turkish authorities among the PKK.

Beyond the necessity of undertaking confidence-building measures to regain the trust of the Kurds, another grave danger awaits if Turkish officials cannot secure a peace with the current PKK administrators: a highly radicalized Kurdish youth. On various occasions, Deniz and some Kurdish politicians have warned the Turkish state officials that the current PKK administrative cadre is likely the last generation that the Turkish government will be able to negotiate with for a peace that includes a democratic union. These PKK seniors have some commonalities with the Turks—they have experiences of living together as they attended the same universities, engaged in activities in the same ideological organizations, or even served together in the Turkish military. By contrast, the Kurdish youths in the southeastern Anatolian cities do not have any commonalities with the Turks that live in the western parts of the country. Even worse, these Kurds have experienced emotional separation from the rest of the country as they grew up seeing their brothers, sisters, and fathers dying at the hands of the Turkish security forces. They are angry with the Turks because ethnic animosity has already started to find a place in their blood.

> If Ankara continues to delay the establishment of a permanent peace, while the wise seniors of the organization, such as Cemil Bayık and Murat Karayılan, are still alive, their chances of making peace with the new radicalized Kurdish generation is extremely low. The new generation considers Turkey an enemy because of the losses they have suffered so far and they are unable to think rationally. They do not want to live within the borders of Turkey, as the seniors of the organization would have them do. Rather, they want to establish a Free Kurdistan by carving territories out of Turkey. If these highly radicalized and politicized Kurdish youth have a voice in those matters in the future, their demands will be different than the demands of the current seniors of the organization. They will say, "We are a distinct society, and each society has the right of governing itself, and determining its own fate. Since we are a society of 40 million, including the Kurds in Syria, Iran, and Iraq, we can also have our own state." The new generation thinks like that! (p. 397)
>
> The Kurdish youth living in the region experienced violence on a daily basis. They all sacrificed their fathers, brothers, sisters, or uncles to this fight. They were in clashes with the police every day. Their psychology and way of thinking was very different from us, old guerillas. (p. 397)

That is why it is crucial that Turkish state officials take meaningful steps to secure a peace with the current generation of PKK leaders before the highly politicized younger generation of Kurds succeed these seniors. The establishment of peace requires Turkey to set aside the counterproductive military measures and embrace other solutions, including the treatment of the Kurds with respect, dignity, and peace. From a rational standpoint, granting the Kurdish people their own cultural and democratic rights would have virtually no negative impact on the Turkish citizenry or society. In fact, the PKK will not feel the need to continue its armed struggle if Kurds are allowed to express themselves freely in the Turkish political domain. Now, let us assume that this transpired. Would any Turks be disadvantaged if the Kurds laid down their arms and became engaged in the political arena—instead of continuing to carry out a violent struggle? No! Would any Turks be disturbed living together with the Kurds under a democratic multi-cultural system based on fraternity and equal citizenship status instead of killing each other? No!

> …there is no other option left between the two communities. Of course, that would be a whole other story, if Turkey should risk division of its territories, chaos in the country, or a turmoil similar to that which erupted in Syria and Iraq. If Ankara cannot settle this problem with this generation of Kurds, they will be unlikely to make peace with the next generation. This is very true, and this is why I have said several times that this peace process is the last opportunity for Turkey. (p. 397)

There is no reason to be so resistant to allowing the Kurds to possess local autonomy, to open their own schools, and to protect and celebrate their heritage. As mentioned previously, the Kurdish issue existed decades before the PKK emerged. Therefore, it is not an issue of terrorism but a broader problem that involves the ethnic, cultural, legal, and political rights of the Kurds. That is, the Kurdish problem will continue to exist no matter how many PKK members are eradicated in the region. By contrast, as Deniz tells us, Turkey will achieve true peace if the negotiations provide the Kurds with their cultural rights and find a way to integrate the PKK members into legitimate politics.

> The PKK is, in fact, a unique force, which could contribute to the military power of Turkey and could potentially side with the Turkish government against all their enemies. If they would just establish the Goddamn, long-delayed peace treaty, and use this ready-trained power for much bigger goals in the Middle East. I cannot readily believe that the Turks have not had one single politician, who had an idea like this. (p. 390)

Finally, there likely will always be those who will portray the PKK as terrorists—and not as "freedom fighters." And there are those who will even resort to violence during talks to create division and incite more conflict. But Deniz is offering a pathway to peace: true mutual understanding and respect. All would do well to listen to his words of wisdom.

Appendix

LIST OF MAJOR INDIVIDUALS AND ABBREVIATIONS IN THE LIFE HISTORY

I Major Individuals

Apo	Abdullah Öcalan. Founder and the leader of the PKK.
Asmin	Deniz's second girlfriend. Committed suicide.
Barzani	Mesud Barzani, the President of the Iraqi Kurdistan.
Cemil Bayık	Code name is Cuma. Number two in the organization.
Deniz Koçer	The interview subject.
Duran Kalkan	Code name is Abbas. Senior member of the KCK Executive Committee.
Erbakan	Former Prime Minister of Turkey.
Erdoğan	The current President of Turkey.
Eşref Bitlis	Deceased commander of the Turkish Gendarmerie.
Fehman Hüseyin	Code name is Bahoz Erdal. Former head of the PKK armed wing.
Hakkı Gabar	The person who caused Deniz to desert the organization.
Halil Ataç	Code name is Ebubekir. Former member of the PKK Presidency Council.
Murat Karayılan	Code name is Cemal. One of the founders of the PKK.
Nizamettin Taş	Code name is Botan. Former head of the PKK military wing.
Şilan	Sevin's best friend. Deserted the PKK after Sevin's suicide.
Şemdin Sakık	Code name is Zeki. Former commander of the PKK.
Sevin	Deniz's girlfriend.
Talabani	Jalal Talabani. A Kurdish Iraqi politician.
Turgut Özal	Former President of Turkey. Died unexpectedly in 1993.
Zeynep Kınacı	Code name is Zilan. The first women suicide bomber of the PKK.

II Abbreviations

AKP	The Justice and Development Party
ANAP	Motherland Party
ARGK	Kurdistan National Liberty Army
BDP	Peace and Democracy Party

DEHAP	Democratic People's Party
DEP	Democracy Party
DTP	Democratic Society Party
EMEP	Labor Party
ERNK	National Liberation Front of Kurdistan
ETA	Basque Country and Freedom
HADEP	People's Democracy Party
HDP	People's Democratic Party
HEP	People's Labor Party
HPG	Kurdish People's Defense Force
IRA	Irish Republican Army
ISIS	Islamic State of Iraq and the Levant
JITEM	Turkish Gendarmerie Intelligence and Counterterrorism
KADEK	Kurdistan Freedom and Democracy Congress
KCK	Kurdistan Communities Union
KDP	Kurdish Democratic Party
KNG	Kurdistan National Congress
KONGRA-GEL	Kurdistan People's Congress
MHP	Nationalist Movement Party
MIT	Turkish National Intelligence Agency
PCDK	Party of Democratic Solution in Kurdistan (Iraq)
PJAK	Party of Free Life in Kurdistan (Iran)
PKK	The Kurdistan Workers Party
PUK	Patriotic Union of Kurdistan
PYD	Democratic Union Party (Syria)
TIKKO	Liberation Army of the Workers and Peasants of Turkey
YDGH	Patriotic Revolutionary Youth Movement
YPG	People's Protection Units

REFERENCES

Ahmed, M. M. & Gunter, M. M. (2005). *The Kurdish Question and the 2003 Iraqi War*. Costa Mesa, CA: Mazda.

Akyol, M. (2015). "Who killed Turkey-PKK peace process?" Al-Monitor. Retrieved June 8, 2016, from www.al-monitor.com/pulse/originals/2015/08/turkey-syria-iraq-pkk-peace-process-who-killed-kurds.html.

Albayrak, A. & Parkinson, J. (2013). "Kurdish Group to Pull Armed Units from Turkey." *The Wall Street Journal*. Retrieved June 18, 2016, from www.wsj.com/articles/SB10001424127887324743704578444463069125276
0.

Allen, J., Kelly, D. H., & Heymann, P. B. (1977). *Assault with a deadly weapon: The Autobiography of a Street Criminal*. New York, NY: Pantheon.

Anna, B., Gordon, M. R., & Smith, E. (2015). "Turkey and U.S. Plan to Create Syria 'Safe Zone' Free of ISIS," *The New York Times*. Retrieved June 24, 2016, from www.nytimes.com/2015/07/28/world/middleeast/turkey-and-us-agree-on-plan-to-clear-isis-from-strip-of-northern-syria.html?_r=0.

Barnard, A., & Gordon, M. R. (2015). "Goals Diverge and Perils Remain as U.S. and Turkey take on ISIS." *The New York Times*. Retrieved June 23, 2016, from www.nytimes.com/2015/07/28/world/middleeast/us-and-turkey-agree-to-create-isis-free-zone-in-syria.html.

Basar, U. (2015). "Turkey Ponders HDP's Role in Kurdish Peace Process." Al Jazeera News. Retrieved June 28, 2016, from www.aljazeera.com/news/2015/10/turkey-ponders-hdp-role-kurdish-peace-process-151026085940919.html.

Baser, B. & Ozturk, A. E. (2015). "Turkey's Snap Elections: Erdoğan is Forcing his People to Take Sides." Retrieved June 16, 2016, from www.juancole.com/2015/08/turkeys-elections-erdogan.html.

Bloor, M. (1997). *Selected Writings in Sociological Research*. Aldershot, UK: Ashgate.

Bois, T. (1966). *The Kurds*. Translated from the French by M. W. M. Welland. Beirut, Lebanon: Khayats.

Cagaptay, S. (2015). "What Turkey's Election Results Mean." The Washington Institute for Near East Policy. 08 June 2015. Retrieved July 03, 2016, from www.washingtoninstitute.org/policy-analysis/view/what-turkeys-election-results-mean.

Çandar, C. (2012). "'Leaving the Mountain': How May the PKK Lay down Arms? Freeing the Kurdish Question from Violence." Istanbul, TR: Turkish Economic and Social Studies Foundation.

Chambliss, W. J. (1990). *Harry King: A professional thief's journey*. New York, NY: MacMillan.

Cloward, R. A. & Ohlin, L. E. (1960). *Delinquency and Opportunity: A Theory of Delinquent Gangs*. Glencoe, ILL: Free Press.

Dalay, G. (2015). "Is Turkey's Kurdish Peace Process on the Brink?" Al Jazeera. Retrieved June 18, 2016, from http://studies.aljazeera.net/en/reports/2015/09/20159813236393942.html.

Dalay, G. (2015). "Regional Kurdish Politics in the Post-ISIS Period." Retrieved June 14, 2016, from Al Jazeera Center for Studies.

Dalay, G. (2015). "Pushing Restart on Turkey's Kurdish Peace Process." Retrieved June 9, 2016, from www.middleeasteye.net/columns/pushing-restart-turkeys-kurdish-peace-process-904758201.

De Bellaigue, C. (2009). *Rebel Land: Among Turkey's Forgotten Peoples.* New York, NY: Bloomsbury.

Dersimi, N. M. (1992). *Hatıratım.* Ankara, TR: Öz-Ge Yayınları.

Dolan, D. & Gumrukcu, T. (2016). "Turkey Health Minister: 155 Wounded, 14 in Intensive Care After Istanbul Blast." Reuters. Retrieved December 11, 2016, from www.reuters.com/article/us-turkey-blast-toll-wounded-idUSKBN1400BL?il=0.

Don, M. (2015). "At Least 97 Killed in Twin Bombings Near Train Station in Turkey's Capital." CNN. Retrieved June 19, 2016, from www.cnn.com/2015/10/10/middleeast/turkey-ankara-bomb-blast/index.html.

Ensaroglu, Y. (2013). "Turkey's Kurdish Question and the Peace Process," Insight Turkey, Vol. 15, No. 2 (Spring 2013), pp. 7–17.

Fanon, F. (1965). *A Dying Colonialism.* New York, NY: Grove Press.

Ferhad, I. & Gurbey, G. (2000). The *Kurdish Conflict in Turkey: Obstacles and Chances for Peace and Democracy.* New York. NY: St. Martins.

Gibbs, J. P. (1989) "Conceptualization of Terrorism." *American Sociological Review* 54–329.

Gibbs, J. P. (2012). "Conceptualization of terrorism." In J. Horgan & K. Braddock (Eds.). *Terrorism Studies: A Reader* (pp.63–76). New York, NY: Routledge.

Goodman, S., Steffensmeier, D. J., & Ulmer, J. T. (2005). *Confessions of a dying thief: Understanding criminal careers and illegal enterprise.* New Brunswick, NJ: Aldine Transaction.

Gottfredson, M. R. & Hirschi, T. (1990). *A General Theory of Crime.* Stanford, CA: Stanford University Press.

Gupta, D. K. (2006). *Who Are the Terrorists?* New York, NY: Chelsea House.

Gupta, D. K. (2008). *Understanding Terrorism and Political Violence: The Life Cycle of Birth, Growth, Transformation, and Demise.* New York, NY: Routledge.

Gursel, Kadri. (2013). "Erdogan Asks 'Wise People' to Make Case for Peace." Al-Monitor. Al-Monitor, 15 April, 2013. Retrieved July 3, 2016, from www.al-monitor.com/pulse/originals/2013/04/erdogan-wise-people-commission-peace-process.html.

Gurr, T. Tobert. (1989). "Political Terrorism: Historical Antecedents and Contemporary trends." In *Violence in America: Protest, Rebellion, Reform,* edited by Ted Robert Gurr. Vol. 2. Newbury Park, CA: Sage.

Hoffman, B. (2006). *Inside Terrorism.* New York: Columbia University Press.

Hoffman, B. (2012). "The Changing Face of Al-Qaeda and the Global War on Terrorism." In J. Horgan & K. Braddock (Eds.). *Terrorism Studies: A Reader* (pp.392–413). New York, NY: Routledge.

Horgan, J. & Braddock, K. (2012). *Terrorism Studies: A Reader.* New York, NY: Routledge.

Hurriyet (2011). "Müthiş iddia: MİT-PKK görüşmesi internete sızdı." Retrieved June 25, 2016, from www.hurriyet.com.tr/muthis-iddia-mit-pkk-gorusmesi-internete-sizdi-18722968.

Imogen, C. (2015). "Turkish Election Result is Hailed a Personal Victory for President Erdogan." *The Daily Mail.* Retrieved June 14, 2016, from www.dailymail.co.uk/news/article-3299300/Shock-Turkish-election-result-hailed-massive-personal-victory-President-Erdogan-party-stuns-pollsters-regain-majority-rule.html.

Izady, M. R. (1992). *The Kurds: A Concise History and Fact Book.* Washington, D.C.: Taylor & Francis.

Johnson, G. (2015). "Two Bomb Blasts Kill 86 at Peace Rally in Turkish Capital." *Los Angeles Times.* Retrieved June 11, 2016, from www.latimes.com/world/europe/la-fg-turkey-bomb-attack-20151010-story.html.

Jones, D. (2016). "Turkish President Rules Out Return to Peace Process With Kurds." Voice of America. Retrieved June 28, 2016, from http://m.voanews.com/a/turkey-president-erdogan-rules-out-peace-process-rebel-kurds-pkk/3154802.html.

Jones, D. (2016). "Amnesty International Condemns Turkey's Treatment of Kurds." Voice of America. Retrieved June 20, 2016, from www.voanews.com/content/amnesty-calls-turkey-campaign-against-kurds-collective-punishment/3155683.html.

Jones, D. (2016). "Turkey Threatens Military Action Against Syrian Kurds." Voice of America. Retrieved June 29, 2016, from www.voanews.com/content/turkey-threatens-military-action-against-syrian-kurds/3167056.html.

Jawideh, W. (2006). *The Kurdish Nationalist Movement: Its origins and development*. Syracuse, NY: Syracuse University Press.

Kendal, N. (1993). "Kurdistan in Turkey." In G. Chaliand (Ed.) *A People Without a Country: The Kurds & Kurdistan* (pp.97–120). New York, NY: Olive Branch Press.

Klockars, C. B. (1974). *The professional fence*. New York, NY: Free Press.

Laciner, S. & Bal, I. (2004). "The Ideological and Historical Roots of the Kurdist Movements in Turkey: Ethnicity, Demography, and Politics." *Nationalism and Ethnic Politics, 10:3*, 473–504.

Letsch, C., & Shaheen, K. (2015). "Turkey Says Islamic State is Main Suspect in Ankara Bombings." *The Guardian*. Retrieved June 25, 2016, from www.theguardian.com/world/2015/oct/12/turkey-blames-ankara-bombings-on-islamic-state.

Lewis, B. (1968). *The Emergence of Modern Turkey*. London, UK: Oxford University Press.

Lizzie, D. (2015). "Ankara Explosions: President Erdogan Vows Turkey Will Stand in 'Unity and Solidarity' After Terror Attack." *The Independent*. Retrieved June 18, 2016, from www.independent.co.uk/news/world/europe/ankara-explosions-president-erdogan-vows-turkey-will-stand-in-unity-and-solidarity-after-terror-a6688931.html.

Marcus, A. (2015). "Turkey's Kurdish Guerrillas are Ready for War, Foreign Policy." Retrieved June 17, 2016, from http://foreignpolicy.com/2015/08/31/turkeys-kurdish-guerillas-are-ready-for-war/.

Mardin, S. (1989). *Religion and Social Change in Modern Turkey: The Case of Bediuzzaman Said Nursi*. New York, NY: SUNY Series in Near Eastern Studies.

Marszal, A. & Akkoc, R. (2015). "Kurdish Militants Claim 'Revenge' Killing of Two Turkish Policemen." *The Telegraph*. Retrieved June 18, 2016, from www.telegraph.co.uk/news/worldnews/europe/turkey/11755018/Two-Turkish-police-officers-killed-close-to-Syria-border.html.

Martin, G. (2016). *Understanding terrorism: Challenges, Perspectives, and Issues* (Fifth Edition). Thousand Oaks: Sage Publications.

McDowall, D. (2000). *A Modern History of the Kurds*. New York, NY: Iradj Bagherzade Tauris.

McKiernan, K. (2006). *The Kurds: A People in Search of their Homeland*. New York, NY: St. Martin's Press.

Miller, A. C. (2013). "PKK Militants Start Withdrawal from Turkey, Fueling Optimism for Peace Process." *The Christian Science Monitor*. Retrieved June 15, 2016, from www.csmonitor.com/World/Europe/2013/0508/PKK-militants-start-withdrawal-from-Turkey-fueling-optimism-for-peace-process.

Milliyet. (2009, October 19). "34 PKK 'lı Habur Sınır Kapısı'ndan girip teslim oldu." Retrieved June 19, 2016, from www.milliyet.com.tr/acilim-da-kritik-an/siyaset/siyasetdetay/19.10.2009/1151953/default.htm.

Milliyet. (2011, September 13). "MİT ve PKK arasındaki görüşme internete sızdı." Retrieved from www.milliyet.com.tr/mit-ve-pkk-arasindaki-gorusme-internete-sizdi/gundem/gundemdetay/13.09.2011/1438049/default.htm.

Moffitt, T. E. (1993). "Adolescence-Limited and Life-Course Persistent Antisocial Behavior: A Developmental Taxonomy." *Psychological Review*, 100.

Nissenbaum, D. (2015). "U.S., Turkey Agree to Keep Syrian Kurds Out of Proposed Border Zone." *The Wall Street Journal*. Retrieved June 5, 2016, from www.wsj.com/articles/u-s-turkey-agree-to-keep-syrian-kurds-out-of-proposed-border-zone-1438641577.

NTV (2011). "MİT-PKK görüşmeleri sızdı." Retrieved June 15, 2016, from www.ntv.com.tr/turkiye/mit-pkk-gorusmeleri-sizdi,a87SUp4ta0akgKLpkhb5-w.

O'Ballance, E. (1996). *The Kurdish Struggle, 1920–94*. New York, NY: Macmillan Press.

Olson, R. W. (1996). *Imperial Meanderings and Republican by-Ways: Essays on Eighteenth Century Ottoman and Twentieth Century History of Turkey*. Istanbul, TR: Isis Press.

Osborne, S. (2016). "Ankara Explosion: Several Feared Dead After 'Large Explosion' in Park in Turkey Capital." *The Independent*. Retrieved June 26, 2016, from www.independent.co.uk/news/world/middle-east/ankara-explosion-several-reportedly-injured-after-big-explosion-in-turkish-capital-a6928926.html.

Peacock, J. L. & Holland, D. C. (1993). "The Narrated Self: Life Stories in Process." *Ethos*, *21*, pp.367–383.

Radikal (2014). "HDP'den Kobani Açıklaması." Radikal. 07 October, 2014. Retrieved July 03, 2016, from www.radikal.com.tr/politika/hdpden-kobani-aciklamasi-1217436/.

Rapoport, D. (2012). "Fear and Trembling: Terrorism in Three Religious Traditions." In J. Horgan & K. Braddock (Eds.), *Terrorism Studies: A Reader* (pp.3–27). New York, NY: Routledge.

Rettig, R. P., Torres, J., & Garrett, G. R. (1977). *Manny: A Criminal-Addict's Story*. Boston, MA: Houghton Mifflin Harcourt.

Richardson, L. (2006). *What Terrorists Want: Understanding the Enemy, Containing the Threat*. New York, NY: Random House.

Romano, D. (2006). *The Kurdish Nationalist movement: Opportunity, Mobilization, and Identity*. Cambridge, UK: Cambridge University Press.

Sampson, R. J. & Laub, J. H. (1993). *Crime in the Making: Pathways and Turning Points Through Life*. Cambridge, MA: Harvard University Press.

Schmid, A. P. (1983). *Political Terrorism: A Research Guide to Concepts, Theories, Data Bases and Literature*. Amsterdam, Holland: North Holland Publishing Co.

Shaheen, K. & Smith, H. (2016). "Turkey Vows Vengeance After Bombing Kills 38 and Wounds 166." *The Guardian*. Retrieved December 11, 2016, from www.theguardian.com/world/2016/dec/10/bomb-outside-istanbul-football-stadium-causes-multiple-casualties.

Shaw, C. R. (1930). *The Jack-Roller: A Delinquent Boy's Own Story*. Chicago, IL: The University of Chicago Press.

Shaw, C. R. & Moore, M. E. (1931). *The Natural History of a Delinquent Career*. Chicago, IL: The University of Chicago Press.

Shaw, C. R. (1938). *Brothers in Crime*. Chicago, IL: The University of Chicago Press.

Silke, A. (2003). *Terrorists, Victims, and Society: Psychological Perspectives on Terrorism and its Consequences*. Hoboken, NJ: Wiley.

Silke, A. (2003). "Becoming a Terrorist." In A. Silke (Ed.). *Terrorists, Victims, and Society: Psychological Perspectives on Terrorism and its Consequences* (pp.29–55). Hoboken, NJ: Wiley.

Snodgrass, J. (1982). *The Jack-Roller at Seventy: A Fifty-Year Follow-Up*. Lexington, MA: Lexington Books.

Srivastava, M. (2016). "Battle Raging in Eastern Turkey Shatters Kurdish Peace Process." *The Financial Times*. Retrieved June 14, 2016, from https://next.ft.com/content/3646d7de-b85a-11e5-b151-8e15c9a029fb.

Steffensmeier, D. J. (1986). *The Fence: In the Shadow of Two Worlds*. Totowa, NJ: Rowman & Littlefield.

Stern, J. (2003). *Terror in the Name of God. Why Religious Militants Kill*. New York, NY: Ecco.

Sutherland, E. H. (1937). *The Professional Thief*. Chicago, IL: University of Chicago Press.

Sutherland, E. H. (1979). *Differential Association Theory, Criminology*. Philadelphia, PA: Lippincott.

TRT (2012). "MİT Müsteşarı Hakan Fidan İfadeye Çağrıldı." TRT, 8 February, 2012. Retrieved June 14, 2016, from www.trthaber.com/haber/gundem/mit-mustesari-hakan-fidan-ifadeye-cagrildi-27602.html.

Uras, U. (2015). "Turkey's AK Party wins back majority in snap election." Al Jazeera News. Retrieved June 14, 2016, from www.aljazeera.com/news/2015/11/turkey-ruling-akp-leads-crucial-snap-elections-151101160104190.htm.

Van Bruinessen, M. (1978). *Agha, Sheikh and State: the Social and Political Structures of Kurdistan*. London, NJ: Zed Books.

Vertigans, S. (2011). *The Sociology of Terrorism: Peoples, Places and Processes*. New York, NY: Routledge.

Waheed, A. (1958). *The Kurds and their Country: A History of the Kurdish people from Earliest Times to Present*. Lahore, Pakistan: University Book Agency.

White, P. J. (2000). *Primitive Rebels or Revolutionary Modernizers?: The Kurdish National Movement in Turkey*. New York, NY: Zed Books.

White, J. R. (2015). *Terrorism and Homeland Security* (Ninth edition.). Belmont, CA: Wadsworth Cengage Learning.

Weinberg, L., Pedahzur, A., & Hoefler, S. H. (2012). "The Challenges of Conceptualizing Terrorism." In J. Horgan & K. Braddock (Eds.). *Terrorism Studies: A Reader* (pp.76–91). New York, NY: Routledge.

Whittaker, D. J. (2003). *The Terrorism Reader*. London: Routledge.

Yeginsu, C. (2015). "Sharp Denials After Arrest of Vice News Journalists in Turkey." *The New York Times*. Retrieved June 14, 2016, from www.nytimes.com/2015/09/02/world/europe/turkey-arrests-3-vice-news-journalists-on-terrorism-charges.html?_r=0.

Yeginsu, C. (2016). "Explosion in Ankara Kills at Least 34, Turkish Officials Say." *The New York Times*. Retrieved June 19, 2016, from www.nytimes.com/2016/03/14/world/middleeast/explosion-ankara-turkey.html?_r=1.

INDEX

 Taylor & Francis eBooks

Helping you to choose the right eBooks for your Library

Add Routledge titles to your library's digital collection today. Taylor and Francis ebooks contains over 50,000 titles in the Humanities, Social Sciences, Behavioural Sciences, Built Environment and Law.

Choose from a range of subject packages or create your own!

Benefits for you

- » Free MARC records
- » COUNTER-compliant usage statistics
- » Flexible purchase and pricing options
- » All titles DRM-free.

Benefits for your user

- » Off-site, anytime access via Athens or referring URL
- » Print or copy pages or chapters
- » Full content search
- » Bookmark, highlight and annotate text
- » Access to thousands of pages of quality research at the click of a button.

 REQUEST YOUR **FREE** INSTITUTIONAL TRIAL TODAY

Free Trials Available
We offer free trials to qualifying academic, corporate and government customers.

eCollections – Choose from over 30 subject eCollections, including:

Archaeology	Language Learning
Architecture	Law
Asian Studies	Literature
Business & Management	Media & Communication
Classical Studies	Middle East Studies
Construction	Music
Creative & Media Arts	Philosophy
Criminology & Criminal Justice	Planning
Economics	Politics
Education	Psychology & Mental Health
Energy	Religion
Engineering	Security
English Language & Linguistics	Social Work
Environment & Sustainability	Sociology
Geography	Sport
Health Studies	Theatre & Performance
History	Tourism, Hospitality & Events

For more information, pricing enquiries or to order a free trial, please contact your local sales team:
www.tandfebooks.com/page/sales

 **Routledge** Taylor & Francis Group | The home of Routledge books

www.tandfebooks.com